- Letting your point unfold gradually (Chapter 20)
- Considering a humorous or playful style (pp. 508–10)
- Using techniques from popular magazines (pp. 510–12)

HOW TO DEVELOP YOUR OWN DRAFTING AND REVISING PROCESS BY:

- Maintaining engagement with your problem (pp. 3–20, 22–26, 427–36)
- Using a variety of exploration techniques (pp. 21–42; Writing Projects chapters)
- Reducing writer's block by lowering expectations for drafts (Chapter 17)
- Using outlines or tree diagrams to visualize structure (pp. 451–55)
- Following revision practices of experienced writers (pp. 428–36)
- Identifying readers and revising with their needs in mind (pp. 437–40; Chapter 19)
- Editing for gracefulness, clarity, and correctness (pp. 432, 434)

HOW TO WORK PRODUCTIVELY IN GROUPS BY:

- Viewing writing as "joining a conversation" (pp. 5–7, 514–15)
- Listening to the views of your classmates (pp. 517–19)
- Working together to brainstorm and solve problems (pp. 524–28)
- Collaborating through electronic media (pp. 597–612)
- Becoming an effective peer reviewer (pp. 524–28; Guidelines for Peer Reviewers in the Writing Projects chapters)
- Using peer feedback to stimulate revision of your drafts (pp. 437–40, 524–28)

HOW TO BECOME AN EFFECTIVE RESEARCHER BY:

- Unlocking resources of libraries (pp. 536–43)
- Finding resources in your community (pp. 543–47)
- Using the Internet and World Wide Web (pp. 613–19)
- Incorporating sources into your writing (pp. 548–62)
- Citing and documenting your sources (pp. 562–96)

HOW TO PERFORM WELL ON ESSAY EXAMS BY:

- Preparing for an essay exam (pp. 626–28)
- Analyzing essay exam questions (pp. 628–36)
- Knowing what instructors look for (pp. 638–47)
- Writing efficiently under pressure (pp. 636–38)

The
Allyn and Bacon
Guide to Writing,
Brief Edition

John D. Ramage
Arizona State University

John C. Bean
Seattle University

ALLYN AND BACON

Boston

London

Toronto

Sydney

Tokyo

Singapore

Vice President: Eben Ludlow
Senior Developmental Editor: Marlene Ellin
Editorial Assistant: Elisabeth Egan
Marketing Manager: Lisa Kimball
Editorial-Production Administrator: Susan Brown
Editorial-Production Service: Saxon House Productions
Text Designer: Melinda Grosser
Composition Buyer: Linda Cox
Manufacturing Buyer: Suzanne Lareau
Cover Administrator: Linda Knowles
Cover Designer: Susan Paradise

Copyright © 1997 by Allyn & Bacon
A Viacom Company
160 Gould Street
Needham Heights, MA 02194
Internet: www.abacon.com
America Online: Keyword: College Online

Library-of-Congress Cataloging-in-Publication Data
Ramage, John D.
    The Allyn and Bacon guide to writing / John D. Ramage, John C.
Bean.
        p.   cm.
    Includes bibliographical references (p.) and index.
    ISBN 0-02-398273-X (notch paper)
    1. English language—Rhetoric.   2. College readers.   I. Bean,
John C.   II. Title.
PE1408.R18   1996
808'.0427—dc20   96-31910
                                                                CIP

Printed in the United States of America
10 9 8 7 6 5 4   01 00 99 98 97

Acknowledgments:
    Page 3. Rodney Kilcup, "A Modest Proposal for Reluctant Writers," *Newsletter of the Pacific North-west Writing Consortium,* Vol. 2, No. 3 (Sept. 1982), p. 5.
    Page 3. Stephen D. Brookfield, *Developing Critical Thinkers: Challenging Adults to Explore Alternative Ways of Thinking and Acting.* San Francisco: Jossey-Bass, 1987, p. 5
    Page 4. Andrea Lunsford and Lisa Ede, *Singular Texts/Plural Authors: Perspective on Collaborative Writing.* Carbondale and Edwardsville, IL: Southern Illinois University Press, 1992, pp. 45–48.

Acknowledgments continue on page 649, which constitutes a continuation of the copyright page.

Brief Contents

p   a   r   t   **T   H   R   E   E**

A Guide to Composing and Revising   425

p   a   r   t   **F   O   U   R**

A Guide to Research   529

p   a   r   t   **F   I   V   E**

A Guide to Writing Under Pressure   621

W R I T I N G   P R O J E C T S

Contents

chapter **3**   *Solving Content Problems: Thesis and Support*   43

chapter **4**   *Solving Rhetorical Problems: Purpose, Audience,
and Genre*   54

p a r t

T W O *Writing Projects* 73

Writing to Learn

Writing to Express

Writing to Explore

Writing to Inform

Writing to Analyze

Writing to Persuade

chapter **14**   *Writing a Classical Argument* 328

chapter 15   *Making an Evaluation*   365

chapter 16   *Proposing a Solution*   389

p a r t

THREE *A Guide to Composing and Revising* 425

chapter **17** *Writing as a Problem-Solving Process* 427

p a r t

FOUR *A Guide to Research* 529

chapter **24**   *Electronic Writing and Research* 597

p a r t

F I V E   *A Guide to Writing Under Pressure* 621

chapter **25**   *Essay Examinations: Writing Polished Prose in a Hurry* 623

Preface

We take seriously the designation of *guide* for our title. For us the word resonates to the core of our experiences over the past 25 years in college writing classrooms and in our collegial friendship, which has spanned two decades and half a continent. We have spent much of our professional lives mapping the territory of rhetoric and composition. The word *guide*, with its connotations of an unknown and alluring realm and of new learners seeking the expertise of those who have traveled before them, summons up the hundreds of questions that we and our students have posed and discussed over the years.

What answers can a guide give to students' questions? Many students enter first-year composition in search of a formula; they seek a single set of directions they might follow to become good writers. A guide's first responsibility is to reveal that there aren't any formulas. However, there is much that a guide can teach about how writers pose and attempt to resolve questions, about the tactics and strategies they use, about the purposes they hope to achieve, and about the processes they follow. Moreover, a guide can help learners discover their own inherent strengths as thinkers and users of language, setting tasks that enhance these strengths and increase students' confidence.

In *The Allyn and Bacon Guide to Writing, Brief Edition*, we talk honestly about what we know and what still mystifies us about writing, inviting students to join in our quest for greater understanding. We intend our book to reflect our experiences as classroom teachers, our study of composition theory and pedagogy, our admiration and empathy for those who teach composition, and our faith in the intelligence and integrity of students. To achieve these ends, we set for ourselves three major goals.

First, we wanted to create a comprehensive rhetoric that integrated up-to-date composition theory with pedagogical research in critical thinking and inquiry. Particularly, we wanted our treatment of critical thinking to reflect the generative sense of problems associated with John Dewey. Rather than regarding problems as annoying blockages to be overcome, Dewey views them as invitations to creative action in the world. When writers respond to a problem, they contribute to an ongoing conversation among a community of readers and provoke further inquiry and dialog. To foster this kind of generative thought among students, we wanted our book to include a sequence of well-designed, class-tested writing assignments that would engage them in the pursuit of interesting problems. Like Dewey, we believe that such pursuits are at the core of a liberating curriculum.

Second, we wanted to create a book that would be a pleasure for teachers to use in the classroom. Such a book had to have a clear, yet flexible organizational structure that would accommodate a range of course designs and include lively collaborative activities for small groups or the whole class. Moreover, the book had to be intellectually stimulating for teachers and capable of guiding students toward composing focused, idea-rich essays that teachers would enjoy reading.

Finally, and most important, we wanted to create a book that first-year college students would value. By making the book friendly and encouraging, we hoped to engage students intellectually in problem-centered activities that would prepare them for academic tasks across the curriculum.

After nearly four years of planning, writing, field testing, and revising, we believe that we have created a text that meets our goals. Like our other Allyn and Bacon text, *Writing Arguments, The Allyn and Bacon Guide to Writing, Brief Edition* represents the best of what we have learned from wrestling throughout our careers with the practical and theoretical issues involved in teaching composition.

DISTINCTIVE FEATURES OF *THE ALLYN AND BACON GUIDE TO WRITING, BRIEF EDITION*

The Allyn and Bacon Guide to Writing, Brief Edition is distinguished by the following features:

- *An emphasis on problem posing and inquiry.* Throughout the text, we show how the impulse to write emerges from the desire to say something new or surprising about a question or problem. Writers must address simultaneously two interrelated kinds of problems: subject-matter problems that drive inquiry and rhetorical problems related to purpose, audience, and genre.
- *An emphasis on writing as a rhetorical act.* This text constantly reminds students that writers direct their work to an audience for a purpose within the conventions of a genre. Writers influence readers by what they include and exclude, by their choice of words and figures of speech, and, more broadly, by their style, point of view, and projected voice.
- *The concept of a continuum from closed to open forms of writing.* Through this continuum we show how the writer's choice of form is always a function of the rhetorical situation. Closed forms, characterized by a problem-thesis-support structure, are the most common forms for academic and professional writing. Open forms, with their stylistic and structural surprises, are the forms of choice for expressive and exploratory writing, personal essays, and belletristic prose.
- *Concentration on academic/professional writing balanced with personal and narrative forms.* Because we want to prepare students for academic writing across the curriculum and for the kinds of writing most frequently encountered in their professional lives, the text provides extensive instruction in problem-thesis-support writing. However, because we also want students to value personal and narrative writing, the text provides instruction and writing

opportunities in these forms as well, encouraging their use for both exploratory and finished pieces.

- *Carefully designed, class-tested writing projects.* These major projects in Part Two, "Writing Projects," guide students through all phases of the writing process, engaging them in group collaboration and peer review. Arranged according to the purposes of writing, these projects are designed to increase students' rhetorical knowledge and skills while promoting habits of inquiry and dialectic thinking valued in college courses.

- *Brief Writing Projects* in Part One, "A Rhetoric for College Writers," help students learn key rhetorical concepts from Chapters 1 to 4 as well as important principles of punctuation, sentence structure, and style. In Part One, these "microthemes" allow instructors to assign writing beginning on the first day of class.

- *An emphasis on collaborative learning and writing.* Throughout the text, "For Writing and Discussion" activities engage students with instructional material and stimulate the kind of rich exploratory writing and talking that leads to deeper inquiry and more complex thinking. Designed either for small groups or for whole class discussion, these exercises focus on key instructional concepts and thinking strategies. Those exercises highlighted with an icon (reproduced here in the margin) call for preliminary freewriting, a technique we encourage students to use throughout the text for generating, clarifying, and deepening ideas.

- *Guidelines for Peer Reviewers at the conclusion of each chapter in Part Two, "Writing Projects."* Posing questions that promote both a fresh view of one's own writing and careful critiquing of others' drafts, these guidelines encapsulate key concepts in the chapter and guide students through the review process.

- *An organizational structure that facilitates coherent course design.* The book's structure also offers instructors flexibility in emphases and selection of major writing projects.

- *Professional and student readings throughout the text.* These readings illustrate a range of rhetorical strategies and structures. Selected to stimulate inquiry and discussion, these essays examine provocative academic and societal issues. In addition, the text illustrates the evolution of two student essays from early exploratory drafts to finished papers. Marginal symbols, like the one reproduced here in the margin, are used to distinguish student writing throughout the text.

STRUCTURE OF *THE ALLYN AND BACON GUIDE TO WRITING, BRIEF EDITION*

Part One, "A Rhetoric for College Writers," provides a conceptual framework for the text by showing how writers pose problems, pursue them through exploratory writing and talking, and try to solve them as they compose and revise. Chapter 1 shows how writers grapple with both subject matter and rhetorical problems, introducing the concept of a continuum from closed to open forms of prose. Chapter 2 presents an array of techniques for exploring ideas and deepening inquiry, including strategies for making exploratory writing and talking a regular habit.

Chapters 3 and 4 together describe the kinds of problems that experienced writers try to solve as they compose. Chapter 3 explains how academic writers pose good questions, formulate a surprising thesis, and support that thesis with strong arguments and convincing detail. Chapter 4 shifts from subject matter problems to rhetorical problems, demonstrating that decisions about content, structure, and style are controlled by a writer's purpose, intended audience, and genre.

Part Two, "Writing Projects," contains twelve self-contained assignment chapters arranged according to purposes for writing: to learn, to express, to explore, to inform, to analyze, and to persuade. Each chapter within this part has a consistent structure that guides students through the process of generating and exploring ideas, composing and drafting, and revising and editing. The heart of each chapter is a writing project designed to teach students new ways of seeing and thinking. The project is defined early in the chapter so that students will be pondering the problem it poses as they absorb the chapter's explanatory material. A special icon next to each project description, like the one reproduced here in the margin, will enable students to refer back to the description easily as they draft.

The exploratory exercises throughout each assignment chapter help students generate ideas for their essays, while developing their skills at posing problems, delaying closure, speaking back to texts, valuing alternative points of view, and thinking dialectically. A set of Guidelines for Peer Reviewers concludes each chapter, showing students how to critique classmates' drafts and revise their own.

Part Three, "A Guide to Composing and Revising," focuses on nuts-and-bolts strategies for composing and revising along the continuum from closed to open forms. Its five self-contained chapters can be read in any sequence at the instructor's discretion.

Chapter 17 explains how experienced writers use multiple drafts to manage the complexities of writing and suggests ways that students can improve their own writing processes. Chapters 18 and 19 focus on structuring and revising thesis-based, closed-form writing. Chapter 18 explains how familiarity with the generic features of closed-form prose can help a writer generate and organize ideas. Chapter 19 teaches how to revise closed-form prose with readers' needs in mind.

In Chapter 20, the focus shifts from closed to open forms that play with conventions in various ways. Exploring major differences between open- and closed-form writing, the chapter offers advice on how to "open up" prose in appropriate rhetorical situations. Finally, Chapter 21 shows students how working in small groups can help them generate ideas, solve problems, and gather feedback for revision.

Part Four, "A Guide to Research," is an introduction to conducting research and incorporating sources into prose. Chapter 22 guides students through the process of posing and focusing a research problem and of unlocking the resources of libraries and one's community. Chapter 23 explains how to summarize, paraphrase, quote sources, and avoid plagiarism. Model MLA and APA formats for citing and documenting sources—including electronic media—are provided. Finally, Chapter 24, written by Daniel Anderson, Assistant Director of the Computer Writing and Research Labs at the University of Texas at Austin, introduces students to a wealth of new on-line resources for writers. Introducing options available through the Internet and World Wide Web, it suggests ways to explore and develop ideas, work collaboratively, conduct research, and evaluate sources.

Part Five, "A Guide to Writing Under Pressure," by Christy Friend, also of the University of Texas at Austin, draws on her extensive research into the demands of timed writing, showing students how to plan and draft an exam essay by applying the principles of rhetorical assessment discussed throughout the text.

STRATEGIES FOR USING *THE ALLYN AND BACON GUIDE TO WRITING, BRIEF EDITION*

The logic of the text's organizational structure makes course design easy. The main rhetorical concepts that students should learn early in the course are developed in Part One; explanations of compositional strategies and skills—which students can use to complete the assignments in Part Two—are placed in Part Three. Additional instructional material related to research and to writing under pressure are included in Parts Four and Five.

We suggest that instructors use the following basic course design:

First, students will read all of Part One, Chapters 1 to 4. The brief write-to-learn projects that engage students with the instructional material in these chapters will also allow teachers to assess students' initial writing skills.

Next, instructors can begin assigning writing project chapters from the array of options available in Part Two, Chapters 5 to 16. While students are engaged with the writing projects in these chapters, instructors can assign material from the compositional chapters in Part Three, or from the additional instructional materials in Parts Four and Five, selected and sequenced according to their own needs (the *Instructor's Resource Manual* suggests several options). While students are working on a writing project, classroom discussion can alternate between issues related directly to the assignment (invention exercises, group brainstorming, peer review workshops) and those focusing on instructional matter from the rest of the text.

USING THE WRITING PROJECTS IN PART TWO

Because each of the twelve assignment chapters in Part Two is self-contained, instructors can select and organize the writing projects in the way that best fits their course goals and students' needs. The projects in Chapters 5 and 6 introduce students to the rhetorical ways of observing and reading that underpin mature academic thinking, showing students how to analyze a text, pose questions about it, and understand and resist the text's rhetorical strategies.

Chapter 7 on autobiographical narrative is the text's primary "open-form" assignment. Introducing students to strategies of plot, character, and dramatic tension, the project typically produces surprisingly sophisticated narratives. Some teachers like to give this assignment early in the course—on the grounds that personal writing should precede more academic forms. Others like to give it last—on the grounds that open-form writing is more complex and subtle than closed-form prose. We have found that either choice can work well.

The assignment in Chapter 8, an exploratory essay, asks students to narrate their engagement with a problem and their attempts to resolve it. Teachers may pair this chapter with Part Four on research writing, using the exploratory essay as the first stage of a major research project. The two student essays in this chapter are in fact early explorations for finished projects that appear later in the text.

Chapter 9 on informative writing urges students to reach beyond straightforward reporting by employing a "surprising reversal" strategy aimed at altering the reader's initial assumptions about the topic. Surprising reversal is a powerful rhetorical move that can be used to enliven almost any kind of informative, analytical, or persuasive prose.

The four writing projects in the analysis section (Chapters 10 to 13) allow instructors to select among different kinds of phenomena for analysis: images in advertising (Chapter 10); numerical data from tables, graphs, and charts (Chapter 11); a short story, with strong emphasis on a reader response approach (Chapter 12); or causes/consequences (Chapter 13). These chapters teach the generic skills of close observation, close reading, and close attention to detail while offering specific guidance in the skills unique to each category of analysis.

The persuasion chapters (Chapters 14 to 16) teach key concepts of argumentation adapted from the third edition of our *Writing Arguments*. Providing a strong introduction to both academic and civil argument, they combine accessible Toulmin and stasis approaches with the traditional approach that focuses on *logos*, *ethos*, and *pathos* as rhetorical appeals.

SUPPLEMENTS FOR *THE ALLYN AND BACON GUIDE TO WRITING, BRIEF EDITION*

Authored by Vicki Byard, Northeastern Illinois University, the *Instructor's Resource Manual for the Allyn and Bacon Guide to Writing, Brief Edition* features a comprehensive section on managing the freshman composition classroom, including topics such as lesson planning, encouraging student participation, designing journal and portfolio assignments, grading, conferencing, and small group workshops. The *Manual* then provides an overview of the text along with an array of sample syllabi tailored to a variety of emphases and course lengths. Chapter-by-chapter coverage of the instructional material and readings, additional discussion questions, and suggestions for possible activities come next, followed by ways to use the text in an electronic classroom. A special section for ESL students, transparency masters for classroom use, and an annotated bibliography are also included.

Two additional Allyn and Bacon publications are available without cost to instructors. The first, *Teaching College Writing* by Maggy Smith, University of Texas at El Paso, presents ideas for organizing and teaching the freshman composition course, identifying research origins for most of the practical suggestions. The second, *The Allyn and Bacon Sourcebook for College Writing Teachers* by James C. McDonald, University of Southwestern Louisiana, is a collection of writings on theories and approaches to composition instruction by some of today's foremost scholars and teachers.

Finally, Allyn and Bacon's new *CompSite* on the World Wide Web (www. abacon. com/compsite) offers a rich array of resources for both students and instructors. Students will find suggestions for conducting and documenting research as well as ongoing discussions devoted to topics that inspire research and writing. Faculty resources include strategies for teaching in the computer classroom and teaching composition for the World Wide Web. In addition, *CompSite* provides hot links to Internet teaching sites, contact information for organizations and individuals concerned with computer pedagogy, and a forum for trading teaching tips with freshman composition instructors around the globe. New information and features will appear regularly at this dynamic site.

ACKNOWLEDGMENTS

Many people have contributed to the development of this text over the past four years. At the outset we would like to express special thanks and appreciation to Daniel Anderson and Christy Friend, both of the University of Texas at Austin, who wrote the chapters on electronic writing and research (Chapter 24) and essay examinations (Chapter 25), respectively. We also thank Rosalie (Kit) Bean for assistance in preparing Chapters 22 and 23 on research writing and the use of sources.

Grateful acknowledgement and thanks go to our editor, Eben Ludlow, Vice-President at Allyn and Bacon, with whom we have worked productively over the last twelve years. Eben deserves his reputation as one of the premier editors in college publishing. Marlene Ellin, Senior Developmental Editor, provided invaluable help in structuring and refining the manuscript as well as skillful project management. Doug Day, English Sales Specialist, and Lisa Kimball, English Marketing Manager, provided helpful suggestions and support. Susan Brown, Editorial-Production Administrator, capably guided the book through its final stages. And Sydney Baily-Gould was a pleasure to work with as she managed many key aspects of production.

To the many scholars and teachers who reviewed the manuscript at its many stages we give special thanks: Elizabeth Addison, Western Carolina University;

Cora Agatucci, Central Oregon Community College; Kathleen L. Bell, University of Central Florida; Vicki Byard, Northeastern Illinois University; Alma G. Bryant, University of South Florida; Richard Bullock, Wright State University; Marilyn Clelland, Purdue University Calumet; Cheryl Abrams Collier, Clemson University; Patricia E. Connors, The University of Memphis; M. C. Flanigan, University of Oklahoma; Christy Friend, The University of Texas, Austin; Maurice Hunt, Baylor University; Charles Kostelnick, Iowa State University; William H. Lay, Kalamazoo Valley Community College; Richard Louth, Southeastern Louisiana University; Irvin Peckham, University of Nebraska, Omaha; Nancy Prosenjak, Metropolitan State College; Charlton Ryan, The University of Memphis; Kathy Overhulse Smith, Indiana University, Bloomington; Beckey Stamm, Columbus State Community College; Susan Taylor, University of Nevada, Las Vegas; Margaret Urie, University of Nevada, Reno; Allison Warriner, California State University, Hayward; Stephen Wilhoit, University of Dayton; Sally B. Young, University of Tennessee, Chattanooga.

We would like to thank Larry Nichols, Director of the Writing Center at Seattle University, for his extensive class testing of materials on exploratory and research writing. We also thank two of his students, Mary Turla and Sheridan Botts, whose writing processes we describe in detail. We are grateful to Andrew, Stephen, and Sarah Bean for their research assistance and for their willingness to respond to this text from students' perspectives.

Most of all, however, we are indebted to the hundreds of students who, over the past quarter-century, have entered our classrooms and shared with us their enthusiasms, quandaries, and revelations as they strove to become better writers. They sustained our love of teaching and inspired us to write this book.

John C. Bean

John D. Ramage

A Rhetoric for College Writers

part O N E

c h a p t e r   **1**

Posing Problems
The Demands of
College Writing

It seems to me, then, that the way to help people become better writers is not to tell them that they must first learn the rules of grammar, that they must develop a four-part outline, that they must consult the experts and collect all the useful information. These things may have their place. But none of them is as crucial as having a good, interesting question.

—Rodney Kilcup, *Historian*

Our purpose in this introductory chapter is to help you see writers as questioners and problem posers—a view that we believe will lead to your growth as a college-level thinker and writer. In particular, we want you to think of writers as people who pose interesting questions and struggle to work out answers or responses to them. As we will show in this chapter, writers pose two sorts of questions: *subject-matter* questions (for example, Can zoos be used to preserve endangered species?) and *rhetorical* questions (for example, How much background information will my readers need about current controversies over zoos?).

We don't mean to make this focus on problems sound scary. Indeed, humans pose and solve problems all the time and often take great pleasure in doing so. Psychologists who study critical and creative thinking see problem solving as a productive and positive activity. According to psychologist Stephen Brookfield, "Critical thinkers are actively engaged with life. . . . They appreciate creativity, they are innovators, and they exude a sense that life is full of possibilities." By focusing first on the kinds of problems that writers pose and struggle with, we hope to increase your own engagement and pleasure in becoming a writer.

This chapter begins with an introductory question: What does it mean to be a writer? We examine how posing subject-matter questions drives the writing process and brings writers into community with readers interested in the same questions. We then introduce you to the kinds of rhetorical problems writers pose by discussing one example, what we call the problem of closed versus open forms. The chapter concludes with a brief writing assignment that asks you to try your own hand at proposing a subject-matter question.

3

WHAT DOES IT MEAN TO BE A WRITER?

Let's begin with a problematic question about writing: What does it mean to be a writer? For some people, being a writer is part of their identity, so much so that when asked, "What do you do?" they are apt to respond, "I'm a writer." Poets, novelists, script writers, journalists, technical writers, grant writers, self-help book authors, and so on see themselves as writers the way other people see themselves as chefs, realtors, bankers, or musicians. But many people who don't think of themselves primarily as writers nevertheless *use* writing—often frequently—throughout their careers. They are engineers writing proposals or project reports; attorneys writing legal briefs; nurses writing patient assessments; business executives writing financial analyses or management reports; accountants writing advisement letters to clients; concerned citizens writing letters to the editor about public affairs; college professors writing articles for scholarly journals; college students writing papers and reports for their classes.

In our view, all these kinds of writing are valuable and qualify their authors as writers. If you already identify yourself as a writer, then you won't need much external motivation for improving your writing. But if you have little interest in writing for its own sake and aspire instead to become a nurse, an engineer, a business executive, a social worker, or a marine biologist, then you might question the benefits of taking a writing course.

Writing skills are essential to most professional careers. To measure how essential, researchers Andrea Lunsford and Lisa Ede surveyed randomly selected members of such professional organizations as the American Consulting Engineers Counsel, the American Institute of Chemists, the American Psychological Association, and the International City Management Association. They discovered that members of these organizations spent, on the average, 44 percent of their professional time writing, most commonly, writing letters, memos, short reports, instructional materials, and professional articles and essays.

Professionals who can write typically advance further and faster than those who can't. Over the past decade, both authors of this text have worked extensively with faculty in every discipline trying to discover ways to teach college writing more effectively. Through this work, we've been in contact with leaders in numerous professional communities, all of whom stress the importance of writing for career success. Having knowledge of a discipline's subject matter, they say, isn't enough. In the workplace, the ability to explain one's knowledge to others and to argue persuasively to different constituencies is critical. Lunsford and Ede, in the same study cited earlier, report numerous on-the-job situations in which written communication skills are crucial. Here, for example, is how one of their respondents, an engineer working as a city planner, described his frustration at his inability to produce adequately persuasive documents.

> After I had been out of school a number of years practicing as a city planner, I had become concerned about why we could develop a good plan for a community and try to explain it to people and they wouldn't seem to understand it. They wouldn't support it for one reason or another. And time and time again we would

see a good plan go down the drain because people didn't agree with it or for some reason didn't actively support it.

This city manager describes a situation often encountered in professional life—the need to explain and sell one's ideas to others. As he implies, those who can write clearly and persuasively contribute invaluably to the success of their organizations.

But career success is only one of the reasons that learning to write well can be valuable to you. As we show throughout this text, writing is closely allied to thinking and to the innate satisfaction you take in exercising your curiosity, creativity, and problem-solving ability. Writing connects you to others and helps you discover and express ideas that you would otherwise never think or say. Unlike speaking, writing gives you time to think deep and long about an idea. Because you can revise writing, it lets you pursue a problem in stages, with each new draft reflecting a deeper, clearer, or more complex level of thought. In other words, writing isn't just a way to express thought; it is a way to do the thinking itself. The act of writing stimulates, challenges, and stretches your mental powers and, when you do it well, is profoundly satisfying.

SUBJECT-MATTER PROBLEMS: THE STARTING POINT OF WRITING

Having made a connection between writing and thinking, we now move to the spirit of inquiry that drives the writing process. Thus far in your writing career, you may have imagined a simple relationship between you and your subject matter. Someone handed you a broad topic area (for example, contemporary urban America or Renaissance love poetry) or a narrower topic area (homelessness or Shakespeare's sonnets), and you collected and wrote information about that topic. In the process of writing your paper, you may have learned some interesting things about your subject matter. But if you approached your writing in this way, you weren't approximating the thinking processes of most experienced writers. Experienced writers usually see their subject matter in terms of questions or problems rather than broad or narrow topic areas. They typically enjoy posing questions and pursuing (and sometimes finding) answers. They write to share their discoveries and insights with readers interested in the same problems.

Shared Problems Unite Writers and Readers

Everywhere we turn, we see writers and readers forming communities based on questions or problems of mutual interest. Perhaps nowhere are such communities more evident than in academe. Many college professors are engaged in research projects stimulated and driven by questions or problems. At a recent workshop for new faculty members, we asked participants to write a brief description of a question or problem that motivated them to write a seminar paper or article. Here is a sampling of their responses.

A Biochemistry Professor   During periods of starvation, the human body makes physiological adaptations to preserve essential protein mass. Unfortunately, these adaptations don't work well during long-term starvation. After the body depletes its carbohydrate storage, it must shift to depleting protein in order to produce glucose. Eventually, this loss of functional protein leads to metabolic dysfunction and death. Interestingly, several animal species are capable of surviving for extensive periods without food and water while conserving protein and maintaining glucose levels. How do the bodies of these animals accomplish this feat? I wanted to investigate the metabolic functioning of these animals, which might lead to insights into the human situation.

A Nursing Professor   Being a nurse who had worked with terminally ill or permanently unconscious patients, I saw doctors and nurses struggle with the question of when to withdraw life-support systems. I wondered how philosophers and ethicists went about deciding these issues and how they thought physicians and other clinicians should make the decision to withdraw life support. I wanted to answer this question: What is the relationship between the way "experts" say we should solve complex ethical problems and the way it actually happens in a clinical context? So I chose to look at this problem by reading what philosophers said about this topic and then by interviewing physicians and nurses in long-term care facilities (nursing homes) in the United States and the Netherlands—asking them how they made decisions to withdraw life support from patients with no hope of recovery.

A Journalism Professor   Several years ago, I knocked on the wooden front door of the home of an elderly woman in Tucson, Arizona. Tears of grief rolled down her cheeks as she opened the door. The tears turned to anger when I explained that I was a reporter and wished to talk with her about her son's death in jail. Her face hardened. "What right do you have coming here?" I recall her saying. "Why are you bothering me?" Those questions have haunted me throughout my journalism career. Do journalists have the right to intrude on a person's grief? Can they exercise it any time they want? What values do journalists use to decide when to intrude and violate someone's privacy?

Of course these are not new college students speaking; these are new college professors recalling problems they posed in graduate school. We share these problems with you to persuade you that most college professors value question asking and want you to be caught up, as they are, in the spirit of inquiry.

As you progress through your college career, you will find yourself increasingly engaged with questions. All around college campuses you'll find clusters of professors and students asking questions about all manner of curious things—questions about the reproductive cycles of worms and bugs, the surface structure of metals, the social significance of obscure poets, gender roles among the Kalahari Bushmen, the meaning of Balinese cockfighting, the effect of tax structure on economies, the rise of labor unions in agriculture, the role of prostitutes in medieval India, the properties of concrete, and almost anything else a human being might wonder about. A quick review of the magazine rack at any large grocery store reveals that similar communities have formed around everything from hot rods to model railroads, from computers to kayaks to cooking.

At the heart of all these communities of writers and readers is an interest in common questions and the hope for better or different answers. Writers write because they have something new or surprising or challenging to say in response to a question. Readers read because they share the writer's interest in the problem and want to deepen their understanding.

The Writer as Problematizer

Few writers discover their "answers" in a blinding flash. And even fewer writers produce a full-blown essay in a moment of inspiration. Professionals may require weeks, months, or years of thinking to produce a single piece of writing.

A new insight may start out as a vague sense of uncertainty, an awareness that you are beginning to see your subject (the metabolism of a starving animal, the decision to let a patient die, a grieving mother's anger at a journalist) differently from how others see it. You feel a gap between your view of a topic and your audience's view of the same topic and write to fill these gaps, to articulate your different view. Rarely, however, do writers know at the outset what they will write in the end. Instead, they clarify and refine their thoughts in the act of writing.

One of the most common causes of weak writing is the writer's tendency to reach closure too quickly. It's difficult, of course, to keep wrestling with a question. It's easier simply to ignore alternative views and material that doesn't fit and to grab hold of the first solution that comes to mind. What characterizes a successful writer is the ability to live with uncertainty and to acknowledge the insufficiency of an answer.

One term that describes serious writers is *problematizers;* that is, serious writers are not merely problem solvers, but problem posers, people who problematize their lives. We learned the term *problematize* from South American educator Paulo Freire, who discovered that adult literacy was best taught as a problem-solving activity tied to essential themes in his students' daily lives. Freire's method contrasts starkly with the traditional mode of teaching literacy, which Freire called the banking method. The goal of the banking method is to deposit knowledge in students' memory banks, not to act or discover or question, just to file away.

The banking method encourages a passive attitude, not only toward learning, but also toward reality. Freire characterized students indoctrinated in such methods as "submerged in reality," unable to distinguish between the way things are and the way things might or should be. When people are taught to read and write by the banking method, they are likely to learn the word *water* by constantly repeating an irrelevant, self-evident sentence, such as "The water is in the well." Using Freire's method of teaching literacy, students might learn the word *water* by asking, "Is the water in our village dirty or clean?" and if the water is dirty, asking, "Why is the water dirty? Who is responsible?" The power of reading and writing lies in making discriminations, in unveiling alternative ways of seeing the world in which we live. By using language to problematize reality, Freire's students learned the meaning of written words because they recognized the power of those words.

Skilled writers, thus, are seekers after alternatives who look deliberately for questions, problems, puzzles, and contradictions. They realize that they can't write anything significant if they don't bring something new or challenging to the reader, something risky enough to spark disagreement or complex enough to be misunderstood. The surest way to improve your writing is to ground your essay in a question or problem that will motivate your thinking and help you establish a purposeful relationship with your audience. In the process, you'll have to live for a while with a sense of incompleteness, ambiguity, and uncertainty—the effects of engagement with any real problem.

POSING A PROBLEM: A CASE STUDY OF A BEGINNING COLLEGE WRITER

So far we have talked about how professional writers pose problems. In this section we show you how student writer Mary Turla posed a problem for an argumentative paper requiring research. (Her final paper is reproduced in Chapter 23, pp. 583–96, as an example of a student research paper.)

At the start of her process, Mary's general topic area was mail-order brides. Her interest in this subject was sparked by a local newspaper story about an American man who gunned down his Filipina mail-order bride outside the courtroom where she was filing for divorce. Although Mary was immediately intrigued by the topic, she didn't initially have a focused question or problem. She began doing library research on the mail-order bride industry and discovered that 75 percent of mail-order brides come from the Philippines. Because Mary is a Filipina American, this statistic bothered her, and she began focusing on the image of Asian women created by the mail-order bride industry. Early in her process, she wrote the following entry in her journal:

Mary's Paper— Early Journal Entry

The mail-order bride industry may create & perpetuate the image of Asian women as commodities, vulnerable, uneducated, subservient; this image is applied to Asian American women or women of Asian descent. . . . Obviously, the mail-order bride is wrong--but what is the statement I want to make about it? Exploits/develops & creates negative image of Asian women. This image passes on to Asian American women. The image makes them sexual objects, "object" period--love as

```
a commodity--exploitation industry--twists our culture--unrealistic
expectations. What is the consequence?: domestic violence, unsatis-
fied partners, multimillion-dollar industry; subtle consequence:
buying/selling people OK; Love/marriage a commodity.
```

This journal entry helped Mary see the more complex aspects of her subject—especially the connection of the mail-order bride industry to the image of Asian or Asian American women—but she was not yet able to define a central question or problem. Shortly after writing this journal entry, Mary discussed the topic with her classmates. After class, Mary wrote again in her journal.

Mary's Paper—
Later Journal Entry

```
    Class was great. We all had a chance to discuss our research so
far and give others input on theirs. It was an extremely helpful ex-
ercise. A few helpful hints I got from the gang: 1) Define partic-
ipants (men/women/business); 2) Are some "brides" there because they
want to be? 3) Find a question! Most everyone (as far as I could
tell) felt the mail-order bride industry was comparable to prosti-
tution or trafficking of women. I have to ask: Is it? If it is, is
it inherently so? Or, is it something about the mechanics of the in-
dustry now that justifies criticism? I could also sense an attitude--
a mix of pity and contempt for the women involved.
```

Shortly thereafter, a conversation between Mary and her mother produced a focusing problem. After Mary complained about the evils of mail-order brides, her mother unexpectedly supported the practice. Women in the Philippines are desperately poor, her mother explained. Marrying a stranger, she said, may be the only way for some women to escape lives of abject poverty. Although Mary disliked the mail-order bride industry, her mother's response gave her pause. Perhaps being treated like a commodity might be a small price to pay for escaping near starvation and an early death.

Mary was now caught in a dilemma between her own gut-level desire to outlaw the mail-order bride industry and her realization that doing so would end many women's only hope of avoiding a life of poverty. She finally posed her problem this way: Should the mail-order bride industry be made illegal? She was no longer certain about her own answer to this question. Her goal was to make up her mind by learning as much as she could about the industry from the perspectives of the husband, the bride, and the industry itself. We return to Mary's story occasionally throughout this text. (You can read her final paper in Chapter 23; you can also read her earlier exploratory paper in Chapter 8, pp. 167–69.)

FOR WRITING AND DISCUSSION

For this exercise, we ask you to try converting a topic area into a field of interesting questions. The topic area for this exercise, as well as for the brief writing assignment at the end of this chapter, is "animals"; we chose this topic because almost everyone has had some experience with animals either through owning a pet, observing a hornets' nest, wondering about dinosaurs, or questioning the ethics of stepping on ants. Moreover, animals are widely studied by university researchers across many disciplines (the metabolism of starvation is just one example).

1. Working in small groups, brainstorm a dozen or so good questions about animals. These should be questions that no one in your group can currently answer authoritatively (that's one of the things that makes them good questions). Imagine that at a later date (after a period of thinking, exploration, and research) you are going to write a paper giving your answer to one of these questions based on your own personal experience, critical thinking, or research. You'll want your paper to be interesting to readers. Here are some examples of questions about animals.
   - Why did dinosaurs become extinct?
   - How do spiders know how to build webs?
   - Is saving the spotted owl worth the economic costs?
   - Is it cruel to put animals in zoos?
   - Should people be allowed to own pit bulls?
   - Why is it that a starfish can regrow an arm, but a mammal can't regrow a limb?
2. After each group has generated a dozen or more questions, try to reach consensus on your group's three best questions to share with the whole class. Be ready to explain to the class why you think some questions are better than others.

RHETORICAL PROBLEMS: REACHING READERS EFFECTIVELY

As we suggested in the introduction, writers wrestle with two categories of problems—subject-matter problems and rhetorical problems. The previous section introduced you to subject-matter problems; we turn now to rhetorical problems.

In their final products, writers need to say something significant about their subjects to an audience, for a purpose, in an appropriate form and style. This network of questions related to audience, purpose, form, and style constitute rhetorical problems, and these problems often loom as large for writers as do the subject-matter problems that drive their writing in the first place. Indeed, rhetorical problems and subject-matter problems are so closely linked that writers can't address one without addressing the other. For example, the very questions you ask about your subject matter are influenced by your audience and purpose. Before you can decide what to say about content, you need to ask: Who am I writing for and why? What does my audience already know (and not know) about my topic? Will the question I pose already interest them, or do I have to hook their interest? What effect do I want my writing to have on that audience? How should I structure my essay and what tone and voice should I adopt?

In Chapter 4, we discuss extensively the rhetorical problems that writers must pose and solve. In this chapter we simply introduce you to one extended example of a rhetorical problem. From a student's point of view, we might call this "the problem of varying rules." From our perspective, we call it "the problem of closed versus open forms."

AN EXAMPLE OF A RHETORICAL PROBLEM: CLOSED VERSUS OPEN FORMS

In our experience, beginning college writers are often bothered by the ambiguity and slipperiness of rules governing writing. Many beginning writers wish that good writing followed consistent rules, such as "Never use 'I' in a formal paper" or "Start every paragraph with a topic sentence." The problem is that different kinds of writing follow different rules, leaving the writer with rhetorical choices rather than with hard and fast formulas for success. To develop this point, we begin by asking you to consider a problem about how writing might be classified.

Read the following short pieces of nonfiction prose. The first is a letter to the editor written by a professional civil engineer in response to a newspaper editorial arguing for the development of wind-generated electricity. The second piece is the opening page of an autobiographical essay by writer Minnie Bruce Pratt about her experiences as a white woman living in a predominantly black neighborhood. After reading the two samples carefully, proceed to the discussion questions that follow.

DAVID ROCKWOOD

A LETTER TO THE EDITOR

1   Your editorial on November 16, "Get Bullish on Wind Power," is based on fantasy rather than fact. There are several basic reasons why wind-generated power can in no way serve as a reasonable major alternative to other electrical energy supply alternatives for the Pacific Northwest power system.

2   First and foremost, wind power is unreliable. Electric power generation is evaluated not only on the amount of energy provided, but also on its ability to meet system peak

load requirements on an hourly, daily, and weekly basis. In other words, an effective power system would have to provide enough electricity to meet peak demands in a situation when the wind energy would be unavailable—either in no wind situations or in severe blizzard conditions, which would shut down the wind generators. Because wind power cannot be relied on at times of peak needs, it would have to be backed up by other power generation resources at great expense and duplication of facilities.

Secondly, there are major unsolved problems involved in the design of wind generation facilities, particularly for those located in rugged mountain areas. Ice storms, in particular, can cause sudden dynamic problems for the rotating blades and mechanisms which could well result in breakdown or failure of the generators. Furthermore, the design of the facilities to meet the stresses imposed by high winds in these remote mountain regions, in the order of 125 miles per hour, would indeed escalate the costs.   3

Thirdly, the environmental impact of constructing wind generation facilities amounting to 28 percent of the region's electrical supply system (as proposed in your editorial) would be tremendous. The Northwest Electrical Power system presently has a capacity of about 37,000 megawatts of hydro power and 10,300 megawatts of thermal, for a total of about 48,000 megawatts. Meeting 28 percent of this capacity by wind power generators would, most optimistically, require about 13,400 wind towers, each with about 1,000 kilowatt (one megawatt) generating capacity. These towers, some 100 to 200 feet high, would have to be located in the mountains of Oregon and Washington. These would encompass hundreds of square miles of pristine mountain area, which, together with interconnecting transmission facilities, control works, and roads would indeed have major adverse environmental impacts on the region.   4

There are many other lesser problems of control and maintenance of such a system. Let it be said that, from my experience and knowledge as a professional engineer, the use of wind power as a major resource in the Pacific Northwest power system, is strictly a pipe dream.   5

MINNIE BRUCE PRATT

FROM "IDENTITY: SKIN BLOOD HEART"

I live in a part of Washington, D.C. that white suburbanites called "the jungle" during the uprising of the '60s—perhaps still do, for all I know. When I walk the two-and-a-half blocks to H St. NE, to stop in at the bank, to leave my boots off at the shoe-repair-and-lock shop, I am most usually the only white person in sight. I've seen two other whites, women, in the year I've lived here. (This does not count white folks in cars, passing through. In official language, H St., NE, is known as "The H Street Corridor," as in something to be passed through quickly, going from your place, on the way to elsewhere.)   1

When I walk three blocks in a slightly different direction, down Maryland Avenue, to go to my lover's house, I pass the yards of Black folks: the yard of the lady who keeps children, with its blue-and-red windmill, its roses-of-sharon; the yard of the man who delivers vegetables with its stacked slatted crates; the yard of the people next to the Righteous Branch Commandment Church-of-God (Seventh Day) with its tomatoes in the summer, its collards in the fall. In the summer, folks sit out on their porches or   2 steps or sidewalks; when I walk by, if I lift my head and look toward them and speak, "Hey," they may speak, say, "Hey" or "How you doing?" or perhaps just nod. In the spring, I was afraid to smile when I spoke, because that might be too familiar, but by the end of summer I had walked back and forth so often, I was familiar, so sometimes we shared comments about the mean weather.

3   I am comforted by any of these speakings for, to tell you the truth, they make me feel at home. I am living far from where I was born; it has been twenty years since I have lived in that place where folks, Black and white, spoke to each other when they met on the street or in the road. So when two Black men dispute country matters, calling across the corners of 8th St—"Hey, Roland, did you ever see a hog catch a rat?"— "I seen a hog catch a *snake*"—"How about a rat? Ever see one catch a *rat*?"—I am grateful to be living within sound of their voices, to hear a joking that reminds me, with a startled pain, of my father, putting on his tales for his friends, the white men gathered at the drugstore.

FOR WRITING AND DISCUSSION

Working in small groups or as a whole class, list the main differences you see between these two pieces of writing. Then try to reach consensus on the following specific tasks:

1. Create a metaphor, simile, or analogy that best sums up your feelings about the most important differences between Rockwood's and Pratt's writing: "Rockwood's writing is like . . . , but Pratt's writing is like . . . ."
2. If you are working in a group, help your group's recorder prepare a brief explanation for why your metaphors are apt. How do your metaphors help clarify or explain the differences between the two pieces of writing?

Now that you have done some thinking on your own about the differences between these two examples, turn to our brief analysis.

Distinctions Between Closed and Open Forms of Writing

David Rockwood's letter and Minnie Pratt's excerpt are both examples of nonfiction prose. But as these examples illustrate, nonfiction prose can vary enormously in form and style. From the perspective of structure, we can place nonfiction prose along a continuum that goes from closed to open forms of writing (see Figure 1.1, on p. 14).

Of our two pieces of prose, Rockwood's letter illustrates tightly closed writing and falls at the far left end of the continuum. The elements that make this writing closed are the presence of an explicit thesis in the introduction (i.e., wind-generated power isn't a reasonable alternative energy source in the Pacific Northwest) and the writer's consistent development of that thesis throughout the body (i.e., "First and foremost, wind power is unreliable. . . . Secondly, there are major unsolved [design] problems. . . . Thirdly, . . ."). Once the thesis is stated, the reader knows the point of the essay and can predict its structure. The reader also knows that the writer's point won't change as the essay progresses. Because its

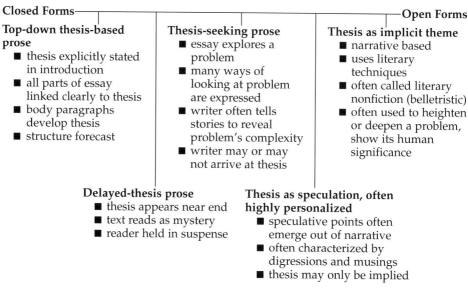

Closed Forms ── Open Forms

Top-down thesis-based prose
- thesis explicitly stated in introduction
- all parts of essay linked clearly to thesis
- body paragraphs develop thesis
- structure forecast

Thesis-seeking prose
- essay explores a problem
- many ways of looking at problem are expressed
- writer often tells stories to reveal problem's complexity
- writer may or may not arrive at thesis

Thesis as implicit theme
- narrative based
- uses literary techniques
- often called literary nonfiction (belletristic)
- often used to heighten or deepen a problem, show its human significance

Delayed-thesis prose
- thesis appears near end
- text reads as mystery
- reader held in suspense

Thesis as speculation, often highly personalized
- speculative points often emerge out of narrative
- often characterized by digressions and musings
- thesis may only be implied

FIGURE 1.1   A Continuum of Essay Types: Closed to Open Forms

structure is transparent and predictable, the success of closed-form prose rests entirely on its ideas, which must "surprise" readers by asserting something new, challenging, doubtful, or controversial. It aims to change the reader's view of the subject through the power of reason, logic, and evidence. Closed-form prose is what most college professors write when doing their own scholarly research, and it is what they most often expect of their students. It is also the most common kind of writing in professional and business contexts.

Pratt's writing falls at the far right of the closed-to-open continuum. It resists reduction to a single, summarizable thesis and leaves the reader in suspense about where it is going. Open-form essays are often organized chronologically; they tell a story rather than support an announced main point. This kind of writing is narrative based rather than thesis based. Narrative-based essays still have a focus, but the focus is more like the theme in a work of fiction than the thesis of an argument. Often the point of a narrative is implied rather than explicitly stated. Readers may argue over the point in the same way that they argue over the meaning of a film or novel.

As you can see from the continuum in Figure 1.1, essays can fall anywhere along the scale. Not all thesis-with-support writing has to be top down, stating its thesis explicitly in the introduction. In some cases writers choose to delay the thesis, creating a more exploratory, open-ended, "let's think through this together" feeling before finally stating the main point late in the essay. In some cases writers explore a problem without *ever* finding a satisfactory thesis, creating an essay that is thesis seeking rather than thesis supporting; that is, aiming at deepening the question, refusing to accept an easy answer. Such essays may replicate their author's process of exploring a problem and include digressions, speculations, conjectures, multiple perspectives, and occasional invitations to the reader to help solve the problem. When writers reach the far right-hand position on the continuum, they no longer state an explicit thesis. Instead, like novelists or short-story writers, they embed their points in plot, imagery, dialogue, and so forth, leaving their readers to *infer* a theme from the text.

How Rules Vary Along the Continuum

Clearly, essays at opposite ends of this continuum operate in different ways and obey different rules. Because each position on the continuum has its appropriate uses, the writer's challenge is to determine which sort of writing is most appropriate for a given situation.

As you will see in later chapters, the kind of writing you choose depends on your purpose, your intended audience, and your genre (a genre is a recurring type of writing with established conventions, such as an academic article, a newspaper feature story, a grant proposal, an article for *Seventeen* or *Rolling Stone*, and so forth). Thus if you were writing an analytical paper for an academic audience, you would typically choose a closed-form structure and your finished product would include such elements as the following:

- an explicit thesis in the introduction
- forecasting of structure
- cohesive and unified paragraphs with topic sentences
- clear transitions between sentences and between parts
- no digressions

But if you were writing an autobiographical narrative about, say, what family means to you, you would probably move toward the open end of the continuum and violate one or more of these conventions (note how extensively Pratt violates them). It's not that open-form prose doesn't have rules; it's that the rules are different, just as the rules for jazz are different from the rules for a classical sonata.

For another perspective on how rules vary, consider two frequently encountered high school writing assignments: the five-paragraph theme and the "What I Did Last Summer" essay. The five-paragraph theme is a by-the-numbers way to teach closed-form, thesis-with-support writing. It emphasizes logical development, unity, and coherence. The five-paragraph structure may emerge naturally if you are writing an argument based on three supporting reasons—an introductory paragraph, three body paragraphs (one for each reason), and a concluding paragraph. Rockwood's letter is a real-world example of a five-paragraph essay, even though Rockwood certainly didn't have that format in mind when writing.

In contrast, the "What I Did Last Summer" assignment calls for a different sort of writing, probably an open-form structure closer to that of Pratt's piece. If you tried to write the "What I Did Last Summer" essay with the thesis-up-front rules of the five-paragraph essay, you would be hamstrung from the start; the summer essay calls not for an argument, but for a well-plotted, vivid story. Whether the writer chooses a closed-form or an open-form approach depends on the intended audience of the piece and the writer's purpose.

FOR WRITING AND DISCUSSION

Do you and your classmates most enjoy writing prose at the closed or more open end of the continuum? Prior to class discussion, work individually by recalling a favorite piece of writing that you have done in the past. Jot down a brief description of the kind of writing this was (a poem, a personal experience essay, a research paper, a newspaper story, a persuasive argument). Then, working in small groups or as a whole class, report one at a time on your favorite piece of writing and speculate where it falls on the continuum from closed to open forms. Are you at your best in closed-form writing that calls for an explicit thesis statement and logical support? Or are you at your best in more open and personal forms?

Is there a wide range of preferences in your class? If so, how do you account for this variance? If not, how do you account for the narrow range?

Summary

This chapter has introduced you to the notion of writers as questioners and problem posers who wrestle with both subject-matter and rhetorical problems. We have shown how writers start with questions or problems about their subject matter, rather than with topic areas, and how they take their time resolving the uncertainties raised by such questions. We saw that writers must ask questions about their rhetorical situation and make decisions about content, form, and style based on their understanding of their purpose and of their audience. We described how the rules governing writing vary as the writer moves along the continuum from closed to open forms.

The next chapter looks closely at how writers pose problems and pursue them in depth through behind-the-scenes exploratory writing and talking.

BRIEF WRITING PROJECT

We close out this chapter with a brief writing project (we like to call it a *microtheme*) designed to help you recognize the elements of a good subject-matter problem. You will write a short piece similar in structure to the introductions of many academic articles.

Write a one-page microtheme that poses a question about animals (or about some other topic provided by your instructor). In addition to explaining your question clearly, you will need to help readers understand three things about it: (1) why you are invested in your question, that is, why it interests you or engages you; (2) why the question is problematic, that is, what makes it a genuine question or problem; and (3) why the question is significant or worth pursuing, that is, what benefit will come from solving it. Your microtheme should NOT answer the question; your purpose is only to ask it.

This assignment builds on the For Writing and Discussion exercise on page 10 which asked you to brainstorm questions about animals and then to establish criteria for selecting the better questions. You should not try to answer your question for this assignment. Indeed, you aren't supposed to know the answer—that's part of what makes it a good question.

To help you understand the assignment more fully, we will give you our own answer to the problem posed earlier: What makes a question a good one? Effective questions meet the following three criteria: (1) the writer is invested in the question; (2) the question is problematic; and (3) the question is significant (worth solving). We now look at each of these criteria in turn.

Becoming Invested in a Question

It is possible to brainstorm questions about animals in a game-playing way without ever becoming interested in them. At some point, however, you should look for ways to make one of the questions matter to you. Sometimes this interest is practical; finding an answer might bring positive consequences to people's lives. Or, your interest can be primarily intellectual; answering the question will advance your knowledge in some useful way, perhaps by filling in a piece of a larger intellectual puzzle. In either case, your personal investment in the question will go a long way toward helping you interest your reader in it. To illustrate personal investment, here is a microtheme based on a question about animals that truly engages coauthor John Bean.

HOW DO YOU GET RID OF YOUR DOG'S FLEAS?

1   A couple months ago we adopted into our family a lovable mutt from the local Pet Protectors Society. Unfortunately, the dog became infested with fleas and started scratching himself miserably day and night. The fleas became a serious problem both for the dog (because constant scratching at fleas leads to painful skin allergies and diseases) and for us (because we worried about him and his scratching was a constant annoyance).

2   We tried everything to get rid of the fleas. First, we shampooed the dog in flea soap, but the fleas were hopping on him again within ten minutes. Then we shampooed him once more, but this time also immersed him in a flea dip guaranteed to last for twenty-one days. Within an hour we were combing live fleas out of his fur. We thought perhaps we were doing the shampooing and dipping wrong, so we hired a professional dog groomer to dip the dog. No luck—the scratching quickly returned.

We then went to our local hardware store, where a clerk told us we needed a three-pronged attack: we had to de-flea the dog, de-flea the house, and de-flea the yard. So we bought an arsenal of flea-poison products (my family and I felt awful about using poisons, but what else to do?). We flea-bombed the house (seven cans of the stuff); we flea-poisoned the yard with a yard insecticide; and again we shampooed and flea-dipped the dog. That night we heard the dog scratching again, and the next morning we were combing live fleas out of his fur. Then we began hearing about alternative approaches. A veterinarian told us about using nematodes (a biological organism) that eat flea larvae. Someone else told us about beating mixtures of diatomaceous earth and borax into our carpet. But these are expensive and time-consuming approaches that may not work. So what can we do to get rid of our dog's fleas?   3

Clearly, Bean would spend good money for an article on how to get rid of fleas. This is a question about animals in which the writer is invested—what you might call an internally motivated question, not simply a game-playing one.

Choosing a Question That Is Problematic

The question about controlling fleas is problematic because the solutions that immediately come to mind, as Bean shows, didn't work. In contrast, a question about how to get dirt off your hands poses no real problem (wash them in soap and water). Bean's microtheme not only states the problem, but also shows *why* it is problematic by describing the family's failed attempts to get rid of fleas. Problematic questions either have no immediately apparent answers or have multiple answers. Some strategies writers use to show that a question is problematic include the following:

- Show your own (or previous researchers') failed attempts to solve the problem. (The passage describing the failed attempts to get rid of fleas uses this strategy.)
- Describe a controversy about the question showing how and why experts disagree. (For example, if the question concerns the value of saving the spotted owl, the writer can summarize opposing arguments.)
- Describe the subject in such a way that the puzzling nature of the question gradually emerges. (For example, in the student microtheme at the end of this chapter the writer describes the swarming behavior of starlings in enough detail to evoke a sense of puzzlement and mystery.)
- Show why an expected or easy answer isn't satisfactory. (For example, you might show why "to keep themselves clean" may not be a satisfactory answer to the question, "Why do cats lick themselves?")
- Narrate your own attempts to think through the problem, revealing how none of the answers you came up with fully satisfied you. (For example, if you ask, "Is it ethical to keep animals in a zoo?" you might describe your previous thinking about the pros and cons of keeping animals in zoos and show why no single position satisfies you.)

Choosing a Question That Is Significant

A question can be problematic without seeming significant to an audience. The writer often needs to point out why a problem is worth pursuing. If readers think that fleas are merely a minor annoyance, they might respond, "Just let the dog scratch" to Bean's query about getting rid of fleas. Consequently, Bean shows the significance of his dog's flea problem by explaining that fleas can cause serious skin diseases for the dog and are a source of constant annoyance and worry for the family. As you develop your essay, be thinking of ways to hook into your readers' concerns and values so that your question's significance is recognizable to them. If the first criterion for a good question is that the writer should be invested in it, our third criterion—significance—aims at getting the reader invested. Here are some typical ways in which writers can show the significance of a problem.

- Show the practical benefits of solving the problem. (For example, knowing why dinosaurs became extinct may help humans better understand how to prepare for and survive environmental disasters.)
- Show the intellectual benefits of solving the problem. (For example, if we understand how spiders "know" how to spin webs, we may be able to understand better how genetic encoding works.)
- Show the negative consequences of not solving the problem, in terms of either actual bad consequences or lost opportunities. (For example, failure to solve the flea problem might lead to serious skin diseases for the dog.)
- Pose the question in such a way that it provokes the reader's natural curiosity. (We are all problem solvers by nature and find an innate satisfaction in resolving a question. Often we seek solutions to problems for the sheer joy of solving them.)

Writing Your Microtheme

A premise throughout this book is that good finished products grow out of a rich exploratory process. We suggest that you make a list of possible questions to share with classmates. As you and your classmates pool your questions, begin looking for those that most intrigue you. Ask each other questions such as:

- Why are you interested in this question? What personal experiences or previous knowledge does it relate to?
- What makes it problematic?
- What makes it significant and worth pursuing?

Choose a question that interests you and write a quick rough draft, remembering that you aren't supposed to know the answer, just the question. Pretend that you are writing under exam conditions and have only twenty minutes to write your microtheme. Then take some time off. When you return to your draft later, revise it to make it as interesting as possible. Ask a friend to read it, and see if your friend can explain to you (without looking at the draft) what your question is, why it is problematic, and why it is significant. Most important, ask your friend if he or she would like to read an essay or article that went on to try to *answer* your question. If your friend says yes, you can be pleased that your microtheme hooked at least one reader.

Student Example

To conclude this chapter, here is an example of a microtheme written by a student in response to the assignment.

The Starling Mystery

Several years ago the Pioneer Square district in Seattle was overrun   1
with starlings. Some friends and I went down to the waterfront area one
evening to watch them come in. Starting just before dusk you could see swarms
of dim specks in the sky coming from all different directions and converg-
ing in the air over Pioneer Square. As the specks got closer, you could see
that they were thousands of birds. They would swoop over a small park in
the center of Pioneer Square and then circle away. They seemed to be waiting until all the starlings in the city joined them. Gradually the swarm of
starlings would get bigger and bigger, and they would fly over the park like
squadrons of airplanes in an air show. They would fly so close together that
you couldn't tell how they signaled each other to turn. Eventually the swarm
got so huge that the sky would darken when they flew by. All of a sudden,
the whole swarm would swoop down on the park and land in the trees so that
the trees were totally infested with the birds, and their squawking sound
would be so loud you could hardly talk.

Ever since that moment, I have wondered what causes starlings to exhibit   2
this strange behavior. When you see starlings in your yard during most of
the year, they are just like robins or sparrows or other normal, ordinary
birds that you see around all the time. But sometimes they exhibit this
swarming, gathering behavior, as if they were all attending some bird convention. What makes them do this? If scientists could find out the answer,
they might learn something about how species of animals are wired geneti-
cally to behave in different ways.

chapter 2

Pursuing Problems
Exploratory Writing and Talking

When Ofelya Bagdasaryan completed her first university exam in the United States, she was confident that she would earn a high grade. "I had studied hard, memorized the material and written it perfectly in the examination book," she recalled.

But Ofelya, 26, a recent immigrant from Armenia in the former Soviet Union, was in for a rude shock. When the exams were returned the following week, she discovered that the professor had given her a D. "But I repeated exactly what the textbook said," she told her teaching assistant. "Yes," he replied, "but you didn't tell us your [judgment of what the book said]."

—David Wallechinsky, *Journalist*

My professor said that I received a low grade on this essay because I just gave my opinion. Then she said that she didn't *care* what my *opinion* was; she wanted an *argument*.

—Student overheard in hallway

"In management, people don't merely 'write papers,' they solve problems," said [business professor Kimbrough Sherman]. . . . He explained that he wanted to construct situations where students would have to "wallow in complexity" and work their way out, as managers must.

—A. Kimbrough Sherman, *Management Professor*

In the previous chapter, we introduced you to the role of the writer as questioner and problem poser. In this chapter and the next, we narrow our focus primarily to academic writing, which most frequently means closed-form, thesis-based essays and articles. Mastering this kind of writing is necessary to your success in college and requires a behind-the-scenes ability to think deeply and rigorously about problems, pursuing them at length. In this chapter we show you how to use exploratory writing and talking to do this behind-the-scenes work. The strategies explained in this chapter will help you develop powerful thinking and studying habits for every discipline.

WHAT DOES A PROFESSOR WANT?

It is important for you to understand the kind of thinking that most college professors look for in student writing. As the first two chapter-opening quotations indicate, many first-year college students are baffled by their professors' responses to their writing. Ofelya Bagdasaryan mistakenly thought her teachers wanted her to rehash her textbook. The second student thought her teacher wanted her to describe how she felt about a subject (opinion), not why someone else ought to feel the same way (argument). But as management professor A. Kimbrough Sherman explains in the third quotation, college instructors expect students to wrestle with problems by applying the concepts, data, and thought processes they learn in a course to new situations. As Sherman puts it, students must learn to "wallow in complexity" and work their way out.

Learning to Wallow in Complexity

Wallowing in complexity is not what most first-year college students aspire to do. (Certainly that wasn't what we, the authors of this text, had uppermost in our minds when we sailed off to college!) New college students tend to shut down their creative thinking processes too quickly and head straight for closure to a problem. Harvard psychologist William Perry, who has studied the intellectual development of college students, found that few of them become skilled wallowers in complexity until late in their college careers. According to Perry, most students come to college as "dualists," believing that all questions have right or wrong answers, that professors know the right answers, and that the student's job is to learn them. Of course, these beliefs are partially correct. First-year students who hope to become second-year students must indeed understand and memorize mounds of facts, data, definitions, and basic concepts.

But true intellectual growth requires the kind of problematizing we discussed in Chapter 1. It requires students to *do* something with their new knowledge, to apply it to new situations, to conduct the kinds of inquiry, research, analysis, and argument pursued by experts in each discipline. Instead of confronting only questions that have right answers, students need to confront what cognitive psychologists call *ill-structured problems*.

An ill-structured problem is one that may not a have single, correct answer. Often these problems require the thinker to operate in the absence of full and complete data. People face ill-structured problems every day in their personal lives: What should I major in? Should I continue to date person X? Should I take this job or keep looking? Likewise, many decisions in professional and public life are excruciatingly difficult precisely because they concern ill-structured problems that are unsolvable in any clear-cut and certain way: What should be done about homelessness? What public policies will best solve the problem of global warming or the national debt or the lack of affordable health care for our citizens?

Similarly, college professors pursue ill-structured problems in their professional writing. The kinds of problems vary from discipline to discipline, but they all require the writer to use reasons and evidence to support a tentative solution. Because your instructors want you to learn how to do the same kind of thinking, they often phrase essay exam questions or writing assignments as ill-structured problems. They are looking not for one right answer, but for well-supported arguments that acknowledge alternative views. A C paper and an A paper may even have the same "answer" (identical thesis statements), but the C writer may have waded only ankle deep into the mud of complexity, whereas the A writer wallowed in it and worked a way out.

What skills are required for successful wallowing? Specialists in critical thinking have identified the following:

1. The ability to pose problematic questions
2. The ability to analyze a problem in all its dimensions—to define its key terms, determine its causes, understand its history, appreciate its human dimension and its connection to one's own personal experience, and appreciate what makes it problematic or complex
3. The ability (and doggedness) to find, gather, and interpret facts, data, and other information relevant to the problem (often involving library or field research)
4. The ability to imagine alternative solutions to the problem, to see different ways in which the question might be answered, and different perspectives for viewing it
5. The ability to analyze competing approaches and answers, to construct arguments for and against alternatives, and to choose the best solution in light of values, objectives, and other criteria that you determine and articulate
6. The ability to write an effective argument justifying your choice while acknowledging counterarguments

We discuss and develop these skills throughout this text.

In addition to these generic thinking abilities, critical thinking requires what psychologists call *domain-specific* skills. Each academic discipline has its own characteristic ways of approaching knowledge and its own specialized habits of mind. The questions asked by psychologists differ from those asked by historians or anthropologists; the evidence and assumptions used to support arguments in literary analysis differ from those in philosophy or sociology.

What all disciplines value, however, is the ability to manage complexity, and this skill marks the final stage of William Perry's developmental scheme. At an intermediate stage of development, after they have moved beyond dualism, students become what Perry calls "multiplists." At this stage students believe that since the experts disagree on many questions, all answers are equally valid. Professors want students merely to have an opinion and to state it strongly. A multiplist believes that a low grade on an essay indicates no more than that the teacher didn't like his or her opinion. Multiplists are often cynical about professors and grades; to them, college is a game of guessing what the teacher wants to hear. Students emerge into Perry's final stages—what he calls "relativism" and "commitment in relativism"—when they are able to take a position in the face of complexity and to justify that decision through reasons and evidence while weighing and acknowledging contrary reasons and counterevidence. The three quotations that open this chapter exemplify Perry's scheme: Whereas the first student sees her task as recalling right answers, the second sees it as forcefully expressing an opinion, and Professor Sherman articulates what is expected at Perry's last stages—wading into the messiness of complexity and working your way back to solid ground.

Seeing Each Academic Discipline as a Field of Inquiry and Argument

When you study a new discipline, you must learn not only the knowledge that scholars in that discipline have acquired over the years, but also the processes they used to discover that knowledge. It is useful to think of each academic discipline as a network of conversations in which participants exchange information, respond to each other's questions, and express agreements and disagreements. The scholarly articles and books that many of your instructors write (or would write if they could find the time) are formal, permanent contributions to an ongoing discussion carried on in print. By extension, your college's or university's library is a huge collection of conversations frozen in time. Each book or article represents a contribution to a conversation; each writer agreed with some of his or her predecessors and disagreed with others.

As each discipline evolves and changes, its central questions evolve also, creating a fascinating, dynamic conversation that defines the discipline. At any given moment, scholars are pursuing hundreds of cutting-edge questions in each discipline. Table 2.1 provides examples of questions that scholars have debated over the years as well as questions they are addressing today.

Of course, students can't immediately address the current, cutting-edge questions of most disciplines, particularly the sciences. But even novice science students can examine historical controversies. Beginning physics students, for example, can wrestle with Archimedes' problem of how to measure the volume of a crown or with other early problems concerning the mechanics of levers, pulleys, and inclined planes. In the humanities and social sciences, beginning students are often asked to study, explore, and debate some of the enduring questions that have puzzled generations of scholars.

- Is there a rational basis for belief in God?
- Why does Hamlet delay?
- Should Truman have dropped the atomic bomb on Hiroshima? On Nagasaki?
- What is the most just economic system?
- Do humans have free will?

As you study a discipline, you are learning how to enter its network of conversations. To do so, you have to build up a base of knowledge about the disci-

TABLE 2.1   Scholarly Questions in Different Disciplines

Field	Examples of Current Cutting-Edge Questions	Examples of Historical Controversies
Anatomy	What is the effect of a pregnant rat's alcohol ingestion on the development of fetal eye tissue?	In 1628, William Harvey produced a treatise arguing that the heart, through repeated contractions, caused blood to circulate through the body. His views were attacked by followers of the Greek physician Galen.
Literature	To what extent does the structure of a work of literature, for example, Conrad's *Heart of Darkness*, reflect the class and gender bias of the author?	In the 1920s a group of New Critics argued that the interpretation of a work of literature should be based on close examination of the work's imagery and form and that the intentions of the writer and the biases of the reader were not important. These views held sway in U.S. universities until the late 1960s, when they came increasingly under attack by deconstructionists and other postmoderns, who claimed that author intentions and reader bias were an important part of the words' meaning.
Linguistics	Do all the languages of the world descend from the same protolanguage or, in the evolution of humankind, did a variety of languages spring up independently around the globe?	Do humans learn language through behavior modification, as proposed by many learning theorists in the 1950s, or is there an innate language-learning center in the brain that is "hard-wired" to learn a language, as proposed by Noam Chomsky?
Psychology	What are the underlying causes of gender identification? To what extent are differences between male and female behavior explainable by nature (genetics, body chemistry) versus nurture (social learning)?	In the early 1900s, under the influence of Sigmund Freud, psychoanalytic psychologists began explaining human behavior in terms of unconscious drives and mental processes that stemmed from repressed childhood experiences. Later, psychoanalysts were opposed by behaviorists, who rejected the notion of the unconscious and explained behavior as responses to environmental stimuli.

pline, learn its terminology, observe its conversations, read its major works, see how it asks questions, learn its methods. To help you get a clearer sense of how written "conversation" works within a discipline—that is, how a writer poses a question and proposes an answer—the next section examines a typical introduction to an academic article.

How a Typical Introduction Poses a Question and Proposes an Answer

To illustrate the typical structure of an academic introduction, we use a psychology article that has generated continuous controversy in the discipline since its publication in the early 1960s—"The Myth of Mental Illness" by Thomas S. Szasz. Szasz's article appeared in a scholarly journal in psychology, but his ideas soon spread into the popular culture and have had a marked effect on popular conceptions of mental illness. Along with Ken Kesey's novel *One Flew over the Cuckoo's Nest* (and the subsequent film of the same name, starring Jack Nicholson), Szasz's ideas helped changed governmental policy toward involuntary hospitalization in mental asylums. We will explain these changes later, but first we want you to understand the elements of a typical introduction to an academic article.

> My aim in this essay is to raise the question "Is there such a thing as mental illness?" and to argue that there is not. Since the notion of mental illness is extremely widely used nowadays, inquiry into the ways in which this term is employed would seem to be especially indicated. Mental illness, of course, is not literally a "thing"—or physical object—and hence it can "exist" only in the same sort of way in which other theoretical concepts exist. Yet, familiar theories are in the habit of posing, sooner or later—at least to those who come to believe in them—as "objective truths" (or "facts"). During certain historical periods, explanatory conceptions such as deities, witches, and microorganisms appeared not only as theories but as self-evident causes of a vast number of events. I submit that today mental illness is widely regarded in a somewhat similar fashion, that is, as the cause of innumerable diverse happenings. As an antidote to the complacent use of the notion of mental illness—whether as a self-evident phenomenon, theory, or cause—let us ask this question: What is meant when it is asserted that someone is mentally ill?
>
> In what follows, I shall describe briefly the main uses to which the concept of mental illness has been put. I shall argue that this notion has outlived whatever usefulness it might have had and that it now functions merely as a convenient myth.
>
> —Thomas S. Szasz, "The Myth of Mental Illness"

This introduction, like most introductions to academic articles, includes the following three features:

1. A question or problem to be investigated, including, if needed, an indication of its problematic nature and its significance. Often the question is explicitly

stated, but sometimes it is only implied. Thomas Szasz states his question directly: "Is there such a thing as mental illness?"

2. The writer's tentative answer to this question (the essay's thesis), which must in some way bring something new or surprising to the audience. In closed-form articles such as this one, the thesis is stated prominently in the introduction. In this instance, Szasz's answer to his opening question— "There is no such thing as 'mental illness' "—goes against the grain of widely accepted theory.

3. A structural or organizational map. Frequently the last section of an academic introduction describes the organizational structure of the essay in order to help the reader navigate through it. The more difficult the ideas, the more readers appreciate a blueprint or map. Szasz's organizational map tells readers that he will first discuss historical uses of the concept of mental illness and then argue that the concept of mental illness is no longer useful.

The body of Szasz's article had to present a strong argument to support his shocking thesis. His reasoning was effective enough to help create a political movement that eventually closed many state-run mental asylums and released thousands of mental patients. Many current analysts believe that the closing of mental hospitals led to a dramatic increase in homelessness because former mental patients had nowhere to go when they left the hospitals. As a consequence, today many observers advocate reopening mental asylums and placing the homeless mentally ill back in hospitals, often involuntarily. In making their case, psychologists and other specialists almost always begin with an attack on Szasz's article, offering their own refutation of his arguments.

Although most scholarly publications don't have the political and social consequences of Szasz's article, they do aim to have an impact on their disciplines either by challenging prevailing beliefs and assumptions (as does Szasz's article) or by contributing to the solution of a problem of interest to the discipline. Many of the papers you will be asked to write in college will require you, in some way, to exhibit the same kind of thinking—to pose a problem, to assert a tentative, risky answer (your thesis), and to support it with reasons and evidence. One of the major aims of this book is to teach you how to do this kind of thinking and writing.

In the rest of this chapter we will explain the behind-the-scenes role of exploratory writing and talking. The neatness of Szasz's introduction—its statement of a focused problem, its confidently asserted thesis, its clear forecasting of structure—masks the messiness of the exploratory process that precedes the actual writing of an academic essay. Szasz began contemplating the problem of mental illness long before he formulated his answer or began writing an article. Underneath the surface of all academic essays is a long process of exploratory writing and talking, including periods of intense thinking, reflecting, studying, researching, notebook or journal writing, and sharing. Through this process, the writer defines the question or problem and eventually works out an answer or response. Some of your professors may build opportunities for exploratory writing and talking directly into their courses in the form of journals, in-class freewriting, collaborative group work, E-mail exchanges, class discussions and debates, and so forth. Other teachers will spend most of the class time lecturing and leave you on your own to explore ideas. The rest of this chapter presents strategies and techniques that many writers have found useful for exploring ideas.

TECHNIQUES FOR EXPLORATORY WRITING AND TALKING

To use language for exploration, you need to imagine a friendly, nonjudgmental audience with whom you can share ideas in a risk-free environment. Perhaps you can imagine yourself as your audience, or, if you prefer, a friend or classmate. Your purpose is to get ideas down on paper to help you see what you are thinking. Exploratory writing jogs your memory, helps you connect disparate ideas, lets you put difficult concepts into your own words, and invites you to see the relevance of your studies to your own life. In this section we describe five useful techniques for exploratory writing and talking: freewriting, thought letters, idea mapping, dialectic discussions, and active reading and research.

Freewriting

Freewriting, also sometimes called nonstop writing or silent, sustained writing, asks you to record your thinking directly. To freewrite, put pen to paper (or sit at your typewriter or computer screen, perhaps turning *off* the monitor so that you can't even see what you are writing) and write rapidly, *nonstop,* for ten to fifteen minutes at a stretch. Don't worry about grammar, spelling, organization, transitions, or other features of edited writing. The object is to think of as many ideas as possible. Some freewriting looks like stream of consciousness. Some is more organized and focused, although it lacks the logical connections and development that would make it suitable for an audience of strangers.

Many freewriters find that their initial reservoir of ideas runs out in three to five minutes. If this happens, force yourself to keep your pen moving. If you can't think of anything to say, write "relax" over and over (or "this is stupid" or "I'm stuck") until new ideas emerge.

What do you write about? The simplest answer is to write about anything—jot down what you are currently thinking and see where it leads. A more focused answer might be that the goal of freewriting—and other forms of exploratory writing and talking—is to pose problems or questions, the responses, answers, or solutions to which you can then explore. Since the authors are avid freewriters, we can use ourselves for illustration. We use freewriting for many purposes in our scholarly work. We freewrite when we are first becoming engaged with a problem. We often pose for ourselves trigger questions: "What really puzzles me about X?" "Why did I react so strongly to what person A said about X?" "How are my ideas about X different from A's?" We also freewrite extensively when doing scholarly reading. Although our note-taking systems differ, we both react strongly to articles or books we are reading and freewrite our own ideas about them into our notes. (See Chapter 6, in which we explain the process we use for "speaking back" to texts.) Finally, both of us freewrite when we get stuck in the process of writing a draft. If we come to a difficult section and find ourselves blocked, we turn away from the draft itself, find a sheet of scratch paper, and freewrite rapidly just to get the ideas flowing.

Many teachers assign freewriting in the form of journals, invention exercises for a formal essay, or in-class explorations. Mary Turla's journal entries, which you read in Chapter 1 (pp. 8–9), are examples of freewriting. Here is another example of a freewrite by a student thinking about the issue of homelessness.

> Let's take a minute and talk about the homeless. Homeless homeless. Today on my way to work I passed a homeless guy who smiled at me and I smiled back though he smelled bad. What are the reasons he was out on the street? Perhaps an extraordinary string of bad luck. Perhaps he was pushed out onto the street. Not a background of work ethic, no place to go, no way to get someplace to live that could be afforded, alcoholism. To what extent do government assistance, social spending, etc, keep people off the street? What benefits could a person get that stops "the cycle"? How does welfare affect homelessness, drug abuse programs, family planning? To what extent does the individual have control over homelessness? This question of course goes to the depth of the question of how community affects the individual. Relax, relax. What about the signs that I see on the way to work posted on the windows of businesses that read, "please don't give to panhandlers it only promotes drug abuse etc" a cheap way of getting homeless out of the way of business? Are homeless the natural end of unrestricted capitalism? What about the homeless people who are mentally ill? How can you maintain a living when haunted by paranoia? How do you decide if someone is mentally ill or just laughs at society? If one can't function obviously. How many mentally ill are out on the street? If you are mentally ill and have

```
lost the connections to others who might take care of you I can see

how you might end up on the street. What would it take to get treat-

ment? To what extent can mentally ill be treated? When I see a home-

less person I want to ask, How do you feel about the rest of society?

When you see "us" walk by how do you think of us? Do you possibly

care how we avoid you?
```

Note how this freewrite rambles, moving associatively from one topic or question to the next. Freewrites often have this kind of loose, associative structure. The value of such freewrites is that they help writers discover areas of interest or rudimentary beginnings of ideas. When you read back over one of your freewrites, try to find places that seem to you worth pursuing. Freewriters call these places hot spots, centers of interest, centers of gravity, or simply nuggets or seeds. The student who wrote the preceding freewrite discovered that he was particularly interested in the cluster of questions beginning "What about the homeless people who are mentally ill?" and he eventually wrote a research paper proposing a public policy for helping the mentally ill homeless.

Because we think this technique is of great value to writers, we suggest that you use it for many assignments and activities throughout this text. Each suggestion is highlighted with a special, freewriting icon, reproduced in the margin.

Informal Thought Letters

The informal *thought letter* is our term for a kind of exploratory writing used frequently by scholars in every discipline. When working on a piece of research, scholars often correspond with colleagues at other institutions who are interested in their work in progress. They exchange letters or E-mail to help them think through their current ideas and get feedback. In writing this text, for example, we exchanged numerous E-mail messages for each chapter; we also occasionally wrote hard-copy letters, running eight or ten pages long, in which we tried to talk on paper as a way of thinking through ideas with which we were wrestling. Most scholars have drawers full of such letters exchanged with colleagues.

An informal thought letter is similar to an extended form of freewriting, but it is usually longer, more detailed, and more focused on one or two key problems or questions. Whereas a ten-minute freewriting session might wander from one topic to another, a thought letter pursues one idea in search of fuller understanding and clarity.

Here is an exchange of E-mail thought letters initiated by a first-year literature student requesting help from her classmate, an international student from Taiwan. The literature student was working on a paper about Amy Tan's novel *The Joy Luck Club*. Note how her classmate's reply might help the writer reshape her thinking about the thesis she has formulated.

1   Hi Wu Li!

2   I finally figured out the questions I wanted to ask you about Chinese women! Thanks for agreeing to help me out. My title question is: "Does Traditional Chinese Culture Repress the Joy Luck Mothers' Expression of Their Senses of Self?" (I'm working on changing that title a bit--it's kind of wordy!)

3   My thesis sentence is: "Traditional Chinese culture seems to stifle a woman's ability to express her sense of self--her hopes, dreams, and goals, her identity, and her feelings of self-worth." I am going to base my paper on what happens in the novel to Lindo Jong, Ying-Ying St. Clair, and An-Mei Hsu.

4   One question I have for you then is, as a Chinese woman, do you agree with my thesis? Do you see this repression of women in your culture? Have you ever felt it yourself?

5   Since I am focusing on the mothers in The Joy Luck Club, I am focusing on a generation before yours. But do you know much about the experiences your mother and grandmother had with this subject? Do you think that Chinese women have traditionally had to give up their hopes, dreams, and goals, or do you see them as having been able to hang on to these in traditional Chinese culture? I have been doing some research, and it seems to me that Chinese females have almost no worth in traditional culture. I've read all these horrible stories about drowning girl babies at birth, or selling young girls for a penny, etc. How common is/was this sort of thing?

6   What do you think about An-Mei's story? Do you think she lost her sense of self? I would certainly say her mother did, but am going back and forth a little with An-Mei. In the "family" she was in (being the daughter of a wealthy man's concubine), what was her worth? In other words, what worth is typically attributed to the children of concubines? I have found nothing about this in my research, and would be curious to know.

7   I guess that's all the questions I have for now. Thanks again for your help! I'll see you in class tomorrow.

8   Linda

Dear Linda, 1

I don't think Chinese women feel repressed like you think. After I read 2
your letter I found myself thinking of the word <u>tradition</u>. This is difficult word to describe, and it seems to me it could have two definitions. It
could mean something old not existing now or exists in some changed way; or
it could mean something that is still carried on, like a custom, like a
Christmas dinner custom. I think of myself as traditional in the second
definition. I have traditions from my family, but I am not seen as old-
fashioned.

I do not know the experiences of my mother and grandmother on this sub- 3
ject of tradition. I don't know if Amy Tan's Chinese women are accurate Chinese history. My grandmother never told stories like Amy Tan has. I think
sometimes tradition in Chinese culture could look like repression in western culture. When I was younger, for example, I would always kneel and give
tea to my grandparents when I visited them. I did this to show respect, but
when I told some of my friends here in America about this custom they thought
I was being put in low place, not seen as equal.

I have difficulty answering your question about how common drowning girl 4
babies at birth was and your question about the worth of children of concubines. All this is complicated. Remember in China that parents' old age
economic survival completely depends on their children caring for them. Boy
child is more important than daughter for old age survival because the daughter traditionally leaves the family when she is married. I am not saying
that I believe this is right; I am saying that there is so much more to the
culture than just "the Chinese repress women."

I also think it is important to keep in mind that I am not the author- 5
ity on Chinese culture. China is big country with many different views on
your questions. However, I hope my views on tradition and repression help
you with your paper.

Wu Li 6

Idea Mapping

Another good technique for exploring ideas is idea mapping, a more visual method than freewriting. To make an idea map, draw a circle in the center of the page and write down your broad topic area (or a triggering question or your thesis) inside the circle. Then record your ideas on branches and subbranches that extend out from the center circle. As long as you pursue one train of thought, keep recording your ideas on subbranches off the main branch. But as soon as that chain of ideas runs dry, go back and start a new branch.

Often your thoughts will jump back and forth between one branch and another. This technique will help you see them as part of an emerging design rather than as strings of unrelated ideas. Additionally, idea mapping establishes at an early stage a sense of hierarchy in your ideas. If you enter an idea on a subbranch, you can see that you are more fully developing a previous idea. If you return to the hub and start a new branch, you can see that you are beginning a new train of thought.

An idea map usually records more ideas than a freewrite, but the ideas are not as fully developed. Writers who practice both techniques report that they can vary the kinds of ideas they generate, depending on which technique they choose. Figure 2.1 (on p. 34) shows an idea map created by the same student who wrote the previous freewrite on homelessness. When the student made this idea map, he had completed approximately ten hours of library research on the issue, What should society do about the mentally ill homeless? He used the idea map to try to find some order in his evolving thoughts on this topic.

Dialectic Discussion

Another effective way to explore the complexity of a topic is through face-to-face discussions with others, whether in class, over coffee in the student union, or late at night in bull sessions. Not all discussions are productive; some are too superficial and scattered, others too heated. Good ones are dialectic—participants with differing views on a topic try to understand each other and resolve their differences by examining contradictions in each person's position. The key to dialectic conversation is careful listening, made possible by an openness to each other's views. A dialectic discussion differs from a classic pro–con debate in which proponents of opposing positions, their views set in stone, attempt to win the argument. In a dialectic discussion, participants assume that each position has strengths and weaknesses and that even the strongest position contains inconsistencies, which should be exposed and examined. When dialectic conversation works well, participants scrutinize their own positions more critically and deeply, and often alter their views. True dialectic conversation implies growth and change, not a hardening of positions. (For more discussion of how to work cooperatively with others through dialectic discussion, see Chapter 21 on working in groups.)

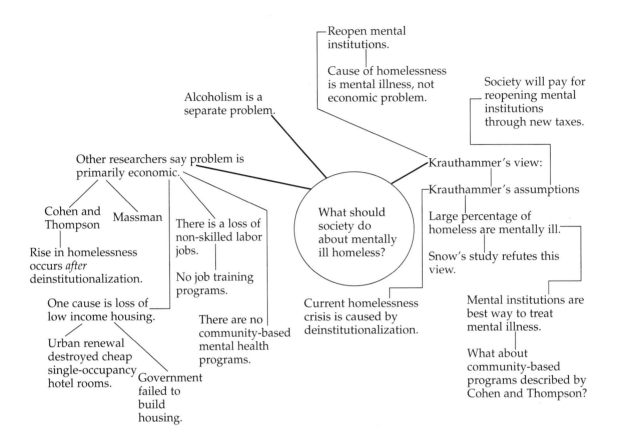

Reopen mental institutions.

Cause of homelessness is mental illness, not economic problem.

Society will pay for reopening mental institutions through new taxes.

Alcoholism is a separate problem.

Other researchers say problem is primarily economic.

Krauthammer's view:

Krauthammer's assumptions

Cohen and Thompson   Massman

There is a loss of non-skilled labor jobs.

What should society do about mentally ill homeless?

Large percentage of homeless are mentally ill.

Rise in homelessness occurs *after* deinstitutionalization.

No job training programs.

Snow's study refutes this view.

One cause is loss of low income housing.

There are no community-based mental health programs.

Current homelessness crisis is caused by deinstitutionalization.

Mental institutions are best way to treat mental illness.

Urban renewal destroyed cheap single-occupancy hotel rooms.

Government failed to build housing.

What about community-based programs described by Cohen and Thompson?

FIGURE 2.1   Idea Map on Homelessness

Active Reading and Research

If dialectic discussion engages you in live, face-to-face conversation with others, active reading and research engage you in conversation with others through reading. The key is to become an *active* reader who both listens to a piece of writing and speaks back to it through imaginative interaction with its author. Chapter 6 offers instruction on becoming an active reader, showing you how to read texts both with the grain and against the grain. In addition, Part Four, "A Guide to Research," describes in detail how to use an academic library as well as computer networking technology (such as the Internet and the World Wide Web) to find sources, how to use those sources to stimulate your own thinking, and how to incorporate them purposefully into your own writing.

When you pursue a question through active reading and research, you join the conversation of others who have contemplated and written about your problem.

Through research, you gather facts, data, and other information relevant to your topic. You learn who the experts are, what is known and unknown about your topic area, what authorities agree on and disagree about, what basic values, beliefs, or assumptions are in dispute, and so forth. In short, you build up a knowledge base about your topic area that makes your thinking deeper and more complex. If you turn back momentarily to the list of critical thinking skills required for wallowing in complexity (p. 23), you will see that many of these skills—and particularly skill 3 (the ability to find, gather, and interpret facts, data, and other information relevant to the problem)—depend on your ability and willingness to do research on your problem.

Not all college writing assignments require library or field research, but many do, and most of the rest can benefit by the process. The writing assignments in Part Two of this text involve varying degrees of research, depending on the assignments selected by your instructor and the problems you choose to pursue.

FOR WRITING AND DISCUSSION

The following exercise is a simulation game that asks you to try some of the exploratory writing and talking techniques we have discussed.

The Situation   The city attorney of a large U.S. city* has proposed a "get-tough" policy on "vagrants and panhandlers" in the city's downtown shopping areas. It is time, says the city attorney, to stand up for the rights of ordinary citizens to enjoy their city. Supported by the mayor, the city attorney is ready to present his proposal to the city council, which will vote to pass or reject the proposal. The details of the proposal are outlined in the following newspaper article:

PROPOSED LAW CALLS FOR FINES, ARRESTS

Proposed public-conduct ordinances before the Seattle City Council focus on repeated drinking in public, urinating in public, sitting or lying on public streets, aggressive panhandling and public drug trafficking. Among their provisions:

- The second and any subsequent drinking-in-public offense becomes a criminal misdemeanor punishable by up to 90 days in jail, a $1,000 fine and up to one year of probation.
- The second and any subsequent offense of urinating or defecating in public becomes a criminal misdemeanor punishable by up to 90 days in jail, a $1,000 fine and up to one year of probation.
- The purchase, possession or consumption of alcohol by those between ages 18 and 21 becomes a criminal misdemeanor punishable by jail, fine and probation.

*The actual city is Seattle, Washington, but this proposal is similar to those being debated in many cities across the United States. For the purposes of this simulation game, assume that the city in question is any city close to your college or university where homelessness is a serious problem.

- Between 7 a.m. and 9 p.m., it would be unlawful to sit or lie on sidewalks in commercial areas, including Broadway, the University District, other neighborhoods and downtown.
- A tighter definition of "intimidation" would be created to make the present law against aggressive panhandling more effective in prosecution.
- Alleys where drug trafficking occurs could be closed for specific periods of the day or night, except for authorized use. Those who enter without permission could be arrested.

The Task   In class, hold a simulated public hearing on this issue. Assign classmates to play the following roles: (1) a homeless person; (2) a downtown store owner; (3) a middle-class suburban home owner who used to shop downtown but hasn't done so for years because of all the "bums" lying on the streets; (4) an attorney from the American Civil Liberties Union who advocates for the civil rights of the homeless; (5) a college student who volunteers in a homeless shelter and knows many of the homeless by name; (6) a city council member supporting the proposal; (7) a city council member opposing it. Every class member should be assigned to one of these roles; later, all students assigned to a role will meet as a group to select the person to participate in the actual simulation.

The Procedure   (1) Begin with five minutes of freewriting. Class members should explore their own personal reactions to this ordinance. (2) Class members should freewrite again, this time from the perspective of the character they have been assigned to play in the simulation. (3) Classmates should meet in groups according to assigned roles in the simulation, share freewrites, and make a group idea map exploring all the arguments that the group's assigned character might make. Group members can choose a person to play the role; those not chosen can play members of the city council. (4) Allow time for people playing the roles to develop their arguments fully and to exchange views. (5) After each participant has spoken, the remaining members of the class, acting as city council members, should sit in a circle and hold a dialectic discussion (listening carefully to each other rather than conducting a shouting match), trying to decide whether to accept or reject the city attorney's proposal. (6) Finally, the class should hold a vote to see whether the proposal is accepted or rejected.

HOW TO MAKE EXPLORATORY WRITING AND TALKING WORK FOR YOU

All the formal writing assignments in Part Two of this text have built-in opportunities for exploratory writing and talking. But we hope you will use the techniques in this chapter in all your college courses as well as in your career. The more you use them, the more natural they will feel. In this final section of the chapter we discuss some of the habits you can cultivate to make exploratory writing and talking a regular part of your intellectual life. We hope that one or more of the following suggestions will work for you through your college years and beyond.

Make Marginal Notes on Readings

Scholars and experienced writers often respond to what they read by writing notes in the margins of books and articles. (If you don't own the book, you will need to write your notes in a journal or reading log.) In Chapter 6 we discuss in detail this method of responding to readings, showing how critical readers regularly write two kinds of marginal notations: (1) *summarizing notes,* which help them understand and recall the gist of the text, and (2) *responding notes,* which help the reader speak back to the text by agreeing or disagreeing, posing questions, drawing connections to other ideas, supplying new examples from the reader's own experience, and so forth. Notes on readings are crucial for persons pursuing an academic problem. Through reading and research you build up an expertise on your subject and become knowledgeable about the conversation your own writing will join. Summarizing notes help you gather data and "listen" to other points of view; responding notes help you carry on a running conversation with your research sources.

Keep a Journal, Daybook, Commonplace Book, or Dialectic Notebook

Another good way to develop the exploratory writing habit is to keep a journal, daybook, or commonplace book. Many teachers assign journals in their courses, providing some guidance about topics to explore. Most professional writers keep regular journals of their own (which they sometimes call daybooks or commonplace books), since they know that their ideas for formal pieces often take root in their journals as they record daily observations, play with ideas, and reflect thoughtfully on the stuff of their lives. You can keep a learning journal for any of your courses by posing questions about course material and then writing out exploratory answers.

If your teacher hasn't specifically assigned a journal for one of your courses, you might also consider keeping a dialectic notebook (sometimes called a double-entry notebook or double-entry journal). Such a notebook makes use of two columns with different purposes. Draw a vertical line down the middle of each notebook page to create a left and right column, or use the right-hand pages of a spiral notebook for one column and the left-hand pages for the other. In the right-hand column, concentrate on learning course material. Record lecture and reading notes, summarize course material and organize it into chunks that make sense to you, and put important concepts into your own words to enhance learning.

Then, in the left-hand column, carry on an interactive commentary on the material, posing questions, raising doubts, making connections, seeing opposing views, linking course material with personal experiences, expressing confusion, and so forth. The kinds of ideas you explore in the left-hand column will vary from course to course. In the sciences, you might use most of the space to explain difficult concepts and to formulate questions that you want to ask the teacher. In a political science class, you might use it to raise doubts or questions about political theories or to draw connections between different theories. The goal in either case is to become actively engaged with the course material. (For an example of a dialectic notebook, see Chapter 8, pp. 184–87.)

Discuss Your Ideas with E-mail Correspondents

At many institutions, teachers use electronic mail (E-mail) to connect students with each other by computer. You can sit at a terminal, type in your exploratory writing, and then send what you have written to a classmate, a group of classmates, or the whole class, and your teacher. The great advantage of E-mail is that it facilitates conversation and dialogue. You can respond to classmates' ideas, and they can respond to yours. At any time the teacher can enter the conversation, asking questions and stimulating further dialogue. If you print out your exchanges or set up a filing system to store them, you can draw on them later when you are exploring ideas for a particular topic.

If your teacher doesn't set up a formal E-mail network for your course, you can set up your own by finding classmates with E-mail accounts. If you are doing research on a particular problem, you may be able to find an international network of people interested in the same topic through an Internet listserve, news group, or chat group. (See Chapter 24 for more suggestions on using electronic media to explore ideas with others.)

Join Focused Study Groups

A focused study group is a collection of individuals who voluntarily come together to study for a course. Such a group can provide an ideal setting for dialectic discussions. Many students do their best work by alternating between private and communal study. Focused study groups work best if members prepare for them in advance. Create a list of questions about course material, concentrating on areas that you have trouble understanding. Then begin by discussing questions that focus on comprehension, generating possible responses to each other's questions. If parts of the material are confusing to everyone in your study group, then you can formulate questions to ask the teacher. Focused study groups also provide good opportunities to predict the kinds of critical thinking questions teachers are apt to ask on exams. When they function effectively, study groups can stimulate thinking about course material and send you back to private study with more confidence and an enhanced appreciation for complexity.

Participate Effectively in Class Discussions

Class discussion provides an excellent opportunity for exploratory talking. The key to effective participation is learning to listen to classmates' ideas and to link your own contributions to what others have said. Often students are so busy rehearsing what they want to say in a class discussion that they fail to listen carefully to other points of view, and their sense of the topic's complexity is diminished. Moreover, such class discussions may lose their dialectic feel and become adversarial shouting matches.

Because it is difficult to take class notes on a good discussion (ideas are flying everywhere, and you don't know what is important and what isn't), many students find it valuable not to take notes in class. Instead, they freewrite their reactions to the discussion as soon as possible after the class ends. They write out all the things they wanted to say in the discussion but didn't, in effect continuing the discussion on their own. Later, rereading the freewrite jogs their memories of the whole discussion, helping them to recover a sense of the topic's complexity.

Summary

In this chapter we looked at the kind of wallowing in complexity that professors expect from students and introduced techniques for exploratory writing and talking that will help you become fully engaged in an academic problem. We saw how an academic essay contributes to a conversation by posing a question and then offering a tentative and risky answer. We also saw how an academic essay is preceded by a long process of thinking, reflecting, studying, researching, and talking. The starting point for such an essay is exploratory writing and talking. We explained five strategies for exploring ideas—freewriting, thought letters, idea mapping, dialectic conversation, and active reading and research—and then offered suggestions for making exploratory writing and talking a regular habit throughout your academic career. In Chapter 3, we examine how to move from exploratory writing and talking to the next step for joining an academic conversation—using the drafting process to seek a surprising thesis and appropriate support.

BRIEF WRITING PROJECT

One of the best ways to dwell with a problem is to play what writing theorist Peter Elbow calls the "believing and doubting game." This game helps you appreciate the power of alternative arguments and points of view by urging you to formulate and explore alternative positions. To play the game, you imagine a possible answer to a problematic question and then systematically try first to believe that answer and then to doubt it.

Play the believing and doubting game with two of the following assertions (or other assertions provided by your instructor). For one of the assertions, play the game by freewriting your believing and doubting responses (following the example on pages 40–42). For your second assertion, use the idea-mapping method. Label one side of your center circle "Believe" and the other side

"Doubt." Spend approximately twenty minutes believing and doubting each assertion for a total of about forty minutes for the whole assignment.

1. State and federal governments should legalize hard drugs.
2. Grades are an effective means of motivating students to do their best work.
3. If I catch someone cheating on an exam or plagiarizing a paper, I should report that person to the instructor.
4. The city council should pass a get-tough policy on vagrants (see For Writing and Discussion, pp. 35–36).
5. In recent years advertising has made enormous gains in portraying women as strong, independent, and intelligent.
6. For grades 1 through 12, the school year should be extended to eleven months.
7. It is a good idea to make children take music lessons.
8. States should legalize marriage for gays and lesbians.
9. Cutting off welfare payments for single mothers will reduce teenage pregnancy.
10. Hate speech should be forbidden on college campuses.

When you play the believing side of this game, you try to become sympathetic to an idea or point of view. You listen carefully to it, opening yourself to the possibility that it is true. You try to appreciate why the idea has force for so many people; you try to accept it by discovering as many reasons as you can for believing it. It is easy to play the believing game with ideas you already believe in, but the game becomes more difficult, sometimes even frightening and dangerous, when you try believing ideas that seem untrue or disturbing.

The doubting game is the opposite of the believing game. It calls for you to be judgmental and critical, to find fault with an idea rather than to accept it. When you doubt a new idea, you try your best to falsify it, to find counterexamples that disprove it, to find flaws in its logic. Again, it is easy to play the doubting game with ideas you don't like, but it, too, can be threatening when you try to doubt ideas that are dear to your heart or central to your own worldview.

Student Example

Here is how one student played the believing and doubting game with the following assertion from professional writer Paul Theroux that emphasizing sports is harmful to boys.

> Just as high school basketball teaches you how to be a poor loser, the manly attitude towards sports seems to be little more than a recipe for creating bad marriages, social misfits, moral degenerates, sadists, latent rapists and just plain louts.
> I regard high school sports as a drug far worse than marijuana.

Believe

Although I am a woman I have a hard time believing this because I was a high school basketball player and believe high school sports are <u>very</u> important. But here goes. I will try to believe this statement even though I hate it. Let's see. It would seem that I wouldn't have much first-hand experience with how society turns boys into men. I do see though that Theroux is right about some major problems. Through my observations, I've seen many young boys go through humiliating experiences with sports that have left them scarred. For example, a 7-year-old boy, Matt, isn't very athletic and when kids in our neighborhood choose teams, they usually choose girls before they choose Matt. I wonder if he sees himself as a sissy and what this does to him? I have also experienced some first-hand adverse affects of society's methods of turning boys into men. In our family, my dad spent much of his time playing football, basketball, and baseball with my brother. I've loved sports since I was very young so I was eager to play. In order to play with them, I had to play like a boy. Being told you threw or played like a girl was the worst possible insult you could receive. The phrase, "be tough" was something I heard repeatedly while I was growing up. Whenever I got hurt, my dad would say, "Be tough." It didn't matter how badly I was hurt, I always heard the same message. Today, I think, I have a very, very difficult time opening up and letting people get to know me, because for so long I was taught to keep everything inside. Maybe sports does have some bad effects.

Doubt

I am glad I get to doubt this too because I have been really mad at all the sports bashing that has been going on in class. I think much of what Theroux says is just a crock. I know that the statement "sports builds character" is a cliché, but I really believe it. It seems to me that the people who lash out at sports clichés are those who never experienced these aspects of athletics and therefore don't understand them. No one can tell me that sports didn't contribute to some of my best and most meaningful friendships and growing experiences. I am convinced that I am a better person because through sports I have had to deal with failure, defeat, frustration, sacrificing individual desires for the benefit of the team, and so on. After my last high school basketball game when after many years of mind games, of hating my coach one minute and the next having deep respect for him, of big games lost on my mistakes, of hours spent alone in the gym, of wondering if the end justifies the means, my coach put his arm around me and told me he was proud. Everything, all the pain, frustration, anxiety, fear, and sacrifice of the past years seemed so worthwhile. You might try to tell me that this story is hackneyed and trite, but I won't listen because it is a part of me, and something you will never be able to damage or take away. I think athletes share a special bond. They know what it is like to go through the physical pain of practice time and again. They understand the wide variety of emotions felt (but rarely expressed). They also know what a big role the friendships of teammates and coaches play in an athlete's life.

We admire this writer a great deal—both for the passion with which she defends sports in her doubting section and for the courage of walking in a sports basher's shoes in the believing section. This exercise clearly engaged and stretched her thinking.

This brief writing assignment asks you to stretch your own thinking by choosing any two of the assigned assertions and practicing believing and doubting each in turn. Use freewriting to explore your first assertion. Spend ten minutes believing the assertion and ten minutes doubting it for a total of twenty minutes. Then choose a second assertion, but this time use idea mapping. Spend ten minutes entering reasons for believing the assertion and then ten minutes for doubting it (or move back and forth between believing and doubting, since an idea map gives you this flexibility), again for a total of twenty minutes. The total assignment should take forty minutes.

chapter 3

Solving Content Problems
Thesis and Support

Tutor: If I said, tell me whether or not this is imperialism, what's your first gut reaction? . . .

Writer: There's very strong arguments for both. It's just all in how you define it.

Tutor: Okay, who's doing the defining?

Writer: Anybody. That's just it, there's no real clear definition. Over time it's been distorted. I mean, before, imperialism used to be like the British who go in and take Hong Kong, set up their own little thing that's their own British government. That's true imperialism. But the definition's been expanded to include indirect control by other means, and what exactly that is, I guess you have to decide. So I don't know. I don't think we really have control in Central America, so that part of me says no that's not imperialism. But other parts of me say we really do control a lot of what is going on in Central America by the amount of dollars and where we put them. So in that essence, we do have imperialism. . . .

Tutor: So you're having a hard time making up your mind whether it is or isn't imperialism?

Writer: Yes! The reason why I'm undecided is because I couldn't create a strong enough argument for either side. There's too many holes in each side. If I were to pick one side, somebody could blow me out of the water.

> —Partial transcript of a Writing Center conference, Seattle University. [The student is responding to a political science assignment: Is U.S. involvement in Central America a case of imperialism?]

The commonsense, conventional understanding of writing is as follows. Writing is a two-step process. First you figure out your meaning, then you put it into language. . . . This idea of writing is backwards. . . . Meaning is not what you start out with but what you end up with.

> —Peter Elbow, *Writing Teacher and Theorist*

Chapter 2 explained how to use exploratory writing and talking to discover and develop ideas. This chapter and the next describe the kinds of problems that experienced writers try to solve as they move beyond exploratory writing and talking to produce a formal finished product. This chapter explains how writers of academic essays seek a final product that poses a good question, has a surprising thesis, and supports that thesis with strong arguments and convincing detail. Chapter 4 shifts from subject-matter problems to rhetorical problems and demonstrates that what writers say and how they say it are controlled by their purpose, intended audience, and genre. In these two chapters we temporarily separate subject-matter problems from rhetorical problems for the sake of instructional clarity. But, like the classic problem of the chicken and the egg, it is impossible to say which should or can be addressed first, subject-matter problems (What's my thesis? What's my supporting evidence?) or rhetorical problems (Who's my audience? What's my purpose?). Throughout the writing process, writers wrestle simultaneously and recursively with both subject-matter problems and rhetorical problems.

DRAFTING AND REVISING AS A PROBLEM-SOLVING PROCESS

Beginning writers often don't appreciate the extent to which experienced writers struggle when they compose. Unlike beginning writers, who often think of revision as cleaning up errors in a rough draft, experienced writers use the writing process to "wallow in complexity." The more experienced the writer, the more likely that he or she will make large-scale, global revisions in a draft rather than local, sentence-level changes. Experienced writers, in fact, often dismantle their first constructions and start fresh. They build on what they learned the first time to create a more appropriate structure the second time around. To help you learn similar skills, Part Three of this text focuses entirely on the processes of composing and revising prose along the continuum from closed to open forms.

One reason writers need multiple drafts is that early in the writing process they may be unsure of what they want to say or where their ideas are headed. As Peter Elbow puts it (in the second epigraph for this chapter), "Meaning is not what you start out with but what you end up with." To appreciate Elbow's point, consider the transcript that precedes his quotation at the head of the chapter. The student writer is blocked because she thinks she has to make up her mind about her issue before she starts writing. The assigned problem requires her both to define imperialism and to argue whether U.S. activity in Central America meets the definition. What we admire about this student is that she is wallowing in complexity, fully aware of the problem's difficulty and actively confronting alternative views. The best way for her to think through these complexities is to start doing exploratory writing—freewriting, idea mapping, a thought letter, or any of the other strategies described in Chapter 2. This exploratory writing can then evolve into a first draft. Our point here is that the act of writing generates thought. The more she writes, the more she will clarify her own ideas. Her first drafts may have to be dismantled once she finally commits herself to a position. But the discarded drafts won't have been wasted; they will have helped her to manage the complexity of the assignment.

This writer needs to realize that her difficulty is a sign of strength. A good thesis statement is a risky one. Knowing that a skeptical reader might "blow you out of the water" motivates you to provide the best support possible for your thesis while acknowledging the power of opposing views. Perhaps this writer hopes that a miraculous insight will give her the "correct" solution, which she can then write out effortlessly. "In your dreams," we reply. Or perhaps she thinks that her present difficulty is a sign of her own inadequacy. To the contrary, her awareness of complexity and risk means that she is on the right track.

TAKING RISKS: SEEKING A SURPRISING THESIS

As we have seen, most academic writing is thesis based. By *thesis based* we mean that the writer aims to support a main point or thesis statement, which is the writer's one-sentence summary answer to the problem or question that the paper addresses. The writer supports the thesis with reasons, explanations, details, and evidence because he or she assumes that the audience will regard it skeptically and will test it against other possible answers. As the quotation from Peter Elbow implies, many writers do not formulate their final arguments until quite late in the writing process because they are constantly testing their ideas as they draft. The underlying motivation for multiple drafting is the search for a strong argument headed by a strong thesis.

But what makes a thesis strong? For one thing, a strong thesis always contains an element of uncertainty, risk, or challenge. A strong thesis implies a counter thesis. According to Elbow, a thesis has "got to stick its neck out, not just hedge or wander. [It is] something that can be quarreled with." Elbow's sticking-its-neck-out metaphor is a good one, but we prefer to say that a strong thesis *surprises* the reader with a new, unexpected, different, or challenging view of the writer's topic. In this section, we present two ways of creating a surprising thesis: (1) trying to change your reader's view of your subject and (2) giving your thesis tension.

Try to Change Your Reader's View of Your Subject

To change your reader's view of your subject, you must first imagine how the reader would view the subject *before* reading your essay. Then you can articulate how you aim to change that view. A useful exercise is to write out the "before" and "after" views of your imagined readers.

Before reading my essay, my readers think this way about my topic: _____.

After reading my essay, my readers will think this different way about my topic: _____.

You can change your reader's view of a subject in several ways.* First, you can enlarge it. Writing that enlarges a view is primarily informational; it provides new ideas and data to add to a reader's store of knowledge about the subject. For example, a research paper on wind-generated electricity might have the following thesis: "The technology for producing wind-generated electricity has improved remarkably in recent years." (Before reading my essay, the reader has only limited, out-of-date knowledge of wind-power technology; after reading my essay, the reader will have up-to-date knowledge.)

Second, you can clarify your reader's view of something that was previously fuzzy, tentative, or uncertain. This kind of writing often explains, analyzes, or interprets. Suppose, for example, that you are an engineering student working on the problem of how rotor blades on a wind tower could adapt to changing wind speed and direction. Through your own critical thinking, you figure out a new design that solves one of the technical problems. You could then write a technical report asserting the following thesis: "The linkage mechanism described in this paper enables rotor blades to adapt quickly to changing wind directions." (Before reading my technical report, the reader may be confused about how rotor blades can adapt to changing wind directions; after reading my report, the reader will understand a workable design.) The technical report thus clarifies a previously confusing aspect of the subject.

Third, you can change your reader's view by doing the opposite of clarifying; you can raise questions or problems that will make your reader feel less certain and more puzzled. Suppose that you are a different engineer responding to the technical report just mentioned. If you were intrigued by the proposed design but saw problems that the original writer overlooked, you might join the conversation with a paper of your own asserting this thesis: "The proposed linkage design, although basically workable, assumes a design for the rotor itself that is inefficient." Your goal isn't to oppose the proposed design, but simply to raise doubts about it. (Before reading my paper, the reader thinks the proposed design fully solves the problem; after reading my paper, the reader will have doubts about this solution.)

Still another kind of change occurs when an essay actually restructures a reader's whole view of a subject. Such essays persuade readers to change their minds or make decisions. They can be threatening to a reader's identity because they shake up closely held beliefs and values. For example, in Chapter 1 we printed a letter to the editor written by a civil engineer who argued that "wind-generated power can in no way serve as a reasonable major alternative [to hydro, coal-fired, or nuclear power]." (Before reading my letter, the reader believes that wind-generated power is a solution to our energy crisis; after reading my letter, the reader will believe that wind-generated power is a pipe dream.) One person we know—a committed environmentalist with high hopes for wind energy—said that this letter persuaded him that large-scale harnessing of wind energy wouldn't work. He was visibly dismayed; the engineer's argument had knocked his view of wind energy off its props. (We aren't saying, of course, that the engineer is *cor-*

---

*Our discussion of how writing changes a reader's view of the world is indebted to Richard Young, Alton Becker, and Kenneth Pike, *Rhetoric: Discovery and Change*, New York: Harcourt Brace & Company, 1971.

rect. We are saying only that his letter persuaded at least one of our acquaintances to change his mind about wind energy.)

Surprise, then, is the measure of change an essay brings about in a reader. (Of course, to bring about such change requires more than just a surprising thesis; the essay itself must persuade the reader that the thesis is sound as well as novel. In the last part of this chapter we talk about how writers support a thesis with details.)

Give Your Thesis Tension

Another element of a surprising thesis is tension. By *tension* we mean the reader's sensation of being stretched from a familiar, unsurprising idea to a new, surprising one or of being twisted by two ideas pushing in opposing directions. Although we describe them individually, the two sensations often overlap.

Theses that induce stretching are compelling because they continually give the reader something new to consider. Often the purpose of these essays is to inform, explain, or analyze. They are satisfying because they fill gaps in knowledge as they take the reader on a journey from old, familiar ground into new territory—stretching the reader, as it were, into a new place. Stretching theses teach readers something they didn't already know about a subject.

A thesis designed to twist a reader sets up an opposition between the writer's claims and various counterclaims. The reader is asked to choose among alternative ways of looking at a topic. Twisting theses argue for a particular view of the subject in the face of alternative or countering views.

One of the best ways to create tension in a thesis statement is to begin the statement with an "although" or "whereas" clause: "Whereas most people believe X, this essay asserts Y." The "whereas" or "although" clause summarizes the reader's "before" view of your topic or the counterclaim that your essay opposes; the main clause states the surprising view or position that your essay will support. You may choose to omit the "although" clause from your actual essay, but formulating it first will help you achieve focus and surprise in your thesis. The examples that follow illustrate the kinds of tension we have been discussing and show why tension is a key requirement for a good thesis.

Question	What effect has the telephone had on our culture?
Thesis Without Tension	The invention of the telephone has brought many advantages to our culture.
Thesis with Tension	Although the telephone has brought many advantages to our culture, it may also have contributed to the increase of violence in our society.
Question	Do reservations serve a useful role in contemporary Native American culture?
Thesis Without Tension	Reservations have good points and bad points.

Thesis with Tension	Although my friend Wilson Real Bird believes that reservations are necessary for Native Americans to preserve their heritage, the continuation of reservations actually degrades Native American culture.

In the first example, the thesis without tension (telephones have brought advantages to our culture) is a truism with which everyone would agree and hence lacks surprise. The thesis with tension places this truism (the reader's "before" view) in an "although" clause and goes on to make a risky assertion. The surprising idea that the telephone contributes to violence stretches our thinking because it shakes up our old, complacent view of the telephone as a beneficent instrument.

In the second example, the thesis without tension may not at first seem tensionless because the writer sets up an opposition between good and bad points. But *almost anything* has good and bad points, so the opposition is not meaningful, and the thesis offers no element of surprise. Substitute virtually any other social institution (marriage, the postal service, the military, prisons), and the statement that it has good and bad points would be equally true. The thesis with tension, in contrast, is risky. It commits the writer to argue that reservations have degraded Native American culture and to oppose the counterthesis that reservations are needed to *preserve* Native American culture. The reader is twisted by the tension between two opposing views.

We have used the terms *stretching* and *twisting* to help you see various ways in which a thesis can have tension, but it is not important to make sharp distinctions between the two. Frequently, a thesis stretches and twists simultaneously. What *is* important is that you see that the writer's goal is to surprise the reader in some way, thereby bringing about some kind of change in the reader's view. A thesis can surprise a reader by doing the following:

- giving the reader new information or clarifying a confusing concept
- posing a dilemma by juxtaposing two or more differing answers to the same question or by finding paradoxes or contradictions in an area that others regard as nonproblematic
- identifying an unexpected effect, implication, or significance of something
- showing underlying differences between two concepts normally thought to be similar or underlying similarities between two concepts normally thought to be different
- showing that a commonly accepted answer to a question isn't satisfactory or that a commonly rejected answer may be satisfactory
- opposing a commonly accepted viewpoint, supporting an unpopular viewpoint, or otherwise taking an argumentative stance on an issue
- providing a new solution for a problem

FOR WRITING AND DISCUSSION

It is difficult to create thesis statements on the spot because a writer's thesis grows out of an exploratory struggle with a problem. However, through brief exploratory writing and talking it is sometimes possible to arrive at a thesis that is both surprising and arguable. Working individually, spend ten minutes freewriting on one of the following topics chosen by your class or the instructor:

competitive sports	television talk shows
commuting by automobile	sex-education classes
homelessness	mathematics education
gangs	zoos

Then, working in small groups or as a whole class, share your freewrites, looking for elements in each person's freewrite that surprise other members of the class. From the ensuing discussion, develop questions or problems that lead to one or more surprising thesis statements. Each thesis should be supportable through personal experiences, previous reading and research, or critical thinking; for example:

Topic	Competitive Sports.
Question	Is it psychologically beneficial to participate in competitive sports?
Surprising Thesis	Although we normally think that participation in competitive sports is psychologically healthy, the psychological traits that coaches try to develop in athletes are similar to the traits exhibited by an anorectic dieter.

SUPPORTING A THESIS WITH CONVINCING DETAILS

A surprising thesis is only one aspect of an effective essay. An essay also must persuade the reader that the thesis is sound. Although tabloid newspapers have shocking headlines ("Thigh Cream a Cheap Alternative to Fossil Fuel!" "Elvis Captains UFO That Buzzes Home of Michael Jackson!"), skepticism quickly replaces surprise when the reader discovers that within the articles the claims are unsupported. A strong thesis must *both* surprise a reader *and* be supported by convincing details.

The flesh and bone of writing is in the details. A thesis statement is only one sentence of many hundreds that constitute an essay. Most of an essay's sentences are detail sentences that support points. In this section, we explore two facets of the relationship between points and particulars: (1) how essays use details to support each point in a network of points, and (2) how essays move up and down the scale of abstraction.

Details Within a Network of Points

In a good essay a writer weaves back and forth between generalizations and details. The generalizations form a network of points that develop the thesis, and the details support each of the points in turn. In closed-form prose, the network of points is easily discernible because the points are clearly highlighted with transitions and are placed prominently at the head of paragraphs. Most paragraphs are composed of detail sentences that support the paragraph's point. When you read closed-form prose, you constantly shift back and forth between generalizations and details, points and particulars. (In open-form prose, generalizations are often left unstated, creating gaps where the reader must actively fill in meaning.)

If you remove most of the details from a closed-form essay, leaving only the network of generalizations, you will have a summary or abstract of the essay. As an example, reread the civil engineer's letter to the editor arguing against the feasibility of wind-generated power (pp. 11–12). The writer's argument can be summarized in a single sentence.

> Wind-generated power is not a reasonable alternative to other forms of power in the Pacific Northwest because wind power is unreliable, because there are major unsolved problems involved in the design of wind-generation facilities, and because the environmental impact of building thousands of wind towers would be enormous.

What we have done in this summary is remove the details, leaving only the high-level generalizations that form the skeleton of the argument. The writer's thesis remains surprising and contains tension, but without the details the reader has no idea whether to believe the generalizations or not. The presence of the details is therefore essential to the success of the argument. In the assignment chapters of Part Two, we provide extensive discussion of the kinds of details needed to support a particular thesis.

FOR WRITING AND DISCUSSION

Compare Rockwood's original letter to the editor with the one-sentence summary; note how Rockwood uses specific details to support each point. How do the details differ from paragraph to paragraph? How are they chosen to support each point?

Moving Up and Down the Scale of Abstraction

We have said that writers weave back and forth between generalizations and details. To help you understand more clearly what we mean by the terms *points* and *particulars* or *generalizations* and *details,* consider the following scale of abstraction descending from the general to the specific:

living creature

animal

mammal

cow

holstein

Twyla

old, sleepy-eyed Twyla chewing her cud

This scale takes you from a general word, encompassing all living creatures, to a specific phrase, the details of which represent one specific cow—old, sleepy-eyed Twyla.

An often-cited piece of writing advice goes something like this: "Use definite, specific, concrete language," or "Support generalizations with colorful details." For many writing situations, this is excellent advice. Note the difference in particularity between the following passages:

General The awkward, badly dressed professor stood at the front of the room.

Particular At the front of the room stood the professor, a tall, gawky man with inch-thick glasses and an enormous Adam's apple, wearing a manure-brown jacket, burgundy-and-gray plaid pants, a silky vest with what appeared to be scenes from an aquarium printed on it, and a polka-dot blue tie.

The details in the particularized passage help you experience the writer's world; they don't just tell you that the professor was dressed weirdly, they *show* you.

In many instances the terms *particular* or *detail* apply to words that convey sensory experience, words that show how something looked or sounded or felt or tasted or smelled. In other cases, particulars can be statistics, facts, quotations used as testimony, or specific examples. Civil engineer David Rockwood uses numerical data about the size and number of wind towers as details to convince readers that wind generation of electricity entails environmental damage.

But detail sentences don't always have to be concrete sensory details (such as the color of the professor's tie) or highly specific factual or numerical details (such as those used in Rockwood's letter). Some kinds of writing, notably, academic prose on theoretical or philosophical topics, remain at fairly high levels of abstraction. The best way to state the rule is not "Use definite, specific, concrete language," but "Move up and down the scale of abstraction, achieving a level of detail appropriate to your purpose, audience, and genre." A philosophical piece will move up and down the scale of abstraction, but rarely will it get to the level of specific examples or sensory details. A descriptive or narrative passage will move up and down the scale, but may never rise much above the level of sensory detail. The kinds of details you use in any particular essay depend on your writing situation. Each of the assignment chapters in Part Two of this text gives advice on finding the right kinds and levels of details to support each essay. (See also the discussion of points and particulars in Chapters 18 and 19.)

FOR WRITING AND DISCUSSION

Working on your own, write out a passage using detail sentences to support each of the points provided. If no details come to mind, invent plausible ones. Then share your results with the whole class or a small group. This exercise is a warm-up for the brief writing assignment at the end of this chapter.

1. The weather was beautiful yesterday.
2. I was shocked by the messiness of Bill's dorm room.

3. The tornado's sweeping through our town caused many hardships.
4. Although freewriting looks easy, it is actually quite difficult.
5. At the introductory level, chemistry is much more abstract than physics.

Summary

In this chapter, we have highlighted the importance of drafting as a problem-solving process in which the writer seeks a surprising thesis and convincing details. To achieve surprise, the writer chooses a thesis that "sticks its neck out" by aiming to change the reader's view of a topic. A surprising thesis is characterized by tension, created either from stretching the reader's understanding in a new direction or from twisting the reader's beliefs in a contrary direction. In addition to presenting a surprising thesis, a writer needs to support the thesis through a network of points, each point backed up by details. The flesh and bone of most writing is in the details. Writers weave back and forth between generalizations and details by moving up and down the ladder of abstraction.

BRIEF WRITING PROJECT

The microtheme assignment for this chapter gives you practice generating details to support a point. To make it easier, we've supplied the point sentence. (In contrast, the closed-form writing projects for Part Two ask you to construct your own surprising thesis, give it tension, and support it with details.) Despite its relative simplicity, however, this assignment teaches an essential concept: effective closed-form writing supports points with particulars.

> Write a one-paragraph microtheme that uses specific details to support the provided point sentence. Begin your microtheme with the point sentence and then use the body of the paragraph to provide specific supporting details. Your microtheme should be between 150 and 250 words in length. For your point sentence, choose any one of the following (or another point sentence provided by your instructor):
>
> - Directly or indirectly, anyone who is not a vegetarian causes animals to suffer.
> - Although the college library looks as though it is a good place to study, it has many distractions that lure you from your work.
> - Although doing X looks easy, it actually requires remarkable skill. (For X, substitute any activity of your choice; for example, "Although playing center midfielder in soccer looks easy, it actually requires remarkable athletic skill.")
> - Although X works reasonably well, it has one major problem—_____. (For X substitute anything of your choice, e.g., "Although the interior of my new car is generally well designed, it has one major problem—awkward controls." or "Although the registration system at

our school works reasonably well, it has one major problem: most students find it almost impossible to locate their advisor." The idea is to use convincing details to persuade readers that a problem exists.

- The most memorable trait of (person's name) is X. (e.g., "The most memorable trait of my grandfather was his sense of humor." or "The most memorable trait of my sister is her incredible athletic ability." Then use specific details to illustrate the trait.)

The purpose of this assignment is to help you appreciate the difference between generalizations and details. This assignment provides you with a generalization or the frame for a generalization that you can apply to your own topic. Your task is to provide the supporting details that convince the reader of the truth of the generalization. For this assignment, your details will probably take the form of specific observations, facts, or examples. Here is a student microtheme written for this assignment.

Student Example

Although my new stereo receiver produces a pleasant sound and has ample power and volume, it has one major problem: poor design of the controls. The on/off switch in the upper left-hand corner is small and easy to confuse with two switches that control the main and remote speakers. If you hit the main speaker switch instead of the on/off switch, the sound will go off and you will think you have turned off the amplifier. When you try to turn it on again (by hitting the on/off switch), you will not hear any sound and will think the system is broken. This problem wouldn't be so bad if the tuning dial were always lit--that way you would know if the amplifier was turned on or not. But no light appears on the face of the receiver unless it is set in the "tuner" mode. Another problem with the controls is that the preset tuning buttons for radio stations are so small and close together that you have to use your little finger to push them. In the dark, they aren't lit, so I have to keep a little flashlight next to the amplifier to change radio stations at night. Finally, the volume control isn't gradual enough. The slightest movement of the knob changes the volume dramatically so that it is very difficult to adjust the sound to just the right level. (236 words)

c h a p t e r 4

Solving Rhetorical Problems

Purpose, Audience, and Genre

It is amazing how much so-called writing problems clear up when the student really cares, when he is realistically put into the drama of somebody with something to say to somebody else.

James Moffett, *Writing Teacher and Theorist*

In Chapter 3, we characterized composing as a problem-solving process requiring multiple drafts. We focused on subject-matter problems, in particular, the writer's struggle to find a surprising thesis and convincing details. In this chapter we explore ways in which writers' structural and stylistic choices are influenced by their rhetorical situations. We begin by discussing occasions that impel people to write. We then analyze three key variables of rhetorical context—purpose, audience, and genre—and show how these variables affect choices about structure and style.

MOTIVATING OCCASIONS, OR WHY AM I WRITING THIS PIECE?

We said in Chapter 1 that people naturally enjoy posing and pursuing subject-matter problems. It is less clear whether people naturally enjoy writing about those problems. It is interesting to ask yourself when putting words on paper, "Why am I sitting here writing an essay when I could be doing something else?"

If asked, Why *do* you write? many of you might well answer, "Because teachers like you tell me to." Perhaps from first grade on, writing—or at least writing for school—has not been pleasant for you. Left to your own desires, you might have avoided school writing as diligently as you avoided canned spinach or bad hair days.

For others, writing school essays may have been—at least on occasion—deeply satisfying. Perhaps there was something about the assignment, the subject matter, or the environment created by the teacher that engaged you. On those occasions you may have immersed yourself in the writing project, written with care, and rewritten until you had fulfilled standards higher than those you would have set on your own. Even when there is an element of compulsion in the writing situation, you can claim ownership of the project and grow in the act of writing.

What we are suggesting is that there are two different motivations for writing—an external compulsion and an internal creative desire. Many of you might think that the first of these motivations—compulsion or coercion—is peculiar to school situations in which teachers assign papers and set deadlines. But you should know that the element of external compulsion felt so keenly in school writing is present in nearly every writing situation. Even poets report that writing can be a laborious process, provoked as often by ego, dumb habit, publishers' deadlines, or even greed, as by a burning vision. Eighteenth-century English writer Samuel Johnson, regarded by many as the first professional writer in Western culture, claimed that "No man but a blockhead ever wrote but for money." Yet he managed to write compellingly and artfully on everything from politics to language.

Most writing, whether it's done by students, artists, or businesspeople, is the product of mixed motives, some more or less voluntary, others downright coercive. Consider a middle manager requested by a company vice-president to write a report explaining why his division's profits are down. The manager is motivated by several factors: he wants to provide sound causal explanations for the financial decline, which will help the company set a course to remedy the situation; he wants to avoid looking bad or at least appearing to be solely responsible for the dip in profits; he wants to impress the vice-president in the hope that she will promote him to upper management; he wants to understand and articulate for himself just how this lamentable state of affairs came about; he wants each sentence to say just what he wants it to say; and so on.

College students' motivations for writing are often as complex as those of our hypothetical middle manager. Perhaps your writing is occasioned by an assignment and a deadline set by an instructor. But that rarely tells the whole story. In part, you write because you are engaged by an intellectual problem and want to say something significant about that problem; in part, you want to produce a well-written essay; in part, you want to please the teacher and get a good grade; in part, you want to improve your writing, and so forth. However arbitrary or artificial a college writing assignment might seem, it is really no more so than the writing occasions you will encounter outside college, when you must often write on tight deadlines for purposes specified by others. Given this fact, we believe that your best chance of writing successfully in college is to become engaged with the intellectual problem specified in the assignment. When you care about your ideas, you begin to imagine readers who care about them also (as opposed to imagining a teacher looking for mistakes), and you write to have an impact on those readers. The external motivations for writing are real and inescapable, but developing an internal motivation for writing—the desire to say something significant about your topic to an audience for a purpose—will help you produce your best work.

FOR WRITING AND DISCUSSION

Think of a time when you actually wanted to write something. What did you write and why did you find it satisfying? If this experience was a school assignment, what was it about the assignment, the subject matter, the classroom environment, the teacher, or you that awakened in you an internal motivation for writing? Prior to class discussion, spend several minutes freewriting about the occasion, exploring what made you feel internally motivated to write. Then, working in small groups or as a whole class, share your experiences with classmates. As a class, can you make any generalizations about the kinds of occasions or experiences that make a person want to write something? (If you cannot recall such an occasion, then recall the most hideous writing experience you've had and recount the elements that made it particularly gruesome. Why did the occasion fail to motivate you internally?)

THE ELEMENTS OF RHETORICAL CONTEXT: PURPOSE, AUDIENCE, AND GENRE

We have said that the best motivation for writing is the desire to say something significant about a substantive problem to an audience that cares about your ideas. But in writing your essay you must also wrestle with rhetorical problems. What you say about your topic, how you organize and develop your ideas, what words you choose, and what voice and tone you adopt are all determined by your rhetorical context. In this section, we discuss in detail three important components of rhetorical context—purpose, audience, and genre.

Purpose

In analyzing your rhetorical context, you should start by asking: What is my purpose? Or, to put it another way: What effect do I want to have on my readers? What change do I want to bring about in their understanding of my subject? In most instances, you can write a one-sentence, nutshell answer to your question about purpose.

My purpose is to share with my reader my successful struggle with dyslexia.

My purpose is to raise serious doubts in my reader's mind about the value of the traditional grading system.

My purpose is to inform my reader about the growth of the marijuana industry in the midwestern farm states.

My purpose is to explain how Northrop Frye's view of *Hamlet* fails to account for several key features of the text.

My purpose is to convince readers that the potential bad consequences of mail-order marriages require governments to regulate the mail-order bride industry.

> My purpose is to persuade the general public that wind-generated electricity is not
> a practical energy alternative in the Pacific Northwest.

In closed-form academic articles, technical reports, and other business and professional pieces, writers typically place explicit purpose statements in the introduction. In most other forms of writing, they formulate purpose statements
behind the scenes—the writer keeps a purpose statement in mind and uses it to
achieve focus and direction, but seldom states it explicitly.

Writers' purposes generally fall into six broad categories. Situating your writing project within one or more of these categories can help you understand how
to approach your task.

Writing to Express or Share (Expressive Purpose)

When you adopt this general purpose, you place your own life—your personal experiences and feelings—at the center of your reader's attention. You express in words what it is like to be you, to see or feel the world your way. Writing
expressively in a diary, journal, or personal notebook has therapeutic value because it gives you the opportunity to vent your feelings and explore your
thoughts. Often, however, you may choose to write expressively to move or touch
a reader, to share your experiences and feelings with others—with friends or relatives through letters or with strangers through formal autobiographical essays or
personal reflections.

Expressive writing usually follows the impulse to share rather than to argue
or disagree. It says, in effect, "While you read my story or my reflections, you can
momentarily cease being you and become me for a while, seeing the world
through my eyes. My words might cause you to see the world differently, but my
goal isn't to change you, just to help you appreciate the uniqueness of my experience." Instead of creating surprise through an argumentative thesis, expressive
writing achieves surprise by offering the reader access to the private experiences
of another human being.

Expressive writing usually falls near the open end of our closed-to-open continuum. When an expressive purpose is joined to a literary one (which we will describe shortly) the writer produces autobiographical pieces that function in a
literary way, using image, plot, character, and symbol.

Writing to Inquire or Explore (Exploratory Purpose)

Although exploratory writing is closely linked to expressive writing, it usually focuses more on subject-matter problems than on the writer's life. You use exploratory writing to wade into complexity via freewriting, idea mapping, journal
keeping, note taking, E-mail exchanges, letter writing, drafting, and any other
writing that probes a subject and deepens your thinking. Its goal is to help you ask
questions, explore possible answers, consider opposing views, pursue conflicting
trains of thought, expand and clarify your thinking, and generally delay closure
on a question in order to work your way through the complexity of your subject.

Exploratory writing is usually unfinished, behind-the-scenes work not intended to be read by others, but it sometimes results in a formal, finished product.
In these cases, the writing aims to *pose* or *deepen a problem*, to muddy waters

that the reader thought were clear. It doesn't *support* a thesis; it *seeks* a thesis. It perplexes the reader by revealing new questions about a topic, by showing how various approaches to that topic are unsatisfactory or how certain aspects of a topic are more problematic than previously supposed. Because exploratory writing often takes a narrative shape, dramatizing the process of the writer's thinking about a subject, it usually falls toward the open end of the closed-to-open continuum.

Writing to Inform or Explain (Informative Purpose)

When your purpose is informative, you see yourself as more knowledgeable than your reader about your topic. You create surprise by enlarging the reader's view of a topic, providing new ideas and information based on your own experiences or research. When you write to inform, you adopt the role of teacher in relation to your reader. You imagine that the reader will trust your authority and not dispute what you say. Although informative writing usually has a closed-form structure, it may fall anywhere along the continuum from closed to open.

Writing to Analyze or Interpret (Analytical Purpose)

When your purpose is analytical, you examine aspects of a subject that puzzle your reader and offer tentative ways to resolve these puzzles. Analytical writing requires you to think critically about a problematic text, set of data, or other phenomenon. Your goal is to clarify your reader's understanding of this problematic subject. You surprise your reader with a new or more illuminating way of seeing, thinking about, or understanding the subject.

Analytical writing, often laced with informative elements, constitutes the most common kind of academic prose. It typically takes a closed-form structure. The introduction poses a question, and the body presents the writer's solution. The reader generally regards the solution as *tentative*, so the writer must support it with reasons and evidence or other justifying arguments. Unlike informative writing, which positions the writer as an expert, analytical writing generally assumes that writer and reader are equally well informed and equally engaged with the puzzling phenomenon. Analytical writing presupposes a more skeptical audience than does informative prose. The writer might not expect readers to argue back, but will certainly expect them to test his or her ideas against their own experience and hypotheses.

Writing to Persuade (Persuasive Purpose)

When your purpose is persuasive, you enter a conversation in which people disagree with each other about answers to a given question. You think of your audience as judges, jurors, or other decision makers, who must be convinced that your answer to the question is sounder than other answers. Persuasive writing addresses a controversial problem, to which there are several alternative answers with supporting reasons and evidence. When you write to persuade, you aim to surprise the reader with your own reasons and evidence or other appeals that will change the reader's beliefs or actions.

Persuasive writing can fall anywhere along the closed-to-open continuum. It may have a closed-form structure of reasons and evidence set out in a logical point-by-point format, or it may have a very open structure—a powerful story or a collage of emotionally charged scenes might be extremely persuasive in influencing a reader's views on an issue.

When writing persuasively, writers usually imagine skeptical readers vigorously questioning their claims. The only way they can effectively anticipate and respond to these questions is to understand alternative positions on the issue—including understanding the values, assumptions, and beliefs of the people who hold alternative views—and either refute these views, concede to them, or compromise with them. This emphasis on countering or accommodating alternative views and on appealing to the values and beliefs of the reader distinguishes persuasive writing from most analytical writing.

Writing to Entertain or Give Aesthetic Pleasure (Literary Purpose)

Sometimes writers focus not on themselves (expressive prose), nor on the subject matter (exploratory, informative, and analytical prose), nor on the reader (persuasive prose), but on the artistic shaping of language. When you adopt a literary purpose, you treat language as a medium, such as paint or bronze. You explore its properties and its sound and rhythms. We typically think of literary writing as fiction or poetry, but nonfiction prose can also use literary techniques. Such prose is often called *literary nonfiction* or *belletristic prose*. Literary nonfiction usually combines a literary purpose with one or more other purposes, for example, an expressive purpose (an autobiographical essay about a turning point in your life) or an exploratory purpose (your contemplation of the cosmic meanings of a spider web).

FOR WRITING AND DISCUSSION

As a class, choose one of the following topic areas or another provided by your instructor. Then imagine six different writing situations in which a hypothetical writer would compose an essay about the selected topic. Let each situation call for a different purpose. How might a person write about the selected topic with an expressive purpose? An exploratory purpose? An informative purpose? An analytical purpose? A persuasive purpose? A literary purpose? How would each essay surprise its readers?

baseball	cats	hospices or nursing homes*
homelessness	garbage	dating or marriage
advertising	newspapers	gays in the military

---

*If this topic interests you, see how student writer Sheridan Botts wrote about hospices, first with an exploratory purpose (Chapter 8, pp. 170–72), and later with a persuasive purpose (Chapter 16, pp. 401–13).

Working on your own or in small groups, create six realistic scenarios, each of which calls for prose in a different category of purpose. Then share your results as a whole class. Here are two examples based on the topic "hospices."

Expressive Purpose	Working one summer as a volunteer in a hospice for dying cancer patients, you befriend a woman whose attitude toward death changes your life. You write an autobiographical essay about your experiences with this remarkable woman.
Analytic Purpose	You are a hospice nurse working in a home-care setting. You and your colleagues note that sometimes family members cannot adjust psychologically to the burden of living with a dying person. You decide to investigate this phenomenon. You interview "reluctant" family members in an attempt to understand the causes of their psychological discomfort so that you can provide better counseling services as a possible solution. You write a paper for a professional audience analyzing the results of your interviews.

Audience

In our discussion of purpose, we have already had a lot to say about audience. What you know about your readers—their closeness to you, their familiarity with your subject matter, their values and beliefs, their methods and reasons for reading—affects most of the choices you make as a writer.

You need to consider the significance of your reader's methods and reasons for reading. Imagine that you are a marketing manager and you want to persuade your harried boss to increase your research budget. You picture your boss sitting at her desk, people waiting to see her, phone ringing, a pile of memos, reports, and proposals in the in box. Consequently, you fashion a budget request with a tightly closed structure. Your document must be clear, concise, and well designed for her immediate comprehension and assent. The same reader in a different mood and setting may turn to a different kind of prose. In the evening, your harried boss might relax in an easy chair, sip a cup of tea, and reach for her favorite magazine. Is she most concerned now with speedy comprehension and quick access to needed information? Probably not. She's more likely to be interested in leisurely reading, perhaps an open-form piece on, say, bicycling in Italy. And she may well savor the way a passage is written, pausing to reflect on the scene it evokes.

Now consider how a change in audience can affect the content of a piece. Suppose you want voters in your city to approve a bond issue to build a new baseball stadium. If most members of your audience are baseball fans, you can appeal to their love of the game, the pleasure of a new facility, and so forth. But non–baseball fans won't be moved by these arguments. To reach them, you must tie the new baseball stadium to their values. You can argue that a new stadium will bring new tax revenues to the city, clean up a run-down area, revitalize local businesses, or stimulate the tourist industry. Your purpose remains the same, to persuade taxpayers to fund the stadium, but the content of your argument changes if your audience changes.

A change in audience can change a writer's purpose as well. A graduate student we know who studies wildlife management developed a technique for using a net gun to capture mountain goats so that researchers could place radio collars around their necks. He wrote several articles based on his expertise. For fellow specialists who studied mountain goats, he wrote a scientific article showing that capturing mountain goats with a net gun was more effective than drugging them with a dart gun (informative and analytical purposes). For the audience of a popular outdoors magazine, he wrote a personal-action narrative about shooting a net gun from a hovering helicopter (expressive and literary purpose). And because he was also concerned with preserving natural habitats for mountain goats, he wrote letters to legislators using data gathered from the radio collars to argue for restrictions on wilderness development (persuasive purpose).

In college, you are often writing for an audience of one—your instructor. However, most instructors try to read as a representative of a broader audience. To help college writers imagine these readers, many instructors try to design writing assignments that provide a fuller sense of audience. They may ask you to write for the readers of a particular magazine or journal, or they may create case assignments with a built-in audience (for example, "You are an accountant in the firm of Numbers and Fudge; one day you receive a letter from . . ."). If your instructor does not specify an audience, you can generally assume what we like to call the generic academic audience—student peers who have approximately the same level of knowledge and expertise in the field as you do, who are engaged by the question you address, and who want to read your writing to be surprised in some way.

Assessing Your Audience

In any writing situation, you can use the following questions to help you make decisions about content, form, and style:

1. Who is going to read what I write? A specific individual? A specific group with special interests? Or a general readership with wide-ranging interests and backgrounds?
2. What relationship do I have with these readers? Do I and my readers have an informal, friendly relationship or a polite, formal one? Is my readers' expertise in my general subject area greater, less, or equal to mine?
3. How much do my readers already know about the specific problem I address? How much background will I have to provide?
4. How much interest do my readers bring to my topic? Do I need to hook readers with a vivid opening and use special techniques to maintain their interest throughout? Or are they interested enough in the problem I am examining that the subject matter itself will drive their reading? (In persuasive writing, particularly in writing that proposes a solution to a problem, you may need to shock your readers into awareness that the problem exists.)
5. What are my audience's values, beliefs, and assumptions in relation to my topic? If I am writing on a controversial issue, will my readers oppose

my position, be neutral to it, or support it? To which of their values, beliefs, or assumptions can I appeal? Will my position unsettle or threaten my audience or stimulate a strong emotional response? (Because a concern for audience is particularly relevant to persuasive writing, we will treat these questions in more depth in Chapters 14 through 16.)

Posing these questions will not lead to any formulaic solutions to your writing problems, but can help you develop strategies that will appeal to your audience and enable you to achieve your purpose.

FOR WRITING AND DISCUSSION

Working on your own, imagine that you enjoyed a fun party last weekend. (a) Describe that party in a letter to a close friend, inventing the details needed to show your friend how great the party was. (b) Describe the same party in a letter to a parent (or some other person whose differences from your friend would lead to a different description.) Note: You may substitute any other event or phenomenon that you would describe in different ways to different audiences.

Then, in small groups or as a class, share excerpts from your two letters. What changes did you make in your description as a result of changes in your audience?

Genre

The term *genre* refers to broad categories of writing that follow certain conventions of style, structure, and approach to subject matter. Literary genres include the short story, the novel, the epic poem, the limerick, the sonnet, and so forth. Nonfiction prose has its own genres: the business memo, the technical manual, the scholarly article, the scientific report, the popular magazine article (each magazine, actually, has its own peculiar conventions), the five-paragraph theme (a school genre), the newspaper editorial, the cover letter for a job application, the legal contract, the advertising brochure, and so forth.

The concept of genre creates strong reader expectations and places specific demands on writers. How you write any given letter, report, or article is influenced by the structure and style of hundreds of previous letters, reports, or articles written in the same genre. If you wanted to write for *Reader's Digest*, for example, you would have to use the conventions that appeal to its older, conservative readers: simple language, subjects with strong human interest, heavy reliance on anecdotal evidence in arguments, an upbeat and optimistic perspective, and an approach that reinforces the conservative ethos of individualism, self-discipline, and family. If you wanted to write for *Seventeen* or *Rolling Stone*, however, you would need to use quite different conventions.

To illustrate the relationship of a writer to a genre, we sometimes draw an analogy with clothing. Although most people have a variety of different types of clothing in their wardrobe, the genre of activity for which they are dressing (Saturday night movie date, job interview, wedding) severely constrains their choice and expression of individuality. A man dressing for a job interview might express his personality through choice of tie or quality and style of business suit; he probably wouldn't express it by wearing a bicycle helmet and mismatched shoes. Even when people deviate from a convention, they tend to do so in a conventional way. For example, teenagers who do not want to follow the genre of "teenager admired by adults" form their own genre of purple hair and pierced body parts. The concept of genre raises intriguing and sometimes unsettling questions about the relationship of the unique self to a social convention or tradition.

These same kinds of questions and constraints perplex writers. For example, academic writers usually follow the genre of the closed-form scholarly article. This highly functional form achieves maximum clarity for readers by orienting them quickly to the article's purpose, content, and structure. Readers expect this format, and writers have the greatest chance of being published if they meet these expectations. In some disciplines, however, scholars are beginning to publish more experimental, open-form articles. They may slowly alter the conventions of the scholarly article, just as fashion designers alter styles of dress.

The genre of the scholarly article varies enormously from discipline to discipline, both in the kinds of questions that specialists pose about their subject matter and in the style and structure of articles. As a specific example of a genre that many college students regularly encounter, we introduce you here to the *experimental report*. This genre is commonly used in fields that conduct empirical research, such as the physical or social sciences, nursing, medicine, business, engineering, education, and other fields.

The Experimental Report

An experimental report, sometimes called a scientific or technical report, is a formal paper addressed primarily to professionals who are interested in the results of an investigation. Its readers want to know why the investigation was undertaken, how it was conducted, what was learned, and whether the findings are significant and useful. Experimental reports usually follow a standard five-part format as shown below.

1. *Introduction.* This section explains the purpose of the investigation, what problem was addressed and what makes the problem both problematic and significant. The introduction often includes a review of the literature, which summarizes previous research addressing the same or a related problem. In many scientific disciplines, it is conventional to conclude the introduction with a hypothesis, a tentative answer to the question, which the investigation confirms or disconfirms.
2. *Methods.* Sometimes called *methodology* or *procedures*, the methods section details in cookbook fashion how the investigators conducted the research. It provides enough details so that other researchers can replicate the investigation. This section usually includes the following subsections: (a) research design; (b) apparatus and materials; and (c) procedures followed.
3. *Findings (results).* This section presents the empirical results of the investigation, the data discovered in the experiment. The findings may be

displayed in figures, tables, graphs, or charts. Usually, the findings are not interpreted in this section.

4. *Discussion of findings.*   This section is the main part of the experimental report—the part that will be read with the most care by other professionals. It explains the significance of the findings by relating what was discovered back to the problem set out in the introduction and detailing how the investigation did or did not accomplish its original purpose, that is, whether it answered the questions outlined in the introduction. (Did it confirm/disconfirm the writer's hypothesis?) This section also discusses the usefulness and significance of the findings and explores new questions raised by the experiment.

5. *Conclusions and recommendations.*   This last section focuses on the main points learned from the investigation and, in some cases, on the practical applications of the investigation. If the investigation was a pure research project, this section often summarizes the most important findings and recommends areas for further research. If the investigation was aimed at making a practical decision (for example, an engineering design decision), this section recommends appropriate actions.

You can tell from this description that the experimental report has a very closed form. Note, however, that the thesis is delayed until the discussion section, which reveals through the writer's analysis of the findings whether the original hypothesis was confirmed or disconfirmed.

FOR WRITING AND DISCUSSION

1. On page 62, we offered you a brief description of the conventions governing *Reader's Digest* articles, which appeal mainly to older, conservative readers. For this exercise, prepare similar descriptions of the conventions that govern articles in several other magazines, such as *Rolling Stone, Sports Illustrated, Cosmopolitan, Details, The New Yorker,* or *Psychology Today.* Each person should bring to class a copy of a magazine that he or she enjoys reading. The class should then divide into small groups according to similar interests. Your instructor may supply a few scholarly journals from different disciplines. In preparing a brief profile of your magazine, consider the following:

   ■ Scan the table of contents. What kinds of subjects or topics does the magazine cover?

   ■ Look at the average length of articles. How much depth and analysis are provided?

   ■ Consider the magazine's readership. Does the magazine appeal to particular political or social groups (liberal/conservative, male/female, young/old, white collar/blue collar, in-group/general readership)?

   ■ Look at the advertisements. What kinds of products are most heavily advertised in the magazine? Who is being targeted by these advertisements? What percentage of the magazine consists of advertisements?

- Read representative pages, including introductions, of some articles. Would you characterize the prose as difficult or easy? Intellectual or popular? Does the prose use the jargon, slang, or other language particular to a group? Are the paragraphs long or short? How are headings, inserts, visuals, and other page-formatting features used? Is the writing formal or informal?
- Think about what advice you would give a person who wanted to write a freelance article for this magazine.

2. Imagine that someone interested in hospices (see the example in the For Writing and Discussion exercise on p. 59) wanted to write an article about hospices for your chosen magazine. What approach would the writer have to take to have a hospice-related article published in your magazine? There may be no chance of this happening, but be creative. Here is an example:

> Ordinarily *Sports Illustrated* would be an unlikely place for an article on hospices. However, *SI* might publish a piece about a dying athlete in a hospice setting. It might also publish a piece about sports memories of dying patients or about watching sports as therapy.

RHETORICAL CONTEXT AND DECISIONS ABOUT STRUCTURE AND STYLE

So far in this chapter we have examined purpose, audience, and genre as components of a writer's rhetorical context. In this section, our goal is to help you appreciate how these variables influence a writer's choices regarding structure and style. Although there is no formula that allows you to determine an appropriate structure and style based on particular purposes, audiences, and genres, there are some rules of thumb that can help you make decisions.

Making Decisions About Structure

Because most academic, business, and professional writing uses a closed-form structure, we spend a significant portion of this text advising you how to write such prose. However, you also need to be able to open up your prose on occasion, and to that end you need to practice writing at different positions on the continuum. The following advice will help you decide when closed or open forms are more appropriate.

When is closed-form prose most appropriate?

- When your focus is on the subject matter itself and your goal is to communicate efficiently to maximize clarity. In these cases, your purpose is usually to inform, to analyze, or to persuade.

■ When you imagine your audience as a busy or harried reader who needs to be able to read quickly and process ideas rapidly. Closed-form prose is easy to summarize; moreover, a reader can speed read closed-form prose by scanning the introduction and then glancing at headings and the openings of paragraphs, where writers place key points.

■ When the conventional genre for your context is closed-form writing, and you choose to meet, rather than break, readers' expectations.

■ When you encounter any rhetorical situation that asks you to assert and support a thesis in response to a problem or question.

When is a more open form desirable?

■ When you want to delay your thesis rather than announce it in the introduction, for example, to create suspense. A delayed thesis structure is less combative and more friendly; it conveys an unfolding "let's think through this together" feeling.

■ When your purpose is expressive, exploratory, or literary. These purposes tend to be served better through narrative rather than through thesis-with-support writing.

■ When you imagine your audience reading primarily for enjoyment and pleasure. In this context you can often wed a literary purpose to another purpose.

■ When the conventional genre calls for open-form writing, for example, autobiographical narratives, character sketches, or personal reflective pieces. Popular magazine articles often have a looser, more open structure than do scholarly articles or business reports.

■ When you are writing about something that is too complex or messy to be captured in a fixed thesis statement, or when you feel constrained by the genre of thesis with support.

Making Decisions About Style

Writers need to make choices not only about structure but also about style. By *style,* we mean the choices you make about how to say something. Writers can say essentially the same thing in a multitude of ways, each placing the material in a slightly different light, subtly altering meaning, and slightly changing the effect on readers. In this section we illustrate more concretely the many stylistic options open to you and explain how you might go about making stylistic choices.

Factors that affect style

We can classify the hundreds of variables that affect style into four broad categories.

1. Ways of shaping each sentence: long/short, simple/complex, many modifiers/few modifiers, detailed/general
2. Types of words: abstract/concrete, formal/colloquial, unusual/ordinary, metaphoric/literal

3. Implied relationship with reader: intimate/distant, personal/impersonal, angry/calm, browbeating/sharing, informative/entertaining
4. Attitudes toward subject: humorous/serious, ironic/straightforward

To help you get a sense of different styles, we try our hand at illustrating a few. Rather than draw examples from published sources, we imitate different styles ourselves—both to show you that doing so can be fun and to let you see how stylistic variations on the same subject matter can produce different effects. Imagine the following scenario: One Farrago Pomp, a rising light in the educational community, has developed a new teaching method that he calls the critical visionary method of instruction. He has conducted several studies to demonstrate its effectiveness, and now other scholars are beginning to join the conversation that Pomp has initiated. First we present the introduction to a hypothetical scholarly article written in a formal academic style.

> Variations in pedagogical methodology are widely reported in the literature, and it is to be assumed that such variations will continue so long as empirical research yields less than unanimous consensus concerning the psychological and environmental factors that influence learning and cognition. Nevertheless, the work of F. Pomp (see especially 1989; 1992b; 1995) has firmly established the trance-inducing methodology embodied in his "Critical Visionary Method of Instruction" as among the most influential of the last two decades. Indeed, a recent review of the literature reveals that eighty-four articles—virtually all of which make elaborate claims for the efficacy of Pomp's approach—were published in the last three years alone. According to the *Citation Index*, nearly 300 additional articles cited Pomp's work during that same time period. Each year nearly 300 academics attend Pomp's training seminars at any one of six regional sites around the country. It would be difficult to overstate the impact of Pomp's pedagogical philosophy on contemporary American higher education.
>
> Yet Pomp's work is being called increasingly into question. Shovit (1994) and Stuffit (1995) recently questioned a number of Pomp's underlying premises, while Ehrbag's (1994) pioneering empirical study raised serious doubts about Pomp's methodology. For that reason a rigorous research agenda was undertaken to put Pomp's claims to a definitive test in 26 college classrooms around the country. The results of this study are reported herein. The findings, while confirming a few of Pomp's less ambitious claims, show significantly sparser learning gains overall than those claimed in the literature.
>
> —Elwit Morganthorpe, "Dimming the Vision: A Critical
> Evaluation of Pomp's 'Visionary Method of Instruction' "

Next is the introduction to a conference presentation addressed to an academic audience. It is a still an academic paper, but in a conversational rather than a formal style.

> A lot of teachers these days have been experimenting with Farrago Pomp's Visionary Method, and many have reported good results. (I am told that more than eighty articles supporting Pomp's work have been published in the last three years.) So I decided to try out some of Pomp's methods myself—with disastrous

results. I admit that I have no weighty evidence to support my own less than en-thusiastic assessment of VM—just one semester's experience with thirty first-year students in a writing class at Weasel College. I sincerely tried to make the method work. I read Pomp meticulously and tried to follow his suggestions exactly when I induced the trances, including use of drums, mantras, and synthetic sea music. In short, I employed Pomp's method with as much conviction as a normally cred-ulous human being could muster.

As I'll show in the rest of this paper, Pomp's method had dismal effects on my students' writing and evoked extremely negative reactions to the more evangeli-cal aspects of the approach. As one of my students put it: "Trances are for summer camp, not the classroom."

—Elmira Eggwhite, "Waking Up From Pomp's Trance"

In our final example, we switch all three variables of rhetorical context: purpose, audience, and genre. In this example the writer's purpose is not to analyze or eval-uate Pomp's methods, but to write an informative piece on the visionary method movement. The audience consists of general readers rather than scholars. The genre is an upbeat popular magazine aimed at a youthful audience.

What's new in the college classroom these days? Retro hairdos and plastic pumps, you say. Tattoos and nose rings? True true, but what are people actually doing in those classrooms? Anything new about the way today's students are being taught?

Most definitely, say our campus correspondents. The latest rage is Vision. Or, more properly, Visionary Method.

According to Farrago Pomp, the man who invented the Visionary Method, his approach will be the mainstay of the 21st century classroom.

The tall, bearded Pomp explained the genesis of his approach at an early morning interview between numerous cups of double espresso.

"The idea for the Visionary Method hit me," says Pomp, "during a drum cer-emony in my men's group."

"I realized that the old methods—tedious studying, often in weary isolation—didn't work. Knowledge should be imbibed, or quaffed in heady drafts, amidst chanting circles of fellow Visionaries," said Pomp, gesturing frantically for an-other espresso.

It appears, however, that not all of Pomp's colleagues are beating the same drum. Professor Elwit Morganthorpe has been leading a pack of educators throw-ing sand and water on Pomp's sacred campfires. "Pomp's methods are bogus," says Morganthorpe, citing his own comprehensive investigation of the Visionary Method. "Drum ceremonies can never replace old-fashioned studying."

In the meantime, thousands of college students are chanting their way through their college courses. Heady stuff indeed for those of us who got through college by memorizing textbooks and solving equations. What we wouldn't have given to be able to walk into our philosophy class and chug-a-lug some Spinoza. . . .

—"Drum Rolls, Please: Learning in the New Age"

FOR WRITING AND DISCUSSION

Working in small groups or as a whole class, analyze the differences in the styles of these three samples. What features of the writing make each voice sound different? How are differences in style a result of differences in the writer's purpose, audience, or genre?

Creating an Effective Style: The "Natural" Voice

In the face of various stylistic choices, we often ask our students to write in their "natural" speaking voices—something similar to the conversational academic style of our second Pomp example—to avoid the stiffness of the formal style or the breezy glibness of the popular magazine style. By *natural*, we mean a voice that strives to be plain and clear while retaining the engaging quality of a person who is enthusiastic about the subject.

Of course, this natural voice is not really all that natural. We know that people talk differently in different situations. "Sounding like me" when I am with my friends at a party is very different from "sounding like me" when I am meeting my true love's parents for the first time. Just as you vary your speaking voice for different purposes, so can you vary your writing voice. With practice, you can even construct an artificial voice that sounds—and even feels—natural even though it isn't "you."

For most college assignments a voice close to your speaking voice is a good choice, for it is generally engaging to readers and avoids such stylistic annoyances as wordiness, excessive nominalization, or monotonic abstractions.

Creating a Persona

Through your stylistic choices, you create an image of yourself in your reader's mind. This image, sometimes called a *persona,* can be cold or warm, humorous or serious, stuffy or lively, and so forth. It is your persona that your reader likes or dislikes, trusts or distrusts. In most rhetorical situations, it is to your advantage to project a trustworthy, credible, well-informed, thoughtful, and fair persona.

Sometimes you can convey these qualities in subtle ways. In an academic article, the overt function of footnotes, citations, and a bibliography is to enable other scholars to track down the cited sources. A covert function, however, is to create an air of authority for you, the writer, to assure readers that you have done your homework and are fully knowledgeable and informed. Judicious use of the discipline's specialized language can have a similar effect.

Your persona is also reflected in your manuscript's form, appearance, and editorial correctness. Sloppy or inappropriately formatted manuscripts, grammatical errors, misspelled words, and other problems send a signal to the reader that you are unprofessional and perhaps untrustworthy and undependable. Printing a manuscript on a dot matrix printer with a worn ribbon might not matter in some situations, but could prove disastrous in others (if the manuscript were a job-application letter, for example). In all contexts, grammatical errors and misspellings signal a lack of care.

Another factor in creating a trustworthy persona, especially in analytical and persuasive writing, is how you treat alternative views. Do you acknowledge the existence of views different from your own? If you do not, readers of analytical prose may sense that you are uninformed or less than rigorous; readers of persuasive prose may perceive you as unfair or not credible. And when you do acknowledge differing views, do you summarize them fairly and treat them with dignity, or do you ridicule them? In some contexts, ridiculing an opponent works well (for example, if you are fanning the enthusiasm of readers who already share your views), but in other contexts it is disastrous (for example, if you want to change the views of those who disagree with you). How you acknowledge differing views is a particularly important concern in persuasive writing, as we explain in detail in Chapter 14.

You need to recognize that almost every choice you make as a writer influences the way readers perceive who you are, what your beliefs and assumptions are, and how you view reality. Once you recognize this perhaps unsettling truth—that your writing always conveys an image of you as the writer—you will be better able to control the choices you make and to construct a persona that fits your purpose, your audience, and your genre.

Summary

In this chapter we have examined how the elements of rhetorical context influence structure and style. We began by looking at the three key variables of rhetorical context—purpose, audience, and genre—and then considered how these variables influence a writer's choices about structure and style. The brief writing assignment that follows will help you experience for yourself the relationship between a writer's context and choices about structure and style.

This chapter concludes Part One, "A Rhetoric for College Writers." The chapters in Part One have given you some background about how writers pose problems, how they pursue them through exploratory writing and talking, and how they try to solve them during the process of composing and revising. You have seen how writers try to solve subject-matter problems by seeking a surprising thesis supported with convincing details, and how they simultaneously try to solve rhetorical problems regarding structure and style by considering issues of purpose, audience, and genre. This knowledge should prepare you to tackle the writing assignments of Part Two. Further help for your Part Two assignments is provided in Part Three, which offers nuts-and-bolts instruction on composing and revising.

BRIEF WRITING PROJECT

This assignment asks you to try your hand at translating a piece of writing from one rhetorical context to another. As background, you need to know that each month's *Reader's Digest* includes a section called "News from the World of Medicine," which contains one or more mini-articles reporting on recent medical research. The writers of these pieces scan articles in medical journals, select items of potential interest to the general public, and translate them from a formal scientific style into a popular style. Here is a typical example of a *Reader's Digest* mini-article.

> Cheese could be one secret of a healthy, cavity-free smile, according to a recent study by a professor of dentistry at the University of Alberta in Edmonton, Canada.
>
> In the study, John Hargreaves found that eating a piece of hard cheese the size of a sugar cube at the end of a meal can retard tooth decay. The calcium and phosphate present in the cheese mix with saliva and linger on the surface of the teeth for up to two hours, providing protection against acid attacks from sweet food or drink.
>
> —Penny Parker, "For Teeth, Say Cheese"

Now compare this style with the formal scientific style in the following excerpts, the introduction and conclusion of an article published in the *New England Journal of Medicine*.

> *Introduction:* The past 10 years have witnessed major changes in our understanding of the pathophysiologic mechanisms underlying vascular occlusion and considerable progress in the clinical assessment of aspirin and other antiplatelet agents. The purpose of this review is to describe a rational basis for antithrombotic prophylaxis and treatment with aspirin. Basic information on the molecular mechanism of action of aspirin in inhibiting platelet function will be integrated with the appropriate clinical pharmacologic data and the results of randomized clinical trials. . . .
>
> *Conclusions:* Aspirin reduces the incidence of occlusive cardiovascular events in patients at variable risk for these events. Progress in our understanding of the molecular mechanism of the action of aspirin, clarification of the clinical pharmacology of its effects on platelets, and clinical testing of its efficacy at low doses have contributed to a downward trend in its recommended daily dose. The present recommendation of a single loading dose of 200–300 mg followed by a daily dose of 75–100 mg is based on findings that this dose is as clinically efficacious as higher doses and is safer than higher doses. The satisfactory safety profile of low-dose aspirin has led to ongoing trials of the efficacy of a combination of aspirin and low-intensity oral anti-coagulants in high-risk patients. Finally, the efficacy of a cheap drug such as aspirin in preventing one fifth to one third of all important cardiovascular events should not discourage the pharmaceutical industry from attempting to develop more effective antithrombotic drugs, since a sizeable proportion of these events continue to occur despite currently available therapy.
>
> —Carlo Patrono, "Aspirin as an Antiplatelet Drug"

Assume that you are a writer of mini-articles for the medical news section of *Reader's Digest*. Translate the findings reported in the article on aspirin into a *Reader's Digest* mini-article.

Although the style of the medical article may seem daunting at first, a little work with a good dictionary will help you decipher the whole passage. The original article by Dr. Patrono followed the experimental report format described on pages 63–64 and included sections entitled "Introduction," "Methods," "Findings," "Discussion," and "Conclusions." We have reprinted here most of the introduction and the complete conclusions section. Because Patrono's conclusion summarizes the important findings reported and analyzed in the body of the report, these two sections provide all the information you need for your mini-article.

Writing Projects

part T W O

c h a p t e r   5

Seeing Rhetorically
The Writer as Observer

ABOUT SEEING RHETORICALLY

One time-honored way to begin a writing course is to have students observe a scene and describe it in dense, sensory language. On the surface, this seems a simple and pleasurable enough exercise. But consider what happens to this traditional task when it is given a rhetorical twist. Suppose we asked you to write *two* descriptions of the same scene from different angles of vision (for example, different perspectives, moods, or rhetorical purposes). We could then ask to what extent your prior experiences and beliefs influence what you see. Recast in this way, the task requires you to reflect on your degree of responsibility for what you see and to acknowledge the impossibility of arriving at a single, objective account of the scene.

We take this self-reflective twist as our point of departure for this chapter. As soon as you realize that your perceptions of the world shape as well as record that world, you are ready to play a more active role in the learning process and to use writing as a way of seeing and a mode of learning. Your writing assignment for this chapter falls into a category that we call *writing to learn*. Such assignments seldom result in self-contained essays. More often they result in thought exercises that help you learn a concept and then reflect on your learning.

One goal of this writing assignment is to raise the issue of angle of vision versus objectivity in writing. Angle of vision is a factor in all kinds of writing, not just in description. Consider an example from the world of statistics. At one point in a recent baseball season, the Seattle Mariners had the following twelve-game sequence of wins and losses: seven consecutive losses; two wins; one loss; two wins. On the same day in the local papers, two different sports writers summed up the Mariners' record as follows:

Reporter 1   The surging Mariners have now won four out of their last five games.

Reporter 2   The struggling Mariners have won only four of their last twelve games.

These two accounts raise some interesting questions. Are they equally factual? Are they equally true? Is there a term that would sum up the Mariners' recent record more accurately than "surging" or "struggling"? (By "recent" do we mean the last five games or the last twelve? Why not the last eight or the last eighteen?)

This example illustrates what we mean by *seeing rhetorically*. To see something rhetorically is to interpret it, that is, to see it as meaningful. To see data as meaningful entails asserting a point about it ("The Mariners are struggling" or "The Mariners are surging") and identifying data that account for that conclusion (to go back twelve games, which explains "struggling," or to go back five games, which explains "surging"). Before we develop this explanation in more detail, we would like you to experience for yourself the dilemma of having to see rhetorically.

EXPLORING RHETORICAL OBSERVATION

You are an assistant professor of management in the School of Business at Ivy Lite College. One day you receive a letter from a local bank requesting a confidential evaluation of a former student, one Neal Weasel, who has applied for a job as a management trainee. The bank wants your assessment of Weasel's intelligence, aptitude, dependability, and ability to work with people. You haven't seen Neal for several years, but you remember him well. Here are some of the facts and impressions you recall about Mr. Weasel.

- Very temperamental student, seemed moody, something of a loner.
- Long hair and very sloppy dress—seemed like a misplaced street person; often twitchy and hyperactive.
- Absolutely brilliant mind; took lots of liberal arts courses and applied them to business.
- Wrote a term paper relating different management styles to modern theories of psychology—the best undergraduate paper you ever received. You gave it an A+ and remember learning a lot from it yourself.
- Had a strong command of language—the paper was very well written.
- Good at mathematics; could easily handle all the statistical aspects of the course.
- Frequently missed class and once told you that your class was boring.
- Didn't show up for the midterm. When he returned to class later, he said only that he had been out of town. You let him make up the midterm, and he got an A.
- Didn't participate in a group project required for your course. He said the other students in his group were idiots.
- You thought at the time that Weasel didn't have a chance of making it in the business world because he had no talent for getting along with people.
- Other professors held similar views of Weasel—brilliant, but rather strange and hard to like; an odd duck.

You are in a dilemma because you want to give Weasel a chance (he's still young and may have had a personality transformation of some sort), but you also don't want to damage your own professional reputation by falsifying your true impression.

Working individually at your desk for ten minutes or so, compose a brief letter assessing Weasel; use details from the list to support your assessment. Try to convey a positive impression, but remain honest. Then, working in small groups or as a whole class, share your letters. Pick out representative examples ranging from most positive to least positive and discuss how the letters achieve their different rhetorical effects. To what extent does honesty compel you to mention some or all of your negative memories? Is it possible to mention negative items without emphasizing them? How?

WRITING PROJECT

Your writing project for this chapter is to write two descriptions and an analysis. The assignment has two parts.*

Part A: Find a place on or near campus where you can sit and observe for fifteen or twenty minutes in preparation for writing a focused description of the scene that will enable your readers to see what you see. Here is the catch. You are to write *two* descriptions of the scene. Your first description must convey a favorable impression of the scene, making it appear pleasing or attractive. The second description must convey a negative, or unfavorable, impression, making the scene appear unpleasant or unattractive. Both descriptions must contain only factual details and must describe exactly the same scene from the same location at the same time. It's not fair, in other words, to describe the scene in sunny weather and then in the rain or otherwise to alter factual details. Each description should be one paragraph long (approximately 125–175 words).

Part B: Attach to your two descriptions an analysis (approximately 400–500 words) that explains how your two equally factual descriptions create two contrasting impressions of the same subject. What did you do differently to create the contrasting effects in the two descriptions? In the conclusion of your analysis, address the question "So what?" by exploring what you have learned about reading and writing from composing your two descriptions. Help your readers see what is significant about your thought exercise.

Part A of the assignment asks you to describe the same scene in two different ways, giving your first description a positive tone and the second description a

*For this assignment, we are indebted to two sources: (1) Richard Braddock, *A Little Casebook in the Rhetoric of Writing*, Englewood Cliffs, NJ: Prentice-Hall, 1971, and (2) Kenneth Dowst, "Kenneth Dowst's Assignment," in William E. Coles, Jr., and James Vopat (eds.), *What Makes Writing Good?*, Lexington, MA: D.C. Heath, 1985, pp. 53–57.

negative one. You can choose from any number of scenes: the lobby of a dormitory or apartment building, a view from a park bench or from your dormitory or apartment window, the entrance to campus, a crowd at a basketball game, a busy street, a local eating or drinking spot, a scene in a lecture hall, a person studying at a library table, whatever. Part B of the assignment asks you to reflect on what you did to convey a positive or negative impression. Did you include different details? Did you choose different wording or alter the sentence structure? Did you arrange details in a different order? The assignment concludes by prompting you to reflect further on what you learned from this exercise about seeing rhetorically.

More discussion of this assignment, as well as a student example of two contrasting descriptions, occurs later in this chapter. As we noted earlier, this assignment results in a thought exercise rather than in a self-contained essay that requires an introduction, transitions between parts, and so forth. You can label your sections simply "Descriptions" and "Analysis."

UNDERSTANDING OBSERVATIONAL WRITING

In this section we explore the extent to which the writer's angle of vision shapes the language he or she chooses, or, to put it inversely, how the chosen language creates an angle of vision. We also explore the complex relationship between perception and belief by showing how previous knowledge, cultural background, interests, values, and beliefs may influence perceptions.

How Observational Writing Reflects an Angle of Vision

To see how observational or descriptive writing reflects an angle of vision, let's look at several examples. Our first is the opening of a newspaper feature article in which a freelance writer describes his bicycle tour through the Prudhoe Bay area of Alaska.

> The temperature is 39 degrees. The going is slow but finally I am in motion. The bike churns through big rocks and thick gravel that occasionally suck the wheels to a dead halt.
>
> Sixty miles to the east lies the Arctic National Wildlife Refuge, a place ARCO describes as "a bleak and forbidding land where temperatures plunge to more than 40 degrees below zero and the sun is not seen for nearly two months each year." To me, the refuge is 19.5 million acres of unspoiled wilderness believed to contain crude oil and natural gas fields.
>
> Prudhoe Bay production is on the decline, and oil corporations are salivating over the prospect of drilling on the 125-mile-long stretch of coastal plain within the refuge.
>
> This area is the principal calving ground for the 180,000-member porcupine caribou herd that annually migrates to this windswept plain, seeking relief from insects.

The refuge also provides habitat for grizzlies, wolves, musk oxen, wolverines and arctic foxes. Polar bears hunt over the ice and come ashore. Millions of waterfowl, seabirds and shorebirds nest here.

—Randal Rubini, "A Vicious Cycle"

The opening of this article juxtaposes the author's view of the Arctic National Wildlife Refuge (ANWR) and ARCO's view. ARCO, a major oil-refining company, describes the ANWR as a "bleak and forbidding land where temperatures plunge to more than 40 degrees below zero and the sun is not seen for nearly two months each year." In contrast, Rubini describes it as "unspoiled wilderness," the habitat of caribou, grizzly bears, shorebirds, and other wildlife.

FOR WRITING AND DISCUSSION

Working as a whole class or in small groups, explain how each description reflects an angle of vision that serves the political interests of each party, that is, explain how ARCO's description makes the ANWR seem like a good place to drill for oil and how Rubini's description makes it seem like a bad place to drill for oil. Also discuss how Rubini's use of "salivating" (third paragraph) serves his interests.

Appreciating how a writer's choice of words and selection of details reflects an angle of vision can help you read any text from a position of strength. One key is to pay attention to what is *omitted* from a text as well as to what is included. For example, ARCO's descriptive passage about the ANWR omits reference to the animals, keeping the reader focused on the bleak and frigid landscape. In contrast, Rubini's description of the ANWR omits references to the Alaskan economy or the U.S. need for domestic oil, keeping the reader focused instead on the ANWR's beauty and wildlife. Neither perspective is necessarily dishonest; each is true in a limited way. In any writing, writers necessarily—whether consciously or unconsciously—include some details and exclude others. Their choices are driven by their sense of audience and purpose and most important, by their "situatedness" in the world, which creates a predisposition toward a particular perspective or angle of vision. By noting what is *not there,* a reader can begin to detect that angle of vision and analyze it. The reader sees the piece of writing not as the whole truth, but as a constructed piece with a rhetorical effect (that is, with a persuasive power) created by its angle of vision.

The rhetorical effect of observational writing is even more clear in our next example, consisting of excerpts from the works of two female anthropologists studying the role of women in the !Kung tribe of the African Kalahari (sometimes called the Bushmen). Anthropologists have long been interested in the !Kung because they still hunt and forage for food in the manner of their prehistoric ancestors.

Here is how anthropologist Lorna Marshal describes !Kung women's work:

Women bring most of the daily food that sustains the life of the people, but the roots and berries that are the principal plant foods of the Nyae Nyae !Kung are apt to be tasteless, harsh and not very satisfying. People crave meat. Furthermore, there is only drudgery in digging roots, picking berries, and trudging back to the encampment with heavy loads and babies sagging in the pouches of the karosses: there is no splendid excitement and triumph in returning with vegetables.

—Lorna Marshal, *The !Kung of Nyae Nyae*

And here is how a second anthropologist describes women's work:

A common sight in the late afternoon is clusters of children standing on the edge of camp, scanning the bush with shaded eyes to see if the returning women are visible. When the slow-moving file of women is finally discerned in the distance, the children leap and exclaim. As the women draw closer, the children speculate as to which figure is whose mother and what the women are carrying in the karosses. . . .

!Kung women impress one as a self-contained people with a high sense of self-esteem. There are exceptions—women who seem forlorn and weary—but for the most part, !Kung women are vivacious and self-confident. Small groups of women forage in the Kalahari at distances of eight to ten miles from home with no thought that they need the protection of the men or of the men's weapons should they encounter any of the several large predators that also inhabit the Kalahari.

—P. Draper, "!Kung Women: Contrasts in Sexual Egalitarianism in Foraging and Sedentary Contexts"

As you can see, these two anthropologists "read" the !Kung society in remarkably different ways. Marshal's thesis is that !Kung women are a subservient class relegated to the heavy, dull, and largely thankless task of gathering vegetables. In contrast, Draper believes that women's work is more interesting and requires more skill than other anthropologists have realized. Her thesis is that there is an egalitarian relationship between men and women in the !Kung society.

The source of data for both anthropologists is careful observation of !Kung women's daily lives. But the anthropologists are clearly not seeing the same thing. When the !Kung women return from the bush at the end of the day, Marshal sees their heavy loads and babies sagging in their pouches, whereas Draper sees the excited children awaiting the women's return.

So, which view is correct? That's a little like asking whether the Mariners are surging or struggling or whether the ANWR is bleak or teeming with animals. All writers necessarily present their own perspectives on their subjects; the alternative would be to list only facts—but even then you would have to decide which facts to list and in what order. As soon as you begin interpreting the facts—making inferences, reaching judgments, asserting meanings—you create a view of your subject from your own angle of vision. As a reader you should realize that all texts filter reality by privileging some aspects of the subject and suppressing others. When you realize that no text gives you the whole truth, but only the author's version of the truth, you can learn to read more critically, to be aware of the writer's point of view, and to be alert to how the writer's choice of words, use of metaphor, style, and arrangement of text urge you to narrow your view of the subject until it coincides with the writer's own angle of vision.

This doesn't mean that there is no such thing as truth. It means that no one writer can give you the complete picture and that you must actively seek alternative points of view, do further research, ask more questions, and confront the subject's complexity. If you wanted to do further study of women's roles in !Kung society, for example, some additional questions you might want to ask are the following: Were the two anthropologists studying the same !Kung groups at the same time? Are there aspects of male and female behaviors in !Kung society on which most anthropologists agree? What other information about male and female roles would be helpful and how could it be obtained? Should some terms, such as *male dominance* and *subservient role*, be defined more clearly?

Conducting a Simple Rhetorical Analysis

Before proceeding to the relationship between perception and interpretation, let's consolidate what we have covered so far and apply it to your writing assignment for this chapter. Your assignment asks you first to compose two contrasting descriptions of the same scene (Part A) and then to explain how your two equally true descriptions create contrasting rhetorical effects (Part B). This latter task constitutes a rhetorical analysis of your two descriptions. We next describe five textual features to consider when writing a rhetorical analysis.

Feature 1: Writer's Overt Statement of Meaning

Writers often state their point or angle of vision openly. In the pieces on the !Kung women, for example, Marshal writes that "there is only drudgery in digging roots," whereas Draper writes, "!Kung women impress one as a self-contained people with a high sense of self-esteem."

Feature 2: Selection or Omission of Details

Another feature that creates an angle of vision (and therefore influences a reader's view) is the writer's selection or omission of details. For example, Marshal focuses on the tastelessness of the vegetables and the heaviness of the women's loads, creating an overall impression of women's work as thankless and exhausting. Draper focuses on the excitement of the children awaiting their mothers' return and the fearlessness of the women as they forage "eight to ten miles from home," creating an impression of self-reliant women performing an essential task.

Feature 3: Choice of Words

Writers can also influence readers through their choice of particular words. Because words carry emotional connotations as well as denotative meanings, any given word is a kind of lens that filters its subject in a certain way. The first anthropologist chooses words that connote listlessness and fatigue, such as "drudgery," "trudging," "heavy," and "sagging." In contrast, the second anthropologist chooses words that connote energy—the children "scan" the bush, "leap and exclaim," and "speculate," while the women "forage."

Feature 4: Use of Figurative Language

Figurative language—metaphors, similes, and analogies that compare or equate their subject to something else—can profoundly affect perception of a subject. When Rubini writes that oil companies are "salivating" for new oil-drilling opportunities, the reader's negative image of drooling and voracious dogs is transferred subconsciously to the oil companies. If those same companies were said to be "exploring new paths toward U.S. independence from foreign oil," the reader might see them in a quite different light.

Feature 5: Sentence Structure

Another subtle way to control the rhetorical effect of a passage is through sentence structure. By placing key words and phrases in emphatic positions (for example, at the end of a long sentence, in a short sentence surrounded by long sentences, or in a main clause rather than a subordinate clause), writers can emphasize some parts of the passage while de-emphasizing others. Consider the difference in emphasis of these two possible sentences for a letter of recommendation for Neal Weasel (from the exercise on pp. 76–77).

> Although Neal Weasel was often moody and brusque in my classes, he is surely a genius.

> Although Neal Weasel is surely a genius, he was often moody and brusque in my classes.

Most readers will agree that the first version emphasizes Neal's brilliance and the second version emphasizes his less than peachy personality. The passages are equally factual—they both contain the same information—but they subtly convey different impressions.

Next consider how Marshal uses sentence structure to create a negative feeling about !Kung women's plant-gathering role:

> Women bring most of the daily food that sustains the life of the people, but the roots and berries that are the principal plant foods of the Nyae Nyae !Kung are apt to be tasteless, harsh and not very satisfying. People crave meat.

Here the writer's emphasis is on meat as highly desirable (the short sentence, "People crave meat," in an environment of long sentences is especially emphatic) and on vegetables as "tasteless, harsh and not very satisfying" (these words occur in the stress position at the end of a long sentence). We could rewrite this passage, keeping the same facts, but creating a quite different rhetorical effect.

Although the !Kung people crave meat and consider the plant food of the Kalahari tasteless, harsh, and not very satisfying, the women nevertheless provide most of the daily food that sustains the life of the people.

In this version, the emphasis is on how the women sustain the life of the people—a point presented in a nonstressed position in the original passage.

FOR WRITING AND DISCUSSION

What follows is a student example of two contrasting descriptions written for the assignment in this chapter. Read the descriptions carefully. Working individually, analyze the descriptions rhetorically to explain how the writer has created contrasting impressions through overt statements of meaning, selection and omission of details, word choice, figurative language, and sentence structure. You will do the same thing for your own two descriptions in Part B of your assignment. Spend approximately ten minutes freewriting your analysis. Then, working in small groups or as a whole class, share your analyses, trying to reach agreement on examples of each of the five features just described.

Light rain gently drops into the puddles that have formed along the curb as I look out my apartment window at the corner of 14th and East John. Pedestrians layered in sweaters, raincoats, and scarves and guarded with shiny rubber boots and colorful umbrellas sip their steaming hot triple-tall lattes. Some share smiles and pleasant exchanges as they hurry down the street, hastening to work where it is warm and dry. Others, smelling the aroma of French roast espresso coming from the coffee bar next to the bus stop, listen for the familiar rumbling sound that will mean the 56 bus has arrived. Radiant orange, yellow, and red leaves blanket the sidewalk in the areas next to the maple trees that line the road. Along the curb a mother holds the hand of her toddler, dressed like a miniature tugboat captain in yellow raincoat and pants, who splashes happily in a puddle.

A solemn grayness hangs in the air, as I peer out the window of my apartment at the corner of 14th and East John. A steady drizzle

of rain leaves boot-drenching puddles for pedestrians to avoid. Bun-
dled in rubber boots, sweaters, coats, and rain-soaked scarves, commuters clutch Styrofoam cups of coffee as a defense against the
biting cold. They lift their heads every so often to take a small
sip of caffeine, but look sleep-swollen nevertheless. Pedestrians
hurry past each other, moving quickly to get away from the dismal
weather, the dull grayness. Some nod a brief hello to a familiar
face, but most clutch their overcoats and tread grimly on, looking
to avoid puddles or spray from passing cars. Others stand at the bus
stop, hunched over, waiting in the drab early morning for the smell
of diesel that means the 56 bus has arrived. Along the curb an impatient mother jerks the hand of a toddler to keep him from stomp-
ing in an oil-streaked puddle.

Using Rhetorical Knowledge to Become a Strong Reader

Knowing how to analyze a text rhetorically can help you become a stronger reader. The more you understand how a text works, the more you can appreciate its particular point of view. Learning to ask what is *not* in the text, why the text is constructed *this* way and not *that* way, or why the writer took this particular point of view and not another enables you to identify the forces that shape what a writer sees and opens up the possibility for you to challenge and speak back to the text.

Reading written texts in this way prepares you to "read" many other human artifacts—body language, advertising images, architecture, classroom seating arrangements, party behaviors—in a similar way. You can learn to ask questions like the following:

What news items are *not* included on page 1 of today's paper? What belief or value system (and whose) causes this story to be front-page news while relegating that story to page 4?

When I read *Mademoiselle* or *Seventeen*, what products are *not* being advertised in its pages? Why? Why are there so few advertisements for stereo equipment in these magazines but so many such ads in *Playboy*?

Why does a party in the Philippines typically include all the host's neighbors and relatives whereas a party in the United States typically includes just one social group (for example, teens, but not uncles, aunts, and neighbors)? How do differences in who is invited or not invited to parties reflect differences in cultures?

We return to such questions in subsequent chapters. For now, keep in mind that the exercise of creating two different descriptions of the same scene can open up new ways of asking questions about countless things in the world around you.

Which Comes First, Perception or Interpretation?

So far we have been examining how writers, in observing a certain scene from their unique angle of vision, create a rhetorical effect through language choices. What we have saved for last is a crucial chicken-and-egg question: Which comes first, the writer's perception or the writer's interpretation? For example, did the two anthropologists begin their observations of the !Kung people with no preconceived theories or notions, letting their interpretations arise from their observations, or did they start with a theory or hypothesis, which in turn determined what they saw? This is a truly knotty problem, for, as we try to show in this section, it is difficult to draw a clear line between observation and interpretation; what you see and what you are predisposed to see are complexly intertwined.

On the face of it, terms such as *observation, perception,* and *seeing* seem nonproblematic. Objects are objects, and the process of perceiving an object—assuming that you aren't imbibing mind-altering drugs—is immediate and automatic. However, perception is never a simple matter. Consider what we call the expert–novice phenomenon. Experts on any given subject notice details about that subject that a novice overlooks. An experienced bird-watcher can distinguish dozens of kinds of swallows by subtle differences in size, markings, and behaviors, whereas a non-bird-watcher sees only a group of birds of similar size and shape. Similarly, people observing an unfamiliar game (for example, an American watching cricket or a Nigerian watching baseball) don't know what actions or events have meaning and hence don't know what to look for. Psychologists have found that after observing an inning of baseball, avid baseball fans remember numerous details about plays on the field, but people unfamiliar with the game remember none of these details, although they may have vivid recollections of people in the stands or of a player's peculiar mannerisms. In short, prior knowledge or absence of it causes people to see different things.

Cultural differences also affect perception. An American watching two Japanese business executives greet each other might not know that they are participating in an elaborate cultural code of bowing, eye contact, speech patterns, and timing of movements that convey meanings about social status. An Ethiopian newly arrived in the United States and an American sitting in a doctor's office will see different things when the nurse points to one of them to come into the examination room. The American notices nothing remarkable about the scene; he or she may remember what the nurse was wearing or something about the wallpaper. The Ethiopian, however, is likely to remember the nurse's act of pointing, a gesture of rudeness used in Ethiopia only to beckon children or discipline dogs. Again, observers of the same scene see different things.

Sometimes your beliefs and values are so powerful that they create blind spots. You won't notice data that contradict them. You may perceive contradictory data at some level, but if they don't register on your mind as significant, you disregard them. In this vein, a syndicated columnist explains why people who favor gun control and people who oppose it have trouble communicating with each other; they each filter out information that contradicts their own beliefs.

> The gun control advocates keep large files on every case of careless gun use they can find.
> But they don't have any records of people successfully defending themselves against criminals.
> At the same time, the National Rifle Association has thick files on honest citizens using guns to kill, wound or capture criminals.
> But under F in its file cabinets, there is nothing about family gun tragedies.
>
> —Mike Royko, *Seattle Times*

The lesson here is that people note and remember whatever is consistent with their worldview much more readily than they note and remember whatever is inconsistent with that view. What you believe is what you see.

To really see something that is familiar to you, to get beyond your beliefs about a subject in order to recognize aspects of it that are inconsistent with those beliefs, you may need to "defamiliarize" it, to make it strange. Many artists try to defamiliarize familiar objects by seeing them from unfamiliar perspectives, sometimes even distorting the object to disrupt ordinary ways of seeing. An artist might draw something upside down, or a writer might write about an event from the point of view of someone he or she considers loathsome—whatever it takes to wipe away "the film of habit" from the object. The writing project for this chapter will get you to see your scene in unfamiliar ways.

READINGS

The two readings in this section raise issues about observation as a rhetorical act. The first, by American humorist Mark Twain, shows how his perception of the Mississippi River changed when he became a steamboat pilot.

MARK TWAIN
TWO WAYS OF SEEING A RIVER

Now when I had mastered the language of this water and had come to know every   1
trifling feature that bordered the great river as familiarly as I knew the letters of the alphabet, I had made a valuable acquisition. But I had lost something, too. I had lost

something which could never be restored to me while I lived. All the grace, the beauty, the poetry, had gone out of the majestic river! I still kept in mind a certain wonderful sunset which I witnessed when steamboating was new to me. A broad expanse of the river was turned to blood, in the middle distance the red hue brightened into gold, through which a solid log came floating, black and conspicuous; in one place a long, slanting mark lay sparkling upon the water; in another the surface was broken by boiling, tumbling rings, that were as many-tinted as an opal; where the ruddy flush was faintest, was a smooth spot that was covered with graceful circles and radiating lines, ever so delicately traced; the shore on our left was densely wooded and the somber shadow that fell from this forest was broken in one place by a long, ruffled trail that shone like silver, and high above the forest wall a clean-stemmed dead tree waved a single leafy bough that glowed like a flame in the unobstructed splendor that was flowing from the sun. There were graceful curves, reflected images, woody heights, soft distances, and over the whole scene, far and near, the dissolving lights drifted steadily, enriching it every passing moment with new marvels of coloring.

2   I stood like one bewitched. I drank it in, in a speechless rapture. The world was new to me and I had never seen anything like this at home. But as I have said, a day came when I began to cease from noting the glories and the charms which the moon and the sun and the twilight wrought upon the river's face; another day came when I ceased altogether to note them. Then, if that sunset scene had been repeated, I should have looked upon it without rapture, and should have commented upon it inwardly after this fashion: "This sun means that we are going to have wind to-morrow; that floating log means that the river is rising, small thanks to it; that slanting mark on the water refers to a bluff reef which is going to kill somebody's steamboat one of these nights, if it keeps on stretching out like that; those tumbling 'boils' show a dissolving bar and a changing channel there; the lines and circles in the slick water over yonder are a warning that that troublesome place is shoaling up dangerously; that silver streak in the shadow of the forest is the 'break' from a new snag and he has located himself in the very best place he could have found to fish for steamboats; that tall dead tree, with a single living branch, is not going to last long, and then how is a body ever going to get through this blind place at night without the friendly old landmark?"

3   No, the romance and beauty were all gone from the river. All the value any feature of it had for me now was the amount of usefulness it could furnish toward compassing the safe piloting of a steamboat. Since those days, I have pitied doctors from my heart. What does the lovely flush in a beauty's cheek mean to a doctor but a "break" that ripples above some deadly disease? Are not all her visible charms sown thick with what are to him the signs and symbols of hidden decay? Does he ever see her beauty at all, or doesn't he simply view her professionally and comment upon her unwholesome condition all to himself? And doesn't he sometimes wonder whether he has gained most or lost most by learning his trade?

Thinking Critically About "Two Ways of Seeing a River"

1. Earlier in this chapter we asked which comes first, knowledge or perception? What seems to be Twain's view of the relationship between knowledge and perception?
2. Do you agree with Twain that professionals such as doctors or riverboat pilots lose the ability to see the beauty in the subjects they study?

The second reading is by a well-known linguist, S. I. Hayakawa, who late in life became a Republican U.S. Senator from California. In this article, Hayakawa addresses one of the problems we have wrestled with throughout this chapter: Is it possible to write a completely objective description uninfluenced by your angle of vision? Whereas we tend toward the rhetorical view that you can never completely escape your own situated perspective, Hayakawa believes that writers can attain a reasonably objective language if they exercise certain cautions. The following piece is excerpted from Hayakawa's *Language in Thought and Action*.

S. I. HAYAKAWA
REPORTS, INFERENCES, JUDGMENTS

For the purposes of the interchange of information, the basic symbolic act is the   1
report of what we have seen, heard, or felt: "There is a ditch on each side of the road." "You can get those at Smith's Hardware Store for $2.75." "There aren't any fish on that side of the lake, but there are on this side." Then there are reports of reports: "The longest waterfall in the world is Victoria Falls." "The Battle of Hastings took place in 1066." "The papers say that there was a smash-up on Highway 41 near Evansville." Reports adhere to the following rules: first, they are *capable of verification;* second, they *exclude,* as far as possible, *inferences and judgments.* (These terms will be defined later.)

Verifiability

Reports are verifiable. We may not always be able to verify them ourselves, since   2
we cannot track down the evidence for every piece of history we know, nor can we all go to Evansville to see the remains of the smash-up before they are cleared away. But if we are roughly agreed upon the names of things, upon what constitutes a "foot," "yard," "bushel," "kilogram," "meter," and so on, and upon how to measure time, there is relatively little danger of our misunderstanding each other. Even in a world such as we have today, in which everybody seems to be quarreling with everybody else, *we still to a surprising degree trust each other's reports.* We ask directions of total strangers when we are traveling. We follow directions on road signs without being suspicious of the people who put them up. We read books of information about science, mathematics, automotive engineering, travel, geography, the history of costume, and other such factual matters, and we usually assume that the author is doing his best to tell us as truly as he can what he knows. And we are safe in so assuming most of the time. With the interest given today to the discussion of biased newspapers, propagandists, and the general untrustworthiness of many of the communications we receive, we are likely to forget that we still have an enormous amount of reliable information available and that deliberate misinformation, except in warfare, is still more the exception than the rule. The desire for self-preservation that compelled men to evolve means for the exchange of information also compels them to regard the giving of false information as profoundly reprehensible.

At its highest development, the language of reports is the language of science. By   3
"highest development" we mean greatest general usefulness. Presbyterian and Catholic,

workingman and capitalist, East German and West German *agree* on the meanings of such symbols as *2 × 2 = 4, 100° C, HNO₃, 3:35 A.M., 1940 A.D., 1,000 kilowatts, Quercus agrifolia,* and so on. But how, it may be asked, can there be agreement about even this much among people who disagree about political philosophies, ethical ideas, religious beliefs, and the survival of my business versus the survival of yours? The answer is that circumstances *compel men to agree,* whether they wish to or not. If, for example, there were a dozen different religious sects in the United States, each insisting on its own way of naming the time of the day and the days of the year, the mere necessity of having a dozen different calendars, a dozen different kinds of watches, and a dozen sets of schedules for business hours, trains, and television programs, to say nothing of the effort that would be required for translating terms from one nomenclature to another, would make life as we know it impossible.

4   The language of reports, then, including the more accurate reports of science, is "map" language, and because it gives us reasonably accurate representations of the "territory," it enables us to get work done. Such language may often be dull reading: one does not usually read logarithmic tables or telephone directories for entertainment. But we could not get along without it. There are numberless occasions in the talking and writing we do in everyday life that *require that we state things in such a way that everybody will be able to understand and agree with our formulation.*

Inferences

5   Not that inferences are not important—we rely in everyday life and in science as much on *inferences* as on reports—in some areas of thought, for example, geology, paleontology, and nuclear physics, reports are the foundations; but inferences (and inferences upon inferences) are the main body of the science. An inference, as we shall use the term, *is a statement about the unknown made on the basis of the known.* We may *infer* from the material and cut of a woman's clothes her wealth or social position; we may *infer* from the character of the ruins the origin of the fire that destroyed the building; we may *infer* from a man's calloused hands the nature of his occupation; we may *infer* from a senator's vote on an armaments bill his attitude toward Russia; we may *infer* from the structure of the land the path of a prehistoric glacier; we may *infer* from a halo on an unexposed photographic plate its past proximity to radioactive materials; we may *infer* from the sound of an engine the condition of its connecting rods. Inferences may be carefully or carelessly made. They may be made on the basis of a broad background of previous experience with the subject matter or with no experience at all. For example, the inferences a good mechanic can make about the internal condition of a motor by listening to it are often startlingly accurate, while the inferences made by an amateur (if he tries to make any) may be entirely wrong. But the common characteristic of inferences is that they are statements about matters which are not directly known, made on the basis of what has been observed.

6   The avoidance of inferences . . . requires that we make no guesses as to what is going on in other people's minds. When we say, "He was angry," we are not reporting; we are making an inference from such observable facts as the following: "He pounded his fist on the table; he swore; he threw the telephone directory at his stenographer." In this particular example, the inference appears to be safe; nevertheless, it is important to remember, especially for the purposes of training oneself, that it is an inference. Such expressions as "He thought a lot of himself," "He was scared of girls," "He has an inferiority complex," made on the basis of casual observation, and "What Russia really wants to do is to establish a communist world dictatorship," made on the basis of casual

reading, are highly inferential. We should keep in mind their inferential character and . . . should substitute for them such statements as "He rarely spoke to subordinates in the plant," "I saw him at a party, and he never danced except when one of the girls asked him to," "He wouldn't apply for the scholarship, although I believe he could have won it easily," and "The Russian delegation to the United Nations has asked for *A, B,* and *C.* Last year they voted against *M* and *N* and voted for *X* and *Y.* On the basis of facts such as these, the newspaper I read makes the inference that what Russia really wants is to establish a communist world dictatorship. I agree."

Even when we exercise every caution to avoid inferences and to report only what 7 we see and experience, we all remain prone to error, since the making of inferences is a quick, almost automatic process. We may watch a car weaving as it goes down the road and say, "Look at that *drunken driver,*" although what we *see* is only *the irregular motion of the car.* I once saw a man leave a dollar at a lunch counter and hurry out. Just as I was wondering why anyone should leave so generous a tip in so modest an establishment, the waitress came, picked up the dollar, put it in the cash register as she punched up ninety cents, and put a dime in her pocket. In other words, my description to myself of the event, "a dollar tip," turned out to be not a report but an inference.

All this is not to say that we should never make inferences. The inability to make 8 inferences is itself a sign of mental disorder. For example, the speech therapist Laura L. Lee writes, "The aphasic [brain-damaged] adult with whom I worked had great difficulty in making inferences about a picture I showed her. She could tell me what was happening at the moment in the picture, but could not tell me what might have happened just before the picture or just afterward." Hence the question is not whether or not we make inferences; the question is whether or not we are aware of the inferences we make. . . .

Judgments

. . . By judgments, we shall mean *all expressions of the writer's approval or disap-* 9 *proval of the occurrences, persons, or objects he is describing.* For example, a report cannot say, "It was a wonderful car," but must say something like this: "It has been driven 50,000 miles and has never required any repairs." Again, statements such as "Jack lied to us" must be avoided in favor of the more verifiable statement, "Jack told us he didn't have the keys to his car with him. However, when he pulled a handkerchief out of his pocket a few minutes later, a bunch of keys fell out." Also a report may not say, "The senator was stubborn, defiant, and uncooperative," or "The senator courageously stood by his principles"; it must say instead, "The senator's vote was the only one against the bill."

Many people regard statements such as the following as statements of "fact": "Jack 10 *lied* to us," "Jerry is a *thief,*" "Tommy is *clever.*" As ordinarily employed, however, the word "lied" involves first an inference (that Jack knew otherwise and deliberately misstated the facts) and second a judgment (that the speaker disapproves of what he has inferred that Jack did). In the other two instances, we may substitute such expressions as, "Jerry was convicted of theft and served two years at Waupun," and "Tommy plays the violin, leads his class in school, and is captain of the debating team." After all, to say of a man that he is a "thief" is to say in effect, "He has stolen *and will steal again*"—which is more of a prediction than a report. Even to say, "He has stolen," is to make an inference (and simultaneously to pass a judgment) on an act about which there may be difference of opinion among those who have examined the evidence upon which the conviction was obtained. But to say that he was "convicted of theft" is to make a statement capable of being agreed upon through verification in court and prison records.

11　　Scientific verifiability rests upon the external observation of facts, not upon the heaping up of judgments. If one person says, "Peter is a dead-beat," and another says, "I think so too," the statement has not been verified. In court cases, considerable trouble is sometimes caused by witnesses who cannot distinguish their judgments from the facts upon which those judgments are based. Cross-examinations under these circumstances go something like this:

> WITNESS: That dirty double-crosser ratted on me.
>
> DEFENSE ATTORNEY: Your honor, I object.
>
> JUDGE: Objection sustained. (Witness's remark is stricken from the record.) Now, try to tell the court exactly what happened.
>
> WITNESS: He double-crossed me, the dirty, lying rat!
>
> DEFENSE ATTORNEY: Your honor, I object!
>
> JUDGE: Objection sustained. (Witness's remark is again stricken from the record.) Will the witness try to stick to the facts.
>
> WITNESS: But I'm telling you the facts, your honor. He did double-cross me.

This can continue indefinitely unless the cross-examiner exercises some ingenuity in order to get at the facts behind the judgment. To the witness it is a "fact" that he was "double-crossed." Often patient questioning is required before the factual bases of the judgment are revealed.

12　　Many words, of course, simultaneously convey a report and a judgment on the fact reported, as will be discussed more fully in a later chapter. For the purposes of a report as here defined, these should be avoided. Instead of "sneaked in," one might say "entered quietly"; instead of "politician," "congressman" or "alderman," or "candidate for office"; instead of "bureaucrat," "public official"; instead of "tramp," "homeless unemployed"; instead of "dictatorial set-up," "centralized authority"; instead of "crackpot," "holder of nonconformist views." A newspaper reporter, for example, is not permitted to write, "A crowd of suckers came to listen to Senator Smith last evening in that rickety fire-trap and ex-dive that disfigures the south edge of town." Instead he says, "Between 75 and 100 people heard an address last evening by Senator Smith at the Evergreen Gardens near the South Side city limits.". . .

How Judgments Stop Thought

13　　A judgment ("He is a fine boy," "It was a beautiful service," "Baseball is a healthful sport," "She is an awful bore") is a conclusion, summing up a large number of previously observed facts. The reader is probably familiar with the fact that students almost always have difficulty in writing themes of the required length because their ideas give out after a paragraph or two. The reason for this is that those early paragraphs contain so many judgments that there is little left to be said. When the conclusions are carefully excluded, however, and observed facts are given instead, there is never any trouble about the length of papers; in fact, they tend to become too long, since inexperienced writers, when told to give facts, often give far more than are necessary, because they lack discrimination between the important and the trivial.

14　　Still another consequence of judgments early into the course of a written exercise—and this applies also to hasty judgments in everyday thought—is the temporary blindness they induce. When, for example, a description starts with the words, "He was a real Madison Avenue executive" or "She was a typical hippie," if we continue writing at all, we must make all our later statements consistent with those judgments. The result is that all the individual characteristics of this particular "executive" or this particular "hippie" are lost sight of; and the rest of the account is likely to deal not with observed facts but the stereotypes and the writer's particular notion (based on previously read stories, movies, pictures, and so forth) of what "Madison Avenue executives" or "typical hippies" are like. The premature judgment, that is, often prevents us from seeing what is directly in front of us, so that clichés take the place of fresh description. Therefore, even if the writer feels sure at the beginning of a written account that the man he is describing is a "real leatherneck" or that the scene he is describing is a "beautiful residential suburb," he will conscientiously keep such notions out of his head, lest his vision be obstructed.

Thinking Critically About "Reports, Inferences, Judgments"

1. Using Hayakawa's definitions and adopting his perspective, analyze the two passages by the anthropologists on the !Kung women (p. 80), pointing out what parts of each passages are observable facts, what parts are inferences, and what parts are judgments.
2. How would the anthropologists' passages have to be rewritten to meet Hayakawa's criteria for a report?
3. The writing assignment for this chapter calls for two descriptions of the same scene, one slanted positively and the other negatively. Hayakawa, we surmise, might ask you instead to observe your scene and then write a descriptive report on what you saw. How would your descriptions of the scene have to be rewritten to qualify as a report? Would your descriptive report, written to meet Hayakawa's criteria, still be slanted?
4. Throughout this book, we have called thesis statements risky or surprising assertions that are in tension with countering assertions. In Hayakawa's terms, a thesis statement is a judgment. Hayakawa makes the surprising claim that "judgments stop thought." What is he getting at, and how would you respond?
5. What parts of Hayakawa's argument do you find most persuasive? Least persuasive?
6. For a view of language remarkably different from Hayakawa's, see the excerpt from Jane Tompkins's "'Indians': Textualism, Morality, and the Problem of History" (Chapter 8, pp. 173–80). To what extent does Tompkins believe it is possible to get a verifiable report on what Native Americans were like when the Puritans arrived in America in the seventeenth century?

COMPOSING YOUR ESSAY

Since the assignment for this chapter has two parts—Part A calling for two contrasting descriptions and Part B calling for a rhetorical analysis—we will address each part separately.

Generating and Exploring Ideas for Your Two Descriptions

When you think about description, it sometimes helps to imagine yourself as the companion of a recently blinded person. Suppose that you were to become that person's eyes, describing your scene so fully that your blind companion could share your experience of seeing it. Then your blind companion, having a newly heightened sense of hearing, touch, and smell, could enrich your own perceptions so that the two of you, pooling your perceptions, could work together to create a richly detailed description of the scene. In your writing, good description should also be packed with sensory detail—sights, sounds, smells, textures, even on occasion tastes—all contributing to a dominant impression that gives the description focus.

After you have chosen a subject for your two descriptions, observe it intensely for fifteen or twenty minutes. One way to train yourself to notice sensory details is to create a sensory chart, with one column for your pleasant description and one column for your unpleasant description.

Pleasant Impression	Unpleasant Impression
Sight/eyes	Sight/eyes
Sound/ears	Sound/ears
Odor/nose	Odor/nose
Touch/fingers	Touch/fingers
Taste/tongue	Taste/tongue

As you observe your scene, note details that appeal to each of the senses and then try describing them first positively (left column) and then negatively (right column). One student, observing a scene in a local tavern, made these notes in her sensory chart:

Taste/tongue	**Taste/tongue**
salted and buttered popcorn	salty, greasy popcorn
frosty pitchers of ice-cold beer	half-drunk pitchers of stale, warm beer
big bowls of salted-in-the-shell peanuts on the tables	mess of peanut shells and discarded pretzel wrappers on tables and floor
Sound/ears	**Sound/ears**
hum of students laughing and chatting	din of high-pitched giggles and various obnoxious frat guys shouting at each other from across the room
the juke box playing oldies but goodies from the early Beatles	juke box blaring out-of-date music

Shaping and Drafting Your Two Descriptions

Once you have observed your scene and made your sensory chart, compose your two descriptions. You will need to decide on an ordering principle for your descriptions. It generally makes sense to begin with an overview of the scene to orient your reader.

> From the park bench near 23rd and Maple, one can watch the people strolling by the duck pond.

> By 8:00 on any Friday night, Pagliacci's Pizzeria on Broadway becomes one of the city's most unusual gathering places.

Then, you need a plan for arranging details. There are no hard and fast rules here, but there are some typical practices. You can arrange details in the following ways:

- by spatially scanning from left to right or from far to near
- by using the written equivalent of a movie zoom shot; begin with a broad overview of the scene, then move to close-up descriptions of specific details

Compose your pleasant description, selecting and focusing on details that convey a positive impression. Then compose your unpleasant description. Each description should comprise one fully developed paragraph (125–175 words).

Revising Your Two Descriptions

Share your drafts with classmates, and use their suggestions to help guide your revision. The following questions will help you and your reviewers.

1. *Do the two descriptions focus on the same scene at the same time?* The rules for the assignment ask you to use only factual details observable in the same scene at the same time. It violates the spirit of the assignment to have one scene in the rain and another in the sunshine, or to have one scene at a winning basketball game and another at a losing game.
2. *Does the writer use plenty of "show" words and few "tell" words?* One of the surest ways to improve description is by showing rather than telling. Words that tell interpret a scene without describing it. They name an interior, mental state, telling the reader what emotional reaction to draw from the scene. In contrast, words that show describe a scene through sensory details that appeal to sight, sound, smell, touch, and even taste. The description itself evokes the desired mental state without requiring the writer to name it.

   In their rough drafts, many writers try to create contrasting impressions of a scene simply by using different tell words, as in the following rough drafts.

Positive Impression	The smiling merchants happily talked with customers trying to get them to buy their products.
Negative Impression	The annoying merchants kept hassling customers trying to convince them to buy their products.

In this example, the negative words "annoying" and "hassling" and the positive words "smiling" and "happily" create a contrast in tone, but neither passage describes the scene. Now read the revised passages that use show words.

Positive Impression   One of the merchants, selling thick-wooled Peruvian sweaters, nodded approvingly as a woman tried on a richly textured, blue cardigan in front of the mirror.

Negative Impression   One of the merchants, hawking those Peruvian sweaters that you find in every open-air market, tried to convince a woman that the lumpy, oversized cardigan she was trying on looked stylish.

Here are some more examples taken from students' drafts before and after revision.

Draft with Tell Words	**Revision with Show Words**
Children laugh and point animatedly at all the surroundings.	Across the way, a small boy taps his friend's shoulder and points at a circus clown.
The wonderful smell of food cooking on the barbecue fills my nose.	The tantalizing smell of grilled hamburgers and buttered corn on the cob wafts from the barbecue area of the park, where men in their cookout aprons wield forks and spatulas and drink Budweisers.
The paintings on the wall are confusing, dark, abstract, demented, and convey feelings of unhappiness and suffering.	The paintings on the wall, viewed through the smoke-filled room, seem confusing and abstract—the work of a demented artist on a bad trip. Splotches of black paint are splattered over a greenish yellow background like bugs on vomit.

3. *Can the focus on a dominant impression be improved through more effective word choice?*   Can you improve the focus on each description's dominant impression (pleasant/unpleasant) by choosing naming and action words with stronger connotations? For example, consider synonyms for the generic word *shoe.* Most people wear shoes, but only certain people on certain occasions wear wing tips or pumps or sandals. Among words for kinds of sandals, *Birkenstocks* carries a different connotation from *Tevas* or *thongs* or *strappy espadrilles with a faux-metallic finish.* Consider possible substitutions for the verb *to laugh.* One can laugh, rejoice, giggle, chuckle, cackle, jeer, joke, guffaw, mock, snort, snicker, sneer, applaud, titter, scoff, flout, ridicule, poke fun at, taunt, hiss, hoot, cheer, razz, squeal. Search your draft for places where you could substitute more colorful or precise words for a generic word to convey your dominant impression more effectively.

Generating and Exploring Ideas for Your Rhetorical Analysis

Part B of the assignment asks you to do a rhetorical analysis of your two passages, focusing on their differences. Follow the suggestions on pages 81–83 for doing a rhetorical analysis, focusing on overt statements, selection or omission of details, word choice, figurative language, and sentence structure.

The last part of the rhetorical analysis should be your reflection on what you learned from doing this assignment. In effect, you are answering your reader's "So what?" question. "So you wrote two different descriptions," your reader might say. "Why are you telling me this? What's your point?" Your reader needs an answer to this question to understand the larger implications—the value—of what he or she has read. In sharing your two descriptions of a scene, what larger point do you want to make about writing and reading? What is the surprise (new knowledge? new understanding about description?) that you want to bring your reader?

What did you learn? To help you generate ideas for this section, try freewriting your responses to the following questions:

1. What are the most important things you learned from reading this chapter and writing your two descriptions?
2. How has reading this chapter and doing this writing project affected the way you now read other texts, for example, the newspaper or readings from your other courses?
3. Did the need to slant your descriptions affect the way you observed? How so? Do you think you could write a single objective description of your scene that would be better than the two paragraphs you wrote? Why?
4. What are the most important questions that this chapter raises in your mind? What does it make you think about?

Freewriting for several minutes in response to each of these questions should give you enough material for your final reflection on what you learned.

Shaping and Drafting Your Rhetorical Analysis

The structure of your analysis is prescribed by the assignment: (a) a rhetorical analysis of the difference between your two descriptions, and (b) a final reflection on what you learned.

Revising Your Rhetorical Analysis

When you have written a draft of your rhetorical analysis, share it with your classmates to get insights about how best to revise it. Your goal at the revision stage is to discover the ideas that you want to communicate and then to make those ideas as clear as possible for readers. The following guidelines for peer reviewers should be helpful.

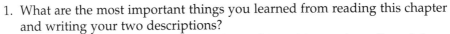

g   u   i   d   e   l   i   n   e   s

for Peer Reviewers

Instructions for peer reviews, including use of these guidelines, are provided in Chapter 21, pages 527–28. To write a peer review for a classmate, use your own paper, numbering your responses to correspond to the questions on the guide-lines. At the head of your paper place the author's name and your own name as shown.

Author's Name: _____

Peer Reviewer's Name: _____

  I. Read the draft at normal reading speed from beginning to end. As you read, do the following:
   A. Place a wavy line in the margin next to any passages that you find con-fusing, or that contain something that doesn't seem to fit, or that other-wise slow down your reading.
   B. Place a "Good!" in the margin next to any passages where you think the writing is particularly strong or interesting.
 II. Read the draft again slowly. Describe for the writer what you currently see in this draft. If you have difficulty answering any of the following questions, explain briefly the source of your difficulty.
   A. If there are any differences in the time or place of the two descriptions or other differences in "fact" (change in the weather, in what people are doing, or so forth), describe these differences.
   B. In the two descriptions, where has the author used show words that ap-peal to the senses?
   C. Where has the author relied primarily on tell words?
   D. In the analysis section, what examples does the writer use from his or her own descriptions to illustrate differences in overt commentary, selec-tion or omission of details, word choice, figurative language, and sen-tence structure?
   E. In the final reflection, what does the writer say that he or she has learned from doing this assignment? What details does the writer use to illustrate these points?
III. What recommendations do you have for improving this draft?
   A. How might the writer improve the two descriptions?
    1. Where could the writer strengthen the show words?
    2. If the writer has relied primarily on one or two methods of creating contrast (overt interpretation, selection or omission of details), how might he or she use other methods (contrasting word choice, contrast-ing figurative language, changes in sentence structure)?
   B. How might the writer improve the rhetorical analysis?
    1. Do you disagree with any of the writer's ideas? Which ones, and why?
    2. Should anything be added to or changed in the analysis? (Could better or different examples be included)?
   C. How might the writer improve the final reflection on what he or she learned?
    1. What might the writer add?
    2. Could any of the writer's points be better developed or illustrated?

       D. Sum up what you see as the chief strengths and problem areas of this draft.
1. Strengths
2. Problem areas
IV. Read the draft one more time. Place a check in the margin wherever you notice problems in grammar, spelling, or mechanics (one check per problem).

c h a p t e r 6

Reading Rhetorically
The Writer as Strong Reader

ABOUT READING RHETORICALLY

Many new college students are surprised by the amount, range, and difficulty of reading they have to do in college. Every day they are challenged by reading assignments ranging from scholarly articles and textbooks on complex subject matter to primary sources, such as Plato's dialogues or Darwin's *Voyage of the Beagle.*

The goal of this chapter is to help you become a more powerful reader of academic texts, prepared to take part in the conversations of the disciplines you study. To this end, we review two skills essential to your college reading: your ability to listen carefully to a text, to summarize its argument, and to see the world through its author's perspective; and your ability to speak back to the text by resisting its argument or by employing its methods in a new way. We say that readers who respond strongly to texts in this manner *read rhetorically;* that is, they are aware of the effect a text is intended to have on them, and they critically consider that effect, resisting, without rejecting, the text's intentions.

EXPLORING RHETORICAL READING

As an introduction to rhetorical reading, we would like you to read Dr. Marcia Angell's "Disease as a Reflection of the Psyche," which appeared in the *New England Journal of Medicine.* Prior to reading the article, complete the following opinion survey. Answer each question using a 1 to 5 scale, with 1 meaning "strongly agree" and 5 meaning "strongly disagree."

1. Stress can cause many diseases, such as high blood pressure, peptic ulcers, and asthma.
2. Certain personality types are prone to certain diseases.
3. Your emotional state influences your physical health.

4. People with a strong will to live and an optimistic attitude toward life recover from diseases faster than do passive or pessimistic people.

When you have finished rating your degree of agreement with these statements, read Angell's article, using whatever note-taking, underlining, or highlighting strategies you normally use when reading for a class. When you have finished reading, complete the exercises that follow.

MARCIA ANGELL

DISEASE AS A REFLECTION OF THE PSYCHE

Is cancer more likely in unhappy people? Can people who have cancer improve their chances of survival by learning to enjoy life and to think optimistically? What about heart attacks, peptic ulcers, asthma, rheumatoid arthritis, and inflammatory bowel disease? Are they caused by stress in certain personality types, and will changing the personality change the course of the disease? A stranger in this country would not have to be here very long to guess that most Americans think the answer to these questions is yes.

The popular media, stirred by occasional reports in the medical literature, remind us incessantly of the hazards of certain personality types. We are told that Type A people are vulnerable to heart attacks, repressed people (especially those who have suffered losses) are at risk of cancer, worry causes peptic ulcers, and so on. The connection between mental state and disease would seem to be direct and overriding. The hard-driving executive has a heart attack *because* he is pushing for promotion; the middle-aged housewife gets breast cancer *because* she is brooding about her empty nest.

Furthermore, we are told that just as mental state causes disease, so can changes in our outlook and approach to life restore health. Books, magazines, and talk shows abound in highly specific advice about achieving the necessary changes, as well as in explanations about how they work. Norman Cousins, for example, tells us how he managed to achieve a remission of his ankylosing spondylitis by means of laughter and vitamin C—the former, he assumes, operating through reversal of "adrenal exhaustion."[1] Carl and Stephanie Simonton prescribe certain techniques of relaxation and imagery as an adjunct to the conventional treatment of cancer.[2] The imagery includes picturing white cells (strong and purposeful) destroying cancer cells (weak and confused).

Clearly, this sort of postulated connection between mental state and disease is not limited to the effect of mood on our sense of physical well-being. Nor are we talking about relaxation as a worthy goal in itself. Cousins, the Simontons, and others of their persuasion advocate a way of thinking not as an end, but rather as a means for defeating disease. The assumption is that mental state is a major factor in causing and curing specific diseases. Is it, and what is the effect of believing that it is?

The notion that certain mental states bring on certain diseases is not new. In her book, *Illness as Metaphor,* Susan Sontag describes the myths surrounding two mysterious and terrifying diseases—tuberculosis in the 19th century and cancer in the 20th.[3] Tuberculosis was thought to be a disease of excessive feeling. Overly passionate artists "consumed" themselves, both emotionally and through the disease. In contrast, cancer is seen today as a disease of depletion. Emotionally spent people no longer have the energy to battle renegade cells. As Sontag points out, myths like these arise when a disease of unknown cause is particularly dreaded. The myth serves as a form of mastery—we can predict where the disease will strike and we can perhaps ward it off by modifying our inner life. Interestingly, when the cause of such a disease is discovered, it is usually relatively simple and does not involve psychological factors. For example, the elaborate construct of a tuberculosis-prone personality evaporated when tuberculosis was found to be caused by the tubercle bacillus.

6   The evidence for mental state as a cause and cure of today's scourges is not much better than it was for the afflictions of earlier centuries. Most reports of such a connection are anecdotal. They usually deal with patients whose disease remitted after some form of positive thinking, and there is no attempt to determine the frequency of remission without positive thinking. Other, more ambitious studies suffer from such serious flaws in design or analysis that bias is nearly inevitable.[4] In some instances, the bias lies in the interpretation. One frequently cited study, for example, reports that the death rate among people who have recently lost their spouses is higher than that among married people.[5] Although the authors were cautious in their interpretation, others have been quick to ascribe the finding to grief rather than to, say, a change in diet or other habits. Similarly, the known physiologic effects of stress on the adrenal glands are often over-interpreted so that it is a short leap to a view of stress as a cause of one disease or another. In short, the literature contains very few scientifically sound studies of the relation, if there is one, between mental states and disease.

7   In this issue of the *Journal,* Cassileth et al. report the results of a careful prospective study of 359 cancer patients, showing no correlation between a number of psychosocial factors and progression of the disease.[6] In an earlier prospective study of another disease, Case et al. found no correlation between Type A personality and recurrence of acute myocardial infarction.[7] The fact that these well-designed studies were negative raises the possibility that we have been too ready to accept the venerable belief that mental state is an important factor in the cause and cure of disease.

8   Is there any harm in this belief, apart from its lack of scientific substantiation? It might be argued that it is not only harmless but beneficial, in that it allows patients some sense of control over their disease. If, for example, patients believe that imagery can help arrest cancer, then they feel less helpless; there is something they can do.

9   On the other hand, if cancer spreads, despite every attempt to think positively, is the patient at fault? It might seem so. According to Robert Mack, a surgeon who has cancer and is an adherent of the methods of the Simontons, "The patients who survive with cancer or with another catastrophic illness, perhaps even in the face of almost insurmountable odds, seem to be those who have developed a very strong will to live and who value each day, one at a time."[8] What about the patients who *don't* survive? Are they lacking the will to live, or perhaps self-discipline or some other personal attribute necessary to hold cancer at bay? After all, a view that attaches credit to patients for controlling their disease also implies blame for the progression of the disease. Katherine Mansfield described the resulting sense of personal inadequacy in an entry in her journal a year before her death from tuberculosis: "A bad day . . . horrible pains and so on, and weakness. I could do nothing. The weakness was not only physical. I must *heal my Self* before I will be well. . . . This must be done alone and at once. It is at the root of my not getting better. My mind is not *controlled.*"[9] In addition to the anguish of personal failure, a further harm to such patients is that they may come to see

medical care as largely irrelevant, as Cassileth et al. point out, and give themselves over completely to some method of thought control.

The medical profession also participates in the tendency to hold the patient re- 10 sponsible for his progress. In our desire to pay tribute to gallantry and grace in the face of hardship, we sometimes credit these qualities with cures, not realizing that we may also be implying blame when there are reverses. William Schroeder, celebrated by the media and his doctors as though he were responsible for his own renascence after implantation of an artificial heart, was later gently scolded for slackening. Dr. Allan Lansing of Humana Heart Institute worried aloud about Schroeder's "ostrich-like" behavior after a stroke and emphasized the importance of "inner strength and determination."[10]

I do not wish to argue that people have no responsibility for their health. On the 11 contrary, there is overwhelming evidence that certain personal habits, such as smoking cigarettes, drinking alcohol, and eating a diet rich in cholesterol and saturated fats, can have great impact on health, and changing our thinking affects these habits. However, it is time to acknowledge that our belief in disease as a direct reflection of mental state is largely folklore. Furthermore, the corollary view of sickness and death as a personal failure is a particularly unfortunate form of blaming the victim. At a time when patients are already burdened by disease, they should not be further burdened by having to accept responsibility for the outcome.

References

1. Cousins N. Anatomy of an illness as perceived by the patient. New York: WW Norton, 1979.
2. Simonton OC, Matthews-Simonton S, Creighton J. Getting well again: a step-by-step, self-help guide to overcoming cancer for patients and their families. Los Angeles: JP Tarcher, 1978.
3. Sontag S. Illness as metaphor. New York: Farrar, Straus and Giroux, 1977.
4. Fox BH. Premorbid psychological factors as related to cancer incidence. J Behav Med 1978; 1:45–133.
5. Kraus AS, Lilienfeld AM. Some epidemiologic aspects of the high mortality rate in the young widowed group. J Chronic Dis 1959; 10:207–17.
6. Cassileth BR, Lusk EJ, Miller DS, Brown LL, Miller C. Psychosocial correlates of survival in advanced malignant disease. N Engl J Med 1985; 312:1551–5.
7. Case RB, Heller SS, Case NB, et al. Type A behavior and survival after acute myocardial infarction. N Engl J Med 1985; 312:737–41.
8. Mack RM. Lessons from living with cancer. N Engl J Med 1985; 311:1640–4.
9. Sontag, S. Illness as metaphor. New York: Farrar, Straus and Giroux, 1977.
10. McLaughlin L. Schroeder kin, doctors try to lift his spirits. Boston Globe. December 17, 1984:1.

Postreading Exercises

1. Summarize in one or two sentences Angell's main argument.
2. Freewrite your response to this question: In what way, if any, has Angell's article caused me to reconsider my answers to the opinion survey?
3. Working in small groups or as a whole class, compare the note-taking strategies you used while reading this piece. (a) How many people wrote marginal notes? How many underlined or highlighted? (b) Compare the contents of these notes. Did people highlight the same passage or different

passages? (c) Individually, look at your annotations and highlights and try to decide why you wrote or marked what you did. Share your reasons for making these annotations. The goal of this exercise is to make you more aware of your thinking processes as you read. Systematically practicing new ways to annotate texts can help make you a stronger reader.

4. Working as a whole class or in small groups, share your responses to the questionnaire and to the postreading questions. To what extent did this article change people's thinking about the psyche's effect on the body? What was most convincing about the article?

5. Assume that you are skeptical of Dr. Angell's ideas. To what parts of her article might you raise objections?

WRITING PROJECT

Part A: Summarize in approximately 250 words a reading specified by your instructor (the reading may be one of the readings in the reading section of this chapter or any other reading chosen by the instructor).

Part B: Write a strong response to this reading by speaking back to the text from your own personal experience, critical thinking, and values.

UNDERSTANDING RHETORICAL READING

In this section we contrast the kinds of difficulties college students encounter when they read academic texts with the fluent reading practices of experts. We then show you how to read a text both with the grain and against the grain—skills you will need to summarize a text and respond to it strongly.

What Makes College-Level Reading Difficult

The difficulty of college-level reading stems in part from the complexity of the subject matter. Whatever the subject—from international monetary policies to cold fusion—you have to wrestle with new and complex materials that might perplex anyone. But in addition to the daunting subject matter, several other factors contribute to the difficulty of college-level reading.

Vocabulary

Many college-level readings—especially primary sources—contain unfamiliar technical language. The Angell text, for example, assumes that you understand such technical terms as "Type A personality," "adrenal exhaustion," and "my-ocardial infarction." In some contexts you can look up a difficult word in the dictionary. But in academia, words often carry specialized meanings that evoke a whole history of conversation and debate that may be inaccessible even through a specialized dictionary. "Existentialism," "neo-Platonic," "postmodernism," "Newtonian," and "Keynesian," for example, are code words for attitudes or positions in a complex conversation. No dictionary could capture all the nuances of meaning that these words carry in those conversations. You will not fully understand them until you are initiated into the disciplinary conversations that gave rise to them.

Unfamiliar Rhetorical Context

Another cause of difficulty, especially in primary materials, is lack of familiarity with the text's original rhetorical context. As we explained in Part One, writers write to an audience for a purpose; the purpose results from some motivating occasion or event. Unless you know something about a text's purpose, occasion, and intended audience (that is, unless you know the conversation to which the text belongs), you may well be left floundering. Sometimes the rhetorical context is easy to figure out, as in the case of the Angell article (she's reacting negatively to the currently popular notion that diseases reflect a person's mental state). But why did Plato write his dialogues? What conversation was Freud joining when he began interpreting dreams? Whom was Einstein opposing when he proposed his theory of relativity? The more you can learn about a text's rhetorical context, through internal clues or through outside research, the easier it is to read and respond to the text.

Unfamiliar Genre

In Chapter 4 we discussed genre in our analysis of a writer's rhetorical context. In your college reading you will encounter a wide range of genres, such as textbooks, scholarly articles, scientific reports, historical documents, newspaper articles, op-ed pieces, and so forth. Each of these genres makes different demands on readers and requires a different reading strategy. An unfamiliar genre adds to the difficulty of reading.

Lack of Background Knowledge

Writers necessarily make assumptions about what their readers know. If you lack background knowledge, you may have trouble interpreting the writer's ideas and fully understanding the text. Your understanding of Angell, for example, would be more complete if you had read Norman Cousins's best-selling book on healing through laughter and knew something about psychological imagery techniques or scientists' reasons for distrusting anecdotal evidence.

FOR WRITING AND DISCUSSION

The importance of background knowledge can be easily demonstrated any time you dip into past issues of a news magazine or try to read articles about an unfamiliar culture. Consider the following passage from a 1986 *Newsweek* article.

How much background knowledge do you need before you can fully comprehend this passage? What cultural knowledge about the United States would a student from Ethiopia or Indonesia need?

> Throughout the NATO countries last week, there were second thoughts about the prospect of a nuclear-free world. For 40 years nuclear weapons have been the backbone of the West's defense. For almost as long American presidents have ritually affirmed their desire to see the world rid of them. Then, suddenly, Ronald Reagan and Mikhail Gorbachev came close to actually doing it. Let's abolish all nuclear ballistic missiles in the next 10 years, Reagan said. Why not all nuclear weapons, countered Gorbachev. OK, the president responded, like a man agreeing to throw in the washer-dryer along with the house.
>
> What if the deal had gone through? On the one hand, Gorbachev would have returned to Moscow a hero. There is a belief in the United States that the Soviets need nuclear arms because nuclear weapons are what make them a superpower. But according to Marxist-Leninist doctrine, capitalism's nuclear capability (unforeseen by Marx and Lenin) is the only thing that can prevent the inevitable triumph of communism. Therefore, an end to nuclear arms would put the engine of history back on its track.
>
> On the other hand, Europeans fear, a nonnuclear United States would be tempted to retreat into neo-isolationism.
>
> —Robert B. Cullen, "Dangers of Disarming," *Newsweek*

Working in small groups or as a class, identify words and passages in this text that depend on background information or knowledge of culture for complete comprehension.

Reading Processes Used by Experienced Readers

In Chapter 17, we describe the difference between the writing processes of experts and those of beginning college writers. There are parallel differences between the reading processes of experienced and inexperienced readers, especially when they encounter complex materials. In this section we discuss some of the skills used by experienced readers.

Varying Strategies to Match Reading Goals

Unlike novices, experienced readers vary their reading speed and strategies according to their goals. Experienced readers sometimes scan texts for a piece of information, and at other times scrutinize every word. Robert Sternberg, a cognitive psychologist, asked subjects to read four different passages for four different purposes: (1) scanning for a piece of information, (2) skimming for main ideas, (3) reading for complete comprehension, and (4) reading for detailed analysis. The researcher discovered that experienced readers varied their reading speed appropriately, spending the most time with passages they had to analyze in detail and the least time with those requiring only scanning or skimming. Inexperienced readers, in contrast, read all four passages at the same speed, spending too much or too little time on three of the four readings.

FOR WRITING AND DISCUSSION

Suppose you are doing a research project on a question of interest to you. So far you have located several books and a dozen or so articles on your topic. Working in small groups or as a whole class, create hypothetical scenarios in which you would, on different occasions, read material at all four reading speeds. When would you scan material? When would you skim for main ideas only? When would you read a text carefully from beginning to end? When would you pore over a text line by line?

Varying Strategies to Match Genre

Experienced readers also match their reading strategies to the genre of the piece being read. They use conventions of the genre to select the portions of the text that are most important to their purposes. To illustrate, let's look at how experienced readers read scientific or technical reports, a genre described in Chapter 4. Such reports typically contain five sections: introduction, methods (procedures), findings, discussion of findings, and conclusions and recommendations. The scientific studies cited by Angell in references 5, 6, and 7, for example, would be written in this format.

Experts seldom read a scientific report from beginning to end. A common approach is to read the introduction section (which explains the research question being examined, often reviews the literature surrounding the question, and presents the hypothesis), move to the discussion section, and then read the conclusions and recommendations section. These sections carry the study's argument by showing to what extent the findings help answer the research question. Most experts would turn to the methods and findings sections only after determining that the research was relevant to their work and generally helpful. They would read these sections primarily to determine how carefully and thoughtfully the research was done. (Debates about scientific research often focus on the research design and methodology.)

Other genres, too, demand special ways of reading, which you will develop through experience. For now, it is important simply to recognize that different genres use different conventions, which, in turn, invite different ways of reading.

Adopting a Multidraft Reading Process

Just as people may mistakenly believe that experienced authors compose effortlessly in one sitting, they also may mistakenly believe that expert readers comprehend a text perfectly with one rapid reading. Deceived by speed-reading advertisements, many students push themselves to read more quickly rather than more carefully. Experts, however, adjust their reading speed to the text's level of difficulty. As they read, they struggle to make the text comprehensible. They hold confusing passages in mental suspension, having faith that later parts of the essay may clarify earlier parts. They "nutshell" passages, often writing gist statements in the margins. A gist statement is a brief summary of the paragraph's content or a brief indication of the paragraph's function or purpose in the argument. Experts reread difficult texts two and three times, treating their first pass as an approximation or rough draft. They interact with the text by asking questions, expressing disagreement, and linking the text with other readings or with personal experience.

Students often don't allot enough study time for this kind of careful reading and rereading, thus depriving themselves of the challenges that will help them grow as readers. The rest of this chapter will show you how to struggle effectively with a challenging text.

Improving Your Own Reading Process

Here are some general strategies you can use to improve your ability to read any kind of college-level material.

1. *Slow down or speed up, depending on your goals.*   First, decide why you are reading the material and what you will need to do with it. If you are looking through several articles to find those that relate to a specific research topic, then you probably want to skim quickly through them. But many of your assignments will demand close, detailed reading. In these instances, follow the strategies of experts, reading with pen in hand and allotting time to reread a text if it is particularly difficult, treating first readings as first drafts.

2. *Reconstruct the rhetorical context.*   Train yourself to ask questions such as these: Who is this author? What audience is the author targeting? What occasion prompted this writing? What is the author's purpose? Any piece of writing makes more sense if you think of its author as a real person writing for some real purpose within a real historical context. Often you can reconstruct the rhetorical context from clues within the text. Encyclopedias and biographical dictionaries can also help you establish a rhetorical context.

3. *Join the text's conversation by exploring your views on the issues before reading.*   To determine the text's issues before reading it through, note the title, read the first few paragraphs carefully, and skim the opening sentences of all paragraphs. Try to appreciate from the outset what conversation the text is joining and consider your own views on the issue. This sort of personal exploration at the prereading stage both increases your readiness to understand the text and enhances your ability to enjoy it. We tried to create this experience for you by designing the brief prereading questionnaire for the Angell piece.

4. *Lose your highlighter; find your pen.*   Relying on those yellow highlighters or underlining with a pen or pencil can be a good strategy when your sole concern is to note main ideas, but in other cases it can make you too passive. When you read for full comprehension and detailed analysis, highlighting can lull you into thinking that you are reading actively when you aren't.

Next time you get the urge to highlight a passage, write in the margin why you think it's important. Is it a major new point in the argument? A significant piece of support? A summary of the opposition? A particularly strong or particularly weak point? Use the margins to summarize, protest, question, or assent—but don't merely color the pages. If you are reading a text that you can't write in (for example, a library book), make your marginal notes in a reading log keyed to the text's pages.

5. *Get the dictionary habit.*   Get in the habit of looking up words when you can't tell their meaning from context. One strategy is to make small tick marks next to words you're unsure of while you're reading and then to go back and look them up after you've finished so that you don't break your concentration.

6. *Recognize when lack of background information is the source of your difficulty.*   Sometimes you simply have to live awhile with fuzzy passages that refer to concepts or phenomena that you don't understand. Write a question in the margin to make note of the concept, term, or reference that you don't understand, and then continue to do the best you can with the rest of the text. After you finish your reading, you can consult encyclopedias, other library resources, or knowledgeable peers to fill gaps in your knowledge.

7. *Try "translating" difficult passages.*   When you stumble over a difficult passage, try translating it into your own words. Converting the passage into your own language will force you to focus on the precise meanings of words. Although your translation may not be exactly what the author intended, you will see more clearly where the sources of confusion lie and what the likely range of meanings might be.

8. *Read both with the grain and against the grain.*   When you read with the grain, you are a compliant reader who tries to read the text as the author intended. When you read against the grain, you are a resistant reader who asks unanticipated questions, pushes back, and reads the text in ways unforeseen by the author. Using the believing-doubting game introduced in Chapter 2 as a metaphor, reading with the grain is to believe the text, reading against the grain is to doubt it. When you share the author's belief system, it is sometimes difficult to resist the text; when you oppose the author's belief system, it is sometimes hard to be compliant. Nevertheless, strong readers try to develop their ability to read in both ways. We explain how to read with the grain in the section on summary writing and how to read against the grain in the section on writing strong responses.

9. *Continue the conversation after you read.*   After you've read a text, try completing the following statements in a journal: The most significant question this essay raises is _____. The most important thing I learned from this essay is _____. I agree with the author about _____; however, I disagree about _____. These questions will help you remember the reading and urge you to respond actively to it.

Reading with the Grain: How to Write a Summary

We turn now to the nuts and bolts of reading a text carefully when your goal is a full and detailed comprehension of its argument. Your first task is to read the text with the grain. When you read with the grain, you practice what psychologist Carl Rogers calls "empathic listening," in which you try to see the world through the author's eyes, role-playing as much as possible the author's intended audience, adopting its beliefs and values, and acquiring its background knowledge. Reading with the grain also requires your willingness to extend the author's project, to support the author's thesis or point of view or method with new evidence from your own personal experiences, other readings, or research.

According to Rogers, the best way to indicate that you have understood another person's view is to summarize that person's argument as completely and fairly as possible. The process of reading with the grain outlined in the following steps will help you read more actively and accurately. As you become a more experienced reader, you'll follow these steps without thinking about them.

1. The first time through, read the text fairly quickly for general meaning. If you get confused, keep going; later parts of the text might clarify earlier parts.
2. Reread the text carefully. As you read, write gist statements in the margins for each paragraph. A gist statement is a brief summary of the paragraph's content or a brief indication of the paragraph's function or purpose in the argument. Sometimes it helps to think of these two kinds of gist statements as "what it says" statements or "what it does" statements. A "what it says" statement summarizes a paragraph's content; a "what it does" statement indicates the paragraph's function, for example, "summarizes an opposing view," "introduces another reason," "presents a supporting example," "provides statistical data in support of a point," and so on.

When you first practice detailed readings of a text, you might find it helpful to write complete "says" and "does" statements on a separate sheet of paper rather than in the margins until you develop the internal habit of appreciating both the content and the function of parts of an essay. Here are says and does statements for selected paragraphs in Angell's essay (see pp. 100–02).

Paragraph 1   *Does:* Asks series of questions to identify issue; presents "common" answer and implies author's opposing answer. *Says:* Are diseases caused by people's mental states? Most Americans think yes.

Paragraph 2   *Does:* Elaborates the common view. *Says:* The media tell us that our personality types and emotional states cause certain diseases.

Paragraph 3   *Does:* Elaborates and expands the common view with more examples. *Says:* As argued by Cousins, the Simontons, and others, a change in one's emotional state can help cure diseases.

Paragraph 7   *Does:* Cites scientific studies that oppose common view. *Says:* Two recent studies—one on cancer and one on heart disease—show no correlation between mental state and the progression of disease.

Paragraph 10   *Does:* Gives examples of how doctors mistakenly contribute to the popular view. *Says:* When doctors praise patients' will to live, they imply blame to patients whose illnesses worsen.

Paragraph 11   *Does:* Qualifies author's stance and then sums up article by stating thesis implied throughout. *Says:* People are responsible for avoiding risky behaviors, but they shouldn't be held responsible for their diseases.

You may occasionally have difficulty writing a says statement for a paragraph because you may have trouble deciding what the main idea is, especially if the paragraph doesn't begin with a closed-form topic sentence. One way to respond to this problem is to formulate the question that you think the paragraph answers. If you think of chunks of the text as answers to a logical progression of questions, you can often follow the main ideas more easily. In addition, research shows that a question triggers a person's ability to recall text better than does a statement. Rather than writing says statements in the margins, therefore, some readers prefer writing says questions. Says questions for the Angell text may include the following: What is the common view of the relationship between health and the psyche? What are the flaws in this common view? What evidence supports the view that the psyche is unrelated to the progression of a disease?

No matter which method you use—says statements or says questions—when you reread a text, perhaps in preparation for an exam, you will appreciate how much more useful than underlining and highlighting such annotations are for helping you recall the text's structure and argument.

3. After you've analyzed the essay paragraph by paragraph, try locating the argument's main divisions or parts. In longer closed-form arguments, writers often forecast the shape of their essays in their introductions or use their conclusions to sum up main points. Although Angell's short article doesn't have an initial forecasting passage, the article is divided into several main chunks as follows:
   - An introduction, which poses the question to be addressed and gives the popular answer (paragraph 1)
   - A section explaining the popular view (paragraphs 2–4)
   - A section refuting the popular view (paragraphs 5–7)
   - A section examining the consequences of the popular view (paragraphs 8–10)
   - A conclusion, which states the thesis explicitly (paragraph 11)

Instead of listing the sections, you might prefer to make an outline or tree diagram of the article showing its main parts and subparts.

Writing Your Summary

Once you have written gist statements or questions in the margins and clarified the text's structure by creating an outline or diagram, you are ready to write a summary (also called an *abstract* or a *précis*). You can probably compose a first draft of your summary rapidly by piecing together your says statements for each paragraph. Then you can pare and polish your draft to fit the required length.

Summaries of articles generally range from 100 to 250 words, but sometimes writers compose summaries as short as one sentence. The order and proportions of your summary can usually follow the order and proportions of the text. However, if the original article has a delayed thesis or other characteristics of open-form writing, you may find it necessary to rearrange the order and begin with the thesis. Consider the following three summaries of Angell's article as examples of how you can write summaries of different lengths.

One-Sentence Abstract   Although the popular belief that one's mental state can cause or cure diseases may have some psychological benefits, this belief is largely folklore and leads to the unfortunate consequence of blaming sick people for their diseases. (36 words)

100–125 Word Abstract   The popular view that one's mental attitude can cause or cure disease is largely folklore and has negative consequences. The popular media, influenced by Cousins, the Simontons, and others whose research is largely anecdotal and seriously flawed, argue that changes in mental state can cure diseases. However, more careful scientific studies on cancer and myocardial infarction recently showed no correlation between mental state and progression of disease. The gravest consequence of the psychological view is that patients suffer guilt when their condition worsens, causing many to avoid medical treatment. Although people are responsible for avoiding high-risk behaviors, they shouldn't be held responsible for their diseases. (106 words)

200–250 Word Abstract   The popular belief that personality types and mental attitude can cause or cure diseases such as cancer, ulcers, and asthma is largely folklore and leads to unfortunate consequences. The popular media, influenced by Cousins's autobiographical account of being healed by laughter and the Simontons' stories of using mental imagery techniques to combat cancer, suggest that changes in mental states can cure diseases. This belief is not new, as illustrated by the nineteenth century belief that an overly passionate temperament, not the tubercle bacillus, caused tuberculosis. Recent studies show that the popular view is based on anecdotal evidence or on research seriously flawed in design or analysis. Two recent studies—one on cancer and one on myocardial infarction—show no correlation between mental state and the progression of disease. Although the psychological view may offer some people hope and a sense of control, its negative consequences render it unacceptable. Patients suffer debilitating guilt if their diseases worsen, causing them to avoid further medical treatment. The medical profession contributes to this problem whenever doctors praise patients for their will to live, implying censure of those who get worse. Although people are responsible for avoiding high-risk behaviors, such as smoking or unhealthy diets, they shouldn't be blamed for their diseases and made to feel guilt when they get worse. (217 words)

Incorporating a Summary into Your Own Writing

Suppose that you want to incorporate Angell's views into your own research paper on alternative medicines. Any of the sample summaries can be adapted to your own essay and introduced with *attributive tags*, such as "Angell says" or "according to Angell," so that your views and Angell's views are clearly distinguished. If you choose to copy any of Angell's words directly from the article you need to use quotation marks and cite the quotation using an appropriate documentation system. Chapter 23 provides a full discussion of how to summarize, paraphrase, or quote sources; work them smoothly into your own writing; and avoid plagiarism. The following example uses the MLA documentation system.*

> The popular view that one's mental attitude can cause or cure disease is sharply attacked by Dr. Marcia Angell (1985), writing in the New England Journal of Medicine. According to Angell, "our belief in disease as a direct reflection of the psyche is largely folklore" (1572). She attacks the claims of Cousins, the Simontons, and others on the grounds that their research is largely anecdotal and seriously flawed. She cites recent scientific studies on cancer and myocardial infarction showing no correlation between mental state and progression of disease. The negative consequences of the psychological view, according to Angell, are that patients suffer guilt when their condition worsens, and that they may not seek medical treatment. "At a time when patients are already burdened by disease, they should not be further burdened by having to accept responsibility for the outcome" (1572).

Works Cited

Angell, Marcia. "Disease as a Reflection of the Psyche." New England Journal of Medicine 312 (1985): 1570–72.

FOR WRITING AND DISCUSSION

Look carefully at the differences between the self-standing abstracts on page 111 and the version in which the summary is worked into the researcher's own writing. Identify the major differences between the two kinds of summaries and explain why these differences occur. For example, describe an attributive tag, locate an example, and explain why attributive tags are needed in one kind of summary but not the other.

Reading Against the Grain: Writing a Strong Response

After you have read a text with the grain, you will want to read it against the grain. Any reading experience places you somewhere on a continuum that ranges from unproblematic assimilating to strong contesting. Unproblematic assimilating is what you do when you become completely absorbed in a pleasurable text, whether it is a book about your favorite hobby or an article that expresses exactly your own views and feelings on a subject. At the other end of the continuum are readings that you contest vigorously every step of the way. Such texts challenge your intellect and your values to the fullest, offering worldviews so hostile or alien to your own that you may feel great discomfort reading them.

---

*Numbers in parentheses indicate page numbers in this text where the quotations can be found. A listing of complete bibliographic information would be included at the end of the essay under the heading "Works Cited." See Chapter 23, Using, Citing, and Documenting Sources, for further discussion of documentation systems. Note that Angell's "References" list (p. 102) is in the particular style used by the *New England Journal of Medicine* in which the article appeared.

In between fall texts that challenge your thinking without necessarily provoking a strong emotional response. Perhaps you agree with some parts of the text and disagree with others. Perhaps the text poses questions you have never considered. Such texts can stretch your thinking, and, if you allow them to, can cause you to grow and change. When we say that a strong response involves resisting a text or speaking back to it, we don't necessarily mean opposing it. We mean joining the conversation the text is part of and adding your own voice.

How do you do so? There is no one right way to speak back to a text. In any group of readers, a series of strong responses is like a series of individual jazz riffs, all responding uniquely to the same initial melody. The key is for each reader to write a response to the reading derived from his or her own background as a person and thinker. As you read, fill the margins with "against the grain" comments to complement your "with the grain" says and does annotations. These comments capture your initial reaction to a text and often form the starting point for a more fully articulated response later. Let's look more closely at how to read a text against the grain.

Write Out Questions Triggered by the Text

Almost any text triggers questions as you read. A good way to begin formulating a strong response is to write out several of these questions and then to explore your responses to those questions through freewriting. Sometimes the freewrite will trigger more questions.

Identify Hot Spots in the Text

In addition to raising questions, most texts will create hot spots for you (each reader's hot spots are apt to be different). By *hot spot* we mean a quotation or passage that you especially notice either because you agree or disagree with it or because it triggers memories or other associations. A hot spot may strike you as particularly thought provoking; or it may raise a problem; or it may be confusing, yet suggestive. Go back through the text and copy out short quotations that intrigue you (or place an asterisk next to longer passages); then freewrite your responses to these hot spots.

Articulate How You Differ from the Intended Audience

In some cases you can read strongly by articulating how you differ from the text's intended audience. In our discussion of the writing process in Chapter 17, we emphasize how experienced writers struggle to imagine their audience. They ask: What are my audience's values? How interested in and knowledgeable about my topic is my audience? Eventually, the writer makes decisions about the audience, in effect, creates the audience, so that the text reveals an image both of the writer and of the intended reader.

Your own experiences, arising from your gender, class, ethnicity, sexual orientation, political and religious beliefs, interests, values, and so forth, may cause you to feel estranged from the author's imagined audience. If the text seems written for straight people and you are gay, or for Christians and you are a Muslim or an atheist, or for environmentalists and you grew up in a small logging community, you may well resist the text.

Sometimes your sense of exclusion from the intended audience makes it difficult to read a text at all. For example, a student we know once brought a class to a standstill by slamming the course anthology on her desk and exclaiming, "How can you people stand reading this patriarchal garbage!" She had become so irritated by the authors' assumption that all readers shared their male-oriented values that she could no longer bear to read the selections.

FOR WRITING AND DISCUSSION

What follows is a short passage by writer Annie Dillard in response to a question about how she chooses to spend her time. This passage often evokes heated responses from our students.

> I don't do housework. Life is too short. . . . I let almost all my indoor plants die from neglect while I was writing the book. There are all kinds of ways to live. You can take your choice. You can keep a tidy house, and when St. Peter asks you what you did with your life, you can say, "I kept a tidy house, I made my own cheese balls."

 Read the passage and briefly freewrite your reaction to it. Then, working in groups or as a whole class, develop answers to the following questions:

1. What values does Dillard assume her audience holds?
2. What kinds of readers are apt to feel excluded from that audience?
3. If you are not part of the intended audience for this passage, what about the text evokes resistance?

Articulate Your Own Purpose for Reading

You may read a text against the grain if your purposes for reading differ from what the author imagined. Normally you read a text because you share the writer's interest in a question and want to know the writer's answer. In other words, you usually read to join the writer's conversation. But suppose that you wish to review the writings of nineteenth-century scientists to figure out what they assumed about nature (or women, or God, or race, or capitalism). Or suppose that you want to examine a politician's metaphors to see what they reveal about his or her values or analyze *National Geographic* for evidence of political bias. In these cases, you will read against the grain of the text. In a sense, you will be blindsiding the authors—while they are talking about topic X, you are observing them for topic Y.

You can see this strategy at work in literary critic Jane Tompkins's "'Indians': Textualism, Morality, and the Problem of History" (see pp. 173–80). Tompkins, assigned to teach a course in early American literature, wanted to find out as much as she could about the relationship between Puritans and Native Americans in colonial New England. So she turned to a famous 1950s scholarly work by Perry Miller on the Puritan mind. Here is her brief account of her reading experience.

My research began with Perry Miller. Early in the preface to *Errand into the Wilderness,* while explaining how he came to write his history of the New England mind, Miller writes a sentence that stopped me dead. He says that what fascinated him as a young man about his country's history was "the massive narrative of the movement of European culture into the vacant wilderness of America." "Vacant?" Miller, writing in 1956, doesn't pause over the word "vacant," but to people who read his preface thirty years later, the word is shocking. In what circumstances could someone proposing to write a history of colonial New England *not* take into account the Indian presence there?

This experience—reading a sentence that "stopped [her] dead"—set Tompkins off on her own research project: How do historians examining colonial New England portray Indians? As she read historian after historian, her interest wasn't in the research problems posed by the authors but in her own research problem: This method of resistant reading is very common in academia.

Ask Generic Strategic Questions

The essence of reading against the grain is to read critically and to pose questions. Here are generic strategic questions you can ask to resist a text.

- How is this author trying to change my view of this topic? What do I have to give up or lose in order to change my view? What do I gain?
- What is excluded from this author's text? (All writers must select certain details to include in their texts and others to exclude. By looking at what is omitted from a text, you can often ascertain something about the writer's value system.)
- How can I question this writer's data, evidence, and supporting arguments? If I am not persuaded by the writer's data and evidence, why not? What is missing? What can be called into question?
- How can I question the writer's values, beliefs, and assumptions, both stated and unstated? Conversely, how does this text cause me to question my own values, beliefs, and assumptions?

As an illustration of how these questions can provoke your own thinking, read what one student freewrote about the Angell text in response to these questions.

1 How is this author trying to change my view of this topic? What do I

have to give up or lose in order to change my view? What do I gain? Marcia

Angell assumes that I as reader start out believing the popular view that

the mind can cause (and cure) various kinds of diseases. If I accept her

view, then I have to accept a much more physical view of medicine and see

my mind and body as separate. I can also remember that my grandmother, who

is 92 years old, fought off a number of diseases in her late 60s and 70s

and doctors always praised her "will to live." In contrast, my grandfather sort of "gave up." I would have to give up this sense of my grandmother's willpower that has always been a comfort to me. On the other hand, she makes me think better of my grandfather at the end. I wonder what Angell would say about prayer?

What is excluded from this author's text? Although Angell mentions Cousins and the Simontons, she dismisses them quickly. We don't really hear their side of the story nor get to judge for ourselves whether Angell accurately characterizes their arguments. What is kept out of this article is all those people who distrust traditional medicine and go to health food stores, value midwives and Indian "medicine men," meditate, etc. Also omitted is much discussion of stress. I have heard that stress causes high blood pressure, asthma attacks, etc. and stress clearly is related to mental states. 2

How can I question this writer's data, evidence, and supporting arguments? In her article, Angell cites two studies that found no correlation between mental state and progress of disease--one on cancer and one on heart disease. I would have to read these studies to see how convincing they seemed. I would also want to look at other studies to see what studies support an opposing view. Angell is not very clear about such studies. She says that most reports are anecdotal, that these studies usually have certain flaws, that very few studies support the popular view, that the popular view is largely folklore. Why this hedging? Is she aware of other studies that make a more positive case for the psychological causes of disease? 3

How can I question the writer's values, beliefs, and assumptions? How does the text cause me to question mine? Dr. Angell seems to be most comfortable with diseases that have a clear physical cause--especially diseases like tuberculosis that are clearly caused by a microbe that shows up under a microscope. She has a strong faith in science and wants the body to be treated like a purely physical thing. I like the sympathy she shows for those whose conditions get worse and who are held "responsible" for their 4 diseases under the popular view. This is a real problem for me: I like to praise people like my grandmother for their fighting spirit, but I don't like blaming grandpa for giving up. At least she is an advocate for my grandpa. She really makes me wonder what the role of the spirit is in the physical universe.

Consider the Purpose of Your Strong Response

In imagining possibilities for different kinds of strong responses, consider again the various purposes for writing that we developed in Chapter 4. Most of these purposes suggest possible approaches for composing a strong response.

Expressive purpose.   Respond to the reading by applying it in some way to your own life.

Exploratory purpose.   Highlight puzzling questions raised by the text and explore possible answers to them based on the your personal experiences or critical thinking.

Analytical purpose.   Analyze or evaluate the reading, examining its rhetorical strategies and effectiveness.

Persuasive purpose.   Argue for or against the text. If you are for the text, support the author's thesis with additional data and evidence and perhaps a new line of argument. If you are against the text, refute it using counter arguments and evidence.

Literary purpose.   Respond to the text with a poem or short story that captures your reaction more evocatively than would discursive prose.

The following example of a strong response to the Angell article was written by the same student who wrote the freewrite beginning on page 115. This student decided to write this response as an exploratory piece organized around several questions.

1   Angell's article raises some thought-provoking questions for me. The first concerns the value of willpower in fighting a disease. My grandmother, who is still alive and kicking at age 92, developed severe asthma in her sixties and was often hospitalized with terrifying wheezing attacks that required paramedics and ambulances in response to my grandfather's panicked calls to 911. In addition, she once had a heart attack that put her in intensive care, difficulty swallowing, which led to an operation, a couple of cases of shingles, and pneumonia, and an accident, which broke her hip at age 87. But she is what the doctors call a "fighter." She has a tenacious

will to live and many doctors have told my parents that she fought her way back to health. In contrast, my grandfather died of congestive heart failure at age 90. When he started getting sick in his late eighties, he just seemed to me to "give up." Watching my grandparents leads me to believe that a will to live really does help you fight a disease. Yet Dr. Angell's article calls this belief into question. I rather like the notion of not blaming my grandfather for his failing health, but my grandmother's will to live has always been an inspiration to me, and I hate to give that up.

Another question raised by Angell is the nature of disease itself. Some 2 diseases are clearly caused by a bacteria or virus, and Dr. Angell seems to be most at ease with these diseases. She likes the tuberculosis example because the cause of tuberculosis turned out to be so clearly a scientifically observable microbe. She would also be happiest if cancer turned out to be caused by a clear external agent--such as a virus or exposure to certain chemicals. But some diseases seem to come from some kind of internal failing of the system, like heart attacks, or from clear mental conditions, like anorexia. I know in reading some of the pamphlets my grandmother got on asthma that stress can trigger asthma attacks. It makes sense to me that stress and worry could have internal effects on your physical body, which could in turn affect the body's ability to fight a disease.

The largest issue raised by Angell's argument is the relationship between 3 the mind and the body. Angell really likes to treat the body as a scientifically observable thing. She is thus in step with the Western scientific notion of science gaining control over the physical world. Part of me doesn't like this view. I like the now popular notion that we have to get back to more spiritual ways of seeing things. But part of me likes Angell's view, at least as it applies to medicine. There is so much emphasis now on being responsible for your health (eating right, exercising right, managing stress) that you start believing that life is rational and that you have complete control over your future. But then something awful happens, like you have a car accident or find out you have multiple sclerosis or leukemia.

It gives you a different feeling about the world if you think of disease as being bad luck rather than the result of a flaw in your personality.

Suggestions for Summarizing Open-Form Prose

In the first part of this chapter, we discussed the challenges of summarizing closed-form prose. In general, the more closed a piece of writing, the easier it is to summarize. Closed prose often includes a summary of the argument built into the introduction or conclusion. And, its points-first organization, along with mapping passages and transitions, makes it relatively easy to see how the parts relate to the whole.

With more open prose, however, a summary is less likely to parallel the organization of the original article. In summarizing a delayed-thesis article, you might choose to begin with the thesis. In very open articles, it may be difficult to distinguish main points from digressions, and different readers will reach different conclusions on what should be highlighted in a summary.

It is not impossible to summarize open-form prose—it is just difficult to do so. Whereas closed-form authors provide numerous textual signals to indicate how the text is to be read to narrow down the possibility of divergent readings, open-form pieces are often marked by the absence of such textual signals. Open-form pieces require you to create the meaning of what you read. When you summarize open-form prose, therefore, what you are summarizing is a jointly constructed reading of the text—jointly constructed by you and the author.

To see what we are getting at here, let's look at Joan Didion's essay "On Going Home." First read the piece, and then respond to the questions that follow.

JOAN DIDION
ON GOING HOME

1   I am home for my daughter's first birthday. By "home" I do not mean the house in Los Angeles where my husband and I and the baby live, but the place where my family is, in the Central Valley of California. It is a vital although troublesome distinction. My husband likes my family but is uneasy in their house, because once there I fall into their ways, which are difficult, oblique, deliberately inarticulate, not my husband's ways. We live in dusty houses ("D-U-S-T," he once wrote with his finger on surfaces all over the house, but no one noticed it) filled with mementos quite without value to him (what could the Canton dessert plates mean to him? how could he have known about the assay scales, why should he care if he did know?), and we appear to talk exclusively about people we know who have been committed to mental hospitals, about people we know who have been booked on drunk-driving charges, and about property, particularly about property, land, price per acre and C-2 zoning and assessments and freeway access. My brother does not understand my husband's inability to perceive the advantage in the rather common real-estate transaction known as "sale-leaseback,"

and my husband in turn does not understand why so many of the people he hears about in my father's house have recently been committed to mental hospitals or booked on drunk-driving charges. Nor does he understand that when we talk about sale-lease-backs and right-of-way condemnations we are talking in code about the things we like best, the yellow fields and the cottonwoods and the rivers rising and falling and the mountain roads closing when the heavy snow comes in. We miss each other's points, have another drink and regard the fire. My brother refers to my husband, in his presence, as "Joan's husband." Marriage is the classic betrayal.

Or perhaps it is not any more. Sometimes I think that those of us who are now in our thirties were born into the last generation to carry the burden of "home," to find in family life the source of all tension and drama. I had by all objective accounts a "normal" and a "happy" family situation, and yet I was almost thirty years old before I could talk to my family on the telephone without crying after I had hung up. We did not fight. Nothing was wrong. And yet some nameless anxiety colored the emotional charges between me and the place that I came from. The question of whether or not you could go home again was a very real part of the sentimental and largely literary baggage with which we left home in the fifties; I suspect that it is irrelevant to the children born of the fragmentation after World War II. A few weeks ago in a San Francisco bar I saw a pretty young girl on crystal take off her clothes and dance for the cash prize in an "amateur-topless" contest. There was no particular sense of moment about this, none of the effect of romantic degradation, of "dark journey," for which my generation strived so assiduously. What sense could that girl possibly make of, say, *Long Day's Journey into Night?* Who is beside the point?

That I am trapped in this particular irrelevancy is never more apparent to me than when I am home. Paralyzed by the neurotic lassitude engendered by meeting one's past at every turn, around every corner, inside every cupboard, I go aimlessly from room to room. I decide to meet it head-on and clean out a drawer, and I spread the contents on the bed. A bathing suit I wore the summer I was seventeen. A letter of rejection from *The Nation,* an aerial photograph of the site for a shopping center my father did not build in 1954. Three teacups hand-painted with cabbage roses and signed "E. M.," my grandmother's initials. There is no final solution for letters of rejection from *The Nation* and teacups hand-painted in 1900. Nor is there any answer to snapshots of one's grandfather as a young man on skis, surveying around Donner Pass in the year 1910. I smooth out the snapshot and look into his face, and do and do not see my own. I close the drawer, and have another cup of coffee with my mother. We get along very well, veterans of a guerrilla war we never understood.

Days pass. I see no one. I come to dread my husband's evening call, not only because he is full of news of what by now seems to me our remote life in Los Angeles, people he has seen, letters which require attention, but because he asks what I have been doing, suggests uneasily that I get out, drive to San Francisco or Berkeley. Instead I drive across the river to a family graveyard. It has been vandalized since my last visit and the monuments are broken, overturned in the dry grass. Because I once saw a rattlesnake in the grass I stay in the car and listen to a country-and-Western station. Later I drive with my father to a ranch he has in the foothills. The man who runs his cattle on it asks us to the roundup, a week from Sunday, and although I know that I will be in Los Angeles I say, in the oblique way my family talks, that I will come. Once home I mention the broken monuments in the graveyard. My mother shrugs.

I go to visit my great-aunts. A few of them think now that I am my cousin, or their daughter who died young. We recall an anecdote about a relative last seen in 1948, and

2

3

4

5

they ask if I still like living in New York City. I have lived in Los Angeles for three years, but I say that I do. The baby is offered a horehound drop, and I am slipped a dollar bill "to buy a treat." Questions trail off, answers are abandoned, the baby plays with the dust motes in a shaft of afternoon sun.

6   It is time for the baby's birthday party: a white cake, strawberry-marshmallow ice cream, a bottle of champagne saved from another party. In the evening, after she has gone to sleep, I kneel beside the crib and touch her face, where it is pressed against the slats, with mine. She is an open and trusting child, unprepared for and unaccustomed to the ambushes of family life, and perhaps it is just as well that I can offer her little of that life. I would like to give her more. I would like to promise her that she will grow up with a sense of her cousins and of rivers and of her great-grandmother's teacups, would like to pledge her a picnic on a river with fried chicken and her hair uncombed, would like to give her *home* for her birthday, but we live differently now and I can promise her nothing like that. I give her a xylophone and a sundress from Madeira, and promise to tell her a funny story.

Postreading Exercises

1. Freewrite briefly on how your experience reading this open-form essay is different from your experience reading Angell's closed-form piece.
2. Summarize in one or two sentences what you think Didion's piece is about.
3. Freewrite your response to Didion's essay.

FOR WRITING AND DISCUSSION

1. Working in small groups or as a whole class, share your responses to the three postreading questions.
2. Working in small groups, create an interview with Joan Didion in which you ask the author several "Why did you . . . " questions about "On Going Home" and then create what you think she would say. For example, you might ask, "Why did you end the piece with a description of your baby's birthday party?" or "Why did you say that you and your mother were 'veterans of a guerrilla war we never understood'?" Then compose the answers you think Didion might give. The best questions involve aspects of the text that truly puzzled you.
3. Small groups should then share their interviews with the whole class.

One way to articulate the difference between highly closed and highly open prose is to show how difficult it is to write "what it does" and "what it says" gist statements about individual paragraphs in open-form prose. At first, the opening paragraph of Didion's essay seems to yield itself to "what it does" and "what it says" gist statements.

What It Does   Sets up the problem of "going home" by presenting examples of things from the author's family that her husband doesn't understand.

What It Says	My family's disregard of dust, our propensity for mementos, and our coded talk about real-estate transactions, make my husband feel like an outsider.

But even here the "what it says" statement doesn't quite sum up Didion's ominous "Marriage is the classic betrayal," nor does it account for why Didion chose certain details, such as her family's habit of discussing acquaintances committed to mental institutions or booked on drunk-driving charges, or what larger meanings are intended in the details about dust and Canton dessert plates. When we come to paragraph 3, no "what it does" or "what is says" statement seems possible. Rather than opening with a point sentence (the hallmark of closed prose), it opens with narrative details. "Days pass. I see no one." What follows is a collage of images and details beginning with telephone calls from her husband and a drive to a family graveyard and ending with her mother's shrug at hearing about the broken monuments. There is nothing to summarize in this series of details (making a "what it says" statement difficult). To establish what the paragraph "does," the reader must first interpret what it means.

This active involvement of the reader gives literary pleasure. Summarizing such a piece is much more demanding than summarizing a closed-form piece with a clear thesis, supporting points, and supporting details. The purpose of the summary, though, is similar: to give a new reader an overview of the piece. Here is one reader's summary of Didion's essay.

> In returning to her family home to celebrate the first birthday of her only child, Didion is alternately repelled by and attracted to her family and its odd ways. On the one hand, she characterizes family life as a "guerrilla war" with "ambushes"; on the other hand, she laments the fact that her daughter will never have the "sense of her cousins and of rivers and her grandmother's teacups" that Didion grew up with. Partly she worries about her family life because of the tremendous importance that she attaches to it. This sense of importance is not shared by the subsequent generation who cast off their family ties as easily as the young topless dancer casts off her clothes. She was thirty, Didion reports, before she could talk with her family on the phone without crying afterwards. The things that tie her family together are unusual—things like their silences, their odd topics of conversation, their weird relatives, their code words. These are the very things that seem to exasperate her not totally sympathetic husband. In the end, Didion can't belong wholly to either her "old" home or her "new" home with her husband and daughter. She can't be wholly comfortable in either role as mother and wife or as daughter and child. She lives instead in the uneasy tension between the two worlds.

If the formula for summarizing a closed-form piece is "Keep the main points and leave out the supporting details," then the formula for summarizing an open-form piece is something like "Use your own interpretive powers to create the unstated main points." The summary provided here is more an interpretation of the piece than a condensation of its argument.

FOR WRITING AND DISCUSSION

1. Working in small groups or as a whole class, select what you see as important aspects of Didion's essay that are omitted from the summary.
2. Share how individual class members' summaries of Didion's essay would be different from the one here. For example, another student began her summary of Didion's piece, "Didion uses her baby at the beginning and end of this essay to symbolize growth and change. The baby is a positive, hopeful symbol in contrast to the deadening, static life of the Didion family."

READINGS

This section contains three essays that invite strong responses. The first is a closed-form piece; the second we would place about midway on the continuum between closed and open forms; the last is open form. Your instructor may choose one of these pieces as the subject of your assignment for this chapter. Because your task is to summarize your assigned piece and respond strongly to it, we omit the questions for analysis that typically accompany readings elsewhere in this text. In a sense, you will be asking your own questions for analysis. Although the assignment asks you to summarize just one reading, your instructor may invite you to incorporate reactions to all three readings into your strong response. You will see that the readings themselves "speak to each other"; they form a conversation about the kinds of underlying values that we choose for our lives.

The first reading is from a recent issue of *Ms.* Its author, Sharon Lerner, is a freelance writer and editor who specializes in health-related topics.

SHARON LERNER

IF WE'VE COME SUCH A LONG WAY, WHY ARE WE STILL SMOKING?

1   Seventy-five years ago, a woman ran for president of the United States on an antismoking platform. Lucy Page Gaston, who ran against known smoker Warren G. Harding, thought that smoking led to drinking, a life of crime, and a condition she called "cigarette face." She objected particularly to smoking by minors and women and, with the support of a substantial turn-of-the-century antismoking movement, she helped restrict smoking in more than 20 states by the mid-1920s. At the time, women accounted for an estimated 5 percent of all tobacco consumers.

2   We've come a long way since then, of course. Women now make up nearly half of all smokers in the U.S. (48 percent), and researchers predict we will soon be the majority. The number of females who begin smoking during high school and college has risen steadily, while the number of males has declined. And recent studies on smoking

trends show that women as a group—in particular women living in poverty and those with less education—are doing worse with smoking than the overall population.

What is perhaps most upsetting about these landmarks is that we reach them in the face of overwhelming evidence that smoking does cause disease—things far worse than "cigarette face." While men have thus far dominated the habit during a period of ignorance about health effects, women are poised to become the majority of smokers at a time when it's absolutely clear that smoking is harmful. 3

Ignoring the Medical Evidence

At least part of the problem is that it's still not widely understood just how harmful it is to smoke. Many people still lump it in with risks like pesticides on fruit or sunbathing. The truth is that smoking kills more women than alcohol, illicit drugs, car accidents, suicide, and homicide—*combined.* It's by far the number one cause of premature death in women, causing approximately 20 percent of *all deaths,* killing roughly one in seven—or 141,832—women annually. Lung cancer, which has increased over 400 percent in women in the past 30 years, is now the biggest cancer killer of women—bigger even than breast cancer. And together, conditions such as emphysema, heart disease, stroke, and various other cancers are responsible for more smoking-related deaths than lung cancer. 4

There is now also overwhelming evidence that women are uniquely vulnerable to certain smoking-related health problems. Women smokers are more susceptible to reproductive tract infections and cervical cancer, and those who use oral contraceptives have an especially high risk of stroke and heart disease. Smoking also wreaks havoc on women's hormonal systems—decreasing fertility, increasing the chances of premature menopause and osteoporosis, and disrupting pregnancy. Women smokers have more preterm stillbirths, and their children are more likely to suffer and die from a variety of birth defects. 5

If the full extent of the above litany is not common knowledge, most of us have gotten the basic message: smoking is bad for you. Nevertheless, the medical news about smoking has had far less impact on women's smoking than on men's. Middle-class white men have stopped smoking in greater numbers than any other group, while women's smoking has gone down only slightly overall. 6

Starting Young

Why have female smokers been so unresponsive to the grim health news? A large part of the answer, according to Jean Forster, a researcher at the University of Minnesota School of Public Health, lies in the fact that most smokers—over 90 percent—take up the habit before age 20. African American girls constitute the one exception to this rule. The smoking rate among black teenagers has dropped in the past 10 to 15 years, but the rate significantly increases for black women later in life. Researchers have yet to reach a consensus as to why African American women often start smoking at a later age. 7

The average teen smoker begins at age 13. "At that point," says Forster, who has conducted focus groups with teenage smokers, "the public health message means nothing to kids. They're simply too young for it." And the earlier people start, the more likely they are to smoke heavily and the harder it will be for them to quit. But according to Forster, most teenagers are not worried about that. They are confident they will quit before they develop health problems, even before they become addicted. And, for 8 teenage girls especially, concerns such as social acceptance, attractiveness, and body image often far outweigh thoughts of serious illness in the far-off future.

9   Cigarette marketers' ability to appeal to these concerns has been critical to their success in replacing the two to three million smokers who either quit or die each year. With the industry now spending over $4 billion annually on advertising and promotion (after cars, cigarettes are the second most advertised consumer product in the U.S.—despite the fact that cigarette advertising is banned from broadcast media), marketing techniques have reached a new level of complexity. Lately, many brands have taken to offering products geared to women that can be bought with proofs of purchase from cigarette packs. These incentives are offered with a time limit, so that you have to buy 400 packs of Merits within six months, for example, to get the "Merit Award" of a suede barn jacket. For the outfit featured in Virginia Slims's V-wear ad, you have to buy about five and a half packs a day for six months, according to the calculations of Dr. Elizabeth Whelan, president of the American Council on Science and Health, who keeps close track of cigarette ads aimed at women.

10   While cigarette companies regularly devise new marketing gimmicks such as these, the main themes of their ads have remained the same since they began marketing to women and girls about 70 years ago. One longtime favorite, the association of smoking with independence, equality, and yes, feminism, dates back to when women's smoking was socially unacceptable. Tobacco marketers capitalized on the allure of breaking that taboo, casting cigarettes as a symbol of women's liberation: one public relations agent even arranged for a contingent of women to march in the 1929 New York City Easter parade carrying "little torches of freedom." To this day, variations on the theme that smoking makes women tough, independent, and equal to men surface in ads—especially in Virginia Slims ads, from "You've come a long way, baby" to the recent "You can do it" slogan.

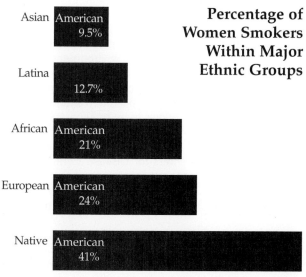

Percentage of Women Smokers Within Major Ethnic Groups

Asian American 9.5%

Latina 12.7%

African American 21%

European American 24%

Native American 41%

Source: Centers for Disease Control

Another recurrent theme of cigarette marketing to women—identifying smoking   11
with being thin—began with Lucky Strikes' 1920s "Reach for a Lucky instead of a
sweet" ad, which featured a slim woman with a shadow of a double chin looming behind her. Female models in cigarette ads still conform to standard ideals of beauty, including thinness. And ads often emphasize the words "slim" and "thin," as in the Capri
slogan "There is no slimmer way to smoke" and Misty's "slim and sassy." As a result,
according to former Surgeon General C. Everett Koop, many young girls are left with
the misconception that taking up smoking will actually make them thin. "Most of the
adolescent female smokers I have talked with tell me they smoke to prevent gaining
weight," says Koop, who has traveled extensively throughout the country interviewing
young smokers. "They believe that if women who stop smoking gain weight, smoking
must be a preventive to weight gain as well."

But regardless of content, the presence of cigarette ads alone influences women by   12
affecting the editorial policies of the publications that carry them. It's now widely known
that magazines that accept cigarette ads are less likely to report on the health effects
of smoking, and studies have shown that tobacco ad revenue has an even greater impact on health reporting in women's magazines than in other publications.

Tobacco funding also complicates antismoking efforts by women's professional   13
and political groups. Unfortunately the practice is unlikely to change given the scarcity
of funding for women's organizations and the good publicity it affords the tobacco companies. Betty Dooley, president of the Women's Research and Education Institute, says
that without the support of the tobacco industry, the organization would be unable to
continue its public policy fellowship program—the only one of its kind for women.
Spokesman K. Richmond Temple insists that Phillip Morris' motivation for funding
women's groups comes from its female employees, who "support women's participation in all aspects of life."

Staying Smoking

While the image of smoking has much to do with its initial appeal, the *experience*   14
of smoking is, of course, why people continue to smoke. Smoking is pleasurable. It can
relax muscles, increase concentration, and relieve anxiety. Because women are more
likely to live in poverty and juggle multiple roles, these physical effects hold particular
appeal as ways to reduce stress and to exert control over their environment. Lorraine
Greaves, vice president of the International Network of Women Against Tobacco and a
sociologist who has analyzed the many ways smoking functions for women, notes that
it can provide them with an escape when no others exist. "Women often smoke to claim
and mark their personal space," says Greaves. "This allows them to separate or break
from partners, children, and workmates whenever desired."

The special social significance of smoking to women may explain the gender   15
differential in quitting success. According to the Centers for Disease Control's 1993
National Health Interview Survey, slightly more women than men want to quit completely (73 percent as opposed to 67 percent, respectively), while slightly fewer
female smokers (46.7 percent as opposed to 51.9 percent) are successful in their
attempts.

But the reality is that it's extraordinarily difficult for anyone to quit, mostly because   16
tobacco is incredibly physically addictive (despite what some tobacco executives
say). As Jack Henningfield, a scientist at the National Institute on Drug Abuse, sees
it, although gender-related pressures may add to women's difficulties in quitting, the

main problem is simply being exposed to nicotine. "All the advertising in the world wouldn't affect women if nicotine weren't addictive," says Henningfield. "Just having a normal, healthy, functioning brain means that you are prewired to be a nicotine addict."

Slaying the Giant

17   Many in the antismoking movement look to regulatory possibilities—such as further restricting advertising, tightening youth access, limiting public smoking, and classifying and regulating tobacco as a drug—as their best hopes. But with annual revenues of $48 billion at stake, the industry is a daunting opponent, and so far it has managed to preserve its profits by creatively circumventing restrictions. When tobacco ads were banned from radio and TV in 1971, for instance, the industry compensated by stepping up other ad efforts; the relative share of tobacco ad revenue in women's magazines soared after this point—it more than tripled from 1967 to 1986. And many see the current trend of expanding sales into the "developing" world as a direct result of increased restrictions in the "developed" world.

18   The recent Republican electoral landslide, made possible in part by $1 million in campaign contributions from tobacco companies, seems to have allowed the industry to yet again avoid serious regulation. In addition to the strong antiregulatory tenor of this current Congress, the November election brought a shift in leadership that bodes badly for tobacco regulation. Representative Henry Waxman (D.-Calif.), who oversaw the recent investigation of industry manipulation of nicotine levels, has been deposed—and the investigation halted. The person who now has control over almost all tobacco-related regulation is Representative Thomas Bliley, Jr. (R.-Va.), who (until redistricting in 1990) represented a congressional district in which Phillip Morris is the largest employer. During the last election, Bliley received more contributions from tobacco industry political action committees than any other member of the House.

19   Although a few optimistic health advocates see potential for bipartisan support of tobacco control by casting it as a "pro-family" issue, most have a grimmer outlook, at least for the moment. But while the possibilities may be bleak in Washington, D.C., women are increasingly active and successful in fighting tobacco on other levels. Such organizations as the Berkeley, California-based Women and Girls Against Tobacco, the American Medical Women's Association, and NOW, as well as a growing network of international women's organizations, have recently begun major outreach projects to raise consciousness about the tobacco issue. And people all over the country are fighting the image war, covering cigarette ads with their own antismoking stickers and putting up counter-ads, such as a "Virginia Slime" campaign that recently ran in the New York City subway system. The point, of course, is to heighten women's personal and collective awareness that smoking has more to do with being exploited than with being liberated.

Our next reading, by writer and journalist Florence King, is a strong response to articles such as the preceding *Ms.* piece. It explains with passion why one woman chooses to smoke. We place King's essay about midway on the continuum between closed and open forms. It combines an explicit thesis (characteristic of closed-form prose) with numerous narrative elements (characteristic of open form).

FLORENCE KING
I'D RATHER SMOKE THAN KISS

I am a woman of 54 who started smoking at the late age of 26. I had no reason to start earlier; smoking as a gesture of teenage rebellion would have been pointless in my family. My mother started at 12. At first her preferred brands were the Fatimas and Sweet Caporals that were all the rage during World War I. Later she switched to Lucky Strike Greens and smoked four packs a day. 1

She made no effort to cut down while she was pregnant with me, but I was not a low-birth-weight baby. The Angel of Death saw the nicotine stains on our door and passed over. I weighed nine pounds. My smoke-filled childhood was remarkably healthy and safe except for the time Mama set fire to my Easter basket. That was all right, however, because I was not the Easter-basket type. 2

I probably wouldn't have started smoking if I had not been a writer. One day in the drugstore I happened to see a display of Du Maurier English cigarettes in pretty red boxes with a tray that slid out like a little drawer. I thought the boxes would be ideal for keeping my paperclips in, so I bought two. 3

When I got home, I emptied out the cigarettes and replaced them with paperclips, putting the loose cigarettes in the desk drawer where the loose paperclips had been scattered. Now the cigarettes were scattered. One day, spurred by two of my best traits, neatness and thrift, I decided that the cigarettes were messing up the desk and going to waste, so I tried one. 4

It never would have happened if I had been able to offer the Du Mauriers to a lover who smoked, but I didn't get an addicted one until after I had become addicted myself. When he entered my life it was the beginning of a uniquely pleasurable footnote to sex, the post-coital cigarette. 5

Today when I see the truculent, joyless faces of anti-tobacco Puritans, I remember those easy-going smoking sessions with that man: the click of the lighter, the brief orange glow in the darkness, the ashtray between us—spilling sometimes because we laughed so much together that the bed shook. 6

A cigarette ad I remember from my childhood said: "One of life's great pleasures is smoking. Camels give you all of the enjoyment of choice tobaccos. Is enjoyment good for you? You just bet it is." My sentiments exactly. I believe life should be savored rather than lengthened, and I am ready to fight the misanthropes among us who are trying to make me switch. 7

A *misanthrope* is someone who hates people. Hatred of smokers is the most popular form of closet misanthropy in America today. Smokists don't hate the sin, they hate the sinner, and they don't care who knows it. 8

Their campaign never would have succeeded so well if the alleged dangers of smoking had remained a problem for smokers alone. We simply would have been allowed to invoke the Right to Die, always a favorite with democratic lovers of mankind, and that would have been that. To put a real damper on smoking and make it stick, the right of others not to die had to be invoked somehow so "passive smoking" was invented. 9

The name was a stroke of genius. Just about everybody in America is passive. Passive Americans have been taking it on the chin for years, but the concept of passive smoking offered them a chance to hate in the land of compulsory love, a chance to dish it out for a change with no fear of being called a bigot. The right of self-defense, long since gone up in smoke, was back. 10

Smokers on the Run

11   The big, brave Passive Americans responded with a vengeance. They began shouting at smokers in restaurants. They shuddered and grimaced and said "Ugh!" as they waved away the impure air. They put up little signs in their cars and homes: at first they said, "Thank You for Not Smoking," but now they feature a cigarette in a circle slashed with a red diagonal. Smokists even issue conditional invitations. I know—I got one. The woman said. "I'd love to have you to dinner, but I don't allow smoking in my home. Do you think you could refrain for a couple of hours?" I said, "Go ---- yourself," and she told everybody I was the rudest person she had ever met.

12   Smokists practice a sadistic brutality that would have done Vlad the Impaler proud. *Washington Times* columnist and smoker Jeremiah O'Leary was the target of two incredibly baleful letters to the editor after he defended the habit. The first letter said, "Smoke yourself to death, but please don't smoke me to death," but it was only a foretaste of the letter that followed:

> Jeremiah O'Leary's March 1 column, "Perilous persuaders . . . tenacious zealots," is a typical statement of a drug addict trying to defend his vice.
>
> To a cigarette smoker, all the world is an ashtray. A person who would never throw a candy wrapper or soda can will drop a lit cigarette without a thought.
>
> Mr. O'Leary is mistaken that nonsmokers are concerned about the damage smokers are inflicting on themselves. What arrogance! We care about living in a pleasant environment without the stench of tobacco smoke or the litter of smokers' trash.
>
> If Mr. O'Leary wants to kill himself, that is his choice. I ask only that he do so without imposing his drug or discarded filth on me. *It would be nice if he would die in such a way that would not increase my health-insurance rates* [my italics].

13   The expendability of smokers has also aroused the tender concern of the Federal Government. I was taking my first drag of the morning when I opened the *Washington Post* and found myself staring at this headline: NOT SMOKING COULD BE HAZARDOUS TO PENSION SYSTEM. MEDICARE, SOCIAL SECURITY MAY BE PINCHED IF ANTI-TOBACCO CAMPAIGN SUCCEEDS, REPORT SAYS.

14   The article explained that since smokers die younger than non-smokers, the Social Security we don't live to collect is put to good use, because we subsidize the pensions of our fellow citizens like a good American should. However, this convenient arrangement could end, for if too many smokers heed the Surgeon General's warnings and stop smoking, they will live too long and break the budget.

15   That, of course, is not how the government economists phrased it. They said:

> The implications of our results are that smokers "save" the Social Security system hundreds of billions of dollars. Certainly this does not mean that decreased smoking would not be socially beneficial. In fact, it is probably one of the most cost-effective ways of increasing average longevity. It does indicate, however, that if people alter their behavior in a manner which extends life expectancy, then this must be recognized by our national retirement program.

16   At this point the reporter steps in with the soothing reminder that "the war on tobacco is more appropriately cast as a public-health crusade than as an attempt to save

money." But then we hear from Health Policy Center economist Gio Gori, who says: "Prevention of disease is obviously something we should strive for. But it's not going to be cheap. We will have to pay for those who survive."

Something darkling crawls out of that last sentence. The whole article has a die-damn-you undertow that would make an honest misanthrope wonder if perhaps a cure for cancer was discovered years ago, but due to cost-effectiveness considerations . . .   17

But honest misanthropes are at a premium that no amount of Raleigh coupons can buy. Instead we have tinpot Torquemadas like Ahron Leichtman, president of Citizens against Tobacco Smoke, who announced after the airline smoking ban: "CATS will next launch its smoke-free airports project, which is the second phase of our smoke-free skies campaign." Representative Richard J. Durbin (D., Ill.) promised the next target will be "other forms of public transportation such as Amtrak, the inter-city bus system, and commuter lines that receive federal funding." His colleague, Senator Frank Lautenberg (D., N.J.), confessed, "We *are* gloating a little bit," and Fran Du Melle of the Coalition on Smoking OR Health, gave an ominous hint of things to come when she heralded the airline ban as "only one encouraging step on the road to a smoke-free society."   18

Health Nazis

These remarks manifest a sly, cowardly form of misanthropy that the Germans call *Schadenfreude:* pleasure in the unhappiness of others. It has always been the chief subconscious motivation of Puritans, but the smokists harbor several other subconscious motivations that are too egregious to bear close examination—which is precisely what I will now conduct.   19

Study their agitprop and you will find the same theme of pitiless revulsion running through nearly all of their so-called public-service ads. One of the earliest showed Brooke Shields toweling her wet hair and saying disgustedly, "I hate it when somebody smokes after I've just washed my hair. Yuk!" Another proclaimed, "Kissing a smoker is like licking an ashtray." The latest, a California radio spot, asks: "Why sell cigarettes? Why not just sell phlegm and cut out the middle man?"   20

Fear of being physically disgusting and smelling bad is the American's worst nightmare, which is why bathsoap commercials never include the controlled-force shower nozzles recommended by environmentalists in *their* public-service ads. The showering American uses oceans of hot water to get "ZESTfully clean" in a sudsy deluge that is often followed by a deodorant commercial.   21

"Raise your hand, raise your hand, raise your hand if you're SURE!" During this jingle we see an ecstatically happy assortment of people from all walks of life and representing every conceivable national origin, all obediently raising their hands, until the ad climaxes with a shot of the Statue of Liberty raising hers.   22

The New Greenhorns

The Statue of Liberty has become a symbol of immigration, the first aspect of American life the huddled masses experienced. The second was being called a "dirty little" something-or-other as soon as they got off the boat. Deodorant companies see the wisdom in reminding their descendants of the dirty-little period. You can sell a lot of deodorant that way. Ethnics get the point directly; WASPs get it by default in the subliminal reminder that, historically speaking, there is no such thing as a dirty little WASP.   23

Smokers have become the new greenhorns in the land of sweetness and health, scapegoats for a quintessentially American need, rooted in our fabled Great Diversity,   24 to identify and punish the undesirables among us. Ethnic tobacco haters can get even for past slurs on their fastidiousness by refusing to inhale around dirty little smokers; WASP tobacco haters can once again savor the joys of being the "real Americans" by hurling with impunity the same dirty little insults their ancestors hurled with impunity.

25   The tobacco pogrom serves additionally as the basis for a class war in a nation afraid to mention the word "class" aloud. Hating smokers is an excellent way to hate the white working class without going on record as hating the white working class.

26   The anti-smoking campaign has enjoyed thumping success among the "data-receptive," a lovely euphemism describing the privilege of spending four years sitting in a classroom. The ubiquitous statistic that college graduates are two-and-a-half times as likely to be non-smokers as those who never went beyond high school is balm to the data-receptive, many of whom are only a generation or two removed from the lunch-bucket that smokers represent. Haunted by a fear of falling back down the ladder, and half-believing that they deserve to, they soothe their anxiety by kicking a smoker as the proverbial hen-pecked husband soothed his by kicking the dog.

27   The earnest shock that greeted the RJR Reynolds Uptown marketing scheme aimed at blacks cramped the vituperative style of the data-receptive. Looking down on blacks as smokers might be interpreted as looking down on blacks as blacks, so they settled for aping the compassionate concern they picked up from the media.

28   They got their sadism-receptive bona fides back when the same company announced plans to target Dakota cigarettes at a fearsome group called "virile females."

29   When I first saw the headline I thought surely they meant me: what other woman writer is sent off to a book-and-author luncheon with the warning, "Watch your language and don't wear your Baltimore Orioles warm-up jacket"? But they didn't. Virile females are "Caucasian females, 18 to 24, with no education beyond high school and entry-level service or factory jobs."

30   Commentators could barely hide their smirks as they listed the tractor pulls, motorcycle races, and macho-man contests that comprise the leisure activities of the target group. Crocodile tears flowed copiously. "It's blue-collar people without enough education to understand what is happening to them," mourned Virginia Ernster of the University of California School of Medicine. "It's pathetic that these companies would work so hard to get these women who may not feel much control over their lives." George Will, winner of the metaphor-man contest, wrote: "They use sophisticated marketing like a sniper's rifle, drawing beads on the most vulnerable, manipulable Americans." (I would walk a mile to see Virginia Ernster riding on the back of George Will's motorcycle.)

31   Hating smokers is also a guiltless way for a youth-worshipping country to hate old people, as well as those who are merely over the hill—especially middle-aged women. Smokers predominate in both groups because we saw Bette Davis's movies the same year they were released. Now we catch *Dark Victory* whenever it comes on television just for the pleasure of watching the scene in the staff lounge at the hospital when Dr. George Brent and all the other doctors light up.

32   Smoking is the only thing that the politically correct can't blame on white males. Red men started it, but the cowardly cossacks of the anti-tobacco crusade don't dare say so because it would be too close for comfort. They see no difference between tobacco and hard drugs like cocaine and crack because they don't wish to see any. Never mind that you will never be mugged by someone needing a cigarette; hatred of smokers is the conformist's substitute for the hatred that dare not speak its name. Condemning "substance abuse" out of hand, without picking and choosing or practicing discrimination, produces lofty sensations of democratic purity in those who keep moving farther and farther out in the suburbs to get away from . . . smokers.

Our last piece is by nature writer and essayist Annie Dillard. This open-form piece, which uses the literary strategies of narrative, imagery, and symbolism, describes a momentary encounter between the author and a weasel and asks what a human life might be like if it could be lived "like a weasel."

ANNIE DILLARD

LIVING LIKE WEASELS

A weasel is wild. Who knows what he thinks? He sleeps in his underground den, his tail draped over his nose. Sometimes he lives in his den for two days without leaving. Outside, he stalks rabbits, mice, muskrats, and birds, killing more bodies than he can eat warm, and often dragging the carcasses home. Obedient to instinct, he bites his prey at the neck, either splitting the jugular vein at the throat or crunching the brain at the base of the skull, and he does not let go. One naturalist refused to kill a weasel who was socketed into his hand deeply as a rattlesnake. The man could in no way pry the tiny weasel off, and he had to walk half a mile to water, the weasel dangling from his palm, and soak him off like a stubborn label. 1

And once, says Ernest Thompson Seton—once, a man shot an eagle out of the sky. He examined the eagle and found the dry skull of a weasel fixed by the jaws to his throat. The supposition is that the eagle had pounced on the weasel and the weasel swiveled and bit as instinct taught him, tooth to neck, and nearly won. I would like to have seen that eagle from the air a few weeks or months before he was shot: was the whole weasel still attached to his feathered throat, a fur pendant? or did the eagle eat what he could reach, gutting the living weasel with his talons before his breast, bending his beak, cleaning the beautiful airborne bones? 2

I have been reading about weasels because I saw one last week. I startled a weasel who startled me, and we exchanged a long glance. 3

Twenty minutes from my house, through the woods by the quarry and across the highway, is Hollins Pond, a remarkable piece of shallowness, where I like to go at sunset and sit on a tree trunk. Hollins Pond is also called Murray's Pond; it covers two acres of bottomland near Tinker Creek with six inches of water and six thousand lily pads. In winter, brown-and-white steers stand in the middle of it, merely dampening their hooves; from the distant shore they look like miracle itself, complete with miracle's nonchalance. Now, in summer, the steers are gone. The water lilies have blossomed and spread to a green horizontal plane that is terra firma to plodding blackbirds, and tremulous ceiling to black leeches, crayfish, and carp. 4

This is, mind you, suburbia. It is a five-minute walk in three directions to rows of houses, though none is visible here. There's a 55 mph highway at one end of the pond, and a nesting pair of wood ducks at the other. Under every bush is a muskrat hole or a beer can. The far end is an alternating series of fields and woods, fields and woods, threaded everywhere with motorcycle tracks—in whose bare clay wild turtles lay eggs. 5

So. I had crossed the highway, stepped over two low barbed-wire fences, and traced the motorcycle path in all gratitude through the wild rose and poison ivy of the pond's shoreline up into high grassy fields. Then I cut down through the woods to the mossy 6 fallen tree where I sit. This tree is excellent. It makes a dry, upholstered bench at the upper, marshy end of the pond, a plush jetty raised from the thorny shore between a shallow blue body of water and a deep blue body of sky.

7   The sun had just set. I was relaxed on the tree trunk, ensconced in the lap of lichen, watching the lily pads at my feet tremble and part dreamily over the thrusting path of a carp. A yellow bird appeared to my right and flew behind me. It caught my eye. I swiveled around—and the next instant, inexplicably, I was looking down at a weasel, who was looking up at me.

8   Weasel! I'd never seen one wild before. He was ten inches long, thin as a curve, a muscled ribbon, brown as fruitwood, soft-furred, alert. His face was fierce, small and pointed as a lizard's; he would have made a good arrowhead. There was just a dot of chin, maybe two brown hairs' worth, and then the pure white fur began that spread down his underside. He had two black eyes I didn't see, any more than you see a window.

9   The weasel was stunned into stillness as he was emerging from beneath an enormous shaggy wild rose bush four feet away. I was stunned into stillness twisted backward on the tree trunk. Our eyes locked, and someone threw away the key.

10   Our look was as if two lovers, or deadly enemies, met unexpectedly on an overgrown path when each had been thinking of something else: a clearing blow to the gut. It was also a bright blow to the brain, or a sudden beating of brains, with all the charge and intimate grate of rubbed balloons. It emptied our lungs. It felled the forest, moved the fields, and drained the pond; the world dismantled and tumbled into that black hole of eyes. If you and I looked at each other that way, our skulls would split and drop to our shoulders. But we don't. We keep our skulls. So.

11   He disappeared. This was only last week, and already I don't remember what shattered the enchantment. I think I blinked, I think I retrieved my brain from the weasel's brain, and tried to memorize what I was seeing, and the weasel felt the yank of separation, the careening splashdown into real life and the urgent current of instinct. He vanished under the wild rose. I waited motionless, my mind suddenly full of data and my spirit with pleadings, but he didn't return.

12   Please do not tell me about "approach-avoidance conflicts." I tell you I've been in that weasel's brain for sixty seconds, and he was in mine. Brains are private places, muttering through unique and secret tapes—but the weasel and I both plugged into another tape simultaneously, for a sweet and shocking time. Can I help it if it was a blank?

      What goes on in his brain the rest of the time? What does a weasel think about? He won't say. His journal is tracks in clay, a spray of feathers, mouse blood and bone: uncollected, unconnected, loose-leaf, and blown.

13   I would like to learn, or remember, how to live. I come to Hollins Pond not so much to learn how to live as, frankly, to forget about it. That is, I don't think I can learn from a wild animal how to live in particular—shall I suck warm blood, hold my tail high, walk with my footprints precisely over the prints of my hands?—but I might learn something of mindlessness, something of the purity of living in the physical senses and the dignity of living without bias or motive. The weasel lives in necessity and we live in choice, hating necessity and dying at the last ignobly in its talons. I would like to live as I should, as the weasel lives as he should. And I suspect that for me the way is like the weasel's: open to time and death painlessly, noticing everything, remembering nothing, choosing the given with a fierce and pointed will.

I missed my chance. I should have gone for the throat. I should have lunged for   14
that streak of white under the weasel's chin and held on, held on through mud and into
the wild rose, held on for a dearer life. We could live under the wild rose wild as weasels,
mute and uncomprehending. I could very calmly go wild. I could live two days in the
den, curled, leaning on mouse fur, sniffing bird bones, blinking, licking, breathing musk,
my hair tangled in the roots of grasses. Down is a good place to go, where the mind is
single. Down is out, out of your ever-loving mind and back to your careless senses. I
remember muteness as a prolonged and giddy fast, where every moment is a feast of
utterance received. Time and events are merely poured, unremarked, and ingested directly, like blood pulsed into my gut through a jugular vein. Could two live that way?
Could two live under the wild rose, and explore by the pond, so that the smooth mind
of each is as everywhere present to the other, and as received and as unchallenged, as
falling snow?

We could, you know. We can live any way we want. People take vows of poverty,   15
chastity, and obedience—even of silence—by choice. The thing is to stalk your calling
in a certain skilled and supple way, to locate the most tender and live spot and plug
into that pulse. This is yielding, not fighting. A weasel doesn't "attack" anything; a
weasel lives as he's meant to, yielding at every moment to the perfect freedom of single necessity.

I think it would be well, and proper, and obedient, and pure, to grasp your one ne-   16
cessity and not let it go, to dangle from it limp wherever it takes you. Then even death,
where you're going no matter how you live, cannot you part. Seize it and let it seize you
up aloft even, till your eyes burn out and drop; let your musky flesh fall off in shreds,
and let your very bones unhinge and scatter, loosened over fields, over fields and
woods, lightly, thoughtless, from any height at all, from as high as eagles.

COMPOSING YOUR SUMMARY
AND STRONG RESPONSE

Generating and Exploring Ideas for Your Summary

Once you have selected the piece you will use for this assignment, your first
task is to read it carefully with the grain. If the piece you are summarizing is relatively closed, you can apply the following steps sequentially. If the piece is more
open, you may have to adapt the steps to a more literary way of reading.

1. The first time through, read the piece for general meaning. Follow the argument's flow without judgment or criticism, trying to see the world as the author sees it.
2. Reread the piece slowly, paragraph by paragraph, writing "what it says" or
   "what it does" gist statements in the margins for each paragraph or representing each paragraph with the question that the paragraph answers. We
   recommend that you supplement these marginal notations by writing out a
   complete paragraph-by-paragraph does/says analysis modeled after our
   example on pages 109–10.

3. After you've analyzed the piece paragraph by paragraph, locate the argument's main divisions or parts and create an outline or tree diagram of the argument.

Shaping and Drafting Your Summary

Once you have read the article carefully paragraph by paragraph and understand its structure, you are ready to write a draft. If the piece you are summarizing is closed form, you can generally follow the order of the original article, keeping the proportions of the summary roughly equivalent to the proportions of the article. Begin with the article's thesis and then summarize the argument part by part. If the article has a delayed thesis or is open form, then you may have to rearrange the original order to create a clear structure for readers.

Revising Your Summary

Because summaries condense the author's argument, the main criteria for excellence are accuracy and clarity. Use the Guidelines for Peer Reviewers (pp. 136–37) as a guide for revision.

Generating and Exploring Ideas for Your Strong Response

After you have written your summary, your next step is to read the piece against the grain and consider your strong response.

1. Begin by making against the grain marginal notations in the text; ask questions, note hot spots, doubt evidence, raise problems, note your reactions, relate text to your own ideas and experiences.
2. Make a list of questions that the text raises in your mind or identify several hot spots that particularly attracted your notice (see p. 113). Pick the most promising of these questions or hot spots and freewrite your responses to them.
3. For some texts it is useful to articulate the differences between you and the text's intended audience. How does your position in terms of gender, class, ethnicity, sexual orientation, or value system make you different from the reader the text assumes?
4. Freewrite your responses to the following generic strategic questions (see pp. 115–17 for examples based on the Angell article):
   a. How is this author trying to change my view of X? What do I have to give up or lose in order to change my view? What do I gain?
   b. What is excluded from this author's text?
   c. How can I question this writer's data, evidence, and supporting arguments?
   d. How can I question the writer's values, beliefs, and assumptions, both stated and unstated? Or, how does this writer make me question my own values and beliefs?

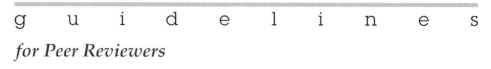

5. Quickly freewrite what you might say in a strong response that adapted each of the following purposes:

   a. *Expressive purpose.* How does this text relate to my own life? What memories or autobiographical stories does it trigger in my mind?

   b. *Exploratory purpose.* What questions, doubts, or uncertainties does this text trigger? What problems does it raise that I could explore?

   c. *Analytical purpose.* What rhetorical strategies does this text use to make its argument? What is omitted from the text? What are its author's values? What are the strong and weak parts of the text's argument? How effective is it?

   d. *Persuasive purpose.* Can I refute this text? Can I rebut its arguments and evidence? Can I argue against its author's values? Conversely, can I support this text with an additional line of argument or with additional data and evidence? Can I extend this author's methods to a new area?

   e. *Literary purpose.* How might I write a poem or short story that captures my reaction to this piece?

Shaping and Drafting Your Strong Response

Based on your explorations, draft a strong response to the reading using whatever strategy and purpose (expressive, exploratory, analytical, persuasive, or literary) that best expresses your own contribution to the conversation. If you are stuck, one approach that almost always produces ideas is to write an exploratory response keyed to several key questions you pose about the text. The student response to Angell's article follows this strategy.

Revising Your Strong Response

Peer reviews are especially helpful in generating ideas for strong responses and identifying areas that need expansion and development. Since strong responses are often written in an expressive or exploratory style, they sometimes lack the tight, closed-form structure of a typical academic essay. What you are shooting for is a response that is thoughtful, interesting, and engaging—something that shows you entering the text's conversation and speaking back to it in your own voice.

g   u   i   d   e   l   i   n   e   s

for Peer Reviewers

Instructions for peer reviews, including use of these guidelines, are provided in Chapter 21, pages 527–28. To write a peer review for a classmate, use your own paper, numbering your responses to correspond to the questions on the guidelines. At the head of your paper, place the author's name and your own name as shown.

Author's Name: _____

Peer Reviewer's Name: _____

   I. Read the draft at normal reading speed from beginning to end. As you read, do the following:
     A. Place a wavy line in the margin next to any passages that you find confusing, that contain something that doesn't seem to fit, or that otherwise slow down your reading.
     B. Place a "Good!" in the margin next to any passages where you think the writing is particularly strong or interesting.
  II. Read the draft again slowly. Describe for the writer what you currently see in this draft. If you have difficulty answering any of the following questions, explain briefly the source of your difficulty.
     A. In the summary, if you think the writer has misunderstood any points from the article, say in your own words what you think those points are.
     B. List the major points from the article cited in the summary.
     C. List any major points in the article that don't appear in the summary.
     D. If the writer has developed any points disproportionately (spent too little or too much time on them relative to their importance), note those points.
     E. How many words are in the summary?
     F. In the strong response, what specifics from his or her life, reading, or research does the writer use to speak back to the text? (Note any places in the text where you'd like more specifics.)
     G. Summarize in your own words the main points the writer makes in his or her strong response.
 III. What recommendations do you have for improving this draft?
     A. Is the summary as comprehensive and accurate as possible, and does it read smoothly with appropriate transitions between ideas? What suggestions do you have for improving the summary?
     B. In the strong response, the writer should apply his or her own critical thinking to the text by questioning it, analyzing it, evaluating it, arguing for and against it, or extending its argument. Suggest to the writer points that might be added to the strong response or a different way to present the arguments. How could the strong response be improved?
     C. Sum up what you see as the chief strengths and problem areas of this draft.
       1. Strengths
       2. Problem areas
 IV. Read the draft one more time. Place a check in the margin wherever you notice problems in grammar, spelling, or mechanics (one check per problem).

c h a p t e r **7**

Writing an Autobiographical Narrative

ABOUT AUTOBIOGRAPHICAL NARRATIVE

The assignment in this chapter asks you to write an autobiographical narrative about something significant from your own life. But rather than state the significance up front in a thesis, you let it unfold in storylike fashion. This narrative base places autobiographical writing on the open end of the closed-to-open prose continuum, making it more like literary nonfiction than like an academic essay. Consequently, we advise you to consult Chapter 20, which discusses the features of open-form prose, prior to writing your assignment for this chapter. The student piece in that chapter ("Berkeley Blues") was written for an assignment like the one in this chapter.

Don't let the term *literary* scare you. It simply refers to basic techniques, such as dialogue, specific language, and scene-by-scene construction, that you use when sharing stories, telling jokes, or recounting experiences to friends. These are the most natural and universal of techniques, the ones that peoples of all cultures have traditionally used to pass on their collective wisdom in myths, legends, and religious narratives.

In addition to telling stories to entertain and to preserve wisdom, we use them to reveal ourselves. In this regard, autobiographical writing, like certain forms of conversation, fills a very basic need in our daily lives—the need for intimacy or nontrivial human contact. One of the best measures we have of our closeness to other human beings is our willingness or reluctance to share with them our significant life stories, the ones that reveal our aspirations or humiliations.

We also use others' stories, particularly during adolescence, to monitor our own growth. Many of us once read (and still read) the stories of such people as Anne Frank, Helen Keller, Malcolm X, and Laura Ingalls Wilder in search of attitudes and behaviors to emulate. Reading their stories becomes a way of critiquing and understanding our own stories.

At this point, you might be thinking that your own life lacks the high drama of these authors' lives. In the context of holocausts and race wars, your own story may seem unworthy of recounting. Perhaps you're thinking that unless you've gone parasailing in the Pacific, bilked a savings and loan, saved a politician from an assassin's bullet, or survived a fall off the Sears Tower, you haven't done anything significant enough to write about. In this chapter we try to give you another view of significance—one that gets at the heart of what it means to write a story.

To our way of thinking, significance is not a quality out there in the events of your life; it's in the sensibility that you bring to those events and the way you write about them. When you mistakenly equate significance with singularity (it never happened to anyone else) or its public importance (what happened here made history), you misunderstand the power of a good writer to render any sort of event significant.

Many of the events your audience will find most interesting are those ordinary occurrences that happen to everyone. All of us have experienced a first day at school, a rival or sibling who seemed to best us at every turn, a conflict with a parent. But everyone enjoys hearing good writers describe their unique methods of coping with and understanding these universal situations. It is precisely because readers have experienced these things that they can project themselves easily into the writer's world. This chapter shows you how to write an autobiographical story by finding a significant moment in your life and by writing about it compellingly using literary techniques.

EXPLORING AUTOBIOGRAPHICAL NARRATIVE

One of the premises of this book is that good writing is rooted in the writer's perception of a problem. Problems are at the center not only of thesis-based writing, but also of narrative writing. In effective narration, the problem usually takes the form of a *contrary,* two or more things in opposition—ideas, characters, expectations, forces, worldviews, or whatever. Three kinds of contraries that frequently form the plots of autobiographical narratives are the following:

1. *Old self versus new self.*   The writer perceives changes in himself or herself as a result of some transforming moment or event.
2. *Old view of person X versus new view of person X.*   The writer's perception of a person (favorite uncle, friend, childhood hero) changes as a result of some revealing moment; the change in the narrator's perception of person X also indicates growth in self-perception.
3. *Old values versus new values that threaten, challenge, or otherwise disrupt the old values.*   The writer confronts an outsider who challenges his or her worldview, or the writer undergoes a crisis that creates a conflict in values.

Prior to class discussion, freewrite for ten minutes about episodes in your own life that fit one or more of these typical plots. Then, working in small groups or as a whole class, share your discoveries. Your goal is to begin seeing that each of your lives is a rich source of stories.

For the moment think of *significant* not as "unusual" or "exciting," but as "revealing" or "conveying an unexpected meaning or insight." Thought of in this way, a significant moment in a story might be a gesture, a remark, a smile, a way of walking or tying a shoe, a piece of clothing, or an object in a purse or pocket. Invent a short scene in which a gesture, smile, or brief action reverses one character's feelings about, or understanding of, another character.

1. You think that Maria has led a sheltered life until _____.
2. You think Pete is a gruff, intimidating thug until _____.
3. Ken (Julia) seemed the perfect date until _____.

In each case, think of specific details about one revealing moment that reverses your understanding. Here is an example of a scene.

> My dad seemed unforgivingly angry at me until he suddenly smiled, turned my baseball cap backward on my head, and held up his open palm for a high five. "Girl, if you don't change your ways, you're going to be as big a high school screw-up as your old man."

WRITING PROJECT

Write a narrative essay about something significant in your life, using the literary strategies of plot, character, and setting. Develop your story through the use of contraries, creating tension that moves the story forward and gives it significance. You can discuss the significance of your story explicitly, perhaps as a revelation, or you can imply it (we discuss and illustrate each of these strategies later in this chapter). Use specific, telling details and develop contraries that create tension.

This assignment calls for a *story.* In Chapter 20, we argue that a narrative qualifies as a story only when it depicts a series of connected events that create for the reader a sense of tension or conflict that is resolved through a new understanding or change in status. (See the discussion of minimal story in Chapter 20, pp. 494–98.) Your goal for this assignment is to write a story about your life that fulfills these criteria. The rest of this chapter will help you every step of the way.

UNDERSTANDING AUTOBIOGRAPHICAL WRITING

Autobiographical writing may include descriptions of places and people and depictions of events that are more entertaining than enlightening. However, the spine of most autobiographical writing is a key moment or event, or a series of key moments or events, that shape or reveal the author's emerging character or growth in understanding.

Autobiographical Tension: The Opposition of Contraries

Key events in autobiography are characterized by a contrariety of opposing values or points of view. These oppositions are typically embodied in conflicts between characters or in divided feelings within the narrator. The contrariety in a story can often be summed up in statements such as these:

> My best friend from the eighth grade was suddenly an embarrassment in high school.

> My parents thought I was too young to drive to the movies when in fact I was ready to ride off with Iggy's Motorcycle Maniacs.

> My boyfriend thought I was mad about his being late for dinner when in fact I was mad about things he could never understand.

An autobiographical piece without tension is like an academic piece without a problem or a surprising thesis. No writing is more tedious than a pointless "So what?" narrative that rambles on without tension. (You can read such a narrative in the discussion of "and then" writing in Chapter 18, pp. 446–48. It's a good example of what *not* to do for this assignment.)

Like the risky thesis statement in closed-form writing, contrariety creates purpose and focus for open-form writing. It functions as an organizing principle, helping the writer determine what to include or omit. It also sets a direction for the writer. When a story is tightly wound and all the details contribute to the story line, the tension moves the plot forward as a mainspring moves the hands of a watch. The tension is typically resolved when the narrator experiences a moment of recognition or insight, vanquishes or is vanquished by a foe, or changes status.

Using the Elements of Literary Narrative to Generate Ideas

In Chapter 20 we describe the basic elements of a literary narrative that work together to create a story: plot, character, setting, and theme. In this section we show how you can use each of these elements to help think of ideas for your autobiographical story. Before doing the exercises in this section, consult the discussion of these concepts in Chapter 20 (pp. 498–500).

Plot

By *plot* we mean the basic action of the story, including the selection and sequencing of scenes and events. Most autobiographical plots revolve around how the writer came to be who he or she is. Often stories don't open with the earliest chronological moment; they may start *in medias res* ("in the middle of things") at a moment of crisis and then flash backward to fill in earlier details that explain the origins of the crisis. What you choose to include in your story and where you place it are concerns of plot. The amount of detail you choose to devote to each scene is also a function of plot. How a writer varies the amount of detail in each scene is referred to as a plot's *pacing*.

As we note in Chapter 20, plots typically unfold in the following stages: (a) an arresting opening scene; (b) the introduction of characters and the filling in of background; (c) the building of tension or conflict through oppositions embedded in a series of events or scenes; (d) the climax or pivotal moment when the tension or conflict comes to a head; and (e) reflection on the events of the plot and their meaning.

To help you recognize story-worthy events in your own life, consider the following list of pivotal moments that have figured in numerous autobiographical narratives:

- Moments of enlightenment or coming to knowledge: understanding a complex idea for the first time, recognizing what is meant by love or jealousy or justice, mastering a complex skill, seeing some truth about yourself or your family that you previously haven't seen
- Passages from one realm to the next: from innocence to experience, from outsider to insider or vice versa, from child to adult, from novice to expert, from what you once were to what you now are
- Confrontation with the unknown or with people or situations that challenged or threatened your old identity and values
- Moments of crisis or critical choice that tested your mettle or your system of values
- Choices about the company you keep (friends, love interests, cliques, larger social groups) and the effects of those choices on your integrity and the persona you project to the world
- Problems maintaining relationships without compromising your own growth or denying your own needs
- Problems accepting limitations and necessities, such as the loss of dreams, the death of intimates, the failure to live up to ideals, or living with a chronic illness or disability
- Contrasts between common wisdom and your own unique knowledge or experience: doing what people said couldn't be done, failing at something others said was easy, finding value in something rejected by society, finding bad consequences in something widely valued

FOR WRITING AND DISCUSSION

Prior to class, use one or more of these pivotal-moment categories as an aid to brainstorm ideas for your own autobiographical essay. Then choose one of your ideas to use for your plot, and freewrite possible answers to the following questions:

1. How might you begin your story?
2. What events and scenes might you include in your story?
3. How might you arrange them?
4. What would be the climax of your story (the pivotal moment or scene)?
5. What insights or meaning might you want your story to suggest?

Then share your ideas and explorations with classmates. Help each other explore possibilities for good autobiographical stories. Of course, you are not yet committed to any pivotal moment or plot.

Character

Which characters from your life will you choose to include in your autobiography? The answer to that question depends on the nature of the tension that moves your story forward. Characters who contribute significantly to that tension or who represent some aspect of that tension with special clarity belong in your story. Whatever the source of tension in a story, a writer typically chooses characters who exemplify the narrator's fears and desires or who forward or frustrate the narrator's growth in a significant way.

Sometimes writers develop characters not through description and sensory detail but through dialogue. Particularly if a story involves conflict between people, dialogue is a powerful means of letting the reader experience that conflict directly. The following piece of dialogue, taken from African American writer Richard Wright's classic autobiography, *Black Boy*, demonstrates how a skilled writer can let dialogue tell the story, without resorting to analysis and abstraction. In the following scene, young Wright approaches a librarian in an attempt to get a book by Baltimore author and journalist H. L. Mencken from a whites-only public library. He has forged a note and borrowed a library card from a sympathetic white coworker and is pretending to borrow the book in his coworker's name.

> "What do you want, boy?"
>
> As though I did not possess the power of speech, I stepped forward and simply handed her the forged note, not parting my lips.
>
> "What books by Mencken does he want?" she asked.
>
> "I don't know ma'am," I said avoiding her eyes.
>
> "Who gave you this card?"
>
> "Mr. Falk," I said.
>
> "Where is he?"
>
> "He's at work, at the M—— Optical Company," I said. "I've been in here for him before."
>
> "I remember," the woman said. "But he never wrote notes like this."
>
> Oh, God, she's suspicious. Perhaps she would not let me have the books? If she had turned her back at that moment, I would have ducked out the door and never gone back. Then I thought of a bold idea.
>
> "You can call him up, ma'am," I said, my heart pounding.
>
> "You're not using these books are you?" she asked pointedly.
>
> "Oh no ma'am. I can't read."
>
> "I don't know what he wants by Mencken," she said under her breath.
>
> I knew I had won; she was thinking of other things and the race question had gone out of her mind.
>
> —Richard Wright, *Black Boy*

It's one thing to hear *about* racial prejudice and discrimination; it's another thing to *hear* it directly through dialogue such as this. In just one hundred or so words of conversation, Wright communicates the anguish and humiliation of being a "black boy" in the United States in the 1920s.

Another way to develop a character is to present a sequence of moments or scenes that reveal a variety of behaviors and moods. Imagine taking ten photographs of your character to represent his or her complexity and variety and then arranging them in a collage. Your narrative can create a similar collage using verbal descriptions. Sheila Madden uses this strategy in "Letting Go of Bart," a story in the Readings section of this chapter.

FOR WRITING AND DISCUSSION

If you currently have ideas for the story you plan to write, consider now the characters who will be in it. If you haven't yet settled on a story idea, think of memorable people in your life. Explore questions such as these: Why are these characters significant to you? What role did they play in forwarding or frustrating your progress? Given that role, which of their traits, mannerisms, modes of dress, and actions might you include in your account? Could you develop your character through dialogue? Through a collage of representative scenes? After you have considered these questions privately, share your responses to them either as a whole class or in groups. Help each other think of details to make your characters vivid and memorable.

Setting

Elements of setting are selected as characters are selected, according to how much they help readers understand the conflict or tension that drives the story. When you write about yourself, what you notice in the external world often reflects your inner world. In some moods you are apt to notice the expansive lawn, beautiful flowers, and swimming ducks in the city park; in other moods you might note the litter of paper cups, the blight on the roses, and the scum on the duck pond. The setting typically relates thematically to the other elements of a story. In "Berkeley Blues" (Chapter 20, pp. 491–94), for example, the author contrasts the swimming pools and sunsets of his hometown to the grit and darkness of inner-city Berkeley. The contrast in settings mirrors the contrast in the worldviews of the high school debaters and the homeless person who confronts them.

FOR WRITING AND DISCUSSION

On your own, freewrite about possible settings to include in your autobiographical narrative. Describe one of these settings fully. What do you see? Hear? Smell? Why is this setting appropriate for your story? Can you imagine two contrasting settings that reflect the contraries or oppositions in your story? Alternatively, picture in your mind one of the characters you thought of in the exercise on page 140. Now, imagine this character in a setting that reveals his or her significance—in a kitchen baking a pie, on the front steps of a porch laughing with neighbors, in an open field running barefoot, in the backyard working on an old engine, in a cluttered office standing by the watercooler. Picture a photograph of your character in this setting. Freewrite your description of that photograph.

Then, share your descriptive freewrites with classmates, discussing how your settings might be used in your autobiographical narrative.

Theme

The word *theme* is difficult to define. Themes, like thesis statements, organize the other elements of the essay. But a theme is seldom stated explicitly and never proved with reasons and factual evidence. Readers ponder—even argue about—themes, and often different readers are affected very differently by the same theme. Some literary critics view theme as simply a different way of thinking about plot. To use a phrase from critic Northrop Frye, a plot is "what happened" in a story, whereas the theme is "what happens" over and over again in the story and others like it. To illustrate this distinction we summarize a part of Maureen Howard's autobiography, which you will read in the next section, from two perspectives:

Plot Perspective   It's the story of a preadolescent girl's encounters with various teachers, especially a dance teacher named Ruby Weinstein. The story ends with the girl's mother's taking her home after a dance recital.

Theme Perspective   It's the story of a preadolescent girl's awakening to the contrast between her conventional, Catholic upbringing and the freedom, beauty, and abandon of art. In the end, the narrator seems caught between opposing identities.

As you can see, the thematic summary goes beyond the events of the story to point toward the larger significance of those events. Although you may choose not to state your theme directly for your readers, you need to understand that theme to organize your story. This understanding usually precedes and guides your decisions about what events and characters to include, what details and dialogue to use, and what elements of setting to describe. But sometimes you need to reverse the process and start out with events and characters that, for whatever reason, force themselves on you, and then figure out your theme after you've written for a while. In other words, theme may be something you discover as you write.

FOR WRITING AND DISCUSSION

Using the ideas you have brainstormed from previous exercises in this chapter, choose two possible ideas for an autobiographical narrative you might write. For each, freewrite your response to this question: What is the significance of this story for me? (Why did I choose this story? Why is it important to me? Why do I want to tell it? What am I trying to show my reader?)

In class, share your freewrites. All the exercises in this section are designed to generate discussion about the elements of autobiographical narrative and to encourage topic exploration.

READINGS

Now that we have examined some of the key elements of autobiographical writing, let's look at some particular examples.

The first reading is taken from basketball player Bill Russell's autobiography, *Second Wind*. In this passage, Russell tells about a life-changing event that happened during his junior year in high school.

BILL RUSSELL
FROM *SECOND WIND*

During my junior year in high school, in 1950, I had a mystical revelation. One day 1
while I was walking down the hall from one class to another, by myself, as usual, it suddenly dawned on me that it was all right to be who I was.

The thought just came to me: "Hey, you're all right. Everything is all right." The 2
idea was hardly earthshaking, but I was a different person by the time I reached the end of the hall. Had I been methodical I would have immediately written down my thoughts. Over and over again I received the idea that everything was all right about me—so vividly that the thought seemed to have colors on it. I remember looking around in class to make sure the other kids didn't think I was acting strange.

Those moments in the hall are the closest I've come to a religious experience. For 3
all I know, it may have actually been one. A warm feeling fell on me out of nowhere. I wondered why the idea hadn't occurred to me before; everything seemed to fall into place, the way it does for a kid when he first understands simple multiplication.

Everybody remembers the "Aha!" sensation when a good idea hits you. I remem- 4
ber sitting in a logic class at the University of San Francisco, puzzling over something the priest had been explaining to us for the previous few days. Then it came to me. Bells went off; the mental pleasure was so great that I jumped as if someone had pinched me and yelled "Hey!"

The priest said, "Congratulations, Mr. Russell. You have just had your first real and 5
complete thought. How does it feel?" He was patronizing me, but I didn't care because he had just given me a new way of seeing things.

What I saw in the hallway at high school that day was more than just an idea; it 6
was a way out of self-rejection. In the four years since my mother had died, everybody I encountered felt that there was something wrong with me. Worse, I *agreed* with them. I was clumsy at everything. When I opened a soup can, it felt as if I was trying to take apart a watch with a sledgehammer. I was insulted all the time. At my first and only football practice the coach lined up players to run over me all afternoon, and then complained to the team that he'd gotten the "bum of the family" instead of my brother, who was a star football player at a rival high school. I dropped football, swallowed my pride and went out for the cheerleading team. I didn't even make that. I was the classic ninety-pound weakling—except that nobody would have dreamed of using my picture in an advertisement.

The white cops in Oakland stopped me on the streets all the time, grilled me and 7
routinely called me "nigger." Whenever they said it, it put me in such a state that I would

shrivel up inside and think, "Oh, God. They're right." I gave everybody the benefit of the doubt—friends who ignored me, strangers who were mean—because I thought they were probably justified.

8   All this changed after that trip down the hall.

Thinking Critically About *Second Wind*

Perhaps the first thing the reader realizes about Russell's narrative is that the significant event is hardly an event at all—just a revelation that came to him while he was walking down the hall. So tiny and noneventful is the event itself that Russell spends very little time describing it. Instead, most of this passage (and the several pages that follow it) recounts Russell's mental journey through the significance of the event; it is short on action and long on reflection. The tension arises from a clash between the poles of a major contrariety: the contrast between Russell's old self and his new self.

Notice that this essay shares many of the features of open-ended, narrative-based prose discussed in Chapters 4 and 20:

- Lack of initial mapping with occasional gaps created by unexpected transitions (Russell's first sentence prepares the reader only for a "mystical revelation," not for the account of self-acceptance that follows)
- Use of flashbacks and flash-forwards (Russell opens the story with a moment of revelation in his junior year of high school, flashes forward to an analogous moment of revelation in a college logic class, then flashes back to events that occurred between the death of his mother when he was twelve and his moment of revelation at sixteen)
- Use of analogy and figurative language ("everything seemed to fall into place, the way it does for a kid when he first understands simple multiplication")
- Use of details more than generalizations to make points (Russell conveys the point that he was a victim of prejudice through specifics: "The white cops in Oakland stopped me on the streets all the time, grilled me and routinely called me 'nigger.' ")

For a much different approach to narrative, one with almost no commentary, consider Maureen Howard's autobiographical account of her evolution from repressed, middle-class, Catholic child to nationally prominent writer. Here is an excerpt from her autobiography, *Facts of Life*.

MAUREEN HOWARD
FROM *FACTS OF LIFE*

1   Our piano lessons, taught by Sister Mary Patronella, a large woman who dosed with Listerine so that she might breathe freely over her pupils, cost fifty cents an hour and

were not worth the price. Then ballet for me, elocution, clarinet for George—none of my mother's efforts to spring us from our cultural poverty or the dim children in our neighborhood came to much. She found extraordinary people to widen our horizons. A distraught mother (with a house full of waifs in undershirts gnawing at pieces of Bond Bread) instructed us in drawing and watercolors. Shading, outline, perspective: the point of each academic exercise was lost in the woman's confusion: our studio her kitchen table, old jelly jars to dip our brushes, chipped saucers to mix our colors and her kids whining in the doorway. For a while our Saturday mornings were a penance.

There followed, for me, a vivid year of modern dance. Only imagine the heroics of it: a tiny Jewish girl in her twenties, tense as a young bird, dedicated to Art, operating out of a storefront behind venetian blinds. A few potted plants, photos of Isadora, Ted Shawn and Ruth St. Denis piously tacked on the Walls. Through her gauze drapery Miss Weinstein was all bone and dancer's muscle. Her body was covered for Bridgeport, though sometimes when the mothers had gone off—they were not allowed to attend class with their clumpy purses and absurdly disguised shapes—sometimes, our teacher would fling off her kimono and reveal herself to us, free and naked under her Grecian dress, leaping, swaying around the shop for her small audience. We felt the walls thrust out beyond the dry cleaners next door. The stamped tin ceiling arched heavenward into the insurance office above. Here was perfect space; and the phonograph playing away. Her breasts were like small muscles, too. Her buttocks and stomach flat. We were to believe the human body was beautiful: Miss Weinstein made it so, her neck tendons stretched to the sublime. The idea was alien to me. My arms and legs and all the mysteries between were called a temple of the Holy Ghost. All the nuns' warnings—never to see, never to touch. One sad warped Sister of Saint Joseph took the girls aside each spring and near to hysteria instructed us in ingenious arrangements of lace handkerchiefs into rosettes that, pinned with a miraculous medal on our more revealing cotton dresses, would distract the eye from our childish bosoms—our very bodies being instruments of the devil. For the school play we had undressed with large white towels held in our teeth, covering our shame. Then came the modern dance. Ruby Weinstein was ridiculous in her abandon, but the ten preadolescent girls in her class never snickered. Nipples and navels were reasonable in the atmosphere she created. I'd never seen pubic hair, but it was quite the right thing on Miss Weinstein as she danced for us.

In our home-sewn togas we expressed ourselves, leaping (as though against the wind), swaying (branches in spring), falling (in death to the cold floor). There was no technique at all, save the perfect imitation of our teacher. There was no critique, no one student singled out for grace or elevation of style. The only choreographed piece, which we danced finally and disastrously for our mothers, was performed to the "Narcissus Song." We rushed from the corners of the store to a round 1930's mirror set on the floor, fell in love with our respective images, tossed our heads, sighed, leapt, swayed, fell to the contemplation of our beauty again and expired, all ten of us, by the side of the reflecting pool.

At home I played my own record of "Narcissus" when "they" were out. I dashed from the sun parlor to the center of the living room carpet timing each move, the coy little testing of the water with my toe, the flirtatious smile. There was no mirror needed. The true narcissism of adolescence lay a few years ahead: the self-enchantment of my dancing was enough. Imagined away the plumpness and pigtails. Turned to dust my colorless school clothes. Fantasies in an empty house. It was the beginning of my long career as an escape artist. Secrecy was important. No one on the block, no one at Saint Patrick's School should know that I studied the modern dance. I was the only Christian in Miss Weinstein's class, and though the girls were friendly I was content to go off alone in the car with my mother. I did not want art confused with real life. The dread ballet classes of former years had been an ordeal—all the little daughters of doctors and dentists, *socialites* from Fairfield in squirrel coats and Tyrolean skirts, the heiress of a girdle empire escorted by a black maid.

5   No, what Ruby Weinstein offered was pure. Art. Freedom.

6   I had come to know in my childish way these grand abstractions. Grace and Beauty. All written on the blossoming soul with an indiscriminate use of capital letters. Such inflation seems horrifying to me now. I have no clear idea what freedom is and grace belongs to children, to one perfect stroke, or to the talented who put in a lifetime of hard work. So I leapt out of Ruby's corner with my illusions on the afternoon of our spring recital to adore myself, pink toga and pigtails, but I was Narcissus no more. They laughed. The mothers, squeezed back against the shop window in a line of folding chairs, swapped smiles and laughed, not cruelly but with a sweet indulgence. We were little girls again, consigned to another clumsy step in our advance toward the womanly state. Someday we would have purses and hats, hateful permanent waves and face powder soiling the collars of our print dresses. We would sit in a row like vegetable women, amused by art, wondering if there was enough in the house for supper. End of the record. I died by the side of the pool.

7   Polite applause, the scraping of chairs and then Miss Weinstein sprang forth wearing underclothes beneath her gauze, decent this day. To urgent unknown music she danced for them, danced against them. Her strong small body became a force: the sequence of leaps, back falls, contractions, spun from her endlessly, like magic scarves. The little studio was charged with her conviction. She was not afraid to expose herself: this was her Art. She danced till the end of the old seventy-eight and danced beyond to silence. Yes, her performance had a manic energy, was routine artsy, but Ruby's dedication was the real thing. Stunned by such beauty I went straight to my dreams again, while the mothers, bewildered but with full respect, clapped and clapped. There was a sudden intimacy in the storefront studio—"It's meant so much." "Next Year, Miss Weinstein," they said, "in the fall." We stood by the jars of lilacs she had placed on the window shelf for our final meeting. There was no next year. Ruby Weinstein was passing through Bridgeport.

8   In the car my mother called me by a pet name. "You were very good, Mimi." That was untrue. She had laughed with the rest. There was no comfort in the old name. I remember this moment and others like it when she would draw away as though the years to come were accomplished and she had lost control of me. "How will it turn out for you?" she seemed to say. Then in a soothing voice she went back, back further to the nursery rhyme that was always mine—"Reeny-Pen-Pone/Lived all alone." I was her strange, fat child, wounded, clutching my toga in a brown paper bag. She had done her best.

Thinking Critically About *Facts of Life*

Unlike Russell, who is more concerned with reflection than with action, Maureen Howard focuses on a few intensely realized scenes. There is little commentary, except for a brief reflection on the thematic significance of Ruby Weinstein, who, Howard tells us flatly, stands for "Art. Freedom." But Howard doesn't tell us explicitly what her story reveals about these abstractions. What will be the place of art and freedom when Howard becomes, as she envisions, a "vegetable woman"—one of those middle-class ladies with "purses and hats, hateful permanent waves and face powder soiling the collars of . . . print dresses"? What ambiguities are buried in the lines that end that paragraph: "End of the record. I died by the side of the pool"? Who is the narrator and what is she becoming? What is the meaning of the last line of the narrative, when Howard says of her mother, "She had done her best"?

These are the kinds of questions readers ask about literary writing that perplexes them. These are exactly the kinds of questions readers *don't* ask about closed-form, thesis-based prose. For a reader of closed-form writing to say, "I didn't understand your last line" signals some failure by the writer. But in open-form prose, such confusion is often the jumping off point for an exploration of the text's larger significance.

FOR WRITING AND DISCUSSION

1. In Chapter 20, we discuss various aspects of narrative-based writing, including memory-soaked words and revelatory words. Read pages 504–06 where these concepts are discussed. Then, working as a whole class or in small groups, find examples of this kind of language in Howard's essay. Explain Howard's choice of details in the following examples.

   a. "The dread ballet classes of former years had been an ordeal—all the little daughters of doctors and dentists, *socialites* from Fairfield in squirrel coats and Tyrolean skirts, the heiress of a girdle empire escorted by a black maid." Why a girdle empire? Why the town Fairfield? Why the black maid? What is a Tyrolean skirt? Why the squirrel coats? Note: Many of these memory-soaked words and revelatory words are from Maureen Howard's generation and may require some historical reconstruction on your part in order to recover their significance.

   b. "A tiny Jewish girl in her twenties, tense as a young bird, dedicated to Art, operating out of a storefront behind venetian blinds. A few potted plants, photos of Isadora, Ted Shawn and Ruth St. Denis piously tacked on the Walls. . . . [The mothers] were not allowed to attend class with their clumpy purses and absurdly disguised shapes." Who are Isadora, Ted Shawn, and Ruth St. Denis? What memory-soaked images are called to mind by "storefront behind venetian blinds"? By "clumpy purses and absurdly disguised shapes"?

2. Imagine yourself twenty years in the future describing the room where you live now (your dorm room or apartment, or, if you live at home, the room that is most your own). What memory-soaked words and revelatory words will be most likely to make this room come to life in your imagination? What details about room decorations, posters or pictures on the wall, furniture, stereo or computer equipment, clothes on the floor or bed, and so on. will most trigger old associations and memories? You probably don't have photos of Isadora Duncan and Ted Shawn on your wall. What, if anything,

do you have on your wall? List some of the memory-soaked details and revelatory words of your room and then share them with classmates.

3. How does the setting of Ruby's studio reveal the contrast between art and ordinary life?

The next example offers more commentary than Howard's with its virtual absence of commentary. It was written by a student writer who wishes to remain anonymous, for a first-year composition class.

MASKS

1   Her soft, blond hair was in piggytails, as usual, with ringlets that bounced whenever she turned her head. As if they were springs, they could stretch, then shrink, then bounce, excited by the merest movement of her head. Never was there a hair that wasn't enclosed in those glossy balls which always matched her dress. I knew the only reason she turned her head was so they'd bounce. Because it was cute. Today, she wore a pink dress with frills and lace and impeccably white tights. Her feet, which swayed back and forth underneath her chair, were pampered with shiny, black shoes without a single scuff. She was very wise, sophisticated beyond her kindergarten years.

2   I gazed at her and then looked down at my clothes. My green and red plaid pants and my yellow shirt with tiny, blue stars showed the day's wear between breakfast, lunch, and recess. Showing through the toe of my tenny runners was my red sock.

3   At paint time, I closely followed behind her, making sure I painted at the easel next to hers. She painted a big, white house with a white picket fence and a family: Mom, Dad, and Daughter. I painted my mom, my brother, and myself. I, then, painted the sky, but blue streaks ran down our faces, then our bodies, ruining the picture.

4   The next day, I wore my hair in piggytails. I had done it all by myself, which was obvious due to my craftsmanship. She pointed and giggled at me when I walked by. I also wore a dress that day but I didn't have any pretty white tights. The boys all gathered underneath me when I went on the monkeybars to peak at my underwear to chant, "I see London, I see France, I see Tiffy's underpants."

5   When the day was done, she ran to the arms of her mother that enveloped her in a loving and nurturing hug. She showed her mother her painting, which had a big, red star on it.

6   "We'll have to put this up on the refrigerator with all of your others," her mother said. I had thrown my painting away. I looked once more at the two of them as they walked hand in hand towards their big, white house with a white picket fence. I trudged to my babysitter's house. I wouldn't see my mother until six o'clock. She had no time for me, for my paintings, for my piggytails. She was too busy working to have enough money to feed my brother and me.

7   Digging absently through books and folders, I secretly stole a glance at her, three lockers down. Today she wore her Calvins and sported a brand new pair of Nikes. As always, at the cutting edge of fashion. If I wanted Nikes, I could pay for them myself, or so said my mother. In the meantime, I had to suffer with my cheap, treadless Scats. As I searched for a pen, her giggle caught my attention. Three of her friends had flocked

around her locker. I continued searching for a pen but to no avail. I thought of approaching and borrowing one but I was fearful that they would make fun of me.

"Jim and Brad called me last night and both of them asked me to go to the show. Which one should I pick?" she asked. My mom wouldn't let me go out on dates until I was a sophomore in high school. We were only in seventh grade and she was always going out with guys. Not that it mattered that I couldn't date, yet. Nobody had ever asked me out.   8

"My hair turned out so yucky today. Ick," she commented. She bent down to grab a book and light danced among the gentle waves of her flowing, blond mane. Her radiant brown eyes and adorable smile captivated all who saw her. Once captured, however, none was allowed past the mask she'd so artfully constructed to lure them to her. We were all so close to her, so far away. She was so elusive, like a beautiful perfume you smell but can't name, like the whisper that wakes you from a dream and turns out to belong to the dream.   9

As she walked into the library, I heard a voice whisper, "There she is. God, She's beautiful." She was wearing her brown and gold cheerleader outfit. Her pleated skirt bounced off her thighs as she strutted by. Her name, "Kathy," was written on her sweater next to her heart and by it hung a corsage. As she rounded the corner, she flicked her long, blond curls and pivoted, sending a ripple through the pleats of the skirt. She held her head up high, befitting one of her social standing: top of the high school food chain. She casually searched the length of the library for friends. When she reached the end of the room, she carefully reexamined every table, this time less casually. Her smile shaded into a pout. She furrowed her face, knitting her eyebrows together, and saddening her eyes. People stared at her until she panicked.   10

She was bolting toward the door when she spotted me. She paused and approached my table. Putting on her biggest smile, she said, "Oh hi! Can I sit by you?" Thrilled at the possibility of at last befriending her, I was only too happy to have her sit with me. As she sat down, she again scanned the expanse of the library.   11

"So, who does the varsity basketball team play tonight?" I asked.   12

"Great Falls Central," she replied. "Make sure you're there! . . . How's the Algebra assignment today?!"   13

"Oh, it's okay. Not too tough," I said.   14

"John always does my assignments for me. I just hate Algebra. It's so hard."   15

We stood up in silence, suddenly painfully aware of our differences. She glanced in the reflection of the window behind us, checked her hair, then again scanned the room.   16

"There's Shelly! Well, I'll see you later," she said.   17

She rose from the table and fled to her more acceptable friend.   18

The next day, she walked down the hall surrounded by a platoon of friends. As we passed, I called out "Hi!" but she turned away as if she didn't know me, as if I didn't exist.   19

I, then, realized her cheerleader outfit, her golden locks, her smile were all a mask. Take them away and nothing but air would remain. Her friends and their adoration were her identity. Without them she was alone and vulnerable. I was the powerful one. I was independent.   20

Thinking Critically About "Masks"

1. What are the main contrarieties in this piece?
2. This piece focuses on the narrator's movement toward a significant recognition. What is it she recognizes? If you were a peer reviewer for this writer,

would you recommend eliminating the last paragraph, expanding it, or leaving it as it is? Why?

3. Where does this writer use details with particular effectiveness?

The final example uses a collage technique (see p. 144). Here the emphasis is so much on the character Bart that the narrator seems relatively unimportant, and you may wonder whether this piece is biography (the story of Bart) or autobiography (the story of the narrator). We include "Letting Go of Bart" in the category of autobiographical narrative because the way in which the writer, Sheila Madden, tells the story reveals her own growth in understanding, her own deepening of character.

SHEILA MADDEN
LETTING GO OF BART

1   Bart lies stiffly in bed, toes pointed downward like a dancer's, but Bart is far from dancing. When he tries to shift position, his limbs obey spasmodically because his nervous system has been whipsawed by the medications he has been taking for years to control the various manifestations of AIDS.

2   He is wearing diapers now, for incontinence—the ultimate indignity. An oxygen tube is hooked into his nose, morphine drips into his arm; his speech is slurred.

3   But Bart is not confused. He is intensely irritable and has been the terror of his nurses. Though he has a great self-deprecating grin, I haven't seen it for weeks.

4   I can't say a proper goodbye because he is never alone. I would like to pray silently by his bedside, meditating; but even if I could, he would barely tolerate it. Bart has no god.

5   I remember the day a tall, good-looking young man popped into the open door of the downstairs apartment I was fixing up in my San Francisco home. That late afternoon, I was tiredly putting the last coat of paint on the walls with the help of a couple of friends. Bart had seen the for-rent sign in the window and just walked in. Within moments he had all three of us laughing uproariously as he put a deposit in my hand. I had asked the angels for help in finding a decent renter; the angels had responded. Bart and I would get on famously.

6   For one thing, Bart managed to fix or overlook the unfinished bits in the apartment. He and his father built a fine, much-needed deck on the back garden, charging me only for the lumber. He made the small apartment look spacious, arranging the furniture skillfully, backlighting the sofas. And he was prompt with the rent.

7   However, Bart was far more than a satisfactory renter. He was a fine singer and a member of the symphony chorus. When he practiced, his rich baritone would sail up the stairs, smoothing the airways, never ruffling them.

8   He asked permission to put a piano in his apartment, and I agreed nervously. Because he was a beginner on the instrument, I feared endless, fumbling scales disturbing my peace. It never happened. He played softly, sensitively, and always at reasonable hours.

I attended some of his concerts and met his friends. At times we joined forces at   9
parties upstairs or downstairs, but somehow we never got in each other's hair.

He was a skillful ballroom dancer. Once he agreed to stand in as partner for my   10
visiting sister when we attended a Friday dance at the Embarcadero Plaza—although
the prospect could not have thrilled him.

Another time I disabled my tape deck by spraying it with WD-40 and ran down-   11
stairs for help. Bart came up immediately, scolding me roundly for putting oil on such
a machine. Then he spent the better part of an hour wrapping matchsticks in cotton
batting (for lack of a better tool), degreasing the heads with rubbing alcohol, and
putting all to rights.

Bart had family problems; I had them. We commiserated. Bart was an ally, a com-   12
patriot, a brother.

I suspected Bart was gay; but we never talked about it, although he knew I was   13
working in the AIDS fields as a counselor and that it was a nonissue with me.

Then one day he got a bad flu, which turned into a deep, wracking cough that did   14
not go away. I worried about it, having heard such coughs in the AIDS patients I dealt
with daily. I encouraged him to see a doctor, and he did, making light of his visit.

Finally the cough receded, but psychically so did Bart. I saw him hardly at all for   15
the next three months. When I did, he seemed somber and abstracted.

However, my life was hectic at the time. I didn't pay attention, assuming his prob-   16
lem was job dissatisfaction; I knew his boss was a constant thorn in his side. One day
he told me that he was changing jobs and moving to Napa, an hour's drive away. I re-
joiced for him and cried for myself. I would miss Bart.

Our lives separated. Napa might as well have been the moon. Over a two-year pe-   17
riod we talked once or twice on the phone, and I met him once for dinner in the city.

Then one night my doorbell rang unexpectedly, and Bart came in to tell me of his   18
recovery from a recent bout of pneumocystis pneumonia. "I'm out of the closet, willy-
nilly," he said.

I was stunned. I had put him in the "safe" category, stuffing my fears about the   19
telltale cough. It must have been then that he learned his diagnosis. For the next 24
hours I cried off and on, inconsolably, for Bart and probably for all the others I had seen
die.

Now he is at the end, an end so fierce there is nothing to do but pray it will come   20
quickly. Bart is courageous, his anger masking fear. He has thus far refused to let the
morphine dull his consciousness. His eyes, hawklike, monitor all that is going on around
him. Angels, who once brought him, take him home.

Thinking Critically About "Letting Go of Bart"

Madden's technique is to create her portrait of Bart through a collection of
scenes: Bart lying stiffly in bed; Bart popping into the apartment to put down a
rent deposit; Bart fixing up the apartment and building a deck with his father;
Bart singing and playing piano; Bart taking Madden's sister to a ballroom dance;
Bart cleaning Madden's tape deck; Bart coughing. The scenes are selected to
show, rather than tell about, Bart's personality. The way in which Madden remembers the scenes and movingly describes them indicates the depth of her own
feelings.

FOR WRITING AND DISCUSSION

As a means of generating more possible topics for an autobiographical narrative, each class member should do the following exercise independently and then share the results with the rest of the class.

1. Have you ever known a person whose presence in your life made an important difference to you, as did Bart to Sheila Madden? If you have, freewrite about this character, imagine a series of scenes that might create a collage effect.
2. Have you ever changed your assessment of a person and consequently of yourself in a way analogous to the narrator's reassessment of the cheerleader in "Masks"? If you have, freewrite about this character, including details that reveal this person before and after your moment of reassessment.
3. Have you ever known a character whose values or way of life differed dramatically from those of your own family as Ruby Weinstein differed from Howard's family? If you have, freewrite about this character, imagining specific details that show the difference between this character's values and those of your family.
4. Have you ever had a moment of revelation when the world suddenly seemed different to you—as did Bill Russell? If you have, freewrite about this experience.

COMPOSING YOUR ESSAY

In deciding what to write about, keep in mind the basic requirement for a good story: it must portray a sequence of connected events driven forward by some tension or conflict that results in a recognition or new understanding. Not every memorable event in your life will lend itself to this sort of structure. The most common failing in faulty narratives is that the meaning of the event is clearer to the narrator than to the audience. "You had to be there," the writer comments, when a story just doesn't have the expected impact on an audience.

But it's the storyteller's job to *put the reader there* by providing enough detail and context for the reader to *see* why the event is significant. If an event didn't lead to any significant insight, understanding, knowledge, change, or other kind of difference in your life, and if you really had to be there to appreciate its significance, then it's a poor candidate for an autobiographical narrative.

Generating and Exploring Ideas

Choosing a Plot

For some of you, identifying a plot—a significant moment or insight arising out of contrariety—will present little problem; perhaps you have already settled on an idea you generated in one of the class discussion exercises earlier in this chapter. However, if you are still searching for a plot idea, you may find the following list helpful:

- A time when you took some sort of test that conferred new status on you (Red Cross lifesaving exam, drivers' test, SAT, important school test, entrance exam, team tryout). If you failed, what did you learn from it or how did it shape you? If you succeeded, did the new status turn out to be as important as you expected it would be?
- A situation in which your normal assumptions about life were challenged (an encounter with a foreign culture, a time when you ran away from home or got lost, a time when a person you'd stereotyped surprised you).
- A time when you left your family for an extended period or forever (going to college, getting married, entering the military, leaving one parent for another after their divorce).
- A time that plunged you into a crisis (being the first person to discover a car crash, seeing a robbery in progress, being thrown in with people who are repugnant to you, facing an emergency).
- A situation in which you didn't fit or didn't fulfill others' expectations of you, or a situation in which you were acknowledged as a leader or exceeded others' expectations of you (a summer job, membership on a team, a tough class, a new role).
- A time when you overcame your fears to do something for the first time (first date, first public presentation).
- A situation in which you learned how to get along amicably with another human being, or a failed relationship that taught you something about life (your first extended romantic relationship, your relationship with a difficult sibling, relative, teacher, or boss).
- A time when a person who mattered to you (parent, romantic interest, authority figure) rejected you or let you down, or a time when you rejected or let down someone who cared for you.
- A time when you made a sacrifice on behalf of someone else or someone else made a sacrifice in your name (parent or spouse who took on a second job to help you through school).
- A time when you were irresponsible or violated a principle or law and thereby caused others pain (you shoplifted or drank when underage and were caught; you failed to look after someone entrusted to your care).
- A time when you were criticized unjustly or given a punishment you didn't deserve (you were accused of plagiarizing a paper that you'd written).
- A time when you were forced to accept defeat or death or the loss of a dream or otherwise learned to live with reduced expectations.
- A time when you lived out a fantasy.

Thickening the Plot

Once you've identified an event about which you'd like to write, you need to develop ways to show readers what makes that event particularly story worthy. In thinking about the event, consider the following questions:

- What makes the event so memorable? What particulars, what physical details come most readily to mind when you think back on the event?
- What are the major contrarieties that gave the event tension? Did it raise a conflict between two or more people? Between their worldviews? Between before and after versions of yourself?
- How can you make the contrarieties memorable and vivid to the reader? What scenes can you create? What words could your characters exchange?
- Is there a moment of insight, recognition, or resolution that would give your plot a climax?
- What is the significance of the story? How does it touch on larger human issues and concerns? What makes it something your reader will relate to? What is its theme?

Shaping and Drafting

When stuck, writers often work their way into a narrative by describing in detail a vividly recalled scene, person, or object. This inductive approach is common with many creative processes. You may or may not include all the descriptive material in your final draft, but in the act of writing exhaustively about this one element, the rest of the story may begin to unfold for you and forgotten items and incidents may resurface. In the course of describing scenes and characters, you will probably also begin reflecting on the significance of what you are saying. Try freewriting answers to such questions as "Why is this important?" and "What am I trying to do here?" Then continue with your rough draft.

Revising

Once you've written a draft, you need to get down to the real work of writing—rewriting. Revisit your prose critically, with an eye toward helping your reader share your experience and recognize its significance. Chapter 20, as well as the following guidelines for peer reviewers, will be of particular help during revision.

g   u   i   d   e   l   i   n   e   s

for Peer Reviewers

Instructions for peer reviews, including use of these guidelines, are provided in Chapter 21, pages 527–28. To write a peer review for a classmate, use your own paper, numbering your responses to correspond to the questions on the guidelines. At the head of your paper place the author's name and your own name as shown.

Author's Name: _____

Peer Reviewer's Name: _____

I. Read the draft at normal reading speed from beginning to end. As you read, do the following:
   A. Place a wavy line in the margin next to any passages that you find confusing, that contain something that doesn't seem to fit, or that otherwise slow down your reading.
   B. Place a "Good!" in the margin next to any passages where you think the writing is particularly strong or interesting.

II. Read the draft again slowly. Describe for the writer what you currently see in this draft. If you have difficulty answering any of the following questions, explain briefly the source of your difficulty.
   A. List the characters in the story and describe the function of each in one sentence.
      1. Which characters do you identify or sympathize with most strongly and why?
      2. Which characters are you least sympathetic toward and why?
   B. List the major events of the story in the order in which they appear. Does the narrative follow chronological order or are there flashbacks and flash-forwards?
   C. Describe the contrarieties, tensions, or conflicts that generate the story. Are these conflicts internal (between opposing values, attitudes, or ideas within the narrative) or external (competition between peers or conflicts with parents)?
   D. What details does the narrator use to describe the setting for the story? If the setting plays an important part in the story, how is it related to the story's theme?
   E. What seems to be the theme of the story? In a sentence or two, describe how you would respond to the question, So what? in regard to the story. Why is the story important to the writer? Why might it be important to someone else?
   F. What does the writer do in the early part of the story to make you want to read on?

III. What recommendations do you have for improving this draft?
   A. How might the writer improve the title?
   B. How might the writer improve the overall quality of the story?
      1. How might the writer portray characters more effectively? Where might the writer use more effective details or include more dialogue?
      2. How might the writer improve the structure or pacing of the plot? If you were to expand or reduce the treatment given to any events, which would you change and why?
      3. How might the writer heighten or clarify tension between contraries? Do you have to wait too long before the essential tension of the story becomes clear?

      4. How might the writer use setting more effectively?

      5. How might the writer clarify the thematic significance of the story?

  C. Sum up what you see as the chief strengths and problem areas of this draft.

      1. Strengths

      2. Problem areas

IV. Read the draft one more time. Place a check in the margin wherever you notice problems in grammar, spelling, or mechanics (one check per problem).

c h a p t e r **8**

Writing an Exploratory Essay

ABOUT EXPLORATORY WRITING

In Chapter 1, we said that to grow as a writer you need to love problems—to pose them and to live with them. Most academic writers testify that writing projects begin when they become engaged with a question or problem and commit themselves to an extensive period of exploration. During exploration, writers may radically redefine the problem and then later alter or even reverse their initial thesis.

As we noted in Chapters 2 and 3, however, inexperienced writers tend to truncate this exploratory process, committing themselves hastily to a thesis to avoid complexity. College professors say this tendency hinders their students' intellectual growth. Asserting a thesis commits you to a position. Asking a question, on the other hand, invites you to contemplate multiple perspectives, entertain new ideas, and let your thinking evolve. As management professor A. Kimbrough Sherman puts it, to grow as thinkers students need "to 'wallow in complexity' and work their way back out" (see p. 21).

To illustrate his point, Sherman cites his experience in a management class where students were asked to write proposals for locating a new sports complex in a major U.S. city. To Sherman's disappointment, many students argued for a location without first considering all the variables—impact on neighborhoods, building costs and zoning, availability of parking, ease of access, attractiveness to tourists, aesthetics, and so forth—and without analyzing how various proposed locations stacked up against the criteria they were supposed to establish. The students reached closure without wallowing in complexity.

The assignment for this chapter asks you to dwell with a problem, even if you can't solve it. You will write an essay with an exploratory purpose; its focus will be a question rather than a thesis. The body of your paper will be a narrative account of your thinking about the problem—your attempt to examine its complexity, to explore alternative solutions, and to arrive at a solution or answer. Your exploration will generally require outside research, so many instructors will assign sections of Part Four, "A Guide to Research," along with this chapter. The paper will be relatively easy to write because it will be organized chronologically, but you will have nothing to say—no process to report—unless you discover and examine the problem's complexity.

EXPLORING EXPLORATORY WRITING

Through our work in writing centers, we often encounter students disappointed with their grades on essay exams or papers. "I worked hard on this paper," they tell us, "but I still got a lousy grade. What am I doing wrong? What do college professors want?"

To help you answer this question, consider the following two essays written for a freshman placement examination in composition at the University of Pittsburgh, in response to the following assignment:

> Describe a time when you did something you felt to be creative. Then, on the basis of the incident you have described, go on to draw some general conclusions about "creativity."

How would you describe the differences in thinking exhibited by the two writers? Which essay do you think professors rated higher?

Essay A

1　　I am very interested in music, and I try to be creative in my interpretation of music. While in high school, I was a member of a jazz ensemble. The members of the ensemble were given chances to improvise and be creative in various songs. I feel that this was a great experience for me, as well as the other members. I was proud to know that I could use my imagination and feelings to create music other than what was written.

2　　Creativity to me means being free to express yourself in a way that is unique to you, not having to conform to certain rules and guidelines. Music is only one of the many areas in which people are given opportunities to show their creativity. Sculpting, carving, building, art, and acting are just a few more areas where people can show their creativity.

3　　Through my music I conveyed feelings and thoughts which were important to me. Music was my means of showing creativity. In whatever form creativity takes, whether it be music, art, or science, it is an important aspect of our lives because it enables us to be individuals.

Essay B

Throughout my life, I have been interested and intrigued by music. My 1
mother has often told me of the times, before I went to school, when I would
"conduct" the orchestra on her records. I continued to listen to music and
eventually started to play the guitar and the clarinet. Finally, at about
the age of twelve, I started to sit down and to try to write songs. Even
though my instrumental skills were far from my own high standards, I would
spend much of my spare time during the day with a guitar around my neck,
trying to produce a piece of music.

Each of these sessions, as I remember them, had a rather set format. I 2
would sit in my bedroom, strumming different combinations of the five or
six chords I could play, until I heard a series which sounded particularly
good to me. After this, I set the music to a suitable rhythm (usually dependent on my mood at the time), and ran through the tune until I could play
it fairly easily. Only after this section was complete did I go on to writing lyrics, which generally followed along the lines of the current popular songs on the radio.

At the time of the writing, I felt that my songs were, in themselves, an 3
original creation of my own; that is, I, alone, made them. However, I now
see that, in this sense of the word, I was not creative. The songs themselves
seem to be an oversimplified form of the music I listened to at the time.

In a more fitting sense, however, I <u>was</u> being creative. Since I did not
purposely copy my favorite songs, I was, effectively, originating my songs
from my own "process of creativity." To achieve my goal, I needed what a
composer would call "inspiration" for my piece. In this case the inspiration was the current hit on the radio. Perhaps, with my present point of
view, I feel that I used too much "inspiration" in my songs, but, at that
time, I did not.

Creativity, therefore, is a process which, in my case, involved a cer- 4
tain series of "small creations" if you like. As well, it is something the

```
appreciation of which varies with one's point of view, that point of view
being set by the person's experience, tastes, and his own personal view of
creativity. The less experienced tend to allow for less originality, while
the more experienced demand real originality to classify something a "cre-
ation." Either way, a term as abstract as this is perfectly correct, and
open to interpretation.
```

Working as a whole class or in small groups, analyze the differences between Essay A and Essay B. What might cause college professors to rate one essay higher than the other? What would the writer of the weaker essay have to do to produce an essay more like the stronger?

WRITING PROJECT

Choose a question, problem, or issue that genuinely perplexes you. At the beginning of your exploratory essay, explain why you are interested in this chosen problem and why you have been unable to reach a satisfactory answer. Then write a first-person, chronologically organized, narrative account of your thinking process as you investigate your question through library research, talking with others, and doing your own reflective thinking. You might also wish to interview people, if appropriate, and to draw on your own personal experiences, memories, and observations. Your goal is to examine your question, problem, or issue from a variety of perspectives, assessing the strengths and weaknesses of different positions and points of view. By the end of your essay, you may or may not have reached a satisfactory solution to your problem. You will be rewarded for the quality of your exploration and thinking processes. In other words, your goal is not to answer your question, but to report on the process of wrestling with it.

This assignment asks you to dwell with a problem—and not necessarily to solve that problem. Your problem may shift and evolve as your thinking progresses. What matters is that you actively engage with your problem and demonstrate why it is problematic.

Your instructor may choose to combine this writing project with a subsequent one (for example, a research paper based on one of the assignments in the remaining chapters in Part Two) to create a sustained project in which you write two pieces on the same topic. If so, then the essay for this chapter will prepare you to write a later analytical or persuasive piece. Check with your instructor to make sure that your chosen question for this project will work for the later assignment.

UNDERSTANDING EXPLORATORY WRITING

As we have explained, this assignment calls for an essay with an *exploratory purpose* (see our discussion of purposes in Chapter 4, pp. 56–59). Exploratory writing generally has an open-form structure; the writer cannot assert a thesis and forecast a structure in the introduction (typical features of closed-form prose) because the thesis is unknown as the essay opens. Instead of following a closed-form, points-first structure, the essay narrates chronologically the process of the author's thinking about the problem. In a sense, an exploratory essay is analogous to those behind-the-scenes films about the making of a movie (*The Making of "Star Wars"* or *The Making of "Jurassic Park"*), in which you get to see the process behind the finished product—how, for example, the crew created and photographed a spaceflight or simulated an encounter with a brontosaurus.

The Essence of Exploratory Prose: Considering Multiple Solutions

The essential move of an exploratory essay is to consider multiple solutions to a problem. The writer defines a problem, poses a possible solution, explores its strengths and weaknesses, and then *moves* on to consider another possible solution.

To show a mind at work examining multiple solutions, let's return to the two student essays you examined in the previous exploratory activity (pp. 161–63). The fundamental difference between Essay A and Essay B is that the writer of Essay B treats the concept of "creativity" as a true problem. Note that the writer of Essay A is satisfied with his or her initial definition.

```
Creativity to me means being free to express yourself in a way that

is unique to you, not having to conform to certain rules and guide-

lines.
```

The writer of Essay B, however, is *not* satisfied with his or her first answer and uses the essay to think through the problem. This writer remembers an early creative experience—composing songs as a twelve-year-old.

```
At the time of the writing, I felt that my songs were, in themselves,

an original creation of my own; that is, I, alone, made them. How-

ever, I now see that, in this sense of the word, I was not creative.

The songs themselves seem to be an oversimplified form of the music

I listened to at the time.
```

This writer distinguishes between two points of view: "On the one hand, I used to think this, but now, in retrospect, I think that." This move forces the writer to go beyond the initial answer to think of alternatives.

The key to effective exploratory writing is to create a tension between alternative views. When you start out, you might not know where your thinking process will end up; at the outset you might not have formulated an opposing, countering, or alternative view. Using a move such as "I used to think . . . , but now I think" or "Part of me thinks this . . . , but another part thinks that . . ." forces you to find something additional to say; writing then becomes a process of inquiry and discovery.

The second writer's dissatisfaction with the initial answer initiates a dialectic process that plays one idea against another, creating a generative tension. In contrast, the writer of Essay A offers no alternative to his or her definition of creativity. This writer presents no specific illustrations of creative activity (such as the specific details in Essay B about strumming the guitar), but presents merely space-filling abstractions ("Sculpting, carving, building, art, and acting are just a few more areas where people can show their creativity."). The writer of Essay B scores a higher grade, not because the essay creates a brilliant (or even particularly clear) explanation of creativity; rather, the writer is rewarded for thinking about the problem dialectically.

We use the term *dialectic* to mean a thinking process often associated with the German philosopher Hegel, who said that each thesis ("My act was creative") gives rise to an antithesis ("My act was not creative") and that the clash of these opposing perspectives leads thinkers to develop a synthesis that incorporates some features of both theses ("My act was a series of 'small creations' "). You initiate dialectic thinking any time you play Elbow's believing and doubting game (see Chapter 2, pp. 39–42) or use other strategies to place opposing possibilities side by side.

Essay B's writer uses a dialectic thinking strategy that we might characterize as follows:

1. Regards the assignment as a genuine problem worth puzzling over
2. Considers alternative views and plays them off against each other
3. Looks at specifics
4. Continues the thinking process in search of some sort of resolution or synthesis of the alternative views
5. Incorporates the stages of this dialectic process into the essay

FOR WRITING AND DISCUSSION

1. According to writing theorist David Bartholomae, who analyzed several hundred student essays in response to the above placement-examination question, almost all the highest scoring essays exhibited a similar kind of dialectic thinking. How might the writer of the first essay expand the essay by using the dialectic thinking processes just described?
2. Working individually, read each of the following questions and write out your initial opinion or one or two answers that come immediately to mind.

- Given the easy availability of birth-control information and the ready availability of condoms, why do you think there are so many teenage pregnancies?
- Why do U.S. students, on the average, lag so far behind their European and Asian counterparts in scholastic achievement?
- Should women be assigned to combat roles in the military?
- The most popular magazines sold on college campuses around the country are women's fashion and lifestyle magazines such as *Glamour, Seventeen, Mademoiselle,* and *Cosmopolitan.* Why are these magazines so popular? Is there a problem with these magazines being so popular? (Two separate questions, both of which are worth exploring dialectically.)

3. Choose one of these questions or one assigned by your instructor and freewrite for five or ten minutes using one or more of the following moves to stimulate dialectic thinking.

I used to think _____ , but now I think _____ .

Part of me thinks _____ , but another part of me thinks _____ .

On some days I think _____ , but on other days I think _____ .

The first answers that come to mind are _____ , but as I think further I see _____ .

My classmate thinks _____ , but I think _____ .

Your goal here is to explore potential weaknesses or inadequacies in your first answers, and then to push beyond them to think of new or different answers. Feel free to be wild and risky in posing possible alternative solutions.

4. As a whole class, take a poll to find out what the most common first-response answers were for each of the questions. Then share alternative solutions generated by class members during the freewriting. The goal is to pose and explore answers that go beyond or against the grain of the common answers. Remember, there is little point in arguing for an answer that everyone else already accepts.

READINGS

To help you appreciate exploratory essays, we include in this section two student essays and a professional article.

In the first essay, student writer Mary Turla explores the problem of mail-order brides. (You read some of Mary's early research journal entries in Chapter 1, pp. 8–9.) She later developed this exploration into a research paper that appears as our student example in Chapter 23 (pp. 583–96).

MARY TURLA (student)

MAIL-ORDER BRIDE ROMANCES: FAIRY TALE, NIGHTMARE, OR SOMEWHERE IN BETWEEN?

Mary's Paper— Exploration

1   I first became interested in the issue of mail-order brides when I picked up the *Seattle Times* one afternoon and read that an angry Timothy Blackwell walked into the King County Courthouse and gunned down his wife, Susanna Remarata Blackwell, a mail-order bride (Haines and Sevens A1). I was outraged mainly because she was Filipina and so am I. I remember asking myself questions like, "Why did she become a mail-order bride? Why did Timothy Blackwell pick a wife out of a mail-order catalog? Is this prostitution?"

2   When I discussed the topic with my friends and fellow Pinays, the general feeling was that the mail-order bride business exploited vulnerable, poor women from the Third World. We felt that men who searched specifically for a foreign Asian bride wanted either a sex slave or a domestic slave, or maybe both. Basically, I felt the mail-order bride business should absolutely be abolished.

3   But then I spoke with my mother. And, I admit I wavered on my absolute intolerance of the process. She grew up in the Philippines and, although she wasn't a mail-order bride, I am sure she has met a few or has heard of such matches. I was surprised to find out that she had once played matchmaker for her friend in the Philippines and a male co-worker here in the States! "Life is so hard there," she explained. "We moved here to give our children a better life . . . opportunities and choices many back home don't have." Although I still did not feel entirely comfortable with the idea, I realized that maybe there were legitimate motivations for people using a mail-order bride service.

4   In my desire to form a justifiable position on the issue, I wanted to find out as much as I could about how the business worked, the profiles of the typical brides and grooms, and the social, cultural, or economic consequences. I also wanted to find out the role of Filipinas as mail-order brides. If this industry does create a negative image of the women involved (as sexual, submissive commodities), I better pay attention because I am Filipina American.

5   I went to the college library to start my investigation with a study of the Susanna Blackwell murder case. The question that kept nagging at me while I was reading the Blackwell articles was: Was the marital violence that led to her murder because she was a Filipina mail-order bride? Based on his testimony, Blackwell's anger toward his wife grew out of his belief that she had used him for his money and for getting American citizenship. "From the beginning she wanted money . . . she wanted a green card," he said (Haines and Sevens A1). Throughout his testimony, Blackwell continually expressed his anger over the money he had spent on her. Susanna testified that Blackwell emotionally and physically abused her, as early as their courtship in 1993. In her statement to the police, Susanna said that she wanted to go back to the Philippines but that Timothy told her "to stay in the U.S. for two years and pay him $500 a month to repay the $10,000 he'd spent on her" (Haines and Sevens A6).

6   Many other questions ran through my mind. Are there many cases where domestic violence and mail-order marriages go hand-in-hand? Why did she marry him? Would Susanna Blackwell be dead if they had met though different means or if she wasn't

Filipina? What are the implications for his emphasis on how much she had cost him? What were they both hoping for in this marriage? What is the new bride's status in her husband's country? After the murder, one *Seattle Times* headline read, "Gunman felt duped." In response, I say: Who was really in control?

7

The next logical piece of the puzzle was to find out what kind of men and women participate in the mail-order business: What are their hopes and expectations? What happens if those dreams aren't met? Unfortunately, I couldn't find any answers to these questions in our college library. Using INFOTRAC and other indexes in the library didn't yield any sources. However, being Filipina, I knew that the Filipino National Historical Society had its own specialized library in Seattle. I headed off to this library in hopes of finding psychological, cultural, or social perspectives on the mail-order industry within its archives. I was lucky because they had a file of information on the mail-order bride industry.

8

I found out that most of the men who subscribe to mail-order bride catalogs are Caucasian. According to a University of Texas study cited by Villipando, the median income of 265 subscribers to these catalogs was higher than average—65 percent with incomes higher than $20,000. The average age was 37 (50 percent being over 37), average height five feet seven inches, and most were college educated. Only five percent never finished high school (Villipando 6).

9

Article after article supported the idea that men choose Asian brides because they long for the traditional woman: she cooks and cleans and is subservient and loyal to her husband. Also the men are burnt out by both the women's movement and the American dating scene. The Japanese American Citizens League, a national civil rights group, confirms these findings in its recent position paper on mail-order brides. The group found the men to be "white, much older than the bride they choose, politically conservative, frustrated by the women's movement. They . . . find the traditional Asian value of deference to men reassuring" (Villipando 6).

10

Most of the women who take part in the mail-order service range from teenagers to women in their 40's. They come from disadvantaged families and may reside within underdeveloped countries. They see America as the land of opportunity and feel that American men may provide better for them and their families than they would be able to for themselves in their own countries. "It is the social and economic conditions in underdeveloped countries that drive women to participate. For many, marrying a North American means marrying upward in society" (Valdez 21).

11

After reading this information, I seriously questioned whether mail-order marriages could be successful based on the vulnerable position in which the woman is placed. She is a foreigner living a new life in a new country with new customs. Most often, she is left without nearby family or community support (vital in most Asian communities). Her immigrant status leaves her vulnerable to the threat of deportation and return to a life of poverty. There is also the question of domestic abuse and who the bride will turn to if it occurs, if she speaks out at all. I also learned from the Blackwell murder case how much the threat of deportation becomes a part of domestic violence.

12

What bothered me most of all were the descriptions of women found in the mail-order catalogs. The brochures put out by the mail-order bride industry create and perpetuate unrealistic images of real people. One brochure that describes Filipino women reads: "They are raised to respect and defer to the male. . . . The young Oriental woman . . . derives her basic satisfactions from serving and pleasing her husband" (Villipando 13). Another brochure reads: "Most, if not all are very feminine, loyal, loving . . . and virgins!" Timothy Blackwell bought into the images: "I had heard so much that these women were very sincere, very loving, very faithful. . . . I always admired Polynesian-type women with very long, straight black hair, and light brown skin" (Haines and Sevens A6).

13   Although there is a sense (thus far) that the women are more vulnerable than the men, I began feeling sympathy for both parties. Both are victims of romantic ideals. He searches for a docile, loyal, family-oriented, exotic, dark-haired fantasy. She longs for a big, strong American to save her from her desperate circumstances.

14   I then had the opportunity to speak with Ellen Ayaberra, commissioner for the Seattle Women's Commission and president of the Filipino American Political Action Group of Washington on her assessment of the issue. She believes that the mail-order bride industry should be abolished for three reasons. First, she sees it as legalized woman trafficking. Second, she adds that the media misrepresent the true image of the Filipino women as uneducated and naive instead of degree-holding professionals, as many of them are. And, third, she fears the consequences of the unrealistic expectations that both husband and bride bring to the relationship. Abeyerra said:

> [A mail-order marriage] is a union based on false expectations. . . . America is not always paradise, American men are not always heros. . . . Filipinas are educated, hardworking professionals who live, with few choices, in poverty . . . we are not dumb country girls.

15   I left the session and leave this paper wondering: Should we try to outlaw the mail-order bride industry completely or should we try to regulate it in some way? In all honesty, I hope to see it abolished because it seems to treat people like commodities or unrealistic romantic figures. It keeps people from being seen as they are: individual human beings. But I can see the other side too.

Works Cited

Ayaberra, Ellen. Personal Interview. 26 April 1995.

Haines, Thomas W., and Richard Sevens. "Gunman Felt Duped by Bride from the Start." *The Seattle Times* 4 Mar. 1995: A1+.

Valdez, Marybeth. "Return to Sender: The Mail-Order Bride Business in the Philippines." *The Philippine Review* May 1995: 5+.

Villipando, Venny. "The Business of Selling Mail-Order Brides." *San Diego Asian Journal* 1 Feb. 1990: 6–16.

Thinking Critically About "Mail-Order Bride Romances"

1. How does Mary Turla's exploratory paper reveal dialectic thinking?
2. What do you see as the chief strengths and weaknesses of Mary's exploration of the mail-order bride industry?
3. Mary uses only four research sources for this paper. In her final researched argument (pp. 583–96), however, she has fourteen sources—indicating that she felt the need to do more research. What additional questions or issues do you think Mary needs to investigate before she can make a strong argument to abolish or regulate the mail-order bride industry?

In this next essay, student writer Sheridan Botts explores problems related to the funding of hospices for the terminally ill. Because her professor assigned the exploratory essay as a first stage in writing a proposal argument (Chapter 16), this writer poses both content-oriented questions about hospices and rhetorical questions about the focus, purpose, and audience for her proposal paper. (Her final version, a proposal argument, appears on pp. 401–13.)

SHERIDAN BOTTS (student)
EXPLORING PROBLEMS ABOUT HOSPICE

*Sheridan's Paper—
Exploration*

Last fall my brother-in-law, Charles, lay dying, and his mother, Betty, was over- 1 whelmed with grief and responsibility. Charles wanted to die at home, not connected to tubes in the hospital, so Betty cared for him in his home with the help of a home care agency. At the same time as she was caring for him—helping him get sips of water, trying to meet his every need—she was terribly depressed. She had already lost one son, and now she was losing another. But she was unable to talk about her depression with her friends. When I called the home care agency to seek counseling help for Betty, they said, "Is she the patient? We can only care for the patient." And then, after Charles died, and Betty was bereft, she was on her own. No services were available to her from the home care agency.

If Charles had been with a hospice agency instead of a home care agency, Betty 2 would have had help. A hospice would have helped Charles stay comfortable at home, and, in addition to the visits by nurses, social workers, and home health aides provided by the home care agency, a hospice would have provided chaplain and volunteer helpers both for Charles and for Betty. Social workers or a chaplain would have helped Betty prepare for Charles' death—and after his death, helped her deal with her tremendous grief. Then, for the following year, a hospice would have offered Betty continuing help with grief—articles, a grief counseling group, and calls from volunteers.

So, this spring, when I started thinking about what to do my paper on, I thought of 3 hospice. I wanted to learn more about the hospice movement and be able to clearly articulate the benefit of hospice programs. I had two interconnected writing assignments—this exploratory paper and then a follow-up persuasive argument. There were a lot of things I wanted to find out about hospice, but what was there to argue about in a persuasive paper? Perhaps I could persuade people about the benefits of hospice. But I already knew the benefits, and almost everyone agrees that hospices are valuable. So what issue about hospices is there to argue about? What persuasive essay is crying to be written?

I decided to find out more about the problems facing hospices, so I looked in the 4 phone book under "Hospice," called Hospice of Seattle, and was referred to the Marketing Coordinator. I asked her if there was a hospice question that needed arguing and she said:

> Yes! Convince the private insurance companies to bill on a per diem basis instead of fee-for-service. Fee-for-service doesn't pay for social work, chaplain visits, volunteers, and grief counseling. You could really help hospices if you wrote a persuasive paper on that subject!

Ah ha! This was it! A meaningful project. Here was an opportunity to make a real difference, have an impact, learn more about hospices, and improve my writing. Here was a subject that was important, and to which I didn't have a ready answer. How could I convince insurance companies to pay for hospice on a per diem basis?

5   I got excited about convincing a real entity to do something real about a real issue. I called the National Hospice Organization and ordered information on hospice care. I then went to the library to see what else I could find. There are so many books in the library on hospice that it was easy to find information on the hospice experience. I especially enjoyed reading moving stories in *Final Passages: Positive Choices for the Dying and Their Loved Ones* (1992) about men and women who had received hospice care and how much it meant to them.

6   Although the library books confirmed the value of hospice, they did not help me understand the problem of funding, and I started feeling frustrated. I skimmed through the computerized article search, looked up "hospice," and read through the headings.

7   The problem was that I didn't quite know what to look for because I didn't fully understand the implications of fee-for-service versus per diem payment. Just what is the difference? Why is there such a distinct preference for fee-for-service by insurance companies, and such a preference for per diem by hospices? Instead of seeking the answers in the library, I decided to try interviews. I made an appointment with a Medical Social Worker at Hospice of Seattle who helped patients sign up for insurance. She was great to talk to because she understood the issue clearly. She explained that with fee-for-service, each visit to the patient's home by a nurse, social worker, home health aide, or therapist is paid for separately, but fee-for-service doesn't pay for everything the patient needs. Fee-for-service doesn't pay for the volunteer program (which has a paid Volunteer Coordinator), chaplains, grief care (the Grief Counselor coordinates volunteers to call on grief-stricken family members and mails packages throughout the year to family members). Also some insurance programs don't pay for social work. Hospice of Seattle pays for all these services, and tries to incorporate the cost into services that insurance *does* pay for. It seemed clear that fee-for-service did not benefit Hospice of Seattle.

8   According to the social worker, per diem payment works better for hospices. With per diem, the patient's insurance pays the hospice for each day of care the patient receives. This covers the costs better because the hospice can budget and plan better, can order the most appropriate services and supplies, can negotiate better rates with medical equipment companies, and can provide services not covered under fee-for-service. Per diem is also better for the family. They can be assured that their medical needs will be covered. There won't be unexpected surprises, or mounting co-payments. This justification of per diem sounded good to me.

9   Per diem did not seem to benefit the insurance company, however. Insurance companies want to minimize the cost for each patient, and get the most for their money. As long as patients are getting the care they need, if the insurance company can get away without paying, well, that sounds pretty good for the insurance company.

10   Uh oh. What if I couldn't come up with good reasons for insurance companies to pay per diem? What if it is to the advantage of the hospice, but *not* to the insurance company, to pay per diem? I asked the Hospice of Seattle Director for help and he gave me a paper, "Accessing Reimbursement: How to Bill Private Insurance," by Brenda Horne. Ms. Horne says, "Billing on a per visit (fee-for-service) basis does not provide adequate reimbursement levels to cover costs for the entire range of hospice services. Only per diem rates take into consideration the fact that hospice offers a unique range of services not available through any other health provider" (2). Unfortunately, the rationale focuses on the value to hospices rather than for insurance companies. The article didn't help me as much as I had hoped it would.

This is where I am now, somewhat discouraged. I have learned quite a bit about   12
hospice care and I am even more convinced of the importance of providing this care
for dying people. I have been frustrated, however, that I was not able to find more literature analyzing per diem billing. I have more papers to read, but I don't think they
will shed light on this subject. The literature seems either to be about hospice care in
general, or on the cost saving of hospice care over traditional medicine. The articles
and books don't get much into the specific question of the benefit of per diem over fee-
for-service billing. Maybe that's why the Marketing Coordinator said that this would be
a good paper to write.

I think my best hope in supporting per diem billing is to talk with more staff peo-   13
ple at Hospice of Seattle. My guess is that per diem billing should have an advantage
in keeping costs down; I need to investigate this justification for per diem billing and try
to find other reasons that will persuade insurance companies to try the per diem approach. Now I have the question, but I still need to find a convincing answer.

Works Cited

Ahronheim, Judith, M.D., and Doron Weber. *Final Passages, Positive Choices for the
  Dying and Their Loved Ones.* New York: Simon & Schuster, 1992.
Friedrichsen, Ann. Medical Social Worker, Hospice of Seattle. Personal interview April
  18, 1995.
Horne, Brenda. "Accessing Reimbursement: How to Bill Private Insurance." Recorded
  at the 14th Annual Meeting and Symposium of the National Hospice Organization.
  Nashville, Tennessee. October 31, 1992.
Smith, Rodney. Hospice Director, Hospice of Seattle. Personal interview May 11, 1995.
Surla, Johanna. Marketing Coordinator, Hospice of Seattle. Personal interview April 14,
  1995.

Thinking Critically About "Exploring Problems About Hospice"

1. In Part One, we distinguished between two kinds of problems that writers
   face: content problems and rhetorical problems. Sheridan Botts wrestles with
   both problems throughout this exploratory paper. In your own words, what
   are the content problems that Sheridan examines and what are the rhetorical
   problems?
2. What are the chief strengths and chief weaknesses of her exploration so far?
3. What further research does Sheridan need to do before she can persuade insurance companies to pay hospices on a per diem basis?

The third example of exploratory writing is an excerpt from a scholarly article
by literary critic Jane Tompkins. First published in the scholarly journal *Critical Inquiry,* Tompkins's article focuses on the problem of how different historians portray Native Americans. This problem was a surprise for Tompkins, who began her
research in pursuit of another topic. Note how deftly Tompkins uses an open-form
structure to recount both personal and scholarly revelations. Although it is too
long to print in full here, the entire article follows the narrative shape of Tompkins's thinking process, beginning with the discovery and evolution of a "problem
of my own."

JANE TOMPKINS

"INDIANS": TEXTUALISM, MORALITY, AND THE PROBLEM OF HISTORY

1   When I was growing up in New York City, my parents used to take me to an event in Inwood Park at which Indians—real American Indians dressed in feathers and blankets—could be seen and touched by children like me. This event was always a disappointment. It was more fun to imagine that you *were* an Indian in one of the caves in Inwood Park than to shake the hand of an old man in a headdress who was not overwhelmed at the opportunity of meeting you. After staring at the Indians for a while, we would take a walk in the woods where the caves were, and once I asked my mother if the remains of a fire I had seen in one of them might have been left by the original inhabitants. After that, wandering up some stone steps cut into the side of the hill, I imagined I was a princess in a rude castle. My Indians, like my princesses, were creatures totally of the imagination, and I did not care to have any real exemplars interfering with what I already knew.

2   I already knew about Indians from having read about them in school. Over and over we were told the story of how Peter Minuit had bought Manhattan Island from the Indians for twenty-four dollars' worth of glass beads. And it was a story we didn't mind hearing because it gave us the rare pleasure of having someone to feel superior to, since the poor Indians had not known (as we eight-year-olds did) how valuable a piece of property Manhattan Island would become. Generally, much was made of the Indian presence in Manhattan; a poem in one of our readers began: "Where we walk to school today / Indian children used to play," and we were encouraged to write poetry on this topic ourselves. So I had a fairly rich relationship with Indians before I ever met the unprepossessing people in Inwood Park. I felt that I had a lot in common with them. They, too, liked animals (they were often named after animals); they, too, made mistakes— they liked the brightly colored trinkets of little value that the white men were always offering them; they were handsome, warlike, and brave and had led an exciting, romantic life in the forest long ago, a life such as I dreamed of leading myself. I felt lucky to be living in one of the places where they had definitely been. Never mind where they were or what they were doing now.

3   My story stands for the relationship most non-Indians have to the people who first populated this continent, a relationship characterized by narcissistic fantasies of freedom and adventure, of a life lived closer to nature and to spirit than the life we lead now. As Vine Deloria, Jr., has pointed out, the American Indian Movement in the early seventies couldn't get people to pay attention to what was happening to Indians who were alive in the present, so powerful was this country's infatuation with people who wore loincloths, lived in tepees, and roamed the plains and forests long ago. The present essay, like these fantasies, doesn't have much to do with actual Indians, though its subject matter is the histories of European-Indian relations in seventeenth-century New England. In a sense, my encounter with Indians as an adult doing "research" replicates the childhood one, for while I started out to learn about Indians, I ended up preoccupied with a problem of my own.

4   This essay enacts a particular instance of the challenge poststructuralism poses to the study of history. In simpler language, it concerns the difference that point of view makes when people are giving accounts of events, whether at first or second hand. The

This passage introduces the problem by relating a childhood memory about Indians.

This section explains the focus of this paper and then makes a transition to the academic problem it will explore.

Poststructuralism is a critical theory that, among other things, denies that

truth can be directly understood and stated clearly.

problem is that if all accounts of events are determined through and through by the observer's frame of reference, then one will never know, in any given case, what really happened.

This section provides an overview of Tompkins's exploration of the problem.

I encountered this problem in concrete terms while preparing to teach a course in   5 colonial American literature. I'd set out to learn what I could about the Puritans' relations with American Indians. All I wanted was a general idea of what had happened between the English settlers and the natives in seventeenth-century New England; poststructuralism and its dilemmas were the furthest thing from my mind. I began, more or less automatically, with Perry Miller, who hardly mentions the Indians at all, then proceeded to the work of historians who had dealt exclusively with the European-Indian encounter. At first, it was a question of deciding which of these authors to believe, for it quickly became apparent that there was no unanimity on the subject. As I read on, however, I discovered that the problem was more complicated than deciding whose version of events was correct. Some of the conflicting accounts were not simply contradictory, they were completely incommensurable, in that their assumptions about what counted as a valid approach to the subject, and what the subject itself was, diverged in fundamental ways. Faced with an array of mutually irreconcilable points of view, points of view which determined what was being discussed as well as the terms of the discussion, I decided to turn to primary sources for clarification, only to discover that the primary sources reproduced the problem all over again. I found myself, in other words, in an epistemological quandary, not only unable to decide among conflicting versions of events but also unable to believe that any such decision could, in principle, be made. It was a moral quandary as well. Knowledge of what really happened when the Europeans and the Indians first met seemed particularly important, since the result of that encounter was virtual genocide. This was the kind of past "mistake" which, presumably, we studied history in order to avoid repeating. If studying history couldn't put us in touch with actual events and their causes, then what was to prevent such atrocities from happening again?

Here Tompkins shows why her problem is problematic.

Here she shows why her problem is significant.

For a while, I remained at this impasse. But through analyzing the process by which   6 I had reached it, I eventually arrived at an understanding which seemed to offer a way out. This essay records the concrete experience of meeting and solving the difficulty I have just described (as an abstract problem, I thought I had solved it long ago). My purpose is not to throw new light on antifoundationalist epistemology—the solution I reached is not a new one—but to dramatize and expose the troubles antifoundationalism gets you into when you meet it, so to speak, in the road.

This paragraph states the purpose of the essay and forecasts its exploratory shape.

Antifoundationalism rejects the notion that truth can be verified using laws, events, or texts.

My research began with Perry Miller. Early in the preface to *Errand into the Wilderness,* while explaining how he came to write his history of the New England mind, Miller   7 writes a sentence that stopped me dead. He says that what fascinated him as a young man about his country's history was "the massive narrative of the movement of European culture into the vacant wilderness of America." "Vacant?" Miller, writing in 1956, doesn't pause over the word "vacant," but to people who read his preface thirty years later, the word is shocking. In what circumstances could someone proposing to write a history of colonial New England *not* take account of the Indian presence there?

Here Tompkins describes the start of her intellectual journey.

The rest of Miller's preface supplies an answer to this question, if one takes the   8 trouble to piece together its details. Miller explains that as a young man, jealous of older compatriots who had had the luck to fight in World War I, he had gone to Africa in search of adventure. "The adventures that Africa afforded," he writes, "were tawdry enough, but it became the setting for a sudden epiphany" (p. vii). "It was given to me," he writes, "disconsolate on the edge of a jungle of central Africa, to have thrust upon me the mission of expounding what I took to be the innermost propulsion of the United States, while supervising, in that barbaric tropic, the unloading of drums of case oil flowing out of the inexhaustible wilderness of America" (p. viii). Miller's picture of himself on the banks of the Congo furnishes a key to the kind of history he will write and to his mental image of a vacant wilderness; it explains why it was just there, under precisely these conditions, that he should have had his epiphany.

9   The fuel drums stand, in Miller's mind, for the popular misconception of what this country is about. They are "tangible symbols of [America's] appalling power," a power that everyone but Miller takes for the ultimate reality (p. ix). To Miller, "the mind of man is the basic factor in human history," and he will plead, all unaccommodated as he is among the fuel drums, for the intellect—the intellect for which his fellow historians, with their chapters on "stoves or bathtubs, or tax laws," "the Wilmot Proviso" and "the chain store," "have so little respect" (p. viii, ix). His preface seethes with a hatred of the merely physical and mechanical, and this hatred, which is really a form of moral outrage, explains not only the contempt with which he mentions the stoves and bathtubs but also the nature of his experience in Africa and its relationship to the "massive narrative" he will write.

In this section, Tompkins presents a series of particulars to illustrate the point that Miller had a biased and limited perspective that prevented him from truly "seeing" the Indians.

10   Miller's experiences in Africa are "tawdry," his tropic is barbaric because the jungle he stands on the edge of means nothing to him, no more, indeed something less, than the case oil. It is the nothingness of Africa that precipitates his vision. It is the barbarity of the "dark continent," the obvious (but superficial) parallelism between the jungle at Matadi and America's "vacant wilderness" that releases in Miller the desire to define and vindicate his country's cultural identity. To the young Miller, colonial Africa and colonial America are—but for the history he will bring to light—mirror images of one another. And what he fails to see in the one landscape is the same thing he overlooks in the other: the human beings who people it. As Miller stood with his back to the jungle, thinking about the role of mind in human history, his failure to see that the land into which European culture had moved was not vacant but already occupied by a varied and numerous population, is of a piece with his failure, in his portrait of himself at Matadi, to notice *who* was carrying the fuel drums he was supervising the unloading of.

11   The point is crucial because it suggests that what is invisible to the historian in his own historical moment remains invisible when he turns his gaze to the past. It isn't that Miller didn't "see" the black men, in a literal sense, any more than it's the case that when he looked back he didn't "see" the Indians, in the sense of not realizing they were there. Rather, it's that neither the Indians nor the blacks *counted* for him, in a fundamental way. The way in which Indians can be seen but not counted is illustrated by an entry in Governor John Winthrop's journal, three hundred years before, when he recorded that there had been a great storm with high winds "yet through God's great mercy it did no hurt, but only killed one Indian with the fall of a tree." The juxtaposition suggests that Miller shared with Winthrop a certain colonial point of view, a point of view from which Indians, though present, do not finally matter.

12   A book entitled *New England Frontier: Puritans and Indians, 1620–1675,* written by Alden Vaughan and published in 1965, promised to rectify Miller's omission. In the outpouring of work on the European-Indian encounter that began in the early sixties, this book is the first major landmark, and to a neophyte it seems definitive. Vaughan acknowledges the absence of Indian sources and emphasizes his use of materials which

Here Tompkins describes the next step in her journey. Vaughan's book is explicitly about Puritans and Indians, so

she expects it to answer questions that Miller didn't address.

catch the Puritans "off guard." His announced conclusion that "the New England Puritans followed a remarkably humane, considerate, and just policy in their dealings with the Indians" seems supported by the scope, documentation, and methodicalness of his project (*NEF,* p. vii). The author's fair-mindedness and equanimity seem everywhere apparent, so that when he asserts "the history of interracial relations from the arrival of the Pilgrims to the outbreak of King Philip's War is a credit to the integrity of both peoples," one is positively reassured (*NEF,* p. viii).

Tompkins begins showing the reader why Vaughan is also not a reliable source of truth about Indians.

But these impressions do not survive an admission that comes late in the book, when, in the course of explaining why works like Helen Hunt Jackson's *Century of Dishonor* had spread misconceptions about Puritan treatment of the Indians, Vaughan finally lays his own cards on the table.

13

> The root of the misunderstanding [about Puritans and Indians] . . . lie[s] in a failure to recognize the nature of the two societies that met in seventeenth century New England. One was unified, visionary, disciplined, and dynamic. The other was divided, self-satisfied, undisciplined, and static. It would be unreasonable to expect that such societies could live side by side indefinitely with no penetration of the more fragmented and passive by the more consolidated and active. What resulted, then, was not—as many have held—a clash of dissimilar ways of life, but rather the expansion of one into the areas in which the other was lacking. [*NEF,* p. 323]

In these transitional paragraphs, Tompkins shows how the reader plays an active role in shaping the meaning of a written text. The perspective, of scholars who were deeply affected by the tumultuous cultural changes of the 1960s exposed Vaughan's racial biases. Finally, Tompkins leaves the scholars of the past behind, preparing us for "an entirely different picture of the European-Indian encounter."

From our present vantage point, these remarks seem culturally biased to an incredible degree, not to mention inaccurate: was Puritan society unified? If so, how does one account for its internal dissensions and obsessive need to cast out deviants? Is "unity" necessarily a positive culture trait? From what standpoint can one say that American Indians were neither disciplined nor visionary, when both these characteristics loom so large in the ethnographies? Is it an accident that ways of describing cultural strength and weakness coincide with gender stereotypes—active/passive, and so on? Why is one culture said to "penetrate" the other? Why is the "other" described in terms of "lack"?

14

Vaughan's fundamental categories of apprehension and judgment will not withstand even the most cursory inspection. For what looked like even-handedness when he was writing *New England Frontier* does not look that way anymore. In his introduction to *New Directions in American Intellectual History,* John Higham writes that by the end of the sixties

15

> the entire conceptual foundation on which [this sort of work] rested [had] crumbled away. . . . Simultaneously, in sociology, anthropology, and history, two working assumptions . . . came under withering attack: first, the assumption that societies tend to be integrated, and second, that a shared culture maintains that integration. . . . By the late 1960s all claims issued in the name of an "American mind" were subject to drastic skepticism.

"Clearly," Higham continues, "the sociocultural upheaval of the sixties created the occasion" for this reaction. Vaughan's book, it seemed, could only have been written before the events of the sixties had sensitized scholars to questions of race and ethnicity. It came as no surprise, therefore, that ten years later there appeared a study of European-Indian relations which reflected the new awareness of social issues the sixties had engendered. And it offered an entirely different picture of the European-Indian encounter.

16   Francis Jennings's *The Invasion of America* (1975) rips wide open the idea that the Puritans were humane and considerate in their dealings with the Indians. In Jennings's account, even more massively documented than Vaughan's, the early settlers lied to the Indians, stole from them, murdered them, scalped them, captured them, tortured them, raped them, sold them into slavery, confiscated their land, destroyed their crops, burned their homes, scattered their possessions, gave them alcohol, undermined their systems of belief, and infected them with diseases that wiped out ninety percent of their numbers within the first hundred years after contact.

Here begins the third stage of Tompkins's journey. Now she is exploring the work of a post-1960s scholar with a radically different perspective on Puritans and Indians.

17   Jennings mounts an all-out attack on the essential decency of the Puritan leadership and their apologists in the twentieth century. The Pequot War, which previous historians had described as an attempt on the part of Massachusetts Bay to protect itself from the fiercest of the New England tribes, becomes, in Jennings's painstakingly researched account, a deliberate war of extermination, waged by whites against Indians. It starts with trumped-up charges, is carried on through a series of increasingly bloody reprisals, and ends in the massacre of scores of Indian men, women, and children, all so that Massachusetts Bay could gain political and economic control of the southern Connecticut Valley. When one reads this and then turns over the page and sees a reproduction of the Bay Colony seal, which depicts an Indian from whose mouth issue the words "Come over and help us," the effect is shattering.

18   But even so powerful an argument as Jennings's did not remain unshaken by subsequent work. Reading on, I discovered that if the events of the sixties had revolutionized the study of European-Indian relations, the events of the seventies produced yet another transformation. The American Indian Movement, and in particular the founding of the Native American Rights Fund in 1971 to finance Indian litigation, and a court decision in 1975 which gave the tribes the right to seek redress for past injustices in federal court, created a climate within which historians began to focus on the Indians themselves. "Almost simultaneously," writes James Axtell, "frontier and colonial historians began to discover the necessity of considering the American natives as real determinants of history and the utility of ethnohistory as a way of ensuring parity of focus and impartiality of judgment." In Miller, Indians had been simply beneath notice; in Vaughan, they belonged to an inferior culture; and in Jennings, they were the more or less innocent prey of power-hungry whites. But in the most original and provocative of the ethnohistories, Calvin Martin's *Keepers of the Game,* Indians became complicated, purposeful human beings, whose lives were spiritually motivated to a high degree. Their relationship to the animals they hunted, to the natural environment, and to the whites with whom they traded became intelligible within a system of beliefs that formed the basis for an entirely new perspective on the European-Indian encounter.

Tompkins begins showing how Jennings's view is also limited by his own perspective.

Before she moves to the fourth stage of her journey, Tompkins helps readers get their bearings by briefly reviewing the path she has taken.

19   Within the broader question of why European contact had such a devastating effect on the Indians, Martin's specific aim is to determine why Indians participated in the fur trade which ultimately led them to the brink of annihilation. The standard answer to this question had always been that once the Indian was introduced to European guns, copper kettles, woolen blankets, and the like, he literally couldn't keep his hands off them. In order to acquire these coveted items, he decimated the animal populations on which his survival depended. In short, the Indian's motivation in participating in the fur trade was assumed to be the same as the white European's—a desire to accumulate material goods. In direct opposition to this thesis, Martin argues that the reason why Indians ruthlessly exploited their own resources had nothing to do with supply and demand, but stemmed rather from a breakdown of the cosmic worldview that tied them to the game they killed in a spiritual relationship of parity and mutual obligation.

Tompkins begins the fourth stage of her journey by summarizing the work of Calvin Martin, a modern scholar motivated by the desire to explore a problem: Why did the Indians willingly participate in the fur trade, a self-destructive pursuit?

The hunt, according to Martin, was conceived not primarily as a physical activity   20
but as a spiritual quest, in which the spirit of the hunter must overmaster the spirit of
the game animal before the kill can take place. The animal, in effect, *allows* itself to be
found and killed, once the hunter has mastered its spirit. The hunter prepared himself
through rituals of fasting, sweating, or dreaming which revealed the identity of his prey
and where he can find it. The physical act of killing is the least important element in
the process. Once the animal is killed, eaten, and its parts used for clothing or imple-
ments, its remains must be disposed of in ritually prescribed fashion, or the game boss,
the "keeper" of that species, will not permit more animals to be killed. The relationship
between Indians and animals, then, is contractual; each side must hold up its end of the
bargain, or no further transactions can occur.

What happened, according to Martin, was that as a result of diseases introduced   21
into the animal population by Europeans, the game suddenly disappeared, began to
act in inexplicable ways, or sickened and died in plain view, and communicated their
diseases to the Indians. The Indians, consequently, believed that their compact with the

Tompkins specu-
lates that Indians'
perceptions of
events differed so
radically from
those of European
settlers' that
"conflict was
inevitable."

animals had been broken and that the keepers of the game, the tutelary spirits of each
animal species whom they had been so careful to propitiate, had betrayed them. And
when missionization, wars with the Europeans, and displacement from their tribal lands
had further weakened Indian society and its belief structure, the Indians, no longer re-
strained by religious sanctions, in effect, turned on the animals in a holy war of revenge.

Whether or not Martin's specific claim about the "holy war" was correct, his analy-   22
sis made it clear to me that, given the Indians' understanding of economic, religious,
and physical processes, an Indian account of what transpired when the European settlers arrived here would look nothing like our own. Their (potential, unwritten) history
of the conflict could bear only a marginal resemblance to Eurocentric views. I began to
think that the key to understanding European-Indian relations was to see them as an
encounter between wholly disparate cultures, and that therefore either defending or attacking the colonists was beside the point since, given the cultural disparity between
the two groups, conflict was inevitable and in large part a product of mutual misunderstanding.

Now Tompkins
begins stage five
of her journey,
summarizing a
collection of
essays that run
counter to
Martin's way
of thinking.

But three years after Martin's book appeared, Shepard Krech III edited a collection   23
of seven essays called *Indians, Animals, and the Fur Trade,* attacking Martin's entire
project. Here the authors argued that we don't need an ideological or religious explanation for the fur trade. As Charles Hudson writes,

> The Southeastern Indians slaughtered deer (and were prompted to enslave
> and kill each other) because of their position on the outer fringes of an ex-
> panding modern world-system. . . . In the modern world-system there is a core
> region which establishes *economic* relations with its colonial periphery. . . . If
> the Indians could not produce commodities, they were on the road to cultural
> extinction. . . . To maximize his chances for survival, an eighteenth-century
> Southeastern Indian had to . . . live in the interior, out of range of European
> cattle, forestry, and agriculture. . . . He had to produce a commodity which was
> valuable enough to earn him some protection from English slavers.

Though we are talking here about Southeastern Indians, rather than the subarctic   24
and Northeastern tribes Martin studied, what really accounts for these divergent explanations of why Indians slaughtered the game are the assumptions that underlie them.
Martin believes that the Indians acted on the basis of perceptions made available to
them by their own cosmology; that is, he explains their behavior as the Indians them-

selves would have explained it (insofar as he can), using a logic and a set of values that are not Eurocentric but derived from within Amerindian culture. Hudson, on the other hand, insists that the Indians' own beliefs are irrelevant to an explanation of how they acted, which can only be understood, as far as he is concerned, in the terms of a Western materialist economic and political analysis. Martin and Hudson, in short, don't agree on what counts as an explanation, and this disagreement sheds light on the preceding accounts as well. From this standpoint, we can see that Vaughan, who thought that the Puritans were superior to the Indians, and Jennings, who thought the reverse, are both, like Hudson, using Eurocentric criteria of description and evaluation. While all three critics (Vaughan, Jennings, and Hudson) acknowledge that Indians and Europeans behave differently from one another, the behavior differs, as it were, within the order of the same: all three assume, though only Hudson makes the assumption explicit, that an understanding of relations between the Europeans and the Indians must be elaborated in European terms. In Martin's analysis, however, what we have are not only two different sets of behavior but two incommensurable ways of describing and assigning meaning to events. This difference at the level of explanation calls into question the possibility of obtaining any theory-independent account of interaction between Indians and Europeans.

25   At this point, dismayed and confused by the wildly divergent views of colonial history the twentieth-century historians had provided, I decided to look at some primary materials. I thought, perhaps, if I looked at some firsthand accounts and at some scholars looking at those accounts, it would be possible to decide which experts were right and which were wrong by comparing their views with the evidence. Captivity narratives seemed a good place to begin, since it was logical to suppose that the records left by whites who had been captured by Indians would furnish the sort of first-hand information I wanted. . . .

26   After a while it began to seem to me that there was something wrong with the way I had formulated the problem. . . .

27   My problem presupposed that I couldn't judge because I didn't know what the facts were. All I had, or could have, was a series of different perspectives, and so nothing that would count as an authoritative source on which moral judgments could be based. But, as I have just shown, I did judge, and that is because, as I now think, I did have some facts. I seemed to accept as facts that ninety percent of the native American population of New England died after the first hundred years of contact, that tribes in eastern Canada and the northeastern United States had a compact with the game they killed, that Comanches had subjected a captive girl to casual cruelty, that King Philip smoked a pipe, and so on. It was only where different versions of the same event came into conflict that I doubted the text was a record of something real. And even then, there was no question about certain major catastrophes. I believed that four hundred Pequots were killed near Saybrook, that Winthrop was the Governor of the Massachusetts Bay Colony when it happened, and so on. My sense that certain events, such as the Pequot War, did occur in no way reflected the indecisiveness that overtook me when I tried to choose among the various historical versions. In fact, the need I felt to make up my mind was impelled by the conviction that certain things *had* happened that shouldn't have happened. Hence it was never the case that "what happened" was completely unknowable or unavailable. It's rather that in the process of reading so many different approaches to the same phenomenon I became aware of the difference in the attitudes that informed these approaches. This awareness of the interests motivating each ver-

Tompkins again helps readers get their bearings by summarizing her understanding of what she has learned up to this point in her journey.

Then she reiterates the basic poststructuralist dilemma posed earlier: How can you get at the truth about an event when every account is biased?

Tompkins describes a new strategy for determining which perspectives are valid.

In the essay's final section, Tompkins works out her solution to the problem she has examined. Here the ellipses indicate a long section we have omitted in which she analyzes a variety of historical documents.

sion cast suspicion over everything, in retrospect, and I ended by claiming that there was nothing I could know. This, I now see, was never really the case. But how did it happen?

Tompkins acknowledges and demonstrates how her own method of reading all these documents reflects her own historical perspective.

Someone else, confronted with the same materials, could have decided that one of these historical accounts was correct. Still another person might have decided that more evidence was needed in order to decide among them. Why did I conclude that none of the accounts was accurate because they were all produced from some particular angle of vision? Presumably there was something in my background that enabled me to see the problem in this way. . . .

28

What this means for the problem I've been addressing is that I must piece together the story of European-Indian relations as best I can, believing this version up to a point, that version not at all, another almost entirely, according to what seems reasonable and plausible, given everything else that I know. And this, as I've shown, is what I was already doing in the back of my mind without realizing it, because there was nothing else I *could* do. If the accounts don't fit together neatly, that is not a reason for rejecting them all in favor of a metadiscourse about epistemology; on the contrary, one encounters contradictory facts and divergent points of view in practically every phase of life, from deciding whom to marry to choosing the right brand of cat food, and one decides as best one can given the evidence available. It is only the nature of the academic situation which makes it appear that one can linger on the threshold of decision in the name of an epistemological principle. What has really happened in such a case is that the subject of debate has changed from the question of what happened in a particular instance to the question of how knowledge is arrived at. The absence of pressure to decide what happened creates the possibility for this change of venue.

29

The change of venue, however, is itself an action taken. In diverting attention from the original problem and placing it where Miller did, on "the mind of man," it once again ignores what happened and still is happening to American Indians. The moral problem that confronts me now is not that I can never have any facts to go on, but that the work I do is not directed toward solving the kinds of problems that studying the history of European-Indian relations has awakened me to.

30

Thinking Critically About " 'Indians': Textualism, Morality, and the Problem of History"

1. Tompkins's essay is about her struggle to find out "what had happened between the English settlers and the natives in seventeenth-century New England." Explain in your own words why Tompkins's study of various historians didn't lead to a direct answer to her question.

2. Tompkins's journey begins with her shocked revelation that historian Perry Miller (one of the great U.S. historians writing in the 1950s) didn't "see" the Indians. He talks instead about the movement of European culture into the "vacant wilderness" of America. To try to understand Miller, Tompkins reads his discussion of his World War I experience in Africa. Tompkins concludes: "[W]hat is invisible to the historian in his own historical moment remains invisible when he turns his gaze to the past." What does Tompkins mean? How does Miller's preface support her claim?

3. Trace the competing theses of each of the historians that Tompkins reads. How does Tompkins show that each thesis is "determined through and through by the observer's frame of reference"?

4. One fact on which historians agree is that Native Americans participated in the fur trade by exchanging furs for guns, copper kettles, and woolen blankets. Historians disagree, however, on why Native Americans sold furs to the white traders. What is the traditional explanation? How does Calvin Martin's explanation (in *Keepers of the Game*) differ from the traditional view? How does Charles Hudson attack Martin?

5. In the final section of her essay, Tompkins explains her own solution to the dilemma she has explored. In your own words, how does she resolve her dilemma? Do you find her resolution satisfactory? How does her resolution give rise to the "moral dilemma" she poses in her last sentence?

COMPOSING YOUR EXPLORATORY ESSAY

Generating and Exploring Ideas

Your process of generating and exploring ideas is, in essence, the *subject matter* of your exploratory paper. This section should help you get started and keep going.

Keeping a Research Log

Since this assignment asks you to create a chronologically organized account of your thinking process, you will need to keep a careful, detailed record of your investigation. The best tool for doing so is a research log or journal in which you take notes on your sources and record your thinking throughout the process.

As you investigate your issue, keep a chronologically organized account that includes notes on your readings, interviews, and significant conversations, plus explorations of how each of these sources, new perspectives, or data influence your current thinking. Many writers use a double-entry notebook system (sometimes called a dialectic journal; see Chapter 2, pp. 37–38) that divides the log pages into two vertical columns. In one column you take notes on your readings or interviews by summarizing arguments, copying quotations, noting data, and so forth. In the other column, you reflect on your thinking, showing how each piece of research advances your thinking or pulls you in one direction or another. (An example of a page from a student's research log will be presented shortly.)

As you write your exploratory essay, your research log will be your main source for details—evidence of what you were thinking at regular intervals throughout the process.*

---

*For those of you majoring in science or engineering, this research log is similar to the laboratory notebooks that are required parts of any original research in science or industry. In addition to recording in detail the progress of your research, these notebooks often serve as crucial data for patent applications or liability lawsuits. Doctors and nurses keep similar logs in their medical records for each patient. This is a time-honored practice. In Mary Shelley's early-nineteenth-century novel *Frankenstein,* the monster learns about the process of his creation by reading Dr. Frankenstein's laboratory journal.

Exploring Possible Problems for Your Essay

Your first step is to choose a question, problem, or issue that currently perplexes you. Perhaps a question is problematic to you because you haven't studied it (How serious is the problem of global warming? Is a salary cap really necessary to save major league baseball?), or because the available factual data seem conflicting and inconclusive (Should postmenopausal women take supplemental estrogen?), or because the problem or issue draws you into an uncomfortable conflict of values (Should we legalize drugs? Where do I stand on abortion?).

The key to this assignment is to choose a question, problem, or issue *that truly perplexes you.* The more clearly readers sense your personal engagement with the problem, the more likely they are to be engaged by your writing. Note: If your instructor pairs this assignment with a later one, be sure that your question is appropriate for the later assignment. Check with your instructor.

Here are several exercises to help you think of ideas for this essay.

Exploration Exercise 1   In your research log, make a list of issues or problems that both interest and perplex you. Then choose two or three of your issues and freewrite about them for five minutes or so, exploring questions such as these: Why am I interested in this problem? What makes the problem problematic? What makes this problem significant? Share your list of questions and your freewrites with friends and classmates. Discussing questions with friends often stimulates you to think of more questions yourself or to sharpen the focus of questions you have already asked.

Exploration Exercise 2   If your exploratory essay is paired with a subsequent assignment, look at the invention exercises for that assignment to help you ask a question that fits the context of the final paper you will write.

Exploration Exercise 3   A particularly valuable kind of problem to explore for this assignment is a public controversy. Often such issues involve complex disagreements about facts and values that merit careful, open-ended exploration. This assignment invites you to explore and clarify where you stand on such complex public issues as gay marriages, overcrowded prisons, the Endangered Species Act, funding of Medicare or Social Security, public funding of the arts, and so forth. These issues make particularly good topics for persuasive papers or formal research papers, if either is required in your course. For this exercise, look through a current newspaper or weekly newsmagazine and in your research log make a list of public issues that you would like to know more about. Use the following trigger question:

> I don't know where I stand on the issue of _____ . Share your list with classmates and friends.

Formulating a Starting Point

After you've chosen a problem or issue, write a research-log entry identifying the problem or issue you have chosen and explaining why you are perplexed by and interested in it. You might start out with a sharp, clearly focused question (for example, "Should the United States eliminate welfare payments for single mothers?"). Often, however, formulating the question turns out to be part of the *process* of writing the exploratory paper. Many writers don't start with a single, focused question but rather with a whole cluster of related questions swimming in their heads. This practice is all right—in fact, it is healthy—as long as you have a direction in which to move after the initial starting point. Even if you do start with a focused question, it is apt to evolve as your thinking progresses.

For this exercise, choose the question, problem, or issue you plan to investigate and write a research-log entry explaining how you got interested in that question and why you find it both problematic and significant. This will be the *starting point* for your essay; it might even serve as the rough draft for your introduction. Many instructors will collect this exploration as a quick check on whether you have formulated a good question that promises fruitful results.

Here is how one student, Sam, wrote the starting-point entry for his research log.

Sam's Paper—Starting Point

    I want to focus on the question of whether women should be allowed to serve in combat units in the military. I became interested in the issue of women in combat through my interest in gays in the military. While I saw that gays in the military was an important political issue for gay rights, I, like many gays, had no real desire to be in such a macho organization. But perhaps that was just the point--we had the opportunity to break stereotypes and attack areas most hostile to us.

    Similarly, I wonder whether feminists see women in combat as a crucial symbolic issue for women's rights. (I wonder too whether it is a <u>good</u> symbol, since many women value a less masculine approach to the world.) I think my instinct right now is that women should be allowed to serve in combat units. I think it is wrong to discriminate against women. Yet I also think America needs to have a strong military. Therefore, I am in a quandary. If putting women in combat wouldn't harm our military power, then I am fully in favor of women in combat. But if it would hurt our military power, then I have to make a value judgment. So I guess I have a lot to think about as I research this issue. I decided to focus on the women issue rather than the gay issue because it poses more of a dilemma for me.

I am absolutely in favor of gays in the military, so I am not very
open-minded about exploring that issue. But the women's issue is more
of a problem for me.

Continuing with Research and Dialectic Thinking

After you have formulated your starting point, you need to proceed with research, keeping a research log that records both your reading notes and your
strong-response reflections to each reading. (See Chapter 6, pp. 109–19 on reading
with and against the grain.) Also keep notes on your research process itself.

After Sam wrote his starting-point entry, he created an initial bibliography by
searching his college library's INFOTRAC. He decided to try keeping his research
log in a dialectic notebook format. What follows is his research-log entry for the
first article he read. His reading notes are in the right column and his exploratory
reflections in the left.

*Sam's Paper—
Research Log*

Reflections	Notes
This article raised some challenging points, but I did not find it completely convincing. First of all I agree that two ideals are at stake in this debate, equality and combat readiness. We could argue over which is of greater importance--our Constitution calls for equality but we also need to be able to defend our Constitution. However, these ideals may not be in conflict. If women in combat improves or doesn't affect our combat readiness we should obviously allow women to fight. If it is only slightly affected for the worse, we may wish to allow women to fight on the grounds that the great improve-	Hackworth, David H. "War and the Second Sex." Newsweek 5 Aug. 1991: 24-28. --Hackworth suggests that the ideals in conflict are equality and combat readiness. "Two sets of values are on a collision course. Equality and opportunity are ideals, but they have little to do with the battlefield, where the issues are living and dying. The question is: what if it turns out that equality and opportunity hurt combat readiness?" (p. 24)

ment in women's equality would be more important.

On to Hackworth's arguments on unit morale. Here he is not so convincing. The Israeli example seems like an odd choice seeing how those soldiers' attitudes in 1948 reflected a much different society. He offers no statistics but more or less leaves it to our intuition to determine whether morale would be affected. Personally, it would seem to me that the camaraderie arising from sharing a common grueling experience would be more of a human bond than a male one. If there are negative feelings toward women we should expect that the army can maintain enough discipline that personal feelings are set aside and the job accomplished. The army successfully integrated African Americans at a time of terrible discrimination against blacks in civilian society.

I am troubled, though, by the issue of pregnancy. A pregnant woman, unlike a father-to-be, cannot continue to fill her role as a

--Acknowledges women's bravery, competence and education (uses the Gulf War as an example).

--Acknowledges that there are some women as strong and fit as the strongest men (gives some examples), but then argues that allowing even these women in combat is the type of experimentation that the army doesn't need right now. (He says women already have plenty of jobs open for them in non-combat units).

--In interviewing "hundreds of service people of both sexes" (p. 25), Hackworth notes that the "biggest complaint" he gets is about "gender norming"--different physical standards. A 22-year-old female is allowed three more minutes than a 22-year-old male to run two miles; men have to climb a 20-foot rope in 30 seconds; women can take 50 seconds.

--One of Hackworth's big issues is male bonding. He points to "male-bonding" as a key to unit cohesion. Men, he argues, have been socialized to think that women must be protected and unless soci-

combat soldier. I was shocked by the number of pregnancies during the Gulf War and by the extent (although Hackworth doesn't give statistics) of the fraternization (he says the army passed out over a million condoms—-p. 28). However, shouldn't a unit be prepared to replace any soldier given the nature of war, and even, as many women have pointed out, such things as mens' sports injuries?

I am also bothered by the gender norming issue. It seems to me that there ought to be some absolute standards of strength and endurance needed for combat duty and the military ought to exclude both men and women who don't meet them. This would mean that a lower percentage of women than men would be eligible, but is that discrimination?

Finally, while fraternization and sexual harassment indeed seem like problems, I think they can be overcome with attentive discipline.

Where do I now stand? Well, I am still leaning toward believing ety changes, cohesiveness and morale will be adversely affected by women in combat. He uses Israel as an example:

> "The Israeli Army put women on the front lines in 1948. The experiment ended disastrously after only three weeks. It wasn't that the women couldn't fight. It was that they got blown apart. Female casualties demoralized the men and gutted unit cohesion." (pp. 26-27)

Says that Israel drafts women but doesn't let them serve in combat units.

--Another major problem is pregnancy causing women to leave a unit. He says that 10 to 15 percent of service women wear maternity uniforms in a given year. During Gulf War pregnancy rates soared. 1200 pregnant women were evacuated from the gulf (p. 28) during the war. On one destroyer tender, 36 female crew members got pregnant (p. 28). These pregnancies leave vacancies in a unit that can destroy its effectiveness.

that women should be allowed to serve in combat, but I see that there are a number of sub-questions involved. Should physical standards for combat positions be the same for men and women? Will the presence of women really hurt morale in a mostly male unit? Should women be given special consideration for their roles as mothers? How serious a problem is pregnancy? I also see another problem: Should physically eligible women be <u>required</u> (e.g., drafted) to serve in combat the same way men are drafted into combat positions? And I still want to know whether this is a crucial issue for the women's rights movement.

--He claims that women soldiers themselves had so many complaints about their experiences in the Gulf War (fraternization, sexual harassment, lack of privacy, primitive living conditions) that they said "don't rush to judgment on women in combat" (p. 28).

In the next section we see how Sam converts material from his research log into a draft of his exploratory essay.

Shaping and Drafting

Your exploratory essay should offer accounts of your search procedures (useful conversations with friends, strategies for tracking down sources, use of indexes or computer searches, strokes of good fortune at stumbling on good leads, and so forth) and your thought processes (what you were discovering, how your ideas were evolving). Drawing on your research log, you can share your frustration when a promising source turned out to be off the mark or your perplexity when a conversation with a friend over late-night espresso forced you to rethink your views. Hook your readers by making your exploratory essay read like a detective story. Consider giving your account immediacy by quoting your thoughts at the very moment you wrote a log entry. The general shape of an exploratory essay can take the following pattern:

1. Starting point: you describe your initial problem, why you are interested in it, why it is problematic, why it is worth pursuing.
2. New input: you read an article, interview someone, pose an alternative solution.
   a. Summarize, describe, or explain the new input.
   b. Discuss the input, analyzing or evaluating it, playing the believing and doubting game with it, exploring how this input affects your thinking.
   c. Decide where to go next—find an alternative view, pursue a subquestion, seek more data, and so forth.
3. More new input: you repeat step 2 for your next piece of research.
4. Still more new input.
5. Ending point: you sum up where you stand at the point when the paper is due, how much your thinking about the issue has changed, whether or not you've reached a satisfactory solution.

Here is how Sam converted his starting-point entry (see pp. 183–84) into the opening pages of his exploratory essay.

Sam Scofield

Should Women Be Allowed
to Serve in Combat Units?

Sam's Paper—
Exploration

At first, I wanted to explore the issue of gays in the military. But since I am a gay man I already knew where I stood on that issue and didn't find it truly problematic <u>for myself</u>. So I decided to shift my question to whether women should be allowed to serve in combat units. I wasn't sure whether feminists see the issue of women in combat the same way that gays see the military issue. Is it important to the feminist cause for women to be in combat? Or should feminists seek a kind of political order that avoids combat and doesn't settle issues through macho male behavior? In my initial thinking, I was also concerned about maintaining our country's military strength. In my "starting point" entry of my research log, I recorded the following thoughts:

> If putting women in combat wouldn't harm our military power, then I
> am fully in favor of women in combat. But if it would hurt our mili-
> tary power, then I have to make a value judgment.

2   So I decided that what I should do first is find some general background reading on the women in combat question. I went to the library and found an open INFOTRAC machine. I plugged in the key words "woman and combat" and, bingo, I had about a dozen entries just for the last two years. I went to the stacks and found the most familiar magazine in my initial list: Newsweek.

3   I began with an article by a retired Air Force colonel, David H. Hackworth. Hackworth was opposed to women in combat and focused mainly on the standard argument I was expecting--namely that women in combat would destroy male bonding. He didn't provide any evidence, however, other than citing the case of Israel in 1948.

> The Israeli Army put women on the front lines in 1948. The experiment ended disastrously after only three weeks. It wasn't that the women couldn't fight. It was that they got blown apart. Female casualties demoralized the men and gutted unit cohesion. (Hackworth 26-27)

However, this argument wasn't very persuasive to me. I thought that men's attitudes had changed a lot since 1948 and that cultural changes would allow us to get used to seeing both men and women as people so that it would be equally bad--or equally bearable--to see either men or women wounded and killed in combat.

4   But Hackworth did raise three points that I hadn't anticipated, and that really set me thinking. First he said that the military had different physical fitness requirements for men and women (for example, women had three minutes longer to run two miles than did men [25]). As I said in my research log, "It seems to me that there ought to be some absolute standards of strength and endurance needed for combat duty and the military ought to exclude both men and women who don't meet them." A second point was that an alarming number of female soldiers got pregnant in the Gulf War (1200 pregnant soldiers had to be evacuated [28]) and that prior to the war about 10-15 percent of female soldiers were pregnant at any given time (28). His

point was that a pregnant woman, unlike a father-to-be, cannot continue to fill her role as a combat soldier. When she leaves her unit, she creates a dangerous gap that makes it hard for the unit to accomplish its mission. Finally, Hackworth cited lots of actual women soldiers in the Gulf War who were opposed to women in combat. They raised issues such as fraternization, sexual harassment, lack of privacy, and primitive living conditions.

Although Hackworth didn't turn me against wanting women to be able to 5 serve in combat, he made the issue much more problematic for me. I now realized that this issue contained a lot of sub-issues, so I decided to focus first on the two major ones for me: (1) How important is this issue to feminists? This concern is crucial for me because I want to support equal rights for women just as I want to do so for gays or ethnic minorities. And (2) How serious are the pregnancy and strength-test issues? I also want to maintain the strength of fighting units, so I had to find out more about whether having women in combat units would harm our ability to carry out a mission. I didn't really buy the "male-bonding" argument, but the pregnancy problem and the gender-norming of strength and endurance tests bothered me.

As I read the rest of the articles on my list, I began paying particu- 6 lar attention to these issues. But first I decided to invite my friend Julie, who is an avid feminist, out for coffee and to interview her. . . .

Revising

Because an exploratory essay describes the writer's research and thinking in chronological order, most writers have little trouble with organization. When they revise, their major concern is often to improve their essay's interest level by keeping it focused and lively. Exploratory essays grow tedious if the pace crawls too slowly or if extraneous details appear. They also tend to become too long, so that condensing and pruning become key revision tasks. The draft here is actually Sam's second draft; the first draft was a page longer and incorporated many more details and quotations from the Hackworth article. Sam eliminated these because he realized that his purpose was not to report on Hackworth, but to describe the evolution of his own thinking. By condensing the Hackworth material, Sam saved room for the ideas he discovered later.

Peer reviewers can give you valuable feedback about the pace and interest level of an exploratory piece. They can also help you achieve the right balance between external details (how you did the research, to whom you talked, where you were) and mental details (what you were thinking about). As you revise, make sure you follow proper stylistic conventions for quotations and citations (see Chapter 23).

g   u   i   d   e   l   i   n   e   s

for Peer Reviewers

Instructions for peer reviews, including use of these guidelines, are provided in Chapter 21, pages 527–28. To write a peer review for a classmate, use your own paper, numbering your responses to correspond to the questions on the guidelines. At the head of your paper place the author's name and your own name as shown.

Author's Name: _____

Peer Reviewer's Name: _____

I. Read the draft at normal reading speed from beginning to end. As you read, do the following:
   A. Place a wavy line in the margin next to any passages that you find confusing, that contain something that doesn't seem to fit, or that otherwise slow down your reading.
   B. Place a "Good!" in the margin next to any passages where you think the writing is particularly strong or interesting.
II. Read the draft again slowly. Describe for the writer what you currently see in this draft. If you have difficulty answering any of the following questions, explain briefly the source of your difficulty.
   A. Describe the initial problem posed by the writer.
   B. Describe in your own words what makes the problem problematic and significant.
   C. Describe how the writer's thinking changes during the exploration process. Chart what you see as the major evolutionary stages in the writer's thinking.
   D. What research did the writer conduct in exploring the problem?
   E. To what extent has the writer resolved his or her problem by the end of the essay?
III. What recommendations do you have for improving this draft?
   A. How might the writer improve the title?

     B. How effectively does the opening interest you in the problem to be ad-
        dressed? What suggestions do you have for improving the interest level
        of the introduction or for showing the reader that the problem is both
        problematic and significant?
     C. What suggestions do you have for improving the content of the essay?
        1. Are there additional ideas that you think the writer should consider?
        2. Could you deepen the writer's thinking by challenging certain ideas?
        3. Can you make suggestions for further research that would improve
           the exploration?
     D. How might the writer improve the clarity or structure of the draft?
     E. Sum up what you see as the chief strengths and problem areas of this
        draft.
        1. Strengths
        2. Problem areas
IV. Read the draft one more time. Place a check in the margin wherever you no-
    tice problems in grammar, spelling, or mechanics (one check per problem).

c h a p t e r 9

Writing an Informative (and Surprising) Essay

ABOUT INFORMATIVE (AND SURPRISING) WRITING

Throughout this text we have encouraged the habit of considering alternative solutions to a problem. This chapter shows you how to amplify that habit through the use of a powerful rhetorical strategy for thesis-based essays: the *problem/ expected answer/surprising reversal* pattern. This pattern creates tension between your own thesis and one or more opposing views.

The concept of *surprising reversal* spurs you to go beyond the commonplace to change your reader's view of a topic. As we discussed in Chapters 3 and 4, writers of thesis-based prose usually approach this task in one of three ways, corresponding to three of the broadly defined purposes of writing.

1. *Informative purpose:* *enlarging* readers' views of a topic by providing new information or otherwise teaching them something about the topic they didn't know ("People my parents' age commonly think that men with tattoos are sleezy, macho bikers or waterfront sailors, but I will show them that many younger people get tattoos for deeply personal and spiritual reasons.")
2. *Analytical or interpretive purpose:* *clarifying* readers' views of a topic by bringing critical thinking to bear on problematic data or on a problematic text ("Most people think that this jeans ad reveals a liberated woman, but on closer inspection we see that the woman fulfills traditional gender stereotypes.")
3. *Persuasive purpose:* *restructuring* readers' views of a topic by causing them to choose the writer's position rather than a competing position on a controversial issue ("Many readers believe that the federal government should legalize cocaine and heroin, but I will show that legalizing such drugs would be disastrous.")

The surprising reversal pattern occurs whenever you contrast your reader's original view of a topic with your own new or surprising view. The pattern's power isn't that it tells you what to say about the topic or how to organize the main body of your essay. Its power is that it automatically gives your thesis tension. It pushes your view up against the commonplace or expected views that are likely to be shared by your audience. Although the assignment for this chapter is limited to the first purpose listed (writing to inform), the surprising reversal pattern works well also for the purposes of analysis or persuasion. You may find yourself using variations of this pattern for the remaining essay assignments in Part Two.

EXPLORING INFORMATIVE (AND SURPRISING) WRITING

Your goal for this activity is to discover unique knowledge or experience that gives each member of your class an uncommon perspective on some topic.

For the first part of this task, work privately at your desk for five or ten minutes. Consider one of the following trigger questions:

> Based on my personal experience, reading, research, or observation, what information or knowledge do I have about X that is different from the popular view of X?

or

> Although people commonly regard X this way, my personal experience, observation, or research shows X to be this other way.

In response to these trigger questions, brainstorm as many possible Xs as you can, using freewriting, idea mapping, or simple list making. Here are some examples from recent students.

Most people think that having an alcoholic mother would be the worst thing that could happen to you, but my mother's disease forced our family closer together.

Most people think that Native Americans lived in simple harmony with the earth, but my research reveals that they often "controlled" nature by setting fire to forests to make farming easier or to improve hunting.

Most people think of pawnshops as sleazy, disreputable places, but my experience shows pawn shops can be honest, wholesome businesses that perform a valuable social service.

The common image of gay men is of swishing queens or black-leather bikers, but my gay brother isn't like that at all.

```
Most people believe that operating your own AM radio station would

be both illegal and expensive, but my research has revealed a cheap

and legal way to become a disk jockey on your own AM station.
```

After everyone has brainstormed at least a few such statements, work in small groups or as a whole class to refine and share ideas. Most people think of many more possibilities once they begin hearing what their classmates are saying. Keep helping classmates until everyone in the class has at least one satisfactory topic.

WRITING PROJECT

Write a short informative essay following the surprising reversal pattern. Imagine an audience of general readers who hold a common view of your topic. Your purpose is to give them a new, surprising view. Pose a question, provide the commonly accepted answer to the question, and then give your own surprising answer, based on information derived from personal experience, observation, or research.

This assignment asks you to use your own personal experiences, observation, or research to enlarge your reader's view of a subject in a surprising way. The introduction of your essay should engage your reader's interest in a question and provide needed background or context. Do not put your thesis early in the introduction; instead, delay it until after you have explained the common, expected answer to your opening question. This delay in presenting the thesis creates a slightly open-form feel that readers often find engaging.

You might wonder why we call this assignment informative writing rather than persuasive writing, since we emphasize reversing a reader's view. The difference is in the kind of question posed and the reader's stance toward the writer. In persuasive writing the question being posed is controversial (Should drugs be legalized? Is the greenhouse effect currently warming the earth?), with strong, rational arguments on all sides. Often, disputes about values are as prevalent as disputes about facts. When writing persuasive prose, you imagine a resistant reader who may argue back.

With informative prose, the stakes are lower, and you can imagine a more trusting reader willing to learn from your experiences or research. You are enlarging your reader's view of the topic by presenting unexpected or surprising information, but you aren't necessarily saying that the common view is wrong, nor are you initiating a debate. In the examples in the preceding exploratory activity, the student writers aren't arguing whether alcoholic mothers are good or bad, whether all pawnshops are honest, or whether it is right to get a tattoo or build a personal radio station. They are simply offering readers new, unexpected, and expanded views of their topics.

For this assignment, avoid controversial issues that engender debate (save these issues for the chapters on persuasion, Chapters 14–16), and focus on how you, through your personal experience or research, can enlarge your reader's view of a topic by providing unexpected or surprising information.

UNDERSTANDING INFORMATIVE (AND SURPRISING) WRITING

When we speak of informative writing aimed at surprise, we mean thesis-based prose that is consciously intended to surprise the reader with an unexpected view. Such an essay represents only one kind of informative writing. Other kinds include encyclopedia articles, technical manuals, budget reports, experimental observations, instruction sheets, and many kinds of college textbooks—all of which convey detailed information without being thesis based and without intending to surprise the reader with an unexpected view. Readers turn to these other forms of informative writing when they need straightforward factual information. Often in your college and professional career you will be called upon to write straightforward informative prose without the surprising reversal pattern.

The essay you will write for this assignment is thus more provocative, more like the kinds of self-contained essays published in magazines or journals, for which the audience isn't ready-made, as it is for a budget report or a case observation in nursing. Your essay will need to hook your readers and sustain their interest by showing them a surprising new way of seeing your subject.

Because of its power to hook and sustain readers, examples of surprising reversal essays can be found in almost any publication—from scholarly journals to easy-reading magazines. Here, for example, are abstracts of several articles from the table of contents pages of recent issues of *Atlantic Monthly.*

"Reefer Madness" by Eric Schlosser

Marijuana has been pushed so far out of the public imagination by other drugs, and its use is so casually taken for granted in some quarters of society, that one might assume it had been effectively decriminalized. In truth, the government has never been tougher on marijuana offenders than it is today. In an era when violent criminals frequently walk free or receive modest jail terms, tens of thousands of people are serving long sentences for breaking marijuana laws.

"The Sex-Bias Myth in Medicine" by Andrew G. Kadar

A view has gained wide currency that men's health complaints are taken more seriously than those of women, and that medical research has benefited men more than it has women. "In fact," the author writes, "one sex does appear to be favored in the amount of attention devoted to its medical needs. . . . That sex is not men, however."

" 'It's Not the Economy, Stupid' " by Charles R. Morris

The conventional assumption, on which national elections often turn, is that one of the President's jobs is to "manage" the American economy: to make detailed economic actions that have precise results. But the truth is, the author writes, that managing the economy in this sense is far beyond any President's power—and, indeed, beyond the power of economics.

"Midlife Myths" by Winifred Gallagher

The idea that middle age is a dismal stage of life—scarred by traumas of personal crisis and physical change—is both firmly entrenched and almost completely untrue. The image in many Americans' minds, the author writes, is derived "not from the ordinary experiences of most people but from the unusual experiences of a few."

Each of these articles asserts a surprising new position that counters a commonly held view.

Common View	Surprising View
Because marijuana laws are no longer enforced, marijuana use has effectively become decriminalized.	The government has never been tougher on marijuana offenders than it is today.
More research dollars are spent on men's diseases than on women's diseases.	The reverse is true: more money is spent on women's diseases.
One of the president's jobs is to manage the economy by taking detailed economic action.	The economy is too complicated to control by presidential action.
Middle age is a dismal stage of life.	The widespread notion of midlife crises is a myth based on the unusual experiences of the few.

A similar pattern is often found in scholarly academic writing, which has the following typical underlying shape:

Whereas scholar A says X, scholar B says Y, and scholar C says Z, my research reveals Q.

Because the purpose of academic research is to advance knowledge, an academic article almost always shows the writer's new view against a background of prevailing views (what previous scholars have said).

READINGS

To help you understand the surprising reversal pattern in more detail, let's look at some complete essays. We begin with an easy-reading piece from *America West Airlines Magazine*. The topic, tarantulas, is particularly relevant to travelers on America West Airlines, which has a hub in Arizona, where tarantulas are plentiful. Note that the writer's strategy is to sum up the common view of these creatures and then to counter it with his own thesis.

LEO W. BANKS

NOT GUILTY: DESPITE ITS FEARSOME IMAGE, THE TARANTULA IS A BENIGN BEAST

If an insect ever had an image problem, it is the tarantula. Big, dark and hairy, tarantulas cause even the bold among us to back up a little and shiver reflexively. 1

No doubt that's part of the reason why Hollywood has made the creepy crawlies a movie-industry tradition. In the not-so-subtle 1955 sci-fi film *Tarantula,* for example, a scientist grows a 100-foot-tall version that chews up cars. The horror doesn't end until air force pilots hose the giant bug with napalm. 2

Science fiction isn't the only culprit. In *Dr. No,* the usually composed James Bond goes into a frenzy after being awakened by a tarantula crawling on his shoulder. Bond won the duel by frantically smashing the bug with a shoe. 3

These days Hollywood pays about $75 a day to rent a tarantula, a cheap price for such a grand and terrifying illusion. Illusion is the key word, for virtually everything the movies want the public to believe about tarantulas is false. The unexciting truth is that they are relatively benign insects. "The occurrence of humans being bitten by tarantulas is almost nonexistent," says Howard Lawler, curator of small animals at the Arizona-Sonora Desert Museum in Tucson, Arizona. "You have to practically hold one against your body or press it in your hand to make it bite you." 4

And when tarantulas do bite, the sensation is about as severe as an ant bite or bee sting. What's more, scientists say tarantula venom isn't especially potent and rarely is employed in defensive bites against humans. Instead, tarantulas save their venom, which is also a digestive enzyme, for use against natural prey. "Some people have a reaction to [the venom], but for others it's no problem," says Mike Carrington, a Tucson pet store owner. "I've been bitten several times and it doesn't bother me at all." 5

Found in much of the Southern and Western United States, tarantulas live in burrows—cylindrical foot-deep holes in the ground that usually are lined with silk. Life expectancy is 10 years for males and 25 years for females, who never venture farther than 6 feet from their burrows. 6

The spiders typically feed on crickets, grasshoppers and even small mice. Because of their bad eyesight, they rely on vibration-sensing organs in their feet to pick up the movements of passing prey. "In the darkness, if you drop a beetle from 6 feet above the head of a tarantula resting near its burrow, the tarantula will, in a millisecond, race out and grab it and return to the burrow," says Steve Prchal, president of Sonoran Arthropod Studies Inc., a non-profit organization in Tucson dedicated to public education about insects. 7

Predators, even large ones, often find tarantulas more than a match. If confronted by a curious fox, for example, a tarantula will scoop the hairs off its abdomen and toss them into the fox's eyes. The hairs, which are sharp and contain a venom, irritate and usually distract the animal long enough to allow the tarantula to escape. 8

Ironically, the male tarantula's worst enemy is probably the female. "If she is hungry enough, the female will sometimes try to eat the male during mating," Prchal says. As a defense, males have small hooks on their forelegs that can be used to grab the female's fangs to keep from being bitten. 9

Besides the bad rap they've received in Hollywood, these easygoing beasts also have been the villains of nursery rhymes—"Little Miss Muffet," for example—and folk- 10 lore. One prominent superstition dates back to the Dark Ages in Europe, when people bitten by wolf spiders thought they had to dance hysterically and sweat out the creature's venom in order to survive. The ritual was called the Tarantula Dance.

11 But probably the biggest reason tarantulas are so feared is their appearance. Besides being ugly, they sport fangs that are sometimes a half-inch long and curled at the bottom. And, by spider standards, tarantulas are huge. "I have one male who, if you laid him flat, would reach 11 inches across," says Carrington, who keeps seven pet tarantulas. "Most people who come to the house don't mind my tarantulas, but my mother-in-law won't go anywhere near them."

12 Pet stores sell tarantulas, a practice discouraged by scientists, for between $7 and $35. But sales are irregular because the insects are commonly found in the wild, especially during the spring-summer mating season.

13 In fact, they're so plentiful that former Tucson bar owner Jack Sheaffer remembers some nights when he couldn't keep tarantulas from coming into his establishment. It made for some interesting encounters that speak not to the insect's Hollywood image, but to its true nature. "Tarantulas never hurt anything," Sheaffer, says. "They just wanted to come in and say hello. Once I found one snoozing in a cash box. He was a friendly little critter."

Thinking Critically About "Not Guilty"

Banks' essay follows a formula frequently used in travel magazines: it gives travelers a new view of a local phenomenon. What popular misconceptions might there be about places, people, ways of life, or other phenomena in your own hometown or region? You might consider a similar topic for your own surprising reversal essay. Working as a whole class or in small groups, brainstorm misconceptions that travelers or newcomers have about phenomena in your area or about another area with which you are familiar.

The next reading is by student writer Cheryl Carp, whose experience doing volunteer outreach in a maximum-security prison enabled her to reverse stereotyped ideas about prisoners. She wrote the following essay for her first-year English class.

CHERYL CARP (student)
BEHIND STONE WALLS

1 For about eight hours out of every month I am behind the stone walls of the Monroe State Penitentiary. No, that's not the sentencing procedure of some lenient judge; I am part of a group of inmates and outsiders who identify themselves as Concerned Lifers. Concerned Lifers is an organization operating both inside and outside of prison walls. Inside Monroe there are close to thirty men who take part in the organization and its activities, all of whom have been given life sentences. Concerned Lifers outside the

Student Writing

prison visit the prisoners, take part in the organization's meetings, and then split into various small groups for personal conversation. I became involved in this exciting group as a personal sponsor (able to visit the prison alone for special activities) after attending my first meeting inside Monroe State Penitentiary. That first drive to Monroe seemed to take forever. Looking out the window of that twelve-seater van filled with apprehensive first-time volunteers, I kept my eyes on the evening sky and tried to imagine what it would be like to be shut up in prison for life, never to see this beautiful scenery again. I was not scared, but I was nervous and could feel my pulse rate steadily rise as I began to see the green and white road signs to the prison. As the van slowly climbed the hill to the guard tower at the top, I wondered what it would be like to visit this maximum security prison.

Many people believe that visiting a prison would be frightening. Most people typically picture dangerous men lurking in every corner. The guards are yelling and the men are fighting; the men are covered with tattoos, probably carrying concealed razor blades and scowling menacingly. People think that prisons are a haven for rampant homosexuality and illegal drugs. Common belief is that the inmates are like locked animals, reaching out between the iron bars of their cages. These men are seen as sex-starved, eagerly waiting for a female body to enter their domain. The atmosphere is one of suspense, with sub-human men ready at any moment to break free and run. People I've spoken to express a fear of danger to themselves and almost a threat to their lives. They wonder how I have the nerve to do it.

But visiting a prison to me is an uplifting experience, far from frightening. Since that initial visit, I have returned many times to organize and participate in a clown group. The clown group is made up of about twenty of the inmates in the Concerned Lifers group and myself. The prisoners meet and rehearse once a week, and I join them every other week to critique their progress, give them pointers, and do various exercises to improve their ability.

The only frightening part of a visit is getting through all the guards and their red tape. Last week I drove up the hill to the guard tower, identified myself and my affiliation, and was told to "park to the left" by a disembodied voice coming from a loudspeaker. After going through many metal security doors, being checked by a metal detector that even picks up the nails in your shoes, and being escorted by numerous guards, I finally got to be with the people I had come to see.

The most enjoyable, exciting, and friendly time I spend at the prison is the time I spend with the boys. These people are no longer "the prisoners" or "the inmates," but are now individuals. Visiting the prison is not a frightening experience because the men inside become people, people full of emotions, creativity, and kindness. These qualities are evident in the activities and projects these men become involved in or initiate themselves. For example, one young lifer named Ken became interested in Japanese paper folding—origami. In order to pursue his interest in origami, he requested a book on the subject from the prison librarian and proceeded to teach himself. A few weeks later, I saw origami creations everywhere—flowers, dragons, and birds—all made by the guys and all done carefully and beautifully. Ken had taught his fellow inmates. Another great thing that this group has undertaken is the sponsorship of four children through an orphan relief program. The men make almost nothing at their various jobs within the prison, but what they do make they are more than willing to share, something many of us never seem to "get around to."

It is true that the men value the presence of a female, but not for sexual reasons. The men inside Monroe are hungry for outside companionship and understanding.

They're hungry for a woman's viewpoint and conversation. They have treated me as a friend, valued my conversation, and never made sexual advances. The men behind the walls are reaching through their bars not menacingly, but pleadingly—begging the outside world to take a good look at them. The men need to be looked at as people and as fellow humans in this world. Most of them are aching for a second chance at life and relationships. This is not a place for outsiders to fear, but a place to which outsiders can bring light, hope, and understanding.

7   My point is not to condone the crimes that these men may have committed in the past, but to look to the present and the future by seeing these men not as "inmates," but as individual people trying to succeed in the kind of life they now have to live.

Thinking Critically About "Behind Stone Walls"

1. What is the common view of prisoners that Cheryl Carp attempts to reverse?
2. What is her own surprising view?
3. What are the strengths and weaknesses of Cheryl's essay?

FOR WRITING AND DISCUSSION

Perhaps reading the essays by Banks and Carp has stimulated you to think of more possible essay topics that employ the surprising reversal pattern. The goal of this exercise is to continue brainstorming possible topics.

Form small groups. Assign a group recorder to make a two-column list, with the left column headed "Common view of X" and the right column headed "Groupmate's surprising view." Brainstorm ideas for surprising reversal essay topics until every group member has generated at least one entry for the right-hand column. Avoid repeating the topics you developed in the opening exploratory activity (pp. 194–95). Here is a sample list entry.

Common View of X	Groupmate's Surprising View
Football offensive lineman is a no-brain, repetitive job requiring size, strength, and only enough brains and athletic ability to push people out of the way.	Jeff can show that being an offensive lineman is an interesting job that requires mental smarts as well as size, strength, and athletic ability.

To help stimulate ideas, you might consider topic areas such as the following:

- *People:* computer programmers, homeless people, cheerleaders, skateboarders, gang members, priests or rabbis, feminists, housespouses, mentally ill or developmentally disabled persons
- *Activities:* washing dishes, climbing mountains, wrestling, modeling, gardening, living with a chronic disease or disability, owning a certain breed of dog, riding a subway at night, entering a dangerous part of a city
- *Places:* particular neighborhoods, particular buildings or parts of buildings, local attractions, junkyards, places of entertainment, summer camps
- *Other similar categories:* groups, animals and plants, and so forth; the list is endless

Next, go around the room sharing the topics you have generated with the entire class. Remember that you are not yet committed to writing about any of these topics.

Before we begin offering suggestions for composing your essay, let's look at one more example of a surprising reversal essay. This one moves up the reading dial a bit from the easy-reading airline-travel piece by Leo Banks to a more serious reading station. The article is by David Quammen, who regularly writes about nature for *Outside* magazine. As you will see shortly, this information is important because it gives you some clues about Quammen's intended audience. This article is also about Arizona spiders—written in Tucson, the same locale used by Banks—yet it couldn't be more different from Banks's article. Whereas Banks writes with a simple informative purpose, Quammen combines his informative purpose with a more complex exploratory one.

DAVID QUAMMEN

THE FACE OF A SPIDER: EYEBALL TO EYEBALL WITH THE GOOD, THE BAD, AND THE UGLY

One evening a few years ago I walked back into my office after dinner and found   1
roughly a hundred black widow spiders frolicking on my desk. I am not speaking
metaphorically and I am not making this up: a hundred black widows. It was a vision
of ghastly, breathtaking beauty, and it brought on me a wave of nausea. It also brought
on a small moral crisis—one that I dealt with briskly, maybe rashly, in the dizziness of
the moment, and that I've been turning back over in my mind ever since. I won't say
I'm *haunted* by those hundred black widows, but I do remember them vividly. To me,
they stand for something. They stand, in their small synecdochical way, for a large and
important question.

The question is, How should a human behave toward the members of other living   2
species?

A hundred black widows probably sounds like a lot. It is—even for Tucson, Arizona,   3
where I was living then, a habitat in which black widows breed like rabbits and prosper
like cockroaches, the females of the species growing plump as huckleberries and
stringing their ragged webs in every free corner of every old shed and basement window. In Tucson, during the height of the season, a person can always on short notice
round up eight or ten big, robust black widows, if that's what a person wants to do. But
a hundred in one room? So all right, yes, there was a catch: These in my office were
newborn babies.

A hundred scuttering bambinos, each one no bigger than a poppyseed. Too small   4
still for red hourglasses, too small even for red egg timers. They had the aesthetic virtue
of being so tiny that even a person of good eyesight and patient disposition could not
make out their hideous little faces.

Their mother had sneaked in when the rains began and set up a web in the corner   5
beside my desk. I knew she was there—I got a reminder every time I dropped a pencil

and went groping for it, jerking my hand back at the first touch of that distinctive, dry, high-strength web. But I hadn't made the necessary decision about dealing with her. I knew she would have to be either murdered or else captured adroitly in a pickle jar for relocation to the wild, and I didn't especially want to do either. (I had already squashed scores of black widows during those Tucson years but by this time, I guess, I was going soft.) In the meantime, she had gotten pregnant. She had laid her eggs into a silken egg sac the size of a Milk Dud and then protected that sac vigilantly, keeping it warm, fending off any threats, as black widow mothers do. While she was waiting for the eggs to come to term, she would have been particularly edgy, particularly unforgiving, and my hand would have been in particular danger each time I reached for a fallen pencil. Then the great day arrived. The spiderlings hatched from their individual eggs, chewed their way out of the sac, and started crawling, brothers and sisters together, up toward the orange tensor lamp that was giving off heat and light on the desk of the nitwit who was their landlord.

6   By the time I stumbled in, fifty or sixty of them had reached the lampshade and rappelled back down on dainty silk lines, leaving a net of gossamer rigging between the lamp and the Darwin book (it happened to be an old edition of *Insectivorous Plants,* with marbled endpapers) that sat on the desk. Some dozen others had already managed dispersal flights, letting out strands of buoyant silk and ballooning away on rising air, as spiderlings do—in this case dispersing as far as the bookshelves. It was too late for one man to face one spider with just a pickle jar and an index card and his two shaky hands. By now I was proprietor of a highly successful black widow hatchery.

7   And the question was, How should a human behave toward the members of other living species?

8   The Jain religion of India has a strong teaching on that question. The Sanskrit word is *ahimsa,* generally rendered in English as "noninjury" or the imperative "do no harm." *Ahimsa* is the ethical centerpiece of Jainism, an absolute stricture against the killing of living beings—*any* living beings—and it led the traditional Jains to some extreme forms of observance. A rigorously devout Jain would burn no candles or lights, for instance, if there was danger a moth might fly into them. The Jain would light no fire for heating or cooking, again because it might cause the death of insects. He would cover his mouth and nose with a cloth mask, so as not to inhale any gnats. He would refrain from cutting his hair, on grounds that the lice hiding in there might be gruesomely injured by the scissors. He could not plow a field, for fear of mutilating worms. He could not work as a carpenter or a mason, with all that dangerous sawing and crunching, nor could he engage in most types of industrial production. Consequently the traditional Jains formed a distinct socioeconomic class, composed almost entirely of monks and merchants. Their ethical canon was not without what you and I might take to be glaring contradictions (vegetarianism was sanctioned, plants as usual getting dismissive treatment in the matter of rights of life), but at least they took it seriously. They lived by it. They tried their best to do no harm.

9   And this in a country, remember, where 10,000 humans died every year from snakebite, almost a million more from malaria carried in the bites of mosquitoes. The black widow spider, compared to those fellow creatures, seems a harmless and innocent beast.

10   But personally I hold no brief for *ahimsa,* because I don't delude myself that it's even theoretically (let alone practically) possible. The basic processes of animal life, human or otherwise, do necessarily entail a fair bit of ruthless squashing and gobbling. Plants can sustain themselves on no more than sunlight and beauty and a hydroponic

diet—but not we animals. I've only mentioned this Jainist ideal to suggest the range of possible viewpoints.

Modern philosophers of the "animal liberation" movement, most notably Peter   11 Singer and Tom Regan, have proposed some other interesting answers to the same question. So have writers like Barry Lopez and Eugene Linden, and (by their example, as well as by their work) scientists like Jane Goodall and John Lilly and Dian Fossey. Most of the attention of each of these thinkers, though, has been devoted to what is popularly (but not necessarily by the thinkers themselves) considered the "upper" end of the "ladder" of life. To my mind, the question of appropriate relations is more tricky and intriguing—also more crucial in the long run, since this group accounts for most of the planet's species—as applied to the "lower" end, down there among the mosquitoes and worms and black widow spiders.

These are the extreme test cases. These are the alien species who experience   12 human malice, or indifference, or tolerance, at its most automatic and elemental. To squash or not to squash? Mohandas Gandhi, whose own ethic of nonviolence owed much to *ahimsa,* was once asked about the propriety of an antimalaria campaign that involved killing mosquitoes with DDT, and he was careful to give no simple, presumptuous answer. These are the creatures whose treatment, by each of us, illuminates not just the strength of emotional affinity but the strength, if any, of principle.

But what is the principle? Pure *ahimsa,* as even Gandhi admitted, is unworkable.   13 Vegetarianism is invidious. Anthropocentrism, conscious or otherwise, is smug and ruinously myopic. What else? Well, I have my own little notion of one measure that might usefully be applied in our relations with other species, and I offer it here seriously despite the fact that it will probably sound godawful stupid.

Eye contact.   14

Make eye contact with the beast, the Other, before you decide upon action. No kid-   15 ding, now, I mean get down on your hands and knees right there in the vegetable garden, and look that snail in the face. Lock eyes with that bull snake. Trade stares with the carp. Gaze for a moment into the many-faceted eyes—the windows to its soul—of the house fly, as it licks its way innocently across your kitchen counter. Look for signs of embarrassment or rancor or guilt. Repeat the following formula silently, like a mantra: "This is some mother's darling, this is some mother's child." *Then* kill if you will, or if it seems you must.

I've been experimenting with the eye-contact approach for some time myself. I   16 don't claim that it has made me gentle or holy or put me in tune with the cosmic hum, but definitely it has been interesting. The hardest cases—and therefore I think the most telling—are the spiders.

The face of a spider is unlike anything else a human will ever see. The word "ugly"   17 doesn't even begin to serve. "Grotesque" and "menacing" are too mild. The only adequate way of communicating the effect of a spiderly countenance is to warn that it is "very different," and then offer a photograph. This trick should not be pulled on loved ones just before bedtime or when trying to persuade them to accompany you to the Amazon.

The special repugnant power of the spider physiognomy derives, I think, from fangs   18 and eyes. The former are too big and the latter are too many. But the fangs (actually the fangs are only terminal barbs on the *chelicerae,* as the real jaw limbs are called) need to be large, because all spiders are predators yet they have no pincers like a lobster or a scorpion, no talons like an eagle, no social behavior like a pack of wolves. Large clasping fangs armed with poison glands are just their required equipment for earning a living. And what about those eight eyes—big ones and little ones, arranged in two rows, all bugged-out and pointing every-whichway? (My wife the biologist offers a theory here: "They have an eye for each leg, like us—so they don't *step* in anything.") Well, a predator does need good eyesight, binocular focus, peripheral vision. Sensory perception is crucial to any animal that lives by the hunt and, unlike insects, arachnids possess no antennae. Beyond that, I don't know. I don't *know* why a spider has eight eyes.

19   I only know that, when I make eye contact with one, I feel a deep physical shudder of revulsion, and of fear, and of fascination; and I am reminded that the human style of face is only one accidental pattern among many, some of the others being quite drastically different. I remember that we aren't alone. I remember that we are the norm of goodness and comeliness only to ourselves. I wonder about how ugly I look to the spider.

20   The hundred baby black widows on my desk were too tiny for eye contact. They were too numerous, it seemed, to be gathered one by one into a pickle jar and carried to freedom in the the backyard. I killed them all with a can of Raid. I confess to that slaughter with more resignation than shame, the jostling struggle for life and space being what it is. I can't swear I would do differently today. But there is this lingering suspicion that I squandered an opportunity for some sort of moral growth.

21   I still keep their dead and dried mother, and their vacated egg sac, in a plastic vial on an office shelf. It is supposed to remind me of something or other.

22   And the question continues to puzzle me: How should a human behave toward the members of other living species?

23   Last week I tried to make eye contact with a tarantula. This was a huge specimen, all hairy and handsomely colored, with a body as big as a hamster and legs the size of Bic pens. I ogled it through a sheet of plate glass. I smiled and winked. But the animal hid its face in distrust.

Thinking Critically About "The Face of a Spider"

This article is meaty enough to justify a closer look. Before we comment on it, take a few moments to explore your own reactions to the following questions:

1. This article is closer to the open end of our closed-to-open continuum than are the other readings in this chapter. Quammen clearly highlights his question up front: "How should a human behave toward the members of other living species?" But he delays his answer—"I sprayed them with a can of Raid"—until the end of the article. Why? How did the absence of a thesis up front affect your experience in reading the article?
2. We sometimes use Quammen's dilemma in our classes without having students read the article. We ask students what they would do if they found hundreds of baby black widow spiders crawling across their desks. The most common answer we get, by margins of 10 to 1, is "Spray those suckers with a can of Raid." In other words, the surprising answer in Quammen's article is really the expected, common answer in our classes. So, to whom is Quammen writing?
3. Quammen's audience is apparently familiar with words such as *synecdochical* (we hope you looked it up), and they apparently know the people

mentioned in paragraph 10 (animal liberationists Peter Singer and Tom Regan; nature writers Barry Lopez and Eugene Linden; and scientists Jane Goodall, John Lilly, and Dian Fossey). Quammen assumes that his readers are so familiar with these people's viewpoints that he needs only a single sentence to refresh their memories:

> Most of the attention of each of these thinkers . . . has been devoted to what is popularly (but not necessarily by the thinkers themselves) considered the 'upper' end of the 'ladder' of life.

Are you familiar with any of these thinkers? If not, then what do you surmise their views are, based on the context of Quammen's piece?

4. What do you think Quammen is getting at when he uses the term "eye contact"? How is this a surprising reversal of what the audience expects? How does it lead to his decision to poison the spiders? How does it lead to his uncertainty as to whether Raid was the right answer?

Quammen's essay can teach us a lot about how writers work. By delaying his thesis, Quammen keeps us in suspense about how he is going to solve his problem and invites us to participate with him in thinking through it. The mood he creates—one of inquiring openness rather than confident certainty—is an effect of shifting from closed-form writing to more open-form writing.

In shaping his essay, Quammen sets up two interrelated problems: the immediate problem of what to do about the spiders, and the broad philosophical problem of how humans should behave toward other living species.

To appreciate this essay's surprising reversal, you have to appreciate Quammen's audience—well-educated, typically liberal environmentalists interested in such issues as the rift between humans and the earth's other living creatures. This audience is likely to be sympathetic toward Peter Singer's arguments against eating animals and to be familiar with Barry Lopez's essays on wolves, Jane Goodall's work with chimpanzees, and Dian Fossey's (*Gorillas in the Mist*) passionate defense of mountain gorillas against bounty hunters. Quammen's intention is to push such readers toward a dilemma. "I know," his prose implies, "that you ecologically minded readers won't bring harm to wolves, or salmon, or spotted owls, or mountain gorillas, but what about a deskful of black widow spiders?" To such an audience, a can of Raid has the same symbolic resonance as a chainsaw. Both symbolize Western man's (we use the patriarchal term intentionally) passion for control over nature. The essay thus raises profound questions about the boundaries of our concern for nonhumans. It surprises us—even haunts us—in any number of ways.

COMPOSING YOUR ESSAY

This assignment asks for an informative essay that surprises the reader with new information. Your new information can come either from your own personal experience (as Cheryl Carp uses her personal experience to reverse the common view of lifers) or from research (as Leo Banks uses both library and interview research to reverse the common view of tarantulas).

As you write your essay, keep in mind that *surprise* is a relative term based on the relationship between you and your intended audience. You don't have to surprise everyone in the world, just those who hold a common view of your topic. Cheryl Carp writes to those classmates who have never been inside a prison; Leo Banks writes to airline travelers who have only a Hollywood understanding of tarantulas; and David Quammen writes to ecologically minded folks with a philosophical bent toward animal liberation.

Additionally, your surprising view doesn't necessarily have to be diametrically opposed to the common view. Perhaps you think the common view is *incomplete* or *insufficient* rather than dead *wrong*. Instead of saying, "View X is wrong, whereas my view, Y, is correct," you can say, "View X is correct and good as far as it goes, but my view, Y, adds a new perspective." In other words, you can also create surprise by going a step beyond the common view to show the reader something new.

Generating and Exploring Ideas

When you write something outside a school setting, you are usually prompted to do so in one of two ways. Sometimes you are prompted by a particular rhetorical occasion that dictates your subject matter and purpose—a notice from a collection agency prompts you to protest a bill; your boss needs a proposal for the next sales meeting; your grandmother complains to your parents that you never write to her. On other occasions, you are motivated to write for your own internal reasons, creating your own context and selecting your own subject matter and purpose—you write in a daily journal to express your ideas and feelings; you write a poem or short story to satisfy a creative urge; you write to your representative in Congress to support or oppose impending legislation; or you write a freelance article on safety tips for hitchhikers to see if you can be published in a magazine.

This present assignment, although it gives you an in-school mandate to write something, is designed to simulate the second kind of prompting. We'd like you to experience what it's like to write when you have an almost unlimited choice of subject matter and potential audiences. Part of the point of this assignment is to help you see how experienced writers finally settle on a particular topic under those circumstances. This assignment encourages you to determine how your unique experiences, observations, or research gives you an angle on a topic that differs from the common view.

The For Writing and Discussion exercises in this chapter have been designed to help you brainstorm and select a topic for this assignment. Look back over these exercises, and see if they help you choose a topic. If not, here is one more exercise that might help you get started.

Exploration Task

With its emphasis on enlarging your audience's view with something unexpected or surprising, this assignment invites you to focus on your audience when selecting your topic. To write a surprising reversal essay, you need to know the common views about a topic, reflected in your audience's conversations. This exercise asks you to eavesdrop on conversations inside and outside class. Instead of entering into a conversation, listen to it intently. What in the conversation leaves you dissatisfied? What are the participants leaving out? Where are they too shallow? Where do they over- or underemphasize a point or focus too narrowly? If you could join this conversation anonymously by saying what you really think at a deep level, what might you say?

Freewrite for several minutes about a conversation that bothered you in some way. When you finish the freewrite, ask yourself if you have a surprising view that you could *add* to that conversation.

Shaping and Drafting

The surprising reversal pattern requires two main movements: an exposition of the common or expected answers to a question, and the development of your own surprising answer to that question. In addition, your essay needs an introduction that presents the question to be addressed and a separate conclusion that finishes it off.

Both Cheryl Carp and David Quammen use distinct introductory sections to provide a context and ask the essay's focusing question. Carp's lead provokes curiosity ("For about eight hours out of every month I am behind the stone walls of the Monroe State Penitentiary"), provides explanatory background on Concerned Lifers, and then poses the question that gave rise to her essay—one that she imagines her readers are asking:

> As the van slowly climbed the hill to the guard tower at the top, I wondered what it would be like to visit this maximum security prison.

Quammen opens his essay with a stunning lead ("One evening a few years ago I walked back into my office after dinner and found roughly a hundred black widow spiders frolicking on my desk"). He then explains how this event created "a small moral crisis" and presents, in its own separate paragraph, the essay's focusing question:

> The question is, How should a human behave toward the members of other living species?

In contrast, Leo Banks uses the common view of tarantulas as his lead, fusing his introduction with his exposition of the common view. Rather than stating the essay's question explicitly ("What is the true nature of the tarantula?"), he simply implies it when he presents his thesis:

> Illusion is the key word, for virtually everything the movies want the public to believe about tarantulas is false.

Both methods are effective.

As you go through these moves in your essay, your principal challenge is to maintain your reader's interest. You can do this by developing general statements with colorful, specific details. Cheryl Carp uses details from personal experience (green-and-white road signs, a disembodied voice emanating from a loudspeaker, origami dragons); Leo Banks uses research data about tarantulas (details about tarantula venom and so forth) as well as quotations from spider experts and local Arizonans; Quammen's essay is distinguished by its precise narrative and its descriptive sensory details (the explanation of how the baby spiders happened to be crawling on his desk and the description of the face of a spider, for example).

All three essays make extensive use of supporting examples. Banks uses a James Bond movie and a 1955 sci-fi film to support his point about the common Hollywood view of tarantulas; Carp uses the story of Ken's teaching his fellow inmates how to make origami flowers and dragons to illustrate her point about the inmates' humanity and creativity; Quammen provides a series of examples to make the point that devout Jains will not harm any animal (for example, they will not cut hair for fear of harming lice). Your essay will need these kinds of supporting examples and details.

As a way of helping you generate ideas and overcome writer's block, we offer the following five questions. Questions 1, 2, and 4 are planning questions that will help you create broad point sentences to form your essay's skeletal framework. These questions call for one-sentence generalizations. Questions 3 and 5 are freewriting prompts to help you generate supporting details. For these questions, freewrite rapidly, either on paper or at your computer. Following each question, we speculate about what Carp, Banks, and Quammen might have written if they had used the same questions to help them get started on their respective essays.

1. *What question does your essay address?*   (Carp might have said, "What is it like to visit lifers in a maximum security prison?" Banks might have said, "Do tarantulas deserve their scary reputation?" Quammen might have said, "How should I treat a deskful of baby black widow spiders? And how should humans behave toward other creatures?")

2. *What is the common, expected, or popular answer to this question?*   (Carp might have said, "Visiting these lifers will be scary because lifers are sex-starved, dangerous people." Banks might have said, "Tarantulas are poisonous, nightmarish creatures." Quammen might have said, "My audience expects me to offer an ecologically sound solution to the spider problem that reflects my respect and concern for all of earth's creatures.")

3. *Why do you believe this is the expected answer? Who holds the views that it reflects?*   Expand on these views by developing them with supporting examples and details. (Carp might have brainstormed details about concealed razor blades, drugs, prison violence, the fear of her friends, and so on. Banks's freewrites might have focused on the sci-fi and James Bond films and other misconceptions about tarantulas. Quammen's freewriting might have centered on the Jain religion and other respect-all-earth's-creatures movements.)

4. ***What is your own surprising view?*** (Carp might have answered, "Visiting the prison is uplifting because prisoners can be kind, creative, and generous." Banks might have answered, "Tarantulas are peaceful creatures with a largely painless bite and harmless venom." Quammen might have answered, "My look-them-in-the-eye theory allows me to spray these spiders with Raid.")

5. ***What examples and details support this view? Why do you hold this view? Why should a reader believe you?*** Writing rapidly, spell out the evidence that supports your point. (Carp would have done a freewrite on all the experiences she had that changed her views about prisoners. Later she would have selected the most powerful ones and refined them for her readers. Banks would have spilled out all his evidence that tarantulas don't deserve their bad reputation. Quammen would have explored his theory about looking creatures in the eye, experimentally applying it to black widows.)

Once you finish exploring your response to these five trigger questions, you will be well on the way to composing a first draft of your essay. Now finish writing your draft fairly rapidly without worrying about perfection.

Revising

Once you have your first draft on paper, the goal is to make it work better first for yourself and then for your readers. If you discovered ideas as you wrote, you may need to do some major restructuring. Check to see that the question you are addressing is clear. Do you state it directly, as do Carp and Quammen, or simply imply it, as does Banks? Make sure that you distinguish between the common view and your own surprising view. Do you put your meanings up front, using point sentences at the head of each section and near the beginning of every paragraph? Carp's and Banks's essays are closed-form pieces with no narrative suspense about the writer's thesis or the essay's structure; Quammen purposely violates some of the rules for closed-form writing to create suspense. Which strategy are you using? Check to see that you have colorful details and plenty of examples and illustrations.

As you revise, follow the suggestions in Chapter 17 for improving your own revising processes. At some point in the middle of your writing process, you will want to road-test your draft by trying it out on readers who can give you valuable insights for further revision. Chapter 21 has suggestions for conducting peer reviews and gives advice on how to incorporate feedback from readers into your subsequent drafts. Remember to save editing matters for late in the process, attending first to the global concerns of ideas, structure, and overall development.

We conclude this chapter with peer review guidelines that sum up the features to look for in your essay and remind you of the criteria your instructor will use in evaluating your work.

g   u   i   d   e   l   i   n   e   s

for Peer Reviewers

Instructions for peer reviews, including use of these guidelines, are provided in Chapter 21, pages 527–28. To write a peer review for a classmate, use your own paper, numbering your responses to correspond to the questions on the guidelines. At the head of your paper place the author's name and your own name as shown.

Author's Name: _____

Peer Reviewer's Name: _____

I. Read the draft at normal reading speed from beginning to end. As you read, do the following:
   A. Place a wavy line in the margin next to any passages that you find confusing, that contain something that doesn't seem to fit, or that otherwise slow down your reading.
   B. Place a "Good!" in the margin next to any passages where you think the writing is particularly strong or interesting. Specifically, place a "Good!" next to sensory details that make the writing vivid and lively.
II. Read the draft again slowly. Describe for the writer what you currently see in this draft. If you have difficulty answering any of these questions, explain briefly the source of your difficulty.
   A. What question does the essay address?
   B. How does the writer try to hook the reader and get the reader interested in this question?
   C. What does the writer say is the expected or common answer to this question?
      1. What would your own answer be to this question?
      2. What differences, if any, are there between the expected answer and your own answer?
   D. What is the writer's surprising answer to this question?
      1. Did you find it surprising and why?
      2. What details, examples, or illustrations does the author include to make the surprising answer convincing and vivid?
III. What recommendations do you have for improving this draft?
   A. How might the writer improve the title?
   B. Does the introduction capture your interest and set up the question to be addressed? How might the writer improve the introduction?
   C. Does the writer effectively describe the common or expected view of the topic? Can you think of any additional supporting examples, illustrations, or details that would help the writer develop the common view more vividly?

D. Does the writer effectively explain his or her surprising view? Can you think of any additional supporting examples, illustrations, or details that would help the writer more vividly develop this surprising view?

E. How might the writer improve the clarity or structure of the draft?

F. Sum up what you see as the chief strengths and problem areas of this draft.

1. Strengths
2. Problem areas

IV. Read the draft one more time. Place a check in the margin wherever you notice problems in grammar, spelling, or mechanics (one check per problem).

chapter 10

Analyzing Images

ABOUT ANALYZING IMAGES

This chapter asks you to analyze the persuasive power of images. We are surrounded by images that have designs on us, that urge us to buy things, go places, believe ideas, and so forth. Often the messages of these images are fairly subtle. Information brochures rely on carefully shot photographs of people and places to enhance a subject's image (consider the photographs of the campus included in your college catalog); news photographs editorialize their content (during the Vietnam War a newspaper photograph of a naked Vietnamese child running screaming toward the photographer turned many Americans against the war); and paintings and visual arts cause us literally to see new things ("There was no yellow fog in London until Turner painted it," according to Oscar Wilde). But the most powerful and pervasive images in our culture come to us through the medium of magazine and television advertisements. This chapter focuses on helping you learn to analyze the persuasive nature of these images.

By *images* we mean both the advertisements' pictures themselves and also the images of self and society that they project. When we discuss the persuasive nature of ads we can ask both: How does this ad persuade me to buy this product? and How does this ad persuade me to be a certain kind of person, to adopt a certain self-image, or to strive for certain values?

This chapter is the first of four chapters on writing to analyze. As you may recall from Chapter 4, when you write to analyze you apply your own critical thinking to a puzzling object or to puzzling data. Your goal is to raise interesting questions about the object or data being analyzed—questions that perhaps your reader hasn't thought to ask—and then to provide tentative answers to those questions through close examination of the object or data. The word *analysis* derives from a Greek word meaning "to dissolve, loosen, or undo." Metaphorically, analysis means to divide or dissolve the whole into its constituent parts, to examine these parts carefully, to look at the relationships among them, and then to use this understanding of the parts to better understand the whole—how it functions or what it means. Synonyms for writing to analyze might be writing to interpret, to clarify, or to explain.

What you will develop through this chapter is the ability to understand and explain the persuasive power of advertisements. We will look at the constituent parts of these advertisements—setting, furnishings, and props; characteristics of the models, including their clothes, gestures, hair, facial expressions, and poses; camera angle and lighting; the interplay between the visual images and the verbal copy—and ask how all these parts working together contribute to the rhetorical effect of the advertisement. Along the way, we raise questions about how advertisements shape our sense of who we are and what we value.

Because advertising is such a broad and complex subject, any discussion of it raises numerous interconnected questions concerning the ethics of advertising, the nature of a consumer economy, the complexity and challenge of running a successful business, and what modern critics sometimes call the "social construction of the self," that is, the way messages in the culture create our sense of self and others. Critics of advertising point to its harmful effects (hooking young women on dieting, inciting young men to steal in order to buy $150 basketball shoes), while supporters of advertising point to its benefits (making capitalism work, funding radio and television, undermining communist economies by creating a longing for Western consumer products). All these are areas for exploration and debate.

EXPLORING IMAGE ANALYSIS

Working on your own, freewrite your responses to the following questions:

1. Can you recall a time when a magazine or TV advertisement directly influenced you to buy a product? Describe the occasion and try to recall the specifics of how the ad influenced you.
2. According to a communications professor, Sut Jhally, many critics of advertising claim that "it is a tool whereby consumers are controlled and manipulated by the producers of goods (on whose behalf advertising is waged) to desire things for which they have no real need." To what extent has advertising made you desire things that you don't need? Give some examples. How did the advertisements work on you? What techniques did they use?
3. Has advertising ever influenced your values or your image of what you want to be? For example, an ad may not have caused you to buy a product (a particular perfume or brand of coffee), but has an ad made you long for certain values or experiences (to ride a horse through the pounding surf, to have a romantic encounter in a European café)? As a specific example, one of the authors of this text remembers one summer morning when he and his seven-year-old daughter ate their breakfast cereal on their front porch, cereal bowls cupped in their hands, as a direct result of a Grapenuts advertisement. Can you think of similar experiences?

In small groups or as a whole class, share your freewrites. From the ensuing discussion, create a list of specific ways in which magazine or TV advertisements have been successful in persuading members of your class (a) to buy a product, (b) to value something they didn't need, and (c) to embrace particular values or long for certain experiences.

For further exploration, read the following introduction to a brief article with the headline "Attention Advertisers: Real Men Do Laundry." This article appeared in a recent issue of *American Demographics,* a magazine that helps advertisers target particular audiences based on demographic analysis of the population.

> Commercials almost never show men doing the laundry, but nearly one-fifth of men do at least seven loads a week. Men don't do as much laundry as women, but the washday gap may be closing. In the dual-career 1990's laundry is going unisex.
>
> Forty-three percent of women wash at least seven loads of laundry a week, compared with 19 percent of men, according to a survey conducted for Lever Brothers Company, manufacturers of Wisk detergent. Men do 29 percent of the 419 million loads of laundry Americans wash each week. Yet virtually all laundry-detergent advertising is aimed at women.

Working in small groups, create an idea for a laundry detergent ad to be placed in a men's magazine such as *Playboy, Sports Illustrated, Field and Stream,* or *Esquire.* Draw a rough sketch of your ad that includes picture, the placement of words, and a rough idea of the content of the words. Pay particular attention to the visual features of your ad—the models, their age, ethnicity, social status or class, and dress; the setting, a self-service laundry, a home laundry room; and other features. When you have designed a possible approach, explain why you think your ad will work.

WRITING PROJECT

> Choose two magazine or TV advertisements that sell the same kind of product but appeal to different audiences (for example, a car advertisement aimed at men and one aimed at women; a cigarette ad aimed at upper-middle-class consumers and one aimed at working-class consumers; a clothing ad from *The New Yorker* and one from *Rolling Stone*). Describe the ads in detail so that an audience can easily visualize them without actually seeing them. Analyze the advertisements and explain how each appeals to its target audience. To what values does each ad appeal? How is each ad constructed to appeal to those values? In addition to analyzing the rhetorical appeals made by each ad, you may also wish to evaluate or criticize the ads, commenting on the images they convey of our culture.

This assignment asks you to analyze two different advertisements that are for the same kind of product but appeal to different audiences. Seeing the contrasts in the ads will heighten your awareness of how advertisers vary their appeals to reach different target audiences. For example, Budweiser beer and Pyramid ale are aimed at two different segments of the beer market and the kinds of appeals they use are very different. Companies often vary their appeals for the same product by gender. The Coors beer advertisements in *Glamour* or *Redbook* often differ from the Coors advertisements in *Playboy* or *Sports Illustrated.* Similarly, advertisers often vary their appeals to reach African American, Hispanic, or Asian markets. This assignment asks you to explain how these appeals are targeted and created.

UNDERSTANDING IMAGE ANALYSIS

Advertisements use images in subtle ways. Although some advertisements are primarily informational—explaining why the company believes its product is superior—most advertisements involve parity products, such as soft drinks, deodorants, breakfast cereals, toothpaste, and jeans. *Parity* products are products that are roughly equal in quality to their competitors and can't be sold through any rational or scientific proof of superiority.

Advertisements for parity products usually use psychological and motivational strategies to associate a product with a target audience's (often subconscious) dreams, hopes, desires, and wishes. The ads play on the idea that the product will magically dispel subconscious fears and anxieties or magically deliver on values, desires, and dreams. Using sophisticated research techniques, advertisers study how people's fears, dreams, and values differ according to their ethnicity, gender, educational level, socioeconomic class, age, and so forth; this research allows advertisers to tailor their appeals precisely to a target audience.

Every feature of an expensive ad, down to the tiniest detail, is the result of conscious choice. Therefore, you must pay close attention to every detail: Why is the hair this way rather than that way? Why these clothes rather than other clothes? Why these body positions rather than other body positions? Why this facial expression rather than another facial expression? Why these words rather than other words? Why this camera angle rather than another camera angle? And so forth.

Targeting Specific Audiences

Much of the market research on which advertisers rely is based on an influential demographic tool developed by SRI Research called the VALS™ (*values and lifestyle system*).* This system divides consumers into three basic categories, with further subdivisions.

1. *Needs-driven consumers.* Poor, with little disposable income, these consumers generally spend their money only on basic necessities.
    - *Survivors:* Live on fixed incomes or have no disposable income. Advertising seldom targets this group.
    - *Sustainers:* Have very little disposable income, but often spend what they have impulsively on low-end, mass-market items.

*Our discussion of the VALS™ is adapted from Harold W. Berkman and Christopher Gibson, *Advertising,* 2d ed. (New York: Random House, 1987), pp. 134–37.

2. ***Outer-directed consumers.***   These consumers want to identify with certain in groups, to "keep up with the Joneses" or to surpass them.
   - *Belongers:* Believe in traditional family values and are conforming, non-experimental, nostalgic, and sentimental. They are typically blue collar or lower middle class, and they buy products associated with mom, apple pie, and the American flag.
   - *Emulators:* Are ambitious and status conscious. They have tremendous desire to associate with currently popular in-groups. They are typically young, have at least moderate disposable income, are urban and up-wardly mobile, and buy conspicuous items that are considered "in."
   - *Achievers:* Have reached the top in a competitive environment. They buy to show off their status and wealth and to reward themselves for their hard climb up the ladder. They have high incomes and buy top-of-the-line luxury items that say "success." They regard themselves as leaders and persons of stature.
3. ***Inner-directed consumers.***   Marching to their own drummers, these consumers are individualistic and buy items to suit their own tastes rather than to symbolize their status.
   - *I-am-me types:* Are young, independent, and often from affluent backgrounds. They typically buy expensive items associated with their individual interests (such as mountain bikes, stereo equipment, or high-end camping gear), but may spend very little on clothes, cars, or furniture.
   - *Experiential types:* Are process-oriented and often reject the values of corporate America in favor of alternative lifestyles. They buy organic foods, make their own bread, do crafts and music, value holistic medicine, and send their children to alternative kindergartens.
   - *Socially conscious types:* Believe in simple living and are concerned about the environment and the poor. They emphasize the social responsibility of corporations, take on community service, and actively promote their favorite causes. They have middle to high incomes and are usually very well educated.

No one fits exactly into any category, and most people exhibit traits of several categories, but advertisers are interested in statistical averages, not individuals. When a company markets an item, it enlists advertising specialists to help target the item to a particular market segment. Budweiser is aimed at belongers, expensive imported beers at achievers, and microbrewery beers at either experiential types or emulators (if microbeers are currently "in"). To understand more precisely the fears and values of a target group, researchers can analyze subgroups within each of these VALS segments by focusing specifically on women, men, children, teenagers, young adults, or retirees or on specified ethnic or regional minorities. Researchers also determine what kinds of families and relationships are valued in each of the VALS segments, who in a family initiates demand for a product, and who in a family makes the actual purchasing decisions. Thus ads aimed at belongers depict traditional families; ads aimed at I-am-me types may depict more ambiguous relationships. Advertisements aimed at women can be particularly complex because of women's conflicting social roles in our society. When advertisers target the broader category of gender, they sometimes sweep away VALS distinctions and try to evoke more deeply embedded emotional and psychological responses.

FOR WRITING AND DISCUSSION

You own a successful futon factory that has marketed its product primarily to experiential types. Your advertisements have associated futons with holistic health, spiritualism (transcendental meditation, yoga), and organic wholesomeness (all-natural materials, gentle people working in the factory, incense and sitar music in your retail stores, and so forth). You have recently expanded your factory and now produce twice as many futons as you did six months ago. Unfortunately, demand hasn't increased correspondingly. Your market research suggests that if you are going to increase demand for futons you have to reach other VALS segments.

Working in small groups, develop ideas for a magazine or TV advertisement that might sell futons to one or more of the other target segments in the VALS system. Your instructor can assign a different target segment to each group, or each group can decide for itself which target segment constitutes the likeliest new market for futons.

Groups should then share their ideas with the whole class.

Analyzing an Advertisement

When you analyze an advertisement, you need to examine it in minute detail. Here are some suggestions for analyzing magazine advertisements. The same strategies can be applied to television advertisements, but TV ads are more complex because they add dialogue, multiple scenes, music, and so forth.

1. *Examine the setting, furnishings, and props.*
   a. List all furnishings and props. If the ad pictures a room, look carefully at such details as the kind and color of the rug; the subject matter of paintings on the walls; the styles of picture frames, curtains, and furniture; the objects on tables; the general arrangement of objects (Is the room neat and tidy or does it have a lived-in look?); the room's feeling (Is it formal? Warm? Casual?); and so forth. Almost all details are purposely chosen; almost nothing is accidental.
   b. What social meanings and values are attached to the objects you listed in (a)? In a den, for example, duck decoys and fishing rods have a connotation different from that of computers and fax machines. It makes a difference whether a dog is a Labrador retriever, an English sheepdog, a toy poodle, or a mutt. What symbolic meanings or associations do various props have? A single rose connotes romance or elegance, a bouquet

of daisies suggests freshness, and a hanging fuchsia suggests earthy naturalness. Always ask why the ad maker includes one particular prop rather than another.

2. *Consider the characters, roles, and actions.*

   a. Create the story of the ad. Who are the people? What are their relationships? Why are they here? What are they doing? Note details about the clothing and accessories of all the models; pay special attention to hairstyles, because popular culture invests hair with great significance (hence the anxiety created by a bad hair day). Note the poses and gestures of models as well as their positioning and relative sizes. For further advice on what to look for when analyzing the people in advertisements, consult Gillian Dyer's discussion of the manner and actions of characters in ads (pp. 227–29).

   b. Ask what social roles are being played and what values appealed to. Are the gender roles traditional or nontraditional? Are the relationships between people romantic, erotic, friendly, formal, uncertain? What are the power relationships between characters? In most ads, men are larger than women and occupy a stronger position (the woman looking up at the man, the man looking directly at someone or into the camera while the woman averts her eyes), but sometimes these roles are reversed. Either choice is deliberate.

3. *Examine the photographic effects.* Some advertisements use highly artistic photographic techniques. Parts of the ad may be in crisp focus and others slightly blurred; camera angle or filters may have been used to create special effects. Why? Frequently, photographs are cropped so that only parts of a body are shown. Research suggests that women's bodies are more often cropped than are men's. It is not unusual to see photographs of women's arms, feet, ears, lips, or eyes, but it is rare to see similar photographs of men. What does this difference suggest about the culture's view of men and women? Many ads consist of a large picture with a small insert picture at the top or bottom; the insert often includes one of the characters from the large picture in a different role or pose. Ask how the insert comments on the large picture or how the insert and the large picture otherwise interrelate.

4. *Analyze words and copy.* The words in advertisements are chosen with extreme care, and special attention is given to connotations, double entendres, and puns. In well-made ads the words and pictures combine for a unified effect. Pay attention to both the message of the words and their visual effect on the page (placement, relative size, and so forth).

Sample Analysis of an Advertisement

As an example of how a specific ad persuades, consider the contrast between the beer ads typically aimed at men (showing women in bikinis fulfilling adolescent male sexual fantasies or men on fishing trips or in sports bars) with the "Sam and Me" Coors Light ad (p. 220), which ran in a variety of women's magazines.

Sam and Me.

Me and Sam? We're just friends. Best friends, actually, since Mrs. Ainsley's first grade class when I let the hamster loose and Sam took the rap for me. I mean Sam's seen me in braces and I've seen him eat pizza. There's just way too much history here. Sam's my friend. The one I go to when I really need someone to talk to. I bring the Coors Light and Sam brings his shoulder. And sometimes it's Sam bringing the Coors Light and I'm doing the listening. Me and Sam? Together? I've never even thought about it. Okay, so I've thought about it.

Coors Light.
Just between friends.

Rather than associate beer drinking with a wild party, this ad associates beer drinking with the warm friendship of a man and woman and with just a hint of potential romance. The ad shows a man and a woman, probably in their early to mid-twenties, in relaxed conversation; they are sitting casually on a tabletop, with their legs resting on chair seats. The woman is wearing casual pants, a summery cotton top, and informal shoes. Her braided, shoulder-length hair has a healthy, messed appearance, and one braid comes across the front of her shoulder. She is turned away from the man, leans on her knees, and holds a bottle of Coors Light. Her sparkling eyes are looking up, and she smiles happily, as if reliving a pleasant memory. The man is wearing slacks, a short-sleeved cotton shirt, and scuffed tennis shoes with white socks. He also has a reminiscing smile on his face, and he leans on the woman's shoulder. The words "Coors Light. Just between friends" appear immediately below the picture next to a Coors Light can.

This ad appeals to women's desire for close friendships and relationships. Everything about the picture signifies long-established closeness and intimacy— old friends rather than lovers. The way the man leans on the woman shows her strength and independence. Additionally, the way they pose, with the woman slightly forward and sitting up more than the man, results in their taking up equal space in the picture. In many ads featuring male-female couples the man appears larger and taller than the woman; this picture signifies mutuality and equality.

The words of the ad help you interpret the relationship. Sam and the woman have been friends since the first grade, and they are reminiscing about old times. The relationship is thoroughly mutual. Sometimes he brings the Coors Light and sometimes she brings it; sometimes she does the listening and sometimes he does; sometimes she leans on his shoulder and sometimes he leans on hers. Sometimes the ad says, "Sam and me"; sometimes it says "me and Sam." Even the "bad grammar" of "Sam and me" (rather than "Sam and I") suggests the lazy, relaxed absence of pretense or formality.

These two are reliable old buddies. But the last three lines of the copy leave just a hint of potential romance. "Me and Sam? Together? I've never even thought about it. Okay, so I've thought about it." Whereas beer ads targeting men portray women as sex objects, this ad appeals to women's desire for relationships and for romance that is rooted in friendship rather than sex.

And why the name Sam? Students in our classes have hypothesized that Sam is a "buddy" kind of name rather than a romantic hero name. Yet it is more modern and more interesting than other buddy names such as Bob or Bill or Dave. "A Sam" said one of our students, "is more mysterious than a Bill." Whatever associations the name strikes in you, be assured that the ad makers spent hours debating possible names until they hit on this one. For additional examples of analysis of ads, see cultural critic Mark Crispin Miller's analysis of a TV soap commercial (pp. 230–34) and the sample student essay (pp. 235–37).

FOR WRITING AND DISCUSSION

Examine any of the other magazine ads reprinted in this chapter, or ads brought to class by students or your instructor, and analyze them in detail, paying particular attention to setting, furnishings, and props; characters, roles, and actions; photographic effects; and words and copy. Prior to discussion, freewrite your own analysis of the chosen ad.

Cultural Issues Raised by Advertisements

There isn't space here to examine in depth the numerous cultural issues raised by advertisements, but we can introduce you to a few of them and provide several tasks for exploratory writing and talking.

In 1979, the influential sociologist and semiotician* Erving Goffman published a book called *Gender Advertisements,* arguing that the way in which women are pictured in advertisements removes them from serious power. In many cases, Goffman's point seems self-evident. Women in advertisements are often depicted in frivolous, childlike, exhibitionistic, sexual, or silly poses that would be considered undignified for a man, such as the "Of Sound Body" Zenith ad (p. 223). Women in advertisements are often fun to look at or enthralling to "gaze" at, but seldom call for serious attention. What distinguishes Goffman's work is his analysis of apparently positive portrayals of women in advertisements. He points out tiny details that differentiate the treatment of men from that of women. For example, when men hold umbrellas in an ad, it is usually raining, but when women hold umbrellas, it is for decoration; men grip objects tightly, but women often caress objects or cup them in a gathering in or nurturing way. Female models dance and jump and wiggle in front of the camera (like children playing); whereas male models generally stand or sit in a dignified manner. Even when trying to portray a powerful and independent woman, ads reveal cultural signs that the woman is subordinate.

FOR WRITING AND DISCUSSION

To see what Goffman is getting at, we invite you to explore this issue in the following sequence of activities, which combine class discussion with invitations for exploratory writing.

1. Bring to class advertisements for clothing, perfumes, or accessories from recent fashion and beauty magazines, such as *Glamour, Elle, Mademoiselle,* and *Vogue.* Ask male students to assume the postures of the women in the ads. How many of the postures, which look natural for women, seem ludicrous when adopted by men? To what extent are these postures really natural for women? Freewrite your responses to this exercise.
2. Examine the Zenith advertisement on page 223. How might Erving Goffman argue that this ad subordinates women? Do you agree that this ad reflects the inferior status of women in U.S. culture? Why or why not? Freewrite your response in preparation for class discussion.
3. A highly popular advertisement for cognac that ran several years ago shows three male business executives, ranging in age from the early thirties to early fifties, sitting in an upscale bar overlooking a subway station (see the "The World's Most Civilized Spirit" Hennessy ad, p. 224). The men are wearing

*A *semiotician* is a person who studies the meanings of signs in a culture. A *sign* is any human-produced artifact or gesture that conveys meaning. It can be anything from a word to a facial expression to the arrangement of chairs at a dinner table.

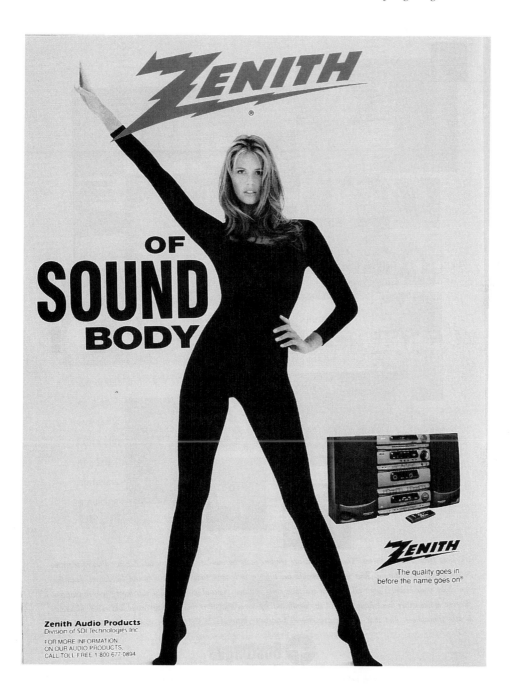

power suits; one man has removed his jacket and rolled up the sleeves on his striped oxford shirt, revealing his power tie and expensive suspenders. He is reaching for cashew nuts in a cut-glass bowl. The three men are sip-

ping cognac from expensive brandy snifters. The copy at the top of the ad reads, "When the 8:05 isn't leaving until 8:55." What the ad reveals, then, are powerful business leaders at the end of a business day, which is—conspicuously—close to 8:00 P.M., not 5:00. Since the 8:05 train has been delayed, the men relax, enjoy each other's company, and sip fine cognac.

Freewrite or discuss your responses to this question: Would this ad work if you replaced the male business executives with female executives? Why or why not?

4. Imagine a comparable ad featuring female models that appeals to women's desire to be seen as competent, empowered corporate leaders in today's business environment. Freewrite your ideas for such an ad, addressing the following questions: (a) What product would the ad be selling? (b) What kind of model or models would you choose for your ad? Of what age? From what ethnic group? With what look? (c) What setting and props would you use? (d) How would the models be dressed? What would their hairstyles be? How would they pose? What would they be doing? (e) What might the ad copy say? (f) In what magazines would you publish your ad?

5. Bring to class examples of advertisements that portray women in a particularly positive and empowered way—ads that you think couldn't be deconstructed even by Erving Goffman, to show the subordination of women in our culture. Share your examples with the class and see if they agree that these ads place women on a par with men.

6. After everyone in the class has examined several recent advertisements in a variety of magazines, ask individuals or groups to look at some advertisements from magazines from the 1950s. (Most college libraries have old copies of *Time* or *Life*.) Then hold a class debate on the following question:

> RESOLVED: In recent years advertising has made enormous gains in portraying women as strong, independent, intelligent, and equal with men in their potential for professional status.

READINGS

Vance Packard's *The Hidden Persuaders* is one of the most significant books ever written on advertising. Published in 1957, it brought to public awareness the extent to which advertisers were applying findings from psychological studies in their attempts to influence consumer behavior. In a chapter entitled "Marketing Eight Hidden Needs," Packard provided convincing evidence that advertisers were trying to manipulate the middle class by appealing to eight psychological needs: emotional security, reassurance of worth, ego gratification, something for moms to love once their kids are grown, a sense of power, a sense of roots, a sense of immortality, and creative outlets. The excerpt that follows focuses on this last need—creative outlets. Although Packard was not a feminist, his observations reveal many of the subtle expectations and limitations that society placed on the roles of middle-class women during the *I Love Lucy*, and *Leave It to Beaver* era. *The Hidden Persuaders* laid the groundwork for subsequent studies of gender and advertising and remains a standard reference for those who pursue this fascinating subject.

VANCE PACKARD
FROM *THE HIDDEN PERSUADERS*

Selling creative outlets.   The director of psychological research at a Chicago ad   1
agency mentioned casually in a conversation that gardening is a "pregnancy activity."
When questioned about this she responded, as if explaining the most obvious thing in
the world, that gardening gives older women a chance to keep on growing things after
they have passed the child-bearing stage. This explains, she said, why gardening has
particular appeal to older women and to men, who of course can't have babies. She
cited the case of a woman with eleven children who, when she passed through menopause, nearly had a nervous collapse until she discovered gardening, which she took
to for the first time in her life and with obvious and intense delight.

Housewives, consistently report that one of the most pleasurable tasks of the home   2
is making a cake. Psychologists were put to work exploring this phenomenon for merchandising clues. James Vicary made a study of cake symbolism and came up with
the conclusion that "baking a cake traditionally is acting out the birth of a child" so that
when a woman bakes a cake for her family she is symbolically presenting the family
with a new baby, an idea she likes very much. Mr. Vicary cited the many jokes and old
wives tales about cake making as evidence: the quip that brides whose cakes fall obviously can't produce a baby yet; the married jest about "leaving a cake in the oven";
the myth that a cake is likely to fall if the woman baking it is menstruating. A psychological consulting firm in Chicago also made a study of cake symbolism and found that
"women experience making a cake as making a gift of themselves to their family,"
which suggests much the same thing.

The food mixes—particularly the cake mixes—soon found themselves deeply in-   3
volved in this problem of feminine creativity and encountered much more resistance
than the makers, being logical people, ever dreamed possible. The makers found themselves trying to cope with negative and guilt feelings on the part of women who felt that
use of ready mixes was a sign of poor housekeeping and threatened to deprive them
of a traditional source of praise.

In the early days the cake-mix packages instructed, "Do not add milk, just add   4
water." Still many wives insisted on adding milk as their creative touch, overloaded the
cakes or muffins with calcium, and often the cakes or muffins fell, and the wives would
blame the cake mix. Or the package would say, "Do not add eggs." Typically the milk
and eggs had already been added by the manufacturer in dried form. But wives who
were interviewed in depth studies would exclaim: "What kind of cake is it if you just need
to add tap water!" Several different psychological firms wrestled with this problem and
came up with essentially the same answer. The mix makers should always leave the
housewife something to do. Thus Dr. Dichter counseled General Mills that it should start
telling the housewife that she and Bisquick *together* could do the job and not Bisquick
alone. Swansdown White Cake Mix began telling wives in large type: "You Add Fresh
Eggs . . . " Some mixes have the wife add both fresh eggs and fresh milk.

Marketers are finding many areas where they can improve sales by urging the   5
prospective customer to add his creative touch. A West Coast firm selling to home
builders found that although its architects and designers could map houses to the last
detail it was wise to leave some places where builders could add their own personal
touch. And Dr. Dichter in his counseling to pharmaceutical houses advised them that
in merchandising ready-mixed medical compounds they would be wise to leave the

doctors ways they could add personal touches so that each doctor could feel the compound was "his own."

Thinking Critically About *The Hidden Persuaders*

1. Packard's explanation of how Bisquick advertisers used psychological research to make their ads more effective suggests both the complexity and the sophistication of the "science" of advertising. Bring to class examples of contemporary advertisements that use psychological motivations in subtle ways. Share your examples with classmates and discuss the strategies employed in the ads.
2. Very few advertisements for stereo equipment are found in women's magazines, although women now constitute a large segment of stereo buyers. Why don't the ads for stereo equipment found in men's magazines, such as *Playboy* and *Esquire,* appeal to women? How might you design a stereo advertisement with a strong appeal to women?

Many of the points addressed in our earlier discussion about analyzing advertisements are explained in greater detail in an influential book published in 1982, *Advertising as Communication,* by Gillian Dyer, a British professor of communication. The following excerpt from that book focuses on what models' nonverbal behaviors are meant to communicate. Again, although Dyer is attempting merely to present observations rather than to promote a feminist point of view, the findings inevitably hone in on gender distinctions and their societal implications. The citations of Erving Goffman refer to the book we mentioned earlier, *Gender Advertisements* (p. 222).

GILLIAN DYER
ON MANNER AND ACTIVITY

Manner

1   Manner indicates behaviour or emotion at any one time, and is manifest in three main codes of non-verbal communication.

2   1. *Expression.* The face and facial expression are a particular focus of attention in ads. Most expressions are based on socially learned, conventionalized cultural codes, which vary from culture to culture. The expression is meant to underwrite the appeal of a product and arouse our emotions. Normally the expression of the "actor" will be positive, contented, purposeful, delighted, happy, gleeful, etc. There is considerable empirical evidence to suggest that in our society women smile more than men—both in reality and in commercial scenes. Women are often depicted in a childlike state of expectation and pleasure. They frequently seem to be too easily pleased in ads, as Goffman suggests:

> If television commercials are to be believed, most American women
> go into uncontrollable ecstasies at the sight and smell of tables and

cabinets that have been lovingly caressed with long-lasting, satin-finish, lemon-scented, spray-on furniture polish. Or they glow with rapture at the blinding whiteness of their wash—and the green-eyed envy of their neighbours . . . (1979, p. 68).

In cosmetic ads in glossy fashion magazines the model's look might be cool and naughty as she looks the reader in the eye. Other typical expressions in ads may be seductive, alluring, coy, kittenish, inwardlooking, thoughtful, pensive, carefree, out-going, comic, maternal or mature.

2. *Eye contact.* The attention of the actor in an ad is significant whether it be directed towards audience/camera (person to viewer eye contact), at an object (product), towards other people in the ad or to the middle-distance (detached, distant). Goffman discusses the ritual of withdrawing one's gaze, mental drifting and social dissociation under the general description *licensed withdrawal.* He remarks that

> Women more than men . . . are pictured engaged in involvements which remove them psychologically from the social situation at large leaving them unoriented in it and to it, and presumably, therefore, dependent on the protectiveness and good will of others who are (or might come to be) present. (1979, p. 57)

Covering the face or mouth with the hands is one way of hiding an emotion like remorse, fear, shyness or laughter. The aversion of the eyes and lowering of the head can indicate withdrawal from a scene and symbolize dependency and submissiveness. In many advertisements women are shown mentally drifting while in close physical contact with a male as if his mental and physical alertness were enough for both of them. Women may focus their attention on the middle distance, on some object (like the product) or on a piece of the man's clothing. Women are sometimes seen with a dreamy luxuriating look in their eyes. Eyes may be covered up or shaded by hair, hats, hands, dark glasses. Similarly, blinking or winking have great cultural significance. However, an equally important feature in ads is the shielding of everything but the eyes so that the person can observe an event without actually participating in it; some ads show women coyly peeping from behind fans, curtains, objects or products.

3. *Pose.* This can be static or active and sometimes corresponds to expression. Poses can be composed, relaxed, leisurely, passive, leaning, seductive, snuggling. Bodies can be vertical or horizontal. An individual can use another to act as a shield or as an object to lean against, or rest hands or legs on. Pose is also related to social position and status, hence women are often seen in a lower position than the man, for instance sitting at their feet.

4. *Clothes.* These are obviously extremely important carriers of meaning in ads, even when they are not the object being sold. They can range from the formal (regimental or work costume), to the informal (leisure, relaxation, sports wear), and can be smart, sophisticated, glamorous, elegant, trendy or comfortable and casual. They can of course sum up a "look," e.g. the "twenties" look.

Activity

Body gestures, movement and posture can be related to what the actor is doing.

1. *Touch.* The finger brought to the mouth or face can signify thoughtfulness but of a dissociated kind; women and children are often shown with the tips of their fin-

gers in the mouth. Finger to finger touching similarly implies dissociation. Women more than men are pictured touching, or delicately fingering objects, tracing their outline, caressing their surfaces. This ritualistic touching is different from functional touching like grasping or holding. Hand-holding can be a signifi- cant gesture in ads and often is used to allow the man to protect or direct the woman. Self-touching is again something that women do more than men; it con- veys the impression of narcissism, admiring one's own body and displaying it to others, so that everyone can share the admiration of this delicate and precious thing. Sometimes the act of touching is displaced onto things—sun, wind or water on the naked body when sunbathing or swimming. The feel of clothes against the skin—satins, silks, furs—is conveyed as a pleasurable thing.

8

2. *Body movement.* This might be quite functional, i.e. simply related to what the actor is doing—cleaning the kitchen floor, making beds, filling up the car with petrol, playing football, gardening. These movements may be exaggerated, ridiculous or child-like, calling into question the competence of the performer. Bodies, particularly women's, are often not treated seriously, either through what Goffmann calls "ritual subordination" (that is lowering the body in front of others more superior, lying or sitting down, ritually bending the knee or lowering the head) *or* through puckishness and clowning. An example of body movement is where two people are engaged in "mock assault" and this is sometimes seen in advertisements, men usually playing these games on women.

9

3. *Positional communication.* The relationships between actors and actors, actors and objects are extremely significant, and are shown by their position within the frame of a picture. Superiority, inferiority, equality, intimacy and rank can be sig- nified by people's position, size, activity and their relationship to the space around them, the furniture and to the viewer/consumer. Close-up shots, for in- stance, are meant to signify more intimacy and identification than long-shots.

Thinking Critically About "On Manner and Activity"

1. Your instructor will choose an advertisement for analysis. Observe the ad closely, paying attention to expression, eye contact, pose, clothes, touch, body movement, and positional communication. How would a change in any of these features affect the ad's impact and "meaning"?

2. Dyer explains that the manner and activity of males and females in adver- tisements differ significantly. What are some of these differences? Can you find these differences illustrated in the advertisements that you and your classmates have been examining?

3. Do you agree with Dyer and Goffman that these differences are culturally significant, that is, that they reveal (and subtly reinforce) a cultural belief that women are subordinate to men?

Cultural critic Mark Crispin Miller examines a wide range of popular media, including TV, rock music, and advertising. Published in 1989 in a volume entitled *Boxed In: The Culture of TV,* the following essay dissects a TV advertisement from a cultural perspective, examining not only gender implications, but also many of the values that define class distinctions in the United States. As you read Miller's description of the ad, think about what VALS categories (see pp. 216–18) the ad is targeting. Also consider ways in which a thirty-second TV commercial can make explicit the messages that a print ad can only imply. What additional elements do TV advertisers have at their disposal?

MARK CRISPIN MILLER
GETTING DIRTY

We are outside a house, looking in the window, and this is what we see: a young 1
man, apparently nude and half-crazed with anxiety, lunging toward the glass. "Gail!" he screams, as he throws the window open and leans outside, over a flowerbox full of geraniums: "The most important shower of my life, and you switch deodorant soap!" He is, we now see, only half-naked, wearing a towel around his waist; and he shakes a packaged bar of soap—"Shield"—in one accusing hand. Gail, wearing a blue man-tailored shirt, stands outside, below the window, clipping a hedge. She handles this reproach with an ease that suggests years of contempt. "Shield is better," she explains patiently, in a voice somewhat deeper than her husband's. "It's extra strength." (Close-up of the package in the husband's hand, Gail's efficient finger gliding along beneath the legend, THE EXTRA STRENGTH DEODORANT SOAP.) "Yeah," whimpers Mr. Gail, "but my first call on J. J. Siss[sie], the company's *toughest customer,* and now *this!*" Gail nods with broad mock-sympathy, and stands firm: "Shield fights odor better, so you'll feel *cleaner,*" she assures her husband, who darts away with a jerk of panic, as Gail rolls her eyes heavenward and gently shakes her head, as if to say, "What a half-wit!"

Cut to our hero, as he takes his important shower. No longer frantic, he now grins 2
down at himself, apparently delighted to be caked with Shield, which, in its detergent state, has the consistency of wet cement. He then goes out of focus, as if glimpsed through a shower door. "Clinical tests prove," proclaims an eager baritone, "Shield fights odor better than the *leading* deodorant soap!" A bar of Shield (green) and a bar of that other soap (yellow) zip up the screen with a festive toot, forming a sort of graph which demonstrates that Shield does, indeed, "fight odor better, so you'll feel *cleaner!*"

This particular contest having been settled, we return to the major one, which has 3
yet to be resolved. Our hero reappears, almost transformed: calmed down, dressed up, his voice at least an octave lower. "I *do* feel cleaner!" he announces cheerily, leaning into the doorway of a room where Gail is arranging flowers. She pretends to be ecstatic at this news and he comes toward her, setting himself up for a profound humiliation by putting on a playful air of suave command. Adjusting his tie like a real man of the world, he saunters over to his wife and her flower bowl, where he plucks a dainty purple flower and lifts it to his lapel: "And," he boasts throughout all this, trying to make his voice sound even deeper, "with old J. J.'s business and my brains—" "—you'll . . . *clean up again?*" Gail asks with suggestive irony, subverting his authoritative pose by leaning against him, draping one hand over his shoulder to dangle a big yellow daisy down his chest. Taken aback, he shoots her a distrustful look, and she titters at him.

Finally, the word SHIELD appears in extreme close-up and the camera pulls back, 4
showing two bars of the soap, one packaged and one not, on display amidst an array of steely bubbles. "Shield fights odor better, so you'll feel *cleaner!*" the baritone reminds

us, and then our hero's face appears once more, in a little square over the unpackaged bar of soap: "I feel *cleaner* than *ever before!*" he insists, sounding faintly unconvinced.

5   Is all this as stupid as it seems at first? Or is there, just beneath the surface of this moronic narrative, some noteworthy design, intended to appeal to (and to worsen) some of the anxieties of modern life? A serious look at this particular trifle might lead us to some strange discoveries.

6   We are struck, first of all, by the commercial's pseudofeminism, an advertising ploy with a long history, and one ubiquitous on television nowadays. Although the whole subject deserves more extended treatment, this commercial offers us an especially rich example of the strategy. Typically, it woos its female viewers—i.e., those who choose the soap in most households—with a fantasy of dominance; and it does so by inverting the actualities of woman's lot through a number of imperceptible details. For instance, in this marriage it is the wife, and not the husband, who gets to keep her name; and Gail's name, moreover, is a potent one, because of its brevity and its homonymic connotation. (If this housewife were more delicately named, called "Lillian" or "Cecilia," it would lessen her illusory strength.) She is also equipped in more noticeable ways: she's the one who wears the button-down shirt in this family, she's the one who's competent both outdoors and in the house, and it is she, and only she, who wields the tool.

7   These visual details imply that Gail is quite a powerful housewife, whereas her nameless mate is a figure of embarrassing impotence. This "man," in fact, is actually Gail's *wife:* he is utterly feminized, striking a posture and displaying attributes which men have long deplored in women. In other words, this commercial, which apparently takes the woman's side, is really the expression (and reflection) of misogyny. Gail's husband is dependent and hysterical entirely without that self-possession which we expect from solid, manly types, like Gail. This is partly the result of his demeanor: in the opening scene, his voice sometimes cracks ludicrously, and he otherwise betrays the shrill desperation of a man who can't remember where he left his scrotum. The comic effect of this frenzy, moreover, is subtly enhanced by the mise-en-scène, which puts the man in a conventionally feminine position—in dishabille, looking down from a window. Thus we infer that he is sheltered and housebound, a modern Juliet calling for his/her Romeo; or—more appropriately—the image suggests a scene in some suburban red-light district, presenting this husband as an item on display, like the flowers just below his stomach, available for anyone's enjoyment, at a certain price. Although in one way contradictory, these implications are actually quite congruous, for they both serve to emasculate the husband, so that the wife might take his place, or play his part.

8   Such details, some might argue, need not have been the conscious work of this commercial's makers. The authors, that is, might have worked by instinct rather than design, and so would have been no more aware of their work's psychosocial import than we ourselves: they just wanted to make the guy look like a wimp, merely for the purposes of domestic comedy. While such an argument certainly does apply to many ads, in this case it is unlikely. Advertising agencies do plenty of research, by which we can assume that they don't select their tactics arbitrarily. They take pains to analyze the culture which they help to sicken, and then, with much wit and cynicism, use their insights in devising their small dramas. This commercial is a subtle and meticulous endorsement of castration, meant to play on certain widespread guilts and insecurities; and all we need to do to demonstrate this fact is to subject the two main scenes to the kind of visual analysis which commercials, so brief and broad, tend to resist (understandably). The ad's visual implications are too carefully achieved to have been merely accidental or unconscious.

The crucial object in the opening shot is that flower box with its bright geraniums, which is placed directly in front of the husband's groin. This clever stroke of composition has the immediate effect of equating our hero's manhood with a bunch of flowers. This is an exquisitely perverse suggestion, rather like using a cigar to represent the Eternal Feminine: flowers are frail, sweet, and largely ornamental, hardly an appropriate phallic symbol, but (of course) a venerable symbol of *maidenhood.* The geraniums stand, then, not for the husband's virility, but for its absence.   9

More than a clever instance of inversion, furthermore, these phallic blossoms tell us something odd about this marital relationship. As Gail, clippers in hand, turns from the hedge to calm her agitated man, she appears entirely capable of calming him quite drastically, if she hasn't done so already (which might explain his hairless chest and high-pitched voice). She has the power, that is, to take away whatever slender potency he may possess, and uses the power repeatedly, trimming her husband (we infer) as diligently as she prunes her foliage. And, as she can snip his manhood, so too can she restore it, which is what the second scene implies. Now the flower bowl has replaced the flower box as the visual crux, dominating the bottom center of the frame with a crowd of blooms. As the husband, cleaned and dressed, comes to stand beside his wife, straining to affect a new authority, the flower bowl too appears directly at his lower center; so that Gail, briskly adding flowers to the bouquet, appears to be replenishing his vacant groin with extra stalks. He has a lot to thank her for, it seems: she is his help-mate, confidante, adviser, she keeps his house and grounds in order, and she is clearly the custodian of the family jewels.   10

Of course, her restoration of his potency cannot be complete, or he might shatter her mastery by growing a bit too masterful himself. He could start choosing his own soap, or take her shears away, or—worst of all—walk out for good. Therefore, she punctures his momentary confidence by taunting him with that big limp daisy, countering his lordly gesture with the boutonniere by flaunting that symbol of his floral status. He can put on whatever airs he likes, but she still has his fragile vigor firmly in her hand.   11

Now what, precisely, motivates this sexless battle of the sexes? That is, what really underlies this tense and hateful marriage, making the man so weak, the woman so contemptuously helpful? The script, seemingly nothing more than a series of inanities, contains the answer to these questions, conveying, as it does, a concern with cleanliness that amounts to an obsession: "Shield fights odor better, so you'll feel cleaner!" "I *do* feel cleaner!" "Shield fights odor better, so you'll feel *cleaner!*" "I feel *cleaner* than *ever before!*" Indeed, the commercial emphasizes the feeling of cleanliness even more pointedly than the name of the product, implying, by its very insistence, a feeling of dirtiness, an apprehension of deep filth.   12

And yet there is not a trace of dirt in the vivid world of this commercial. Unlike many ads for other soaps, this one shows no sloppy children, no sweatsoaked workingmen with blackened hands, not even a bleary housewife in need of her morning shower. We never even glimpse the ground in Gail's world, nor is her husband even faintly smudged. In fact, the filth which Shield supposedly "fights" is not physical but psychological besmirchment: Gail's husband feels soiled because of what he has to do for a living, in order to keep Gail in that nice big house, happily supplied with shirts and shears.   13

"My first call on J. J. Siss, the company's *toughest customer,* and now *this!*" The man's anxiety is yet another feminizing trait, for it is generally women, and not men, who are consumed by doubts about the sweetness of their bodies, which must never be   14 offensive to the guys who run the world. (This real anxiety is itself aggravated by commercials.) Gail's husband must play the female to the mighty J. J. Siss, a name whose oxymoronic character implies perversion: "J. J." is a stereotype nickname for the potent boss, while "Sis" is a term of endearment, short for "sister" (and perhaps implying "sissy," too, in this case). Gail's husband must do his boyish best to please the voracious J. J. Siss, just as a prostitute must satisfy a demanding trick, or "tough customer." It is therefore perfectly fitting that this employee refer to the encounter, not as a "meeting" or "appointment," but as a "call"; and his demeaning posture in the window—half dressed and bent over—conveys, we now see, a definitive implication.

15   Gail's job as the "understanding wife" is not to rescue her husband from these sordid obligations, but to help him meet them successfully. She may seem coolly self-sufficient, but she actually depends on her husband's attractiveness, just as a pimp relies on the charm of his whore. And, also like a pimp, she has to keep her girl in line with occasional reminders of who's boss. When her husband starts getting uppity *après la douche,* she jars him from the very self-assurance which she had helped him to discover, piercing that "shield" which was her gift.

16   "And, with old J. J.'s business and my brains—" "—you'll . . . *clean up again?*" He means, of course, that he'll work fiscal wonders with old J. J.'s account, but his fragmentary boast contains a deeper significance, upon which Gail plays with sadistic cleverness. "Old J. J.'s business and my brains" implies a feminine self-description, since it suggests a variation on the old commonplace of "brains vs. brawn": J. J.'s money, in the world of this commercial (as in ours), amounts to brute strength, which the flexible husband intends to complement with his mother wit. Gail's retort broadens this unconscious hint of homosexuality: "—you'll . . . *clean up again?*" Given the monetary nature of her husband's truncated remark, the retort must mean primarily, "You'll make a lot of money." If this were all it meant, however, it would not be a joke, nor would the husband find it so upsetting. Moreover, we have no evidence that Gail's husband ever "cleaned up"—i.e., made a sudden fortune—in the past. Rather, the ad's milieu and *dramatis personae* suggest upward mobility, gradual savings and a yearly raise, rather than one prior killing. What Gail is referring to, in fact, with that "again," is her husband's shower: she implies that what he'll have to do, after his "call" on J. J. Siss, is, quite literally, wash himself off. Like any other tidy hooker, this man will have to clean up after taking on a tough customer, so that he might be ready to take on someone else.

17   These suggestions of pederasty are intended, not as a literal characterization of the husband's job, but as a metaphor for what it takes to get ahead: Gail's husband, like most white-collar workers, must debase himself to make a good impression, toadying to his superiors, offering himself, body and soul, to the corporation. Maybe, therefore, it isn't really Gail who has neutered him; it may be his way of life that has wrought the ugly change. How, then, are women represented here? The commercial does deliberately appeal to women, offering them a sad fantasy of control; but it also, perhaps inadvertently, illuminates the unhappiness which makes that fantasy attractive.

18   The husband's status, it would seem, should make Gail happy, since it makes her physically comfortable, and yet Gail can't help loathing her husband for the degradations which she helps him undergo. For her part of the bargain is, ultimately, no less painful than his. She has to do more than put up with him; she has to prepare him for his world of affairs, and then must help to conceal the shame. Of course, it's all quite hopeless. She clearly despises the man whom she would bolster; and the thing which

she provides to help him "feel cleaner than every before" is precisely what has helped him do the job that's always made him feel so dirty. "A little water clears us of this deed" is her promise, which is false, for she is just as soiled as her doomed husband, however fresh and well-ironed she may look.

Of course, the ad not only illuminates this mess, but helps perpetuate it, by obliquely gratifying the guilts, terrors, and resentments that underlie it and arise from it. The strategy is not meant to be noticed, but works through the apparent comedy, which must therefore be studied carefully, not passively received. Thus, thirty seconds of ingenious advertising, which we can barely stand to watch, tell us something more than we might want to know about the souls of men and women under corporate capitalism.   19

Thinking Critically About "Getting Dirty"

1. Because Miller's essay becomes more complex as it progresses, it may help to look carefully at each of its parts.
   a. In the opening movement of the essay (paragraphs 1–4), Miller describes the advertisement. What happens in the ad?
   b. In the second movement (paragraphs 6–11), Miller analyzes the advertisement's "pseudofeminism." How, according to Miller, is the ad constructed to make the wife superior to her husband? Why does Miller call the ad's feminism "pseudo"? In other words, why does he say that this commercial, "which apparently takes the woman's side, is really the expression (and reflection) of misogyny"?
   c. In the third movement (paragraphs 12–16), Miller claims that the ad is not about actual dirt but about psychological or spiritual dirt. How does he make this argument? (Consider Miller's analysis of the name "J. J. Siss" and of the ad's subtext of male prostitution.)
   d. In the essay's concluding movement (paragraphs 17–19), Miller relates the advertisement to the shame and debasement of being (or being married to) a white-collar worker in a modern corporation. Summarize Miller's argument in this concluding section.
2. In the 7 June 1982 issue of *Advertising Age*, columnist Fred Danzig lampooned Miller's essay, calling it the result of a "mind spasm" and "hallucination" from watching the ad too many times. Danzig claims that such ads as the Shield commercial are just humorous "trifles" and that one shouldn't read so much into them. Do you agree with Danzig?
3. Miller responded that ad makers don't want the general public to delve deeply into ads or to apply to them the techniques of critical analysis. How might it serve the ad makers' interests to dismiss Miller and others like him? How would you defend Miller against Danzig's charges?

The final reading is a student essay written in response to the assignment in this chapter. It contrasts the strategies of two different cigarette ads to make smoking appear socially desirable despite public sentiment to the contrary.

STEPHEN BEAN (student)
HOW CIGARETTE ADVERTISERS ADDRESS THE STIGMA AGAINST SMOKING: A TALE OF TWO ADS

1   Any smoker can tell you there's a social stigma attached to smoking in this country. With smokers being pushed out of restaurants, airports, and many office buildings, how could anyone not feel like a pariah lighting up? While never associated with the churchgoing crowd, smoking is increasingly viewed as lower class or as a symbol of rebellion. Smoking has significantly decreased among adults while increasing among teenagers and young adults in recent years—a testament to its growing status as an affront to middle- and upper-class values. Cigarette advertisers are sharply tuned into this cultural attitude. They must decide whether to overcome the working-class/rebellious image of smoking in their advertisements or use it to their advantage. The answer to this question lies in what type of people they want an ad to target—the young? the rich? the poor?—and in what values, insecurities, and desires they think this group shares. Two contrasting answers to these questions are apparent in recent magazine ads for Benson and Hedges cigarettes and for Richland cigarettes.

2   The ad for Benson and Hedges consists of a main picture and a small insert picture below the main one. The main picture shows five women (perhaps thirty years old) sitting around, talking, and laughing in the living room of a comfortable and urbane home or upscale apartment. The room is filled with natural light and is tastefully decorated with antique lamps and Persian rugs. The women have opened a bottle of wine, and a couple of glasses have been poured. They are dressed casually but fashionably, ranging from slightly hip to slightly conservative. One woman wears a loose, black, sleeveless dress; another wears grungesque boots with a sweater and skirt. One of the women, apparently the hostess, sits on a sofa a bit apart from the others, smiles with pleasure at the conversation and laughter of her friends, and knits. Two of the women are smoking, and three aren't. No smoke is visible coming from the cigarettes. Underneath the main picture is a small insert photograph of the hostess—the one knitting in the main picture—in a different pose. She is now leaning back in pleasure, apparently after the party, and this time she is smoking a cigarette. Underneath the photos reads the slogan "For people who like to smoke."

3   The ad for Richland cigarettes shows a couple in their late twenties sitting in a diner or perhaps a tavern off the freeway. The remains of their lunch—empty burger and fries baskets, a couple of beer bottles—lie on the table. They seem to be talking leisurely, sharing an after-meal smoke. The man is wearing black jeans and a black T-shirt. The woman is wearing a pinkish skirt and tank top. Leaning back with her legs apart she sits in a position that signals sexuality. The slogan reads, "It's all right here." And at the bottom of the ad, "Classic taste. Right price." Outside the window of the diner you can see a freeway sign slightly blurred as if from heated air currents.

4   Whom do these different advertisements target? What about them might people find appealing? Clearly the Benson and Hedges ad is aimed at women, especially upper-middle-class women who wish to appear successful. As the media have noted lately, the social stigma against smoking is strongest among middle- and upper-class adults. My sense of the B&H ad is that it is targeting younger, college-educated women who feel social pressure to quit smoking. To them the ad is saying, "Smoking makes

you no less sophisticated; it only shows that you have a fun side too. Be comfortable doing whatever makes you happy."

What choices did the advertisers make in constructing this scene to create this message? The living room—with its antique lamps and vases, its Persian rugs and hard-cover books, and its wall hanging thrown over what appears to be an old trunk—creates a sense of comfortable, tasteful, upscale living. But figuring out the people in the room is more difficult. Who are these women? What is their story? What brought them together this afternoon? Where did their money come from? Are these professional women with high-paying jobs, or are they the wives of young bankers, attorneys, and stockbrokers? One woman has a strong business look—short hair feathered back, black sleeveless dress—but why is she dressed this way on what is apparently a Saturday afternoon? In contrast, another woman has a more hip, almost grunge look—slightly spiky hair that's long in the back, a loose sweater, a black skirt, and heavy black boots. Only one woman wears a wedding ring. It seems everything about these women resists easy definition or categorization. The most striking image in the ad is the hostess knitting. She looks remarkably domestic, almost motherly, with her knees drawn close, leaning over her knitting and smiling to herself as others laugh out loud. Her presence gives the scene a feeling of safety and old-fashioned values amidst the images of independence. Interestingly, we get a much different image of the hostess in the second insert picture placed just above the B&H logo. This picture shows the hostess leaning back pleasurably on the couch and smoking. The image is undeniably sexual. Her arms are back; she's deeply relaxed; the two top buttons of her blouse are open; her hair is slightly mussed; she smokes languidly, taking full pleasure in the cigarette, basking in the party's afterglow.

The opposing images in the advertisement (knitting/smoking, conservative/hip, wife/career, safe/independent, domestic/sexual) mean that these women can't easily be defined—as smokers or as anything else. For an ad promoting smoking, the cigarettes themselves take a back seat. In the main picture the cigarettes are hardly noticeable; the two women holding cigarettes do so inconspicuously and there is no visible smoke. The ad doesn't say so much that it is good to smoke, but that it is okay to smoke. Smoking will not make you less sophisticated. If anything, it only shows that you have an element of youth and fun. The slogan, "For people who like to smoke," targets nonsmokers as much as it does smokers—not so much to take up smoking but to be more tolerant of those who choose to smoke. The emphasis is on choice, independence, and acceptance of others' choices. The ad attacks the social stigma against smoking; it eases the conscience of "people who like to smoke."

While the B&H ad hopes to remove the stigma attached to smoking, the Richland ad feasts on it. Richland cigarettes aren't for those cultivating the upper-class look. The ad goes for a rebellious, gritty image, for beer drinkers, not wine sippers. While the story of the women in the B&H ad is difficult to figure out, the Richland ad gives us a classic image: a couple on the road who have stopped at a diner or tavern. Here the story is simpler: a man and woman being cool. They are going down the freeway to the big city. I picture a heavy American cruising car parked out front. Everything about the ad has a gritty, blue-collar feel. They sit at a booth with a Formica tabletop; the walls are bare, green-painted wood. The man is dressed in black with a combed-back, James Dean haircut. The woman wears a pink skirt with a tank top; her shoulder-length hair hasn't been fussed over, and she wears a touch of makeup. Empty baskets and bottles cluttering the table indicate they had a classic American meal—hamburgers, fries, and a beer—eaten for pleasure without politically correct worries about calories, polyunsaturated fats, cruelty to animals, or cancer. While the sexual imagery in the B&H ad is subtle, in the Richland ad it is blatant. The man is leaning forward with his elbows on the table; the woman is leaning back with her legs spread and her skirt pushed up slightly. Her eyes are closed. They smoke leisurely, and the woman holds the cigarette a couple of inches from her expecting lips. The slogan, "It's all right here," is centered beneath the woman's skirt. Smoking, like sex, is about pure pleasure—something to be done slowly. Far from avoiding working-class associations with smoking, this ad aims to reinforce them. The cigarettes are clearly visible, and, unlike the cigarettes in the B&H ad, show rings of rising smoke. This ad promotes living for the moment. The more rebellious, the better.

8   So we see, then, two different ways that cigarette companies address the stigma against smoking. The B&H ad tries to eliminate it by targeting middle-class, college-educated women. It appeals to upscale values, associating cigarette smoking with choice, and showing that "people who like to smoke" can also knit (evoking warm, safe images of domestic life) or lean back in postparty pleasure (evoking a somewhat wilder, more sexual image). In contrast, the Richland ad exploits the stigma. It associates smoking with on-the-road freedom, rebellion, sexuality, and enjoyment of the moment. The smoke visibly rising from the cigarettes in the Richland ad and noticeably absent from the Benson and Hedges ad tells the difference.

Thinking Critically About "How Cigarette Advertisers Address the Stigma Against Smoking"

1. Stephen Bean argues that the Benson and Hedges and the Richland ads use very different appeals to encourage their target audiences to smoke. What are the appeals he cites? Do you agree with Stephen's analysis?
2. In Chapter 6, we include an article from *Ms.* entitled "If We've Come Such a Long Way, Why Are We Still Smoking?" (pp. 123–27). In that essay, author Sharon Lerner writes that cigarette companies have been remarkably successful at creating advertisements that appeal to women's psychological longings. Collect a variety of cigarette ads from current magazines and analyze their various appeals. How do the ads vary according to their intended audience? Consider ads targeted at men versus women or at audiences from different VALS segments.
3. What do you see as the strengths and weaknesses of Stephen's essay?

COMPOSING YOUR ESSAY

Generating and Exploring Ideas

Your first task is to find two ads that sell the same general product to different target audiences or that make appeals to noticeably different value systems. Look for ads that are complex enough to invite detailed analysis. Then, analyze the ads carefully, using the strategies suggested in Analyzing an Advertisement (pp. 218–19) and Dyer's ideas from "On Manner and Activity" (pp. 227–29). The sample student essay (pp. 235–37) and Miller's analysis of the television adver-tisement for soap (pp. 230–34) provide examples of the kinds of approaches you can take.

If you get stuck, try freewriting your responses to the following questions: (a) What attracted your attention to this ad? (b) Whom do you think this ad tar-gets? Why? (c) What props and furnishings are in this ad, and what values or meanings are attached to them? (d) What are the characters like, what are they doing, and why are they wearing what they are wearing and posed the way they are posed? (e) Is there anything worth noting about camera angle or photographic effects? (f) How do the words of the ad interplay with the picture? (g) How would the ad be less effective if its key features were changed in some way? (h) Overall, to what fears, values, hopes, or dreams is this ad appealing?

Shaping and Drafting

Your essay should be fairly easy to organize at the big-picture level, but each part will require its own organic organization depending on the main points of your analysis. At the big-picture level, you can generally follow a structure like this:

I. Introduction (hooks readers' interest, gives background on how ads vary their appeals, asks the question your paper will address, and ends with ini-tial mapping in the form of a purpose or thesis statement)
II. General description of the two ads
   A. Description of ad 1
   B. Description of ad 2
III. Analysis of the two ads
   A. Analysis of ad 1
   B. Analysis of ad 2
IV. Conclusion (returns to the big picture for a sense of closure; makes final comments about the significance of your analysis or touches in some way on larger issues raised by the analysis)

We recommend that you write your rough draft rapidly, without worrying about gracefulness or about correctness or even about getting all your ideas said at once. Many people like to begin with the description of the ads and then write the analy-sis before writing the introduction and conclusion. After you have written your draft, put it aside for a while before you begin revising. We recommend that you ask classmates for a peer review of your draft early in the revising process.

Revising

Most experienced writers have to make global changes in their final drafts when they revise, especially when they are doing analytical writing. The act of writing a rough draft generally leads to the discovery of more ideas. You may also realize that many of your original ideas aren't clearly developed or that the draft feels scattered and unorganized.

When you write an analytical paper, therefore, the revision process usually involves several stages. Your first revision may be aimed primarily at expanding and developing your first draft, putting in more ideas, adding supporting arguments, making more references to the ads, and so forth. Later in the revising process you need to make your prose clear for readers, following the conventions of closed-form prose (see Chapters 18 and 19). Peer reviews can be especially useful early in the revising process because they give you a reader's-eye view of your draft. The following guidelines can help you and your classmates conduct successful peer reviews.

g u i d e l i n e s

for Peer Reviewers

Instructions for peer reviews, including use of these guidelines, are provided in Chapter 21, pages 527–28. To write a peer review for a classmate, use your own paper, numbering your responses to correspond to the questions on the guidelines. At the head of your paper place the author's name and your own name as shown.

Author's Name: _____

Peer Reviewer's Name: _____

I. Read the draft at normal reading speed from beginning to end. As you read, do the following:
   A. Place a wavy line in the margin next to any passages that you find confusing, that contain something that doesn't seem to fit, or that otherwise slow down your reading.
   B. Place a "Good!" in the margin next to any passages where you think the writing is particularly strong or interesting.
II. Read the draft again slowly. Describe for the writer what you currently see in this draft. If you have difficulty answering any of the following questions, explain briefly the source of your difficulty.
   A. Where does the writer describe the two ads? In what way do the ads appeal to different audiences or different value systems? What makes the ads complex enough to justify an analysis?
   B. Where does the writer analyze each ad? Which of the following does the writer discuss in his or her analysis?
      1. Setting, props, and furnishings: how they indicate lifestyle and socioeconomic status; appeal to certain values; carry certain cultural associations or meanings; serve as symbols, and so forth
      2. Characters, roles, and actions: the story of the ad; power relationships and status of the characters; gender, age, or ethnic roles followed or

violated; the significance of clothing and accessories, of hair and facial expressions, and of posing, positioning, and gestures

3. Photographic effects: lighting, camera angle, cropping, focus
4. Copy, language, and wording: overt message of the copy; feelings, mood, and values communicated through connotations, double-entendres, and so forth; visual layout of the copy

III. What recommendations do you have for improving this draft?
   A. How might the writer improve the title?
   B. Does the introduction capture your interest, provide needed background, set up the question to be addressed, and provide the big picture through a thesis statement, purpose statement, or blueprint statement (see Chapter 19)? How might the writer improve the introduction?
   C. If you were to add one or more points to the writer's analysis, what would they be?
   D. If you were to add additional details from the ads to bolster the writer's analysis, what would you add?
   E. If you were to select one or more details from the ad that contradict the writer's analysis, what would you select?
   F. What suggestions can you make for improving the analysis of the advertisement?
   G. Where do you disagree with the writer or have doubts?
   H. Can you follow the writer's argument? Do you have any suggestions for making the body of the paper clearer, better organized, or easier to follow? Where, for example, might the writer better apply the principles of clarity from Chapter 19: giving the big picture first, putting points before particulars, using transitions, and following the old/new contract?
   I. Sum up what you see as the chief strengths and problem areas of this draft.
      1. Strengths
      2. Problem areas

IV. Read the draft one more time. Place a check in the margin wherever you notice problems in grammar, spelling, or mechanics (one check per problem).

chapter 11

Analyzing Numerical Data

ABOUT NUMERICAL ANALYSIS

Most people have mixed feelings about numerical and graphic data. On the one hand, people venerate these data for their capacity to express large chunks of reality economically and impartially and respect their unique power to persuade. If an outside consultant were to tell a board of directors that a company was in difficulty because it was out of touch with its customer base, the board might or might not listen, but if the consultant told the board that the company's sales were projected to drop off by 50 percent in the current quarter, the directors would take notice. Statistics offer a grainy, black-and-white snapshot of reality in a world full of funhouse mirrors. On the other hand, people also harbor a deep suspicion of numbers. Everyone has seen hucksters and self-promoters manipulate data for their own ends.

Our goal in this chapter grows out of this ambivalence and is basically twofold. We want (1) to make you more respectful of the unique power of numerical data to represent reality broadly and objectively, and (2) to nurture in you a healthy skepticism about conclusions drawn from numbers.

Let's begin by examining how variations in the presentation of data can affect perceptions. Consider the following three stories and accompanying graphics that appeared in two daily newspapers in the same city on the same day, February 4, 1995.

MINIMUM WAGE CALLED DEFINING ISSUE

1   WASHINGTON—President Clinton invited skeptical Republicans on Friday to join him in raising the minimum wage. Congressional Democrats seized the issue as a way to portray GOP opponents as indifferent to struggling working people.

2   At a Rose Garden ceremony, Clinton proposed raising the minimum wage by 90 cents an hour over two years, from $4.25 to $5.15.

3   "This has always been a bipartisan issue," he said, noting that the last increase was enacted in 1990 by a Republican president—George Bush—and lawmakers of both parties in a Democratic-controlled Congress.

Labor Secretary Robert Reich said a majority of Republicans—including House 4
Speaker Newt Gingrich, R-Ga., and Senate Majority Leader Bob Dole of Kansas—voted
for the increase the last time.

"If you did it before, why wouldn't you do it now?" Reich asked. 5

But, in a sign of the difficulty the proposal will face, not one GOP legislator attended 6
the ceremony.

House Majority Leader Dick Armey, R-Texas, previously has vowed to fight the in- 7
crease with "every fiber of my being."

Gingrich promised Clinton "the courtesy of having some serious hearings" but said 8
he was "personally very skeptical of it." He said he thought it would "kill jobs, particularly . . . for minority teenagers" and could widen the wage gap between the United
States and Mexico.

He said Republicans would explore alternatives for helping low-wage workers, such 9
as enterprise zones offering corporations zero capital gains taxes in exchange for locating factories in poor inner-city and rural areas.

In the first hour of House floor action Friday, Democrats applauded and cheered 10
one another as they delivered a series of coordinated one-minute speeches supporting
Clinton and attacking Republicans.

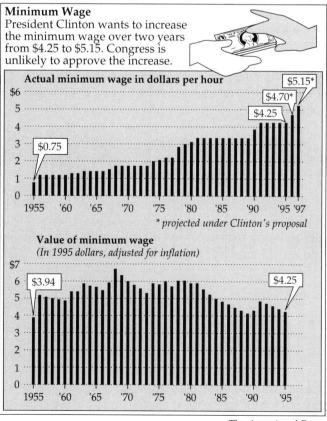

The Associated Press

11   "Democrats finally have a defining issue," said Rep. Bill Richardson, D-N.M.

12   They contrasted Republican opposition to the wage increase with the party's plans to trim welfare rolls and cut capital-gains taxes for stock and bond investors.

13   "The same Republican Party which reveres family values refuses a minimum-wage increase to the working mother trying to help her kids," said Rep. Richard Durbin, D-Ill. "The same Republicans who promised welfare reform would rather build orphanages than create a minimum wage so people can lift themselves off of the dole."

14   House Minority Whip David Bonior, D-Mich., seized on Gingrich's comment on the gap between U.S. and Mexican wages.

15   "Does the speaker and the Republican Party really believe we should tie American wages to Mexican wages, that the standard of living of American working families should be driven down to the standard of a living wage in Mexico?" he asked.

16   But Republicans argued a higher minimum wage can actually hurt the people it is intended to help by foreclosing job opportunities.

17   "Raising the minimum wage will only shut the door on those trying to get started," said Sen. Nancy Kassebaum, R-Kan., chairman of the Labor and Human Resources Committee.

18   However, Sen. Edward Kennedy, D-Mass., said Princeton University research on state minimum-wage increases in New Jersey "found no negative impact on employment and . . . some evidence . . . people who were outside the labor market came back because they could make a decent living."

MINIMUM-WAGE RAISE WOULD BUY
EXTRA BAG OF GROCERIES A WEEK

1   NEW YORK—Raising the minimum wage by 90 cents a hour would buy an extra bag of groceries a week or two tickets to the movies for the estimated 4.2 million Americans who toil for the lowest allowable hourly pay.

2   President Clinton's wage-increase proposal, announced Friday, would add 45 cents an hour, or $18 a week, to the take-home pay of these low-wage workers. Government taxes would get the other 45 cents.

3   Clinton proposed boosting the rate $5.15 an hour from $4.25 over two years through two increases.

4   Who would benefit from the proposal? According to industry statistics, mostly white women who work in unskilled, entry-level jobs, such as department store clerks, hotel maids or cooks.

5   A lot of teenagers and minorities work in minimum-wage jobs, but researchers say overall more white women are in low-paying jobs than any other group.

6   The Center on Budget and Policy Priorities estimates that 4.2 million workers paid by the hour in 1993 earned minimum wage or less, representing 6.6 percent of all hourly workers.

7   The center estimates that 70 percent of minimum-wage earners are white and more than three out of five—or 62 percent—are women.

8   Thirty-one percent of the workers are teenagers, 22 percent are between ages 20 and 24 and 47 percent were 25 or older.

9   Eighteen dollars a week may not seem like a lot. But advocates of the proposal say the extra money would be a boon to low-paid workers.

"To people in small towns earning minimum wage at a factory, it could make a real   10
difference," said Carl Fillichio, a spokesman for the Laborers International Union of
North America.

The increase translates to roughly $72 a month—enough to sign up a child for two   11
months of swimming lessons or buy a new winter coat.

"It would allow people to buy something they might not normally buy," said Mitchell   12
Fromstein, chief executive officer of Manpower Inc., a leading temporary help service.

Fromstein points out that many entry-level or low-wage jobs actually pay more   13
than the minimum wage. Manpower's lowest-paying job—general factory work—pays
$6 an hour or more.

Fromstein said that employers offering minimum wage have a hard time attracting   14
and keeping workers, and raising the wage to $5.15 probably won't make it any easier.

"The market is already ahead of the government in terms of setting a minimum,"   15
he said.

But unions say raising the minimum wage would benefit even those who make   16
more because it raises the floor on wages.

"Everyone benefits from it," said Lenore Miller, president of the Hotel and Restau-   17
rant Employees union.

Lobbyists for retailers, one of the biggest employers of minimum-wage workers,   18
said the proposal will put many low-paying jobs in jeopardy because companies can't
afford to pay the extra 90 cents an hour.

"Retailers just can't absorb the costs or sell that sweater for more," said Steven   19
Pfister, director of political affairs for the National Retail Federation.

About 40 percent of all entry-level jobs are in retailing, the NRF estimates, and many   20
of those positions would be eliminated if stores had to pay people more, he said.

"Many retailers just wouldn't hire that student or that spouse looking for a sec-   21
ondary income," he said.

The Center on Budget and Policy Priorities said studies vary on how many jobs would   22
be lost if the minimum wage goes up, but most indicate modest or negligible job loss.

GOP COOL TO CLINTON CALL TO RAISE MINIMUM PAY

WASHINGTON—Although it faces likely death in the Republican-majority Con-   1
gress, President Clinton on Friday proposed raising the minimum wage by 90 cents
over two years, to $5.15 an hour.

"The only way to grow the middle class and shrink the underclass is to make work   2
pay," Clinton said. "And in terms of real buying power, the minimum wage will be at a
40-year low next year if we do not raise it above $4.25 an hour."

The proposal's likely fate was symbolized when not a single Republican lawmaker,   3
despite weeks of courting by administration officials, joined Clinton at a frosty ceremony in the White House Rose Garden.

Most Republicans, citing many studies and backed by business groups, believe it   4
would result in a net loss of jobs and raise inflation. Democrats cite studies disputing
those conclusions.

In hopes of rebuilding a majority coalition of voters, Clinton is using the minimum-   5
wage proposal as part of a larger political strategy to help define how Democrats differ from Republicans.

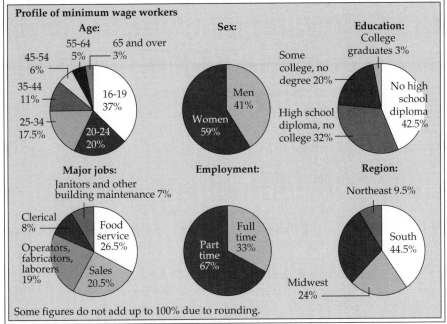

MINIMUM WAGE
Most of America's 2.5 million minimum-wage workers are looking for better wages, because the full-time salary is no longer enough to lift a family out of poverty, as it once was and still is in some countries.

Profile of minimum wage workers

Age:
45-54 6%
55-64 5%
65 and over 3%
35-44 11%
16-19 37%
25-34 17.5%
20-24 20%

Sex:
Men 41%
Women 59%

Education:
College graduates 3%
Some college, no degree 20%
High school diploma, no college 32%
No high school diploma 42.5%

Major jobs:
Janitors and other building maintenance 7%
Clerical 8%
Food service 26.5%
Operators, fabricators, laborers 19%
Sales 20.5%

Employment:
Part time 67%
Full time 33%

Region:
Northeast 9.5%
South 44.5%
Midwest 24%

Some figures do not add up to 100% due to rounding.

Source: Bureau of Labor Statistics   AP/World Wide Photos

6   Clinton made clear that increasing the minimum wage fit his goal of using government to help raise living standards for working people and to give people on welfare an incentive to seek work. It is a theme the president uses increasingly to justify using government as a catalyst.

7   "Our job is to create enough opportunity for people to earn a living, if they'll exercise the responsibility to work," Clinton said.

8   Nearly two-thirds of minimum-wage workers are adults, and more than one-third are their families' sole breadwinners. A 90-cent increase in the minimum wage would raise yearly income by $1,800.

9   An increase in the minimum wage would affect not only the 11 million workers earning $4.25 to $5.14 an hour, but nearly 4 million workers earning up to $5.65 an hour who likely would see their wages bumped up, the administration estimates.

10   Republican leaders gave Clinton's minimum-wage pitch a polite but unenthusiastic response.

11   "I personally am very skeptical of it and I think it will kill jobs, and particularly will kill jobs for minority teenagers," said House Speaker Newt Gingrich, R-Ga. Nevertheless, he emphasized, Congress should not just reject Clinton's proposal out of hand.

12   "Unlike the way the Democrats often treated (former Republican Presidents) Reagan and Bush, I think we owe him the courtesy of having some serious hearings," Gingrich said.

Notice what's at stake in this discussion and how much is riding on the analysis of the data. At the time these articles were written, an estimated eleven million people earned less than the proposed minimum wage of $5.15 per hour and would therefore receive some sort of raise; the proposed increase could also result in higher unemployment, job loss to Mexico, and consumer price hikes. Note how differently each story presents these possibilities.

EXPLORING NUMERICAL ANALYSIS

1. Review the three news stories about the proposed minimum wage hike. In general terms, how would you characterize the different goals of each story? Hint: Because news stories compress much information into a small space and because reporters know that readers skim articles, reporters often convey their intent through headlines, lead paragraphs, and concluding paragraphs.

2. Do the stories cite different data to make their points? If so, how important are the differences? How do the graphical displays affect the presentations? The first article uses two bar graphs to highlight information relevant to the wage hike, whereas the third article uses pie charts. How do the effects of these two graphics differ? What do you think about when you study the bar graphs? The pie charts? Because these are news stories rather than editorials, the writers try to balance the arguments for and against the minimum wage hike. But no writing can achieve complete neutrality. Which story places the proposed minimum wage hike in the most favorable light? In the most negative light? How so? What additional data would you need to make up your own mind on the minimum wage issue?

    After answering these questions for yourself, discuss them in groups and report your conclusions to the class.

3. Suppose that you wanted to write a short argument (say, a letter to the editor) in support of an increase in the minimum wage and that you could cite information from these three stories. What information would you select for your argument and why? Suppose that you wanted to argue against the minimum wage. What information from these articles would you use and why?

WRITING PROJECT

Write an essay that provides your thoughtful answer to either of the following questions:

1. Have women made substantial progress toward job equality since the early 1970s?

2. To what extent did African Americans make progress toward job equality between 1983 and 1993?

Base your essay on the statistical data from Table 11.1 (on pp. 248–51), about employment of women in 1972, 1983, and 1993 and employment of African Americans in 1983 and 1993. Assume that your audience does not have access to this table. To give your reader a visual picture of your data, create figures or abbreviated tables to supplement your analysis. Your paper must include at least one bar graph and one line graph; it may also include a pie chart or a simplified table. Label your graphics as Figure 1, Figure 2, and so on; label tables as Table 1, Table 2, and so on. Insert your visuals at appropriate places in your analysis and refer to them explicitly in your text.

The economic data contained in Table 11.1 can be used to support both optimistic and pessimistic views of the progress made by women and African Americans toward job equality. In Chapter 5 you saw how the writer of a description can shape a reader's response through selection or omission of details, word choice, sentence structure, and other rhetorical strategies. Similarly, you can use this table to create either a rosy or a gloomy picture of the economic progress of women or African Americans, depending on how you select and represent the data (for example whether as raw numbers or as percentages), and how you define progress.

To acknowledge the complexity and ambiguity of the data, you need to show how the data can support both rosy and gloomy views, but you should shape your analysis so that your own position is clearly presented. Your thesis could assert that your selected group, on the whole, has made little progress, some progress, or great progress toward job equality. Likewise, you could argue that your selected group has made substantial progress in some areas but not in others.

Unless they are writing scholarly reports in technical fields, writers rarely include in an essay such highly detailed tables as Table 11.1. Rather, writers extract relevant data from such tables to construct rhetorically effective visuals: pie charts, line graphs, bar graphs, or simplified tables. By saying that a visual is *rhetorically effective*, we mean that it is constructed to support or illustrate one or more of the writer's points. This assignment asks you to recast the tabular data to make it more rhetorically effective.

UNDERSTANDING NUMERICAL ANALYSIS

What Do We Mean by "Data"?

Before we discuss more specifically the basic tools of data analysis and how to get data to "talk," we need to explain what we mean by data and where they fit into the realm of understanding. *Data* are representations, in the form of numbers, words, or graphics, of facts or events in the real world. For the purposes of this chapter, we focus on data in their numeric and graphical forms. In its raw form, each piece of data represents one fact or event. For example, each piece of raw data used to calculate the Consumer Price Index (CPI) represents the current price of

TABLE 11.1 Employed Persons, by Sex, Race, and Selected Occupations: 1972, 1983, and 1993 (Civilians 16 years old and older)

| | 1972 | | |
| | | Percent of Total | |
Occupation	Total Employed (1,000)	Female	African American and Other
Professional, technical, and kindred workers	**11,538**	**39.3**	—
Accountants	720	21.7	
Engineers	1,111	0.8	
Civil	156	0.6	
Electrical and electronic	289	0.7	
Industrial	171	2.4	
Mechanical	192	—	
Lawyers and judges	322	3.8	
Librarians, archivists, and curators	158	81.6	
Life and physical scientists	232	10.0	
Physicians, dentists, and related practitioners	630	9.3	
Dentists	108	1.9	
Pharmacists	127	12.7	
Physicians, medical and osteopathic	332	10.1	
Registered nurses	807	97.6	
Therapists	117	59.1	
Health technologists and technicians	319	69.5	
Teachers, college and university	464	28.0	
Teachers, other	2,852	70.0	
Elementary	1,256	85.1	
Pre-kindergarten and kindergarten	186	96.8	
Secondary	1,118	49.6	
Engineering and science technicians	835	9.1	
Drafters	288	6.3	
Electrical and electronic engineering technicians	166	5.5	
Managers and administrators, except farm	**8,081**	**17.6**	
Health administrators	119	46.6	
School administrators	384	26.0	
Sales workers	**5,383**	**41.6**	
Insurance agents, brokers, and underwriters	443	11.6	
Real estate agents and brokers	352	36.7	
Sales clerks, retail trade	2,359	68.9	

1983			1993		
	Percent of Total			Percent of Total	
Total Employed (1,000)	Female	African American and Other	Total Employed (1,000)	Female	African American and Other
23,592	**40.9**	**5.6**	**32,280**	**47.8**	**6.6**
1,105	38.7	5.5	1,387	49.2	7.0
1,572	5.8	2.7	1,716	8.6	3.7
211	4.0	1.9	221	9.4	4.7
450	6.1	3.4	533	7.6	4.5
210	11.0	3.3	201	16.4	3.4
259	2.8	3.2	296	5.2	4.4
651	15.8	2.7	815	22.8	2.8
213	84.4	7.8	223	83.5	6.2
357	20.5	2.6	531	30.1	3.6
735	13.3	2.7	909	20.5	3.0
126	6.7	2.4	152	10.5	1.9
158	26.7	3.8	187	38.1	6.1
519	15.8	3.2	605	21.8	3.7
1,372	95.8	6.7	1,859	94.4	8.4
247	76.3	7.6	416	74.9	6.9
1,111	84.3	12.7	1,522	81.0	12.4
606	36.3	4.4	772	42.5	4.8
3,365	70.9	9.1	4,397	75.1	8.6
1,350	83.3	11.1	1,688	85.9	9.3
299	98.2	11.8	501	97.7	11.7
1,209	51.8	7.2	1,237	57.5	6.9
822	18.4	6.1	870	17.8	7.4
273	17.5	5.5	244	18.1	6.9
260	12.5	8.2	297	15.5	7.4
10,772	**32.4**	**4.7**	**15,376**	**42.0**	**6.2**
219	57.0	5.0	450	70.5	6.5
415	41.4	11.3	635	59.9	13.0
11,818	**47.5**	**4.7**	**14,245**	**48.1**	**6.7**
551	25.1	3.8	583	33.3	5.1
570	48.9	1.3	710	51.4	2.5
2,009	84.4	10.1	2,581	78.4	13.2

continued

TABLE 11.1 Employed Persons, by Sex, Race, and Selected Occupations: 1972, 1983, and 1993 (Civilians 16 years old and older) *continued*

	1972		
		Percent of Total	
Occupation	Total Employed (1,000)	Female	African American and Other
Clerical and kindred workers	**14,329**	**75.6**	
Bank tellers	290	87.5	
Billing clerks	149	84.6	
Bookkeepers	1,592	87.9	
Cashiers	998	86.6	
Clerical supervisors, not elsewhere classified	200	57.8	
File clerks	274	84.9	
Insurance adjusters, examiners, and investigators	109	34.3	
Mail carriers, post office	271	6.7	
Postal clerks	282	26.7	
Receptionists	439	97.0	
Secretaries	2,964	99.1	
Telephone operators	394	96.7	
Typists	1,025	96.1	
Craft and kindred workers	**10,867**	**3.6**	
Carpenters	1,052	0.5	
Other construction craftworkers	2,261	0.6	
Mechanics, automobile	1,040	0.5	
Transport equipment operatives	**3,223**	**4.2**	
Truck drivers	1,449	0.6	
Service workers	**9,584**	**57.0**	
Food service workers	3,286	69.8	
Nurses aides, orderlies, practical nurses	1,513	87.0	
Childcare workers	358	95.8	
Firefighters, police	1,150	5.7	
Domestic cleaners and servants	715	97.2	
Total	**82,153**	**38.0**	—

Source: U.S. Bureau of Labor Statistics

	1983			1993	
	Percent of Total			Percent of Total	
Total Employed (1,000)	Female	African American and Other	Total Employed (1,000)	Female	African American and Other
31,265	**64.6**	**7.6**	**36,814**	**63.8**	**9.3**
480	91.0	7.5	446	88.4	6.9
146	88.4	6.2	160	88.5	8.4
2,009	84.4	10.1	2,581	78.4	13.2
676	53.4	9.3	778	58.4	11.9
887	83.5	16.7	288	79.6	15.0
199	65.0	11.5	372	71.5	12.1
259	17.1	12.5	333	28.4	12.6
248	36.7	26.2	297	44.8	26.8
602	96.8	7.5	899	97.2	8.6
3,891	99.0	5.8	3,586	98.9	7.7
244	90.4	17.0	197	86.9	21.0
906	95.6	13.8	494	94.3	18.8
12,328	**8.1**	**6.8**	**13,326**	**8.6**	**7.4**
1,160	1.4	5.0	1,276	0.9	4.5
4,289	1.8	6.6	5,004	1.9	6.5
800	0.5	7.8	854	0.6	6.4
4,201	**7.8**	**13.0**	**5,004**	**9.3**	**14.0**
2,195	3.1	12.3	2,786	4.5	12.3
13,857	**60.1**	**16.6**	**16,522**	**59.5**	**17.3**
4,860	63.3	10.5	5,691	58.4	12.8
1,269	88.7	27.3	1,719	87.9	30.7
408	96.9	7.9	345	97.2	9.0
1,672	12.8	13.6	2,152	17.2	17.4
512	95.8	42.4	534	94.0	21.6
100,834	**43.0**	**9.3**	**119,306**	**45.8**	**10.2**

one of several hundred types of consumer goods based on a sampling from a variety of stores.

Data are rarely used in raw form. The power of data derives from your ability to compress and combine them, to express a profusion of raw data as a single datum. As Figure 11.1 shows, raw data undergo several transformations before they emerge as a single number, such as the CPI.

The Consumer Price Index is a single number that allows us to compare over time the cost of buying the basic goods that Americans routinely consume. The starting point for the index is 100, which currently signifies the CPI for the base period of 1982–1984. A CPI of 150 means that basic living expenses—food, transportation, housing, medical care, and so on—cost one-and-a-half times more than they did in the 1982–1984 base period.

The value of a figure such as the CPI is that it functions as a gauge by which to measure large-scale economic change. Workers in many industries use the CPI to determine whether their wages are keeping up with increases in the cost of living. For instance, the CPI has increased by 20 percent since the last contract, but wages have increased by only 10 percent during the same period, workers will use these data to negotiate salary increases in their next contract to make up that gap.

The representative nature of data allows a writer to deal with facts and events economically. By comparing the CPI at two points in time, as we just did, we conveyed a great deal in a few words. Figure 11.2 uses fictional data to plot CPI against wages for a single occupational category. This graph presents data even more economically. If we wanted to see the implications of our comparison for workers in a particular field, we could create a graph with two lines, one tracing the growth of the CPI over the past several years, the other tracing the growth of wages in the particular field. At a glance the reader would know a great deal about how these workers had been doing for an extended period of time.

FIGURE 11.1   Types of Data

Raw Data	Bread X	Detergent Y
Store A	$1.04	$1.89
Store B	1.29	1.75
Store C	1.43	1.59

Intermediate Data	Bread X	Detergent Y
Average price,		
Stores A–Z	$1.25	$1.74

Cumulative Data

Combined average current price of all sampled products.

Comparative Data

Current average combined price of all sampled products measured against average combined price of similarly sampled products in months or years past.

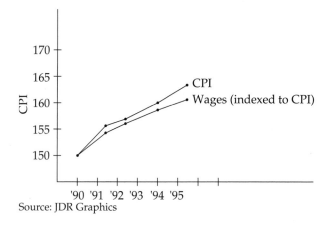

FIGURE 11.2 A Graph Comparing the Consumer Price Index and Growth in Wages for a Single Occupational Category

Source: JDR Graphics

This economy of expression also poses some real dangers. Because it reveals so much with so few words or lines, data can be used to misrepresent—intentionally or unintentionally—a large number of facts or events at a single stroke. This power accounts for public mistrust of numerical data and those who use them, embodied in popular sayings such as, "Figures don't lie, but liars do figure" and "There are three kinds of lies: lies, damned lies, and statistics."

Those who gather, use, and analyze data regularly have their own language for expressing degrees of data manipulation. *Teasing* and *tweaking* data are usually legitimate attempts to portray data in a better light; *massaging* data may involve a bit of subterfuge, but is still within acceptable limits; when the line is crossed and manipulation turns into outright, conscious misrepresentation, however, people say the data have been *cooked*—an unsavory fate for data and people alike. The existence of a well-developed language for describing degrees of manipulation underscores the prevalence of such practices. If you are to use data responsibly and protect yourself from others' abuses of them, it's important to understand how to analyze them.

Basic Tools of Data Analysis

In this section, we discuss some of the most common tools for data analysis and offer advice on when to use them and how to read them. We consider the most basic forms of graphic representations—tables, line graphs, bar graphs, and pie charts—and in the process introduce several basic statistical concepts such as average, correlation, parameters, and independent and dependent variables.

Tables

One of the simplest means of making data visible to your audience is a table. Halfway between a picture and a list, a table presents numerical data in columns (vertical groupings) and rows (horizontal groupings), allowing the viewer to see relationships relatively quickly.

Figure 11.3 depicts a table that is intended to help people perceive how much progress a large southwestern university (SSU) has made toward diversifying its faculty during a given decade. It offers snapshots of the faculty's ethnic composition in 1984 and again in 1994, followed by a summary of the changes that took place in between.

You read tables in two directions: from the top down and from left to right. The title of the table is usually at the top. In this case the title, "Southwest State University: A Historical Review of Minority Students, Faculty, and Staff," indicates the most general content of the table—the change over time of the ethnic makeup of the university community. Directly below, the subtitle, "Full-time Faculty by Tenure Status: Fall 1984 and Fall 1994," reveals the subject of the table—SSU faculty—and the principle means used to organize the table's contents—tenure status and time.

Continuing down, you see the first row of categories, which list the major ethnic groups on SSU's faculty. Now, move to the top of the far left column, labeled "Tenure Status." There are three variations of tenure status: tenured; on track (to be tenured), which comprises faculty, typically in their first six years of employment, who have not yet come up for tenure but will be eligible in the future; and not on track, which comprises adjunct faculty who were hired with no expectation of a long-term contractual commitment from the university.

In the far left of the column immediately below "Tenure Status" the data are broken down into three groups: "1984 Total," "1994 Total," and "10-Year % Change." Reading across each row, you see a series of numbers telling you the number of people in each category and the percentage of the whole that that number represents. The whole is the number in the "Total" column on the right. For example, in 1984 there were 6 tenured Native American faculty members, representing 0.6 percent of the 937 tenured faculty in the university.

When you read a table, avoid the temptation to plunge into all the numbers. After you've read the title and headings to make basic sense of what the table is telling you, try randomly selecting several numbers in the table and saying aloud what those numbers "mean" to be sure you understand what the table is really about.

FOR WRITING AND DISCUSSION

Pretend for a moment that you are a college administrator defending the effectiveness of SSU's diversity hiring program. Which pieces of data would you point toward as the most persuasive evidence of the university's good-faith effort to diversify its faculty? Now put yourself in the position of a member of the Minority Student Caucus who is unhappy with the university's progress on diversifying its faculty. Which pieces of data in the table would you focus on?

Line Graphs

At first glance, line graphs seem significantly simpler to read than tables. You can sometimes see the significance of a line graph at a glance. A line graph con-

Southwest State University: A Historical Review of Minority Students, Faculty, and Staff

Full-Time Faculty by Tenure Status, Fall 1984 and Fall 1994

Tenure Status	Native Amer.		Asian Amer.		African Amer.		Hispanic		White		Total		Minority	
	No.	%	No.	%	No.	%	No.	%	No.	%	No.	%	No.	%
1984 Total	9	0.6	64	4.2	21	1.4	44	2.9	1,371	90.9	1,509	100.0	138	9.1
Tenured	6	0.6	30	3.2	10	1.1	24	2.6	867	92.5	937	100.0	70	7.5
On track	2	0.7	15	5.5	5	1.8	13	4.7	240	87.3	275	100.0	35	12.7
Not on track	1	0.3	19	6.4	6	2.0	7	2.4	264	88.9	297	100.0	33	11.1
1994 Total	15	0.8	137	7.5	37	2.0	102	5.6	1,533	84.0	1,824	100.0	291	16.0
Tenured	6	0.5	54	4.9	15	1.4	49	4.5	973	88.7	1,097	100.0	124	11.3
On track	8	2.5	32	9.9	11	3.4	39	12.1	232	72.0	322	100.0	90	28.0
Not on track	1	0.2	51	12.6	11	2.7	14	3.5	328	81.0	405	100.0	77	19.0
10-Year % Change	6	66.7	73	114.1	16	76.2	58	131.8	162	11.8	315	20.9	153	110.9
Tenured	0	0.0	24	80.0	5	50.0	25	104.2	106	12.2	160	17.1	54	77.1
On track	6	300.0	17	113.3	6	120.0	26	200.0	-8	-3.3	47	17.1	55	157.1
Not on track	0	0.0	32	168.4	5	83.3	7	100.0	64	24.2	108	36.4	44	133.3

Source: SSU Office of Institutional Analysis

FIGURE 11.3   A Table Showing Relationships Among Numerical Data

verts numerical data into a series of points on an imaginary grid formed by horizontal and vertical axes and then connects those points. The resulting line gives a picture of the relationship between whatever is represented on the horizontal (x) axis and whatever is represented on the vertical (y) axis. Although they are extremely economical, graphs can't convey the same richness of information that tables can convey. They are most useful when your focus is on a single relationship.

To see how graphs work, consider Figure 11.4, which contains a graphical representation of a learning curve for assembly-line workers. To determine what this graph is telling you, you must first clarify what is represented on the two axes: In this case the x-axis represents units produced and the y-axis represents the average number of hours of labor required to produce each unit. The first point on the x-axis indicates that it takes a worker 100 hours to produce the first unit; by the time a worker gets to the 20th unit, the number of hours required per unit is down to 63; and by the 140th unit, production time is down to only 48 hours per unit.

So, what does this graph tell you? How would you characterize the nature of the relationship between the x-axis and the y-axis? In this case, x and y are *inversely related,* that is, as x gets greater, y gets smaller. This general description holds for all line graphs that slope downward from left to right.

In simple English, we might translate this relationship to something like the following: "As you produce more units of anything, you learn how to produce

FIGURE 11.4   A Graph Depicting a Dynamic Relationship Between Two Variables

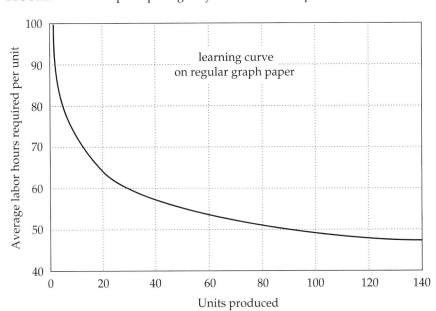

those units more efficiently and spend less time producing each one." But note that the line's slope (its angle of ascent or descent) flattens out as it moves to the right, suggesting that over time the *rate* at which efficiency improves slows down. In the language of data analysis, the flattened slope indicates that changes in y are less and less *sensitive* to changes in x. At some point, presumably, there would be no further increases in efficiency, and the learning curve would be perfectly parallel to the x-axis, meaning that y was no longer sensitive to x.

You can apply the truth of this graph to your own situation. Any time you begin learning a new subject, you spend a great deal of time acquiring relatively small amounts of knowledge. The less efficient you are at acquiring knowledge initially, the steeper the learning curve will be for you. Over time, as you become more familiar with the subject, its terms and basic concepts, you can more quickly build on your base of knowledge and flatten the learning curve.

One important advantage of expressing this relationship graphically is that you can see it dynamically—changing at different rates over time. Expressing that same relationship as a numerical average might lead you to distort it. If, for example, you chose to freeze the line early in its descent and ask, How many units on average have been produced? you would come up with a very low number. Assuming that the purpose of asking the question in the first place is to project the future cost of producing units, an average will never be as helpful as a graph. The graph not only shows the relationship between two variables up to a given point, it also indicates the probable future direction of that relationship.

FOR WRITING AND DISCUSSION

The line graphs in Figure 11.5 (on p. 258) depict several possible ways to express the relationship between age and happiness. Your task is to put in words the concept that is represented visually on each graph and then to compare your translation with those of others in your group. Which representation best reflects your view and why? How might you account for how different members of your group arrive at different views on the relationship between age and happiness?

To get you started, here are our explanations of the first two graphs.

(a) As you get older, your happiness level (as measured in daily chuckle units) increases at a constant rate.

(b) Bad news. Your happiness is at a peak in early childhood; then as you get older your happiness level decreases at a constant rate.

To understand line graphs, it's helpful to know the following key terms.

Independent variable: a variable in a relationship that effects a change in another variable. In layperson's terms, the independent variable is the cause.

Dependent variable: a variable in a relationship that is acted on and changed by another variable. In layperson's terms, the dependent variable is the effect.

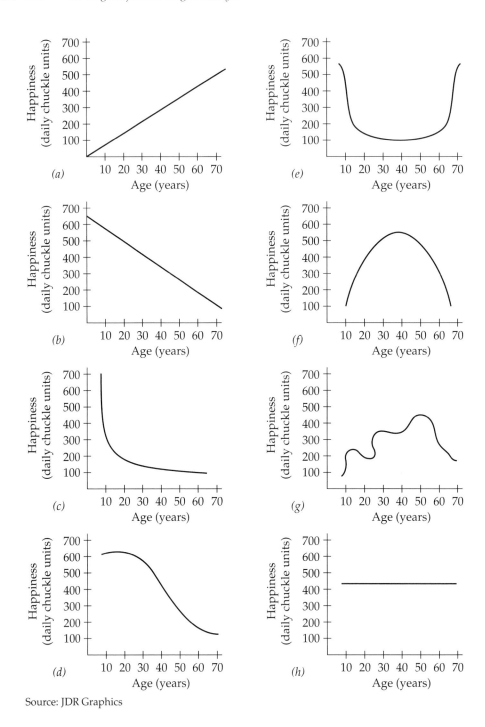

Source: JDR Graphics

FIGURE 11.5   Line Graphs Showing Happiness as a Function of Age

Parameter: an "invisible" variable not depicted on the graph. In layperson's terms, a parameter is an underlying cause.

If you think of the relationship between the x-axis and the y-axis as a causal relationship, x is always the independent variable and y is always the dependent variable. Put another way, variables that effect a change are always plotted on the x-axis and variables that are changed are always plotted on the y-axis. In Figure 11.5, age, because it isn't affected by happiness, is plotted on the x-axis, whereas happiness, because it is affected by age, is depicted on the y-axis. Graphs that depict changes over time always mark the passage of time on the x-axis and whatever is changing over time on the y-axis.

It's important, however, to avoid jumping to the conclusion that because x and y are apparently related, x *causes y.* The two variables may be correlated positively (y grows as x grows; x is smaller as y is smaller) or negatively (y diminishes as x grows; y grows as x diminishes) without one's causing the other. A third, fourth, or fifth variable not shown in the graph may explain both changes. For example, if age and happiness really were positively correlated (a line sloping sharply upward, as in Figure 11.5a), the underlying cause of the happiness could be financial security; that is, as people get older they grow more financially secure, and financial security makes them happy. Financial security in this case would be a parameter of happiness and a correlate of age.

Bar Graphs

Bar graphs use bars of varying length and width, extending either horizontally or vertically, to contrast two or more quantities. As with any graphic presentation, you read bar graphs from the top down. Be sure to note the graph's title. Most bar graphs include *legends,* or explanations of how to read them. Bars are usually shaded or colored, crosshatched, left clear, or filled in with slanting lines to differentiate among the quantities or items being compared. The legend identifies what quantity or item each bar represents.

The bar graph in Figure 11.6 (on p. 260) is from the national newspaper *USA Today,* well-known for its extensive use of graphics as a means of simplifying complex concepts for a broad audience. The caption tells you that the purpose of the graph is to illustrate "How Congress could solve the deficit problem in seven years by holding spending to the projected 3% inflation rate" instead of spending at the rate projected by the Congressional Budget Office (CBO). The legend indicates what each of the bars in the graph represents: the clear bar represents revenues, the dark bar represents the CBO's projected spending, and the lightly colored bar represents spending at the 3 percent inflation rate.

Reading across the x-axis gives you the independent variable, time—in this case a year-by-year comparison of the three quantities from 1995 to 2002. The y-axis gives you the dependent variable, dollars received and expended. As you move from left to right, the revenue bar and the 3 percent growth bar gradually move closer together, until by 2002 they are exactly equal, meaning that revenue and spending are balanced. The black middle bar, the CBO's estimated spending,

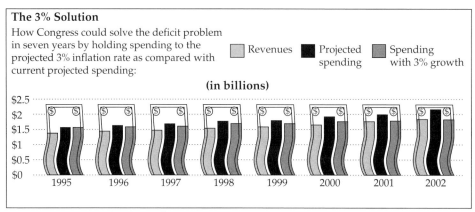

Sources: Congressional Budget Office, USA TODAY research   By Elys A. McLean, USA TODAY

FIGURE 11.6   A Bar Graph That Simplifies a Complex Concept

moves beyond the other two bars until it represents a significant imbalance between revenue and spending.

The power of this visual is that it takes a particularly dodgy set of figures and gives them the certitude of an accomplished fact. National revenue and spending figures are notoriously difficult to project. Both can be markedly affected by a number of economic factors over which people have very limited control. And, the farther out the projections, the more problematic they become. In the world of macroeconomics, eight years is an extraordinarily long projection. But cast into a series of bars, each only slightly different from the previous one, the change seems not only plausible, but almost inevitable. Hey, that 3 percent solution is a great idea!

Pie Charts

Pie charts, as their name suggests, depict different percentages of a total (the pie) in the form of slices. At tax time, pie charts are a favorite way of depicting all the different uses for your tax dollars. If your goal is to show that a particular portion of a whole is disproportionately large—perhaps you're arguing that too many tax dollars are spent on Medicaid or defense—a pie chart can demonstrate your point at a glance. A pie chart can also demonstrate that some part of the whole is undersized relative to other shares. The effectiveness of a pie chart diminishes as you add more slices. In most cases, you begin to confuse readers if you include more than five or six slices.

Figure 11.7 shows a pie chart from *USA Today* that, in combination with a line graph, effectively illustrates the size of three parts relative to one another.

Note how the editors of *USA Today* use a line graph to plot the growth in collections of child-support payments from 1984 to 1993. The impressive upward slope of the line nicely underscores the editors' point that child-support collec-

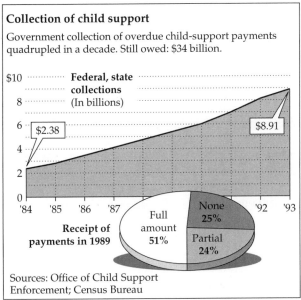

Collection of child support

Government collection of overdue child-support payments quadrupled in a decade. Still owed: $34 billion.

Federal, state collections
(In billions)

$2.38

$8.91

Receipt of payments in 1989

Full amount 51%

None 25%

Partial 24%

Sources: Office of Child Support Enforcement; Census Bureau

By Cliff Vancura, USA TODAY

FIGURE 11.7   Pie Chart Showing Relative Sizes of Three Parts

tions nearly quadrupled during that time period. The line graph does what line graphs do best—it illustrates change over time for a given dependent variable. But when they wanted to depict a static relationship, the editors naturally chose a pie chart to show that a great deal of support is still owed. In 1989, only 51 percent of children granted child support in a divorce settlement received the full amount, and 25 percent received nothing. In lieu of a legend, each slice of the pie is labeled.

Shaping Data for Specific Effects

As a reader and daily consumer of numerical data (and as a user of numerical data on many occasions as a writer), you need to be acutely aware of the ways in which data can sometimes entice you into drawing hasty and erroneous conclusions about the world. You must also take care not to be fooled by people who intentionally manipulate data to lead you to a wrong conclusion. In what follows we review several choices writers make in shaping data for a desired rhetorical effect. The difference between shaping such data legitimately and shaping it intentionally to mislead an audience is a matter of degree, not kind. Everyone inevitably *shapes* data according to his or her goals and perspectives; the question is, How much shaping is legitimate?

Using Data Selectively

Throughout this book, we've remarked on the human tendency to see the world selectively, depending on the viewer's situatedness and purposes in observing or seeking out information. From the mountains of evidence showing salutary and destructive effects of alcohol consumption, teetotalers enthusiastically notice, retain, and quote the latest tidbits about rates of liver destruction among drinkers, along with supporting anecdotes from their personal experience about those who lost everything thanks to Demon Rum. Drinkers, meanwhile, just as enthusiastically clip out the latest research (often from France) extolling the virtues of moderate alcohol consumption and happily supplement these with stories of fabled relatives who drank copiously for eighty or more years with no apparent negative side effects.

Whether conducting secondary research by examining numerical data gathered by others or conducting primary research by gathering the data themselves, people tend to select data that support their points. In selecting data to support your argument (and in analyzing data used by others), you should apply the time-honored criteria for evaluating data: *recency, scope,* and *relevance.*

Recency is an important criterion first, because the subjects that people research (crime rates, economic trends, public opinions, etc.) tend to change over time, and, second, because data-based studies build on earlier studies. If a recent study contradicts an earlier study, then the writers of the later study typically base their rejection of the earlier study on such factors as flawed methodology or technical improvements in data gathering unavailable to earlier researchers.

However, newer isn't *always* better. A later study may ignore earlier studies or may not have been as rigorously conducted. Conscientious writers cite the latest *reliable* studies, whereas manipulative writers cite the latest studies that support their position.

Scope is also a significant measure of a study's value. In most cases, the greater the scope of the research, the more cases, respondents, or experiments it's based on, the more likely that its conclusions are valid. Some small, well-crafted studies are perfectly legitimate also. Bigger isn't *always* better. The care with which a study's subjects are chosen and with which various variables are taken into account is more critical than size. For example, consider a recent controversy about the relationship between estrogen therapy and cancer in women. A study of tens of thousands of women concluded that estrogen therapy substantially increases risk of cancer. In contrast, a much smaller study of several hundred women concluded that there is no significant risk attached to estrogen therapy and that there is even some significant lessening of cancer risk among women who undergo prolonged estrogen therapy.

The scientific community, acknowledging the care with which both studies were conducted, attributed the contrary results to the vagaries of "an emerging science." People on either side of the controversy might be tempted to select the study that supports their view and argue that it is more legitimate either because of its methodological sophistication (the smaller study) or because of its considerably greater scope (the larger study).

Relevance is the third vital criterion for data selection. Charging data with irrelevance is probably the most common critique offered. In arguments about handgun controls, for example, proponents cite studies of low homicide rates in countries with strong gun-control laws, whereas opponents reject the relevance of such studies on the grounds that many cultural differences, and not differences in laws, account for the disparate homicide rates.

Using Graphics for Effect

Anytime you present numerical data pictorially, the potential for enhancing the rhetorical presence of your argument or for manipulating your audience outright, increases markedly. By *presence*, we mean the immediacy and impact of your material. As you have seen, raw numbers by their nature are abstract. But numbers turned into pictures are very immediate. Graphs, charts, and tables help an audience see at a glance what long strings of statistics can only hint at.

You can have markedly different effects on your audience according to how you design and construct a graphic. For example, by coloring one variable prominently and enlarging it slightly, a graphic artist can greatly distort the importance of that variable. Although such depictions may carry warnings that they are not to scale, the visual impact is often more memorable than the warning.

One of the subtlest ways of controlling an audience's perception of a numerical relationship is through the presentation of the grids on the *x*- and *y*-axes of a line graph. Consider the graph in Figure 11.8, which depicts the monthly net profits of an ice cream sandwich retailer. Looking at this graph, you'd think that the net profits of Bite O' Heaven were themselves shooting heavenward. But if you were considering investing in an ice cream sandwich franchise yourself, you would want to consider how the graph was constructed. Note the quantity assigned to each square on the grid. Although the graph does represent the correct quantities, the designer's choice of increments leads to a wildly inflated depiction of success. If the Bite O' Heaven folks had chosen a larger increment for each square on the vertical axis, say, $5,000 instead of $1,000, the company's rise in profitability would appear as in Figure 11.9. You can easily distort or overstate a rate of change on a graph by consciously selecting the quantities assigned to each scale unit on the horizontal or vertical axis.

Another way to create a rhetorical effect with a line graph is to vary the scope of time it covers. Note that the graphs in Figures 11.8 and 11.9 (on p. 264) cover net sales from January through August. What do you think might be typical sales figures for this company from September through December?

FOR WRITING AND DISCUSSION

In small groups, create a line graph for the net profits of the Bite O' Heaven company for a year, based on your best estimates of when people are most apt to buy ice cream sandwiches. Then draw graphs of net profits, quarter by quarter, over a three-year period to represent the following conditions:

1. The Bite O' Heaven company maintains a stable market share with no increase or decrease in the rate of profits over the three years.

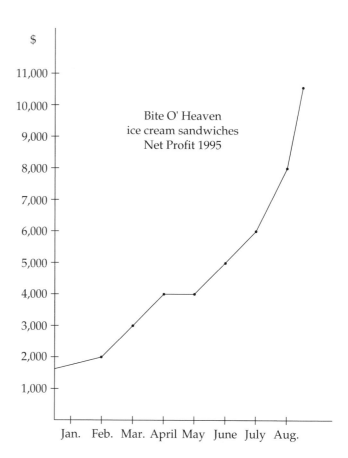

FIGURE 11.8 A Line Graph That Distorts the Data

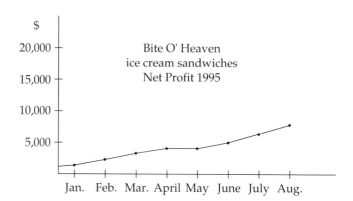

FIGURE 11.9 A Line Graph That More Accurately Depicts Data

2. The Bite O' Heaven company increases its market share, with each year more profitable than the preceding one.
3. The Bite O' Heaven company loses market share, with each year leaner than the previous one.

Using Numbers Strategically

The choice and design of a graphic can markedly affect your audience's perception of your subject. You can also influence your audience through the kinds of numbers you use: raw numbers versus percentages; raw numbers versus adjusted numbers (for example, wages "adjusted for inflation"); or a statistical presentation versus a narrative one. The choice always depends on the audience you are addressing and the purpose you want to achieve.

One of the most frequent choices you have to make as a writer is whether to cite raw numbers or percentages, rates, or some sort of adjusted numbers. In some cases a raw number will be more persuasive than a percentage. If you were to say that the cost of attending a state college would increase at a rate 15 percent greater than the CPI over the next decade, most audiences would be lost—few would know how to translate that number into terms they could understand. But if you said that in the year 2007, the cost of attending a state college for one year would be about $21,000, you would surely grab your audience's attention. So, if you were a financial planner trying to talk a young couple into saving money for their children's college education, you would be more prone to use the raw number than the percentage increase; but if you were a college administrator trying to play down the increasing costs of college to a hostile legislator, you might well use the percentage increase.

FOR WRITING AND DISCUSSION

A recent proposal to build a new ballpark in Seattle, Washington, yielded a wide range of statistical arguments. The following statements are all reasonably faithful to the same facts:

- The ballpark will be funded by raising the sales tax from 8.2 percent to 8.3 percent over a twenty-year period.
- The sales tax increase is one-tenth of one percent.
- This increase represents an average of $7.50 per person per year—about the price of a movie ticket.
- This increase represents $750 per five-person family over the twenty-year period of the tax.
- This is a $250-million tax increase for the residents of the Seattle area.

How would you describe the costs of the proposed ballpark if you opposed the proposal? How would you describe the costs if you supported the proposal?

Similar to the choice between raw numbers and percentages is the choice between raw numbers and adjusted numbers. Again, your audience and purpose will help you make the choice. Let's return to the two bar graphs in the first news article on the minimum wage hike (p. 242). The top graph displays minimum wage increases in raw numbers, whereas the bottom graph displays changes in the minimum wage in numbers adjusted for inflation. Although the first graph shows growth in the minimum wage, the second graph shows that in real dollars the minimum wage has actually *decreased*. The bottom graph would be a powerful tool for those who support a minimum-wage increase; the first graph would be the visual of choice for someone opposing the wage hike.

Finally, you must often decide whether to focus on the numbers themselves or on their human significance. Again, the decision depends on your audience and purpose. Suppose you are trying to convince people to contribute money to help war victims. Your audience might well respond more charitably to a detailed story about one family's travails rather than to a litany of data about the war's casualties. On the other hand, if you were a UN consultant preparing a briefing on the war for the Security Council, you would probably choose to use the data.

FOR WRITING AND DISCUSSION

Consider the rhetorical effect of this author's use of numerical data in the opening of his newsmagazine editorial.

> Of all the grim facts surrounding Oklahoma City [the bombing of a federal building in April of 1995], perhaps the grimmest is the one nobody talks about: against the backdrop of everyday American tragedy, 167 deaths is not many. Even if the darker fears now circulating were realized and this new form of murder began striking once or twice a year, the overall picture of violent death in America would barely change. In a typical year, guns kill 38,000 Americans and about that many die on our roads. These numbers routinely go up or down 2% or 3%— half a dozen Oklahoma bombings—without making the front page.
>
> —Robert Wright, "What Do 167 Deaths Justify?"

In a focused freewrite, try redescribing the Oklahoma City bombing to create support for an argument that the United States needs to take immediate and drastic measures to protect its federal workers from terrorists. Whereas Wright uses statistics to minimize the significance of the bombing, try using a different rhetorical strategy to maximize the bombing's significance. Share your freewrites in class.

READINGS

The first reading is taken from a question–answer column in which science writer Bryant Stamford explains how the labels on low-fat milk can mislead consumers.

BRYANT STAMFORD

UNDERSTAND CALORIES, FAT CONTENT IN FOOD

1 Q: There was a story in the national news on 2 percent low-fat milk. I think I understand the concept about the difference between fat content as weight and as calories. Something about this conversion still escapes me, however. In plain English, can you explain the conflict surrounding low-fat milk?

—J. H., *St. Johns, Mich.*

2 A: Millions of Americans think that 2 percent milk is low in fat. The label even says "low-fat." Sorry, but 2 percent milk actually is very high in fat, with 37.5 percent of its calories (kcals) coming from fat.

3 How can they get away with trying to pass off this fatty product as low-fat? The answer has to do with how the fat content is reported. Food manufacturers who don't want you to know their products are loaded with fat will report the fat content by weight.

4 Here is a simple example: Let's assume a bottle contains 99 grams of water. Water has no calories and passes through the body quickly and easily. We add 1 gram of fat to the water, making 100 total grams. The 1 gram of fat contains calories and stays in the body after being digested. The water, in effect, serves merely as a carrier for the fat.

5 In reporting the fat content of this watery mix, we can report it by weight or by calories. The choice makes a profound difference in our perception of the mix.

6 If we report fat content by weight, we see that, because only 1 gram out of 100 is fat, the mix is only 1 percent fat, or 99 percent fat-free. This is the way a manufacturer would want you to see it, and that's why they would tell you the fat content by weight.

7 But when fat is reported by calories, it is a much different story. This product contains 9 calories, because 1 gram of fat contains 9 calories.

8 Since all 9 calories are in the form of fat, this product is 100 percent fat. The difference between reporting a product as 1 percent fat (by weight) vs. 100 percent fat (by calories) speaks for itself.

9 Now let's apply this concept to milk. Since milk is mostly water, reporting fat by weight will always grossly underestimate the actual fat content. In 2 percent milk, out of 100 grams of total weight, 2 grams will be fat. Thus, it can be reported as 98 percent fat-free.

10 It's an entirely different story when reporting fat content by calories.

11 One cup of 2 percent milk contains 5 grams of fat and 120 calories. Here is the calculation for determining fat content by calories.

12 Five grams of fat times 9 calories equal 45 calories of fat. Of the 120 total calories, 45 are from fat. Forty-five divided by 120 equals .375. Then, .375 times 100 equals 37.5 percent fat.

13 The story is just as bad for whole milk, which is 3.3 percent fat by weight, but 48 percent fat by calories.

14 You can apply this formula to other food as well.

15 Meat, for example, may contain a high proportion of water, and, therefore, reporting fat content by weight grossly underestimates the actual fat content. Your confusion may arise from the fact that there is no "typical" conversion factor, or constant, that can be applied to all food to convert the fat content by weight to fat content by calories.

The reason is that foods vary in water content. The greater the water content, the   16
more diluted will be the fat content when reported by weight.

Thus, you must use the formula for each food to determine the actual fat content   17
by calories.

The bottom line is buyer beware. Unless you are armed with a little information,   18
chances are you will be misled every time.

Thinking Critically About "Understand Calories, Fat Content in Food"

1. In calling 2 percent milk "low fat," do you think the manufacturer is telling the truth, tweaking the data, massaging the data, or cooking the data? Why?
2. Reporting fat content as a percentage of weight or calories is analogous to numerous other statistical dilemmas. What other situations can you think of in which different ways of calculating the numbers will lead to significant differences in results?

In the following essay, mathematician John Paulos offers a number of cautionary notes about the unreliability of social and economic forecasting. Paulos is a professor of mathematics at Temple University in Philadelphia. He has written widely about the importance of "numeracy" to the average U.S. citizen.

JOHN PAULOS
RECESSION FORECAST IF STEPS NOT TAKEN

This first paragraph introduces a topic (political and economic analyses in the media) and an argumentative thesis (media analyses are worthless because they assume that economic and political systems are predictable).

I find reading old newspaper analyses, government press releases, and bygone bits   1
of punditry both sobering and entertaining. They often seem to presuppose that political and economic matters are, with a little thought and perhaps some calculation, more or less predictable. Obviously, such matters are not very predictable, and there are some surprising mathematical reasons why they are not.

These mathematical reasons ensure that much economic and political commen-   2
tary and forecast are fatuous nonsense, no more on target than the farmer marksman with hundreds of chalked bull's-eyes on the wall of his barn, each with a bullet hole in its center. When asked how he could be so accurate, the farmer, who had perhaps read Ionesco, admitted that he first made the shot and then drew the bull's-eye around it.

The analogy in the second paragraph brings humor and substance to Paulos's view that social forecasting is bogus—a view that he states more explicitly in the third paragraph.

In fact, stripped to their essence, many social forecasts may be paraphrased in one   3
of two ways. The first is: "Things will continue roughly as they have been." When pressed, the pooh-bahs and prognosticators admit a further clause: "until something changes." The other way is equivalent, but puts the emphasis on the change: "Things will change." Here again, when pressed, the pooh-bahs and prognosticators admit a further clause, "after an indeterminate period of stability." But THINGS TO STAY SAME UNTIL CHANGE or THINGS TO CHANGE EVENTUALLY are too obviously hollow and unfalsifiable to be suitable for the headline of a news analysis or a columnist's essay. Their emptiness has to be disguised.

4   Consider the typical analysis of the economy. It generally isolates one or two factors (or their absence) as the cause of this or that malady. There is generally more sophistication in football play-by-play broadcasting.

5   The economic cornerstone of Reaganomics, the economist Arthur Laffer's appropriately named Laffer curve, provides a good example. Laffer and others made the obvious point that a 100 percent tax rate would bring in almost no revenue for the government; few of us would have any incentive to work if all our money were being confiscated by the government. At the other extreme, a 0 percent tax rate would clearly bring in no revenue for the government either. Furthermore, if the tax rate were very low, say, 3 percent, doubling it to 6 percent would almost double the government's revenues. If the rate were a little higher, however, around 15 percent, say, doubling it would not have such a pronounced effect; revenues would increase more modestly (see diagram).

Paulos narrows his focus to the reductionist tendencies of economic analysis.

Paulos supports his skepticism about economic predictions by discrediting a popular forecasting tool. The complexity of our economic system, he argues, makes it impossible to determine an optimum tax rate.

Revenue versus Tax Rate

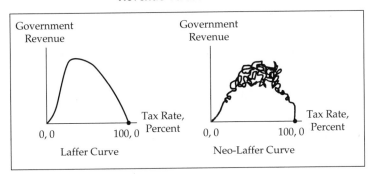

Laffer Curve

Neo-Laffer Curve

6   Likewise, at the other end of the tax rate spectrum. A government whose tax rate was 97 percent would be larcenous, but if it lowered the rate to 94 percent it would likely provide enough incentive for workers to increase their output and thus swell government revenues significantly. However, if the tax rate were lower, say, 85 percent, and the government decreased it to 70 percent, the increase in government revenue would likely not be as dramatic. Revenues increase when high rates are lowered as well as when low rates are raised but, in each case, to a lesser degree as diminishing returns set in.

7   Now it only seems reasonable and a matter of geometric necessity that a tax rate somewhere between 0 and 100 percent should bring in the maximum government revenue. The result of this line of argument is the Laffer curve pictured in the illustration. Many people find the argument convincing and, believing that the economy is on the right side of the hump, argue that a decrease in tax rates would notably raise government revenues.

8   But is what happens in the middle of the curve really as clear as what happens at its extremes? Martin Gardner in a somewhat derisive *Scientific American* article constructed a neo-Laffer curve whose interior is a whirlpool of snarls and convolutions but whose extremes are nevertheless identical to those of the Laffer curve. Gardner's curve has many different points of maximum revenue and which one of them, if any, is

Martin Gardner's dismissive treatment of the Laffer Curve reinforces Paulos's own view of this tool.

achieved depends on an indeterminate number of historical and economic contingencies. These factors and their interaction are too complicated to be determined by variation in any single variable such as the tax rate.

In general, too little notice is taken of the interconnectedness of the variables in question. Interest rates have an impact on unemployment rates, which in turn influence revenues; budget deficits affect trade deficits, which sway interest rates and exchange rates; consumer confidence may rouse the stock market, which alters other indices; natural business cycles of various periods are superimposed on one another; an increase in some quantity or index positively (or negatively) feeds back on another, reinforcing (weakening) it and being in turn reinforced (weakened) by it. These and a myriad of more complicated interactions characterize the economy.

The notion of a nonlinear dynamical system can be used to model such interconnections and, more important for my purposes, helps clarify why we should not expect to predict political or economic developments with any exactitude. Before I define such systems, I want you to picture a more tangible artifact: a pool table. Imagine that approximately twenty to thirty round obstacles are securely fastened to it in haphazard placement (see diagram). Your challenge is to hire the best pool player you can find and ask him to place the ball at a particular spot on the table and take a shot toward one of the round obstacles. After he's done so, ask him to make exactly the same shot from the same spot with another ball. Even if his angle on this second shot is off by the merest fraction of a degree, the trajectories of these two balls will very soon diverge considerably. An infinitesimal difference in the angle of impact will be magnified by successive hits of the obstacles. Soon one of the trajectories will hit an obstacle that the other missed entirely, at which point all similarity between the two trajectories ends.

Billiards—Magnification of Small Differences

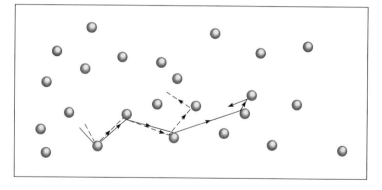

The sensitivity of the billiard balls' paths to minuscule variations in their initial angles is not totally unlike, say, the dependence of one's genetics on which zigzagging sperm cell reaches the egg. This chanciness also brings to mind the disproportionate effect of seemingly inconsequential events: the missed planes, serendipitous meetings, and odd mistakes that shape and reshape our lives. (A job recruiter I know once rejected a well-qualified French applicant because in a discussion of tabloids and pornography, he laughingly mentioned that his mother's picture had once appeared in *Peep*

This section marks a shift in Paulos's analytical argument— from discrediting existing forecasting tools and practices to explaining the nature of the phenomena they attempt to predict. He begins by showing the interconnectedness of economic variables, then introduces the concept of a nonlinear dynamical system to model the interconnections.

To illustrate his definition of a nonlinear dynamical system, Paulos uses a series of analogies. First, the example of two billiard balls illustrates the significance of infinitesimal variations.

He then likens these variations to those in other scientific (sperm motility) and everyday (odd mistakes) phenomena. Finally, he likens variations in all of these phenomena to those that affect the economy.

9

10

11

Hole magazine. She thought it was either true or a poor joke. Later she realized he meant *People* magazine.) The inevitable amplification of tiny differences in detail is just one of the factors suggesting that the economy is almost invulnerable to dependable forecast.

12   Technically, nonlinear dynamical systems are not billiard tables or economic systems, but mathematical spaces on which vector fields are defined. A vector field may be thought of as a *rule f* saying, in effect, that "if an object is currently at a point x, it moves next to point f(x), then to point f(f(x)), and so on." The rule f is nonlinear if, for example, the variables involved are squared or multiplied together and the sequence of the object's positions is its trajectory. A mathematical subterfuge allows us to consider the movement of a fictitious object around a very high dimensional space instead of the movement of many objects around a lower-dimensional space.

To lend credibility to the analogies he has just drawn Paulos shows how their complex variables might be expressed in a mathematical model.

13   For rough expository purposes, we can collapse the important distinction between a mathematical model and a part of reality and think of a system as any collection of parts whose movements and interaction can be described by rules and/or equations, however imprecise. The postal service, the human circulatory system, the local ecology, and the operating system of the computer on which I write are all examples of this loose notion of a system. A nonlinear system is one whose elements—again, I'm writing quite loosely—are not linked in a linear or proportional manner. They are not linked, for example, as they are in a bathroom scale or a thermometer; doubling the magnitude of one part will not double that of another, nor is the output proportional to the input. Linear systems involve equations like Z = 7X + 2Y; nonlinear systems have equations like $Z = 5X^2 + 3XY$.

Here Paulos extends his model to real examples, contrasting the behavior of elements within linear and nonlinear systems.

14   Chaos theory (and, to a lesser extent, the study of nonlinear systems) may be said to have been born in 1960 when the meteorologist Edward Lorenz was playing with a computer model of a simple weather system. Plugging numbers into his model, he derived a set of weather projections. Later, when he ran his program again, he plugged in numbers that had been rounded off to three decimal places instead of six and noticed that the resulting weather projections soon diverged from the original ones and that the two sets of projections soon bore no discernible relation to each other.

In this paragraph, Paulos discusses an overarching chaos theory that attempts to explain (without predicting) the kinds of behaviors that occur within nonlinear dynamical systems.

15   Although Lorenz's nonlinear model was simplistic (it involved only three equations and three variables) and his computer equipment was primitive, he drew the correct inference from this divergence of computer-simulated weathers: It was not a fluke. It was caused by the tiny variations in the system's initial conditions. In fact, the weather, even this simplified model of it, is not susceptible to precise long-range prediction because it, like the billiard table, is sensitive to almost imperceptible changes in the initial conditions. These changes lead to slightly bigger ones a minute later or a foot away, which lead to yet more substantial deviations, the whole process cascading over time into an aperiodic, nonrepetitive unpredictability. Of course, there are certain general constraints that are satisfied (no ice storms in Tanzania, little rain in the desert, rough seasonal temperature gradients, for example), but specific long-range forecasts are virtually worthless.

16   The sensitive dependence of nonlinear systems on their initial conditions has been called the Butterfly Effect, from the idea that a butterfly flapping its wings in China, say, might spell the difference several months later between a hurricane and a balmy day along the eastern U.S. seaboard.

The striking imagery of the Butterfly Effect deepens our understanding of nonlinear systems.

17   Since Lorenz's work, there have been many manifestations of the Butterfly Effect in disciplines ranging from hydrodynamics (turbulence and fluid flow) to physics (nonlinear oscillators), from biology (heart fibrillations and epilepsy) to ecology (population

changes). Furthermore, these nonlinear systems demonstrate a complex unpredictability that seems to arise even when the systems are defined by quite elementary, nonlinear rules and equations. Their trajectories in mathematical space are fractals, astoundingly intricate and self-similar.

Here Paulos introduces a final mathematical concept to describe behaviors in nonlinear systems: the fractal.

A *fractal* is a wispy, tangled curve (or surface, solid, or higher-dimensional object) that contains more, but similar, complexity the closer one looks. The shoreline, to cite a standard example, has a typical jagged shape at whatever scale we draw it—that is, whether we use satellite photos to sketch the whole coast or the detailed observations of someone walking along a stretch of beach. Similarly, the surface of a mountain looks roughly the same whether seen from a height of 200 feet by a giant or up close by an insect. Moreover, as their discoverer Benoit Mandelbrot has stressed, clouds are not circular or elliptical, tree bark is not smooth, lightning does not travel in a straight line, and snowflakes are not hexagons. Rather, these and many other shapes in nature—the surfaces of battery electrodes, the spongy interior of intestines and lung tissue, the diffusion of a liquid through semiporous clays, the variation of commodities prices over time—are near fractals and have the characteristic zigzags, push/pulls, and bump/dents at almost every size scale, greater magnification yielding similar, but ever more complicated, convolutions. 18

In this paragraph, Paulos loops back to his original topic and summarizes the points in his discussion of complex systems that apply to economic forecasting.

This is all very interesting, but what lessons should newspaper readers take away from the discussion? I hope that even a loose, intuitive understanding of the behavior of many interacting variables, the Butterfly Effect, complex nonlinear systems, positive and negative feedback, and so on, should arouse a certain wariness of glib and simplistic diagnoses. Our standard economic statistics are notoriously imprecise and unreliable, and this imprecision and unreliability propagates. The reader should be more mindful of stories where the effect of small differences—say, decreases in a couple of indices—seems to be magnified; of articles about the frenzied selling of stocks feeding self-fulfillingly upon itself; of accounts pointing to single causes or immediate consequences. 19

You should observe that the accuracy of social forecasts and predictions is vastly greater *if* the predictions are short-term rather than long-term; *if* they deal with simple rather than complex phenomena, with pairs of closely associated variables rather than many subtly interacting ones; *if* they're hazy anticipations rather than precise assertions; and *if* they are not colored by the participants' intentions. Note how few political and economic predictions meet the conditions of these "ifs"—those are the ones to take seriously. 20

The blank space between paragraphs signals that Paulos is beginning a summation of his analytical argument. First, he offers an explanation for the media's attachment to linear models: the math is easier.

Lest by these brief suggestions I be accused of ignoring my own misgivings about simplistic brevity (or of offering the paradoxical slogan: No More Slogans), I should mention that there is a body of research, both mathematical and empirical that supports this counsel. Mathematical models of the economy, for example, are only awkwardly cast in a linear framework. The variables in realistic models interact in strongly nonlinear ways that give rise to the phenomena described here. Linear models are used regularly not because they are more accurate but because they are easier to handle mathematically. (Economists and physicists sometimes adopt the same research policy as the proverbial drunkard. Asked why he was looking for his keys under the streetlamp when he lost them up the block, the drunkard replied that the light was better there.) 21

Furthermore, empirical macroeconomic studies by Mosekilde, Larsen, Sterman, Brock, LeBaron, Woodford, and others suggest that chaos can be induced in the labo- 22 ratory. The first three of these researchers, for example, set up a gamelike beer production and distribution system with mock factories, wholesalers, and retailers. They placed plausible constraints on orders, inventory, and time and asked managers, trainees, and people in other roles to play the game realistically and to make reasonable business decisions. They found that these people often interacted in such a way as to produce chaos: aperiodic, unpredictable variations in inventory, huge time lags in fulfilling orders, and extreme sensitivity to small changes in conditions.

23   Of course, it's always dangerous and often idiotic to apply technical results outside their original domain, especially when much mathematical work remains to be done. Nevertheless, I think chaos theory (and much else) counsels that skepticism should guide us when we read about any political, economic, or military policy of any complexity. Much simpler systems governed by transparent and deterministic laws are skittishly unpredictable.

24   Although chaos theory casts doubt on the long-term validity of many social forecasts, it also suggests some constructive, albeit vague, ideas to keep in mind while reading stories on the economy and other social systems. One is that real change in systems often requires a reorganization of their structure. Another is that to effect change in a given system, we must search for points of maximum leverage, points that are often not obvious and are sometimes many steps removed from their intended effects. A third idea is that there is evidence that some chaos is necessary for the stability and resilience of systems.

Paulos cites a study confirming that "rational" behavior can produce unpredictable results.

Paulos adds a standard scientific qualifier: a model developed in one context may not apply in others.

Paulos concludes with lessons to be learned from his analysis: Achieving change in a system often requires radical restructuring, and we must consider variables that seem far removed from the desired change. Moreover, some measure of chaos actually insures a system's resiliency and stability.

Thinking Critically About "Recession Forecast If Steps Not Taken"

1. Restate in your own words Paulos's explanation of the differences between the Laffer curve and the neo-Laffer curve shown in the "Revenue versus Tax Rate" graphs on page 269.
2. Often writers use simple analogies to explain complex subjects. Explain in your own words the point that Paulos makes with his billiard ball analogy.
3. Someone with a strong background in mathematics will be able to read Paulos's article more easily than someone whose eyes glaze over at such equations as $Z = 7X + 2Y$. Identify any parts of this article that you found difficult to understand. Can math experts in your class clarify these passages for you? If you are a math expert, how can you best explain these passages to your classmates?
4. What is the butterfly effect and what is a fractal? How are these concepts related to Paulos's argument?
5. Near the end of his article, Paulos states that "the accuracy of social forecasts and predictions is vastly greater *if*" certain conditions are met ("*if* the predictions are short-term rather than long-term;" and so on). Look through recent newspapers or newsmagazines for articles that attempt to predict the future consequences of some event or proposed event (for example, articles about balancing the budget, changing a tax law, and so forth). To what extent do these articles observe or violate Paulos's conditions? Bring your examples to class to share with your other group members.

COMPOSING YOUR ESSAY

Generating and Exploring Ideas

The first step in writing this essay is to look carefully at Table 11.1 on pages 248–51, making sure that you understand how to read it. Using a calculator, you should be able to convert percentages to raw numbers if you choose. You could say that from 1983 to 1993 the percentage of African American lawyers rose from 2.7 percent to 2.8 percent. Cast this way, the increase seems almost negligible. However, you could cast the same data somewhat more positively by using raw numbers. In 1983 there were approximately 16,500 African American lawyers (612,000 × 2.7 percent), whereas in 1993 there were approximately 21,750 (770,000 × 2.8 percent)—an increase of more than 5,000 in ten years. As you read the table, take notes on positive and negative data, recognizing the different rhetorical effects achieved by using raw numbers versus percentages.

Play the Believing and Doubting Game with the Data

Imagine how you would use these data to make the most positive case possible—arguing, for example, that women have made substantial progress toward job equality. What data would you select? How would you use the data persuasively? When would you use percentages and when would you use raw numbers? What visuals could you develop to put the economic data in the most positive light?

Now do the same thing for the opposite case. How would you argue that women have made only the tiniest progress in the last two decades? Which data would you select? How would you use them persuasively? What kind of visuals could you construct?

Consider the Position You Want to Take

After looking carefully at how the data can be used to support highly rosy or highly gloomy pictures, decide the thesis that you want to support in your analysis. If you choose, you can take a middle position rather than a simple pro or con position. Your goal is to interpret these data for your readers, explaining your own answer to your question and using selected data to support your argument. You also need to show your awareness of the data's complexity and to give voice to possible interpretations different from your own.

Shaping and Drafting

This essay will be clearest for your readers if you follow a closed-form pattern that includes the following:

- An introduction that poses the question your essay will address, engages your readers' interest in that question, presents your thesis, and forecasts a structure for your argument

- A body that develops and supports your thesis, following the structure predicted in the introduction
- A conclusion that returns to the big picture

Creating a Thesis Statement for Your Essay

The main body of your essay will be shaped by the structure of your thesis statement. We recommend that you formulate a detailed behind-the-scenes thesis statement that sums up in one sentence your answer to the question, Have women (or African Americans) made substantial progress toward job equality? Consider beginning your thesis with an "although clause," as recommended in Chapter 3 (pp. 47–48). Typical theses might be as follows:

> Although women have made substantial progress toward job equality in some fields, they lag behind men in most areas of employment.

or

> Although many people believe that the condition of women's employment hasn't changed much in the last two decades, it is surprising how extensively women are now represented in fields formerly dominated by men.

Once you have developed a thesis statement, the body of your essay can follow the structure that your thesis predicts. Typically, you develop your "although" clause first and then devote the last part of your essay to developing the main clause.

Avoiding an Overload of Statistical Data

Readers generally find statistical data rough going. A beginning writer's tendency is to fill sentence after sentence with data from statistical tables, overloading the reader's ability to process all the numbers. You need to be selective in your use of data and to make sure that you use the data to support or illustrate a point that you have already made explicit. Your reader can most easily process essays using statistics if you use a clearly mapped, points-first structure (see Chapter 19, pp. 475–77).

Designing and Referencing Visuals

When you use pie charts, line graphs, or bar graphs to support your analysis, make sure that they can be easily deciphered. Each figure should have a complete title that allows the reader to tell at a glance what it is illustrating. The visual should be referenced in the text. To see how to reference a visual, imagine that you are giving an oral report and have placed your visual on an overhead projector. You would use a pointer to talk your audience through the visual, explaining what it shows and highlighting the most significant details. The body of your paper should do in writing what you imagine yourself doing orally. Here is a typical example of a passage referencing a figure.

The most shocking difference between developed and undeveloped countries is the rate of maternal and infant mortality—that is, the rate at which women die during pregnancy or childbirth or the rate at which infants die within a year of birth. As can be seen in Figure 1, developed countries such as Canada, the United States, or Japan have relatively low rates of maternal and infant mortality. In Canada, for example, only 3 of 10,000 pregnant women die from childbirth, and only 7 of 10,000 infants die during their first year. In contrast, many undeveloped countries have devastatingly high rates of maternal and infant mortality. In Nepal, 830 of 10,000 pregnant women die from pregnancy, and 171 of 10,000 infants die before age one. Expressed as a ratio, a pregnant woman in Nepal has a 1 in 12 chance of dying in childbirth.

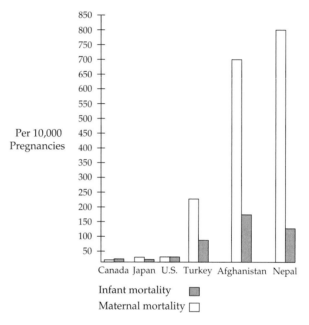

FIGURE 1. Infant and Maternal Mortality Rates in Selected Countries

Revising

Once you've developed a thesis, written a draft, and made rough drawings of your visuals, you are ready to road test your draft on readers to determine what works and what is confusing or undeveloped. Ask outside readers to comment on your draft, using the guidelines for peer reviewers here and following the advice in Chapter 21 for conducting peer reviews. Once you have received their feedback, you're ready to do the major work of revising—converting your draft from something that works for you to something that works for readers. Because your analysis should be written in closed-form style, the revision suggestions in Chapter 19 are especially relevant: give the big picture first and refer to it often; place points before particulars (ensuring that paragraphs open with topic sentences); use frequent transitions; and follow the old/new contract.

g u i d e l i n e s

for Peer Reviewers

Instructions for peer reviews, including use of these guidelines, are provided in Chapter 21, pp. 527–28. To write a peer review for a classmate, use your own paper, numbering your responses to correspond to the questions on the guidelines. At the head of your paper place the author's name and your own name as shown.

Author's Name: _____

Peer Reviewer's Name: _____

I. Read the draft at normal reading speed from beginning to end. As you read, do the following:
   A. Place a wavy line in the margin next to any passages that you find confusing, that contain something that doesn't seem to fit, or that otherwise slow down your reading.
   B. Place a "Good!" in the margin next to any passages where you think the writing is particularly strong or interesting.
II. Read the draft again slowly. Describe for the writer what you currently see in this draft. If you have difficulty answering any of the following questions, explain briefly the source of your difficulty.
   A. What is the writer's thesis?
      1. What data from the tables does the writer use to support the thesis? How does the writer cast the data to make the best case for the thesis (percentages versus raw numbers, selection of key data, and so forth)?
      2. Where does the writer acknowledge opposing views (support for the "although" clause in the thesis)? How does the writer cast data that support the opposing view?
   B. What sort of visuals (bar graph, line graph, pie chart, table) has the writer constructed to support that thesis?
      1. Describe your experience "reading" the visuals. Were they easy to follow? Did you have trouble in any way seeing the point of the visuals? Were the titles and labels clear?
      2. Where and how is each visual referenced in the text? Is the visual's relevance to the text clear?

III. What recommendations do you have for improving this draft?
  A. How might the writer improve the title?
  B. Does the introduction engage your interest, provide a clear thesis, and adequately forecast what's coming? Does the thesis create tension by adequately developing opposing or alternative ways to read the data (for example, by using an "although clause")? How might the writer improve the introduction?
  C. Does the body of the essay follow the structure predicted in the introduction? What advice do you have for clarifying the structure of the argument?
  D. Does the writer use numerical data effectively to support the analysis? Are all the data linked effectively to points so that the reader isn't overwhelmed with data? Are the data cast in rhetorically effective ways? What suggestions do you have for improving the writer's use of data?
  E. Are the visuals clear, accurately referenced, and rhetorically effective? What suggestions do you have for improving the visuals?
  F. If you were to select from the table one or more additional pieces of data to persuade you of the writer's thesis, what would you select?
  G. Which piece(s) of data is least pertinent to the writer's thesis?
  H. Sum up what you see as the chief strengths and problem areas of this draft:
    1. Strengths
    2. Problem areas
IV. Read the draft one more time. Place a check in the margin wherever you notice problems in grammar, spelling, or mechanics (one check per problem).

c h a p t e r **12**

Analyzing a Short Story

ABOUT LITERARY ANALYSIS

You've no doubt had more than one experience analyzing literature. Unhappily, some of these experiences were probably unenlightening, even exasperating. Perhaps the whole process struck you as arbitrary; the teacher assigned one meaning to a work or passage when many others seemed equally possible. Or perhaps your teacher chose to discuss a work whose contents seemed far removed from your own experience and whose language sounded like some sort of Klingon code. Our goal in this chapter is to demonstrate that analyzing literature is neither arbitrary nor useless, and—done right—can even be pleasurable. Analyzing literature isn't all that different from analyzing other texts or events, so you already have most of the skills you need to do it well.

To begin understanding literary analysis, try to think of literature not so much as a collection of great books to be read, but rather as a way of reading. Or, put another way, you can choose to read anything literally or literarily. When you read something *literally,* you attempt to reduce its meaning to one clear set of statements and disregard other possible ways of reading the text. When you read something *literarily,* you read it playfully and openly, trying to see in it a wide range of possible meanings. When you read literarily, you can convert almost anything into literature—at least in a playful sense—even the back of a cereal box.

To help you understand the distinction we're drawing, consider the following analogy. A literal reading of an imaginative text is like a bad package tour of an exotic land. Picture a bus filled with bored American tourists slowly making its way through winding, narrow streets in search of the local Hilton. Centuries-old architectural wonders slip past unnoticed; the raucous sounds and pungent smells of the marketplace go unremarked.

As the few who aren't dozing stare out the windows, they catch glimpses of men in flowing robes greeting each other with embraces and kisses to the cheek— the tourists are perplexed. This is not how members of the class "male" are supposed to dress and act. Later, when they pass women haggling with street vendors, they are appalled. "They wouldn't last long with that sort of attitude at our local supermarket," one tourist assures another. They agree that this is a very strange place and they'll be glad to get back to the normal world where men touch hands, not cheeks, to greet each other and women use coupons, not persuasion, to get a deal on food.

The first step in moving beyond a literal to a literary reading of a text, or a country, is to get off the bus and open yourself up to the otherness of the text. You have to experience it on its own terms, which means reading it carefully, then noticing and examining your reactions to what you have read. You have to stop being a tourist and become instead a traveler, who goes alone, by foot, into foreign lands and lives for an extended time among the natives, trying to learn their language and ways. Travelers aren't driven by a desire to have been somewhere so they can tell others that they were there. Instead, they are driven by curiosity, a sense of wonder, a knack for recognizing resemblances in a world of apparent differences, and a capacity for being enthralled by the differences they do find.

To be a traveler rather than a tourist, you need to be an active participant in the process of constructing meaning from a text. Whereas tourists tend to write brief "We're here!" notes on postcards to friends, travelers are more likely to keep extensive journals to help them remember and understand their experiences. They reflect on what they see and on relationships between what they see, do, and feel one day to what they've seen, done, or felt in the past or to what others have reported seeing, doing, and feeling in the same place.

In this way, travelers interpret what they experience. Interpretative writing differs from other forms of writing most notably in its degree of tentativeness. An interpretation considers several possible meanings of an experience or a text and says, "Here's what I think is most probable." Unlike a classic argument, which obligates the writer to refute other points of view, an interpretation may simply point out alternative views of a text, allowing the reader to consider each in turn and then to explain how the writer arrived at his or her own interpretation. The writer often is an almost tangible presence in an interpretative passage, expressing his or her own thoughts about whether an alternative reading might make better sense and the like.

EXPLORING LITERARY ANALYSIS

As we have noted, any sort of text can be read either literally or literarily. However, texts do tend to invite one kind of reading over another. The following Navajo legend contains several signals that invite us to read literarily rather than literally. As you read through this piece, note where those signals occur.

RETOLD BY EVELYN DAHL REED
THE MEDICINE MAN

There is a telling that, in the beginning, when the animals first came up from the   1
darkness to live above the ground, Coyote was sent ahead by Thought Woman to carry a buckskin pouch far to the south.

2   "You must be very careful not to open the pouch," she told him, "or you will be punished."

3   For many days, Coyote ran southward with the pouch on his back. But the world was new, and there was nothing to eat along the way, so he grew very hungry. He wondered if there might be food in the pouch. At last, he took it from his back and untied the thongs. He looked inside and saw nothing but stars. Of course, as soon as he opened the pouch the stars all flew up into the sky, and there they are to this day.

4   "Now look what you've done," said Thought Woman. "For now you shall always get into trouble everywhere you go."

5   And because Coyote disobeyed, he was also made to suffer with the toothache. When the other animals were asleep, he could only sit and howl at the stars. Thus, he has been crying ever since the beginning of the world.

6   Sometimes he would ask the other animals to cure him, but they would only catch the toothache from him, and they, too, would cry.

7   One day he met Mouse, who lived in a little mound under the chaparral bush. "Friend Mouse," begged Coyote, "can you cure me of this toothache?"

8   Now it happened that while digging underground, as is his habit, Mouse had come upon a sweet-smelling root and had put it with the other herbs in the pouch he always carried. He was said to be very wise in the use of herbs.

9   "I don't know," said Mouse, "but I have just found a new root, and it may be that it will help you." He rubbed the root on Coyote's swollen cheek, and in a little while the toothache was gone.

10   This is how it happened that coyotes never hunt or kill field mice.

1. List the signals in the text that led you to read this story literarily as opposed to literally. Summarize the most important differences between how you read this story and how you read the introduction to this chapter.
2. Devise questions about the legend that you think might produce different responses among your classmates. For example: Why is the woman named Thought Woman? Why is Thought Woman a female and not a male?
3. Explain why you think these questions will evoke different responses.

WRITING PROJECT

Your writing project for this chapter has two parts—a formal essay and a series of reading-log entries that will prepare you to write your formal essay. Here is the formal assignment:

For this assignment, all class members will analyze the same story, Alice Walker's "Everyday Use (for your grandmama)," which appears in the Readings section of this chapter (pp. 292–97), or a short story chosen by your instructor. Your task is not to discover the right way to interpret the text, but to explain *your* way of reading or interpreting it. How is your reading of the text different from that of other members of your class and why? Begin by posing an interesting, problematic, and significant question about the story, one that will lead to differences of opinion among your classmates. In the introduction to your paper, make clear just what question you are putting to the text and why. Then, in the body of your paper, explain your own answer to this question, contrasting your answer with alternative interpretations proposed by other members of your class. Without disputing alternative interpretations, help your reader understand how you arrived at *your* interpretation, using details from the story for support.

To help you settle on a good question and to explore and share ideas, we have interspersed throughout the chapter a series of reading-log questions for you to use in exploring the text.

This assignment asks you to analyze a short story by posing a problematic question about it and then building an analysis of the text around your answer. Your success will hinge on the quality of the question you pose at the beginning. Good literary questions call attention to problematic details of the text, stimulate conversation, and provoke readers to return to the text to reread and rethink. You know you will have a good question if your classmates disagree about the answer and contribute their own differing views to the conversation.

Before writing your formal essay, you'll have an opportunity, through the reading-log entries, to explore your ways of reading and responding to the text and to compare your interpretations with those of your classmates. You will write your formal essay, which will give your own answer or interpretation to your problematic question, as a traditional closed-form essay. We ask you to do each reading-log entry when you come to it in the text. The sequence and timing is important, so try not to read ahead. Keep your notebook and pen with you as you read, and when you come to a reading-log question, stop and respond to it at that time.

UNDERSTANDING LITERARY ANALYSIS

The Truth of Literary Events

As an introduction to literary analysis, let's return to "Medicine Man" and consider several questions that it, and other texts of its sort, pose to the reader. First, in what sense is the story true? What advantages are there to expressing a view of truth in a literary, rather than in a literal way? Why might someone choose to tell such a story rather than to approach the world scientifically? What other stories does "Medicine Man" remind you of? How is it different from those stories? How are the characters in the story like and unlike characters you've known in real life?

"Medicine Man" is immediately recognizable as literary; it's difficult, if not impossible, to read it literally. Animals can't talk, and galaxies can't be carted about in a buckskin pouch. We either make a leap of faith and license the author to play fast and loose with our conventional understanding of reality, or we put the story down, dismayed that anyone could think we'd be gullible enough to buy this twaddle.

The events of the story are presented to us as if they actually happened. We know better, but we go along with the ruse in order to enjoy the story. We know that when we read these sorts of texts, we can't demand a one-to-one correspondence between the words we read and the things, persons, and events to which they supposedly refer. We must read instead with what the poet Coleridge called "a Willing Suspension of Disbelief."

Suspending disbelief does not mean erasing it. While we're reading literarily, we are to some degree consciously suppressing skepticism and nagging doubts, leftovers of our literal-minded selves. While we're reading "Medicine Man," we never really forget that coyotes can't talk. But if coyotes could talk, we can imagine them talking as this coyote talks. The coyote in this story is true not because it literally existed, but because it resembles coyotes of our world and coyotes in other stories we've read. So we put aside our skepticism and focus on the resemblance.

Both ways of looking at the story—literal and literary—are open to us, and we consciously choose one over the other. Choosing between a literary and a literal reading is similar to choosing between two ways of looking at an optical illusion. For example, you can look at the drawing in Figure 12.1 as either two profiles or a vase—but you can't see both at once. Until you see both possibilities, you might get stuck seeing it literally as one thing and one thing only. After you've seen it both ways, you're always conscious of that other way of seeing it.

This both/and principle applies not only to the events of a fictional story, but also to the language of literature. When we encounter a simile announcing that "love is like a red, red rose," we never quite forget that roses aren't really love; we know that the word *like* keeps love and roses forever apart in the very act of bringing them together. To read literarily isn't to cease reading literally so much as it is to read both/and—*both* literally *and* literarily. The stories we read are both true and false; the metaphors we encounter are both one thing (loveredredrose) and two different things (love [an abstract noun] and red, red rose [two adjectives intensifying a concrete noun]); the optical illusion in Figure 12.1 is both two profiles and a vase—we just can't see it both ways simultaneously.

FIGURE 12.1   A Reversible Figure

We read *as if* normally suspicious stories were true and *as if* metaphoric language allowed members of two completely different classes to hop their categorical fences and become some barely imaginable third thing. In this regard, the "as if" of literary language is like the magical "let's pretend" of childhood, which allowed us to become action heroes, televison characters, or historical or legendary figures; to die, marry, become parents, and have careers; to talk freely in character and out—and then to pop back to reality for a peanut butter sandwich and a nap.

Reading the Story

We ask you now to read the short story "Everyday Use (for your grandmama)" (pp. 292–97) or the story chosen by your instructor. Let the following reading-log tasks help you become a traveler in the story rather than a tourist. Task 1 asks you to stop several times along the way as you read. Tasks 2 and 3 should be written immediately after you finish reading.

Reading-Log Task 1	As you read your assigned story, stop at several points and predict what you think will happen in the rest of the story. Make your first stop fairly early in the story, choose a second stopping place in the middle, and stop a third time near the end. In each case, predict what is going to happen in the rest of the story and note what in the text causes you to make your prediction. Freewrite for three or four minutes each time you stop.
Reading-Log Task 2	As soon as you finish your reading, write down your immediate responses to the text—how it made you feel or think, what emotions it triggered, what issues it raised. Freewrite for five minutes.
Reading-Log Task 3	Write down (a) what most interested you about the story and (b) the most important question you're left with after reading the text. Freewrite for a couple of minutes after several minutes of reflecting.

FOR WRITING AND DISCUSSION

As a whole class or in small groups, share your responses to the reading-log tasks. Because you will need to begin your formal essay for this assignment with a problematic question, pay particular attention to the responses to (b) in Task 3— the most important question raised by the text. Perhaps you have a tentative answer you would like to propose to someone's question.

Writing (About) Literature

We put "about" in parentheses in this heading because in a sense, to write about literature is to write literature. When you read literarily you are an active cocreator of the text just as a musician is a cocreator of a concerto. Musicians and literary readers don't completely reinvent composers' notes and authors' words every time they play or read them. Composers and writers provide abundant cues to signal how they wish to be played or read and to limit possible interpretations of their work. But in the process of performing another's text, readers and musicians give those words and notes a meaning unique to that particular performance. And in some cases, their renditions may depart considerably from the originator's intentions.

This reading as performance is quite different from the more passive process of literal reading. Whereas the literal reader expects to find unambiguous, universally shared meaning in the text, the literary reader anticipates having to create meaning, which then must be justified to other readers and modified by them. For the literal reader, meaning is a commodity that is extracted intact from the text much as gold nuggets are sluiced from a stream. For the literary reader, meaning is more like a quilt constructed from bits and pieces of the text by many people, who consult and argue and admire each others' skill and change each others' minds about which pieces to include and where to put them.

To participate in the reading process actively, to "write" your version of a text, you need to know the kinds of questions you might ask of it. To help you, we briefly summarize four critical elements of a literary text and the kinds of questions each element suggests. (For a fuller discussion of these elements, and of open-form writing in general, refer to Chapter 7, pp. 141–45, and Chapter 20, pp. 498–500.)

Asking Questions About Plot

Plot refers to the sequence of critical events in the story. The key term here is *critical.* A plot summary does not include everything that happens in a story; it focuses on the elements that most directly move the action of the story forward. One method of analyzing the plot is to begin by identifying what you see as the most critical single event or moment in a story. What is the most pivotal point, the one that prior events lead up to and that subsequent events derive from? Different readers are apt to pick different moments, indicating differences in the way they read the story. Your task is to identify your own choice and to be prepared to defend it. Remember, you are *performing* the story, not trying to figure out some unambiguous right meaning. As long as you have a rationale for your decision, you are acting as a literary critic.

Reading-Log Task 4   What is the single most important moment or event in your assigned story? Why do you see this moment as important or crucial? Freewrite for about ten minutes.

FOR WRITING AND DISCUSSION

As a whole class or in small groups, share your responses to Task 4. Which events did you choose and what are your arguments for selecting them? Take notes about how your classmates' interpretations differ.

Asking Questions About Characters

Characters are the people who make the decisions that forward the plot and whose fortunes change as a result of the plot. You can understand characters in a text only in relationship to each other and to the direction of change in the text. The major character, sometimes called the *protagonist,* is typically the one most responsible for forwarding the plot. In action stories, these characters are pretty static; Dirty Harry or Batman may undergo occasional physical changes and disguises, but their characters tend not to grow or deepen. In other kinds of stories, the major character may change significantly in terms of fortune, insight, or understanding. Which characters change in the story you are examining? How do they change? Which characters do not change? Why do the characters change or not change?

To examine the characters' relationships with each other, you might start with the protagonist and consider the other characters according to how they help or hinder the protagonist. Characters may contribute to the plot by overt action or inaction, by recognizing or failing to recognize something of significance, by adapting to the situation of the story or by being inflexible. They can guide or misguide the protagonist, be a friend or foe, share or threaten the protagonist's values or beliefs, and so forth. What tensions, contrasts, and differing points of view do you see among the characters?

Reading-Log Task 5   Who do you think is the most important character in the story? How does this character change or grow as the story progresses? How do the other characters promote or inhibit change in the main character? How do they help you see and understand the changes? Freewrite for 20 minutes.

FOR WRITING AND DISCUSSION

Share your reading-log entries and note differences in the interpretations of various members of the class. Remember that you are not seeking the one right answer to these questions. You are trying to determine how *you* read this story and how you might reconcile your interpretation with those of your classmates.

Asking Questions About Setting

Although a setting is sometimes little more than a backdrop, like a black curtain behind a speaker on a stage, it can also serve to amplify or help explain the events and motivations of a story. Sometimes the setting acts as a symbol or serves the same function in a story that theme music serves in a movie, underscoring the text's primary themes and moods. A story could be set at the edge of a dark forest, on an ascent up a mountain, or in an inner city, with action moving back and forth between remote vacant lots and a warm kitchen. Sometimes setting plays an active role in the text, functioning almost as a character. A setting could thwart the protagonist's efforts to bring about change or to survive; for example, the collapse of a bridge could prevent a character from crossing a river. Does setting play a role in the story you are analyzing? If so, how would you characterize that role? Could you picture the events of the text taking place in a significantly different setting? Why or why not?

Asking Questions About Point of View

Perhaps the toughest element to perceive in a fictional work is point of view. It does not exist out there on the page, as do character and plot. Point of view is the filter through which the reader views the action of a story. In some cases the impact of point of view on your perception of a character or event is obvious; in other cases it is not. The point of view can trick you into seeing an event in a particular way that you will have to revise when you realize that the narrator's perspective was limited, biased, or ironic. Often the narrator's values and perceptions are different from those of the author; you should never assume that the narrator of the story and the author are the same.

The two primary elements of point of view are time and person. Most stories are told in the past tense, a significant number in the present tense, and a few in the future tense. An almost equal number of stories are told in the first person (in which case the narrator is usually an actor in the story, although not always the main character) as in the third person (in which case the narrator tells the story from a position outside the tale). All choices of tense and person affect the reader's perception of a story. For example, a story told in the first-person present tense ("We ride back from the hunt at dusk") has an immediacy that a story told in the third-person past ("They rode back from the hunt at dusk") does not have. You learn about a first-person narrator both from what the narrator does or says in the plot and from how the narrator tells the story—what he or she includes or omits, the sentence structure, tone, or figures of speech that he or she adopts, and so forth. A third person narrator may be objective (the narrator sees only the external actions of characters) or omniscient (the narrator can enter the minds and feelings of various characters). Sometimes a third-person narrator is omniscient with respect to one character but objective toward others.

Narrators can provide a full and complete sense of a given character (by entering that character's mind as an omniscient narrator) or a partial view only (by observing the character from the outside). Some stories feature multiple points of view through multiple narrators. For example, one character may discover a journal written by another character or may listen to a story told by another character.

The surest path to understanding point of view is to start with your feelings and attitudes toward characters and events and then to examine the extent to which point of view contributes to those attitudes. Do you trust the narrator? Do you like the narrator? Has the narrator loaded the dice, causing you to see characters or events in strongly slanted ways? Is the narrator scrupulously objective or ironic to the point that you're not quite sure what to make of his or her observations?

To ask questions about point of view, begin by asking whether the narrative is first or third person. Then ask whether the narrator's perspective is omniscient or limited. Does the narrator reveal bias or irony? Do you sense that there is more to the story than the narrator is telling you? What does the narrator leave out? How are the narrator's perceptions different from your own?

Reading-Log Task 6 Is there anything worth noting about your assigned story's setting or point of view? What is the story's setting, how do settings change, and what role do these settings play in your reading of the story? What is the story's point of view? Does the narrator play a role in the story? Is the narrator's way of seeing part of what the story is about? Freewrite for fifteen minutes on any ideas generated by contemplating setting and point of view.

FOR WRITING AND DISCUSSION

Share your reading-log entries with your class and note differences in interpretations.

Asking Questions About Theme

If a plot is what happens in a story, then theme is the significance of what happens. Your response to the question "So what?" after reading a story represents your notion of the story's theme. Sometimes, a theme is obvious—the main characters might discuss it, or the author might even state it outright. Often, however, a theme is veiled, and you have to infer it from the words and deeds of the characters.

One way to discover theme is simply to reflect on your immediate responses to characters or on passages that affected you particularly strongly. Consider questions such as these: How did this story change your view of something or the way you feel about something? Is this story trying to reveal something about racism? About endurance in time of trial? About growth from one phase of life to another? About appearance versus reality? About conflicts between the individual and family? About exterior loss and interior gain? About rebellion from society? About what's really valuable versus what appears to be valuable? About establishing values in a confusing world?

Reading-Log Task 7 Reread your response to Task 2, your first attempt to articulate ideas related to the story's theme. Then complete one of the following statements: (a) After further reflection on my assigned story, I think the author is trying to say something to readers about _____. (b) Here is what this story makes me think about and see: _____. Freewrite for fifteen minutes.

FOR WRITING AND DISCUSSION

Share your responses with your class and note differences in the ways in which members of the class read this story.

READINGS

We include in this section two short stories to test your analytical skills. Because analyzing short stories requires you to pose your own interesting questions about a text, we do not provide any analysis questions following the stories. In addition, we include a student essay written to the same assignment. The first reading is "Moonlight," written in the nineteenth century by French author Guy de Maupassant, one of the early masters of the short story genre.

GUY DE MAUPASSANT
MOONLIGHT

1   His warlike name well suited the Abbé Marignan. He was a tall thin priest, full of zeal, his soul always exalted but just. All his beliefs were fixed; they never wavered. He sincerely believed that he understood his God, entered into His plans, His wishes, His intentions.

2   As he strode down the aisle of his little country church, sometimes a question would take shape in his mind: "Now why has God done that?" He would seek the answer stubbornly, putting himself in God's place, and he nearly always found it. He was not one of those who murmur with an air of pious humility, "O Lord, your designs are impenetrable!" He would say to himself: "I am the servant of God, I should know His purposes, and if I don't know them I should divine them."

3   Everything in nature seemed to him created with an absolute and admirable logic. The "why" and the "because" always balanced out. Dawns existed to make waking up a pleasure, days to ripen the crops, rain to water them, evening to prepare for slumber, and the night was dark for sleeping.

4   The four seasons were perfectly fitted to all the needs of agriculture; and it would never have occurred to the priest to suspect that nature has no intentions at all, and that, on the contrary, every living thing has bowed to the hard necessities of times, climates, and matter itself.

5   But he hated women, he hated them unconsciously and despised them by instinct. He often repeated the words of Christ: "Woman, what have I to do with thee?" and he added, "You'd think that not even God himself was happy with that particular piece of work." Woman for him was precisely that child twelve times unclean of whom the poet speaks. She was the temptress who had ensnared the first man and who still continued her damnable work—a weak creature, dangerous, curiously disturbing. And even more than her devilish body he hated her loving soul.

6   He had often felt the yearning affection of women, and, even though he knew himself invulnerable, he was exasperated by this need to love which always trembled in them.

7   God, in his opinion, had made woman only to tempt man and test him. Thus man should approach her with great care, ever fearful of traps. She was, in fact, even shaped like a trap, with her arms extended and her lips parted for a man.

8   He was indulgent only of nuns, made inoffensive by their vows; and he treated even them severely, because he felt stirring in the depths of their fettered hearts—those

hearts so humbled—that eternal yearning which still sought him out, even though he was a priest. He felt it in their gaze—more steeped in piety than that of monks—in their religious ecstasy tainted with sex, in their transports of love for Christ, which infuriated him because it was woman's love, fleshly love. He felt it—this wicked yearning—even in their docility, in the sweetness of their voices in talking to him, in their lowered eyes, and in their submissive tears when he rebuffed them rudely.

And he shook out his soutane on leaving the gates of a convent and strode quickly away as though fleeing from danger.   9

He had a niece who lived with her mother in a little house nearby. He was determined to make her a Sister of Charity.   10

She was pretty, light-headed, and impish. When the Abbé preached, she laughed; and when he got angry at her she kissed him eagerly, clasping him to her heart while he tried instinctively to escape this embrace which nevertheless gave him a taste of sweet happiness, waking deep within him those paternal impulses which slumber in every man.   11

Often he spoke to her of God—of his God—while walking beside her along country lanes. She scarcely listened but looked at the sky, the grass, the flowers, with a lively joy which showed in her eyes. Sometimes she leaped to catch some flying thing and brought it back to him, crying: "Look, uncle, how pretty it is. I want to pet it." And this impulse to "pet bugs" or nuzzle lilac blossoms disturbed, annoyed, sickened the priest, who discerned in it that ineradicable yearning which always springs up in the female heart.   12

Then, it happened that one day the sacristan's wife, who kept house for the Abbé Marignan, cautiously told him that his niece had a lover. The news shocked him terribly and he stopped, choking, with his face full of soap, for he was busy shaving.   13

When he recovered so that he could think and speak, he shouted: "It is not true, you are lying, Mélanie!"   14

But the good woman put her hand on her heart: "May the Good Lord strike me dead if I'm lying, M. Le Curé. She goes out there every night, I tell you, as soon as your sister's in bed. They meet down by the river. You've only to go and watch there between ten and midnight."   15

He stopped scraping his chin and started walking up and down violently, as he always did in his hours of solemn meditation. When he tried to finish shaving he cut himself three times between the nose and the ear.   16

All day he was silenced, swollen with indignation and rage. To his fury as a priest, confronted by love, the invincible, was added the exasperation of a strict father, of a guardian, of a confessor fooled, cheated, tricked by a child. He shared that self-centered feeling of suffocation experienced by parents whose daughter tells them she has—without them and despite them—chosen a husband.   17

After dinner he tried to read a bit, but he could not get into it. He got more and more exasperated. When ten o'clock struck he took down his walking stick, a formidable oaken cudgel he always used when making his evening rounds to visit the sick. And he smiled as he looked at this big club, whirling it about fiercely in his great countryman's fist. Then, suddenly, he raised it and, gritting his teeth, brought it down on a chair, knocking its splintered back to the floor.   18

He opened the door to go out, but stopped on the sill, surprised by a splendor of moonlight such as he had rarely seen.   19

And, endowed as he was with an exalted spirit—such as those poetical dreamers the Fathers of the Church might have had—he was immediately distracted, moved by the glorious and serene beauty of the pale night.   20

21   In his little garden, all bathed in soft light, the ordered ranks of his fruit trees traced on the path the shadows of their slender limbs, lightly veiled with foliage, while the giant honeysuckle, clinging to the wall of the house, exhaled a delicious, sugary breath that floated through the calm clear air like a ghostly perfume.

22   He began to breathe deeply, drinking the air as a drunkard drinks wine, and he took a few slow, dreaming, wondering steps, almost forgetting his niece.

23   When he reached the open country, he stopped to contemplate the fields all flooded with tender light, bathed in the delicate and languid charm that calm nights have. Incessantly the frogs gave out their short metallic note, and distant nightingales, inspiring dream not thought, blended their unstrung tune—a rapid throbbing music made for kisses—with the enchantment of the moonlight.

24   The Abbé pressed on, losing heart, though he could not tell why. He felt feeble, suddenly drained; he wanted to sit down, to stay there, to contemplate, to admire God in His handiwork.

25   Below, following the undulations of the little river, a tall line of poplars wound like a snake. A fine mist, a white vapor which the moonbeams pierced and turned to glowing silver, hung around and above the banks wrapping the whole tortuous watercourse in a sort of delicate and transparent gauze.

26   The priest halted again, struck to the depths of his soul by an irresistible wave of yearning.

27   And a doubt, a vague disturbance, came over him. He sensed within himself another of those questions he sometimes posed.

28   Why had God done this? Since the night is intended for sleep, for unconsciousness, for repose, for oblivion, why make it more charming than the day, sweeter than dawn or evening? And why this slow and seductive moon, which is more poetic than the sun and seems extended by its very delicacy to illuminate things too fragile and mysterious for daylight, why should it come to make the shadows so transparent?

29   Why should the loveliest of songbirds not go to sleep with the others but linger on to sing in the disturbing shade?

30   Why this half-veil thrown over the world? Why this thrill in the heart, this stirring of the soul, this languor of the flesh?

31   Why this display of delights that men never see, since they are asleep in their beds? For whom was it intended, this sublime spectacle, this flood of poetry poured from the sky over the earth?

32   And the Abbé found no answer.

33   But then, down below, on the edge of the fields, under the vault of trees drenched with glowing mist, two shadows appeared, walking side by side.

34   The man was taller and held the neck of his lover and sometimes kissed her forehead. Their sudden appearance brought the still countryside to life, and it enfolded the young lovers like a setting divinely made for them. They seemed, the pair, a single being, the being for whom this calm and silent night was intended, and they moved toward the priest like a living answer, the answer to his question, flung back by his Master.

35   He stood still, his heart pounding in confusion, and he felt as if he were looking at a biblical scene, like the love of Ruth and Boaz, like the accomplishment of the will of God as presented in one of the great scenes of holy scripture. In his head echoed verses of the Song of Songs: the passionate cries, the calls of the flesh, all the ardent poetry of this poem that seethes with passionate yearning.

36   And he said to himself: "Perhaps God has made such nights to veil the loves of men with ideal beauty."

He recoiled before the couple who kept walking arm in arm. It was certainly his 37 niece. But he asked himself now if he was not on the verge of disobeying God. Must not God permit love since He lavished upon it such visible splendor?

And he fled, distraught, almost ashamed, as it he had entered a temple where he 38 had no right to be.

The second reading is "Everyday Use (for your grandmama)" by contemporary African American writer Alice Walker.

ALICE WALKER
EVERYDAY USE (FOR YOUR GRANDMAMA)

I will wait for her in the yard that Maggie and I made so clean and wavy yesterday 1 afternoon. A yard like this is more comfortable than most people know. It is not just a yard. It is like an extended living room. When the hard clay is swept clean as a floor and the fine sand around the edges lined with tiny, irregular grooves, anyone can come and sit and look up into the elm tree and wait for the breezes that never come inside the house.

Maggie will be nervous until after her sister goes: she will stand hopelessly in cor- 2 ners, homely and ashamed of the burn scars down her arms and legs, eying her sister with a mixture of envy and awe. She thinks her sister has held life always in the palm of one hand, that "no" is a word the world never learned to say to her.

You've no doubt seen those TV shows where the child who has "made it" is con- 3 fronted, as a surprise, by her own mother and father, tottering in weakly from back-stage. (A pleasant surprise, of course: What would they do if parent and child came on the show only to curse out and insult each other?) On TV mother and child embrace and smile into each other's faces. Sometimes the mother and father weep; the child wraps them in her arms and leans across the table to tell how she would not have made it without their help. I have seen these programs.

Sometimes I dream a dream in which Dee and I are suddenly brought together on 4 a TV program of this sort. Out of a dark and soft-seated limousine I am ushered into a bright room filled with many people. There I meet a smiling, gray, sporty man like Johnny Carson who shakes my hand and tells me what a fine girl I have. Then we are on the stage and Dee is embracing me with tears in her eyes. She pins on my dress a large orchid, even though she has told me once that she thinks orchids are tacky flowers.

In real life I am a large, big-boned woman with rough, man-working hands. In the 5 winter I wear flannel nightgowns to bed and overalls during the day. I can kill and clean a hog as mercilessly as a man. My fat keeps me hot in zero weather. I can work out-side all day, breaking once to get water for washing; I can eat pork liver cooked over the open fire minutes after it comes steaming from the hog. One winter I knocked a bull calf straight in the brain between the eyes with a sledge hammer and had the meat hung up to chill before nightfall. But of course all this does not show on television. I am the way my daughter would want me to be: a hundred pounds lighter, my skin like an uncooked barley pancake. My hair glistens in the hot bright lights. Johnny Carson has much to do to keep up with my quick and witty tongue.

6   But that is a mistake. I know even before I wake up. Who ever knew a Johnson with a quick tongue? Who can even imagine me looking a strange white man in the eye? It seems to me I have talked to them always with one foot raised in flight, with my head turned in whichever way is farthest from them. Dee, though. She would always look anyone in the eye. Hesitation was no part of her nature.

7   "How do I look, Mama?" Maggie says, showing just enough of her thin body enveloped in pink skirt and red blouse for me to know she's there, almost hidden by the door.

8   "Come out into the yard," I say.

9   Have you ever seen a lame animal, perhaps a dog run over by some careless person rich enough to own a car, sidle up to someone who is ignorant enough to be kind to him? That is the way my Maggie walks. She has been like this, chin on chest, eyes on ground, feet in shuffle, ever since the fire that burned the other house to the ground.

10   Dee is lighter than Maggie, with nicer hair and a fuller figure. She's a woman now, though sometimes I forget. How long ago was it that the other house burned? Ten, twelve years? Sometimes I can still hear the flames and feel Maggie's arms sticking to me, her hair smoking and her dress falling off her in little black papery flakes. Her eyes seemed stretched open, blazed open by the flames reflected in them. And Dee. I see her standing off under the sweet gum tree she used to dig gum out of; a look of concentration on her face as she watched the last dingy gray board of the house fall in toward the red-hot brick chimney. Why don't you do a dance around the ashes? I'd wanted to ask her. She had hated the house that much.

11   I used to think she hated Maggie, too. But that was before we raised the money, the church and me, to send her to Augusta to school. She used to read to us without pity; forcing words, lies, other folks' habits, whole lives upon us two, sitting trapped and ignorant underneath her voice. She washed us in a river of make-believe, burned us with a lot of knowledge we didn't necessarily need to know. Pressed us to her with the serious way she read, to shove us away at just the moment, like dimwits, we seemed about to understand.

12   Dee wanted nice things. A yellow organdy dress to wear to her graduation from high school; black pumps to match a green suit she'd made from an old suit somebody gave me. She was determined to stare down any disaster in her efforts. Her eyelids would not flicker for minutes at a time. Often I fought off the temptation to shake her. At sixteen she had a style of her own: and she knew what style was.

13   I never had an education myself. After second grade the school was closed down. Don't ask my why: in 1927 colored asked fewer questions than they do now. Sometimes Maggie reads to me. She stumbles along good-naturedly but can't see well. She knows she is not bright. Like good looks and money, quickness passed her by. She will marry John Thomas (who has mossy teeth in an earnest face) and then I'll be free to sit here and I guess just sing church songs to myself. Although I never was a good singer. Never could carry a tune. I was always better at a man's job. I used to love to milk till I was hooked in the side in '49. Cows are soothing and slow and don't bother you, unless you try to milk them the wrong way.

14   I have deliberately turned my back on the house. It is three rooms, just like the one that burned, except the roof is tin; they don't make shingle roofs any more. There are no real windows, just some holes cut in the sides, like the portholes in a ship, but not

round and not square, with rawhide holding the shutters up on the outside. This house is in a pasture, too, like the other one. No doubt when Dee sees it she will want to tear it down. She wrote me once that no matter where we "choose" to live, she will manage to come see us. But she will never bring her friends. Maggie and I thought about this and Maggie asked me, "Mama, when did Dee ever *have* any friends?"

She had a few. Furtive boys in pink shirts hanging about on washday after school.   15
Nervous girls who never laughed. Impressed with her they worshiped the well-turned phrase, the cute shape, the scalding humor that erupted like bubbles in lye. She read to them.

When she was courting Jimmy T she didn't have much time to pay to us, but turned   16
all her faultfinding power on him. He *flew* to marry a cheap city girl from a family of ignorant flashy people. She hardly had time to recompose herself.

When she comes I will meet—but there they are!   17

Maggie attempts to make a dash for the house, in her shuffling way, but I stay her   18
with my hand. "Come back here," I say. And she stops and tries to dig a well in the sand with her toe.

It is hard to see them clearly through the strong sun. But even the first glimpse of   19
leg out of the car tells me it is Dee. Her feet were always neat-looking, as if God himself had shaped them with a certain style. From the other side of the car comes a short, stocky man. Hair is all over his head a foot long and hanging from his chin like a kinky mule tail. I hear Maggie suck in her breath. "Uhnnnh," is what it sounds like. Like when you see the wriggling end of a snake just in front of your foot on the road. "Uhnnnh."

Dee next. A dress down to the ground, in this hot weather. A dress so loud it hurts   20
my eyes. There are yellows and oranges enough to throw back the light of the sun. I feel my whole face warming from the heat waves it throws out. Earrings gold, too, and hanging down to her shoulders. Bracelets dangling and making noises when she moves her arm up to shake the folds of the dress out of her armpits. The dress is loose and flows, and as she walks closer, I like it. I hear Maggie go "Uhnnnh" again. It is her sister's hair. It stands straight up like the wool on a sheep. It is black as night and around the edges are two long ponytails that rope about like small lizards disappearing behind her ears.

"Wa-su-zo-Tean-o!" she says, coming in on that gliding way the dress makes her   21
move. The short stocky fellow with the hair to his navel is all grinning and he follows up with "Asalamalakim, my mother and sister!" He moves to hug Maggie but she falls back, right up against the back of my chair. I feel her trembling there and when I look up I see the perspiration falling off her chin.

"Don't get up," says Dee. Since I am stout it takes something of a push. You can   22
see me trying to move a second or two before I make it. She turns, showing white heels through her sandals, and goes back to the car. Out she peeks next with a Polaroid. She stoops down quickly and lines up picture after picture of me sitting there in front of the house with Maggie cowering behind me. She never takes a shot without making sure the house is included. When a cow comes nibbling around the edge of the yard she snaps it and me and Maggie *and* the house. Then she puts the Polaroid in the back seat of the car, and comes up and kisses me on the forehead.

Meanwhile Asalamalakim is going through the motions with Maggie's hand. Maggie's   23
hand is as limp as a fish, and probably cold, despite the sweat, and she keeps trying to pull it back. It looks like Asalamalakim wants to shake hands but wants to do it fancy. Or maybe he don't know how people shake hands. Anyhow, he soon gives up on Maggie.

24 "Well," I say. "Dee."

25 "No, Mama," she says. "Not 'Dee,' Wangero Leewanika Kemanjo!"

26 "What happened to 'Dee'?" I wanted to know.

27 "She's dead," Wangero said. "I couldn't bear it any longer, being named after the people who oppress me."

28 "You know as well as me you was named after your aunt Dicie," I said. Dicie is my sister. She named Dee. We called her "Big Dee" after Dee was born.

29 "But who was *she* named after?" asked Wangero.

30 "I guess after Grandma Dee," I said.

31 "And who was she named after?" asked Wangero.

32 "Her mother," I said, and saw Wangero was getting tired. "That's about as far back as I can trace it," I said. Though, in fact, I probably could have carried it back beyond the Civil War through the branches.

33 "Well," said Asalamalakim, "there you are."

34 "Uhnnnh," I heard Maggie say.

35 "There I was not," I said, "before 'Dicie' cropped up in our family, so why should I try to trace it that far back?"

36 He just stood there grinning, looking down on me like somebody inspecting a Model A car. Every once in a while he and Wangero sent eye signals over my head.

37 "How do you pronounce this name?" I asked.

38 "You don't have to call me by it if you don't want to," said Wangero.

39 "Why shouldn't I?" I asked. "If that's what you want us to call you, we'll call you."

40 "I know it might sound awkward at first," said Wangero.

41 "I'll get used to it," I said. "Ream it out again."

42 Well, soon we got the name out of the way. Asalamalakim had a name twice as long and three times as hard. After I tripped over it two or three times he told me to just call him Hakim-a-barber. I wanted to ask him was he a barber, but I didn't really think he was, so I didn't ask.

43 "You must belong to those beef-cattle peoples down the road," I said. They said "Asalamalakim" when they met you, too, but they didn't shake hands. Always too busy: feeding the cattle, fixing the fences, putting up salt-lick shelters, throwing down hay. When the white folks poisoned some of the herd the men stayed up all night with rifles in their hands. I walked a mile and a half just to see the sight.

44 Hakim-a-barber said, "I accept some of their doctrines, but farming and raising cattle is not my style." (They didn't tell me, and I didn't ask, whether Wangero (Dee) had really gone and married him.)

45 We sat down to eat and right away he said he didn't eat collards and pork was unclean. Wangero, though, went on through the chitlins and corn bread, the greens and everything else. She talked a blue streak over the sweet potatoes. Everything delighted her. Even the fact that we still used the benches her daddy made for the table when we couldn't afford to buy chairs.

46 "Oh, Mama!" she cried. Then turned to Hakim-a-barber. "I never knew how lovely these benches are. You can feel the rump prints," she said, running her hands underneath her and along the bench. Then she gave a sigh and her hand closed over Grandma Dee's butter dish. "That's it!" she said. "I knew there was something I wanted to ask you if I could have." She jumped up from the table and went over in the corner where the churn stood, the milk in it clabber by now. She looked at the churn and looked at it.

"This churn top is what I need," she said. "Didn't Uncle Buddy whittle it out of a   47
tree you all used to have?"

"Yes," I said.   48

"Uh huh," she said happily. "And I want the dasher, too."   49

"Uncle Buddy whittle that, too?" asked the barber.   50

Dee (Wangero) looked up at me.   51

"Aunt Dee's first husband whittled the dash," said Maggie so low you almost   52
couldn't hear her. "His name was Henry, but they called him Stash."

"Maggie's brain is like an elephant's," Wangero said, laughing. "I can use the churn   53
top as a centerpiece for the alcove table," she said, sliding a plate over the churn, "and
I'll think of something artistic to do with the dasher."

When she finished wrapping the dasher the handle stuck out. I took it for a moment   54
in my hands. You didn't even have to look close to see where hands pushing the dasher
up and down to make butter had left a kind of sink in the wood. In fact, there were a
lot of small sinks; you could see where thumbs and fingers had sunk into the wood. It
was beautiful light yellow wood, from a tree that grew in the yard where Big Dee and
Stash had lived.

After dinner Dee (Wangero) went to the trunk at the foot of my bed and started   55
rifling through it. Maggie hung back in the kitchen over the dishpan. Out came Wangero
with two quilts. They had been pieced by Grandma Dee and then Big Dee and me had
hung them on the quilt frames on the front porch and quilted them. One was in the Lone
Star pattern. The other was Walk Around the Mountain. In both of them were scraps of
dresses Grandma Dee had worn fifty and more years ago. Bits and pieces of Grandma
Jarrell's Paisley shirts. And one teeny faded blue piece, about the size of a penny
matchbox, that was from Great Grandpa Ezra's uniform that he wore in the Civil War.

"Mama," Wangero said sweet as a bird. "Can I have these old quilts?"   56

I heard something fall in the kitchen, and a minute later the kitchen door slammed.   57

"Why don't you take one or two of the others?" I asked. "These old things was just   58
done by me and Big Dee from some tops your grandma pieced before she died."

"No," said Wangero. "I don't want those. They are stitched around the borders by   59
machine."

"That'll make them last better," I said.   60

"That's not the point," said Wangero. "These are all pieces of dresses Grandma   61
used to wear. She did all this stitching by hand. Imagine!" She held the quilts securely
in her arms, stroking them.

"Some of the pieces, like those lavender ones, come from old clothes her mother   62
handed down to her," I said, moving up to touch the quilts. Dee (Wangero) moved back
just enough so that I couldn't reach the quilts. They already belonged to her.

"Imagine!" she breathed again, clutching them closely to her bosom.   63

"The truth is," I said, "I promised to give them quillts to Maggie, for when she mar-   64
ries John Thomas."

She gasped like a bee had stung her.   65

"Maggie can't appreciate these quilts!" she said. "She'd probably be backward   66
enough to put them to everyday use."

"I reckon she would," I said. "God knows I been saving 'em for long enough with   67
nobody using 'em. I hope she will!" I didn't want to bring up how I had offered Dee
(Wangero) a quilt when she went away to college. Then she had told me they were old-
fashioned, out of style.

68   "But they're *priceless!*" she was saying now, furiously; for she has a temper. "Maggie would put them on the bed and in five years they'd be in rags. Less than that!"

69   "She can always make some more," I said. "Maggie knows how to quilt."

70   Dee (Wangero) looked at me with hatred. "You just will not understand. The point is these quilts, *these* quilts!"

71   "Well," I said, stumped. "What would *you* do with them?"

72   "Hang them," she said. As if that was the only thing you *could* do with quilts.

73   Maggie by now was standing in the door. I could almost hear the sound her feet made as they scraped over each other.

74   "She can have them, Mama," she said, like somebody used to never winning anything, or having anything reserved for her. "I can 'member Grandma Dee without the quilts."

75   I looked at her hard. She had filled her bottom lip with checkerberry snuff and it gave her face a kind of dopey, hangdog look. It was Grandma Dee and Big Dee who taught her how to quilt herself. She stood there with her hands hidden in the folds of her skirt. She looked at her sister with something like fear but she wasn't mad at her. This was Maggie's portion. This was the way she knew God to work.

76   When I looked at her like that something hit me in the top of my head and ran down to the soles of my feet. Just like when I'm in church and the spirit of God touches me and I get happy and shout. I did something I never had done before: hugged Maggie to me, then dragged her on into the room, snatched the quilts out of Miss Wangero's hands and dumped them into Maggie's lap. Maggie just sat there on my bed with her mouth open.

77   "Take one or two of the others," I said to Dee.

78   But she turned without a word and went out to Hakim-a-barber.

79   "You just don't understand," she said, as Maggie and I came out to the car.

80   "What don't I understand?" I wanted to know.

81   "Your heritage," she said. And then she turned to Maggie, kissed her, and said, "You ought to try to make something of yourself, too, Maggie. It's really a new day for us. But from the way you and Mama still live you'd never know it."

82   She put on some sunglasses that hid everything above the tip of her nose and her chin.

83   Maggie smiled; maybe at the sunglasses. But a real smile, not scared. After we watched the car dust settle I asked Maggie to me bring me a dip of snuff. And then the two of us sat there just enjoying, until it was time to go in the house and go to bed.

    The following student essay, written in response to this chapter's assignment, analyzes a short story by Flannery O'Connor entitled "Everything That Rises Must Converge." The story, set in an unnamed southern city, describes a bus trip taken by the protagonist, Julian, a young, unemployed college graduate, and his mother, with whom Julian still lives and whom he is accompanying to her weight-reducing class. Julian loathes his mother and hates his dependence on her. Much of the story depicts the mother as Julian sees her—garrulous, bigoted, living in the past. Julian, meanwhile, is bright, but unsuccessful and bitter, not so far above his mother as he would have you—and himself—believe.

When an African American woman and her child get on the bus, Julian is amused by the fact that she is wearing the same one-of-a-kind hat that his mother has recently purchased. But when Julian and his mother get off at the same stop as the African American woman and her son, Julian is appalled that his mother tries to give the child a penny. In response to what she perceives as a white person's act of condescension toward her and her child, the African American woman hits Julian's mother with her purse, knocking her to the ground and perhaps killing her. The story ends with a remorseful Julian desperately calling to his mother.

HOLLY BURKETT (student)
THE JULIAN WITHIN

I must confess that when the class first discussed this story, I had some trouble   1
tracking the discussion. You see, I hadn't yet finished reading the story. The one thing I gained from listening to my classmates was that Julian had somehow killed his mother. Their reactions to the story led me to believe that Julian was a horrid character.

When I went back to the story later that evening, I made predictions about the end-   2
ing based on my class experience. I was surprised, thus, when Julian did not push his mother in front of the bus as I had expected. Instead, what I found was Julian trying to help his mother understand his view of the world after years of having her view of it forced on him. Within the first two pages of the text, I found myself identifying with Julian. Like Julian, I understand what it's like to be closely related to someone who has a completely different view of the world than I do.

So why did most of my classmates react to Julian so differently than I had? Why   3
did they feel so much hostility toward him and why did they find it so hard to tolerate his view of the world? After some thought, I realized that everyone obtains their understanding of a text from their own experiences and background. So what were those differences? I queried several students about their responses to the story trying to discover the reasons behind our dichotomous responses.

"Why do you think Julian is so terrible?" I asked one classmate. "Because," he   4
replied, "he did such awful things to his mother." This response was typical; everyone seemed to believe that Julian had behaved badly toward his mother and had somehow harmed her by his actions. But had he really *done* anything bad? No. After reading the text several times, it was clear to me that Julian's offenses against his mother weren't in what he did to her, but how he thought about her.

Julian is a victim of author Flannery O'Connor's use of point of view. As readers,   5
we get to see many of Julian's thoughts and feelings. But what about his mother's thoughts and feelings? What we're shown is a loud, negative person imposing her views on her son and everyone within hearing distance. As desensitized Americans, do we fall into the trap of allowing her to express harmful prejudices because she is old, feeble and a mother? Many of us have been socialized to revere motherhood and to ignore or soft-peddle negative aspects of mothers. If Julian's mother was Julian's sister or cousin would we react to her in the same way?

6   Julian is presented to us as a young failure who hates his mother. This aspect alone incites a negative response to Julian's character. But there are reasons for his hatred. For one thing, he suspects his mother is the cause of their struggles:

> The law of [her world] was to sacrifice herself for him after she had first created the necessity to do so by making a mess of things. If he had permitted her sacrifices, it was only because her lack of foresight had made them necessary. (O'Connor 450)

The narrator does not tell us the details of her failures or even if they are true. That is not important. It is Julian's perception of these shortcomings and prejudices that causes his anger. It is his anger that we're exposed to. In turn, we're socialized to see bitter anger toward one's mother as reprehensible. But can any of us honestly say we have not been at odds with a family member or close friend to the point that, for a time at least, we felt hatred toward them? Can any one of us say that we have never wanted to teach another person a well-deserved lesson? The difference between Julian and the rest of us is that Julian's thoughts are exposed to us for judgment, without much explanation or defense, while our own dark thoughts remain our secret.

7   In truth, Julian and his mother are more alike than we might realize on first reading. Both of them believe strongly in the rightness of their views and make it a goal to make the other concede.

> "True culture is in the mind," he said.
> "It's in the heart," she said, "and in how you do things and how you do things is because of who you are." (O'Connor 449)

8   Much of the reason we don't see their similarities is because each character is presented so differently. The mother is a flat, typecast character. We only see her thoughts and feelings through Julian's eyes. The narrator doesn't give any individual attention to the mother's character unless it directly affects Julian. Julian, meanwhile, gets lots of individual attention from the narrator. He is presented as a "gloomy," "frustrated" young "failure," with "no future ahead of him." In turn, O'Connor uses words like "scowled," "hissed," "evil urge," and "monster" to characterize Julian.

9   Julian, in short, is presented in negative language as a character who has violated a major social code (honor thy father and mother). This explains much of my classmates' hostile reaction to him. But if we look beyond the author's word choices and our own social taboos, what we see is not one character torturing another but two characters locked pitifully in each others' lives. Neither has the strength to let go of the illusions that sustain them. For the mother, her sustaining illusion is the world she once knew, the old South with its class structure and its racial boundaries where everyone knew their "place." Julian's sustaining illusion, meanwhile, is that his mother is responsible for his failures. But if he lets go of her and her lost world, he will be the only one responsible for his own failures. More than his negative treatment of his mother, it's Julian's pettinesses and failures and his skill at hiding them from himself that we hate. We hate him because in Julian we see ourselves.

Thinking Critically About "The Julian Within"

1. The assignment for this chapter asks the following question: How do you read this text differently from other members of your class and why? How

does Holly's essay follow these instructions? What is the question she poses? How do some of her classmates answer this question? How does she answer the question differently? What is the thesis statement for Burkett's essay and where does she place it?

2. Holly contends that much of her classmates' unsympathetic response to Julian can be traced to their feeling that he violates a powerful social code, encapsulated in the biblical phrase "Honor thy father and mother." To what extent do you agree that this honoring of parents is still an important part of Americans' social code?

3. Flannery O'Connor's narrators are often white American southerners living in the 1950s. In keeping with their point of view, O'Connor's African American characters are usually described in flat, stereotypical terms. In your view, are writers justified in using racial epithets and presenting characters stereotypically in the name of "realism" (in O'Connor's case, to be true to the perceptions of the racist narrators)? (Remember that the narrator's point of view can be very different from the author's; O'Connor herself seems to have been deeply opposed to racism.)

4. What are the strengths and weaknesses of Holly's essay?

COMPOSING YOUR ESSAY

The reading-log entries you've completed in conjunction with your assigned story should help you considerably when you start planning your essay. Begin by posing a good question about the story—one that you have discussed with classmates and that promotes engaged conversation and differing points of view. The additional reading-log tasks in this section will help you decide on a question to pose. You will then need to explore ways to answer your question, using textual details for support and contrasting your answer with one or more differing views expressed by your classmates.

Generating and Exploring Ideas

To help you settle on a good problematic question for the introduction of your formal essay, we list several starter questions that focus on *turning points*— major changes in a story's character, plot, language, and point of view. You may want to begin with one of these questions and then refine it to make it more specific to the story.

After reviewing these questions, complete the two reading-log tasks that follow.

Turning-Point Starter Questions About a Short Story

1. Changes in character
   a. How do circumstances change for each character? What sets each change of circumstance in motion?

    b. How does each character's understanding or knowledge change?

    c. How does your attitude toward each character change?

    d. How does each character's relationship to other characters change?

2. Changes in language

    a. How does the dialogue change? Do characters talk to each other differently at any point?

    b. How does the tone of the language change? Does it become lighter or darker at given points?

    c. How do the metaphors and similes change? Is there a pattern to that change?

3. Changes in point of view

    a. How does the narrator's attitude toward the characters and events change? Does the narrator move closer or farther away from characters and events at any point?

    b. How credible is the narrator? If the narrator is not credible, at what point do you first suspect him or her of unreliability?

4. Changes in setting

    a. How does the time or place depicted in the text change? How are other changes in the text related to these changes?

Reading-Log Task 8	Using the turning-point starter questions to stimulate your thinking, pose five or six specific turning-point questions about your assigned story. Freewrite for about ten minutes.

Reading-Log Task 9	Choose one of our turning-point questions and explore your own answer to it. Freewrite for ten minutes.

    Looking at turning points is not the only way to pose questions about a text. A second list of starter questions focuses on other considerations, such as theme, values, and character. Review the questions and then complete the two reading log tasks that follow.

Additional Starter Questions

1. Why is the story's title appropriate (or inappropriate) in your view?

2. What does each of the major characters seek and want? What are each character's values?

3. Which character's beliefs and values are closest to your own? How so?

4. What or who blocks the characters from reaching their goals (remember, sometimes what blocks them may be inside them), and how much control do they have over achieving their ends?

5. How successful are the characters in achieving their goals and how do they respond to the outcome?

6. Among all the characters, who seems best to understand what happens and why?

Reading-Log Task 10	Pose two or three specific questions about your assigned story using these additional starter questions. Freewrite for five minutes.

Reading-Log Task 11 Choose one of these questions and explore your responses to it through freewriting or idea mapping. Write for ten minutes.

Choosing Your Problematic Question and Exploring Your Answer

You're now ready to choose the question that will initiate your essay and to explore your answer. For the final reading-log tasks, freewrite rapidly to spill your ideas onto the paper and avoid writer's block. Before you begin, read over what you have written so far in your reading log to help you get the juices flowing.

Reading-Log Task 12 Write out the question that you want to ask about your assigned short story. What makes this an interesting and problematic question? Why don't you and your classmates immediately agree on the answer? Freewrite for ten minutes.

Reading-Log Task 13 Freewriting as rapidly as you can, explore your answer to the question you asked in Task 12. Use textual details and your own critical thinking to create an argument supporting your answer. Freewrite for thirty minutes.

Reading-Log Task 14 How is the answer you explored in Task 13 different from the views of some of your classmates? What do they emphasize in this text that you don't emphasize? For example, do you focus on character whereas some of your classmates focus on language? Do you most identify with one of the characters whereas some of your classmates identify with other characters? Do you disagree on where the main turning point of the story occurs? Freewrite for ten minutes.

Shaping and Drafting

Reading-log Tasks 12, 13, and 14 give you a head start on a rough draft. The best way to organize your literary analysis is to follow the problem-thesis pattern of closed-form prose:

First, begin with an introduction that poses your question about the text and shows the reader why it is an interesting, problematic, and significant question. If you choose, you can summarize the differing views of your classmates at this point to show why your question is problematic. At the end of your introduction, be sure to include a thesis statement—a one-sentence summary answer to your question. Early in the introduction you may need to supply background about the story so that your reader can understand your question.

Second, write the main body of your essay, in which you develop and support your thesis using textual details and argument. There is no formula for organizing the body. The major sections will depend on your argument and the steps needed to make your case. If you haven't already summarized the differing views of your classmates in the introduction, you may choose to do so in the body, showing how and why your argument differs from theirs. The key here is to create tension for your thesis.

Conclude by returning to your essay's big picture and suggesting why your answer to your opening question is significant. Does your analysis have larger implications for the story? What are they? What kind of changed view of the story do you want to effect in your readers' minds? Why is this view important to you? You may choose to write about the different value systems or different ways of reading that distinguish *your* analysis of the story from that of some of your classmates.

Revising

After you have produced a good rough draft, let it sit for a while. Then try it out on readers, who can follow the Guidelines for Peer Reviewers. Based on your readers' advice, begin revising your draft, making it as clear as possible for your readers. Remember to start with the big issues and major changes and then to work your way down to the smaller issues and minor changes.

g u i d e l i n e s

for Peer Reviewers

Instructions for peer reviews, including use of these guidelines, are provided in Chapter 21, pages 527–28. To write a peer review for a classmate, use your own paper, numbering your responses to correspond to the questions on the guidelines. At the head of your paper place the author's name and your own name as shown.

Author's Name: _____

Peer Reviewer's Name: _____

I. Read the draft at normal reading speed from beginning to end. As you read, do the following:
   A. Place a wavy line in the margin next to any passages that you find confusing, that contain something that doesn't seem to fit, or that otherwise slow down your reading.
   B. Place a "Good!" in the margin next to any passages where you think the writing is particularly strong or interesting.
II. Read the draft again slowly. Describe for the writer what you currently see in this draft. If you have difficulty answering any of the following questions, explain briefly the source of your difficulty.
   A. What question does the author address?

B. Where does the author show that the question is problematic?

C. Where does the writer summarize the differing views of classmates?

D. What is the writer's thesis? What do you find surprising about the thesis?

E. Where in the body does the writer use textual detail from the short story to support the thesis?

III. What recommendations do you have for improving this draft?

A. How might the writer improve the title?

B. Does the introduction capture your interest and set up the question to be addressed? How might the writer improve the introduction?

C. Is the organization clear? Does the writer follow the principles of presenting the big picture first, putting points before particulars, using transitions, and following the old/new contract as explained in Chapter 19?

D. Has the writer quoted from the story (or used paraphrase or other specific references to the text) sufficiently for you to understand how each point is grounded in the text? Are there passages not cited that you think might better support the argument? What recommendations do you have for improving the writer's use of supporting details?

E. Has the writer effectively shown how the thesis is in tension with differing views? Could the piece benefit from additional citations of classmates' views for contrast?

F. Where do you disagree with the author's analysis? What aspects of the story are left unexplained or unremarked in the writer's essay?

G. Sum up what you see as the chief strengths and problem areas of this draft.

1. Strengths
2. Problem areas

IV. Read the draft one more time. Place a check in the margin wherever you notice problems in grammar, spelling, or mechanics (one check per problem).

c h a p t e r   **13**

Investigating Questions
About Cause
and Consequence

ABOUT CAUSAL ANALYSIS

Questions about causes and consequences crop up everywhere. University researchers often spend their careers pursuing causal questions: What physical processes cause the HIV virus to destroy the immune system? Why are white teenage females seven times more likely than black teenage females to smoke? What effects do changes in the money supply have on an economy? What causes differences in sexual orientation? What is causing the decline of frog populations worldwide? Why do so many people believe in conspiracy theories?

Similarly, questions about cause and consequence dominate business and public life, where answers to these questions shape decisions about what a company or a government ought to do. What effects will privatization of prisons have on our penal system? Will curtailment of government welfare payments discourage teenage pregnancy? Will allowing oil drilling in the Alaska National Wildlife Reserve harm animal populations? To what extent will oil drilling stimulate the Alaskan economy and reduce dependence on foreign oil?

And people face cause and consequence issues all the time in their own lives. What effect will changing majors have on my life? Why did Carlos stomp out of the room like that? What will Danielle do if she finds out that Eric has been cheating on her? And what caused Eric to cheat?

Many college assignments will ask you to investigate questions about causes and consequences. Perhaps you will conduct scientific experiments to establish whether a particular variable causes a phenomenon, or you may study statistical methods for testing causal links between two phenomena. You will also engage in a variety of other activities—observing, reading, testing, surveying, comparing—to help you understand why and how things happen in nature and in culture. In this chapter, we prepare you for these activities by exploring how causal arguments are constructed and how they sometimes go awry.

EXPLORING CAUSAL ANALYSIS

Working as a whole class or in small groups, brainstorm a list of cause or consequence questions about puzzling phenomena. Consider three broad categories of phenomena that raise causal questions.

1. *One-time events*   (the puzzling crash of an airplane; the extinction of dinosaurs; the collapse of communism worldwide)
2. *Repeatable events or recurring phenomena*   (cancer; math anxiety among females; high levels of diabetes among certain minority groups; the attraction of many adolescent boys to violence)
3. *Trends*   (a decline in liquor sales nationwide; an increase in the number of men who buy designer shirts; the increasing number of rap lyrics expressing contempt for women)

Try to brainstorm causal questions in each of these categories, but also include a fourth, miscellaneous category for causal questions that don't seem to fit into these three. We'll start you off with a few more examples in each category, and then you can continue on your own.

One-time events: Why were the 1992 Los Angeles riots that followed the Rodney King trial so widespread and intense? What made Volkswagen lose its once overwhelming market share of foreign-car sales in the United States?

Repeatable events or recurring phenomena: Why do teenagers start smoking? Why do white, middle-class women develop a different relationship with food than do women in most nonwhite or non-middle-class cultures?

Trends: Why has there been such a remarkable growth in the microbrewery industry? Why are convertibles making a comeback? Why are tabloid talk shows so popular?

Miscellaneous: Why don't stereo system advertisers place ads in women's magazines such as *Mademoiselle*? Why does the United States set speed limits on freeways, whereas Germany has no speed limits on its autobahns?

As a class, choose one or two of the most interesting causal questions that you came up with. Make a list of all the possible causes (or consequences) you can imagine. Then see if the class can reach consensus on the best causal explanations for the event, trend, or phenomenon. As you reject some possible causes and agree on others, what factors are you considering? What makes one explanation more plausible or likely than another?

WRITING PROJECT

Write an essay in which you analyze the causes or consequences of a puzzling event, trend, or phenomenon, or in which you argue for an unusual, overlooked, or unexpected cause or consequence. Your instructor will specify a length for your essay.

Your writing assignment for this chapter is to pose a question about the causes or consequences of a puzzling or controversial event, trend, or phenomenon. The introduction to your essay should capture your reader's interest. Describe the event, trend, or phenomenon you are about to investigate and explain why it is intriguing or controversial. In the body of your essay, present your own causal analysis, in which you identify and support each proposed cause or consequence one at a time. If your opening question is particularly controversial, you may wish to begin by summarizing and rejecting views with which you disagree. In this case, your essay uses a *surprising reversal* strategy, in which you pose your thesis against a counterthesis: "You may believe that the causes of this phenomenon are X and Y; however, I am going to argue for an unusual or unexpected cause—Z." Your goal is to restructure your audience's understanding of the causes or consequences of the phenomenon. In selecting your causal question, try to find something local and of manageable size—perhaps something that you have personally experienced or observed. For example, you are more likely to succeed in analyzing why your college's female athletes graduate at a higher rate than male athletes or why local voters turned down the last school bond levy than why the Bosnians and the Serbs don't get along.

The rest of this chapter provides more background about causal analysis and suggestions for each stage of the writing process.

UNDERSTANDING CAUSAL ANALYSIS

In thinking about causal phenomena, we need to distinguish between one-time events and recurrent events. Because one-time events have usually come and gone by the time we study them, it can be especially difficult to determine their causes. Some evidence may have disappeared, or witnesses may have faulty or conflicting memories of what happened. Moreover, we usually can't study the event scientifically by repeating it with different variables. Nor can we study multiple cases over long periods of time and establish sophisticated mathematical correlations between the outcome and various suspected causes.

As a further complication, many one-time events involve human beings, which raises a second set of nettlesome causal questions. First, humans have (or appear to have) free will, which means they don't always respond to external forces predictably. Whereas any two rocks dropped from a roof will fall at precisely thirty-two feet per second squared, any two human beings, placed in any two identical circumstances, may react in a bewildering variety of ways. Sometimes human beings respond oddly out of pure perversity, precisely to disappoint expectations.

Second, even when forces outside their control act on human beings, it may be difficult to determine whether the humans' responses are a result of nurture (how they were raised or influenced by their environment) or nature (their genetic dispositions and body chemistry) or some combination of both. For example, why does person A become an alcoholic but person B does not?

Trends represent middle ground between one-time events and repeatable events. Many trends happen only once (the hula hoop craze in the 1950s, the loss of TV revenues for baseball in 1995), but because they involve so many people it is possible to conduct interviews and to study trends as if they were repeatable events.

With these distinctions and cautions in mind, let's turn to the various ways of arguing that one event causes another.

Three Methods of Developing Causal Arguments

In this section we examine three different ways to construct a causal argument: directly, inductively, or analogically.

Method One: Explain the Causal Mechanism Directly

The most compelling form of causal argument explains directly, step by step, how a given event came (or comes) to be. For example, in a recent newspaper article on the health problems of female athletes, the writer, Monica Yant, noted the alarming tendency of top female athletes to develop severe health problems. This claim is surprising because people typically associate athletes with vigorous health. Yant used a carefully constructed argument to show how a successful young female athlete could become a victim of osteoporosis, a disease of the bones associated with elderly females. She forged the following chain of causes and consequences.

Starting Point	Successful young female athletes are driven by a fierce competitiveness to achieve at the highest levels.
Link A	A female athlete may diet rigorously to keep her weight down to give her an edge over the competition and to please her coach.
Link B	Rigorous dieting gradually becomes obsessive, leading to an abnormal loss of body fat.
Link C	Loss of body fat leads to decreased production of estrogen, which leads in turn to amenorrhea, an absence or marked decrease in menstrual periods.
Link D	Amenorrhea leads to a further drop in the woman's estrogen levels.
End Point	A low estrogen level leads to diminished bone mass and in extreme cases to osteoporosis.

Certainly you could raise additional questions about this causal chain. You could start further back, asking how these young athletes became so competitive and so concerned with their achievements, why they care so much about what their coaches think of them and why they need that external validation. Or, you might want to know more precisely *how* low body fat leads to low estrogen and *how* low estrogen brings about low bone mass.

But the argument as it stands seems pretty persuasive, particularly because it is punctuated by quotations from authorities and examples of individual athletes.

The writer's decisions about which causal links to include and where to start along the chain were based primarily on her perceptions of her audience. She knew she was writing for a general audience of newspaper readers, not a cadre of medical experts or psychologists, so she limited the technical information and began by discussing the medical problems of mature athletes rather than the psychological intricacies of their formative years.

FOR WRITING AND DISCUSSION

Working as a whole class or in small groups, try developing a chain of causal links to connect the following starting points with their specified end points.

Starting Point	**End Point**
Invention of the automobile	Redesign of cities
Invention of the automobile	Changes in sexual mores
Popularity of beef in the U.S.	Global warming
Invention of the cotton gin	American Civil War
Popularity of aerosol sprays	Increase in skin cancer

Method Two: Explain the Causal Link Through Inductive Methods

Induction is a form of reasoning by generalizing from a limited number of specific cases. If you regularly get a headache after eating white rice but not after eating brown rice, you might conclude *inductively* that white rice causes you to get headaches, even though you can't explain the causal mechanism directly. However, it is also possible that unusual coincidences are at work. Because inductive reasoning yields only probable truths, not certain ones, it can mislead you into false assumptions. We discuss this caution in more detail later in this chapter.

When you conduct an investigation of causes using inductive methods, you can take one of several approaches.

Naturalistic Inquiry   In most cases, naturalistic inquiry involves first-person observation, supplemented by interviews and other sources of data. Although naturalistic inquiry is not as rigorous or objective as a controlled scientific experiment, it can offer powerful validation of hypotheses. If you wanted to figure out why people subject themselves to nosh pits at rock concerts or fly around campus on in-line skates, you could hurl yourself into a nosh pit or interview some skaters and undoubtedly reveal insights unavailable to researchers who work at arm's length from their subjects.

For example, two German neurologists, puzzled by the fact that so many teenage girls faint at rock concerts, attended a concert and interviewed nearly four hundred fainters. Their conclusion? The biggest culprit was lack of sleep—the fainters had been too excited to sleep the night before the concert.

Scientific Experimentation   You can reach more precise inductive conclusions by designing scientific experiments to control variables and test them one at a time. For example, scientists conducted a study to determine whether a tendency toward obesity is caused by some inherited metabolic defect, by lifestyle and diet choices, or by some combination of both. The medical team randomly selected people to participate in an experiment designed to identify which of many variables affect weight gain. Researchers placed all subjects in the same environment and gave each the same amount of food, proportioned by body weight, for a prolonged period of time. Some subjects gained weight; others lost weight.

The team noticed that two important variables seemed to have the greatest effect on weight gain or loss: gender and activity level. Women tended to gain more weight than men because they burned fewer calories (a finding that was already well established), and those who lost weight moved around more than those who gained weight (a finding that was less well established and, thanks to the study, assumed greater importance).

Correlation   Correlation is a statistical method of determining whether a relationship between two phenomena is coincidental. Using sophisticated statistical methods, you can determine the probability that when X occurs Y will also occur. Correlation studies tell you whether the tendency of X and Y to occur together is a coincidence or not, but they can't tell you the direction of causality; X may cause Y, Y may cause X, or some unknown factor Z may cause both X and Y.

For example, various historical studies have shown a correlation between creativity and left-handedness. When the percentage of left-handed people in the general population is compared with the percentage of left-handed people in the population of creative people, the latter percentage is two or three times higher than expected—too high to be coincidental. (Folk wisdom appears to have arrived at a similar conclusion: in folktales left-handedness is often associated with eccentricity and imaginative behavior.) But does creativity cause left-handedness or vice versa? Or is there some third factor that accounts for both? Some researchers have suggested that right-brain dominance accounts for both left-handedness and creativity, although many scientists are unsatisfied with that explanation.

In drawing correlations among various phenomena, it is important to identify those that are most relevant to your issue. In the trial of former football star O. J. Simpson, the prosecution established that Simpson had battered his wife, murder victim Nicole Brown Simpson. The defense conceded that fact, but pointed out that only one in every thousand men guilty of assaulting their spouses goes on to murder his spouse. A University of Virginia statistician retorted that the defense was making a wrongheaded correlation. Since in this case the spouse had been murdered, the more relevant question was, When a battered spouse is murdered, how frequently is the batterer responsible for her death? The answer to the latter question, according to the statistician, is that the batterer is also the murderer in one of every three cases. Clearly the latter figure supports the prosecution's case better than does the former figure.

FOR WRITING AND DISCUSSION

Working individually or in small groups, develop plausible causal explanations for correlations between the following pairs of phenomena:

1. Blond or red hair
2. Second born in large family
3. High family income
4. Member of National Rifle Association
5. Blond or red hair

Tendency to develop skin cancer
Tendency to be a peacemaker
Tendency for children to do well in school
Tendency to favor mandatory sentencing of criminals
Tendency toward alcoholism

Method Three: Cite Precedents or Analogies

One of the most common ways to construct a causal argument is to compare the case you are analyzing to something else that is better known and less controversial to your audience. For example, when baseball fans in Seattle and Cincinnati wanted to build a new ballpark, they argued that new ballparks can revitalize downtown areas. As proof, they cited the Baltimore Orioles' Camden Yards ballpark, which had spurred a dramatic revitalization in Baltimore. Or to take an example from analogy, rather than precedent, people who argue that high-density apartments can cause stress disorders in humans cite studies that prove that mice develop stress disorders when placed in overcrowded cages. Causal arguments by analogy and precedent usually are logically weaker than direct or inductive arguments because the *dissimilarities* between the things being compared often outweigh the similarities. Seattle and Cincinnati might be very different from Baltimore; humans are not mice.

But for all their logical and empirical limitations, analogies and precedents often have a great emotional impact in that they explain unfamiliar or puzzling phenomena by connecting them to phenomena that people understand well. So long as they are plausible, analogies and precedents can be extremely persuasive. To make an important point, however, a writer rarely relies on analogy or precedent alone. Most writers provide additional evidence from direct or inductive arguments to strengthen a case.

The Los Angeles Riots: A Causal Case Study

For an extended example of a causal analysis, let's consider one particularly complex causal issue from recent history—the 1992 LA riots that followed the pronouncement of an innocent verdict (later overturned) for four white police officers accused of beating African American motorist Rodney King.

Overview of Competing Theories

In the aftermath of the riots, many people—politicians, journalists, academics, and bureaucrats—offered their own explanations for why the riots occurred. Initially, most people blamed pent-up outrage within the African American community: because the widely aired videotape of the officers beating Rodney King seemed to show excessive force, the community anticipated a guilty verdict; when the officers were found innocent, violence erupted in protest of a racist and inequitable system of justice.

Over time people realized that other causal factors also played a role in the riots. There were not enough local police to cope with a public emergency, police failed to respond to the initial flare-ups in a timely fashion, and the National Guard was unprepared to assist. Moreover, the lingering economic recession had consigned huge numbers of young minority males—the bulk of the rioters—to seemingly permanent unemployment. In south central Los Angeles, racial tensions between longtime African American and Hispanic residents and newer Korean immigrants were running high well before the Rodney King verdict.

Still later, theories about the causes of the riots began to focus on ever more remote factors. People began to discuss the effects of two decades of state tax cuts on the infrastructure of Los Angeles, particularly on social services and police protection. Others mentioned the dwindling federal monies available to cities and city dwellers and the consequent deterioration of the quality of inner-city life. Others cited evidence of increasing racism throughout the country, including a growing number of racial incidents on college campuses, the near election of a former high Ku Klux Klan official to the governorship of a southern state, and the growing numbers of white supremacist hate groups.

One of the more surprising claims was that the failure of social reform programs begun nearly thirty years earlier, under President Lyndon Baines Johnson, was the underlying cause of the LA riots. Proponents of this idea contended that the so-called Great Society programs had cost nearly a trillion dollars over the previous twenty-five years without noticeably improving the lot of urban Americans, that they had merely raised false expectations among the poor and created jobs for bureaucrats. What is surprising about this claim is that it focused on government attempts to alleviate the problem rather than on government failure to address the problem. It argued that the supposed cure for the disease actually nurtured its poisonous progress.

Investigating the "Defective Welfare Program" Claim

Let's examine what a proponent of this claim, which we call the "defective welfare program" claim, would have to do to convince readers that the claim was both plausible and more convincing than rival claims defending the welfare program.

To show that the "defective welfare program" claim was plausible, the writer would have to show that it could explain what happened without stretching the reader's credulity or imagination too far. The writer would have to demonstrate that events resulting from the Great Society legislation in the mid-1960s were connected to the violence in Los Angeles in 1992. One actual argument took the following tack: Welfare legislation of the sixties focused on giving aid to dependent children (ADC), in large part by giving additional money to single mothers for every child they bore. This practice encouraged single mothers to have more children and also encouraged welfare fathers to abandon their families so that the families would be eligible for ADC. Family life and family values decayed; children were less likely to get through school and off welfare. According to this argument, those who rioted in LA were simply the products of this misguided social welfare program.

On first reading, this causal chain, based mainly on inductive reasoning, appears plausible enough. It *could* be true. But when you begin testing one causal claim against alternative explanations, you can more clearly see its vulnerability. Defenders of the Great Society programs were quick to point out that during the same time period the number of single-parent families had also increased markedly among the middle and upper classes. How could the welfare system be responsible for such a phenomenon? And couldn't the factors that had caused middle- and upper-class families to break down (increasing numbers of two-income families, increased emphasis on consumerism, dwindling church membership, and so forth) also have contributed to the breakdown of poor families?

These critics also noted that the Great Society programs had not created steadily worsening conditions since their inception. Statistics from the first four years of the program indicated that economic conditions had improved markedly for poor, urban African Americans. People argued that economic conditions in urban ghettos had subsequently stagnated because of program cuts initiated by a succession of Republican presidents. The program's early success supported their case that underfunding, not an inherent program flaw, was to blame.

One of the major problems with the "defective welfare program" claim is the number of links in its causal chain. In most cases, the simpler and more direct the causal relationship, the more powerful the claim. Those who argue that a quick and decisive response by the police could have stopped the LA riots or that high unemployment created preconditions for rioting had much less to prove than those who make the "defective welfare program" claim. By the same token, the argument that high unemployment created the conditions for rioting is more direct and requires fewer steps than the claim that defective welfare programs led to breakdowns in the family, which led to inadequately educated people, which led to an unskilled labor force, which led to unemployment, which led to poverty, which was a contributing cause of the riots.

Theoretically, all these claims could, to varying degrees, be true. But if you wanted to take action to prevent such riots in the future, you would be forced to rank them. Suppose you were to ask, Now that we've identified the causes of this terrible event, what do we do to insure that something like this doesn't recur? As soon as you move from a discussion of causes to a proposal for preventive action, you have to choose the most plausible explanation. In most instances, the most plausible explanation is the analysis with the fewest causal links.

Glossary of Causal Terms

Now that you've considered one causal argument, let's take a closer look at some of the language that has grown up around causal debates.

The fallacy of the oversimplified cause.   When conducting a causal analysis, a great temptation is to look for *the* cause of a phenomenon. But rarely is an event or phenomenon caused by a single factor; almost always, multiple factors work together. A carefully constructed causal analysis explains why one causal factor made a more or less important contribution than another; rarely does the writer try to convince the reader that a single factor is solely responsible for an effect.

Immediate versus remote causes.   Every causal chain links backward to the indefinite past. Immediate causes are those closest in time to the effect you are studying; remote causes are those further away in time. An immediate cause of the LA riots would be the verdict in the Rodney King trial; a remote cause would be the launching of the Great Society programs in the sixties. The more remote in time the cause is from its purported effect, the greater the arguer's burden of proof. On the flip side, it is all too easy to place too much emphasis on an immediate cause and to treat it as *the* cause rather than as one among many.

Precipitating versus contributing causes.   Whereas remote and immediate causes have different temporal relations to effects, precipitating and contributing causes may coexist simultaneously. Contributing causes are the set of conditions that give rise to a precipitating cause, which helps trigger the effect. In the case of the LA riots, all the conditions that contributed to a sense of injustice in the affected community—lack of job opportunities, inferior schools, uneven police protection, and dwindling governmental support—could be considered contributing causes of the riots. All these conditions might have given rise to the anger that followed the verdict in the King case—the precipitating cause.

Necessary versus sufficient causes.   A necessary cause is a cause that must be present for a given effect to occur. A sufficient cause is a cause that, if present, always triggers the given effect. For example, electricity in a circuit is a *necessary* cause for a refrigerator to run, but it is not a *sufficient* cause; other factors must also be present (a working motor, for example). A cause can be sufficient without being necessary. Lack of water is a sufficient cause for a plant's death, but it is not a necessary cause (plants may die from other causes).

Constraints.   Sometimes an effect occurs not because X happened, but because another factor, a constraint, was removed. A constraint is a kind of negative cause, a factor whose presence limits possibilities and choices. In the aftermath of the LA riots, many nearby communities immediately imposed curfews in their communities. Those curfews were constraints that prevented the riots from spreading.

The *post hoc, ergo propter hoc* fallacy ("after this, therefore because of this").   The *post hoc* fallacy is the most common reasoning fallacy associated with causal arguments. It is tempting to assume that if event A occurs and event B follows, then event A must have caused event B. But chronological sequence does not guarantee causality. (For further discussion and an illustration of the *post hoc* fallacy, see p. 343.)

READINGS

The readings, one by a professional writer and one by a student, provide examples of writers' analyzing causal questions and proposing causal claims.* The first essay, by paleontologist and science writer Stephen Jay Gould, is from his book *The Flamingo's Smile: Reflections in Natural History.*

STEPHEN JAY GOULD

SEX, DRUGS, DISASTERS, AND THE EXTINCTION OF DINOSAURS

1   Science, in its most fundamental definition, is a fruitful mode of inquiry, not a list of enticing conclusions. The conclusions are the consequence, not the essence.

2   My greatest unhappiness with most popular presentations of science concerns their failure to separate fascinating claims from the methods that scientists use to establish the facts of nature. Journalists, and the public, thrive on controversial and stunning statements. But science is, basically, a way of knowing—in P. B. Medawar's apt words, "the art of the soluble." If the growing corps of popular science writers would focus on *how* scientists develop and defend those fascinating claims, they would make their greatest possible contribution to public understanding.

3   Consider three ideas, proposed in perfect seriousness to explain the greatest of all titillating puzzles—the extinction of dinosaurs. Since these three notions invoke the primally fascinating themes of our culture—sex, drugs, and violence—they surely reside in the category of fascinating claims. I want to show why two of them rank as silly speculation, while the other represents science at its grandest and most useful.

4   Science works with testable proposals. If, after much compilation and scrutiny of data, new information continues to affirm a hypothesis, we may accept it provisionally and gain confidence as further evidence mounts. We can never be completely sure that a hypothesis is right, though we may be able to show with confidence that it is wrong. The best scientific hypotheses are also generous and expansive: they suggest extensions and implications that enlighten related, and even far distant, subjects. Simply consider how the idea of evolution has influenced virtually every intellectual field.

5   Useless speculation, on the other hand, is restrictive. It generates no testable hypothesis, and offers no way to obtain potentially refuting evidence. Please note that I am not speaking of truth or falsity. The speculation may well be true; still, if it provides, in principle, no material for affirmation or rejection, we can make nothing of it. It must simply stand forever as an intriguing idea. Useless speculation turns in on itself and leads nowhere; good science, containing both seeds for its potential refutation and implications for more and different testable knowledge, reaches out. But, enough preaching. Let's move on to dinosaurs, and the three proposals for their extinction.

---

*For an additional example of causal analysis, see Sharon Lerner's "If We've Come Such a Long Way, Why Are We Still Smoking?" in Chapter 6, pages 123–27.

1. Sex: Testes function in a narrow range of temperature (those of mammals hang externally in a scrotal sac because internal body temperatures are too high for their proper function). A worldwide rise in temperature at the close of the Cretaceous period caused the testes of dinosaurs to stop functioning and led to their extinction by sterilization of males.
2. Drugs: Angiosperms (flowering plants) first evolved toward the end of the dinosaurs' reign. Many of these plants contain psychoactive agents, avoided by mammals today as a result of their bitter taste. Dinosaurs had neither means to taste the bitterness nor livers effective enough to detoxify the substances. They died of massive overdoses.
3. Disasters: A large comet or asteroid struck the earth some 65 million years ago, lofting a cloud of dust into the sky and blocking sunlight, thereby suppressing photosynthesis and so drastically lowering world temperatures that dinosaurs and hosts of other creatures became extinct.

Before analyzing these three tantalizing statements, we must establish a basic ground rule often violated in proposals for the dinosaurs' demise. *There is no separate problem of the extinction of dinosaurs.* Too often we divorce specific events from their wider contexts and systems of cause and effect. The fundamental fact of dinosaur extinction is its synchrony with the demise of so many other groups across a wide range of habitats, from terrestrial to marine.

The history of life has been punctuated by brief episodes of mass extinction. A recent analysis by University of Chicago paleontologists Jack Sepkoski and Dave Raup, based on the best and most exhaustive tabulation of data ever assembled, shows clearly that five episodes of mass dying stand well above the "background" extinctions of normal times (when we consider all mass extinctions, large and small, they seem to fall in a regular 26-million-year cycle). The *Cretaceous* debacle, occurring 65 million years ago and separating the Mesozoic and Cenozoic eras of our geological time scale, ranks prominently among the five. Nearly all the marine plankton (single-celled floating creatures) died with geological suddenness; among marine invertebrates, nearly 15 percent of all families perished, including many previously dominant groups, especially the ammonites (relatives of squids and coiled shells). On land, the dinosaurs disappeared after more than 100 million years of unchallenged domination. 6

In this context, speculations limited to dinosaurs alone ignore the larger phenomenon. We need a coordinated explanation for a system of events that includes the extinction of dinosaurs as one component. Thus, it makes little sense, though it may fuel our desire to view mammals as inevitable inheritors of the earth, to guess that dinosaurs died because small mammals ate their eggs (a perennial favorite among untestable speculations). It seems most unlikely that some disaster peculiar to dinosaurs befell these massive beasts—and that the debacles happened to strike just when one of history's five great dyings had enveloped the earth for completely different reasons. 7

The testicular theory, an old favorite from the 1940s, had it root in an interesting and thoroughly respectable study of temperature tolerances in the American alligator, published in the staid *Bulletin of the American Museum of Natural History* in 1946 by three experts on living and fossil reptiles—E. H. Colbert, my own first teacher in paleontology; R. B. Cowles; and C. M. Bogert. 8

The first sentence of their summary reveals a purpose beyond alligators: "This report describes an attempt to infer the reactions of extinct reptiles, especially the dinosaurs, to high temperatures as based upon reactions observed in the modern 9 alligator." They studied, by rectal thermometry, the body temperatures of alligators under changing conditions of heating and cooling. (Well, let's face it, you wouldn't want to try sticking a thermometer under a 'gator's tongue.) The predictions under test go way back to an old theory first stated by Galileo in the 1630s—the unequal scaling of surfaces and volumes. As an animal, or any object, grows (provided its shape doesn't change), surface areas must increase more slowly than volumes—since surfaces get larger as length squared, while volumes increased much more rapidly, as length cubed. Therefore, small animals have high ratios of surface to volume, while large animals cover themselves with relatively little surface.

10   Among cold-blooded animals lacking any physiological mechanism for keeping their temperatures constant, small creatures have a hell of a time keeping warm—because they lose so much heat through their relatively large surfaces. On the other hand, large animals, with their relatively small surfaces, may lose heat so slowly that, once warm, they may maintain effectively constant temperatures against ordinary fluctuations of climate. (In fact, the resolution of the "hot-blooded dinosaur" controversy that burned so brightly a few years back may simply be that, while large dinosaurs possessed no physiological mechanism for constant temperature, and were not therefore warm-blooded in the technical sense, their large size and relatively small surface area kept them warm.)

11   Colbert, Cowles, and Bogert compared the warming rates of small and large alligators. As predicted, the small fellows heated up (and cooled down) more quickly. When exposed to a warm sun, a tiny 50-gram (1.76-ounce) alligator heated up one degree Celsius every minute and a half, while a large alligator, 260 times bigger at 13,000 grams (28.7 pounds), took seven and a half minutes to gain a degree. Extrapolating up to an adult 10-ton dinosaur, they concluded that a one-degree rise in body temperature would take eighty-six hours. If large animals absorb heat so slowly (through their relatively small surfaces), they will also be unable to shed any excess heat gained when temperatures rise above a favorable level.

12   The authors then guessed that large dinosaurs lived at or near their optimum temperatures; Cowles suggested that a rise in global temperatures just before the Cretaceous extinction caused the dinosaurs to heat up beyond their optimal tolerance—and, being so large, they couldn't shed the unwanted heat. (In a most unusual statement within a scientific paper, Colbert and Bogert then explicitly disavowed this speculative extension of their empirical work on alligators.) Cowles conceded that this excess heat probably wasn't enough to kill or even to enervate the great beasts, but since testes often function only within a narrow range of temperature, he proposed that this global rise might have sterilized all the males, causing extinction by natural contraception.

13   The overdose theory has recently been supported by UCLA psychiatrist Ronald K. Siegel. Siegal has gathered, he claims, more than 2,000 records or animals who, when given access, administer various drugs to themselves—from a mere swig of alcohol to massive doses of the big H. Elephants will swill the equivalent of twenty beers at a time, but do not like alcohol in concentrations greater than 7 percent. In a silly bit of anthropocentric speculation, Siegel states that "elephants drink, perhaps, to forget . . . the anxiety produced by a shrinking rangeland and the competition for food."

14   Since fertile imaginations can apply almost any hot idea to the extinction of dinosaurs, Siegel found a way. Flowering plants did not evolve until late in the dinosaur's reign. These plants also produced an array of aromatic, amino-acid-based alkaloids—the major group of psychoactive agents. Most mammals are "smart" enough to avoid these potential poisons. The alkaloids simply don't taste good (they are bitter); in any

case, we mammals have livers happily supplied with the capacity to detoxify them. But, Siegel speculates, perhaps dinosaurs could neither taste the bitterness nor detoxify the substances once ingested. He recently told members of the American Psychological Association: "I'm not suggesting that all dinosaurs OD'd on plant drugs, but it certainly was a factor." He also argued that death by overdose may help explain why so many dinosaur fossils are found in contorted positions. (Do not go gentle into that good night.)

Extraterrestrial catastrophes have long pedigrees in the popular literatures of extinction, but the subject exploded again in 1979, after a long lull, when the father-son, physicist-geologist team of Luis and Walter Alvarez proposed that an asteroid, some 10km in diameter, struck the earth 65 million years ago (comets, rather than asteroids, have since gained favor. Good science is self-corrective).   15

The force of such a collision would be immense, greater by far than the megaton-nage of all the world's nuclear weapons. In trying to reconstruct a scenario that would explain the simultaneous dying of dinosaurs on land and so many creatures in the sea, the Alvarezes proposed that a gigantic dust cloud, generated by particles blown aloft in the impact, would so darken the earth that photosynthesis would cease and temperatures drop precipitously. (Rage, rage against the dying of the light.) The single-celled photosynthetic oceanic plankton, with life cycles measured in weeks, would perish outright, but land plants might survive through the dormancy of their seeds (land plants were not much affected by the Cretaceous extinction, and any adequate theory must account for the curious pattern of differential survival). Dinosaurs would die by starvation and freezing; small, warm-blooded mammals, with more modest requirements for food and better regulation of body temperature, would squeak through. "Let the bastards freeze in the dark," as bumper stickers of our chauvinistic neighbors in sunbelt states proclaimed several years ago during the Northeast's winter oil crisis.   16

All three categories, testicular malfunction, psychoactive overdosing, and aster-oidal zapping, grab our attention mightily. As pure phenomenology, they rank about equally high on any hit parade of primal fascination. Yet one represents expansive science, the others restrictive and untestable speculation. The proper criterion lies in evidence and methodology; we must probe behind the superficial fascination of particular claims.   17

How could we possibly decide whether the hypothesis of testicular frying is right or wrong? We would have to know things that the fossil record cannot provide. What temperatures were optimal for dinosaurs? Could they avoid the absorption of heat by staying in the shade, or in caves? At what temperatures did their testicles cease to function? Were late Cretaceous climates ever warm enough to drive the internal temperatures of dinosaurs close to this ceiling? Testicles simply don't fossilize, and how could we infer their temperature tolerances even if they did? In short, Cowles's hypothesis is only an intriguing speculation leading nowhere. The most damning statement against it appeared right in the conclusion of Colbert, Cowles, and Bogert's paper, when they admitted: "It is difficult to advance any definite arguments against this hypothesis." My statement may seem paradoxical—isn't a hypothesis really good if you can't devise any arguments against it? Quite the contrary. It is simply untestable and unusable.   18

Siegel's overdosing has even less going for it. At least Cowles extrapolated his conclusion from some good data on alligators. And he didn't completely violate the primary guideline of siting dinosaur extinction in the context of a general mass dying—for rise in temperature could be the root cause of a general catastrophe, zapping dinosaurs by testicular malfunction and different groups for other reasons. But Siegel's specula-   19 tion cannot touch the extinction of ammonites or oceanic plankton (diatoms make their own food with good sweet sunlight; they don't OD on the chemicals of terrestrial plants). It is simply a gratuitous, attention-grabbing guess. It cannot be tested, for how can we know what dinosaurs tasted and what their livers could do? Livers don't fossilize any better than testicles.

20   The hypothesis doesn't even make any sense in its own context. Angiosperms were in full flower ten million years before dinosaurs went the way of all flesh. Why did it take so long? As for the pains of a chemical death recorded in the contortions of fossils, I regret to say (or rather I'm pleased to note for the dinosaurs' sake) that Siegel's knowledge of geology must be a bit deficient: muscles contract after death and geological strata rise and fall with motions of the earth's crust after burial—more than enough reason to distort a fossil's pristine appearance.

21   The impact story, on the other hand, has a sound basis in evidence. It can be tested, extended, refined and, if wrong, disproved. The Alvarezes did not just construct an arresting guess for public consumption. They proposed their hypothesis after laborious geochemical studies with Frank Asaro and Helen Michael had revealed a massive increase of iridium in rocks deposited right at the time of extinction. Iridium, a rare metal of the platinum group, is virtually absent from indigenous rocks of the earth's crust; most of our iridium arrives on extraterrestrial objects that strike the earth.

22   The Alvarez hypothesis bore immediate fruit. Based originally on evidence from two European localities, it led geochemists throughout the world to examine other sediments of the same age. They found abnormally high amounts of iridium everywhere—from continental rocks of the western United States to deep sea cores from the South Atlantic.

23   Cowles proposed his testicular hypothesis in the mid-1940s. Where has it gone since then? Absolutely nowhere, because scientists can do nothing with it. The hypothesis must stand as a curious appendage to a solid study of alligators. Siegel's overdose scenario will also win a few press notices and fade into oblivion. The Alvarezes' asteroid falls into a different category altogether, and much of the popular commentary has missed this essential distinction by focusing on the impact and its attendant results, and forgetting what really matters to a scientist—the iridium. If you talk just about asteroids, dust, and darkness, you tell stories no better and no more entertaining than fried testicles or terminal trips. It is the iridium—the source of testable evidence—that counts and forges the crucial distinction between speculation and science.

24   The proof, to twist a phrase, lies in the doing. Cowles's hypothesis has generated nothing in thirty-five years. Since its proposal in 1979, the Alvarez hypothesis has spawned hundreds of studies, a major conference, and attendant publications. Geologists are fired up. They are looking for iridium at all other extinction boundaries. Every week exposes a new wrinkle in the scientific press. Further evidence that the Cretaceous iridium represents extraterrestrial impact and not indigenous volcanism continues to accumulate. As I revise this essay in November 1984 (this paragraph will be out of date when the book is published), new data include chemical "signatures" of other isotopes indicating unearthly provenance, glass spherules of a size and sort produced by impact and not by volcanic eruptions, and high-pressure varieties of silica formed (so far as we know) only under the tremendous shock of impact.

25   My point is simply this: Whatever the eventual outcome (I suspect it will be positive), the Alvarez hypothesis is exciting, fruitful science because it generates tests, provides us with things to do, and expands outward. We are having fun, battling back and

forth, moving toward a resolution, and extending the hypothesis beyond its original scope.

As just one example of the unexpected, distant cross-fertilization that good science   26
engenders, the Alvarez hypothesis made a major contribution to a theme that has riveted public attention in the past few months—so-called nuclear winter. In a speech delivered in April 1982, Luis Alvarez calculated the energy that a ten-kilometer asteroid would release on impact. He compared such an explosion with a full nuclear exchange and implied that all-out atomic war might unleash similar consequences.   27

This theme of impact leading to massive dust clouds and falling temperatures formed an important input to the decision of Carl Sagan and a group of colleagues to model the climatic consequences of nuclear holocaust. Full nuclear exchange would probably generate the same kind of dust cloud and darkening that may have wiped out the dinosaurs. Temperatures would drop precipitously and agriculture might become impossible. Avoidance of nuclear warfare is fundamentally an ethical and political imperative, but we must know the factual consequences to make firm judgments. I am heartened by a final link across disciplines and deep concerns—another criterion, by the way, of science at its best: A recognition of the very phenomenon that made our evolution possible by exterminating the previously dominant dinosaurs and clearing a way for the evolution of large mammals, including us, might actually help to save us from joining those magnificent beasts in contorted poses among the strata of earth.

Thinking Critically About "Sex, Drugs, Disasters, and the Extinction of Dinosaurs"

1. Name Gould's criteria for sound hypotheses and explain how his defense of the asteroid theory fits his criteria.
2. Summarize Gould's reasons for rejecting the drug-plant thesis and the overheated testes theories as explanations for the extinction of dinosaurs.
3. Apply Gould's criteria for a scientifically sound hypothesis to an explanation offered for a current causal puzzle in the local or national news.

In the following essay, basketball maven Ron Witten analyzes the causes behind the downfall of the Phoenix Suns basketball team in the 1995–1996 season.

RON WITTEN (student)
SUNS SET IN WEST: WAIT UNTIL MOURNING

Student Essay

As I write this essay, the once proud Phoenix Suns basketball team is next to last   1
in the NBA West Division. Their record is a woeful 14–21. They have gone from being one of the most successful teams in the NBA over the past five years to being one of the worst teams in the league. Overnight, they went from dominance to doormats without ever passing through mediocrity. Like so many of the Suns' loyal fans, I'm stunned, confused, and looking for answers. What caused the demise of Phoenix basketball?

2   The usual answer, the one Suns' coach Paul Westphal kept handing out right up to the point of his abrupt dismissal two losses ago, was injuries. The Suns have lots of them. For most of the past ten games, the team has been without four of its starting five, including center John "Hot Rod" Williams, forwards Charles Barkley and Danny Manning, and point guard Kevin Johnson. In terms of both quantity and quality, their being gone has been a major loss. The four injured players are probably their four best: Barkley is a sure Hall of Famer, Manning and Johnson could reach that level if their careers last long enough, and Williams is a star-quality player. With so many injuries, the Suns were able to suit up only seven players for several games during their slide. It's tough to win with two subs in the NBA no matter who you have on the floor.

3   No one could say these injuries haven't been a major factor in the Suns' decline. But injuries can't explain all these losses, so some people blame the coach. They particularly point to last week's loss to the Cleveland Cavaliers. The Cavs, short on talent in the first place and themselves lacking a couple of starters, destroyed Phoenix on the Suns' home court. The Cavs forced Phoenix to play at a deliberate pace unsuited to the Suns' up-tempo offense, pressured Phoenix into over twenty turnovers, passed the Suns' dizzy, and by the end of the evening left them looking confused and demoralized. The Suns' porous defense was even more accommodating than usual; players were slow to rotate or switch off. Cleveland coach Mike Fratello put on a coaching clinic for Westphal, but by then it was too late for Paul to learn from his betters. He was fired the next day.

4   But before we think that dumping Paul Westphal will improve the Suns, let's keep in mind that over the past three years, he managed to win over 70 percent of his games, one of the best starts to a coaching career in NBA history. He didn't get stupid all of a sudden. Through most of the team's losing streak, they played hard and there were few signs of dissension among the players. Firing Westphal is a classic case of firing the coach only because you can't fire the team.

5   So if we can't blame it all on coaching and injuries, what's left? Perhaps it's the "age thing." For years, there have been whispers about the aging Suns' roster. Five of their top eight players are over thirty. And in the NBA, with its merciless schedule, constant travel, and relentless physical pounding, thirty can be very old. Probably the injury problems are closely related to the aging factor. Older players tend to get hurt more and to need more rest. But age is a double-edged sword. What you lose in physical sharpness, you get back in guile. Some of the greatest NBA teams ever—the Celtics of the late sixties and the Lakers of the late seventies—were older teams. And besides, however old the team Phoenix put on the floor during its swoon, they were losing to some of the worst teams in the NBA. In fact, they lost twice to the Los Angeles Clippers, a team that would probably lose to most NBA Old-Timers teams.

6   Age, injuries, and coaching have surely played a role in the Suns' downfall. The rate of their decline has certainly been speeded up by these factors. But there is another, less obvious factor that the current situation has obscured. Whatever happens to the Suns in the short run, in the long run they still have a fatal weakness that good health, sound coaching, and youth can't cure. In a word—three words actually—the Suns' biggest problem is: No Big Man. To be a consistent winner in the NBA, to have a shot at getting through the play-offs into the championship, you've got to have what TV analyst Al McGuire calls "an aircraft carrier," a large, physical center who can block out, rebound, block shots, neutralize the other team's big guy one-on-one, while forcing the other team to double-team him.

The Suns don't have that now (Williams is a good offensive player who can run the   7
floor and block shots, but not go head-to-head against the best of the NBA big men),
and haven't ever had it. This raises a question. How come their record has been so good
without a true big man? The answer is that their record is deceptive. They've played in
a division that hasn't had a dominant big man in it for many years. The Suns have always done well against teams in their division, but not so well against opponents outside the division with talented big men.

But some people will still question the crucial importance of a big man. Some will   8
cite the success of the Chicago Bulls despite the presence of Will "Still Clueless" Per-
due in the pivot. The Bulls are the exception that proves the rule in my book. If you replaced the two best players on any other team in the NBA with the Bulls' Michael
Jordan and Scottie Pippen, that team would have a legitimate shot at the title. That's
how good Pippen and Jordan are. The chances of any team ever having two similarly
talented players on their team at the same time are virtually nil.

So, in April, when all the Suns' players are back, and the old guys are once again   9
being referred to as our "veterans," and the longtime successful NBA coach Cotton
Fitzsimmons is firmly in control, we still won't be quite good enough. We'll be out of the
play-offs by the time the baseball races start heating up. And unless we get a Patrick
Ewing, a Shaquille O'Neal, a Hakeem Olajuwon, or an Alonzo Mourning in the middle,
we'll continue to slide, however slowly, out of real contention for an NBA championship.

Thinking Critically About "Suns Set in West: Wait Until Mourning"

1. If Ron Witten can so readily recognize the reason for the demise of his
   beloved Suns, what's wrong with Suns' ownership? If you are a basketball
   fan, can you think of any reasons that the Suns' ownership might not share
   Ron's views on (a) the importance of a big man to NBA success or (b) the
   feasibility of acquiring a premier NBA center? Can you cite other situations
   in which teams followed Ron's prescription for success and fell short? Why?
2. If you are not a basketball fan, you can still appreciate the structure of this
   argument. What question does Ron pose? What are the common answers to
   this question? What is Ron's surprising answer?
3. What do you see as the major strengths and weaknesses of Ron's argument?

COMPOSING YOUR ESSAY

This assignment asks you to write a causal analysis in which you pose a question about a puzzling event, trend, or phenomenon and then explain and support
your own understanding of its causes or consequences.

Generating and Exploring Ideas

Your first step is to select the event, trend, or phenomenon you intend to analyze. Your goal is to find a topic that is both puzzling enough and significant
enough to engage your readers' interest and yet gives you plenty to say. Often it is
helpful to explore several possibilities through freewriting or idea mapping before
you settle on a final topic. The following suggestions will help you with the process.

Make a List of People's Unusual Likes and Dislikes

One fruitful subject for a causal argument is the causes of people's unusual likes or dislikes. For example: Why are people afraid of snakes (spiders, bats)? Why do many people fear public speaking (writing, computers)? Why do people like stamp collecting (rock climbing, raising tropical fish)? Make a list of unusual things that people you know like or dislike and freewrite about them for five minutes or so, speculating on the causes of this peculiar behavior. Naturalistic observation can help; or, you can interview people who have these puzzling tastes.

Make Lists of Puzzling Trends, One-Time Events, or Repeatable Phenomena

Another helpful brainstorming activity is to expand the lists of trends, one-time events, and repeatable phenomena that you generated in the exploratory activity on page 306. Think of as many ideas as you can and then select several to explore in more depth through freewriting. Consider working together with classmates since two heads (or three or four) are often better than one at the brainstorming stage.

Create Idea Maps to Explore Causes or Consequences

For this exercise we provide you with two columns; one lists events or trends for which you are to think of causes; the other lists hypothetical events for which you are to think of consequences. Create idea maps of causes or consequences for the problems or events. Begin by placing on your idea map the causes or consequences that people would commonly think of; then search for possible causes or consequences that the average person might not think of.

Think of the Causes of

- the increase in smoking among children and teenagers
- the opposition of many Americans to gun-control legislation
- the urge to write graffiti on walls and in subway stations
- the small number of women in the skilled trades of carpentry, bricklaying, or plumbing
- the appeal of certain print or TV advertisements (choose some specific ads)
- the failure of soccer to capture a wide sports audience in the United States
- the popularity of TV talk shows
- the existence of homophobia or racism
- the failure or success of a TV series (choose one)

Think of the Consequences of

- a cure for cancer
- universal health care in the United States
- increased social acceptance of suicide by the elderly or by persons with serious diseases
- a heavy tax on families with more than two children
- elimination of welfare benefits for unwed mothers
- a four-day workweek
- widespread use of the information highway
- legalizing marijuana, cocaine, and heroin
- allowing gay and lesbian marriages
- exhaustion of the world's supply of petroleum
- a change in a rule or regulation for a sport (choose a specific example)

Explore Your Chosen Phenomenon Through Rapid Freewriting

Once you have chosen a puzzling phenomenon for your causal analysis paper, you can explore ideas and avoid writer's block by freewriting rapidly, spilling your initial ideas onto paper. These freewrites will make it easier to write a first draft and can reveal areas that may require more research or additional ideas. Try freewriting your responses to the following invention questions:

1. What is your chosen phenomenon? Describe it. If it is a trend, what is your evidence that the trend exists?
2. What personal experiences have you had with this phenomenon, either as a participant or as an observer? Describe those experiences.
3. Why are the causes of your phenomenon puzzling? Why is this an interesting or significant phenomenon to analyze?
4. What are the most common explanations for this phenomenon? What explanations do you think will first pop into your readers' minds?
5. Do you think these causes fully explain your phenomenon? What may be wrong, missing, or inadequate?
6. What do you see as the most important causes of this phenomenon? What is your evidence or support?
7. Are there alternative explanations that you think need to be examined and rejected? Why?
8. My ideas about the causes of this phenomenon will surprise my reader because _____. (Explore.)

Develop Ideas and Supporting Arguments Through Observation, Interviewing, or Other Forms of Research

Often your own personal experiences and critical thinking are all you need for a causal analysis. In other cases, research is necessary. It may be helpful to read about how other people have analyzed the causes of your phenomenon. (See Part Four for advice on research.)

You can also gather inductive evidence through naturalistic observation—by living among the people you are investigating, taking notes on their behavior, and asking them questions (see p. 309). Although a tape recorder might come in handy, all you really need to conduct a naturalistic inquiry is a pen and a notebook. Be sure to write down your impressions and quotations on the spot and carefully to note the time, place, and people involved. Soon after you're through observing, review your notes while they're still fresh in your mind and annotate them in the margins or on the facing page, categorizing them according to how they support or refute your initial hypotheses about causes.

Shaping and Drafting

Because your goal at this early discovery stage of drafting is to put your developing argument on paper, it will be useful for you to know some of the standard ways of organizing a causal argument. Later on, you may decide to adopt a different organizational pattern, but these standard ways will help you get started.

1. When your intention is to link your phenomenon to a cause (or consequence) by describing and explaining the links in a causal chain
   - Introduce the phenomenon, establishing (a) that it exists and (b) that it is worthy of analysis by being problematic and significant. Concentrate on engaging your reader's interest. Often readers need to be convinced that a problematic phenomenon exists before they become interested in its causes or consequences.
   - Present your thesis that this phenomenon has a surprising cause (or consequence).
   - Describe and explain each link in the causal chain.
2. When your intention is to explore the relative contribution of all causes to a phenomenon or all consequences of an event
   - Introduce the phenomenon, again demonstrating that it exists and showing why it is problematic or controversial. Engage your reader's interest.
   - Devote one section to each possible cause or consequence and support it with evidence. Arrange sections to present those causes most familiar to the audience first and those most surprising last.
   - If appropriate, describe alternative hypotheses and show why you are rejecting them.
3. When your purpose is to change your reader's view by arguing for a surprising or unexpected cause or consequence
   - Introduce your phenomenon, establishing that it exists and may be even more prevalent than your reader thought, engage your reader's interest in the question, and summarize the commonplace explanation of causes that you assume your reader holds.
   - One by one examine and reject, or show as inadequate or insufficient, the causes or consequences that your audience would normally assume or expect.
   - Introduce your unexpected or surprising cause or consequence and argue for it.

Patterns 2 and 3 are similar in that they examine numerous possible causes or consequences. Pattern 2, however, tries to establish the relative importance of each cause or consequence, whereas Pattern 3 tries to discredit the audience's preconceived notions about these causes or consequences and then argues for a new, surprising cause or consequence.

Revising

Once you've selected your topic, written your draft, and discussed it with a member of your group, you're ready to do the major work of revising—converting your draft from something that works for you to something that works for readers. Because you will probably choose to write this paper near the closed end of the closed-to-open continuum, the revision suggestions in Chapter 19 are especially relevant: give the big picture first and refer to it often; place points before particulars (ensuring that paragraphs have topic sentences); use frequent transitions; and follow the old/new contract.

You should also seek out peer reviews, using the following guidelines.

g   u   i   d   e   l   i   n   e   s
for Peer Reviewers

Instructions for peer reviews, including use of these guidelines, are provided in Chapter 21, pages 527–28. To write a peer review for a classmate, use your own paper, numbering your responses to correspond to the questions on the guidelines. At the head of your paper place the author's name and your own name as shown.

Author's Name: _____

Peer Reviewer's Name: _____

I. Read the draft at normal reading speed from beginning to end. As you read, do the following:
  A. Place a wavy line in the margin next to any passages that you find confusing, that contain something that doesn't seem to fit, or that otherwise slow down your reading.
  B. Place a "Good!" in the margin next to any passages where you think the writing is particularly strong or interesting.
II. Read the draft again slowly. Describe for the writer what you currently see in this draft. If you have difficulty answering any of the following questions, explain briefly the source of your difficulty.
  A. What is the writer's causal question? Why is the question significant? What would happen if the question weren't answered? How will answering the question prove useful or further your understanding?
  B. What is the writer's thesis in response to the question?
  C. What alternative explanations of the phenomenon does the writer mention?
    1. What arguments does the writer use to persuade you to prefer his or her explanation to the alternatives?
    2. What did you find most surprising about the writer's thesis? Can you imagine anyone who would not be surprised by the thesis?
  D. If the writer describes the links in the causal chain, count how many links there are.
    1. How is each link in the chain supported? If you were to bolster the support for one link in the chain, which would you choose and why?
    2. What alternative causal chains can you imagine?

   E. If the writer uses correlations, try reversing the direction of cause and
       ask, Why isn't it just as probable for Y to cause X as it is for X to cause Y?
       1. What arguments could you make for this reversed direction of causal-
           ity?
       2. What unnamed third factors might cause both X and Y?
   F. If the writer uses analogy, cite all the elements of the analogy that are dif-
       ferent from the phenomenon in question. How might these differences
       lead to different consequences?
III. What recommendations do you have for improving this draft?
   A. How might the writer improve the title?
   B. Does the introduction capture your interest and set up the question to be
       addressed? Does it convince you that the phenomenon to be examined
       really exists? How might the writer improve the introduction?
   C. How might the writer improve the structure of the draft?
   D. Can you point out areas where the writer might specifically apply the
       principles of clarity from Chapter 19 (giving the big picture first and re-
       ferring back to it often; placing points before particulars; using frequent
       transitions; and following the old/new contract)?
   E. If you could ask for one or more additional pieces of support for the
       writer's argument, what would you ask for?
   F. Where do you disagree with the writer's argument or have doubts or
       queries?
   G. Sum up what you see as the chief strengths and problem areas of this
       draft.
       1. Strengths
       2. Problem areas
IV. Read the draft one more time. Place a check in the margin wherever you no-
    tice problems in grammar, spelling, or mechanics (one check per problem).

c h a p t e r **14**

Writing a Classical Argument

ABOUT CLASSICAL ARGUMENT

The assignment for this chapter introduces you to a classical way of arguing in which you take a stand on an issue, offer reasons and evidence in support of your position, and summarize and refute opposing views. Some argumentative issues are two-sided, calling for a yes-or-no response: Should gay marriage be legalized? Should the city pass the new school bond proposal? More often argumentative issues are multisided, requiring the writer to select from a wide variety of possibilities one claim to defend: What kind of computer network should the company install? What should the state government do about prison overcrowding? How can children be kept away from pornography on the Internet?

Whereas all writing involves some degree of persuasion, *writing to persuade* entails a purposeful attempt to move readers from their initial position on a controversy toward your own position. Most arguments are aimed at those who disagree with or are neutral toward the writer's positions, although some arguments preach to the converted in order to whip up extra enthusiasm for a cause or to move supporters from belief to action.

We cannot overemphasize the importance of learning to write persuasively. Everyone has the power to influence public policy by writing persuasive letters to the editor or by drafting convincing position papers for business or professional organizations. Whenever an organization needs to make a major decision, those who can write persuasively can wield great influence.

EXPLORING CLASSICAL ARGUMENT

You are a member of a planning committee to develop a *Campus Forum* TV show on a local public-access channel. The show—modeled after Oprah or Phil Donahue—is supposed to stimulate intense conversation and audience participation without the titillating revelations or brain-dead insult swapping typical of talk shows. You want intelligent, multisided discussions of significant issues ranging from the national—What can be done to reduce sexual harassment in the workplace?—to the local—Should students publish their own ratings of faculty?

Working in small groups, develop a list of ten good issues for the show. Then rank the list in order of preference. Explain why your top-ranked issues make especially good questions for discussion. Each group should then place its top three issues on the board. As a class, select the most promising issue. Choose a student as host to lead the class in its own *Campus Forum* on this issue.

WRITING PROJECT

> Write a position paper that takes a stand on a controversial issue. Your introduction will present your issue, provide background, and state the claim you intend to support. The body of your argument will summarize and respond to opposing views as well as present reasons and evidence in support of your own position. You will choose whether to summarize and refute opposing views before or after you have made your own case. Try to end your essay with your strongest arguments.

We sometimes call this assignment an argument in the *classical style* because it is patterned after the persuasive speeches of ancient Greek and Roman orators. In the terms of ancient rhetoricians, the main parts of a persuasive speech are the *exordium*, in which the speaker gets the audience's attention; the *narratio*, which provides needed background; the *propositio*, the speaker's proposition or thesis; the *partitio*, a forecast of the main parts of the speech, equivalent to a blueprint statement; the *confirmatio*, the speaker's arguments in favor of the proposition; the *confutatio*, the refutation of opposing views; and the *peroratio*, the conclusion that sums up the argument, calls for action, and leaves a strong last impression.

We cite these tongue-twisting Latin terms only to assure you that in writing a classical argument you are joining a time-honored tradition that links you to Roman senators on the capitol steps. From their discourse arose the ideal of a democratic society based on superior arguments rather than on superior weaponry. Although there are many other ways to persuade audiences, the classical approach is a particularly effective introduction to persuasive writing.

UNDERSTANDING CLASSICAL ARGUMENT

Having reviewed the basic purpose of persuasive writing, we will now look closely at its features and strategies.

What Is an Arguable Issue?

At the heart of any argument is an issue. We define an *issue* as a question to which there can be more than one reasonable answer supported by reasons and evidence. This requirement excludes disagreements based on personal opinion. Consider the difference between these two questions:

1. Which tastes better, whole milk or skim milk?
2. Which is better for you, whole milk or skim milk?

The first question might produce a dispute, but not an argument. Taste is a personal preference arising from subjective experience. You can't persuade someone to enjoy the taste of something because subjective experience can't be shared in the way in which reasons and evidence are shared. The second question, however, can lead to rational argument, assuming that the disputants can agree what "better for you" means. If "better" means "more apt to contribute to long-range health," you could use medical and nutritional studies, along with testimony from dieticians, to argue the superiority of one kind of milk over the other. The test for an arguable issue is whether reasonable cases can be developed for at least two opposing views.

Truth Issues and Value Issues

Most arguable issues fall into one of two categories: truth issues and value issues.

Truth Issues

Truth issues stem from questions about the way reality is (or was or will be). Unlike questions of fact, which can be proved or disproved by agreed-on empirical measures, issues of truth require interpretation of the facts. Does Linda smoke an average of twenty or more cigarettes per day? is a question of fact, answerable with a yes or a no. But the question, Why did Linda start smoking when she was fifteen? is a question of truth with many possible answers. Was it because of cigarette advertising? Peer pressure? The dynamics of Linda's family? Dynamics in the culture (for example, white American youths are seven times more likely to smoke than are African American youths)? Truth issues generally take one of the three following forms:

1. *Definitional issues.*   Does this particular case fit into a particular category? (Is bungee jumping a "carnival ride" for purposes of state safety regulations? Is tobacco a "drug" and therefore under the jurisdiction of the Federal Drug Administration?)
2. *Causal issues.*   What are the causes or consequences of this phenomenon? (Does the current welfare system encourage teenage pregnancy? Will the "three strikes and you're out" rule reduce violent crime?*)

---

*Although we placed our chapter on causes and consequences (Chapter 13) in the "writing to analyze" category, we could have placed it just as logically under "writing to persuade." The difference concerns the writer's perceived relationship to the audience. If you imagine your readers as decidedly skeptical of your thesis and actively weighing alternative theses, then your purpose is persuasive. However, if you imagine your readers as puzzled and curious—reading your essay primarily to clarify their own thinking on a causal question—then your purpose is analytical. The distinction here is a matter of degree, not of kind.

3. *Resemblance or precedence issues.* Is this phenomenon like or analogous to some other phenomenon?. (Is U. S. involvement in Bosnia like U. S. involvement in Vietnam? Is the anti-AIDS campaign proposed by this administration analogous to putting a Band-Aid on a hemorrhage?)

Value Issues

Rational arguments can involve disputes about values as well as truth. Family disagreements about what car to buy typically revolve around competing values: What is most important? Looks? Performance? Safety? Economy? Comfort? Dependability? Prestige? Similarly, many public issues ask people to choose among competing value systems: Whose values should be adopted in a given situation? Those of corporations or environmentalists? Of the fetus or the pregnant woman? Of owners or laborers? Of the individual or the state? Value issues usually fall in one of the following two categories:

1. *Evaluation issues.* How good is this particular member of its class? Is this action morally good or bad? (How effective was President Clinton's first year in office? Which computer system best meets the company's needs? Is the death penalty morally wrong? [See Chapter 15 for a fuller discussion of evaluation arguments.])
2. *Policy issues.* Should we take this action? (Should Congress pass stricter gun-control laws? Should health-insurance policies cover eating disorders? [See Chapter 16 for a fuller discussion of policy issues.])

An Argument's Skeleton: A Claim Supported by Reasons

The skeleton of an argument is a claim supported by reasons. Your claim is the position you take on an issue. A reason, sometimes called a premise, is a subclaim that supports your main claim. Reasons are usually linked to their claims by such words as "because," "therefore," "so," "consequently," and "thus." For planning purposes, it is often helpful to state your reasons as "because" clauses attached to the claim.

Suppose that you are debating the following issue: Should the government legalize hard drugs such as heroin and cocaine? Figure 14.1 (on p. 332) shows skeletons in the form of tree diagrams (see Chapter 18) for possible pro and con arguments on this issue.

Formulating your reasons as "because" clauses allows you to break your argument into a series of smaller parts, with each part developing one of the clauses.

FOR WRITING AND DISCUSSION

Working as a whole class or in small groups, generate a list of reasons for and against one or more of the following claims. State your reasons as "because" clauses. Here is an example:

Claim   Pornography serves a beneficial function in society.

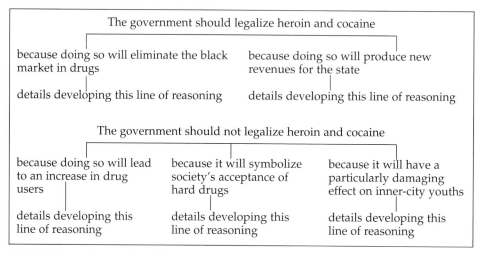

FIGURE 14.1   Sample Tree Diagrams for Pro and Con Arguments

Pro

- because it provides a sexual outlet for lonely people
- because what some people call pornography might really be an art form
- because it helps society overcome Victorian repression
- because many people obviously enjoy it
- because it may relieve the sexual frustration of a person who would otherwise turn to rape or child molestation

Con

- because it is degrading and oppressive to women
- because it depersonalizes and dehumanizes sexuality
- because it gives teenagers many wrong concepts about loving sexuality
- because it is linked with racketeering and crime and destroys neighborhoods
- because it often exploits children
- because it might incite some people to commit rape and violence (serial murderer Ted Bundy's claim)

1. Women should be assigned to combat duty.
2. The school year for grades 1 through 12 should be lengthened to eleven months.
3. A skilled video-game player is an athlete.
4. Writing courses should be pass–fail.
5. The United States should replace its income tax with a national sales tax.

Developing Lines of Reasoning: Toulmin Analysis

You must now transform your persuasive skeleton—a claim with supporting reasons—into a full-bodied argument. You will achieve this transformation by turning each "because" clause into a fully developed *line of reasoning*.

To help you develop lines of reasoning, we look at philosopher Stephen Toulmin's legal model of argument, in which opposing attorneys present their cases before a neutral judge and jury. The Toulmin terms we examine are *warrant, grounds, backing, conditions of rebuttal,* and *qualifier.*

Warrants: Unstated Assumptions That Link Reasons to Claims

Central to Toulmin's system is his recognition that behind every supporting reason lies an assumption, usually unstated, which he calls a warrant. Consider the following line of reasoning:

Claim with Reason   You should buy this car because it is economical.

This argument has force only if the audience believes that economy is an important criterion for choosing a car. The warrant for this line of reasoning is the following:

Warrant   Buying an economical car is valuable or good.

Toulmin derives his term *warrant* from the concept of warranty or guarantee. The warrant is the value or belief that the audience must hold if the stated reason is to have any force. If the audience doesn't care whether a car is economical, then the argument "You should buy this car because it is economical" lacks power. Let's consider another example.

Claim with Reason   We should strengthen the Endangered Species Act because doing so will preserve genetic diversity on the planet.

Warrant   Preserving genetic diversity on the planet is a good/necessary/valuable thing to do.

If the audience doesn't value genetic diversity, then arguments about preserving genetic diversity will have no force. The warrant is the underlying belief that warrants or guarantees the argument's persuasiveness to any audience sharing that belief.

What makes Toulmin's concept of the warrant so valuable is that it requires you as the writer to understand and validate your audience's worldview and to create reasons that have force *for the audience*. If readers don't accept your warrant, you must either abandon your line of reasoning or create an argument supporting the warrant itself (see later discussion of backing).

FOR WRITING AND DISCUSSION

Identify the warrants for each of the following lines of reasoning. Below is an example.

Claim with Reason   People should not own pit bulls because they are so vicious.

Warrant   It is bad to own a vicious pet.

1. You should make your children take music lessons because daily practicing teaches discipline.
2. The government should eliminate welfare payments to unwed mothers because doing so would reduce the illegitimacy rate.

3. After-school jobs are bad for high school students because they use up valuable study time.
4. The government should legalize heroin and cocaine because doing so would end the black market in drugs.
5. *Playboy* magazine should not be sold in the university bookstore because it exploits women.

You have seen that three elements—*claims, reasons,* and *warrants*—underpin each line of reasoning in an argument. But these elements alone aren't enough. To persuade most audiences, you need two additional elements: *grounds,* evidence and arguments in support of the reason; and *backing,* evidence and arguments in support of the warrant.

Grounds: Evidence and Arguments That Support the Reason

To convince a skeptical audience that a reason is true, you need to support it with grounds—facts, data, statistics, testimony, examples, and other details.

Claim with Reason	You should buy this car *because it is economical.*
Grounds	Evidence that the car is economical (statistics on miles per gallon in highway and city driving; testimony from mechanics on its durability and ease of repair; data on resale value)

Grounds constitute all the evidence you can gather in support of your reason.

FOR WRITING AND DISCUSSION

For each line of reasoning presented in the For Writing and Discussion exercises on pages 333-34, suggest what grounds might be used to support the reason. Following is an example.

Claim with Reason	People should not own pit bulls *because they are so vicious.*
Grounds	Evidence that pit bulls are vicious (testimony from people who have been attacked by pit bulls, stories about how they have mauled children, descriptions of pit bulls in dog books and so forth)

Backing: Evidence and Arguments That Support the Warrant

If an audience accepts your warrant, then your claim, reason, and grounds constitute a complete line of reasoning. But if your audience questions your warrant, then the warrant requires backing. *Backing* comprises the data, evidence, and supporting arguments used to gain audience support for the warrant. A writer often needs to show why this warrant is more important than some alternative warrant (why economy is more important than comfort in choosing a car; why preserving genetic diversity is more important than preserving the economy). Here is an example of backing.

Warrant	Buying an economical car is good.
Backing	Arguments and evidence showing why the reader should value economy (statistics showing how much money would be saved over a five-year period by purchasing an economical versus a muscle or flashy car; reminders of what other good things could be purchased with the money saved; arguments showing how economical cars help preserve the environment by burning less fuel—whatever works to convince your intended audience of the value of an economical car)

FOR WRITING AND DISCUSSION

Suggest backing that might be used to support each of the following warrants from the lines of reasoning in the For Writing and Discussion exercise on pages 333–34. Use the following example as a guide.

Warrant	It is bad to own a vicious pet.
Backing	Evidence of the harm that comes from owning a vicious pet (problems with neighbors, public liability if your pet causes damage, potential for serious injury or death to children)

1. Teaching discipline to children is good.
2. It is good to reduce the illegitimacy rate.
3. It is bad to use up valuable study time.
4. It would be good to end the black market in drugs.
5. Magazines that exploit women should not be sold on campus.

Conditions of Rebuttal: Anticipating Weaknesses in Your Argument

Toulmin's system also asks you to imagine a vigilant adversary or opposing counsel questioning each line of reasoning. Imagining their questions will help you recognize what elements of your argument most need bolstering.

For example, consider how adversaries might rebut the argument "You should buy this car because it is economical." They might accept your warrant but question your grounds: "I agree that economy is important, but the specific car you are recommending isn't as economical as you say." They might then offer conflicting data on the car's fuel economy or concede that fuel economy is high but show that the car's repair record is lousy. Or they might accept your grounds but question your argument's warrant: "I agree that the car you are recommending is economical, but economy is less important than safety. What's the value of a few dollars when people's lives are at stake?"

FOR WRITING AND DISCUSSION

Choosing one or more of the lines of reasoning from the For Writing and Discussion exercise on pages 333–34, pretend that you are an adversary bent on rejecting each argument. How might you rebut the reason and grounds or the warrant and backing for each argument? Here is an example.

Claim with Reason	People should not own pit bulls because they are so vicious.
Conditions of Rebuttal	1. *Rebuttals of reasons and grounds*: Provide evidence that pit bulls aren't necessarily vicious; provide examples of gentle pit bulls; argue that training, not breed, determines viciousness. 2. *Rebuttals of warrant and backing*: Argue that a dog with a reputation for viciousness is needed for protection of life and property (refer to the high crime rate in the neighborhood); do a cost–benefit analysis showing that the security a vicious dog provides outweighs the costs.

Qualifier: Limiting Your Claim

Toulmin's final term, *qualifier*, refers to words that limit the scope or force of a claim to make it less sweeping and therefore less vulnerable. Consider the difference between the sentences "After-school jobs are bad for teenagers" and "After-school jobs are often bad for teenagers." The first claim can be refuted by one counterexample of a teenager who benefited from an after-school job. Because the second claim admits exceptions, it is much harder to refute. Unless your argument is airtight, you will want to limit your claim with qualifiers such as the following:

perhaps	maybe
in many cases	generally
tentatively	sometimes
often	usually
probably	likely
may or might (rather than is)	

You can also qualify a claim with an opening "unless" clause ("*Unless* your apartment is well soundproofed, you should not buy such a powerful stereo system.").

FOR WRITING AND DISCUSSION

Based on what you view as the strength of the supporting argument, qualify the claims in the arguments in the For Writing and Discussion exercise on pages 333–34, using the following example:

Claim	People should not own pit bulls.
Qualified	Unless a person really needs the protection of a vicious dog, it is best not to own pit bulls.

Planning Your Argument

Once you have created a skeleton for an argument by establishing one or more lines of reasoning, you can use Toulmin's system to help you develop each major chunk of your argument. In the following case a student writer attending college on an ROTC scholarship wanted to argue that ROTC classes should not receive academic credit. One of his reasons was that ROTC instructors give out As for little work or thought. Following are the student's Toulmin planning notes for this section of his argument.

CLAIM: *ROTC courses should not get academic credit.*

REASON: *because ROTC courses are not academically strenuous.*

GROUNDS: *What's my evidence?*

--*grades in some ROTC classes based on physical activity*

--*everyone I know gets A's (maybe I could take a survey)*

--*we just memorize and regurgitate, unlike my other courses that require critical thinking and lots of writing (in one of my courses I had to memorize preamble to Constitution)*

WARRANT: *Courses that aren't academically strenuous shouldn't get academic credit.*

BACKING: *How can I show it is bad for a course not to be strenuous?*

--*gives cadets a higher GPA, which is unfair in competing for honors, etc.*

--*allows me to devote time to other classes, which is again an unfair advantage*

CONDITIONS OF REBUTTAL: *How could someone doubt my reason and grounds?*

--*Are there any examples of difficult ROTC courses? Could anyone show that ROTC courses require critical thinking and high-level reasoning rather than memory and regurgitation? (I don't think so, but I will take a survey) How could anyone doubt my warrant and survey?*

--*Analogy to other easy courses? Are there any other Mickey Mouse courses on campus equivalent to ROTC? Music courses (but these require extensive practice and skill, unlike ROTC)*

--*ROTC students might object because they believe it is good to have Mickey Mouse courses (it helps their GPA) but they are arguing from self-interest, not from what's right.*

QUALIFIER? *I don't need one. Every ROTC course I can think of is an easy A.*

Based on these planning notes, the student eventually wrote the following paragraph. Although not all the ideas on the planning sheet found their way into this paragraph, the paragraph does include grounds to support the reason and backing to support the warrant.

Another reason that Army ROTC courses do not deserve academic credit is that the classes are not academically strenuous, thus giving cadets a higher GPA and an unfair advantage over their peers. In conducting an informal survey of 10 upperclassmen, I found out that none of them has ever gotten anything lower than an A in a military science class and they do not know of anyone who got anything lower than an A. One third-year cadet stated that "the classes are basic. A monkey coming out of the zoo could get college credit for a military science class." Unlike a typical college class, which requires much thought, questioning, and analysis, an ROTC course requires "regurgitated knowledge"; you just memorize information and feed it back at any time without thought or question. A good example is in my class on basic officership. Our first assignment is to memorize and recite in front of the class the preamble to the Constitution of the United States. The purpose of doing so doesn't seem to be to understand or analyze the Constitution because we never talk about that. In fact, I don't know what the purpose is. I just do it because I am told to. Because the A is so easy to get in my ROTC class, I spend all my time studying for my other classes. I am a step ahead of my peers in the competition for a high GPA, even though I am not getting as good an education.

Supporting Your Argument

Evidence

Some arguments can be fleshed out based solely on your personal experience and observation. But most arguments require more formal evidence—the kind you gather from library or field research. In this section we survey some of the different kinds of evidence and show you how to incorporate that evidence into an argument, either as grounds to support a reason or as backing to support a warrant. (See Chapter 23 for a more elaborate treatment of how to use research sources in your own writing.)

The kinds of evidence most often used for the grounds and backing of an argument are the following:

Examples.   To support his point that ROTC courses don't require critical thinking, the ROTC critic recalled the example of being asked to memorize the preamble to the Constitution. (See the discussion of the "for example" move in Chapter 18, pp. 455–57.)

Summaries of research.   Another common way to support an argument is to summarize or quote summary statements from research studies. Here is how a student writer used a summary statement to support his opposition to mandatory helmet laws for motorcycle riders.

> However, a helmet won't protect against head injury when one is traveling at normal traffic speeds. According to a U.S. Department of Transportation study, "There is no evidence that any helmet thus far, regardless of cost or design, is capable of rejecting impact stress above 13 mph" (Transportation Study, p. 8).

Statistics.   Another common form of evidence is statistics. (For a detailed discussion of statistical data in arguments, see Chapter 11.) Here is how one writer used statistics to argue that alcohol poses a more serious social problem than does heroin or cocaine.

The uproar about drugs is itself odd. In 1987, according to the Kerry sub-committee, there were 1,400 deaths from cocaine; in 1988, that figure had increased to 3,308. Deaths from *all* forms of illegal drugs total under 6,000. By contrast, 320,000 to 390,000 people die prematurely each year from tobacco and 100,000 to 200,000 from misuse of alcohol. Alcohol is associated with 40 percent of all suicide attempts, 40 percent of all traffic deaths, 54 percent of all violent crimes and 10 percent of all work-related injuries. (From Walter Wink, "Biting the Bullet: The Case for Legalizing Drugs," *The Christian Century*, August 8–15, 1990)

Testimony.   Writers often use expert testimony to bolster a case. The following student essay uses testimony to support comparable worth—an economic policy intended to redress salary inequities between traditionally "male" and traditionally "female" job fields.

Barbara Bergmann, professor of economics at the University of Maryland, has studied the comparable worth issue at length. If comparable worth were enacted, she points out, "Nobody's pay need go down. Nor will budgets or profits be wiped out" (9).

You can ensure that any of these forms of evidence is persuasive by monitoring its recency, relevance, impartiality, and scope.

1. *Recency.*   As much as possible, and especially if you are addressing current issues in science, technology, politics, or social trends, use the most recent evidence you can find.
2. *Relevance.*   Ensure that the evidence you cite is relevant to the point you are making. For example, for many decades the medical profession offered advice about heart disease to their female patients based on studies of male subjects. No matter how extensive or how recent those studies, some of their conclusions are bound to be irrelevant for female patients.
3. *Impartiality.*   Although all data must be interpreted and hence are never completely impartial, careful readers are aware of how easily data can be skewed. Newspapers, magazines, and journals often have political biases and different levels of respectability. Evidence you take from *Reader's Digest* or *The National Review* is apt to have a conservative bias, whereas evidence from *The New Republic* or *Mother Jones* is apt to have a liberal bias. These sources often provide excellent data, but be aware that readers may be wary of their objectivity. Generally, evidence associated with scientifically conducted studies is more highly regarded than evidence taken from second- or third-hand sources.
4. *Scope.*   One of the most common reasoning fallacies is to make a sweeping generalization based on only one or two instances. Most claims are persuasive only if based on a wide range of data.

Appeals to Ethos

So far we have focused primarily on what the Greeks called the *logos* of argument—its structure of reasons and evidence. We now turn our attention to another means of supporting your argument, what the Greeks called *ethos*—the reader's confidence in the credibility and trustworthiness of the writer. In Chapter 4 we discussed how readers develop an image of the writer, the writer's persona, based on features of the writer's prose. For readers to accept your argument, they must perceive a persona that's knowledgeable, trustworthy, and fair. We suggest three ways to enhance your argument's ethos.

1. Demonstrate to your reader that you know your subject well. If you have personal experience with the subject, cite that experience. Reflect thoughtfully on your subject, citing research as well as personal experience, and summarize accurately and carefully a range of viewpoints.
2. Be fair to alternative points of view. Scorning an opposing view may occasionally win you favor with an audience predisposed toward your position, but it will offend others and hinder critical analysis. As a general rule, treating opposing views respectfully is the best strategy.
3. Build bridges toward your audience by grounding your argument in shared values and assumptions. Doing so will demonstrate your concern for your audience and enhance your trustworthiness. Moreover, rooting your argument in the audience's values and assumptions has a strong emotional appeal, as we explain in the next section.

Appeals to Pathos

Besides basing your argument on appeals to logos and ethos, you might also base it on an appeal to what the Greeks called *pathos*. Sometimes pathos is interpreted narrowly as an appeal to the emotions. This interpretation effectively devalues pathos because popular culture generally values reason above emotion. Although emotional appeals can be irrational and irrelevant ("You can't give me a C! I need a B to get into med school, and if I don't I'll break my ill grandmother's heart."), they can also arouse audience interest and deepen understanding of an argument's human dimensions. Here are some ways to use pathos in your arguments.

Use Vivid Language and Examples   One way to create pathos is to use vivid language and powerful examples. If you are arguing in favor of homeless shelters, for example, you can humanize your appeal by describing one homeless person.

> He is huddled over the sewer grate, his feet wrapped in newspapers. He blows on his hands, then tucks them under his armpits and lies down on the sidewalk with his shoulders over the grate, his bed for the night.

But if you are arguing for tougher laws against panhandling, you might let your reader see the issue through the eyes of downtown shoppers intimidated by "ratty, urine-soaked derelicts drinking fortified wine from a shared sack."

Find Audience-Based Reasons   The best definition of pathos is not an appeal to emotions but rather an appeal to the audience's values and beliefs. With its emphasis on warrants, Toulmin's system of analysis naturally encourages this kind of appeal.

As you search for reasons to support your claim, you need to consider at the outset your audience's values, assumptions, and beliefs. Suppose that you are advocating the legalization of heroin and cocaine. If you know your audience is concerned about crime in the streets, you might argue as follows:

> We should legalize drugs because doing so will make our streets safer. It will cut down radically on street criminals seeking drug money, and it will free up narcotics police to focus on other kinds of crime.

If your audience is also concerned about the quality of life in inner cities, you might say

> We should legalize drugs because doing so will eliminate the lure of drug trafficking that tempts so many inner-city youth away from honest jobs and into crime.

Or, if your audience is concerned about high taxes and government debt, you might say

> We should legalize drugs because doing so will help us balance federal and state budgets. It will decrease police and prison costs by decriminalizing narcotics; and it will eliminate the black market in drugs, allowing us to collect taxes on drug sales.

In each case, you would move people toward your position by connecting your argument to their beliefs and values.

Addressing Counterarguments

Good arguments anticipate opposing views and respond to them. Often they begin by summarizing opposing views fairly and charitably, and then either rebut or concede to those views.

Summarizing Opposing Views Charitably   Surprisingly, one of the best ways to disarm opposing views is to summarize their best case fairly. By resisting the temptation to distort an opposing argument, you demonstrate a willingness to consider the issue from all sides. Moreover, summarizing opposing views reduces your reader's tendency to say, "Yes, but have you thought of . . . ?" (For an example of a summary of an opposing view using the "summary/however" move, see Chapter 18, p. 457.)

Rebutting Opposing Views   When rebutting or refuting an argument, summarize the view briefly and then show what's wrong with it. In the following student example, the writer summarizes her classmates' objections to abstract art and then analyzes shortcomings in their reasons and grounds.

```
     Some of my classmates object to abstract art because it appar-

ently takes no technical drawing talent. They feel that artists turn

abstract because they are not capable of the technical drafting
```

skills that appear in Remington, Russell, and Rockwell pieces. Therefore they created an art form that anyone was capable of and that was less time-consuming, and then they paraded it as artistic progress. But I object to the notion that these artists turned to abstraction because they lacked the ability to do representative drawing. Many abstract artists, such as Picasso, are excellent draftsmen, and their early pieces show very realistic drawing skill. As his work matured, Picasso became more abstract in order to increase the expressive quality of his work. Guernica was meant as a protest against the bombing of that city by the Germans. To express the terror and suffering of the victims more vividly, he distorted the figures and presented them in a black and white journalistic manner. If he had used representational images and color--which he had the skill to do--much of the emotional content would have been lost and the piece probably would not have caused the demand for justice that it did.

In the next example, an advocate for university-subsidized bus passes focuses on the inadequacies of his opponents' warrant and backing.

Finally, some students who would not ride the bus, even if bus passes were subsidized, worry that they would be helping to pay for a benefit that they would be getting no share of. This is an important concern and a very good point against bus subsidies. But few benefits from tuition dollars are distributed equally to all students. An English major's tuition helps fund science laboratories. Commuters' tuition helps fund on-campus recreational facilities that commuters seldom use. Moreover, as I have shown, the bus pass subsidy will significantly reduce the number of students driving to campus, thereby helping the environment while reducing traffic congestion and the squeeze on parking.

The writer accepts his opponents' reason (students will have to pay for the bus subsidy whether or not they benefit from it), but undercuts their warrant (unequal distribution of student revenues is wrong) by citing precedents for the practice.

Conceding to Opposing Views   In some cases, your opponents' views will be right. If so, don't hide them from your reader; summarize them and concede to them.

Making concessions to opposing views is not necessarily a sign of weakness; in many cases, a concession simply acknowledges that the issue is complex and that your position is tentative. In turn, a concession can enhance your own ethos and invite the reader to follow your example and weigh the strengths of your own argument charitably. Writers typically concede to opposing views with transitional expressions such as the following:

admittedly	I must admit that	I agree that	granted
even though	I concede that	while it is true that	

After conceding to an opposing view, you should immediately remind your reader about the strength of your own argument. For example, adversaries of drug legalization argue plausibly that legalizing drugs would increase the number of users and addicts. If you support legalization, here is how you might deal with this point without fatally damaging your own argument:

> Opponents of legalization claim—and rightly so—that legalization will lead to an increase in drug users and addicts. I wish this weren't so, but it is. Nevertheless, the other benefits of legalizing drugs—eliminating the black market, reducing street crime, and freeing up thousands of police from fighting the war on drugs—more than outweigh the social costs of increased drug use and addiction, especially if tax revenues from drug sales are plowed back into drug education and rehabilitation programs.

The writer concedes that legalization will increase addiction (one reason for opposing legalization) and that drug addiction is bad (the warrant for that reason). But then the writer redeems the case for legalization by shifting the argument to another field of values (the benefits of eliminating the black market, reducing crime, and so forth).

Avoiding Informal Fallacies

Informal fallacies are instances of murky reasoning that can cloud an argument and lead to unsound conclusions. Because they can crop up unintentionally in anyone's writing, and because advertisers and hucksters often use them intentionally to deceive, it is a good idea to learn to recognize the more common fallacies.

Post hoc, ergo proper hoc ("after this, therefore because of this").   This fallacy involves mistaking sequence for cause. Just because one event happens before another event doesn't mean the first event caused the second. The connection may be coincidental, or some unknown third event may have caused both of these events.

Example   For years I suffered from agonizing abdominal itching. Then I tried Jones pills. Almost overnight my abdominal itching ceased. Jones pills work wonders.

Hasty generalization.   Closely related to the *post hoc* fallacy is the hasty generalization, which refers to claims based on insufficient or unrepresentative data.

Example   The food-stamp program supports mostly freeloaders. Let me tell you about my worthless neighbor.

False analogy.   Analogical arguments are tricky because there are almost always significant differences between the two things being compared. If the two things differ greatly, the analogy can mislead rather than clarify.

Example   You can't force a kid to become a musician any more than you can force a tulip to become a rose.

Either/or reasoning.   This fallacy occurs when a complex, multisided issue is reduced to two positions without acknowledging the possibility of other alternatives.

Example   Either you are pro-choice on abortion or you are against the advancement of women in our culture.

Ad hominem ("against the person").   When people can't find fault with an argument, they sometimes attack the arguer, substituting irrelevant assertions about that person's character for an analysis of the argument itself.

Example   Don't pay any attention to Fulke's views on sexual harassment in the workplace. I just learned that he subscribes to *Playboy*.

Appeals to false authority and bandwagon appeals.   These fallacies offer as support for an argument the fact that a famous person or "many people" already support it. Unless the supporters are themselves authorities in the field, their support is irrelevant.

Example   Buy Freeble oil because Joe Quarterback always uses it in his fleet of cars.

Example   How can abortion be wrong if millions of people support a woman's right to choose?

Non sequitur ("it does not follow").   This fallacy occurs when there is no evident connection between a claim and its reason. Sometimes a *non sequitur* can be repaired by filling in gaps in the reasoning; at other times, the reasoning is simply fallacious.

Example   I don't deserve a B for this course because I am a straight-A student.

Circular reasoning.   This fallacy occurs when you state your claim and then, usually after rewording it, you state it again as your reason.

Example   Marijuana is injurious to your health because it harms your body.

Red herring.   This fallacy refers to the practice of raising an unrelated or irrelevant point deliberately to throw an audience off the track. Politicians often employ this fallacy when they field questions from the public or press.

Example   You raise a good question about my support for continuing air strikes in Bosnia. Let me tell you about my admiration for the bravery of our pilots.

Slippery slope.   The slippery slope fallacy is based on the fear that one step in a direction we don't like inevitably leads to the next with no stopping place.

Example   We don't dare send weapons to these guerrillas. If we do, we will next send in military advisers, then a special forces battalion, and then large numbers of troops. Finally, we will be in all-out war.

READINGS

We begin with an argument by Robert B. Reich, secretary of labor under President Bill Clinton. Reich addresses the issue of corporate downsizing—the practice of laying off workers to create a leaner-and-meaner, more efficient business operation. Here Reich looks at downsizing from the workers' perspective and raises issues about corporate responsibility to its employees.

ROBERT B. REICH
COMPANIES ARE CUTTING THEIR HEARTS OUT

1   There used to be an unwritten contract in America between top managers and workers: If you did your job conscientiously, you could count on having that job as long as the company stayed in business. But that implicit contract is being abandoned, at an ever-faster pace. Even reasonably healthy companies are cutting their payrolls.

2   For the past four months, American businesses have been slashing jobs by more than 2,000 a day, a 30 percent higher rate than a year ago, when the nation was still in recession. From the standpoint of investors, this trend seems to make sense. Stock prices often spike upward after the announcement of a major cut in payrolls, even among companies that are showing no sign of bottom-line distress. The butcher metaphor of modern management seems apt: It's time to cut the fat, slash the excess, get lean and mean.

3   Enthusiasm for corporate downsizing is particularly strong among large institutional investors like pension funds, which are exerting increasing influence within corporate board rooms. Pension fund managers are quick to defend their new appetite for corporate downsizing, even though they represent the retirement incomes of workers who may lose their jobs as a result of the cutting. Making American companies more productive is in everyone's long-term interest, or so the argument goes.

4   But I want to sound a cautionary note. Are we in danger of overdoing it?

5   A recent study of 531 mostly large companies by the Wyatt Company, business management consultants, found that although three-quarters of the companies had cut their payrolls, most reported that the cuts had failed to achieve their expected results. Of the companies surveyed, earnings increased for just 46 percent of them; while 58

percent expected higher productivity, only 34 percent experienced it; while 61 percent sought to improve customer service, only 33 percent concluded that they'd achieved it. Even more tellingly, within a year after making the cuts, more than half of the companies had refilled some of the positions.

The results of the Wyatt survey are corroborated by another recent study, by Ken-   6
neth De Meuse, who teaches management at the University of Wisconsin at Eau Claire. De Meuse found no evidence that large layoffs improved, or even stemmed the decline in companies' financial performance. Now, of course, it may have been that these companies were already heading for trouble before they made the cuts, and would have been far worse off had they not made them. But, together with the Wyatt results, De Meuse's conclusion certainly raises the question whether the typical upturn in stock prices immediately upon announcement of layoff is based more on a collective antici- pation by investors that other investors will respond positively to the same news, than it is on any change in the fundamentals.

Perhaps radical surgery needs time to take hold. I know of no reliable studies of   7
the long-term effects of deep cutbacks, but there is cause for concern in the here and now. The first casualties are the morale and loyalty of the employees who remain on the payrolls. Although they do not register directly on balance sheets, high employee morale and loyalty are often among the most important of a firm's assets. Paring the payroll may imperil these assets in ways that escape profit and loss statements but pro- foundly affect competitive advantage.

Visiting many American workplaces, I have heard the same refrain: "Every-   8
body's scared. . . . I don't know how long they'll keep me. . . ." Employees fearful of getting the ax are hardly likely to pursue labor-saving innovations. Nor are they likely to volunteer that extra time and energy that so often makes a difference in productivity.

Another casualty is the cumulative experience of those whose jobs are eliminated.   9
Knowledge that comes from years of hands-on work with products or technologies, or years of dealing with certain customers, is often the key to discovering needed improvements. But financial officers tend to see only the wages and benefits paid to an employee, narrowly weighing them against the value of that employee's current output.

Several years ago, I was asked by a group of design engineers at a large computer   10
company to help devise a strategy for convincing their financial officers why the com- pany should manufacture rather than purchase a particular component. "They think it's cheaper to buy rather than build," one of the engineers complained, "and it is today. But if we don't make it in-house, we don't gain the experience and knowledge that goes with making it. And then we can't develop a whole range of technologies that are likely to evolve from that component."

Some would argue, of course, that downsizing strategies are still preferable to the   11
alternative of allowing companies to continue their slothful ways. So long as the cuts result in greater output per employee, downsizing would seem to make sense even at the cost of some employee morale, loyalty, knowledge and experience. The test, after all, is profitability.

This argument would be a stronger one if the only means of improving productiv-   12
ity was by way of the butcher. But another approach is possible. At the risk of stretch- ing metaphors, let me describe it as the way of the baker. The butcher improves productivity by cutting away whatever seems unnecessary; the baker improves it by enhancing the value of all the ingredients.

13   The baker strategy is to invest in the skills of employees by providing them with training, both on and off the job. It provides front-line workers with substantial authority, so they can make decisions about how to improve the production process and increase sales. And it gives employees a degree of employment security by tying their wages to profits or to productivity gains. That way, when hard times come, they are shared by everyone rather than only by those who were axed. When profits return, everyone will share in them as well.

14   Does the baker approach really work? A number of independent studies provide hard-nosed evidence that it does. An extensive review of 27 econometric studies concludes that the introduction of profit-sharing typically yielded 3 to 5 percent higher productivity. Of 29 studies examining employee participation in company decision-making, 14 showed positive effects on productivity, 2 showed negative effects and 13 had ambiguous results.

15   The implementation of employee training also seems to boost productivity. One study found that companies that introduced a formal training program had at least a 17 percent larger rise in productivity than companies that did not.

16   Last year M.I.T. researchers compared two groups of automobile factories that were similar in every respect except that in the first set, all three practices—employee involvement, profit-sharing or productivity gain-sharing, and training—were followed; in the second, none. The study found that workers in the first set of factories manufactured vehicles 8 hours faster, on average, than workers in the second, and with fewer defects per car.

17   Higher productivity through baking rather than butchering translates directly into higher profits. In a recent survey of more than 700 companies from all major industries, researchers from Rutgers University found that businesses that used one or more employee-friendly strategies had higher annual shareholder returns, and higher gross return on capital, than companies that did not.

18   How do these opposing approaches affect the economy as a whole—a question of critical importance to pension funds and other large institutional investors that have broad holdings across American industry? Consider the effect of widespread downsizing on consumer confidence: workers who have lost their jobs and not yet found new ones tend to consume less than those who are fully employed. Even full-time employees watch their wallets when they're worried that their job may be the next to go. The current recovery would be more buoyant were it not for such anxieties.

19   Even when a company becomes more productive by trimming its payrolls, America as a whole does not necessarily become more productive. A company's books may show an increase in output for each worker remaining on the payroll after others have been let go; but the output of the nation as a whole must also take into account the fates of the workers who have been forced to leave. If they promptly found new jobs where they could be at least as productive, the nation's total output would be enhanced. But fewer and fewer Americans who lose their jobs are finding new jobs this easily.

20   The typical duration of unemployment continues to grow. In the 1970's, an average of 11 percent of the nation's unemployed were out of work for six months or longer; in the 1980's, 15 percent were jobless for half a year or more; thus far in the 1990's, 16 percent. Last year, 21 percent of the unemployed had not worked for six months or longer—the second-highest annual level since the end of World War II.

21   We all pay the price, not only in lost output and potential tax revenues. Regular unemployment insurance benefits, paid for by payroll taxes, have averaged $22 billion annually (adjusted for inflation) over the past five years. Federal extended benefits for

those who have used up their regular six-month insurance have cost an additional $12 billion in each of the last two years.

The Clinton Administration is designing a comprehensive re-employment system   22
to help these Americans get good jobs as quickly as possible after being laid off. Job search assistance, job counseling, job retraining and extra income support during re-training—all are urgently needed because of changes in technologies and global markets that require Americans to move from job to job at a faster pace than before. The current wave of downsizing makes these re-employment reforms even more necessary.

Downsizing can, of course, be an efficient means of moving the nation's workers   23
to jobs where they can be most productive with their existing skills. But downsizing does not increase the value a worker contributes to the economy, because it does not enhance the worker's skills. It merely reallocates work.

It is difficult to have it both ways. The more we butcher, the less we bake. Other   24
advanced industrial countries face the same choice, but have tended to do more baking. Look behind their current recessions and you see highly competitive work forces. A recent study by the Organization for Economic Cooperation and Development is revealing. In 1991, 27 percent of American workers had been with their current employer for less than one year; 62 percent for less than five years. At the other extreme is Japan, where only 10 percent of workers had been with an employer for less than a year, and 37 percent less than five years. Only 25 percent of American workers had been employed by the same employer longer than 10 years, compared with more than 40 percent in Japan, Germany and France.

Average length of stay in the job is in direct proportion to the amount of training   25
provided on the job to young employees. The correlation is logical. Before a company will invest in training, it must be confident that the worker will be around years from now when the training will fully pay off. In the United States, only about 10 percent of young workers receive any formal company training, compared with more than 50 percent in Japan and Germany.

I do not mean to overstate the case. Many fine companies in the United States are   26
reducing their payrolls while at the same time seeking to enhance the skills and involvement of workers who remain. Moreover, one of the great strengths of the American economy—in contrast to that of Japan and most of industrialized Europe—is a highly mobile labor market, and we must do nothing to reduce that flexibility. I simply wish to urge investors—especially the large institutional investors like pension funds—to reconsider their assumptions. Rather than pressure firms to cut payrolls, they may do better to insist that companies invest more in their workers.

Thinking Critically About "Companies Are Cutting Their Hearts Out"

1. What is Reich's claim? List the reasons he develops either to support the claim or to refute opposing views. Can you summarize each line of reasoning as a "because" clause?
2. Where does Reich summarize opposing views? How does he respond to them? What are the strengths and weaknesses of his response?
3. Reich uses various kinds of supporting evidence, including personal observations and anecdotes, research data, and a striking analogy (butchering versus baking). For each line of reasoning that you identified in Question 1,

analyze the kind of evidence that Reich uses for support. In your view, how effective is his evidence?

4. What do you think would be Reich's most effective line of reasoning for a corporate executive contemplating downsizing? Why?

In the following argument, nature writer Edward Abbey argues against the value of dams. Abbey was one of the nation's most prolific environmental writers.

EDWARD ABBEY
THE DAMNATION OF A CANYON

1   There was a time when, in my search for essences, I concluded that the canyon-land country has no heart. I was wrong. The canyonlands did have a heart, a living heart, and that heart was Glen Canyon and the golden, flowing Colorado River.

2   In the summer of 1959 a friend and I made a float trip in little rubber rafts down through the length of Glen Canyon, starting at Hite and getting off the river near Gunsight Butte—The Crossing of the Fathers. In this voyage of some 150 miles and ten days our only motive power, and all that we needed, was the current of the Colorado River.

3   In the summer and fall of 1967 I worked as a seasonal park ranger at the new Glen Canyon National Recreation Area. During my five-month tour of duty I worked at the main marina and headquarters area called Wahweap, at Bullfrog Basin toward the upper end of the reservoir, and finally at Lee's Ferry downriver from Glen Canyon Dam. In a number of powerboat tours I was privileged to see almost all of our nation's newest, biggest and most impressive "recreational facility."

4   Having thus seen Glen Canyon both before and after what we may fairly call its damnation, I feel that I am in a position to evaluate the transformation of the region caused by construction of the dam. I have had the unique opportunity to observe first-hand some of the differences between the environment of a free river and a powerplant reservoir.

5   One should admit at the outset to a certain bias. Indeed I am a "butterfly chaser, googly eyed bleeding heart and wild conservative." I take a dim view of dams; I find it hard to learn to love cement; I am poorly impressed by concrete aggregates and statistics in the cubic tons. But in this weakness I am not alone, for I belong to that ever-growing number of Americans, probably a good majority now, who have become aware that a fully industrialized, thoroughly urbanized, elegantly computerized social system is not suitable for human habitation. Great for machines, yes: But unfit for people.

6   Lake Powell, formed by Glen Canyon Dam, is not a lake. It is a reservoir, with a constantly fluctuating water level—more like a bathtub that is never drained than a true lake. As at Hoover (or Boulder) Dam, the sole practical function of this impounded water is to drive the turbines that generate electricity in the powerhouse at the base of the dam. Recreational benefits were of secondary importance in the minds of those who conceived and built this dam. As a result the volume of water in the reservoir is continually being increased or decreased according to the requirements of the Basin States Compact and the power-grid system of which Glen Canyon Dam is a component.

The rising and falling water level entails various consequences. One of the most   7
obvious, well known to all who have seen Lake Mead, is the "bathtub ring" left on the
canyon walls after each drawdown of water, or what rangers at Glen Canyon call the
Bathtub Foundation. This phenomenon is perhaps of no more than aesthetic importance; yet it is sufficient to dispel any illusion one might have, in contemplating the
scene, that you are looking upon a natural lake.

The utter barrenness of the reservoir shoreline recalls by contrast the aspect of   8
things before the dam, when Glen Canyon formed the course of the untamed Colorado.
Then we had a wild and flowing river lined by boulder-strewn shores, sandy beaches,
thickets of tamarisk and willow, and glades of cottonwoods.

The thickets teemed with songbirds: vireos, warblers, mockingbirds and thrushes.   9
On the open beaches were killdeer, sandpipers, herons, ibises, egrets. Living in grot-
toes in the canyon walls were swallows, swifts, hawks, wrens and owls. Beaver were
common if not abundant: not an evening would pass, in drifting down the river, that we
did not see them or at least hear the whack of their flat tails on the water. Above the
river shores were the great recessed alcoves where water seeped from the sandstone,
nourishing the semi-tropical hanging gardens of orchid, ivy and columbine, with their
associated swarms of insects and birdlife.

Up most of the side canyon, before damnation, there were springs, sometimes   10
flowing streams, waterfalls and plunge pools—the kind of marvels you can now find
only in such small scale remnants of Glen Canyon as the Escalante area. In the rich
flora of these laterals the larger mammals—mule deer, coyote, bobcat, ring-tailed cat,
gray fox, kit fox, skunk, badger and others—found a home. When the river was dammed
almost all of these things were lost. Crowded out—or drowned and buried under mud.

The difference between the present reservoir, with its silent sterile shores and debris choked side canyons, and the original Glen Canyon, is the difference between
death and life. Glen Canyon was alive. Lake Powell is a graveyard.

For those who may think I exaggerate the contrast between the former river canyon   11
and the present man-made impoundment, I suggest a trip on Lake Powell followed immediately by another boat trip on the river below the dam. Take a boat from Lee's Ferry
up the river to within sight of the dam, then shut off the motor and allow yourself the
rare delight of a quiet, effortless drifting down the stream. In that twelve-mile stretch of
living green, singing birds, flowing water and untarnished canyon walls—sights and
sounds a million years older and infinitely lovelier than the roar of motorboats—you will
rediscover a small and imperfect sampling of the kind of experience that was taken
away from everybody when the oligarchs and politicians condemned our river for purposes of their own.

Lake Powell, though not a lake, may well be as its defenders assert the most beau-   12
tiful reservoir in the world. Certainly it has a photogenic backdrop of buttes and mesas
projecting above the expansive surface of stagnant waters where the speedboats,
houseboats and cabin cruisers play. But it is no longer a wilderness. It is no longer a
place of natural life. It is no longer Glen Canyon.

The defenders of the dam argue that the recreational benefits available on the sur-   13
face of the reservoir outweigh the loss of Indian ruins, historical sites, wildlife and
wilderness adventure. Relying on the familiar quantitative logic of business and bu-
reaucracy, they assert that whereas only a few thousand citizens even ventured down
the river through Glen Canyon, now millions can—or will—enjoy the motorized boating
and hatchery fishing available on the reservoir. They will also argue that the rising
waters behind the dam have made such places as Rainbow Bridge accessible by powerboat. Formerly you could get there only by walking (six miles).

14   This argument appeals to the wheelchair ethos of the wealthy, upper-middle-class American slob. If Rainbow Bridge is worth seeing at all, then by God it should be easily, readily, immediately available to everybody with the money to buy a big powerboat. Why should a trip to such a place be the privilege only of those who are willing to walk six miles? Or if Pikes Peak is worth getting to, then why not build a highway to the top of it so that anyone can get there? Anytime? Without effort? Or as my old man would say, "By Christ, one man's just as good as another—if not a damn sight better."

15   It is quite true that the flooding of Glen Canyon has opened up to the motorboat explorer parts of side canyons that formerly could be reached only by people able to walk. But the sum total of terrain visible to the eye and touchable by hand and foot has been greatly diminished, not increased. Because of the dam the river is gone, the inner canyon is gone, the best parts of the numerous side canyons are gone—all hidden beneath hundreds of feet of polluted water, accumulating silt, and mounting tons of trash. This portion of Glen Canyon—and who can estimate how many cubic miles were lost?—*is no longer accessible to anybody.* (Except scuba divers.) And this, do not forget, was the most valuable part of Glen Canyon, richest in scenery, archaeology, history, flora and fauna.

16   Not only has the heart of Glen Canyon been buried, but many of the side canyons above the fluctuating waterline are now rendered more difficult, not easier, to get into. This because the debris brought down into them by desert storms, no longer carried away by the river, must unavoidably build up in the area where flood meets reservoir. Narrow Canyon, for example, at the head of the impounded waters, is already beginning to silt up and to amass huge quantities of driftwood, some of it floating on the surface, some of it half afloat beneath the surface. Anyone who has tried to pilot a motorboat through a raft of half-sunken logs and bloated dead cows will have his own thoughts on the accessibility of these waters.

17   Second, the question of costs. It is often stated that the dam and its reservoir have opened up to the many what was formerly restricted to the few, implying in this case that what was once expensive has now been made cheap. Exactly the opposite is true.

18   Before the dam, a float trip down the river through Glen Canyon would cost you a minimum of seven days' time, well within anyone's vacation allotment and a capital outlay of about forty dollars—the prevailing price of a two-man rubber boat with oars, available at any army-navy surplus store. A life jacket might be useful but not required, for there were no dangerous rapids in the 150 miles of Glen Canyon. As the name implies, this stretch of the river was in fact so easy and gentle that the trip could be and was made by all sorts of amateurs: by Boy Scouts, Camp Fire Girls, stenographers, schoolteachers, students, little old ladies in inner tubes. Guides, professional boatmen, giant pontoons, outboard motors, radios, rescue equipment were not needed. The Glen Canyon float trip was an adventure anyone could enjoy, on his own, for a cost less than that of spending two days and nights in a Page motel. Even food was there, in the water: the channel catfish were easier to catch and a lot better eating than the striped bass and rainbow trout dumped by the ton into the reservoir these days. And one other thing: at the end of the float trip you still owned your boat, usable for many more such casual and carefree expeditions.

19   What is the situation now? Float trips are no longer possible. The only way left for the exploration of the reservoir and what remains of Glen Canyon demands the use of a powerboat. Here you have three options: (1) buy your own boat and engine, the necessary auxiliary equipment, the fuel to keep it moving, the parts and repairs to keep it running, the permits and licenses required for legal operation, the trailer to transport it;

(2) rent a boat; or (3) go on a commercial excursion boat, packed in with other sightseers, following a preplanned itinerary. This kind of play is only for the affluent.

The inescapable conclusion is that no matter how one attempts to calculate the cost in dollars and cents, a float trip down Glen Canyon was much cheaper than a powerboat tour of the reservoir. Being less expensive, as well as safer and easier, the float trip was an adventure open to far more people than will ever be able to afford motorboat excursions in the area now. 20

All of the foregoing would be nothing but a futile exercise in nostalgia (so much water over the dam) if I had nothing constructive and concrete to offer. But I do. As alternate methods of power generation are developed, such as solar, and as the nation establishes a way of life adapted to actual resources and basic needs, so that the demand for electrical power begins to diminish, we can shut down the Glen Canyon power plant, open the diversion tunnels, and drain the reservoir. 21

This will no doubt expose a dreary and hideous scene: immense mud flats and whole plateaus of sodden garbage strewn with dead trees, sunken boats, the skeletons of long-forgotten, decomposing water-skiers. But to those who find the prospect too appalling, I say give nature a little time. In five years, at most in ten, the sun and wind and storms will cleanse and sterilize the repellent mess. The inevitable floods will soon remove all that does not belong within the canyons. Fresh green willow, box elder and redbud will reappear; and the ancient drowned cottonwoods (noble monuments to themselves) will be replaced by young of their own kind. With the renewal of plant life will come the insects, the birds, the lizards and snakes, the mammals. Within a generation—thirty years—I predict the river and canyons will bear a decent resemblance to their former selves. Within the lifetime of our children Glen Canyon and the living river, heart of the canyonlands, will be restored to us. The wilderness will again belong to God, the people and the wild things that call it home. 22

Thinking Critically About "The Damnation of a Canyon"

1. What is Abbey's claim? List the reasons he develops either in support of the claim or in refuting opposing views. Can you summarize each line of reasoning as a "because" clause?
2. Where does Abbey summarize opposing views? How does he respond to them? What are the strengths and weaknesses of his response?
3. How effective is Abbey in developing audience-based reasons? Whom do you think he pictures as his audience? Do you think his argument is enhanced or weakened when he says that arguments supporting Lake Powell appeal "to the wheelchair ethos of the wealthy, upper-middle-class American slob"?
4. Where does Abbey use appeals to ethos? Where does he use appeals to pathos? How effective are these appeals?
5. What does Abbey use as supporting evidence for his reasons? Which line of reasoning do you find most effective, and which least effective?
6. If you were a proponent of dams—either because of the recreational value of reservoirs or because of the electrical power, irrigation, or flood control that dams provide, would you feel that Abbey fairly summarized and addressed your views? How would you refute Abbey's argument?

In the following article, science writer David S. Bennahum attacks a proposal to outlaw pornography on the Internet. Entitled "Getting Cyber Smart," this essay originally appeared as an Op-Ed piece in *The New York Times*.

DAVID S. BENNAHUM
GETTING CYBER SMART

1   "We cannot stand idly by while children are subjected to pornography and smut on the Internet," Senator Jim Exon warns. His proposed solution, hastily debated and passed by the Senate Commerce Committee, will do little to curb people intent on abusing children or purposefully exposing them to pornography in cyberspace. It will, however, fundamentally change the nature of a global medium in which what is obscene anywhere becomes obscene everywhere.

2   The bill, known as the Communications Decency Act, is scheduled to reach the Senate floor in early June as part of the mammoth telecommunications bill. It would punish anyone convicted of sending obscene material through computer networks with up to a $100,000 fine and two years in prison. That doesn't only mean individuals distributing pornography; it could also mean erotic love letters distributed by E-mail or sexually explicit fiction.

3   According to Senator Exon, Democrat of Nebraska, cyberspace is a dangerous jungle of interconnected networks where pedophiles and pornographers roam freely. By stopping obscenity in cyberspace, you protect children, the logic goes.

4   In the meantime, little attention is being paid to the constituency this legislation is supposed to protect: children. To understand the real magnitude of the supposed problem, and the foolishness of the solution, you have to speak with children, go on line and experience cyberspace with them. You'll find a world far different than the jungle Senator Exon perceives.

5   Cyberspace is their world. Of the 6.8 million households with on-line accounts, 35 percent have a youngster under 18, and the average age on the Internet is 23 and falling. So how are children handling themselves in this environment?

6   Pretty well, it seems. With such a dense concentration of children in one "place," picking up kids in cyberspace should be like "shooting fish in a barrel," according to Fred Cotton of Search, an organization that deals with computer crime. Yet, for all the talk of adults stalking children on line, there are few cases of actual face-to-face contact initiated by a meeting in cyberspace, according to Ernie Allan, the director of the National Center for Missing or Abused Children. The numbers are low because, for the most part, children know enough not to give their addresses to strangers or agree to meet with them.

7   "You can really get into serious situations when people ask you questions on line," a 15-year-old girl explained to me on line, "You have to think about that before answering. You have to be street smart and cyber smart."

8   While the specifics of Senator Exon's concerns reflect the environment of the Information Age, the underlying fear behind the bill taps into ageless stories we've all grown up with. Like the wolf in Little Red Riding Hood, the cyber-stalker, we are told, comes disguised as a friend, even another child, and sneaks undetected into the most

secure of domestic settings—the bedroom—while the parents go about their business, oblivious to what's happening. Today's version makes much of the fact that in cyberspace there are no walls or doors for parents to lock. Today's wolf comes home through the innocuous copper filament in the bedroom wall.

Yet the Exon bill would do nothing to stop pedophiles from seducing children in cyberspace. Pedophiles do not harass or send obscene material to their intended victims; they form friendships. Sending vulgar messages erodes the essential ingredient required for a meeting—trust. For things to get out of hand, children must make the essential move, agreeing to a fact-to-face meeting. Stopping that from happening is beyond the reach of Federal law. It requires parents and children to set rules about meeting friends made on line. Common sense and parental involvement is the way to foil pedophiles.   9

And it turns out that the technology that allows the wolf to hide behind a friendly face is the same technology that protects children. In a text-based medium like cyberspace, children hold all the cards: they can conceal their sex, age and location. This privacy not only protects them from physical harm, it is also powerfully liberating. In such an environment, role-playing thrives. Children can represent themselves as adults, adults assume the person they're chatting with is a peer. This bends the boundaries normally erected between adults and children.   10

Most of the time the collapse of these boundaries is not harmful. I recently found myself in an on-line forum discussing poetry with someone I assumed was an adult. It turned out that it was a 15-year-old boy. Only after I asked did he reveal his age. These kinds of discussions abound in cyberspace.   11

Children, like adults, go on line to communicate and explore, but they also use resources like forums devoted to specific subjects, electronic libraries and encyclopedias. When obscene material comes over the Net, it's usually spontaneous and unexpected— like an obscene phone call. For example, you may be discussing baseball on line, and suddenly a new arrival makes offensive remarks. You can always leave the discussion, and in any case cyberspace has its own restraints; harassers face the scorn of the crowd and the possibility of their on-line account getting revoked.   12

As in real life, kids form cliques and circles of friends. Word-of-mouth and group opinion serve as a potent and protective barrier. And stopping repeated harassment is easy, thanks to the technology of cyberspace. You can block the receipt of private messages and electronic mail from specific people.   13

If children actively seek out obscene material, stopping them is much more difficult. But as a 14-year-old girl pointed out to me, "If a kid wants to look at dirty pictures and he can't find them on line, he'll find them somewhere else." Senator Exon's proposal doesn't address the real problem of pornography in cyberspace—namely, that since a lot of material inappropriate for children isn't legally obscene, it would be as available in cyberspace as it is on a newsstand. The Communications Decency Act says nothing about rating systems.   14

Cyberspace, with 20 million users worldwide, connecting 145 nations, is too rich and complex an environment for a law as general and misinformed as the Communications Decency Act.   15

The Clinton Administration, concerned that the Senate will vote without a real understanding of the issues at stake, let alone knowledge of how cyberspace functions, asked the Senate to hold hearings on the act before voting. At the moment, the Senate has no formal plans to do so. That's a mistake. Cyberspace is a national resource too   16 precious to submit to dangerously simplistic legislation. Congress should educate itself on this environment before considering Senator Exon's indecent proposal.

Thinking Critically About "Getting Cyber Smart"

1. What is Bennahum's claim? List the reasons he develops to support the claim or to refute opposing views. Can you summarize each line of reasoning as a "because" clause?
2. Where does Bennahum summarize opposing views? How does he respond to them? What are the strengths and weaknesses of his response?
3. One of Bennahum's arguments is that children don't need protection from cyberspace because they are cyber smart as well as street-smart. Do you agree with Bennahum? How might a concerned parent respond?
4. Bennahum speaks approvingly of the anonymity and privacy that cyberspace gives children, who can role-play being adults. Do you share Bennahum's belief that this privacy is "powerfully liberating"? Why or why not?
5. Do you think whatever is legally available in a bookstore or on a magazine rack ought to be legally available on the Internet? Why or why not?

In the next essay, Walt Spady, the owner of a boat dealership, opposes a local county's ban on "personal watercraft" (small, one-person powerboats analogous to motorcycles or snowmobiles) on lakes and bays. Spady's argument appeared as a guest editorial in a statewide newspaper.

WALT SPADY
A MISGUIDED BAN ON PERSONAL WATERCRAFT

1   Well, they've gone and done it. The _____ County commissioners have passed an ordinance that excludes personal watercraft from their county. Effective last week, they've told me that if I operate my personal watercraft inside the county's boundaries, I'll be fined $50 the first time, $100 the second, and $250 the next.

2   It is the equivalent of the city of _____ saying that I can't ride a motorcycle down Main Street. And we're not talking about speeding or reckless behavior or endangering anyone. We're talking just operating a personal watercraft in _____ County, period.

3   This is a decision based on emotion and arrogance. It is a decision that is unilateral and confrontational, rather than cooperative and aimed at problem-solving. The County commissioners—at least the two who passed this measure—have said simply: "Go away."

4   They have said this to a segment of the boating population that now makes up one-third of all boating units sold [in this region]. There are about 17,000 owners of these small craft in [this state] and the number is growing. The commissioners have also said to a rental business in _____ County and to a number of family businesses all over the state that sell and service personal watercraft: "Go away."

They have said to large boats that use these craft for tenders: "Go away." These   5
convenient and efficient little boats are used as tenders, for pleasure or beach cleanups,
for skiing and for search-and-rescue and law enforcement. Are we all just to "Go
away"?

A total ban on a widely used mode of transportation and recreation can hardly be   6
considered a solution that serves a whole community. It's just not wise. It draws a line
in the sand and provokes an adversarial response, which this action surely will.

A lot of reaction, and overreaction, to personal watercraft is based on two factors: 7
noise and harm to the environment.

The fact is that a personal watercraft is no louder than a household vacuum . . .   8
75 dB's. The fact is that the _____ commissioners could cite no study that says personal watercraft are harmful to whales, dolphins, seals, or any other form of life, no
more harmful than any other type of boat. Because they have no exposed prop, they
are a great deal safer and more environmentally friendly than most boats.

The issue with personal watercraft, as it is with motorcycles, cars, trucks, airplanes,   9
and hang gliders, is safe, responsible operation. The issue lies within the operator and
not inherently in the vehicle itself.

I'd like to ask the county commissioners what they have tried first, in the way of   10
training, education, signing, and public information, instead of jumping to a total ban.
I also wonder what hotels, restaurants, campgrounds, and other tourist-oriented businesses think of banning such a large group of people.

The path that _____ County has taken is one of prohibition and punishment as   11
opposed to education and regulation.

Last fall, the dealers in the state formed a network called the Personal Watercraft   12
Safety Project. It is dedicated to safe, responsible use of personal watercraft. In the
larger picture, we feel that boaters in general could use education in the areas of state
law, tradition, and "rules of the road."

Our goal is to put as much information as we can into the hands of personal   13
watercraft operators. We do that through person-to-person contact at the time of sale,
videos, and brochures provided by manufacturers, safety checklists, posters, and instructional flyers. We'd like every personal watercraft operator in this state to have a
short course on operation and safety, a wallet card, and a laminated on-board checklist.

This approach, we strongly believe, is much more effective, and in the interest of   14
all of the citizens in this statewide community. It addresses an issue through education
at a person-to-person and community level rather than simply saying: "Go away."

Thinking Critically About "A Misguided Ban on Personal Watercraft"

1. What is Spady's claim? How many supporting lines of reasoning does he
   develop? Can you summarize his supporting reasons as "because" clauses?
2. Where does Spady summarize opposing views? How does he respond to
   them? What are the strengths and weaknesses of his response?
3. Spady is the owner of a boat dealership, so he has an economic investment
   in promoting sales of personal watercraft. To what extent does your knowledge of Spady's profession color your reading of his argument? How successful is Spady in establishing an effective ethos? Is Spady's argument any
   more biased than Abbey's (Abbey identifies himself openly as a "googly
   eyed bleeding heart") or Reich's (as secretary of labor)?

4. Have you or anyone else in your class ever operated a personal watercraft (or seen or heard one)? If so, explain why they are controversial. (Who do you imagine raised the complaints that led the county to ban personal watercraft from county waters?)

5. The complaint against personal watercraft is analogous to the complaints that cross-country skiers make against snowmobilers or hikers against motorized trail bikes or motorcycles. At a more remote level, it is the complaint that neighbors make against blaring stereo systems. How do you draw the line between individual and community rights in these issues?

6. How might you refute Spady's argument?

In this last essay, a first-year college student responds to a heated issue being debated in his hometown—a proposal to change the local high school's traditional two-semester schedule with six 55-minute periods to an innovative block schedule with four 90-minute periods.

ELIJAH ISAACSON (student)
THE PROPOSED "BLOCK SCHEDULE" IS A BAD IDEA

Student Essay

1   What's the best way to schedule classes in a high school? During my four years at Wilson High, we attended six 55-minute periods per day. It seemed like the "natural" system for a high school, and I find that most of my classmates here at college had a similar high school schedule. But now the faculty at my old high school are proposing a radical new approach that would consist of four 90-minute periods each day on a semester schedule, with students earning two semesters' credit for a one-semester course. Those who support the idea say that it would provide a more concentrated focus on subject matter and allow for more in-depth study. Student support for the proposal is currently running high. According to my hometown paper, 74 percent of the students thought the block system would improve the quality of education, while 69 percent thought that the new schedule would reduce student stress. However, I have serious doubts about this program. Since I have younger siblings coming up through the school system, I am concerned that the proposed block schedule will damage their education. The block schedule should be rejected.

2   While I see many advantages to changing—the shaking up of taken-for-granted teaching methods and opportunity for students to gain greater connection with subject matter—I fear too little has been made of the plan's disadvantages and potential problems. My first objection to the proposed plan is that it involves too many logistical uncertainties. It is not clear, for example, what will be done with electives like band and journalism, which require year-round participation by students. Whereas a course like band is now one-sixth of a student's schedule, it would have to be one-fourth of the schedule in the new system. Band students would be taking six years of band during their three years of high school.

3   A more serious reason to reject the plan is that a year's study of math or science would have to be compressed into one semester. Is it possible to learn complicated topics like calculus or chemistry at such a rapid pace? And what about the opportunity to

forget material during the enormous "dead" time, between math or science classes. (A student might have sophomore math during the first semester of the sophomore year and then not take math again until the second semester of the junior year—a full twelve months with no math.)

Another reason to fear the new plan is the uncertainty whether faculty can make   4
the transition to teaching 90-minute classes. Advocates maintain that teachers would not just "jump in" to the new schedule but that there would be training sessions to help faculty get a feel for such things as cooperative learning and other strategies for filling 90 minutes of class time. But how effective can two-day or week-long seminars in August be? Many faculty have worked in our present schedule for years, and teaching in this system has become instinctual. Changing these instincts could take years, not days. The quest for different teaching methods—for more hands-on teaching methods— will not come easy. Actual practice won't come close to the romanticized view of "active learning" paraded forth by supporters of the block schedule. It takes an amazingly skilled teacher to come up with 90 minutes of useful classroom activities. My instinctual fear with the block schedule is that teachers will end up using "filler" activities to use up the time. Videos, for example, will have a tremendous opportunity to be abused.

Another potential problem is the attention span of the average high school student.   5
In high school, I had trouble staying tuned in for 55 minutes of calculus (and I was a pretty good math student); I shudder to think how I would have done for 90 minutes. What about the students who have a lot of trouble paying attention in the current system? Clearly the limits of students' attention spans will prevent them from achieving one necessary goal of the block schedule—to learn twice as much in a 90-minute class as they do in a 55-minute one. Some may argue that college classes are often 90 minutes long. First, longer classes might work in college simply because college classes don't meet daily and thus the students do not become overwhelmed. Secondly, it may be that longer classes are appropriate for the educational development of college students, but are simply too long for the attention span of many high school students. Finally, my own experience with 90-minute classes in college increases my skepticism. I have a hard time sitting still for 90 minutes. Consequently, my college teachers give us a break half-way through, cutting the course from 90 to 80 or even 75 minutes.

Advocates of the block schedule claim that one of the great benefits of changing   6
is a decrease in stress levels for both teachers and students. Teachers in pilot programs that have used the block schedule report a noticeable decrease in stress for both teachers and students. One can easily see why Wilson faculty would be attracted to this new schedule. Instead of having to prepare for five classes, they would have to prepare for only three. The problem is, this touted decrease in stress comes primarily from reducing the teacher's workload. Teachers are also unlikely to double students' homework under the new system, so students too will experience a decrease in stress as they have to study for only four courses each semester rather than six. How can this reduced work lead to equivalent learning?

Advocates of the block schedule might reply that the decrease in stress comes   7
from a focus on fewer ideas for a longer time instead of more ideas for a shorter time, and not from a decrease in work. In light of my experiences as a student, I am not satisfied with this explanation. I have found school work easier if it comes in more manageable chunks. I would rather have an hour of math and an hour of reading than two hours of math or two hours of reading. In fact, just the idea of being a high school student who must learn two math concepts a day instead of one seems to increase my stress. Thus, if students really did the same amount of work in the block schedule as

in the present one, I doubt their stress level would decrease at all. The argument that there will be a decrease in stress, then, leads me to the conclusion that classes won't, or couldn't, move twice as fast in the new schedule. In other words, students would never cover 36 weeks of math in 18 weeks simply by increasing class lengths to 90 minutes.

8   But stress-level reports aren't the only reason I think students wouldn't cover as much territory in the block schedule. First of all, the year-long courses (math, history, English, science, etc.) would simply have less class time under the new system. One English teacher worked out that she would lose 33 hours of class time. Consequently, she would have to cut a large amount of material.

9   In short, the proposed block plan is a bad idea. Students would lose class hours in important courses such as English, math, and science. Moreover, students' inability to concentrate for 90 minutes combined with the difficulty teachers will have filling the 90 minutes with meaningful activity will reduce the rigor of courses. Finally, the simple fact that teachers have the trained instinct of assigning homework based on the present schedule would only serve to make classes easier.

10   Although some of these problems may be worked out over time, it isn't fair to ask students coming to Wilson High in the next few years to act as guinea pigs in an un-tried program fraught with problems. Their education may be irreparably damaged. Wilson High School must be careful that it does not change to a new system merely for the sake of changing.

Thinking Critically About "The Proposed 'Block Schedule' Is a Bad Idea"

1. What is Elijah Isaacson's claim? List the reasons he develops in support of the claim or in refuting opposing views. Can you summarize each line of reasoning as a "because" clause?
2. Where does Elijah summarize opposing views? How does he respond to them? What are the strengths and weaknesses of his response?
3. How persuasive do you find Elijah's argument and why?
4. If you were a supporter of the block system, how would you refute this argument?
5. This argument uses no library or field research data. Look carefully at Elijah's evidence for each of his lines of reasoning. What does he use for evidence and supporting details? (For a researched argument written for the same assignment, see Mary Turla's paper in Chapter 23, pp. 583–96).

COMPOSING YOUR ESSAY

Writing arguments deepens writers' thinking by forcing them to consider opposing views and to question the assumptions underlying their reasons and claim. Consequently, it is not unusual for a writer's position on an issue to shift—and even to reverse itself—during the writing process. If this happens to you, take it as a healthy sign of your openness to change, complexity, and alternative points of view. If writing a draft causes you to modify your views, it will be an act of discovery, not a concession of defeat.

Generating and Exploring Ideas

The tasks that follow are intended to help you generate ideas for your argument. Our goal is to help you build up a storehouse of possible issues, to explore several of these possibilities, and then to choose one for deeper exploration before you write your initial draft.

Make an Inventory of Issues That Interest You

Using one or more of the following trigger statements, make a list of ten to fifteen issues that you might like to write about. As much as possible, think of current issues being debated locally, regionally, or nationally. Imagine that you intend to publish your argument as a guest column in a campus or local newspaper. Share your list with classmates, adding to your list ideas from theirs.

As I listened in class today, I wanted to voice my opinion on _____.

As I read my campus newspaper (or read the local or national news), I wanted to voice my opinion on _____.

When I look at legislation being proposed by (campus government, city, state, federal government), I feel especially strongly about _____.

Person X believes _____; however, I believe _____.

When people discuss X (plug in different possible topic areas), what do they disagree about (for example, money, cars, baseball, guns, cooking)?

Explore Several Issues

For this task, choose two or three possible issues from your list and explore them through freewriting or idea mapping. Try responding quickly to the following questions:

1. What is my position on this issue and why?
2. What are opposing positions on this issue?
3. Why do people disagree about this issue? Do people disagree about the facts of the case? About definitions or analogies? About underlying values, assumptions, and beliefs?
4. If I were to argue my position on this issue, what evidence would I need to gather and what research might I need to do?

Brainstorm Pro and Con Reasons

Choose one issue that particularly interests you and work with a group to brainstorm pro and con reasons. First, each group member should write out a possible claim for an issue that he or she is considering. Then all members of the group should generate as many reasons for and against the claim as possible. State the reasons as "because" clauses. Continue the group work until you have brainstormed pro and con reasons for each group member's claim.

Conduct and Respond to Initial Research

If your issue requires research, do a quick bibliographic survey of what is available (see Chapter 22 if you need help with the library) and do enough initial reading to get a good sense of the kinds of arguments that surround your issue and of the alternative views that people hold. Then freewrite your responses to the following questions:

1. What are the different points of view on this issue? Why do people disagree with each other?
2. Explore the evolution of your thinking as you did your initial reading. What new questions did the readings raise for you? What changes occurred in your own thinking?

Conduct an In-Depth Exploration Prior to Drafting

The following set of tasks is designed to help you explore your issue in depth. Most students take one or two hours to complete these tasks; the time will pay off, however, because most of the ideas you will need for your rough draft will then be on paper.

1. Write out the issue your argument will address. Try phrasing your issue as a single question.
2. Now write out your tentative answer to the question. This will be your beginning thesis statement or claim. Put a box around this answer. Next write out one or more different answers to your question. These will be alternative claims that a neutral audience might consider.
3. Why is this a controversial issue? Is there insufficient evidence to resolve the issue, or is the evidence ambiguous or contradictory? Are definitions in dispute? Do the parties disagree about basic values, assumptions, or beliefs?
4. What personal interest do you have in this issue? How does the issue affect you? Why do you care about it? Knowing why you care about it might help you get your audience to care about it.
5. What reasons and evidence support your position on this issue? Freewrite everything that comes to mind that might help you support your case. This freewrite will eventually provide the bulk of your argument. Freewrite rapidly without worrying whether your argument makes sense. Just get ideas on paper.
6. Imagine all the counterarguments your audience might make. Summarize the main arguments against your position and then freewrite your response to each of the counterarguments. What are the flaws in the alternative points of view?
7. What kinds of appeals to ethos and pathos might you use to support your argument? How can you increase your credibility and trustworthiness in the

eyes of your audience? How can you tie your argument to your audience's beliefs and values?

8. Why is this an important issue? What are broader implications and consequences? To what other issues does this issue relate? Thinking of possible answers to these questions may prove useful when you write your introduction or conclusion.

Shaping and Drafting

Once you have explored your ideas, create a plan. Here is a suggested procedure.

1. Create a skeleton, tree diagram, or outline for your argument by stating your reasons as one or more "because" clauses attached to your claim. Each "because" clause will become the head of a main section or line of reasoning in your argument.

2. Use Toulmin analysis to plan each line of reasoning. If your audience accepts your warrant, concentrate on supporting your reason with grounds. If your warrant is doubtful, support it with backing. Try to anticipate audience objections by exploring conditions for rebuttal, and brainstorm ways of addressing those objections.

3. Using the skeleton you created for number 1, finish developing an outline or tree diagram for your argument. Although the organization for each part of your argument will grow organically from its content, the main parts of your classical argument will be as follows:

   a. *Introduction,* in which you engage your reader's attention, introduce your issue, and state your own position.

   b. *Background and preliminary material,* in which you place your issue in a current context and provide whatever background knowledge and definitions of key terms or concepts your reader will need. If this background is short, it can often be incorporated into the introduction.

   c. *Arguments supporting your own position,* in which you make the best case possible for your views by developing your claim with reasons and evidence. This is usually the longest part of your argument, with a separate section for each line of reasoning.

   d. *Anticipation of objections and summary of opposing views,* in which you summarize fairly the arguments against your position. This section not only helps the reader understand the issue more clearly, but establishes your ethos as a fair-minded writer willing to acknowledge complexity.

   e. *Rebuttal of objections to your argument,* in which you respond to anticipated objections to your views by pointing out weaknesses in opposing arguments while conceding to their strengths.

   f. *Conclusion,* in which you place your argument in a larger context, perhaps by summarizing your main points and showing why this issue is an important one or by issuing a call to action.

This classical model can be modified in numerous ways; for example, you might choose to summarize and examine weaknesses in opposing views before you present your own position. However, most classical arguments include all these traditional elements somewhere.

Revising

As you revise your argument you need to attend to both the clarity of your writing (all the principles of closed-form prose described in Chapters 18 and 19) and the persuasiveness of your argument. As always, peer reviews are valuable, and especially so in argumentation if you ask your peer reviewers to role-play a skeptical audience. The following guidelines for peer reviewers can both assist your peer reviewers and help you with revision.

g   u   i   d   e   l   i   n   e   s

for Peer Reviewers

Instructions for peer reviews, including use of these guidelines, are provided in Chapter 21, pages 527–28. To write a peer review for a classmate, use your own paper, numbering your responses to correspond to the questions on the guidelines. At the head of your paper place the author's name and your own name as shown.

Author's Name: _____

Peer Reviewer's Name: _____

I. Read the draft at normal reading speed from beginning to end. As you read, do the following:
   A. Place a wavy line in the margin next to any passages that you find confusing, that contain something that doesn't seem to fit, or that otherwise slow down your reading.
   B. Place a "Good!" in the margin next to any passages where you think the writing is particularly strong or interesting.
II. Read the draft again slowly. Describe for the writer what you currently see in this draft. If you have difficulty answering any of the following questions, explain briefly the source of your difficulty.
   A. What issue does this argument address? How does the writer convince you that the issue is significant and problematic?
   B. What is the essay's major claim?
   C. What reasons does the writer cite in support of the major claim?
      1. Which of the writer's reasons is in your view the least important or well supported? Why?

     2. Where does the writer place the weakest reason in the argument? If you were to move it, where would you move it and why?

    D. What opposing arguments does the writer cite?

     1. How does the writer refute each opposing argument?

     2. Which of those refutations is least well developed or persuasive? Why?

    E. What does the writer do to ensure that he or she is perceived as trustworthy and credible?

    F. Cite those places in the argument where the writer makes the strongest appeal to the audience's beliefs, values, or emotions.

III. What recommendations do you have for improving this draft?

    A. How might the writer improve the title?.

    B. Consider the writer's introduction. Does the introduction engage your interest in the issue, help you understand what issue is being debated, provide a clear thesis, and adequately forecast what's coming? What advice do you have for improving the introduction?

    C. Consider the overall structure. Can you discern the argument's main parts—introduction, background (if needed), supporting reasons (a main section for each line of reasoning), summary and refutation of opposing views, and conclusion? How might the writer improve the structure of this draft?

    D. Consider the support. For each line of reasoning, does the writer provide adequate grounds in the form of facts, examples, statistics, testimony, or other supporting details? Does the writer need to state warrants and develop backing? Does the writer establish a trustworthy and credible persona? Where could the writer better appeal to readers' emotions, beliefs, and values? What recommendations do you have for improving support for the writer's case?

    E. Consider the writer's summary and refutation of opposing views. Does the writer summarize opposing arguments fairly? Are there any important opposing arguments that the writer hasn't considered? Does the writer offer adequate refutation of each opposing argument or otherwise respond to it effectively? How might the writer improve his or her refutation of opposing views?

    F. How might the writer improve the clarity of the draft? Where might the writer better apply the principles of clarity from Chapter 19 (starting with the big picture; placing points before particulars; using transitions; and following the old/new contract)?

    G. Sum up what you see as the chief strengths and problem areas of this draft.

     1. Strengths

     2. Problem areas

IV. Read the draft one more time. Place a check in the margin wherever you notice problems in grammar, spelling, or mechanics (one check per problem).

Making an Evaluation

ABOUT EVALUATIVE WRITING

You confront issues of evaluation every day. Which word-processing program should I buy? What classes should I take next term? Where should we go for spring vacation? Which candidate will make the best senator? Is the B-2 (Stealth) bomber worth funding? Is a light-rail system or an expanded bus system the better transportation choice for our city? Should our company choose marketing plan A or plan B? All these choices involve evaluation issues.

Research suggests that evaluation questions form the core of many college critical-thinking tasks. According to one study, college assignments typically involve evaluative thinking of the good/better/best variety.

Good   Is X good or bad?

Better   Which is better, X or Y?

Best   Which is the best among available options? What is the best solution to a given problem?*

Good/better/best tasks invariably call for arguments. For example, business and engineering proposals often use a "better or best" argument, in which the writer outlines several possible solutions, develops criteria for choosing the best solution, and then demonstrates which solution most fully meets the criteria.

The writing project for this chapter asks you to construct a "good" argument. You will evaluate something controversial to determine the extent to which it is good or bad. The thinking skills you develop in this chapter can be applied to many of the writing tasks you will be assigned in other college courses and throughout your professional career.

---

*The good/better/best example comes from Barbara E. Walvoord and Lucille P. McCarthy, *Thinking and Writing in College: A Naturalistic Study of Students in Four Disciplines.* Urbana, IL: National Council of Teachers of English, 1990, p. 7.

EXPLORING EVALUATIVE WRITING

Whenever you evaluate something you need to establish criteria—that is, for any given class of items, you have to determine the qualities, traits, behaviors, or features that a member of that class must have to fulfill its purposes. Working as a whole class or in small groups, develop criteria to evaluate one or more of the following:

a good leader

a good lecturer

a good class discussion

a good boss

a good basketball coach

a good college library

a good college-registration system

a good city-transportation system

a good ethnic restaurant (specify Italian, Chinese, etc.)

a good sex-education program

a good horror film

To develop criteria, think of the qualities one or more of these items must have to be considered a good member of its class. Display on the board a master list of the criteria developed by your classmates. How hard was it to develop criteria? How difficult was it to achieve consensus?

WRITING PROJECT

Write an argument in which you evaluate something controversial. The opening of your essay should introduce your reader to the person, place, thing, event, or phenomenon that you are going to evaluate and show why its value is controversial or problematic. The body of your argument should establish criteria for evaluating your subject, and then show how your subject meets or does not meet the criteria. As with most other arguments, you should summarize opposing views and respond to them through either concession or refutation.

For this assignment, you need to find an evaluative question that invites controversy. For example: Is a flat income tax (graduated income tax, sales tax, sin tax on cigarettes) a good method of taxation? How effective is your school's general studies curriculum (football program, service learning program, writing center, registration system)? Are TV talk shows (news programs, sitcoms, soap operas) helpful or harmful to society? Is homeopathic medicine (chiropractic medicine, psychic healing) an effective approach to healing? Has the effect of the "three strikes and you're out" law (sexual predator laws, affirmative action, juvenile curfews, public-school dress codes) been good or bad?

The specific person, event, or phenomenon you choose to evaluate should be controversial or problematic, that is, there should be defensible evaluations of your subject that differ from your own evaluation. You must demonstrate that your evaluation makes more sense than these alternative evaluations. Thus this assignment asks you to produce something that is different from a typical movie, restaurant, or consumer-product review, which simply describes the subject being evaluated and explains its strengths and weaknesses. This assignment asks you to change your reader's mind about the evaluation of your subject.

UNDERSTANDING EVALUATION ARGUMENTS

Evaluation arguments involve what we call a *criteria-match* process. The first step in this process is to establish criteria; the second step is to show how well your subject matches these criteria. Sometimes your greatest challenge is to persuade your audience to accept your criteria; at other times, it is to persuade your audience that your specific case matches the criteria.

Here are several examples.

> **Evaluation Issue**   Is Brad Pitt a good actor?
> *Criteria task*: What are the criteria for a good actor?
> *Match task*: Does Brad Pitt meet these criteria?

> **Evaluation Issue**   Was President Clinton's policy on Bosnia effective?
> *Criteria task*: What are the criteria for an effective policy on Bosnia?
> *Match task*: Did President Clinton's policy meet these criteria?

For a more extended illustration, suppose that you are a student representative on a committee charged with selecting the Teacher of the Year. After considerable debate, your committee decides to base its selection on the following criteria:

1. Positive student opinion as measured by student evaluations
2. Rigorous academic standards as measured by amount and difficulty of required work and by grading standards
3. Effective student learning as measured by quality of work produced by students

Your committee has asked finalists for the award to submit portfolios containing evidence related to each criterion.

Your committee's next task is to match the candidates' records against each criterion. Your committee will accept or reject candidates based on the following kind of reasoning:

> Teacher X is (is not) a good teacher because he/she does (does not) meet criterion 1, because he/she does (does not) meet criterion 2, and so forth.

For example:

> Although Professor Jones receives the highest student evaluations on campus (meets criterion 1), she does not deserve the Teacher of the Year award because her academic standards are insufficiently rigorous (fails to meet criterion 2) and because the quality of student performance in her classes is not impressive (fails to meet criterion 3).

Using Toulmin's System to Develop Evaluation Arguments

A typical evaluation argument asks you to develop both a criteria argument and a match argument. Following Toulmin's system of argument analysis (explained in Chapter 14), the criteria argument is equivalent to an argument's warrants and backings, and the match argument is the equivalent to its reasons and grounds. Suppose, for example, that some members of the Teacher-of-the-Year committee want to give the award to Professor Jones because of her uncommonly strong student evaluations, but that you want to argue against Jones because in your view her academic standards are insufficiently rigorous. Your argument will have the following skeleton:

Claim   Jones doesn't deserve the Teacher of the Year award.

Reason   Because her academic standards aren't rigorous.

Warrant   Rigorous academic standards are a criterion for this award.

To develop this argument you need to supply grounds to support the reason (the match argument) and backing to support the warrant (the criteria argument).

Match Argument

Reason   Jones's academic standards aren't rigorous.

Grounds   Evidence that Jones's standards are not rigorous (80 percent of students get As; a review of syllabi shows that she requires little outside reading and no papers; many former students testify that Jones's courses are fun but really easy).

Criteria Argument

Warrant   Rigorous academic standards are a criterion for this award.

Backing   Argument showing why rigorous academic standards are an important criterion (quality of teaching should be measured by quality of students' learning; good teaching is more than a popularity contest; good teachers get a lot of work out of their students; they motivate them to put time and energy into learning; high standards lead to quality performance).

Of course, you don't need to use Toulmin's terminology to understand the principle involved here. Our point is that in making an evaluation writers need to establish and justify criteria (criteria argument) and supply evidence that the thing being evaluated does or does not meet those criteria (match argument).

FOR WRITING AND DISCUSSION

Toulmin's system also asks the writer to consider the conditions for rebuttal of an argument. How might a supporter of Jones rebut the writer's reason and grounds (the match argument)? That is, how might an opponent argue that Jones actually does have high academic standards? How might a supporter of Jones rebut the writer's warrant and backing (the criteria argument)? That is, how might a supporter of Jones argue that high academic standards should not be a criterion for the Teacher of the Year award?

Special Difficulties of Evaluation Arguments

Establishing the criteria for evaluation arguments sometimes entails special difficulties, which we describe in this section.

The Problem of Apples Versus Oranges

You may have occasion to argue that X is excellent, while a friend argues with equal passion that X is lousy. Back and forth you go, both of you equally frustrated at the other's inability to recognize the merits of your case. And then it may suddenly dawn on you that you are claiming that X is a wonderful Y, whereas your friend is claiming that X is a lousy Z. Unless you agree on what class X belongs to, you are engaging in an apples-and-oranges dispute.

For example, suppose that a local eatery is not a good place for gourmet cuisine but it is a wonderful place for sipping coffee and studying on a rainy afternoon. It flops as a member of the class "gourmet restaurant," but it excels as a member of the class "atmospheric study place." Often, to determine in which class to place your subject, you must first consider the interests of your intended audience. For example, a penniless student would probably be more interested in the class "atmospheric study place," whereas readers of a newspaper's restaurant reviews would be more interested in the class "gourmet restaurant."

To avoid the apples-and-oranges problem, try to judge any X according to the smallest applicable class. That is, try to avoid judging apples as members either of the next larger class, "fruit" (where they must compete with grapefruits and bananas), or of a neighboring class, "orange." Better yet, identify an appropriate subclass, say, "eating apple" versus "pie apple," to avoid condemning a great, juicy eating apple, such as a Red Delicious, for its failure to be a good, tart pie apple, such as a Granny Smith.

The Problem of Standards

When you determine criteria, you also encounter the problem of deciding upon standards: what's normal versus what's ideal. Should you measure something against the average performance of members of its class or against your vision of an ideal performance? This is the dilemma between absolutes and situational standards, between rules and ordinary practice. Should teachers grade on an absolute scale or on the curve? Should a TV police drama be praised for its gritty street language (this is the way people *really* talk), or condemned for violating mainstream U.S. values (people *shouldn't* talk that way)? Is it better for high schools to pass out free contraceptives because teenagers are having sex anyway (what's *normal*), or is it better to support abstinence by not making contraceptives available (what's *ideal*)?

There is no easy way to decide which standard to use. The problem with the ideal is that nothing may ever measure up. You might never approve of any compromise that fails to meet your standards. The problem with the normal is that you may lower your standards and slip into a morally dangerous relativism. Would you want to argue, for example, that female infanticide in China is acceptable because it's normal practice there? In deciding which standard to follow, you need to recognize the limitations of each, to make the best choice you can, and to use the same standard for all the items you are evaluating.

The Problem of Seductive Empirical Measures

Empirical data can help you evaluate all sorts of things. If you are buying an automobile, you can be helped a great deal by knowing the numbers for its horsepower and acceleration, for its fuel economy and frequency-of-repair record, and for its potential resale value. But sometimes the need to make defensible evaluative decisions leads people to empirical measures that disastrously oversimplify complex matters. Every year, for example, new crops of potential professional athletes are scrutinized minutely for their records in the forty-yard dash, the bench press, the vertical leap, and so forth. Every year, some of the people who max out on these empirical measures flop ingloriously in actual competition because they lack qualities that are difficult if not impossible to measure empirically, whereas other athletes, with more modest scores, achieve great success thanks to these same invisible qualities.

Quantifiable measures can be helpful, of course. But they are so concrete and they make comparisons so easy that they can seduce you into believing that you can make complex judgments by comparing numbers. It's all too easy to fall into the trap of basing college admissions on SAT scores, scholarships on grade-point averages, or the success of a government policy on tax dollars saved.

The Problem of Cost

A final problem in establishing criteria is cost. A given X may be far superior to any other X's in its class, but it may also cost far more. Before you move from evaluating an X to acting on your evaluation (by buying, hiring, or doing X), you must consider cost, whether it is expressed as dollars, time, or lost opportunity. There's little question, for example, that a Lexus is superior to a Nissan Sentra according to most automotive criteria. But are the differences sufficient to justify the additional thirty thousand or so dollars that the Lexus costs?

CONDUCTING AN EVALUATION ARGUMENT: AN EXTENDED EXAMPLE

Now that we have explored some potential difficulties in establishing and defending criteria for an evaluation, let's consider in more detail the process of making an evaluation argument. For illustration, let's assume that you've been appointed to a committee to determine which resident assistants (RAs) in a first-year college dormitory should be retained. Since your school has never evaluated RAs before, your committee sets as its first task the development of consistent criteria.

Step 1: Determine the Purposes of the Class to Which X Belongs

The first step in the process is to determine the *purpose* of the class "RA": Why do RAs exist? What do you want them to accomplish? Despite the importance of this step, evaluators often fail to ask these kinds of questions. When they do pose such questions, they often discover unexpected disagreement as to the purpose of the class they are evaluating. If your committee members fail to agree about the purpose of RAs, you will not be able to compare them systematically or weigh the relative importance of their strengths and weaknesses. You may end up introducing as virtues qualities that are not clearly relevant to the purposes of the class ("What a sense of style! She was the best-accessorized finalist we interviewed.") and indicting as major vices features that are barely relevant to the class ("For crying out loud, he's a PE major!").

So what is it that RAs are supposed to do? They are supposed to live in dormitories with younger students and help those students adjust to college. So far so good. But what's entailed in helping people adjust to college? What are RAs actually supposed to *do* to realize that goal? If you live in a dorm, you'll probably start by thinking about your own experience. What things do you like about or expect from your RA?

For one thing, your RA can help when people get homesick. When someone gets dumped by a boyfriend or girlfriend back home, the RA can provide some solace and advice; when money gets tight, or parents separate, the RA can step in with some emotional support. And what about that poor girl in your dorm who stopped eating? Your RA may have referred her early on for some serious counseling. Clearly, there's one important purpose for an RA: To provide personal counseling and emotional support

Another desirable feature of an RA is an ability to enforce rules. If your RA is in one of her endless labs, does chaos reign all around you? Do people hold parties and crank their stereos up during quiet hours? Does your roommate smuggle her boyfriend in and throw you out of the room? Does the cleaning go undone and does the place look like a sty? Maybe you've given up trying to work in the dorm and are going off to the library every night. So, here's a second purpose for an RA: To enforce the rules necessary for a large group of strangers to live together harmoniously and to be able to get their schoolwork done

Maybe your RA is good at giving advice about how to study and how to use the university system. He knows all the ins and outs of classes, which teachers to request and which to avoid, how to withdraw from classes after the deadline, where to get the best deals on textbooks. Maybe he knows a lot more about how to make things work from a student's point of view than does your academic adviser, who never seems to remember your name. Okay, that's an important purpose: To help people deal with academic matters and minimize the amount of friction a student experiences getting through the system

When you are satisfied that you have articulated the major purposes of the class "RA," it is time to move on to the second step in the development of criteria.

Step 2: Determine Criteria Based on the Purposes of the Class to Which X Belongs

Having established the purposes of the class "RA," you need to turn your attention back to the members of the class who are supposed to realize those purposes. What specific qualities help potential RAs fulfill the purposes of the class? You will derive your criteria for assessing RAs directly from these qualities.

The first purpose you established was counseling students. What are the qualities or features of a good counselor? One quality is sensitivity toward other people. How can a person be a good counselor if he or she can't "read" other people and seems totally unapproachable? You can also think of other related qualities of a good counselor.

1. Sensitivity
2. Ability to listen well
3. Availablity and approachability
4. Discretion, reliability, and ability to maintain confidentiality

In addition to being a counselor, an RA must be able to lay down the law to people who violate dorm rules and group norms and to arbitrate disputes. Based on this second purpose for the class "RA," you decide on two more qualities important to RA success:

5. Ability to apply rules and norms fairly
6. Diplomacy in enforcing rules and getting people to acknowledge other points of view and others' needs

Beyond counseling people and keeping order, you have determined that a good RA must help new students understand how a university system works. An RA should be able to tell students where to go to get their problems solved and help them think of strategies for solving problems on their own. Qualities that would help an RA realize this third purpose include

7. Familiarity with the procedures and resources of the university
8. Ability to articulate knowledge to other people
9. Creativity in solving problems

At this point, you feel that your list is pretty exhaustive, so you decide to share it with a friend who is also a member of the committee. Your friend has pretty much the same list except for one feature that didn't occur to you. It seems that your friend's RA is not only helpful, fair, and knowledgeable, but also lots of fun. She organizes parties and outings and spontaneous get-togethers. Through her, many of your friend's dormmates have gotten to be quite close.

As a result of this conversation, you decide that you need a fourth purpose for the class "RA": To encourage camaraderie and high morale among dorm members. The qualities that would help an individual RA realize this purpose include

10. Sociability that helps people feel comfortable with each other
11. Ability to organize and involve others in social events

Having explicated the purposes of the class "RA" and having identified qualities most important to realizing those purposes, you are now ready to state your criteria. A good RA should effectively meet the following criteria:

1. Be a counselor (be sensitive; listen well; be available and approachable; be discrete, confidential, and reliable)
2. Apply and enforce rules consistently and fairly (be diplomatic and effective in getting people to acknowledge each others' needs and points of view)
3. Give appropriate advice about school and academics (be familiar with procedures and resources; be able to explain knowledge; be creative in solving problems)
4. Promote a comfortable and enjoyable social life (have good social skills and the ability to make people feel comfortable with each other; be able to organize and involve others in social events)

Step 3: Give Relative Weightings to the Criteria

Next you must rank your criteria in order of importance and develop a justification for your ranking. At this point we want to engage you and your classmates in weighing the relative importance of the criteria you've established.

FOR WRITING AND DISCUSSION

Your committee is now meeting to give relative weightings to the criteria. Individually, look back over the criteria established in Step 2 and rank them in order of importance according to your personal sense of what an RA should be. Freewrite your justification for this ranking.

Working in groups or as a whole class, see if you can reach consensus on the relative weighting of the criteria.

Step 4: Determine the Extent to Which a Specific X Meets the Criteria

Your final step is to determine how well any given X meets your criteria. You'll need to gather evidence, examples, and other data to serve as grounds for your argument.

FOR WRITING AND DISCUSSION

In this exercise we offer you an opportunity to play the role of a committee member charged to hire the new RAs. We provide the profiles of two RAs for you to evaluate according to the criteria and relative weightings you've already developed. Here's how we suggest you proceed.

1. Each member of your group should read over the following profiles and independently assess the performances of the RAs according to the criteria developed in Step 2 and ordered in Step 3. Freewrite the justification for your decision.
2. Working in a group, reach consensus on which of the two RA candidates best meets your committee's criteria.

RA #1   Sheila is very outgoing and personable. She has a great sense of humor and is the life of every party. And she makes sure there are lots of parties. Every weekend, she has arranged exchanges with other dorms, field trips, and contests. Few of those in her charge dislike her and many consider her their best friend at college. Her "door is always open," and, in fact, she goes out of her way to find out what people are up to, making nightly rounds to see how people are. When there's a crisis, Sheila's "there" for people. She stayed up all night with a young woman whose father died unexpectedly. When another woman had a fight with her boyfriend, Sheila organized a "wake" to console her for the loss of her love.

On the other hand, Sheila isn't much of an academic model. About the only academic thing she's really knowledgeable about is how to find the easiest classes. And sometimes she overestimates her ability to deal with people's problems. When a young woman began showing signs of depression, Sheila tried to cheer her up by going out for coffee with her and encouraging her to attend more parties. When the depression got worse, she waited too long before talking her into seeing a counselor. Finally, when it comes to rule enforcement, Sheila tends to be lax, and the study environment in the dorms is not what it should be. Her dorm had the lowest overall GPA on campus last semester.

RA #2   Velda is extremely well organized and efficient. She's a Phi Beta Kappa in microbiology and credits her academic success almost entirely to hard work and discipline. "If I can be a high achiever, anyone can," she says modestly. Before taking on the RA job, she made a thorough study of the university system and put together an "insiders' guide to the university" for her students. It lists all the best general studies courses and the most effective teachers in the university. It explains how to get through registration most efficiently. It explains where student health services are, what they do and don't do, and names the best doctors to see for various ailments. It also explains what student health insurance covers and who to talk to when insurance questions arise. Everyone agrees it's far more thorough and helpful than anything the university provided. In addition, Velda holds regular study skills seminars, which her students universally praise. She helps people with homework questions and maintains very strict study hours. Her dorm floor consistently maintains the highest GPA on campus.

On the other hand, Velda is not a very sociable creature. On the party animal scale, she ranks somewhere between a paramecium and a barnacle. She achieved her own academic success at the expense of a social life, which she claims not to miss. She organizes no get-togethers for her students, though she urges them to "get together now and again" on the grounds that being well-rounded will help them later in life. Consequently, few of her students get to know many people other than their immediate neighbors. And while Velda is a stickler for the rules, she imposes them heavy-handedly, making no allowances for particular circumstances. When a young woman went home to attend a funeral for a high school friend and failed to check out properly, Velda reported her to the University Standards Committee. She's always in her room during her "office hours," but any other time she's in the library. And while she always knows where to refer people, she's not very good at comforting people and gets impatient if they take too much of her time. If students need counseling, she immediately refers them to the counseling center, saying that professionals will give them more help than an RA.

READINGS

In the following student essay, Gabriel Judet-Weinshel evaluates an elementary school's DARE (Drug Abuse Resistance Education) program on the basis of testimonial letters by fifth graders published in his hometown newspaper. Notice how he sets up criteria for the program in his introductory paragraph, then provides evidence throughout the body to show that the program is not meeting those criteria.

GABRIEL JUDET-WEINSHEL (student)
INADEQUACIES OF THE DARE PROGRAM

Student Essay

1   Last week my hometown newspaper featured a series of essays written by fifth-grade alumni of Lincoln Elementary School's DARE (Drug Abuse Resistance Education) program. Although it is a good idea to educate students against drugs, these letters suggest an inadequacy in the effectiveness of the program. The essays reveal a failure in the program both to educate its students properly about drugs and to allow them to think for themselves. Consequently, I feel that the central purpose of the program—to engender in young people the knowledge necessary to make intelligent choices concerning drugs and thus to avoid abuse—is not being met.

2   The lack of proper education about drugs is evidenced in the misconceptions and misinformation that run rampant throughout all six of the printed essays. Inaccurate ideas about drugs, so fallacious as to be comparable to reasoning that babies come from the stork, are incorporated into all the pieces.

3   For example, in the essay entitled "I Think My Life Is Special Because I'm Free of Drugs," a student writes, "Beer makes you see things that aren't really there." Here the writer has connected the effects of hallucinogenic drugs with alcohol, although there is no proven correlation. In fact, the only incidents of people "seeing things" in connection with alcohol occur during delirium tremens, a complication of withdrawal whose occurrence is as rare as one case in every 1,000 reforming alcoholics ("House Call" Medical Dictionary).

4   In another student essay entitled "With Drugs Your Ideas Go Bad; Everything Goes Bad," the student states (and so apparently has been taught) that if one involves oneself

with drugs, one loses all of one's old friends and acquires new ones. These "new, 'drug user' friends are most definitely trashy," she reasons. Here propaganda and scare tactics have obviously taken the place of research. I am appalled by DARE's assumption that drug users are "trashy," implying a social class stigma. The program is teaching its disciples to stereotype rather than to make intelligent decisions concerning drug use.

It seems as if the program assured its students that whatever they held dear in their 5 lives would be irrevocably lost upon contact with drugs. One student is convinced that if she took drugs she would "smell bad" and "be rude." Another DARE graduate believes that if she tried drugs her friends would immediately not trust her any more and that she would also hit any of her companions "for no real reason" upon seeing them in the hall. A third student would no doubt lose his "freedom, self-respect, dignity, ability to be a friend, sense of humor, creativity, and talent for video games." Finally, one all-inclusive statement reads, "Drugs are fatal."

Supporters of the DARE program might say that these "scare tactics" work by successfully associating drugs with "bad things" in young, impressionable minds. There are many powerful, convincing, and accurate arguments against taking drugs, but the DARE program has taught its students few of them. Instead, it has provided them with unfounded propaganda, which, when easily proven false, could lead students to believe that drugs are benign. Also, by providing misinformation, students might, contrary to the efforts of their educators, go directly to the source of their questions—drugs—to find the truths.

In addition to the blatant fallacies expressed in the students' essays, I am disappointed by DARE educators' failure to instill in their students an ability to discern between "hard drugs," such as heroin and cocaine, and "soft drugs," such as marijuana and alcohol. In all of the essays, "drugs" are "Drugs" with a capital D; not once do the essays illustrate an understanding of the vast array of substances available and their differing potencies and effects. This generalization makes pot as pernicious as crack cocaine.

One might argue that as long as DARE graduates can say "no" to any drugs, discerning between them might not matter. But the program is not effectively taking into account the sort of drug use occurring in [the writer's hometown]—that "softer" drugs like marijuana are often dabbled with, especially in high school, and that those experimenting may not be "addicts." Because the program teaches that marijuana and heroin are interchangeable, a proud DARE graduate, who is now in high school and flirting cautiously with drugs and who has not found the effects of marijuana overly harmful (he has not lost his freedom or his ability to play video games), may argue that heroin is equally innocuous. This is the danger of the "ignorance is bliss" adage, which the DARE program seems to promote.

Such mentality also leads to the subject of brainwashing. What struck me in this 9 supposedly eclectic selection of essays was their similarity, the way they were each more or less a carbon copy of one another, all spewing out a resounding and mindless "no" to the issue of drugs. By not allowing students to think and come to their own educated conclusions about drugs, the DARE program is lessening its chances of fostering successful graduates. As a person comes of age, the decision to take or not take drugs becomes an entirely personal one, despite what the program might like to think. It is not a decision that can be made by any organization, nor a decision as simple as an all-dismissing "no." By forcing this "no" on its students, the DARE program is only encouraging an inevitable rebellion, a breaking-away from this strict structure.

DARE might consider telling its students, "This is what is out there. These are the 10 dangers. We wish you wouldn't, and here's why, but this is a decision we can't make for you."

11   In view of the essays, the DARE program has much to improve upon before it can honestly say it has contributed to alleviating the problems of drug abuse or educating those who are "at risk." Therefore, I implore the DARE educators at Lincoln to rid their program of propaganda, scare tactics, and brainwashing and replace them with viable, thought-inducing information if they wish to wield any positive results from their efforts.

Thinking Critically About "Inadequacies of the DARE Program"

1. What criteria does Gabriel Judet-Weinshel use for evaluating the DARE program?
2. What evidence does he provide to show that the DARE program does not meet his criteria?
3. If you were a supporter of the DARE program's current curriculum and approach, how might you rebut Gabriel's argument?
4. What do you see as the main strengths and weaknesses of Gabriel's essay?

In the next reading, Charles Krauthammer evaluates the B-2 bomber. Krauthammer, a former Rhodes Scholar and a medical doctor with a specialty in psychiatry, is a widely syndicated columnist who writes from Washington, D.C.

CHARLES KRAUTHAMMER
B-2 OR NOT B-2? THAT'S AN IMPORTANT QUESTION

1   We hear endless blather about how new and complicated the post-Cold War world is. Hence the endless confusion about what weapons to build, forces to deploy, contingency to anticipate. But there are three simple, glaringly obvious facts about this new era:

2   (1) America is coming home. The day of the overseas base is over. In 1960, the U.S. had 90 major Air Force bases overseas. Today, we have 17. Decolonization is one reason. Newly emerging countries like the Philippines do not want the kind of Big Brother domination that comes with facilities like Clark Air Base and Subic Bay. The other reason has to do with us: With the Soviets gone, we do not want the huge expense of maintaining a far-flung, global military establishment.

3   (2) America cannot endure casualties. It is inconceivable that the U.S., or any other Western country, could ever again fight a war of attrition like Korea or Vietnam. One reason is the CNN effect. TV brings home the reality of battle with a graphic immediacy unprecedented in human history. The other reason, as strategist Edward Luttwak has pointed out, is demographic: Advanced industrial countries have very small families, and small families are less willing than the large families of the past to risk their only children in combat.

4   (3) America's next war will be a surprise. Nothing new here. Our last one was too. Who expected Saddam to invade Kuwait? And even after he did, who really expected the U.S. to send a half-million man expeditionary force to roll him back? Then again, who predicted Pearl Harbor, the invasion of South Korea, the Falklands War?

5   What kind of weapon, then, is needed by a country that is losing its foreign bases, is allergic to casualties, and will have little time to mobilize for tomorrow's unexpected provocation?

Answer: A weapon that can be deployed at very long distances from secure Amer-   6
ican bases, is invulnerable to enemy counterattack and is deployable instantly. You
would want, in other words, the B-2 stealth bomber.

We have it. Yet, amazingly, Congress may be on the verge of killing it. After over   7
$20 billion in development costs—costs irrecoverable whether we build another B-2 or
not—the B-2 is facing a series of crucial votes in Congress that could dismantle its assembly lines once and for all.

The B-2 is not a partisan project. Its development was begun under Jimmy Carter.   8
And, as an urgent letter to President Clinton makes clear, it is today supported by seven
secretaries of defense representing every administration going back to 1969.

They support it because it is the perfect weapon for the post-Cold War world. It has   9
a range of about 7,000 miles. It can be launched instantly—no need to beg foreign dic-
tators for base rights; no need for weeks of advance warning, mobilization and forward
deployment of troops. And because it is invisible to enemy detection, its two pilots are
virtually invulnerable.

This is especially important in view of the B-2's very high cost, perhaps   10
$750,000,000 to $1 billion each. The cost is, of course, what has turned swing Republican votes—the so-called "cheap hawks"—against the B-2.

But the more important calculation is cost in American lives. Weapons cheap in   11
dollars but costly in lives are, in the current and coming environment, literally useless:
We will not use them. A country that so values the life of every Capt. O'Grady is a country that cannot keep blindly relying on non-stealthy aircraft over enemy territory.

In the Gulf War, the stealthy F-117 fighter flew only 2 percent of the missions, but   12
hit 40 percent of the targets. It was, in effect, about 30 times as productive as non-
stealthy planes. The F-117, however, has a short range and thus must be deployed from
forward bases. The B-2 can take off from home. Moreover, the B-2 carries about eight
times the payload of the F-117. Which means that the one B-2 can strike, without es-
cort and with impunity, as many targets as vast fleets of conventional aircraft. Factor
in these costs, and the B-2 becomes cost-effective even in dollar terms.

The final truth of the post-Cold War world is that someday someone is going to at-   13
tack some safe haven we feel compelled to defend, or invade a country whose security is important to us, or build an underground nuclear bomb factory that threatens
millions of Americans. We are going to want a way to attack instantly, massively and
invisibly. We have the weapon to do it, a weapon that no one else has and that no one
can stop. Except a "cheap hawk," shortsighted Republican Congress.

Thinking Critically About "B-2 or Not B-2?"

1. At the beginning of his article, Krauthammer develops criteria for evaluating a weapons system under present political conditions.
   a. What are the facts about the "new era" on which Krauthammer bases
      his criteria?
   b. What are his criteria?
2. What additional criteria, not mentioned by Krauthammer, might be cited for
   selection of defense weapons? Offer conjectures on how well the B-2 meets
   these additional criteria.
3. What technological developments might render the Stealth bomber less
   desirable?

4. Can you think of any characteristics of the "new era" not mentioned by Krauthammer that might render the B-2 less attractive as a defense weapon?
5. In your view, which of Krauthammer's reasons for supporting continued development of the B-2 is most persuasive? Why? Which is least persuasive and why?
6. How might opponents of the B-2 bomber refute Krauthammer's argument?

In the final reading, Corby Kummer, a senior editor for *The Atlantic,* evaluates coffee in light of scientific studies of caffeine and decaffeination.

CORBY KUMMER

IS COFFEE HARMFUL?

1   You can learn what fine coffee is and brew it far better than you ever did before. You can really like the taste of the stuff. But the reason most people drink coffee, of course, is the caffeine. Caffeine may do a wonderful job of fortifying you to face the day. You may think you couldn't live without it. But is it bad for you?

2   Frank evaluation of its hazards is not easy. There is a vast literature on the effects of caffeine on the body, and for every study reaching one conclusion, seemingly there is another that contradicts it. Although most major health risks have been ruled out, research continues at a steady clip. I'll summarize here the work done recently.

3   The first indictment of caffeine in recent years came in 1972, when a Boston group found an association between heavy coffee drinking (more than six cups a day) and elevated risk of heart attack. The association was never confirmed by other studies, however, and the first studies were shown to have been flawed. In 1974 a twelve-year review by the Framingham Heart Study concluded that there was no association between coffee consumption and heart attacks, coronary heart disease, angina pectoris, or sudden death.

4   Today the possible link between caffeine and heart disease is still controversial, and remains the most widely studied aspect of caffeine; recent studies have separated out other risk factors, chiefly smoking, that misled researchers in the past. They have so far come up pretty much undecided. Because very high doses of caffeine can provoke arrhythmia (irregular heartbeat), the danger to people who already suffered from arrhythmia was for a while widely researched, but a study reported last year in the *Archives of Internal Medicine* concluded that moderate doses of caffeine did not pose a danger even to people with life-threatening arrhythmia. Last fall a widely publicized study suggested that people who drink decaffeinated coffee experience a rise in serum cholesterol, but the medical community has largely dismissed the study as preliminary and inconclusive, and no supporting studies have appeared. A recent study in the Netherlands, reported last winter in the *New England Journal of Medicine,* found a significant increase in serum cholesterol among drinkers of boiled coffee, still popular there but made very little here; filtered coffee, which is what most Americans drink, had no effect.

5   A famous health scare associating caffeine with pancreatic cancer turned out to be another case of the missing link: cigarette smoking was the important risk factor, and

five years after publication of the study its authors reversed their original findings. Studies associating coffee with bladder, urinary-tract, and kidney cancer have also been inconsistent and inconclusive.

No link to breast cancer has been proved, although whether a link exists between coffee drinking and benign breast disease, or fibrocystic disease, is still controversial. Large and well-controlled studies have virtually ruled out any link between caffeine consumption and the development of fibrocystic disease, but abstaining from caffeine as a way of treating the disease has been less thoroughly studied. Although the studies conducted so far suggest that no significant lessening of fibrocystic disease occurs when women give up caffeine, many women believe that doing so is an effective treatment. 6

Pregnant women were told in 1980 by the Food and Drug Administration that they should avoid caffeine, on the basis of an FDA experiment in which pregnant rats were force-fed the equivalent of 56 to 87 cups of strong coffee at a time through a stomach tube, and gave birth to offspring with missing toes or parts of toes. A later study giving rats the same exaggerated doses, but orally, in drinking water and at a steadier rate over a day, resulted in none of the birth defects. No later studies on human beings have linked coffee-drinking to any birth defects. 7

The subject for further study seems to be the connection between heavy consumption—more than six or seven cups a day—and low birth weight or birth defects. The average half-life of caffeine in the body, meaning the time it takes the body to get rid of half the caffeine consumed, is three to six hours. Women in the second and third trimesters of pregnancy clear it half as fast, and caffeine, which passes easily through the placenta, can remain in an unborn child for as long as a hundred hours. (Heavy smokers, in contrast, clear caffeine twice as fast.) Although no dangers to infants have been found when pregnant women or nursing mothers drink moderate amounts of coffee, many doctors recommend on principle that pregnant and nursing women avoid caffeine. 8

How caffeine works is still incompletely understood, and the prevailing theory took shape only in the early seventies. The theory holds that caffeine acts less by starting than by stopping something, the something being the depressant effects of adenosine, one of the chemicals the body makes to control neural activity. Caffeine blocks the adenosine receptor sites in cells. This theory is not perfect, for reasons including that there are different types of adenosine receptors, but it is widely accepted. 9

Proponents of caffeine emphasize its ability to increase alertness and enhance performance on various tasks. Its effects are most pronounced, however, on performance levels that are low because of fatigue or boredom. Also, caffeine seems to affect people to a degree that varies according to personality type. For example, it appears to help extroverts keep performing tasks requiring vigilance more than it helps introverts, who are evidently able to plow through such tasks unassisted. Despite the generations of writers who have assumed that coffee helps them think more clearly, caffeine seems to increase only intellectual speed, not intellectual power. Subjects in experiments do things like read and complete crossword puzzles faster but not more accurately. 10

Some studies reveal a curious fact. One recent study found that people who were given doses of caffeine varying from none to high and at the same time allowed to drink their normal amount of coffee each day had no idea how much caffeine they were consuming overall or whether they were consuming any additional caffeine. Even at the highest additional doses people who ordinarily drank small amounts of coffee reported 11 no irritability, nervousness, or tremors. Numerous other studies reinforce the idea that people respond to caffeine more in relation to how much they think they have consumed than to how much they actually have.

12   This is not to say that the effects of caffeine are imaginary. Many studies confirm what most people know—coffee keeps you awake. It also often decreases total sleep time and increases the number of times you wake in the night, depending on how much you drink and on how sensitive you are. Variation among people is great. Everyone knows someone like the woman I met in Brazil who told me, "If I'm sleepy, I take a coffee. If I wake up at night, I take a coffee to go back to sleep." Although caffeine does interfere with some phases of sleep, it has in many studies been shown not to decrease rapid-eye-movement sleep, as alcohol and barbiturates do. The sleep disturbance it causes seems to be more severe in older people, which may be one reason why consumption of decaffeinated coffee increases with age.

13   That caffeine interferes with sleep doesn't mean that it reliably makes you snap to. It doesn't sober you up, black or with milk—your motor functions are just as badly impaired by alcohol as they were before you drank two cups of black coffee, and even if you feel more awake you're just as dangerous a driver. Similarly, caffeine does not counteract phenobarbital or other barbiturates. But it does help reverse the impairment of cognitive activity caused by diazepam, the chemical that is the basis of Valium and many other tranquilizers.

14   Caffeine speeds up the metabolism and makes you burn calories faster, although not significantly for purposes of weight loss, as amphetamine does. The body metabolizes caffeine almost completely, and it appears in all tissue fluids about five minutes after ingestion, reaching its highest levels after twenty to thirty minutes. Caffeine is a diuretic and thus dehydrating, so don't think that drinking coffee will slake your thirst. Coffee, both regular and decaffeinated, has a laxative effect.

15   And coffee can cause stomach pain and heartburn. The exact roles played by caffeine and other substances in coffee in stimulating the secretion of gastric acids remains in question, because there has been proof that both caffeinated and decaffeinated coffee can affect the gastrointestinal tract. One study found that regular and decaffeinated coffee each had twice as much effect on the gastrointestinal tract as caffeine alone. Although coffee, with or without caffeine, and caffeine itself are not thought to cause ulcers, their role has been little studied, and both are known to make ulcers worse.

16   A source of confusion for anyone trying to learn how much caffeine he consumes is the conflicting estimates that appear in studies. Most say that a five-ounce cup of coffee contains from 80 to 100 milligrams of caffeine, although in fact the variation can be much greater, depending on the strength of the coffee. The same amount of tea, brewed for five minutes, has from 20 to 50 milligrams of caffeine; a cup of tea usually contains less caffeine than a cup of coffee because less tea is used per cup. A twelve-ounce serving of cola generally contains 38 (for Pepsi) to 45 (for Coke) milligrams of caffeine. Some studies say that for caffeine to have its effects the minimum oral dose is 85 milligrams, but this too depends on individual sensitivity.

17   The question of addiction is similarly thorny. According to a review of the literature on caffeine and the central nervous system by Kenneth Hirsh, in *Methylxanthine Beverages and Foods*, recent data show that tolerance to caffeine develops in the central nervous system and in many organ systems. Tolerance has been better studied than its ugly corollary, withdrawal. In sleep studies researchers noticed that heavy coffee drinkers were less disturbed than light or moderate coffee drinkers by drinking coffee

before going to sleep and, if they had had no coffee the night before, felt more in need of a cup in the morning. Those little accustomed to caffeine suffer "caffeinism," or coffee nerves, when they have a high dose. Those accustomed to but deprived of it report, and experiments confirm, irritability, inability to work well, nervousness, restlessness, and lethargy.

Worst, and most common, is the headache that comes with giving up caffeine. The   18 headache can be severe and often lasts for one or two days. The adenosine-receptor theory holds that long-term caffeine consumption creates more adenosine receptor sites, and thus sudden abstention from caffeine means unusual sensitivity to adenosine. This could explain withdrawal headache: overreactivity to adenosine in blood vessels in the scalp and cranium can dilate them, and cause a headache. One very effective way to treat the headache, unsurprisingly, is with caffeine, which constricts the blood vessels in the brain; this effect is why caffeine has long been used to treat migraines. (In contrast, caffeine dilates coronary arteries.) The reason so many over-the-counter headache remedies include caffeine, though, is that it is thought to enhance the effects of the other drugs in them—something that has never been proved. Kenneth Hirsh optimistically thinks that because the body is more sensitive to adenosine after caffeine withdrawal, it will compensate by reducing the number of adenosine receptors to the number that existed before caffeine tolerance developed.

If caffeine is so painful to give up, can caffeine tolerance be compared to addiction   19 to other drugs? Hirsh, like many other scientists, wants to avoid the comparison. "All definitions of addiction . . . eventually boil down to compulsion with and for a drug," he writes. Caffeine, he concludes, just doesn't result in addictive behavior. He points to rat and baboon studies in which animals regularly gave themselves doses of morphine, cocaine, and amphetamine but gave themselves caffeine no more often than saline placebos. Some animals in the experiment seemed more eager for caffeine than others, which supports the idea that individual variation is important. Hirsh, it must be noted, worked for General Foods when he wrote his study, but he is not alone in his conclusions.

However fine one draws the distinction, caffeine use does fit several standards of   20 drug addiction, which include compulsion to continue use, tolerance for the drug, and withdrawal. It is silly to invoke the argument, as caffeine apologists often do, that truly addictive drugs impel their users to commit any act, however violent, to obtain them. You don't have to mug someone in a park at night to get money for a cup of coffee. You can stand on a corner and ask for it.

Whether or not caffeine is hazardous or truly addictive, becoming habituated to it   21 and suffering coffee nerves or caffeine withdrawal are no fun, and many people have chosen to drink decaffeinated coffee instead. In 1962, the peak year for American coffee consumption, decaffeinated coffee made up only three percent of coffee sales; today it accounts for more than 20 percent. It's a shame that most decaffeinated coffee is so terrible, because it doesn't have to be. Traditionally, the inferior robusta species of bean has been decaffeinated, not only because it is cheaper but also because it yields more caffeine, which can be sold to soft-drink and patent-medicine companies, and because it has more body and so can better withstand decaffeination processes. Arabica beans, which are of higher quality, are now being decaffeinated. But the public buys the vastly inferior water-process decaf, because it suffers from an unwarranted fear of chemical decaffeination.

Decaffeination has been practiced since the turn of the century, mostly using   22 chemicals. Every process starts with steaming the beans, to loosen the bond of caffeine to the coffee bean. Then, in the "direct" process, a chemical solvent is circulated through the beans. The beans are again steamed to remove any residual solvent, and dried; the solvent is mixed with water and the caffeine extracted. In the water process, after beans are first steamed they soak in water, which removes not only caffeine but all the other solids that flavor a cup of coffee. Caffeine is removed from the solution, which is reduced to a slurry that is returned to soak with the still-wet beans and give them back some of the lost solids.

23   The problems of water-process decaffeination are obvious. The water strips out most of the body and the flavoring compounds. What goes back is sometimes from the previous batch of beans, and it won't all go back anyway. Jacobs Suchard, a large Swiss company, has made improvements in the water process that keep more solids intact in the beans. It has mounted a new campaign to promote the Swiss process, in which caffeine is extracted from the water-solids solution with carbon filters rather than with the chemicals that are sometimes used. Specialty coffee decaffeinated at Jacobs Suchard's new factory in Vancouver has made strong showings in taste tests. But most water-process decaffeinated coffee is still a shadow of its former self and must be over-roasted, to give the false impression that it has body and flavor.

24   The most efficient chemical solvent, methylene chloride, is what people think they should avoid. Methylene chloride has been banned for use in hair sprays since it was shown in animal studies to be dangerous when inhaled. But mice fed methylene chloride in drinking water at doses equivalent to 4.4 million cups of decaf a day showed none of the toxicological or carcinogenic response that had occurred when mice had inhaled it in much smaller quantities. In 1985 the FDA said that the risk from using methylene chloride in decaffeination is so low "as to be essentially non-existent." Methylene chloride evaporates at 100° to 120°F. Beans are usually roasted at a temperature of 350° to 425°, coffee brewed at 190° to 212°. The amount of methylene chloride left in brewed coffee, then, must be measured in parts per billion—comparable to what is in the air of many cities. Even Michael Jacobson, the crusading leader of the consumer-advocacy group Center for Science in the Public Interest, says that caffeine is more dangerous than any chemical residues in decaffeinated coffee. Coffee decaffeinated with methylene chloride certainly tastes better.

25   A new process, using "supercritical" carbon dioxide, shows great promise. The supercritical fluid, in a state between liquid and gas, is produced under extremely high pressure. It can pass through steamed coffee beans and remove the caffeine without removing other solids, vaporizing when its work is done and leaving not a trace. So far General Foods is the only company using the process, and its production capacity allows it to decaffeinate only its Sanka brand (not its Maxwell House decaf) and Private Collection, a smaller GF venture into specialty coffee. A new processing plant is being built independently in northern California, and when completed (in about two years) it will decaffeinate beans from specialty roasters using supercritical carbon dioxide, which Marc Sims, a consultant in Berkeley, California, who is involved with the plant, prefers to call "natural effervescence."

26   "Regular, decaf—it's all caf," a woman said dismissively when I recently offered her a choice of coffees after dinner. She was not entirely wrong. Advertisements for coffee that is "97 percent caffeine-free" might as well describe any coffee, since the caffeine content of coffee beans varies from 1.1 to 2.6 percent. It would be better to say "de-caffeinated," since the FDA requires that 97 percent of caffeine be removed from un-roasted beans. (It has no requirements for brewed coffee.) Coffee decaffeinated by careful firms like Jacobs Suchard and KVW, near Hamburg, which uses methylene

chloride, yields 0.03 percent or less caffeine in unroasted beans. Brewed decaf can thus have one to five milligrams of caffeine per cup, and however little that sounds compared with the supposed minimum 85-milligram dose, it can keep some people—me, for instance—going.

You can rate the processes for yourself. The Coffee Connection (800-284-5282) will send you Jacobs Suchard water decaf. Starbucks, an excellent roaster in Seattle (800-445-3428), and Thanksgiving (800-648-6491) will send you that or KVW chemical decaf. Any of these beans will prove that you don't have to give up what you love about coffee if you give up caffeine.   27

Not only are people turning away from caffeine, they're turning away from coffee, and in more significant numbers. Since 1962 per capita coffee consumption has fallen by more than a third, from 3.12 to 1.75 cups a day. At the same time, per capita consumption of soft drinks has nearly tripled. The decline can't accurately be attributed to fears about caffeine, because two thirds of it occurred before the first health scare about caffeine, in 1972. The culprit is soft drinks, whose manufacturers spend much more on promotion than coffee companies do. Young people drink cola to wake themselves up, and so do many former coffee drinkers. Pepsi recently test-marketed Pepsi A.M., a cola with more than the usual amount of caffeine.   28

The coffee trade has naturally been alarmed by this trend, but no one quite knows what to do about it. The big fear is that coffee will go the way of tea—now considered (when served hot, at any rate) to be an old person's drink. Big companies have tried to compete with specialty roasters, as General Foods did when it started its Private Collection line of whole-bean and ground coffee, because the specialty-coffee market has been growing by 15 to 20 percent a year while the mass coffee market has been shrinking.   29

A recent article in *Tea & Coffee Trade Journal* suggested various ways to combat the decrease: trying to break the coffee-caffeine association, both conceptual and aural, by using brand names to refer to coffee, as with soft drinks; trying to give coffee a youthful image in advertisements, rather than relying on a logo to sell the product; promoting coffee at colleges; dyeing plain old styrofoam cups so they'll look zippy, like soda cans. The Coffee Development Group, an organization dedicated to increasing the consumption of coffee by improving its quality, thinks that one answer is in promoting iced coffee and sweetened coffee drinks, to compete directly with soda. In fact, the fastest-growing part of the specialty-coffee market is coffee mixed with bits of nuts and dried fruit and stirred with flavoring extracts, making really awful combinations that roasters disdain but stock—"those yucky flavors that sell," in the words of Dan Cox, of Green Mountain Coffee, in Vermont, who is the current chairman of the Coffee Development Group.   30

Yucky they are. Better to drink straight coffee, with or without caffeine, that tastes good.   31

Thinking Critically About "Is Coffee Harmful?"

1. Briefly summarize the pluses and minuses of coffee consumption cited by Kummer. Order them in terms of their importance to you.
2. Since 1990, when Kummer's article was written, consumption of coffee has risen dramatically in the United States. Keeping in mind the pros and cons

of coffee consumption cited by Kummer, why do you think so much more coffee is being consumed today? What factors not mentioned by Kummer might account for the current caffeine mania?

3. Should a sin tax similar to that placed on alcohol and tobacco be placed on caffeinated products?

COMPOSING YOUR ESSAY

Generating and Exploring Ideas

If you have not already chosen an evaluation issue, try creating idea maps with spokes chosen from among the following (or any other categories you can think of):

People: athletes, political leaders, musicians, entertainers, clergy

Science and technology: weapons systems, word-processing programs, spreadsheets, automotive advancements, treatments for diseases

Media: news programs, TV shows, radio stations, advertisements

Government and world affairs: economic policies, Supreme Court decisions, laws or legal practices, government customs or practices, foreign policies

The arts: movies, books, buildings, paintings, music

Your college or university: courses, teachers, curricula, administrative policies, financial aid systems

The world of work: jobs, company operations, dress codes, systems of compensation, hiring policies, supervisors

Another good idea for finding a topic is to think of a recent review with which you disagree—a movie review, a restaurant review, a review of an art exhibit or play, or a sportswriter's assessment of a team or player.

Once you have chosen a possible topic, freewrite your responses to each of the following questions as a means of exploring ideas for your argument.

1. To what class does your X belong? Choose the smallest relevant class. (Instead of asking, "Is Joe Smith a good athlete?" ask "Is Joe Smith a good college basketball player?" or, even better, "Is Joe Smith a good college point guard?")

2. Determine the criteria you will use for your evaluation. Begin by listing the purposes of the class and then use freewriting or idea mapping to explore the qualities a member of that class has to have to achieve those purposes. What objections is your audience likely to raise about your criteria? How will you justify your criteria?

3. Which of your criteria is the most important? Why?

4. Evaluate your subject by matching it to each of the criteria. Explore why your subject does or does not match each of the criteria. Your freewriting for this exercise will yield most of the ideas you will need for your argument.

Shaping and Drafting

For your first draft, consider using the following format. Many evaluation arguments follow this shape, and you can always alter it later if it seems too formulaic for you.

1. Introduce your issue and show why evaluating X is problematic or controversial
2. Present your own argument
   a. State criterion 1 and defend it if necessary
   b. Show that X meets/does not meet the criterion
   c. State criterion 2 and defend it if necessary
   d. Show that X meets/does not meet the criterion
   e. Continue with additional criteria and match arguments
3. Summarize opposing views
4. Refute or concede to opposing views
5. Sum up your evaluation

Revising

As always, test your draft on a reader by exchanging work with a classmate. Once you've received feedback from your partner, you are ready to begin revising your draft. As you revise, remember that you're not necessarily through getting reader feedback. Don't limit yourself arbitrarily to resources within the class. Find other audiences for your paper if you can; roommates, relatives, and friends can be excellent editorial resources. If you have access to trained tutors in a writing center, use them.

In getting advice from peers, encourage them not so much to tell you what's wrong or right with your paper, but rather to report what happens as they read. When are they confused? When do they find it hard to believe you or your sources? Where do they need more evidence or information or examples? When are they enjoying the reading and when are they bored? Remember, peers aren't teacher substitutes, so much as audience substitutes.

Most evaluation arguments work best as closed-form pieces that follow the advice presented in Chapters 18 and 19. When you revise, remember to start with the big issues, the major changes, and then work your way to the smaller issues and changes. In the process of revising at the global level, you may well solve many of the local problems. Troublesome sentences may disappear in the process of fixing a shaky argument. If you start trying to fix the paper sentence by sentence, some of your best editing may turn out to have been wasted on passages that were doomed anyway.

g u i d e l i n e s

for Peer Reviewers

Instructions for peer reviews, including use of these guidelines, are provided in Chapter 21, pages 527–28. To write a peer review for a classmate, use your own paper, numbering your responses to correspond to the questions on the guidelines. At the head of your paper place the author's name and your own name as shown.

Author's Name: _____

Peer Reviewer's Name: _____

I. Read the draft at normal reading speed from beginning to end. As you read, do the following:
   A. Place a wavy line in the margin next to any passages that you find confusing, that contain something that doesn't seem to fit, or that otherwise slow down your reading.
   B. Place a "Good!" in the margin next to any passages where you think the writing is particularly strong or interesting.
II. Read the draft again slowly. Describe for the writer what you currently see in this draft. If you have difficulty answering any of the following questions, explain briefly the source of your difficulty.
   A. What is the writer's major claim?
   B. Who disagrees with this claim and why? If nobody could conceivably disagree, the writer should rethink the claim.
   C. To what class of things does X belong? If you were to place X in a broader or narrower class, in which direction would you go and why?
   D. What criteria does the writer use for evaluating X?
   E. What evidence does the writer present to show that the item being evaluated meets or fails to meet each of the criteria?
   F. Where does the writer summarize opposing viewpoints? How does the writer respond to these opposing views?
III. What recommendations do you have for improving this draft?
   A. How might the writer improve the title?
   B. Does the introduction capture your interest and set up the question to be addressed, showing why it is both problematic and significant? How might the writer improve the introduction?
   C. Do you agree with the writer's criteria and with the way the writer has weighted their relative importance? Why? What suggestions do you have for improving the writer's criteria argument?
   D. Do you agree with the writer's match argument and find the writer's use of evidence persuasive? Why? What suggestions do you have for improving the writer's match argument?

      E. How would you refute the writer's argument?

      F. How might the writer improve the structure of the draft? Where might the writer better apply the principles of clarity from Chapter 19 (start with the big picture; place points before particulars; use helpful transitions; and follow the old/new contract)?

      G. Sum up what you see as the chief strengths and problem areas of this draft.

        1. Strengths

        2. Problem areas

IV. Read the draft one more time. Place a check in the margin wherever you notice problems in grammar, spelling, or mechanics (one check per problem).

c h a p t e r   16

Proposing a Solution

ABOUT PROPOSAL WRITING

Proposal arguments call an audience to action. They go beyond truth claims (the grading system creates student stress) and values claims (the grading system is harmful) to action claims (the grading system should be abolished).

Some proposals aim to solve local, practical matters. For example, one of the student proposals in this chapter advocates that a soundproof door be installed in a dorm recreation room to create a quiet study area (pp. 395–400). Practical proposals generally target a specific audience (usually the person with power to act on the proposal) and are often introduced with a *letter of transmittal,* in which the writer briefly summarizes the proposal, explains its purpose, and courteously invites the reader to consider it. The rhetorical context of practical proposals makes effective document design essential. An effective design (layout, neatness, clear headings, flawless editing) helps establish the writer's ethos as a quality-oriented professional and facilitates reading the proposal. In many areas of business and industry, effective practical proposals are crucial to financial success. Many kinds of businesses—construction and engineering firms, ad agencies, university research teams, nonprofit agencies, and others—generate most of their revenue from projects obtained through writing effective, winning proposals.

Other kinds of proposals, often called *policy proposals,* are aimed at more general audiences. These proposals usually address issues of public policy with the intent of swaying public support toward the writer's proposed solution. How can we solve the problem of prison overcrowding (of skyrocketing health-care costs, of gang violence, of declining SAT scores, of caring for infants with fetal alcohol syndrome)? How do we keep pornography off the Internet? How do we prevent the spread of AIDS?

Sometimes proposal writers join an ongoing debate. In such cases the writer can follow the shape of the classical argument described in Chapter 14: introduce the issue; present the claim; provide supporting reasons for the claim; summarize and rebut opposing views; provide a conclusion.

In many cases, however, the proposal writer initiates a debate; the writer in effect *creates* the issue being addressed, by calling the reader's attention to a problem and then proposing a course of action. The rest of this chapter focuses on strategies for this latter type of proposal, which, along with practical proposals, requires a structure slightly different from that of the classical argument.

EXPLORING PROPOSAL WRITING

The following activity introduces you to the thinking processes involved in writing a proposal argument.

1. In small groups, identify and list several major problems facing students in your college or university.
2. Decide among yourselves which problems are most important and rank them in order of importance.
3. Choose your group's number one problem and explore answers to the following questions. Group recorders should be prepared to present answers to the class as a whole.
   a. Why is the problem a problem?
   b. For whom is the problem a problem?
   c. How will these people suffer if the problem is not solved? Give specific examples.
   d. Who has the power to solve the problem?
   e. Why hasn't the problem been solved up to this point?
   f. How can the problem be solved? Create a proposal for a solution.
   g. What are the probable benefits of acting on your proposal?
   h. What costs are associated with your proposal?
   i. Who will bear these costs?
   j. Why should this proposal be enacted?
   k. What makes this proposal better than alternative proposals?
4. As a group, draft an outline for a proposal argument in which you do the following:
   a. Describe the problem and its significance.
   b. Propose your solution to the problem.
   c. Justify your proposal by showing how the benefits of adopting it outweigh the costs.
5. Recorders for each group should write the group's outline on the board and be prepared to present the group's argument orally to the class.

WRITING PROJECT

Call your audience's attention to a problem, propose a solution to that problem, and present a justification for your solution. You have two choices (your instructor may limit you to just one): (a) create a *practical* proposal, with a letter of transmittal proposing a nuts-and-bolts solution to a local problem; or (b) write a more general *policy* proposal, addressing a public issue, in the form of a bylined feature editorial for a particular (state, local, or college) newspaper. For (b), your instructor might ask you to do substantial research and model your proposal after a magazine or journal article.

All proposals have one feature in common—they offer a solution to a problem. For every proposal, there is always an alternative course of action, including doing nothing. Your task as a proposal writer is fourfold: You must demonstrate that a significant problem exists; propose a solution to the problem; justify the solution and its costs; and show that the proposed solution will fix the problem better than alternative solutions would. Accordingly, a proposal argument typically has four main parts.

1. *Description of the problem.*   The description often begins with background. Where does the problem show up? Who is affected by the problem? How long has the problem been around? Is it getting worse? You may add an anecdote or some kind of startling information or statistics to give the problem *presence*. Typically, this section also analyzes the problem. What are its elements? What are its causes? Why hasn't it been solved before? Why are obvious solutions not adequate or workable? Finally, the description shows the problem's significance. What are the negative consequences of not solving the problem?
2. *Proposal for a solution.*   This section describes your solution and shows how it would work. If you don't yet have a solution, you may choose to generate a *planning proposal*, calling for a committee or task force to study the problem and propose solutions at a later date. The purpose of a planning proposal is to call attention to a serious problem. In most cases, however, this section should propose a detailed solution, showing step-by-step how it would solve the problem and at what cost.
3. *Justification.*   This section persuades the audience that the benefits of enacting your solution outweigh the costs. As we explain later in this chapter, justification arguments are typically based on principle, consequences, precedent, or analogy.
4. *Comparison with alternative solutions.*   The purpose of the comparison is to show why your solution is better than alternative solutions. This section explains why each alternative would not solve the problem, would provide fewer benefits, and/or would cost significantly more than your proposal.

UNDERSTANDING PROPOSAL WRITING

As we have noted, proposal arguments differ from other kinds of arguments in both purpose and structure. In this section we look at some of the distinctive demands of proposal writing and then examine a strategy for developing the justification section of a proposal.

Special Demands of Proposal Arguments

To get the reader to take action—the ultimate purpose of a proposal—requires you to overcome some difficult challenges. Here we examine the special demands that proposal arguments make on writers and offer suggestions for meeting them.

Creating Presence

To convince readers that a problem really exists, you must give it *presence*, that is, you must help readers *see* and *feel* the problem. Writers often use anecdotes or examples of people suffering from the problem or cite startling facts or statistics to dramatize the problem. For example, a student proposing streamlined checkout procedures in the hotel where she worked gave her problem presence by describing a family that missed its flight home because of an agonizingly slow checkout line. Her description of this family's frustration—including angry complaints overheard by people waiting to check in—convinced her boss that the problem was worth solving. To persuade your readers to act on your proposal, you need to involve them both mentally *and* emotionally in your argument.

Appealing to the Interest and Values of Decision Makers

Proposal writers sometimes appeal directly to readers' idealism, urging them to do the right thing. But writers also need to show how doing the right thing converges with their readers' own best interests. Show decision makers how acting on your proposal will benefit *them* directly. The author of the hotel checkout proposal argued that her solution would enhance customer satisfaction, an idea that her boss would find more compelling than the notion of making life easier for desk clerks.

Overcoming Inherent Conservatism

People are inherently resistant to change. One of the most famous proposals of all time, the Declaration of Independence, is notable for the way in which it anticipates its audience's resistance to change: "Prudence, indeed, will dictate that governments long established should not be changed for light and transient causes; and accordingly, all experience hath shown, that mankind are more disposed to suffer, while evils are sufferable, than to right themselves by abolishing the forms to which they are accustomed."

To restate this passage as folk wisdom, "Better the devil you know than the one you don't know." Most people expect the *status quo* to have its problems, flaws, and frustrations. They live with and adapt to familiar imperfections. Unless they can be persuaded that change will make things markedly better, they will "suffer, while evils are sufferable" rather than risk creating new, possibly insufferable evils.

The challenge of proving that something needs changing is compounded by the fact that the *status quo* often appears to be working. If its shortcomings were readily apparent, people would probably already have fixed them. It is much harder to stir an audience to action when the problem you depict entails lost potential (things could be better), rather than palpable evil (look at all the suffering).

Predicting Consequences

People also resist change because they fear unforeseen bad consequences and doubt predictions of good consequences. Everyone has experienced the disappointment of failed proposals: your favorite sports team makes a major trade—

and finishes with a record worse than the one it had before the trade; a company you invested in went through a major reorganization—and promptly went into the red; voters elect a new leader who promises major reforms—and nothing happens. Although most people do not become true cynics, they are understandably cautious about accepting the rosy scenarios contained in most proposals.

To persuade your audience that your predictions are realistic, follow the strategies outlined in Chapter 13 for causal arguments. The more uncertain your proposal's consequences, the more clearly you must show *how* the proposal will bring about the consequences. Show the links in the chain and how each one leads to the next. Whenever possible, cite similar proposals that yielded the sorts of results you are predicting.

Evaluating Consequences

Compounding the problem of predicting consequences is the difficulty of figuring out whether those consequences are good or bad and for whom. For example, any alternative to the current health care system will contain changes that simultaneously advantage one segment of your audience (say, patients) and disadvantage another (say, doctors, insurance companies, or taxpayers). Indeed, if any health care proposal benefited all segments of your audience, it would probably have been adopted long ago. Although proposal makers sometimes mask this difficulty by offering universally laudable, if vague, proposals ("We need to provide health care for all our citizens"), an audience will eventually demand to know all those pesky details that harbor the devil ("We need to raise taxes and have insurance companies authorize all procedures in advance").

It can be difficult to identify the appropriate standard of measure to use in calculating a proposal's costs and benefits. Often you must try to balance benefits measured in apples against costs measured in oranges. For instance, suppose that a health care proposal will reduce the cost of insurance by limiting benefits. How would you balance the dollars saved on insurance payments against the suffering of persons denied a potentially life-saving medical procedure? Some cost–benefit analyses try to reduce all consequences to one scale of measure—usually money. This scale may work well in some circumstances, but it can lead to grotesquely inappropriate conclusions in others.

These, then, are some of the challenges that face the proposal writer. With these in mind, we now set forth some strategies for making proposals as effective as possible.

Developing an Effective Justification Section

The distinctions between proposals and other kinds of arguments dictate a special variety of support for proposals. Experienced proposal writers often use a *three-approaches* strategy to help them develop their justification sections. They brainstorm justifying reasons by focusing sequentially on principles, consequences, and precedents or analogies. Figure 16.1 (on p. 394) explains each element in the sequence.

Approach 1: *Argument from Principle*

Using this strategy, you argue that a particular action should be taken because doing so is right according to some value, assumption, principle, or belief that you share with your audience. For example, you might argue, "We should create publicly financed jobs for poor people because doing so is both charitable and just." The formula for this strategy is as follows:

We should (should not) do (this action) because (this action) is _____.

Fill in the blank with an appropriate adjective or noun specifying a belief or value that the audience holds: good, just, right, ethical, honest, charitable, equitable, fair, and so forth.

Approach 2: *Argument from Consequence*

Using this strategy, you argue that a particular action should (should not) be taken because doing so will lead to consequences that you and your audience believe are good (bad). For example, you might say, "We should create publicly financed jobs for poor people because doing so will provide them money for food and housing, promote a work ethic, and produce needed goods and services." The formula for this strategy is as follows:

We should (should not) do (this action) because (this action) will lead to these good (bad) consequences: _____, _____, _____, etc.

Think of consequences that your audience will agree are good or bad, as your argument requires.

Approach 3: *Argument from Precedent or Analogy*

Using a precedent strategy, you argue that a particular action should (should not) be taken because doing so is similar to what was done in another case, which proved to be successful (unsuccessful). For example, you might say, "We should create publicly financed jobs for poor people because doing so will alleviate poverty in this country just as a similar program has helped poor people in Upper Magnesia." Using an analogy strategy, you compare the proposed action with a similar action that your audience already accepts as good or bad. For example, "We should create publicly financed jobs for poor people because doing so is like teaching the poor how to fish rather than giving them fish." The formula for either strategy is as follows:

We should (should not) do (this action) because doing (this action) is like _____, which turned out to be good (bad).

Think of precedents or analogies that are similar to your proposed action and that have definite good (bad) associations for your audience.

FIGURE 16.1   The Three Approaches Strategy for a Justification Section

Each of these argumentation strategies was clearly evident in a recent public debate in Seattle, Washington, over a proposal to raise county sales taxes to build a new baseball stadium. Those favoring the stadium put forth arguments such as these:

> We should build the new stadium because preserving our national pastime for our children is important (*argument from principle*), because building the stadium will create new jobs and revitalize the adjacent Pioneer Square district (*arguments from consequence*), and because building the stadium will have the same beneficial effects on the city that building Camden Yards had in Baltimore (*argument from precedent*).

Those opposing the stadium created arguments using the same strategies:

> We should not build the stadium because it is wrong to subsidize rich owners and players with tax dollars (*argument from principle*), because building a stadium diverts tax money from more important concerns such as low income housing (*argument from consequence*), and because Toronto's experience with Skydome shows that once the novelty of a new stadium wears off attendance declines dramatically (*argument from precedent*).

READINGS

The first reading is a practical proposal by a student writer. Because practical proposals are aimed at a specific audience, they are often accompanied by a letter of transmittal that introduces the writer, sets the context, and summarizes the proposal.

```
                         Campwell Hall, Room 1209

                         February 5, 1995


Ms. Terri Halliwell

Director of Residences

_____ University

City, State  Zip

Dear Ms. Halliwell:
```

1   I am a student in Campwell Hall. Please find enclosed a proposal to make the study lounge on the twelfth floor more quiet. Although I enjoy living in Campwell Hall very much, I and many other students are frustrated by the absence of adequate quiet study areas for its residents. It is particularly difficult to concentrate in the twelfth floor study lounge because of dis-

ruptive noise from hallways, from elevators, and from students who are talking and watching television in the adjoining recreational lounge. My proposed solution is to add a soundproof door between the twelfth floor
recreational lounge and the study lounge. This low-cost addition will create a quiet study place for twelfth floor residents.

    Thank you for your consideration of my ideas.   2

Sincerely,

Theresa LaPorte

Following the letter of transmittal is the proposal's cover or title page.

A PROPOSAL TO CREATE A QUIET STUDY LOUNGE

ON THE TWELFTH FLOOR OF CAMPWELL HALL

Submitted to Ms. Terri Halliwell

Director of Residences

Theresa LaPorte

Campwell Resident

    If this were the actual proposal, the first page would begin on a new page fol-
lowing the cover page.

Problem

    Campwell Hall does not have adequate study areas for its residents. Al-   1
though there are many places for students to study at Campwell, I will examine each area, then show how it is an unacceptable option.

2   The most common studying place for students is their dorm rooms. Unfortunately, though, many students cannot study in their rooms because noise carries easily through the thin, uninsulated walls. Also, students have different study habits from each other. For example, while one student may need silence, her roommate may need music in order to concentrate.

3   The floor lounges are another alternative. Occasionally, students can study in the floor lounges if the television is turned off and if no other students are taking study breaks. However, most floors have ruled that television watchers have priority in the lounges because other study rooms are available, and lounges are meant for relaxation. Therefore, floor lounges are rarely an option.

4   Another alternative might be the study lounge on the first floor of Campwell, but it is also an acceptable option for several reasons. It is located in a corner on the ground floor, well beyond the normal flow of traffic. The room is out of both sight and sound ranges to anyone who is not in the study lounge. The west hall is lined by unprotected windows that can be opened enough to allow a fully grown person easily to crawl in or out. Also, to leave this room, one must exit through another empty room. Because of its location and because it is usually empty, this lounge is potentially dangerous at night, and it can be frightening, especially for women who are alone.

5   The final option is the twelfth floor study lounge. This lounge has four small study rooms and one large community study room. Although this lounge is safe and has many nice features, it is impossible to concentrate in the study lounge because of external noises. The students themselves are usually quiet because they have come to this lounge to study. The problem is that there is no door between the twelfth floor recreational lounge and the study lounge (see diagram).

6   Consequently, frustrated students not only hear twelfth floor residents talking in the recreational lounge, but also elevators dinging, doors open-

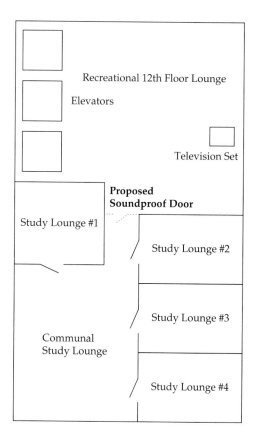

Recreational 12th Floor Lounge

Elevators

Television Set

**Proposed
Soundproof Door**

Study Lounge #1

Study Lounge #2

Study Lounge #3

Communal
Study Lounge

Study Lounge #4

Twelfth Floor Recreational Lounge and Study

Lounge Area

ing, and the television blaring. All of these external noises are magnified in a room that is otherwise silent.

In an informal survey of ten residents, I found that eight out of the   7 ten thought that the communal study lounge on the twelfth floor was too noisy. Five out of ten students interviewed said that they often tried to study in the lounge, even though it was too noisy. An additional three out of ten students did not use the study lounge because it was so noisy.

Proposed Solution

The most practical solution to this problem is to soundproof the twelfth   8 floor study lounge. According to Rick Smith, the Residence Hall Coordinator, building the door is a relatively simple process that could be completed by a single person. The carpenter would first need to build an insulated wall around the door. Because the doorway is about twelve feet high, this wall would cost approximately $300. Next, the carpenter would put in a solid core door and frame. This would cost about $400 for the door, and $80 for the enclosure around it. The only additional charge would be for labor, which would cost approximately $800. The total proposed cost, therefore, is $1,580.

Justification

9   The room cannot be completely soundproofed because the twelfth floor has a false ceiling that is merely plasterboard, but a hard core door and insulated wall would significantly reduce noises that come into the communal study lounge. This action would effectively solve the problem, as the small study rooms are already soundproofed, and no further repairs would be necessary.

10   Although building a soundproof door would cost the Residence Hall Association of _____ University $1,580, other options which provide acceptable solutions to this problem are far less practical and much more expensive. For instance, the most effective solution would be to insulate and carpet each dorm room to eliminate noises coming from other rooms. This option is impractical because of the tremendous labor and expense. Another possible solution to the problem is to make the ground floor study lounge acceptable to all students by hiring a 24-hour monitor and possibly adding bars to cover the windows. This plan, too, is impractical because of its cost, since the expenses of a monitor for one year alone would exceed the one-time cost of a door. The last solution is to make the twelfth floor study lounge quieter without any remodeling. It would entail closing the twelfth floor lounge, removing the television, and banning conversation from the area. This option, too, is impractical. Twelfth floor residents would

resent this decision, no one would be able to enforce the ruling, and the noise from the elevators and hallways would still remain. In comparison, building a soundproof door and wall is the most practical and least expensive choice.

This new door would not only benefit the students who live in Campwell 11 Hall, but it might also make life at _____ University more appealing to potential students. Campwell residents would then have the option of studying in a quiet, yet safe environment in their own hall. More importantly, though, this addition would demonstrate to Campwell residents, as well as potential students, that _____ University takes a serious approach to the academic goals of its students and wants them to get as much out of college and residential life as possible.

Thinking Critically About "A Proposal to Create a Quiet Study Lounge"

1. What strategies does Theresa LaPorte use to convince the residence director that a problem exists?
2. What strategies does Theresa use to convince administrators that the proposed solution is practical and cost-effective?
3. How does Theresa try to tie her proposal to the values and beliefs of her audience—the director of residences in particular and university administrators in general?
4. If you were Ms. Terri Halliwell, the director of residences to whom this proposal is addressed (see Theresa's letter of transmittal), how effective would you find this proposal? What are its chief strengths and weaknesses?

The next proposal, also by a student writer, is a much longer, researched policy argument that addresses the issue of funding for hospices. To appreciate the origins of Sheridan Botts's argument, read her exploratory essay in Chapter 8 (pp. 170–72). The exploratory essay describes how Botts became interested in hospices, how she discovered the issue of funding (fee-for-service versus per diem funding), and how she wrestled to find an appropriate audience and focus for her ideas. The exploratory essay shows the writer struggling with a problem. The proposal argument that follows is the final product that emerged from that struggle. The citation and reference formats in this paper follow the conventions of the American Psychological Association (APA). (See Chapter 23 for a discussion of this citation system.)

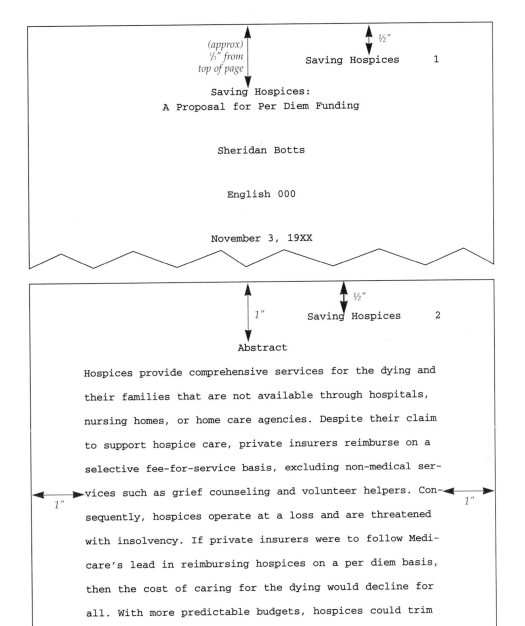

*(approx)
⅓" from
top of page*

½"

Saving Hospices   1

Saving Hospices:
A Proposal for Per Diem Funding

Sheridan Botts

English 000

November 3, 19XX

1"

½"

Saving Hospices   2

Abstract

Hospices provide comprehensive services for the dying and their families that are not available through hospitals, nursing homes, or home care agencies. Despite their claim to support hospice care, private insurers reimburse on a selective fee-for-service basis, excluding non-medical services such as grief counseling and volunteer helpers. Consequently, hospices operate at a loss and are threatened with insolvency. If private insurers were to follow Medicare's lead in reimbursing hospices on a per diem basis, then the cost of caring for the dying would decline for all. With more predictable budgets, hospices could trim expenses and negotiate better rates with suppliers. Since hospice care usually keeps patients at home, insurers could avoid reimbursing costly hospital stays. Moreover, a per diem policy would validate insurers' verbal endorsements of a holistic approach to terminal care.

1"   1"

Saving Hospices:

A Proposal for Per Diem Funding

Sheridan's Paper—Final Proposal

Last fall my brother-in-law, Charles, lay dying, and
his mother, Betty, was overwhelmed with grief and responsibility. Charles wanted to die at home, not connected
to tubes in the hospital, so Betty cared for him in his
home with the help of a home care agency. While caring
for him--helping him get sips of water, trying to meet
his every need--she became terribly depressed. She had
already lost one son, and now she was losing another.
When I called the home care agency to ask for counseling
help for Betty, they said, "Is she the patient? We can
only care for the patient." And then, after Charles
died, and Betty was bereft, she was on her own. No services were available to her from the home care agency.

If Charles had been with a hospice agency instead of
a home care agency, Betty would have had help. A hospice
would have helped Charles stay comfortable at home, and,
in addition to the visits by nurses, social workers, and
home health aides provided by the home care agency, a
hospice would have provided chaplain and volunteer helpers
both for Charles and for Betty. Social workers or a chaplain would have helped Betty prepare for Charles' death--
and after his death, helped her deal with her tremendous
grief. Then, for the following year, a hospice would have
offered Betty continuing help with grief--articles, a
grief counseling group, and calls from volunteers.

1

2

Saving Hospices   4

3   But these extra services cost money, and hospices lose money for each patient they care for under private insurance (Rutchik, 1995). Hospices continue these services because they are committed to caring for the patients and their families regardless of the family's ability to pay. They are able to stay in business, however, only by billing other services at a higher rate. As the cost of medical care increases, hospices risk insolvency if private insurance companies won't reimburse them fairly for their services. The purpose of this essay is to inform the general public that private insurance doesn't adequately cover the costs of hospice care and to propose a fair solution. If enough private insurance customers complain loudly enough, perhaps insurance companies will hear the message.

Background

4   Hospice care is a compassionate way of caring for terminally ill people and their families (Ahronheim & Weber, 1992). Its emphasis is on pain and symptom control, not on trying to cure the patient, and its goal is to allow patients to die in dignity and comfort at home or in a homelike setting. Historically, hospice care started as a reaction to high technology care. Prior to hospice care, many patients were isolated in hospitals, in unfamiliar surroundings, often in pain, and with their lives prolonged with as many treatments as possible. The first hospice in the United States opened in

Saving Hospices   5

1974 (Berry & Lynn, 1993, p. 221). The first hospice
programs were all volunteer—volunteers coming to homes
of patients, providing education about the dying
process, and providing grief services. As hospice programs became more sophisticated, they moved toward hiring professional clinical staff, but still provided the
care in the home.

    Today, someone who is dying has three options: a
hospital or nursing home, home care, or hospice. The
first option, hospital or nursing home care, is appropriate for the person who wants to do everything possible to cure the illness or prolong life and for patients
whose families can't, or don't want to, care for the patient at home. Hospital or nursing home care is by far
the most expensive option and often the most dehumaniz-
ing for the patient.

    The second option, home care, provides nursing, some
social work, and personal attendant care through clinicians visiting the patient at home. Home care is generally directed toward helping the patient get better, and
is strictly oriented toward the patient, not the family.

    The third option, hospice, provides nursing, social
work, personal attendant care, chaplain care, volunteers, and grief counseling. This care is generally provided in the patient's home, although some hospice
services are provided in hospitals or in a special
place. Hospice care is holistic, comprehensive, and

5

6

7

interrelated. Hospice care includes addressing emotional
needs and family needs, as well as patient medical
needs.

Problem

8   Clearly, then, hospices provide more comprehensive
services than home care. The problem is that private insurance companies proclaim that they cover hospice care
when in fact they fund only home care. They will pay
only for medically necessary visits for the dying person
and only on a fee-for-service basis. With fee-for-service, each visit to the patient's home by a nurse, social worker, home health aide, or therapist is paid for
separately, but fee-for-service doesn't pay for everything the patient needs. Fee-for-service doesn't pay for
the volunteer program (which has a paid volunteer coordinator), chaplains, grief care (the grief counselor
conducts support groups, coordinates volunteers to call
on grief-stricken family members, and mails packages
throughout the year to family members). Also, some insurance programs don't pay for social work.

9   Hospices lose money under such a system. For example, according to Rodney Smith (1995), Hospice Director
at Hospice of Seattle, the agency loses $900 per month
for each hospice patient served on a fee-for-service
basis. As health care costs increase, hospices cannot
afford to lose money in this way. According to Zail S.
Berry, M.D., and Joanne Lynn, M.D., who have studied the

Saving Hospices   7

funding problems of hospices, "Insurance payments rarely
cover the full cost of hospice care, and inadequate or
absent insurance coverage serves as a disincentive to
providers, patients, and families" (1993, p. 222). It
follows then that Hospice of Seattle and other hospices
cannot stay in business if they continue to subsidize
insurance companies by providing un-reimbursed services.

Solution

The solution is for private insurance companies to
pay hospices on a per diem rather than fee-for-service
basis. With per diem, the patient's insurance pays the
hospice for each day of care the patient receives. This
covers the costs better because the hospice can budget
and plan better, can order the most appropriate services
and supplies, can negotiate better rates with medical
equipment companies, and can provide services not covered under fee-for-service. Per diem is also better for
family members, who can be assured that their needs will
be covered. With per diem, there won't be unexpected
surprises or mounting co-payments.

There is a strong precedent for per diem payments,
since Medicare (the primary insurer of citizens 65 and
older) has for many years reimbursed hospices on a per
diem basis. Currently Medicare pays hospices $94.02 per
day, which covers all the care that patients need. Per
diem rates established by Medicare are based on the
total costs of providing hospice services divided by the

10

11

total number of patients and days that services are provided. The fair and equitable system pioneered by
Medicare now needs to be adopted by private insurance
companies.

Justification

12   To appreciate the issues involved here, one needs to
understand why private insurance companies have lagged
behind Medicare and still reimburse hospices on a fee-
for-service basis. I interviewed claims representatives
from two medical insurance companies. They explained two
main reasons that insurance companies insist on fee-for-
service rather than per diem payments to hospices.

13   First, they say that fee-for-service provides better
cost control. Paying on a per diem basis, insurance companies claim, would be giving hospices blank checks to
provide all kinds of unnecessary services. Insurance companies do not want to give up their role as overseers of
medical care. To keep the hospice from providing too many
services (in the view of the insurance company), the insurance company currently authorizes a limited number of
visits of nurses, social workers, home health aides, or
therapists in a given time period. To get re-authoriza-
tion when the time period runs out, the hospice has to
request additional services. With this supervision, the
insurance company feels confident that the hospice
patient is getting adequate care and costs are controlled. Thus insurers claim that fee-for-service is

Saving Hospices   9

cost-effective, especially for patients who need only minimal care. Insurance company representatives say that paying per diem would drive up insurance costs and give hospices more money than they need to provide hospice services.

Later I will show that paying hospices on a per diem basis will *save* insurance companies money. At this point, however, I would like to respond just to the objection that per diem would give hospices more money than they need. The per diem rate paid by Medicare averages the costs of care for patients who need few services with patients who need many services. It is true that a per diem rate would give hospices too much money for <u>some</u> patients, but also not nearly enough for other patients. Fair rates could be established that provided hospices with average costs.

14

The second objection to per diem payments raised by insurance companies is their belief that medical insurance should pay only for the medical needs of the insured patient. They say that it is simply beyond the intended scope of medical insurance to pay for non-medical care or for counseling for the patient's family.

15

I would say that this objection is based on an outdated view of medicine that treats the patient as an isolated entity rather than as a human being in a network of family. Moreover, this view is shortsighted, since providing non-medical services to the family can

16

keep the patient at home, where costs are relatively
cheap, rather than sending the patient to the hospital.
As an example of how helping the family can save an insurance company money, consider the case of Randy (not
his real name) as told to me by Hospice of Seattle staff
(Wicks, 1995).

17   Randy was 85 years old when he started hospice care.
He was dying of heart and lung disease and he wanted to
live his last days at home. He was cared for mostly by
his daughter Sharon, who tended to panic in emergencies
and who couldn't accept the fact that her father was
dying. Hospice of Seattle provided Sharon with nursing
consultation twenty-four hours a day, seven days a week.
Several times she called Hospice of Seattle in the middle of the night, in terror. "I think Dad needs to go
back to the hospital," she would say. "He's looking
really bad."

18   Over the telephone the on-call nurse would calm her
down by saying, "Let's see if we can find out what's
happening and treat it so he can stay at home." The on-
call nurse helped Sharon figure out the right dose of
pain medication and convinced her that Randy would be
better off at home. Moreover, counseling from a social
worker helped Sharon accept the process of her father's
dying. Without on-call nursing and counseling help--
provided by hospice but not paid for by private insurance companies--Sharon would have called 911 during

these emergencies and Randy would have been back in the hospital.

Based on this case, it is easy to see how insurance companies are cheating hospices. Hospice care is saving insurance companies enormous sums of money by keeping patients out of hospitals, and yet these companies—in looking only at short-term costs--are reimbursing hospices at home care rates. Fortunately for the future of hospices, current studies are beginning to provide convincing data that per diem reimbursement is cheaper for insurance companies in the long run. For example, a few private insurance companies have recently adopted per diem hospice plans; according to a study by Manard and Perrone (1994), these companies saved money while providing a set of benefits more appropriate to what the terminally ill patient actually needed (p. 13).

In another study, Mitchell (1994) compared hospice and non-hospice patient costs in the last three months of life. The average cost of medical care for hospice patients was $986, compared with $7,731 for non-hospice patients (p. 1576). These cost savings were attributed to the hospice team's teaching the family how to manage the patient at home (a non-medical cost), providing constant, ongoing support for the family (another non-medical cost), and providing optimal comfort care for the patient in the home setting. The enormous cost for non-hospice patients was due to the frequency with which

19

20

families sent the patient back to the hospital. Another
study, "An Analysis of the Cost Savings of the Medicare
Hospice Benefit," by Lewin-VHI, Inc. (1995), shows savings of $1.65 for each $1.00 spent in the last month of
life on patients who received per diem hospice services
(p. 7); again these savings were largely due to the patient's receiving home care days instead of inpatient
(hospital) days (p. 1). Still another study, cited by
Manard and Perrone (1994, p. 13), found that the grief
counseling and support services offered to primary caregivers by hospices led to reduced use of hospital and
clinic services by caregivers.

21   This evidence shows that insurance companies will
save money in the long run by paying hospice services on
a per diem basis. But there is another reason why insurance companies should reimburse hospices equitably: it
is the right and just thing to do. The psychological
value of hospice care for the terminally ill and their
families is undisputed. It is time that insurance companies recognized the value of psychological as well as
physical care. There is something wrong with current
medical practice when insurance companies will fund
without question expensive technological treatments for
a dying patient but will quibble at paying for grief
counseling for the patient's loved ones. The general
public finds hospice care very valuable, and most private insurance companies boast of covering hospice care

Saving Hospices 13

in their advertising brochures. By excluding "non-medical" services, however, they actually provide only home
care, not hospice. If insurance companies claim they believe in the holistic care of hospices, then they ought
to pay for it.

Saving Hospices 14

References

Ahronheim, J., & Weber, D. (1992). Final passages: Positive choices for the dying and their loved ones. New
York: Simon & Schuster.

Berry, Z., & Lynn, J. (1993). Hospice medicine. Journal
of the American Medical Association, 270(2), 221-222.

Lewin-VHI, Inc. (1995). An analysis of the cost savings
of the Medicare hospice benefit. National Hospice
Organization.

Manard, B., & Perrone, C. (1994). Hospice care: An introduction and review of the evidence. National
Hospice Organization.

Mitchell, A. (1994). Hospice care: The cheaper alternative. Journal of the American Medical Association,
271(20), 1576.

Rutchik, P. (1995, May 16). [Personal interview].

Smith, R. (1995, May 11). [Personal interview].

Wicks, M. (1995, May 16). [Personal telephone interview].

```
(In addition, interviews of case managers from two major

health insurance companies, May 16, 1995. I agreed to

keep the interviews anonymous.)
```

Thinking Critically About "Saving Hospices"

1. Compare Sheridan Botts's proposal argument with her exploratory essay on pages 170–72. How did she solve the problems she confronted in the exploratory essay? In your view, how effective are these solutions?
2. One of Sheridan's rhetorical problems is that few audiences are inherently interested in technical issues such as fee-for-service versus per diem payments. Moreover, differences between the two forms of payment are hard to explain succinctly. How does Sheridan try to make her proposal interesting? Does she succeed?
3. Another rhetorical problem is how to make the argument appeal to the values of insurance companies. It is easy to see how this proposal could benefit hospices, patients, and patients' families, but since it would increase the direct costs of hospice care for insurance companies, Sheridan must show how it would benefit insurance companies. Does she do so successfully?
4. How persuasive do you find Sheridan's argument? From your perspective, what are the strengths and weaknesses of her proposal?

The next piece is a short proposal argument by Richard Wade, a professor of history at the Graduate Center of the City University of New York and chair of the Governor's Commission on Libraries for the state of New York. He argues that jail terms for prisoners ought to be reduced in exchange for prisoners' achieving literacy.

RICHARD WADE

REDUCE JAIL TERMS IN EXCHANGE FOR BECOMING LITERATE

1   In our efforts to combat escalating crime, we have failed to acknowledge an elementary fact: one out of every five adult Americans is functionally illiterate.

2   A substantial number of violent criminals are in prison for good reasons and should remain there. Yet many can be returned to society without jeopardizing the public's

safety—they can even learn to lead useful and productive lives. A renewed emphasis on literacy in prisons would enhance this prospect.

3 The functionally illiterate cannot read want ads or fill out job applications, they cannot do elementary banking, read their children's report cards or their own indictments.

4 The cost of illiteracy is up to $200 billion annually, if we take into account unemployment, health, welfare and incarceration. New York State's bill alone is about $20 billion, in large part the result of an overburdened criminal justice system. Each inmate costs the state $150 a day, more than $50,000 a year. By every estimate, the majority of the 60,000 prisoners in New York State and the 21,000 in New York City are functionally illiterate. They enter illiterate, leave illiterate and more often than not return illiterate.

5 A literacy program not only has the value of introducing prisoners to a world they never knew, it also gives them a chance for gainful employment. If they lack these skills and face diminished opportunities, should we be surprised that they revert to crime and wind up back in prison?

6 This has been the experience of the last two decades, during which more than 40 percent returned to jail within three years, and 20 percent more within five years. In Japan, by contrast, convicts cannot get out of prison until they can read and write. The recidivism rate there is 5 percent. Of course, in this country we cannot condone such compulsion, but we can make literacy an attractive option for the incarcerated.

7 Almost all maximum- and medium-security institutions have some library resources, programs to encourage inmates to use such materials and volunteers to help. Support for this effort, however, is erratic and modest. More disconcerting is the fact that participation is voluntary and requires the inmate to request the service, a procedure that generally filters out functional illiterates.

8 This has to change. The Governor's Commission on Libraries is expected to recommend to Mario Cuomo next month that literacy be placed into the sentencing system for convicted criminals. Currently, a period of inquiry between the guilty verdict and sentencing produces a profile of the prisoner for the judge to use in determining the terms of imprisonment. The question on education now establishes the length of schooling, not the ability to read and write. The commission will suggest that a literacy test be given to prisoners before sentencing.

9 To take literacy into account, the judge could declare that if the prisoner goes into a literacy program and successfully completes it, the sentence will be reduced. This proposal requires no new legislation because it falls within present judicial discretion. We reduce sentences for good behavior and community service; there is no reason why the acquisition of literacy should not yield the same reward.

10 In addition, this incentive can be extended to prisoners who already read and write well. There is no reason why a highly literate inmate cannot get a reduced sentence for teaching fellow prisoners basic literacy skills. Educated white collar criminals also cost the system $50,000 a year.

11 This proposal assumes that libraries play a central role. Every corrections institution holding prisoners sentenced to three years or more should have adequate facilities to operate a literacy program. It would also mean attracting additional staff and volunteers to teach and assist in instruction.

12 For such a small investment, it is hard to see where the public could get a larger return. It takes $2,000 to teach an adult to read and write: it costs $8,000 to put him on welfare and $50,000 to put him in jail. What should a prudent society do?

Thinking Critically About "Reduce Jail Terms in Exchange for Becoming Literate"

1. If you were to limit Wade's proposal in any way, how would you do so and why?
2. If you were governor of New York, reading over the Library Commission's recommendation, what sorts of evidence might you ask the commission to provide?
3. Can you see ways of extending the logic of Wade's proposals to other areas? What other behaviors from what other sectors of government clientele might be rewarded in the name of the public good?

In the final reading, policy analysts Stephen Moore and Dean Stansel of the Cato Institute in Washington, D. C., call for a halt to tax breaks for U.S. corporations.

STEPHEN MOORE AND DEAN STANSEL
LET'S STOP CORPORATE WELFARE

1   Secretary of Labor Robert Reich was right on target late in 1994 when he identified "Federal aid to dependent corporations" as a major contributor to the budget crisis. He also was correct to challenge Congressional Republicans and Washington think tanks to propose termination of Federal activities that fall into the category of "corporate welfare."

2   The list of corporate subsidy programs is longer and the dollar expenditures are far greater than most members of Congress and the Clinton Administration suspect. Corporate pork is pervasive. For instance, Congress funds more than 125 programs that subsidize private businesses. Subsidy programs to such businesses cost Federal taxpayers more than $85,000,000,000 annually, and the dollar amount has been growing substantially in recent years. Every major Cabinet department has become a conduit for government funding of private industry. Within some Cabinet agencies, such as the Departments of Agriculture and Commerce, almost every spending program underwrites private businesses.

3   The following list includes some of the more egregious taxpayer subsidies to industries and firms:

- Through Sematech, a consortium of very large U.S. computer microchip producers, the Pentagon provides nearly $100,000,000 a year of support to the industry. However, of the more than 200 chip makers in the U.S., only the 14 largest, including Intel and National Semiconductor, receive Federal support from Sematech. Originally designed to help U.S. firms compete against foreign competition, it now subsidizes the largest producers to help fend off smaller domestic competition.

- An estimated 40% of the $1,400,000,000 sugar price support program benefits the largest one percent of sugar farms. The 33 biggest sugar cane plantations each receive more than $1,000,000.

- Through the Rural Electrification Administration and the Federal power marketing administrations, the government provides about $2,000,000,000 in subsidies each year to large and profitable electric utility cooperatives, such as ALLTEL, which had sales of $2,300,000,000 in 1994. Federally subsidized electricity holds down the costs of running ski resorts in Aspen, Colo.; five-star hotels in Hilton Head, S.C.; and gambling casinos in Las Vegas, Nev.

- During 1994, the Forest Service spent $140,000,000 building roads in national forests, thus subsidizing the removal of timber from Federal lands by multi-million-dollar timber companies. Over the past 20 years, the Forest Service has built 340,000 miles of roads—more than eight times the length of the interstate highway system—primarily for the benefit of logging companies.

- The Department of Agriculture Market Promotion Program spends $110,000,000 per year underwriting the cost of advertising American products abroad.

- In 1994, a House of Representatives investigative team discovered that Federal environmental cleanup and defense contractors had been milking taxpayers for millions of dollars in entertainment, recreation, and party expenses. Martin Marietta Corp. charged the Pentagon $263,000 for a Smokey Robinson concert, $20,000 for the purchase of golf balls, and $7,500 for a 1993 office Christmas party. Ecology and Environment, Inc., of Lancaster, N.Y., spent $243,000 of funds designated for environmental cleanup on "employee morale" and $37,000 on tennis lessons, bike races, golf tournaments, and other entertainment.

Congress no longer can afford to ignore the growing scourge of corporate welfare. Any serious attempt to balance the budget will require a strategy for getting businesses off the $85,000,000,000 annual dole.   4

The Clinton Administration and other proponents of Federal subsidies to the private sector often maintain government support of American business is in the national interest. A multitude of economic, national security, and social arguments are voiced to justify corporate aid. Government support is said to protect industries from failure to preserve high-paying American jobs; subsidize research activities that private industries would not finance themselves; counteract the business subsidies of foreign governments to ensure a "level playing field"; boost high-technology companies whose profitability is vital to American economic success in the 21st century; maintain the viability of "strategic industries" that are essential to national security; finance ventures that otherwise would be considered too risky for private capital markets; assist socially disadvantaged groups, such as minorities and women, to establish new businesses.   5

On the surface, that kind of policy may seem to promote America's economic interest. However, there are at least eight reasons such policies are misguided and dangerous.   6

The Federal government has a disappointing record of picking industrial winners and losers. The function of private capital markets is to direct billions of dollars of capital to industries and firms that offer the highest potential rate of return. The capital markets, in effect, are in the business of selecting corporate winners and losers. The underlying premise of Federal business subsidies is that the government can direct the limited pool of capital funds more effectively than venture and private money managers can. Decades of experience, though, prove that government agencies have a much less successful track record than private money managers of correctly selecting winners. The average delinquency rate is higher for government loan programs (eight percent) than for commercial lenders (three percent). The Small Business Administration delin-   7 quency rates reached over 20% in the early and mid 1980s; the Farmers Home Administration delinquency rate has approached 50%.

8   **Corporate welfare is a huge drain on the Federal treasury for little economic benefit.** It is supposed to offer a positive long-term economic return for taxpayers, but the evidence shows that government "investments" have a low or negative rate of return. In the late 1960s, the Federal government spent nearly $1,000,000,000 on the Supersonic Transport, which experts in Washington expected would revolutionize air travel. Instead, the project went bankrupt and never flew a single passenger. In the late 1970s, the Federal government expended more than $2,000,000,000 of taxpayer money on the Synthetic Fuels Corporation—a public-private project that Department of Energy officials thought would provide new sources of energy for America. The SFC was closed down in the 1980s, never having produced a single kilowatt of electricity.

9   **Corporate welfare creates an uneven playing field.** Business subsidies—often said to be justified because they correct distortions in the marketplace—create huge market distortions of their own. The major effect of corporate subsidies is to divert credit and capital to politically well-connected firms at the expense of their politically less influential competitors. Sematech, for example, was launched to promote the U.S. microchip industry over rivals in Japan and Germany. In practice, it has become a cartel of the large U.S. chip producers—such as Intel—that unfairly handicaps the hundreds of smaller American producers. Farm subsidies create another arbitrary distortion. Agricultural price supports are alleged to be critical to the survival of American farmers. The truth is that, of the 400 classified farm commodities, about two dozen receive more than 90% of the assistance funds. Over 80% of the subsidies enrich farmers with a net worth of more than $500,000.

10   **Corporate welfare fosters an incestuous relationship between government and business.** Government and politics are inseparable. Much of what passes today as benign industrial policy is little more than a political payoff to favored industries or businesses. Taxpayer dollars that are used to subsidize private firms routinely are returned to Washington in the form of political contributions and lobbying activities to secure even more tax dollars. For instance, the outdated Rural Electrification Administration survives primarily because of the lobbying efforts of the National Rural Electrical Cooperative Association in America. With a $78,000,000 budget, that association is one of the most influential and heavily financed lobbying groups in Washington.

11   During the 1992 presidential campaign, Vice Pres. Dan Quayle traveled to Michigan to announce a $250,000,000 plan to upgrade the M-1 tank. It just happened to be built by General Dynamics in Sterling Heights, Mich. Before the campaign, the Bush Administration had argued convincingly that, in the post-Cold War era, the more expensive tank was unnecessary.

12   Many of the top recipients of technology research grants awarded by the Clinton Administration were substantial contributors to the Clinton campaign or the Democratic National Committee. For example, eight Fortune 500 firms that were multi-million-dollar award-winners of the Advanced Technology Program or the Technology Reinvestment Project in 1994 also were large Democratic campaign contributors, according to Federal Election Commission data compiled by Common Cause. These included AT&T, Boeing, Chevron, General Electric, McDonnell Douglas, Shell, Texaco, and United Technology. At the very least, such golden handshake programs create an impression that government is for sale.

13   **Corporate welfare is anti-consumer.** One of the main effects of many corporate subsidy programs is to raise costs to consumers. Trade restrictions, often sought by

politically powerful industries, are estimated to cost consumers $80,000,000,000 a year. The sugar program is estimated to cost consumers several billion dollars a year, according to a U.S. Department of Commerce study that concluded: "Because sugar is an ingredient in many food items, the effect of the sugar program is similar to a regressive sales tax, which hits lower-income families harder than upper-income families."

The most efficient way to promote business in America is to reduce the overall cost and regulatory burden of government. Corporate welfare is predicated on the misguided notion that the best way to enhance business profitability in America is to do so one firm at a time. A much more effective way to boost the competitiveness and productivity of American industry is to create a level playing field, thus minimizing government interference in the marketplace and substantially reducing tax rates and regulatory burdens. For example, all the Federal government's efforts to promote the big three U.S. automobile companies are insignificant compared with the regulatory burden on that industry, which now adds an estimated $3,000 to the sticker price of a new car. Eliminating just half the business subsidies in the Federal budget would generate enough savings to pay for the entire elimination of the capital gains tax. Clearly, a zero capital gains tax would generate far more jobs and business startups than the scores of targeted business handouts in the Federal budget. 14

Corporate welfare is anti-capitalist. It converts the American businessman from a capitalist into a lobbyist. Corporate welfare, notes Wall Street financier Theodore J. Forstmann, has led to the creation of the "statist businessman in America." The statist businessman is "a conservator, not a creator; a caretaker, not a risk taker; an argument against capitalism even though he is not a capitalist at all." For instance, the Fanjul family, owner of several large sugar farms in the Florida Everglades, earns an estimated $60,000,000 a year in artificial profits thanks to price supports and import quotas. The Fanjul family is a fierce defender of the sugar program and, in 1992, contributed $350,000 to political campaigns. All of that has a corrosive effect on the American free enterprise system. 15

Corporate welfare is unconstitutional. The most critical reason government should end corporate subsidy programs is that they lie outside Congress' limited spending authority under the Constitution. Nowhere in the Constitution is Congress granted the authority to spend funds to subsidize the computer industry, enter into joint ventures with automobile companies, or guarantee loans to favored business owners. 16

Government provides special benefits to individual industries and companies through a vast array of policy levers. The three major business benefits come in the forms of special tax breaks, trade policies, and spending programs. 17

When Reich protested against "aid to dependent corporations," his criticism was directed toward "special tax benefits for particular industries." The Democratic Leadership Council's Progressive Policy Institute has specified some 30 such "tax subsidies" that led to a loss of $134,000,000,000 in Federal revenues over five years. 18

Inefficient Subsidization—The Ethanol Example

One of the most inefficient tax subsidies is that for the production of ethanol—a corn-based gasoline substitute. The industry enjoys a tax credit for companies that blend ethanol and an exemption from Federal excise taxes. The tax breaks allegedly are justified on the grounds that they reduce pollution and U.S. dependence on foreign oil. Yet, a U.S. Department of Agriculture study finds that the $500,000,000 subsidy for ethanol "represents an inefficient use of our nation's resources." It concludes, "When all economic costs and benefits are tallied, an ethanol subsidy program is not cost effective." 19

As for the supposed energy conservation and environmental benefits, a study by agricultural economist David Pimental at Cornell University discovered: "About 72% more energy is used to produce a gallon of ethanol than the energy in a gallon of ethanol."

20   Politics, not economics, is the principal motivation behind the ethanol subsidies. Archer Daniels Midland (ADM), a $10,000,000,000 agribusiness based in Decatur, Ill., produces 70% of the ethanol used in the U.S. An estimated 25% of its sales are of ethanol and corn sweetener (another highly subsidized farm product). ADM and its CEO, Dwayne Andreas, have been among the nation's most generous campaign contributors, with more than $150,000 in lifetime contributions to Senate Majority Leader Bob Dole alone.

21   Most targeted tax breaks create similar economic inefficiencies. Nonetheless, we reject the notion that allowing a company to keep its earnings and pay less in taxes somehow is a "subsidy." Furthermore, with the Federal government already collecting $1.3 trillion in revenues each year, we oppose any policy that would give Congress more tax dollars to spend. Research suggests that policies that would bring additional dollars into the Federal treasury would invite higher Congressional spending, not lower budget deficits.

22   Our recommendation is that Congress abolish all tax deductions, including all the special tax breaks for industries identified by the Progressive Policy Institute, in exchange for lower overall corporate and personal tax rates on business and personal taxpayers. That could be accomplished through Rep. Dick Armey's (R.-Tex.) flat tax proposal or Rep. Bill Archer's (R.-Tex.) retail sales tax concept. Any such tax policy reform should be made on a revenue-neutral basis or as a net tax cut.

23   As for trade barriers, according to Benjamin Franklin, "Most of the statutes, or acts, edicts, and placards of parliaments, and states for regulating and directing of trade have been either political blunders or obtained by artful men for private advantage under pretense of public good." In 1991, there were more than 8,000 product tariffs imposed by Washington, all obtained for private advantage under pretense of public good.

24   By erecting trade barriers, the government rewards one industry at the direct expense of another. For instance, in 1991, prohibitive duties were placed on low-cost Japanese computer parts. The motivation was to save jobs in U.S. factories that make computer circuit boards. However, the decision to keep out foreign parts inflated by almost $1,000 the cost per personal computer manufactured by U.S. companies, such as IBM, Apple, and Compaq. That gave a huge advantage to Japanese computer companies, significantly reduced sales of the U.S. computer firms, and, worst of all, thousands of American jobs were *lost*.

25   Steel import quotas are equally injurious economically to American manufacturers. Trade specialists believe that the inflated steel prices paid by U.S. firms have contributed to the competitive decline of several American industries, including automobiles. The cost to the American economy of steel quotas is estimated at $7,000,000,000 per year.

26   No one knows precisely the total cost to American consumers of barriers to free trade, but several authoritative sources place the figure at $80,000,000,000 per year. There is virtually no specific U.S. trade restriction for which the economy-wide costs do not exceed the industry-specific benefits. Therefore, Congress immediately should lift all barriers to free trade.

27   There are at least 125 separate programs providing subsidies to particular industries and firms with a price tag exceeding $85,000,000,000 per year. We recommend the immediate abolition of all such programs.

Because they intermingle government dollars with corporate political clout, busi-   28
ness subsidies have a corrupting influence on America's system of democratic government and entrepreneurial capitalism. Despite the conventional orthodoxy in
Washington that the nation needs an even closer alliance between business and politics, the truth is that both government and the marketplace would work better if they
kept a healthy distance from each other.

It is ironic that at a time when the Federal government is in litigation with Microsoft,   29
perhaps America's most innovative and profitable high-technology corporation in
decades, for successfully dominating the software industry, Congress is spending hundreds of millions of dollars trying to prop up the firm's less efficient computer industry
rivals. A situation exists whereby Federal regulatory policies increasingly are geared toward punishing success, while Federal corporate welfare policies increasingly reward
failure. That is not the way to preserve America's industrial might.

Thinking Critically About "Let's Stop Corporate Welfare"

1. Select one target of Moore and Stansel's attack on corporate welfare and
   come up with as many reasons as you can why favorable tax treatment
   might be justified.
2. Moore and Stansel suggest several ways in which the $85 billion in savings
   gained from their proposal might be spent. List some other possibilities and
   suggest how your choices might constitute better investments.

COMPOSING YOUR ESSAY

Generating and Exploring Ideas

If you are having trouble thinking of a proposal topic, try making an idea map
of local problems you would like to see solved. For your spokes, consider some of
the following starting points:

Problems at your university: dorm, parking, registration system, grading
system, campus appearance, clubs, curriculum, intramural program

Problems in your city or town: dangerous intersections, ugly areas, inadequate lighting, a poorly designed store, a shopping center that needs a specific improvement

Problems at your place of work: office design, flow of customer traffic,
merchandise display, company policies, customer relations

Problems related to other aspects of your life: hobbies, recreational time,
life as a consumer, and so forth

Another approach is to freewrite your response to these trigger statements:

I would really like to solve the problem of _____.

I believe that X should _____. (Substitute for X words such as *my*
teacher, the president, the school administration, Congress, my boss, and so forth.)

Note that the problem you pose for this paper can be personal, but shouldn't be private; that is, others should be able to benefit from a solution to your personal problem. For example, your inability to find child care for your daughter is a private problem. But if you focus your proposal on how zoning laws discourage development of in-home day care—and propose a change in those zoning laws to permit more in-home day-care centers—then your proposal will benefit others.

Once you have decided on a proposal issue, explore it by freewriting your responses to the following questions. These questions are often called *stock issues*, since they represent generic, or stock, questions that apply to almost any kind of proposal.

1. Is there a problem here that has to be solved?
2. Will the proposed solution really solve this problem?
3. Can the problem be solved in a simpler way without disturbing the status quo?
4. Is the proposed solution practical enough that it really stands a chance of being implemented?
5. What will be the positive and negative consequences of the proposal?

You might also try freewriting your responses to number 3 (a–k) in the exploratory exercise on page 390. Although these questions cover much the same territory as the stock issues, their different presentation might stimulate additional thought.

Finally, try thinking of justifications for your solution by using the three approaches strategy described earlier in this chapter.

Shaping and Drafting

The following is a typical organizational plan for a proposal argument you might turn to if you get stuck in composing the first draft of your essay.

1. Presentation of a problem that needs solving
   a. Description of the problem (give it presence)
   b. Additional background, including previous attempts to solve the problem
   c. Argument that the problem is solvable (optional)
2. Presentation of the proposed solution
   a. Succinct statement of the proposed solution
   b. Explanation of specifics for the proposed solution
3. Summary and rebuttal of opposing views (in practical proposals, this section is often a summary and rejection of alternative ways of solving the problem)
4. Justification—persuades reader that proposal should be enacted
   a. Reason 1 presented and developed
   b. Reason 2 presented and developed
   c. and so forth
5. Conclusion—exhorts audience to act (sometimes incorporated into the last sentences of the final supporting reason)

Revising

After you have completed your first draft and begun to clarify your argument for yourself, you are ready to start making your argument clear and persuasive for your readers. Use the strategies for clear closed-form prose outlined in Chapters 18 and 19. At this stage, feedback from peer readers can be very helpful. Use the following guidelines for peer reviewers.

g   u   i   d   e   l   i   n   e   s

for Peer Reviewers

Instructions for peer reviews, including use of these guidelines, are provided in Chapter 21, pages 527–28. To write a peer review for a classmate, use your own paper, numbering your paper to correspond to the questions on the guidelines. At the head of your paper place the author's name and your own name as shown.

Author's Name: _____

Peer Reviewer's Name: _____

I. Read the draft at normal reading speed from beginning to end. As you read, do the following:
   A. Place a wavy line in the margin next to any passages that you find confusing, that contain something that doesn't seem to fit, or that otherwise slow down your reading.
   B. Place a "Good!" in the margin next to any passages where you think the writing is particularly strong or interesting.
II. Read the draft again slowly. Describe for the writer what you currently see in this draft. If you have difficulty answering any of the following questions, explain briefly the source of your difficulty.
   A. Describe the problem addressed in the essay.
      1. How does the writer give the problem presence?
      2. Why does the writer believe the problem is solvable and not simply inherent in the nature of things?
      3. How does the writer show that the problem is significant and serious enough to demand attention?
   B. Summarize the writer's proposed solution.
      1. Where does the writer provide specific details about the workings of the solution?
      2. If you could ask for more detailed information about the workings of the solution, what information would you request?
      3. Do you think the writer's solution will work? Why or why not?

    C. Summarize the writer's justification for the proposal. How many reasons are provided? What are they?

        1. Where does the writer address opposing views or alternative solutions? In what way is the writer's proposed solution superior to alternative solutions?

        2. What are the costs and benefits of the solution being proposed?

        3. Who will pay the costs and who will get the benefits? When?

        4. What possible unforeseen costs and benefits could you mention to the writer?

    D. Has the writer persuaded you that the benefits of this proposal will outweigh the costs? What do you think the gut reaction of a typical decision maker (or of an initially neutral or skeptical member of the general public) will be to the writer's proposal?

        1. If you raised objections to the proposal, how could the writer respond to these objections?

        2. Can you help the writer think of additional justifying arguments (arguments from principle, from consequence, from precedent or analogy)?

III. What recommendations do you have for improving this draft?

    A. How might the writer improve the title?

    B. Does the introduction convince you that a problem exists and that it is significant (worth solving) and solvable? Does the writer give the problem presence? How might the writer improve the presentation of the problem?

    C. Does the writer give you enough details about the solution so that you can understand it and see how it works? How could the writer make the solution clearer or more convincing?

    D. In the justification section does the writer provide strong reasons for acting on the proposal? Are the reasons supported with details and evidence, and do they appeal to the values and beliefs of the audience? Does the writer show why the proposed solution is superior to other possible ways of solving the problem? What suggestions do you have for improving the justification section?

    E. How might the writer improve the clarity of the argument? Where might the writer better apply the principles of clarity from Chapter 19 (starting with the big picture; placing points before particulars; using transitions; and following the old/new contract)?

    F. Sum up what you see as the chief strengths and problem areas of this draft.

        1. Strengths

        2. Problem areas

IV. Read the draft one more time. Place a check in the margin wherever you notice problems in grammar, spelling, or mechanics (one check per problem).

A Guide to Composing and Revising

part THREE

c h a p t e r 17

Writing as a Problem-Solving Process

I rewrite as I write. It is hard to tell what is a first draft because it is not determined by time. In one draft, I might cross out three pages, write two, cross out a fourth, rewrite it, and call it a draft. I am constantly writing and rewriting. I can only conceptualize so much in my first draft—only so much information can be held in my head at one time; my rewriting efforts are a reflection of how much information I can encompass at one time. There are levels and agenda which I have to attend to in each draft.

—Description of revision by an experienced writer

I read what I have written and I cross out a word and put another word in; a more decent word or a better word. Then if there is somewhere to use a sentence that I have crossed out, I will put it there.*

—Description of revision by an inexperienced writer

Blot out, correct, insert, refine,
Enlarge, diminish, interline;
Be mindful, when invention fails,
To scratch your head, and bite your nails.

—Jonathan Swift

In Part One of this text we focused on writing as a problem-solving process in which writers pose and solve both subject-matter problems and rhetorical problems. Part Three shows you how to translate these basic principles into effective strategies for composing and revising your writing along the continuum from closed to open forms. The five self-contained chapters, which can be read in whatever sequence best fits you instructor's course plan, will help you compose and revise the essays you write for the assignments in Part Two.

This chapter explains how experienced writers use multiple drafts to manage the complexities of writing and suggests ways for you to improve your own writ-

---

*From Nancy Sommers, "Revision Strategies of Student Writers and Experienced Adult Writers," *College Composition and Communication,* 31 (October, 1980), 291–300.

ing processes. Chapter 18 shows how you can use your knowledge of the structure and style of closed-form prose to generate and organize ideas. Chapter 19 teaches you how to revise closed-form prose with readers' needs in mind. Chapter 20 switches from closed to open forms, showing you how, when appropriate, to open your prose by creating surprises of style and structure that engage readers and involve them in the process of completing your text's meaning. Finally, Chapter 21 explains how you can improve your writing processes by working in small groups to solve problems, help each other generate ideas, and provide feedback for revision.

UNDERSTANDING HOW EXPERTS COMPOSE AND REVISE

We begin this chapter with a close look at how experienced writers compose, explaining what they think about when they write and why they often need multiple drafts. In Chapter 3 we quoted Peter Elbow's assertion that "meaning is not what you start out with" but "what you end up with." Thus composing is a discovery process. In the early stages of writing, experienced writers typically discover what they are trying to say, often deepening and complicating their ideas rather than clarifying them. Only in the last drafts will such writers be in sufficient control of their ideas to shape them elegantly for readers.

It's important not to over-generalize, however, because no two writers compose exactly the same way; moreover, the same writer may use different processes for different kinds of prose. Some writers outline their ideas before they write; others need to write extensively before they can outline. Some write their first drafts very slowly, devoting extensive thought and planning to each emerging paragraph; others write first drafts rapidly, to be sure to get all their ideas on paper, and then rework the material part by part. Some prefer to work independently, without discussing or sharing their ideas; others seek out classmates or colleagues to help them hash out ideas and rehearse their arguments before writing them down. Some seek out the stillness of a library or private room; others do their best writing in noisy cafeterias or coffee shops.

The actual mechanics of composing differ from writer to writer as well. Some writers create first drafts directly at a keyboard, whereas others require the reassuring heft of a pen or pencil. Among writers who begin by planning the structure of their work, some make traditional outlines (perhaps using the flexible outline feature on their word processors), whereas others prefer tree diagrams or flowcharts. Some of those who use word processors revise directly at the computer, whereas others print out a hard copy, revise with pen and ink, and then type the changes into the computer.

Also, writers often vary their composing processes from project to project. A writer might complete one project with a single draft and a quick editing job, but produce a half dozen or more drafts for another project.

What experienced writers do have in common is a willingness to keep revising their work until they feel it is ready to go public. They typically work much harder at drafting and revising than do inexperienced writers, taking more runs at their subject. And experienced writers generally make more substantial alterations in their drafts during revision. (Compare the first two quotations that open this chapter—one from an experienced and one from an inexperienced writer.) An experienced writer will sometimes throw away a first draft and start over; a beginning writer tends to be more satisfied with early drafts and to think of revision as primarily cleaning up errors. Figure 17.1 (on p. 430) shows the first page of a first draft for a magazine article written by an experienced writer.

WHY EXPERIENCED WRITERS REVISE SO EXTENSIVELY

To help you understand the puzzling difference between beginning and experienced writers, let's consider *why* experienced writers revise. If they are such good writers, why don't they get it right the first time? Why so many drafts? To use the language of Part One, experienced writers need multiple drafts to help them pose, pursue, and solve problems—both subject-matter problems and related rhetorical problems. Faced with many choices, experienced writers use multiple drafts to break a complex task into manageable subtasks. Let's look more closely at some of the functions that revising can perform for writers.

Multiple Drafts and the Limits of Short-Term Memory

A writer's need for multiple drafts results partly from the limitations of memory. Cognitive psychologists have shown that working memory—often called short-term memory—has remarkably little storage space. People use short-term memory to hold the data on which they are actively focusing at any given moment while solving problems, reading texts, writing a draft, or performing other cognitive tasks. People also have long-term memories, which can store an almost infinite amount of material. The trouble is that much of the material held temporarily in short-term memory never gets transferred to long-term memory. (Try closing this book for a moment and writing out this paragraph from memory.)

You can conceptualize short-term memory as a small tabletop surrounded by filing cabinets (long-term memory). To use the ideas and data you generate while writing a draft, you have to place them on the tabletop, which can hold only a few items at once.* Some of the material you place on the tabletop might come from your long-term memory (past experiences and previous knowledge stored in your brain's filing cabinets); other material might come from a passage in a book or a note card you are currently reading; still other material might take the form of new

---

*A famous study conducted by psychologist George Miller revealed that the average person's short-term memory can hold "seven plus or minus two" chunks of information at a time. When given, say, a thirty-item list of random words of numbers, the average person can remember between five and nine of them. The items will quickly be lost from short-term memory unless the person actively rehearses them over and over (as when you repeat a new phone number to yourself so that you won't forget it before you write it down).

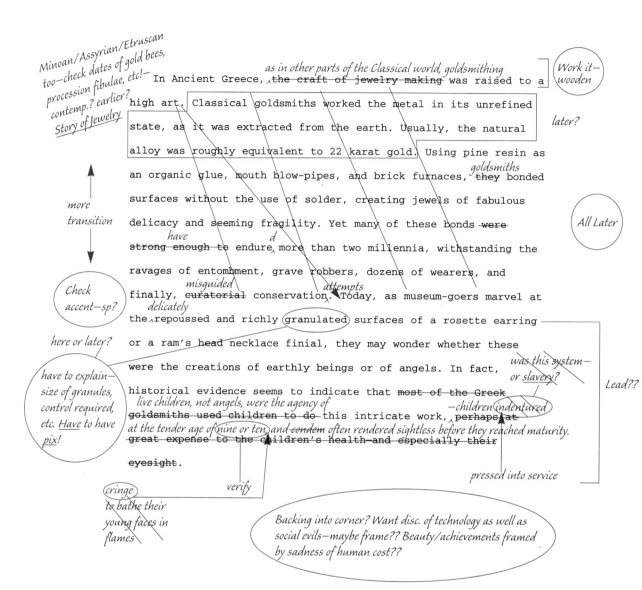

FIGURE 17.1   Draft Page of an Experienced Writer

ideas generated from your earlier ideas. Unfortunately, since every idea belongs to a network of related ideas and experiences, close consideration of even a single idea soon produces more information than your poor tabletop can hold. You need some means of holding it all together, lest ideas spill off the table and become permanently lost.

This analogy illustrates why experienced writers rely on multiple drafts. Because of the limitations of short-term memory, you can actively engage only a few chunks of material at any given moment—a few sentences of a draft or several ideas in an outline. The remaining portions of the evolving essay quickly recede from consciousness without being stored in long-term memory. (Think of your horror when your computer eats your draft or when you accidently leave your nearly finished term paper on the bus—proof that you can't rely on long-term memory to restore what you wrote.) Writing a draft, however, captures these ideas from short-term memory and stores them on paper. When you reread these stored ideas, you can note problem areas, think of new ideas, see material that doesn't fit, recall additional information, and so forth. You can then begin working on a new draft, focusing on one problem at a time.

What kinds of problems do experienced writers locate in a draft? What triggers further rounds of rewriting? We continue with more reasons why experienced writers revise.

Revising to Shift and Change a Writer's Ideas

Early in the writing process, experienced writers often are unsure of what they want to say or where their ideas are leading; they find their ideas shifting and evolving as their drafts progress. Sometimes writing a draft leads the writer to reformulate the initial problem. Just as frequently, the solution that may have seemed exciting at the beginning of the process may seem less satisfactory once it is written out. A writer's ideas deepen or shift under pressure of new insights stimulated by the act of writing. A professional writer's finished product often is radically different from the first draft—not simply in form and style but in actual content.

Revising to Clarify Audience and Purpose

As we noted in Chapter 1, writers need to say something significant to an audience for a purpose. When a writer's sense of audience or purpose shifts, an entire piece may need to be restructured. As they draft, experienced writers pose questions such as these: Who am I picturing as my readers? What is my purpose in writing to them? What effect do I want this piece of writing to have on them? How much background will they need? To which of their values and beliefs should I appeal? What tone and style are appropriate for this audience? What objections will they raise to my argument? In the process of writing, the answers to these questions may evolve so that each new draft reflects a deeper or clearer understanding of audience and purpose.

Revising to Clarify Structure and Create Coherence

Few writers can create detailed outlines before drafting. Those who can, typically set aside their outlines as their drafts take on lives of their own, spilling over the boundaries the writers have laid out. Whereas early drafts usually reflect the order in which writers conceived their ideas, later drafts are often reordered—sometimes radically—in consideration of readers' needs. To help them see their drafts from a reader's perspective, experienced writers regularly put aside those drafts for a time. When they return to a draft, the ideas no longer so familiar, they can more readily see where the material is disjointed, underdeveloped, or irrelevant. They can also see where they need to provide cues to help readers navigate the flow of their essay. At the global level such cues include point sentences, transitions, and forecasting and summarizing statements. In many types of technical or professional writing, writers may also cue their readers with headings and subheadings. At a more local level, writers can increase coherence by putting familiar material near the beginning of sentences and new material in emphatic positions near the end. Such refinements of form are a predominant concern of writers as they revise. (See Chapters 18 and 19 for a detailed discussion of these issues in closed-form prose.)

Revising to Improve Gracefulness and Correctness

Finally, writers have to get their grammar right, punctuate effectively, spell correctly, and compose sentences that are concise, clear, graceful, and pleasing to the ear. Late in the revision process, experienced writers focus extensively on these matters. Often this stage of revision involves more than stylistic polishing. Making a single sentence more graceful may entail rewriting surrounding sentences. If an awkward sentence is symptomatic of confused thinking, correcting the sentence may require generating and exploring more ideas.

A WORKING DESCRIPTION OF THE WRITING PROCESS

The writing process we have just described may be considerably different from what you have previously been taught. For many years—before researchers began studying the composing processes of experienced writers—writing teachers typically taught a model something like this:

1. Choose a topic
2. Narrow it
3. Write a thesis
4. Make an outline
5. Write a draft
6. Revise
7. Edit

The major problem with this model is that hardly anyone writes this way. Few experienced writers begin by choosing a topic and then narrowing it. Rather, they begin by posing problems and exploring ideas, by looking at the world with a wondering and critical eye, by noodling and doodling around. Nor do writers progress sequentially through linear stages, visiting each stage just once. Particularly misleading is this model's oversimplification of how writers get from a topic to a thesis (choose a topic, narrow it, write a thesis). As we explained in Chapters 1, 2, and 3, experienced academic writers become engaged with subject-matter problems that impel them to add their voice to a conversation. Sometimes writers settle on a thesis early in the writing process. But just as frequently they formulate a thesis during an "Aha!" moment of discovery and clarification later in the process, perhaps after several drafts (So *this* is my point! Here is my argument in a nutshell!).

Rather than divide the writing process into distinct, sequential steps, let's review the kinds of things experienced writers are likely to do early, midway, and late in the process of writing an essay.

Early in the Process

The activities in which writers engage early in the process are recursive—writing a draft sends the writer back for further exploring, researching, and talking.

Writers sense a question or problem.   Initially, the question or problem may not be well-defined, but the writer senses something unknown about the topic, sees it in an unusual way, disagrees with someone else's view of it, doubts a theory, notes a piece of unexplained data, or otherwise notices something confusing or problematic. In college, the instructor often assigns the problem or question to be addressed. Sometimes, the instructor assigns only a general topic area, leaving writers to find their own questions or problems.

Writers explore the problem, seeking focus.   The writers gather data from various sources, including readings, laboratory or field research, experience, conversation, and memory. Through exploratory writing and talking, writers analyze, compare, puzzle, and probe, searching for an effective response to the problem. They consider why they are writing, what they want their readers to know about the topic, and how their ideas might surprise the readers, given the readers' background knowledge and point of view. Often writers explore ideas in a journal, research log, or thought letters to colleagues. Writers may also take time off from the problem and do other things, letting ideas cook in the unconscious.

Writers compose a first draft.   At some point writers put ideas on paper in a whole or partial draft. Some writers make an informal outline or tree diagram prior to writing. Others discover direction as they write, putting aside concerns about coherence to pursue different branches of ideas. In either case, they don't try to make the draft perfect as they go. One of the major causes of writer's block among less-experienced writers is the inability to live with temporary imperfection and confusion. Experienced writers know their first drafts are often times awful, and they lower their expectations accordingly. Writing a first draft often leads writers to discover new ideas, to complicate or refocus the problem, to reimagine audience or purpose, and sometimes to change directions.

Midway Through the Process

Writers begin to revise and reformulate.   Once they have written a first draft, writers are in a better position to view the whole territory and are better able to recognize relationships among the parts. Some writers begin again, selecting insights and perspectives from the first draft and reshaping them into a new draft with a different approach and structure; others keep much of the original draft, but incorporate their newfound perspectives. Writers often find that the conclusion of the first draft is much clearer than its introduction—proof that they discovered and clarified their ideas as they wrote. At this point writers begin a second draft, often by going slowly through the first draft, adding, deleting, reordering, or completely rewriting passages. As writers revise, they ask themselves questions such as, What is my point here? Does this material really fit? What am I really trying to say? To help them see the relationship between the parts and the whole, writers often make new outlines or tree diagrams to clarify the shape of their thinking.

Writers increasingly consider the needs of readers.   As writers clarify their ideas for themselves, they increasingly focus on their readers' needs. They reorganize material and insert mapping statements, transitions, and cue words to help readers follow their ideas. In particular, they try to write effective introductions to hook readers' attention, explain the problem to be examined, and preview the whole of the essay.

Writers seek feedback from readers.   Midway through the writing process, experienced writers often ask colleagues to read their drafts and offer feedback. They seek readers' responses to such questions as these: Where do you get lost or confused? Where do you disagree with my ideas? Where do I need to put in more evidence or support?

Writers rewrite in response to feedback from readers.   Readers' responses can often help writers locate confusing spots and better anticipate readers' objections or the need for background. Different readers sometimes respond differently to a draft and offer conflicting advice. Considering the differing responses of multiple readers may allow writers to formulate their own ideas more clearly and may lead to further revisions.

Late in the Process

Writers begin to shift from discovery, shaping, and development to editing. Eventually, the writer's sense of purpose and audience stabilizes and the ideas become increasingly clear, well organized, and developed. At this point writers begin shifting their attention to the craft of writing—getting each word, phrase, sentence, and paragraph just right, so that the prose is clear, graceful, lively, and correct. Even as writers struggle with issues of style and correctness, however, they may discover new meanings and intentions that impel them to rethink parts of the essay.

FOR WRITING AND DISCUSSION

When you write, do you follow a process resembling the one we just described? Have you ever

- had a writing project grow out of your engagement with a problem or question?
- explored ideas by talking with others or by doing exploratory writing?
- made major changes to a draft because you changed your mind or otherwise discovered new ideas?
- revised a draft from a reader's perspective by consciously trying to imagine and respond to a reader's questions, confusions, and other reactions?
- road tested a draft by trying it out on readers and then revising it as a result of what they told you?

Working in groups or as a whole class, share stories about previous writing experiences that match or do not match the description of experienced writers' processes. To the extent that your present process differs, what strategies of experienced writers might you like to try?

IMPROVING YOUR OWN WRITING PROCESSES

The previous section describes the many ways in which experienced writers compose. Although it is difficult for beginning writers simply to duplicate these processes, which evolve from much experience and practice, and trial and error, beginning writers can take steps to develop more effective composing habits. Some nuts-and-bolts suggestions for improving your writing processes are given next.

Recognizing Kinds of Changes Typically Made in Drafts

We begin by classifying the kinds of changes writers typically make in drafts and explaining their reasons for making each sort of change.

Kinds of Changes	Reasons for Change
Crossing out whole passage and rewriting from scratch	Original passage was unfocused; ideas have changed.
	New sense of purpose or point meant whole passage needed reshaping.
	Original passage was too confused or jumbled merely to be edited.
Cutting and pasting; moving parts around	Original was disorganized.
	Points weren't connected to particulars.
	Conclusion was clearer than introduction; part of conclusion had to be moved to introduction.
	Rewriting introduction led to discovery of more effective plan of development; new forecasting required different order in body.
Deletions	Material not needed or irrelevant.
	Deleted material was good but went off on a tangent.

Kinds of Changes *(cont.)*	Reasons for Change *(cont.)*
Additions	Supporting particulars needed to be added: examples, facts, illustrations, statistics, evidence (usually added to bodies of paragraphs).
	Points and transitions needed to be supplied (often added to openings of paragraphs).
	New section needed to be added or a brief point expanded.
Recasting of sentences (crossing out and rewriting portions of sentences; combining sentences; rephrasing; starting sentences with a different grammatical structure)	Passage violated old/new contract (see pp. 481–88).
	Passage was wordy or choppy.
	Passage lacked rhythm and voice.
	Grammar was tangled, diction odd, meaning confused.
Editing sentences to correct mistakes	Words were misspelled or mistyped.
	Writer found comma splices, fragments, dangling participles, other grammatical errors.

FOR WRITING AND DISCUSSION

Choose an important paragraph in the body of a draft you are currently working on. Then write out your answers to these questions about that paragraph.

1. Why is this an important paragraph?

2. What is its main point?

3. Where is that main point stated?

Now—as an exercise only—write the main point at the top of a blank sheet of paper, put away your original draft, and, without looking at the original, write a new paragraph with the sole purpose of developing the point you wrote at the top of the page.

When you are finished, compare your new paragraph to the original. What have you learned that might help you revise your original?

Here are some typical responses of writers who have tried this exercise:

I recognized that my original paragraph was unfocused. I couldn't find a main point.

I recognized that my original paragraph was underdeveloped. I had a main point but not enough particulars supporting it.

I began to see that my draft was scattered and that I had too many short paragraphs.

I recognized that I was making a couple of different points in my original paragraph and that I needed to break it into separate paragraphs.

I recognized that I hadn't stated my main point (or, that I buried it in the middle of the paragraph).

I recognized that there was a big difference in style between my two versions and that I had to choose which version I liked best (it's not always the new version!).

Becoming an Effective Reader of Classmates' Drafts

One of the best ways to become a better reviser is to see your draft from a *reader's* rather than from a writer's perspective. As writer, you know what you mean; you are already inside your own head. But you need to see what your draft is like to someone outside your head.

The best way to learn this skill is to practice reading your classmates' drafts. Chapter 21 focuses on the process of conducting peer reviews—giving written and oral feedback on your classmates' drafts in progress. Each of the assignment chapters in Part Two concludes with Guidelines for Peer Reviewers, which take you through the process of reading and commenting on a particular draft for a particular assignment. These guidelines urge you to comment first on higher-order concerns, such as ideas, organization, development, and overall clarity, rather than on lower-order concerns, such as style, sentence correctness, spelling, and punctuation. The lower-order concerns are lower not because they are unimportant, but because they cannot be efficiently addressed until after the higher-order concerns are met. Why worry about punctuation errors in a paragraph that needs to be completely rewritten?

Whereas Chapter 21 focuses on the mechanics of peer reviews, in this section we want to focus on strategies for responding candidly and helpfully to any draft with the goal of helping the writer make substantive revisions. Using these same strategies on your own drafts (as you role-play being a reader) will help you improve your own revising process.

When you respond to a writer's draft, learn to make readerly rather than writerly comments; describe your mental experience in trying to understand the draft rather than pointing out problems or errors in the draft. For example, instead of saying, "Your draft is disorganized," say, "I got lost when . . . ." Instead of saying, "This paragraph needs a topic sentence," say, "I had trouble seeing the point of this paragraph."

When you help a writer with a draft, your goal is both to point out where the draft needs more work and to brainstorm with the writer possible ways to improve the draft. Begin by reading the draft all the way through at a normal reading speed. As you read, take mental notes to help focus your feedback. We suggest that you make wavy lines in the margin next to passages that you find confusing; write "Good!" in the margin where you like something; and write "?" in the margin where you want to ask questions.

After you have read the draft, use the following strategies for making helpful responses.

If the ideas in the draft seem thin or undeveloped, or if the draft is too short:

■ help the writer brainstorm for more ideas
■ help the writer add more examples, better details, more supporting data or arguments

If you get confused or lost:

■ have the writer talk through ideas to clear up confusing spots
■ help the writer sharpen the thesis: suggest that the writer view the thesis as the answer to a controversial or problematic question; ask the writer to articulate the question that the thesis answers
■ help the writer create an outline or tree diagram (see Chapter 18, pp. 451–54).
■ help the writer clarify the focus by asking him or her to complete these statements about purpose:

My purpose in this paper is _____.
My purpose in this section (paragraph) is _____.
Before reading my paper, the reader will have this view of my topic: _____; after reading my paper, my reader will have this different view of my topic: _____.

■ show the writer where you get confused or miscued in reading the draft ("I started getting lost here because I couldn't see why you were giving me this information" or "I thought you were going to say X, but then you said Y")

If you can understand the sentences but can't see the point:

■ help the writer articulate the meaning by asking "So what?" questions, making the writer bring the point to the surface by stating it directly ("I can understand what you are saying here but I don't quite understand why you are saying it. I read all these facts, and I say 'So what?' What do these facts have to do with your thesis?")

If you disagree with the ideas or think the writer has avoided alternative points of view:

■ play devil's advocate to help the writer deepen and complicate ideas
■ show the writer specific places where you had queries or doubts

FOR WRITING AND DISCUSSION

In the following exercise, we ask you to respond to a student's draft ("Should the University Carpet the Dorm," on pp. 439–40). The assignment asked students to take a stand on a local campus issue. Imagine that you have exchanged drafts with this student and that your task is to help this student improve the draft.

Read the draft carefully; make wavy lines in the margins where you get confused, write "Good!" for something you like, and write "?" where you want to ask questions.

On your own, complete the following tasks:

1. Identify one specific place in the draft where you got confused. Freewrite a brief explanation for why you got confused. Make readerly rather than writerly comments.

2. Identify one place in the draft where you think the ideas are thin or need more development.
3. Identify one place where you might write "So what?" in the margins. These are places where you understand the sentences but don't see what the writer is getting at, the point.
4. Identify at least one place where you could play devil's advocate or otherwise object to the writer's ideas. Freewrite your objections.

In groups or as a whole class share your responses. Then turn to the following tasks:

1. With the instructor serving as a guide, practice explaining to the writer where or how you got confused while reading the draft. Readers often have difficulty explaining their reading experience to a writer. Let several class members role-play being the reader. Practice using language such as "I like the way this draft started because . . . " "I got confused when . . . " "I had to back up and reread when . . . " "I saw your point here, but then I got lost again because . . . ." Writing theorist Peter Elbow calls such language a "movie of your mind."
2. Have several class members role-play being devil's advocates by arguing against the writer's thesis. Where are the ideas thin or weak?

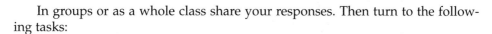

Should the University Carpet the Dorm Rooms?

1   Tricia, a University student, came home exhausted from her work-study job. She took a blueberry pie from the refrigerator to satisfy her hunger and a tall glass of milk to quench her thirst. While trying to get comfortable on her bed, she tipped her snack over onto the floor. She cleaned the mess, but the blueberry and milk stains on her brand new carpet could not be removed.

2   Tricia didn't realize how hard it was to clean up stains on a carpet. Luckily this was her own carpet.

3   A lot of students don't want carpets. Students constantly change rooms. The next person may not want carpet.

4   Some students say that since they pay to live on campus, the rooms should reflect a comfortable home atmosphere. Carpets will make the dorm more comfortable. The carpet will act as insulation and as a soundproofing system.

Paint stains cannot be removed from carpets. If the university carpets   5
the rooms, the students will lose the privilege they have of painting their
rooms any color. This would limit students' self-expression.

The carpets would be an institutional brown or gray. This would be ugly.   6
With tile floors, the students can choose and purchase their own carpets to
match their taste. You can't be an individual if you can't decorate your
room to fit your personality.

According to Rachel Jones, Assistant Director of Housing Services, the   7
cost will be $300 per room for the carpet and installation. Also the univer-
sity will have to buy more vacuum cleaners. But will vacuum cleaners be all
that is necessary to keep the carpets clean? We'll need shampoo machines too.

What about those stains that won't come off even with a shampoo machine?   8
That's where the student will have to pay damage deposit costs.

There will be many stains on the carpet due to shaving cream fights, food   9
fights, beverage parties, and smoking, all of which can damage the carpets.

Students don't take care of the dorms now. They don't follow the rules   10
of maintaining their rooms. They drill holes into the walls, break mirrors,
beds, and closet doors, and leave their food trays all over the floor.

If the university buys carpets our room rates will skyrocket. In con-   11
clusion, it is a bad idea for the university to buy carpets.

Practicing Various Composing Strategies

In addition to knowing the kinds of changes writers typically make in drafts
and seeing your draft from a reader's perspective, you can improve your composing processes by practicing the following strategies.

Use Expressive Writing for Discovery and Exploration

Use the exploratory strategies described in detail in Chapter 2. Don't let your
first draft be the first time you put pencil to paper. Each assignment chapter in Part
Two includes exploratory exercises that will help you generate ideas and overcome writer's block.

Talk About Your Ideas

Talk your draft. Good writing grows out of good talking. Seek out opportunities to talk about your ideas with classmates or friends. Exchange ideas on topics

so that you can appreciate alternative points of view. Whenever possible, talk through your draft with a friend; rehearse your argument in conversation as practice for putting it in writing.

Invent with Research

Depending on your topic, audience, purpose, and genre, you will frequently need to do outside reading and research. In the process of finding new information and exploring the multisided conversation surrounding your subject, you will be deepening your understanding of the topic and reshaping your thinking.

Schedule Your Time

Plan for exploration, drafting, revision, and editing. Don't begin your paper the night before it is due. Talk about your ideas and do exploratory writing before writing a rough draft. Give ideas time to ruminate in your mind. Recognize that your ideas will shift, branch out, even turn around as you write. Allow some time off between writing the first draft and beginning revision.

Exchange Drafts with Others

Get other people's reactions to your work in exchange for your reactions to theirs. Chapter 21 suggests procedures for peer review of drafts.

Discover What Methods of Drafting Work Best for You

Some people compose rough drafts directly on a computer; others write longhand. Of those who write longhand, some find that a certain kind of paper or pen best stimulates thought. Different people prefer different surroundings, also. One of the writers of this text works best in a noisy bagel shop or coffeehouse; the other prefers sitting on a sofa with a legal pad in hand. Discover what works best for you.

Revise on Double- or Triple-Spaced Hard Copy

Although some people can revise directly at the computer, research suggests that writers are more apt to make large-scale changes in a draft if they work from hard copy. Double- or triple-space your drafts and write on one side of the page only. Cross out text to be changed and write new text in the blank spaces between the lines. When a draft gets too messy, write revised passages on a separate sheet and tape that sheet to the hard-copy draft. Then, if you are working on a computer, enter your changes into the computer and print out another hard copy for another round of revision.

Save Correctness for Last

To revise productively, concentrate first on the big questions: Do I have good ideas in this draft? Am I responding appropriately to the assignment? Are my ideas adequately organized and developed? Save questions about exact wording, grammar, and mechanics for later. These concerns are important, but they cannot be efficiently attended to until after higher-order concerns are met. Your first goal is to create a thoughtful, richly developed draft.

To Meet Deadlines, Learn to "Satisfice"

Our description of the writing process may seem pretty formidable. Potentially, it seems, you could go on revising forever. How can you ever know when to stop? There's no ready answer to that question, but in our opinion it is much more a psychological than a technical problem. The best advice we can offer is to "satisfice."

Satisficing doesn't require that you be perfectly satisfied with your writing. Of course, it can always be better. To *satisfice* is to make it as good as you can under the circumstances—your rhetorical situation, your time constraints, and the pressures of other demands on you.

The best advice we can give you for finishing a project is to write a rough draft as early in the process as possible and to allow time for feedback from peers or other readers. Then let the deadline give you energy. In some cases, this approach means letting the paper sit until the day before it's due and then returning to it for intensive revision.

This advice may seem to fly in the face of counsel offered in some study-skills handbooks and courses that promote doing everything well in advance of deadlines through prudent time management. We aren't encouraging procrastination (you should be well along by the time the deadline approaches); we simply recognize that an impending deadline can help writers reach closure on a paper. From lawyers preparing briefs for court to engineers developing design proposals, writers have used deadlines to help them put aside doubts and anxieties and to conclude their work, as every writer must. Satisficing is saying, "Okay, it's not perfect, but it's the best I can do."

Many late papers are, paradoxically, the result of too much rather than too little time. That is, people who hand in work late (or in extreme cases not at all) are often those who agonize over all the arbitrary aspects of writing, the innumerable ways of saying something, the countless choices about theses or details of support, the multiple possible audiences, and so on. They want to do away with all arbitrariness and write The Right Paper. That's impossible. And there's nothing like a deadline, an unwavering due date, to give you that rush of adrenaline, that clarity of purpose, that will allow you to make all those final choices economically and to achieve a Zen-like state of self-acceptance. In this state, you can enjoy the certainty that the paper you'll turn in tomorrow will be the right paper . . . for now.

Summary

This chapter has focused on the writing processes of experts, showing how experienced writers use multiple drafts to solve subject-matter and rhetorical problems. We have also offered advice on how to improve your own writing processes. In particular, beginning college writers need to understand the kinds of changes writers typically make in drafts and to role-play a reader's perspective when they revise. To this end we showed you how to make readerly rather than writerly comments on a rough draft. Finally, we suggested that you practice different kinds of strategies for enriching your own writing processes.

chapter 18

Composing Closed-Form Prose

> [Form is] an arousing and fulfillment of desires. A work has form insofar as one part of it leads a reader to anticipate another part, to be gratified by the sequence.
>
> —Kenneth Burke, *Rhetorician*

Chapter 17 explained the composing processes of experienced writers and suggested ways that you could improve your own writing processes. This chapter and the next will help you compose and revise closed-form prose.

In this chapter, we examine closely the structure and style of closed-form prose, showing you how such knowledge can help you generate and organize ideas. First, we describe the points-first structure of closed-form prose—a structure that requires a risky thesis—and contrast it with the riskless structures of "and then," "all about," and "engfish" writing. Next, we show how outlines and tree diagrams are powerful tools for designing a closed-form structure and explain how writers use four common organizational moves to generate and develop ideas. Finally, we offer a brief discussion of the clear, coherent, and transparent prose style to which closed-form writers typically aspire.

CLOSED-FORM STRUCTURE: ORDERING OF POINTS AND PARTICULARS

We begin by identifying two basic organizational tools of writing: points and particulars. Consider the following lists of data. Column 1 was compiled from a passage in Norman Mailer's *Of a Fire on the Moon* that describes the Vehicle Assembly Building in which the U.S. space program builds its rockets and moon landers. Column 2 provides data about the production of electrical power in the Pacific Northwest. Read each list separately.

NASA Building

Is 526 feet high

Covers an area of 8 acres

Encloses 129 million cubic feet

Without windows

Covered with concentric rectangles painted shades of green, gray, and blue

Northwest Electrical Power

The Northwest Electrical power system has a capacity to generate 37,000. megawatts of hydro power and 10,300 megawatts of thermal power.

This leads to a total of 47,300 megawatts.

Meeting 28 percent of this total with wind power would require 13,400 wind towers.

These 100–200 foot towers would be located in the mountains of Oregon and Washington and would take up an area of hundreds of square miles.

They would be connected by a network of roads and transmission lines.

As a reader, your mind quickly tires of particulars such as these. "So what?" you are apt to ask about either list. "What's your point?" Your frustration reveals that the human mind doesn't like particulars by themselves. It can't hold them for long in short-term memory, and it doesn't know where or why to store them in long-term memory. To show readers the *meaning* of particulars, writers need to connect them to points—that is, to generalizations that the particulars support or develop. It is these points that readers store in memory.

Open-Form Order: From Particulars to Points

Keeping these reader needs in mind, we can now return to the two columns of particulars without points. The information in column 1 apparently supports some point Mailer wants to make about NASA's Vehicle Assembly Building. If you had to hazard a guess about the point based on these data, you might say, "It's amazingly big." But this point leaves out pertinent particulars in the list, for example, the absence of windows and the details about the colored rectangles.

In the sentence that follows this sequence of particulars, Mailer takes an initial run at making a point: "It looked like a block of wood colored by an Op Art painter, but since it was over fifty stories high, it also looked like the walls of a gargantuan suburban department store." Mailer's uncertainty over what point to make about this strange building suggests that he, himself, is trying to figure out while he writes what these details add up to. Finally, in the last sentence of his paragraph, he arrives at an emphatic point: "Viewed from any external approach it was the architectural fungoid of them all." In sum, whatever else it may be, this thing is ugly.

This *discovering-while-writing* structure is characteristic of an open-form style. By putting his point last, Mailer invites his readers to muse along with him in his search for an interpretation of this huge and strange building.

Closed-Form Order: From Points to Particulars

In contrast, closed-form writers place points first and then support them with particulars. They do their musing behind the scenes and offer their conclusions up front to speed reader comprehension. Whereas an open-form text often re-creates and foregrounds the author's discovery process, a closed-form text foregrounds the author's conclusions, not his or her mental process in reaching them. For example, here is the actual paragraph that uses the data in column 2. Notice that the writer *begins* with the point.

> Thirdly, **the environmental impact of constructing wind generation facilities amounting to 28 percent of the region's electrical supply system . . . would be tremendous.** The Northwest Electrical Power system presently has a capacity of about 37,000 megawatts of hydro power. . . .

The paragraph then uses the particulars from the list as supporting data. (To read the whole paragraph, see page 12.) When a writer begins with a point, readers interpret the ensuing particulars not as random data, but rather as *evidence* in support of that point. The writer depends on the particulars to make the point credible and persuasive.

This insight may help you clarify two of the most common kinds of marginal comments that readers (or teachers) place on writers' early drafts. If your draft has a string of sentences giving data or information unconnected to any stated point, your reader is apt to write in the margin "What's your point here?" or "Why are you telling me this information?" Conversely, if your draft tries to make a point that isn't developed with particulars, your reader is apt to write marginal comments such as "Evidence?" "Development?" "Could you give an example?" "More details needed."

Don't be put off by these requests; they are a gift. It is common in first drafts for main points to be unstated, buried, or otherwise disconnected from their particulars, and for particulars to be scattered through the draft or missing entirely. In the following exercise, we ask you to return to the student draft on dorm-room carpets in Chapter 17. One of the causes of confusion in this draft is the lack of clear connection between points and particulars.

FOR WRITING AND DISCUSSION

1. Reread the student draft on pages 439–40. As you read, pay particular attention to any difficulty you have identifying points and linking them clearly to their supporting particulars. Working individually, write out what you see as the writer's main points. Because this is an argumentative essay, the argument's main points will be the reasons that the writer wants to put forward against university funding of dorm-room carpets. It sometimes helps to state each reason as a "because" clause: "The university should not carpet the dorms *because* . . . , because . . . , because . . . ."
2. Working in small groups or as a whole class, develop consensus on the main reasons the writer wants to give for not carpeting the dorms. These are the writer's main-point sentences.

3. Once you have formulated the writer's main reasons, help locate particulars from the draft that could be used as evidence or support for each point. Where might the writer need to add more particulars?

4. The carpets draft has a number of short, undeveloped paragraphs. Such paragraphs are commonly used in newspapers and popular magazines as a means of breaking up long stretches of multicolumned text. But closed-form writing generally calls for longer and more developed paragraphs. Readers expect each paragraph of closed-form writing to be a meaningful unit, with its own point sentence and supporting particulars. How many paragraph units do you envision for a revised draft of the carpets argument?

RETREATING FROM COMPLEXITY: THREE RISKLESS STRUCTURES TO AVOID

Whatever its current limitations, the carpets draft could clearly be revised into an effective closed-form argument. We are optimistic here because the draft has the one critical component of good closed-form writing—a risky thesis. A *thesis*, as we said in Chapter 3, is an assertion that "sticks its neck out," "surprises" readers, or creates "tension." Because developing and supporting a risky thesis is hard work, requiring much critical thought, it is no surprise that writers sometimes retreat into structures that are easier to compose than a thesis-based argument with points and particulars.

In this next section we want to help you better understand thesis-based writing by contrasting it with prose that looks like thesis-based writing but isn't. We show you three common ways in which inexperienced writers give the appearance of writing thesis-based prose while actually retreating from the rigors of making and developing an argument. Avoiding the pitfalls of riskless structures can go a long way toward improving your performance on most college writing assignments.

"And Then" Writing, or Chronological Structure

Chronological structure, often called *narrative*, is the most common organizing principle of open-form prose. It may also be used selectively in closed-form prose to support a point. Sometimes, however, a writer begins recounting the details of a story until chronological order takes over, driving out the thesis-based structure of points and particulars.

To a large degree, chronological order is the default mode writers fall into when they aren't sure how to organize material. For example, if you were asked to analyze a fictional character, you might write a plot summary of the story instead. In much the same way, you might substitute historical chronology ("First A happened, then B happened") for historical analysis ("B happened because A happened"), or you might give a chronological recounting of your research ("First I discovered A, then I discovered B") instead of organizing your material into an argument ("I question A's account of this phenomenon on the grounds of B's recent findings").

The tendency to lapse into inappropriate chronological structure is revealed in the following example. The student was asked to introduce the reader to a problem and then explain how the writer solved it.

1   Last Fall and Winter I was living in Spokane with my brother, who during this time had a platonic girl friend come over from Seattle and stay for a weekend. Her name was Karen, and we became interested in each other and I went over to see her at the first of the year. She then invited me to supposedly, the biggest party of the year, called the Aristocrat's Ball. I said sure and made my way back to Seattle in February. It started out bad on Friday, the day my brother and I left Spokane. We left town an hour late, but what's new. Then my brother had to stop along the way and pick up some parts; we stayed there for an hour trying to find this guy. It all started out bad because we arrived in Seattle and I forgot to call Karen. We were staying at her brother's house and after we brought all our things in, we decided to go to a few bars. Later that night we ran into Karen in one of the bars, and needless to say she was not happy with me. When I got up the next morning I knew I should of stayed in Spokane, because I felt bad vibes. Karen made it over about a hour before the party. By the time we reached the party, which drove me crazy, she wound up with another guy, so her friends and I decided to go to a few bars. The next morning when I was packing, I could not find my watch and decided that someone had to of taken it. We decided that it had to of been the goon that Karen had wound up with the night before, because she was at her brother's house with him before she went home. So how was I going to get my watch back?

2   We decided the direct and honest approach to the problem would work out the best. We got in contact and confronted him. This turned out to be quite a chore. It turned out that he was visiting some of his family during that weekend and lived in Little Harbor, California. It turned out that Karen

knew his half brother and got some information on him, which was not pretty. He had just been released by the army and was trained in a special forces unit, in the fields of Martial Arts. He was a trained killer! This information did not help matters at all, but the next bit of information was just as bad if not worse. Believe it or not, he was up on charges of attempted murder and breaking and entering. In a way, it turned out lucky for me, because he was in enough trouble with the police and did not need any more. Karen got in contact with him and threatened him that I would bring him up on charges, if he did not return the watch. His mother decided, that he was in enough trouble and sent me the watch. I was astounded, it was still working and looked fine. The moral of the story is don't drive 400 miles to see a girl you hardly know, and whatever you do, don't leave your valuables out in the open.

Although this draft does eventually pose a problem (how to get your watch back from a trained killer) and offer a potentially humorous solution (tell the killer's mother), it is a rambling "what happened to me" narrative full of extraneous details about Karen and the writer's trip to Spokane.

How should the writer go about improving this draft? One solution might be to transform it into a sophisticated, open-form narrative with pacing, drama, and focus—that is, turn it into a really good story. But the assignment calls for a thesis-based problem–solution essay. So the writer's first job is to define the problem clearly. From a thesis-based perspective, the author's problem is that he has to choose among a number of options in response to discovering that his watch was stolen. Should he call the police? Forget the watch? Get a bunch of burly buddies to go with him to confront the thief? Send the thug a polite note? After the writer defines the problem, he must explain his solution and justify it as a reasoned choice rather than blind luck.

This revision would require considerable mental effort. Because recounting events chronologically is far easier, many writers—even experienced ones—lapse into long stretches of "and then" writing in their rough drafts. In fact, researchers have shown that chronological thinking provides a natural way for all writers to retrieve ideas and details from long-term memory. But experienced writers have learned to recognize these "and then" sections in their drafts and to rework this material into a closed-form, thesis-based structure.

"All About" Writing, or Encyclopedic Structure

Whereas "and then" writing turns essays into stories by organizing details chronologically, "all about" writing turns essays into encyclopedia articles by piling up details in heaps. When "all about" writing organizes these heaps into categories, it can appear to be well organized: "Having told you everything I learned about educational opportunities in Cleveland, I will now tell you everything I learned about the Rock and Roll Hall of Fame." But the categories do not function as points and particulars in support of a thesis. Rather, like the shelving system in a library, they are simply ways of arranging information for convenient retrieval, not a means of building a hierarchical structure.

If you've ever paraphrased an encyclopedia for a report on some hefty topic, such as "earthquakes" or "North Dakota," you'll know what we mean by "all about" writing. Because such reports usually don't require a risky thesis about earthquakes or North Dakota, they invite you simply to crank out information.

To illustrate the differences between "all about" writing and thesis-based writing, consider the case of two students asked to write term papers on the subject of, for example, female police officers. One student is asked simply to write "all about" the topic; the other is asked to pose and investigate some problem related to female police officers and to support a thesis addressing that problem. In all likelihood, the first student would produce an initial outline with headings such as the following:

I. History of women in police roles
   A. female police or soldiers in ancient times
   B. 19th century (Calamity Jane)
   C. 1900s–1960
   D. 1960–present
II. How female police officers are selected and trained
III. A typical day in the life of a female police officer
IV. Achievements and acts of heroism of female police officers
V. What the future holds for female police officers

Such a paper promises to be either long and boring or short and superficial. In either case, it will be riskless, and, except for occasional new information, surpriseless. In contrast, when a student focuses on a significant question—one that grows out of the writer's own interests and demands engagement—the writing can be quite compelling.

Consider the case of a student, Lynnea, who wrote a research paper entitled "Women Police Officers: Should Size and Strength Be Criteria for Patrol Duty?" Her essay begins with a group of male police officers complaining about being assigned to patrol duty with a new female officer, Connie Jones (not her real name), who is four feet ten inches tall and weighs ninety pounds. Here is the rest of the introduction to Lynnea's essay.

    Connie Jones has just completed police academy training and has

    been assigned to patrol duty in _____. Because she is so small,

    she has to have a booster seat in her patrol car and has been given

    a special gun, since she can barely manage to pull the trigger of a

```
standard police-issue .38 revolver. Although she passed the physi-
cal requirements at the academy, which involved speed and endurance
running, situps, and monkey bar tests, most of the officers in her
department doubt her ability to perform competently as a patrol of-
ficer. But nevertheless she is on patrol because men and women re-
ceive equal assignments in most of today's police forces. But is this
a good policy? Can a person who is significantly smaller and weaker
than her peers make an effective patrol officer?
```

Lynnea examined all the evidence she could find—through library and field research (interviewing police officers) and arrived at the following thesis: "Because concern for public safety overrides all other concerns, police departments should set stringent size and strength requirements for patrol officers, even if these criteria exclude many women." This thesis has plenty of tension because it sets limits on equal rights for women. Because Lynnea considers herself a feminist, it caused her considerable distress to advocate setting these limits and placing public safety ahead of gender equity. The resulting essay is engaging precisely because of the tension it creates and the controversy it engenders.

Engfish Writing, or Structure Without Surprise

Unlike the chronological story and the "all about" paper, the *engfish* essay has a thesis.* But the thesis is a riskless truism supported with predictable reasons—often structured as three supports in a traditional five-paragraph theme. It is fill-in-the-blanks writing: "The food service is bad for three reasons. First, it is bad because the food is not tasty. Blah, blah, blah about tasteless food. Second, it is bad because it is too expensive. Blah, blah, blah about the expense." And so on. The writer is on autopilot and is not contributing to a real conversation about a real question. In some situations, writers use engfish intentionally: bureaucrats and politicians may want to avoid saying something risky; students may want to avoid writing about complex matters that they fear they do not fully understand. In the end, using engfish is bad not because what you say is *wrong;* it's because what you say couldn't *possibly be* wrong. To avoid engfish, stay focused on the need to surprise your reader.

---

*The term *engfish* was coined by the textbook writer Ken Macrorie to describe a fishy kind of canned prose that bright but bored students mechanically produce to please their writing teachers. See *Telling Writing*. Rochelle Park, NJ: Hayden Press, 1970.

VISUALIZING YOUR STRUCTURE

Now that you have a clearer idea of what thesis-governed writing is—writing that uses points and particulars to support a risky thesis—let's return to the problem of how to create a coherent, closed-form structure. You saw in the opening section of this chapter how closed-form writers state a point and then support it with particulars. For the whole essay to make sense to a reader, these chunks of related material must be arranged in a logical sequence. In planning your writing, you need to visualize the hierarchical structure of parts and subparts. The traditional method of displaying this structure is an outline, which uses letters and numerals to indicate levels of points, subpoints, and particulars. An alternative method, which some writers find more powerful, is the tree diagram, which relies on spatial locations to indicate relationships.

How to Make a Tree Diagram

A tree diagram is more visual and more flexible than a traditional outline. It is a powerful planning tool that you can use throughout the writing process. To illustrate how tree diagrams work, we use a short anti-euthanasia argument by a Vietnamese student, Dao. Dao opposes the pro-euthanasia view of her friend, Martha, who described in a class discussion what she considered the needless suffering of her aunt in the late stages of a fatal kidney disease. A tree diagram of Dao's final draft is shown in Figure 18.1 (on p. 452). Her introduction is at the top of the tree, above the thesis. Her main reasons, written as point sentences, appear as branches beneath her claim that "euthanasia is wrong." Supporting evidence and arguments are displayed as subbranches beneath each reason.

The same argument presented in Dao's tree diagram when displayed in outline form looks like this:

Thesis: Despite Martha's strong argument for legalizing euthanasia, euthanasia is wrong for several reasons.

    I. First, I object to euthanasia because it benefits survivors more than the sick person.
       A. Pain can be controlled by modern drugs so sick people don't have to suffer.
       B. Euthanasia most benefits survivors because it saves them worry and money.
   II. Second, I oppose euthanasia because of its unfavorable consequences.
       A. Euthanasia would tempt people to murder for inheritance.
       B. Euthanasia would lead to discrimination against those with "unpopular diseases," such as AIDS.
  III. Third, I oppose euthanasia because it fails to see the value in suffering (supported by example of my grandmother's caring for my crippled uncle in Vietnam).

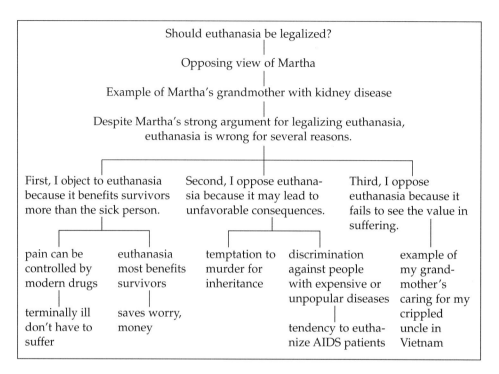

FIGURE 18.1   Dao's Tree Diagram

Although traditional outlines may look more familiar to you, tree diagrams enable you to *see* the interrelated parts of an essay more clearly. When you develop a point with subpoints or particulars, you move down the tree. When you switch to a new point, you move across the tree to make a new branch. Our own teaching experience suggests that this visual-spatial technique, which engages more areas of the brain than does the more purely verbal outline, leads many writers to produce fuller, more detailed, and more logical arguments.

Using Tree Diagrams to Generate Ideas

Tree diagrams may also be more powerful than traditional outlines in helping you think of ideas. These diagrams can stimulate the generation of ideas because they let you literally *see* gaps in your reasoning. For example, the first tree diagram that Dao made for her euthanasia argument had only two main supporting reasons and neither reason was fully developed. During a conference, her teacher encouraged her to place question marks on her tree to represent the points and particulars that might be added to make her argument more persuasive. Figure 18.2 shows what her original tree diagram looked like with these place-holding question marks (compare this with Figure 18.1, her final diagram).

The question marks along the top horizontal line encouraged Dao to search for additional reasons in support of the thesis, and the question mark beneath her

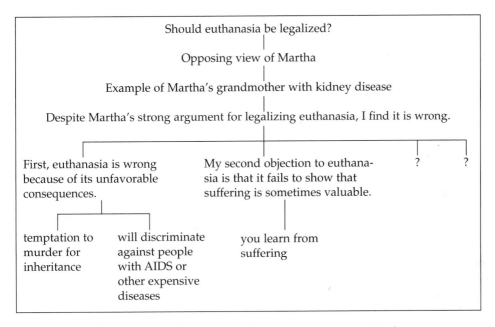

FIGURE 18.2   Dao's Original Diagram with Placeholding Question Marks

second reason urged her to think of a way to support her stated belief that suffering can be valuable. As she brainstormed ideas to replace the question marks, she recalled her grandmother's experience in caring for her congenitally crippled child, Dao's uncle. The example was so powerful that she decided to save it for the last point in her argument. Meanwhile, in response to the question marks along the horizontal line, Dao thought of the notion that euthanasia benefits survivors more than patients, an idea she developed more fully, and then shifted in her final draft to the first-reason slot.

You can also use a question mark to represent a generalization or point sentence that will make sense out of particulars. If your draft includes particulars unrelated to a point, put them on lower branches descending from the question mark.

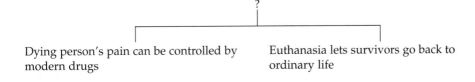

FOR WRITING AND DISCUSSION

1. Trace the development of Dao's ideas by comparing her original tree diagram (Figure 18.2) with her final version (Figure 18.1). Classmates should

help each other "read" the tree diagrams, checking each other's understanding of the logic for each entry.

2. Working individually or in groups, make a tree diagram of David Rockwood's argument against wind-generated electricity in his letter to the editor on pages 11–12. Then make a traditional outline of the same argument. Which method of representing structure works better for you?

3. Working individually or in groups, make a tree diagram with place-holding question marks to guide a next draft for the carpets essay on pags 439–40.

Using Complete Sentences at the Top Levels of the Tree Diagram

The final tree diagram for Dao's essay (Figure 18.1) has complete sentences at the top levels of the tree, which represent the main points and subpoints of the argument. Whether you use trees or traditional outlines, we strongly recommend that you write out your key points and subpoints as complete sentences. You can see why we make this recommendation if you compare the tree diagram in Figure 18.1 (p. 452) with the phrase-only version in Figure 18.3.

Phrases identify topics, but they don't create meanings. Sentences combine topic-identifying subjects with assertion-making predicates. The *meaning* arises from the assertion-making predicate.

Name something	Make an assertion about it
Fat	is an essential dietary ingredient without which we would die.
Justice	is hard to get if you are poor or black.
Television	may cause some children to act violently.

Because topic phrases don't have predicates, they don't have clear meanings. If you already know what you intend to say, a phrase-only tree or outline can be useful as a shorthand way to jog your memory. But if you are trying to discover and create meanings, writing out complete sentences for main points and subpoints makes a tree diagram or an outline a far more powerful tool.

FIGURE 18.3   Dao's Phrase-Only Tree Diagram

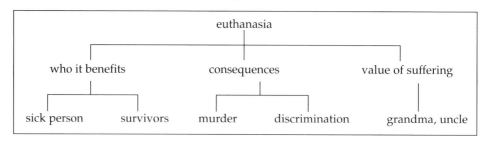

COMMON ORGANIZATIONAL MOVES IN CLOSED-FORM WRITING

In Part One we noted that the structure of an essay is a function of its subject matter, purpose, audience, and genre. The example we gave to illustrate tree diagrams—Dao's anti-euthanasia argument—is a relatively simple structure that uses three main reasons to support a thesis. We want to caution you against thinking of this structure as a ready-made form. Note that Dao started off with two reasons rather than three and that she developed her third reason by considering how best to persuade her audience. In composing her essay, Dao focused on the subject-matter problem of euthanasia and on the rhetorical problems of finding effective reasons and evidence. She did *not* focus on filling out a three-part structure. Most pieces of closed-form writing will have a structure different from this; you should never assume that your ideas will fit neatly into a preexisting shape as if they were plaster poured into a mold.

Nevertheless, writers often do draw on a conventional set of moves to organize their ideas, especially in closed-form writing. In using the term *moves*, we are making an analogy with the "set moves" or "set plays" in such sports as basketball, volleyball, and soccer. For example, a common set move in basketball is the "pick," in which an offensive player without the ball stands motionless in order to block the path of a defensive player who is guarding the dribbler. Similarly, certain organizational patterns in writing occur frequently enough to act as set plays for writers. These patterns set up expectations in the reader's mind about the shape of an upcoming stretch of prose, anything from a few sentences to a paragraph to a large block of paragraphs. As you will see, these moves also stimulate the invention of ideas. Next, we describe four of the most powerful set plays.*

The For Example Move

Perhaps the most common set play occurs when a writer makes an assertion and then illustrates it with one or more examples, often signaling the move explicitly with transitions such as *for example, for instance,* or *a case in point is . . . .* Once the move starts, readers can anticipate how it will unfold, just as experienced basketball fans can anticipate a pick as soon as they see a dribbler swerve toward a stationary teammate. You can probably sense this move unfolding now as you wait for us to give an example of the *for example move.* We have aroused an expectation; now we will fulfill it.

---

*You might find it helpful to follow the set plays we used to write this section. This last sentence is the opening move of a play we call "division into parts." It sets up the expectation that we will develop four set plays in order. Watch for the way we chunk them and signal transitions between them.

A good example of the for example move occurs in the paragraph Dao wrote to support her third reason for opposing euthanasia (see Figure 18.1, p. 452, for the tree diagram of Dao's essay).

Dao's Paper—"For Example" Paragraph

```
My third objection to euthanasia is that it fails to see the
value in suffering. Suffering is a part of life. We only see the
value of suffering if we look deeply within our suffering. For ex-
ample, I never thought my crippled uncle from Vietnam was a bless-
ing to my grandmother until I talked to her. My mother's little
brother was born prematurely. As a result of oxygen and nutrition
deficiency, he was born crippled. His tiny arms and legs were twisted
around his body, preventing him from any normal movements such as
walking, picking up things, and lying down. He could only sit. There-
fore, his world was very limited, for it consisted of his own room
and the garden viewed through his window. Because of his disabili-
ties, my grandmother had to wash him, feed him, and watch him con-
stantly. It was hard, but she managed to care for him for forty-three
years. He passed away after the death of my grandfather in 1982.
Bringing this situation out of Vietnam and into Western society shows
the difference between Vietnamese and Western views. In West, my
uncle might have been euthanized as a baby. Supporters of euthana-
sia would have said he wouldn't have any quality of life and that
he would have been a great burden. But he was not a burden on my
grandmother. She enjoyed taking care of him, and he was always her
company after her other children got married and moved away. Neither
one of them saw his defect as meaningless suffering because it
brought them closer together.
```

This passage uses a single, extended example to support a point. You could also use several shorter examples or other kinds of illustrating evidence, such as facts or statistics. In all cases the for example move creates a pattern of expectation and fulfillment. This pattern drives the invention of ideas in one of two ways: it urges the writer either to find examples to develop a generalization or to formulate a generalization that shows the point of an example.

FOR WRITING AND DISCUSSION

Working individually or in groups, develop a plan for supporting one or more of the following generalizations using the for example move.

1. Another objection to state sales taxes is that they are so annoying.
2. Although assertiveness training has definite benefits, it can sometimes get you into real trouble.
3. People say large cars are generally safer than small ones, but that is not always the case.
4. Sometimes effective leaders are indecisive.
5. Sometimes writing multiple drafts can make your essay worse rather than better.

The Summary/However Move

This move occurs whenever a writer sums up another person's viewpoint in order to qualify or contradict it or to introduce an opposing view. Typically, writers use transition words such as *but, however, in contrast,* or *on the other hand* between the parts of this move. This move is particularly common in academic writing, which often contrasts the writer's new view with prevailing views. Here is how Dao uses a *summary/however move* in the introduction of her essay opposing euthanasia.

> Should euthanasia be legalized? My classmate Martha and her family think it should be. Martha's grandmother was blind from diabetes. For three years she was constantly in and out of the hospital, but then her kidneys shut down and she became a victim of life supports. After three months of suffering, she finally gave up. Martha believes this three-month period was unnecessary, for her grandmother didn't have to go through all of that suffering. If euthanasia were legalized, her family would have put her to sleep the minute her condition worsened. Then, she wouldn't have had to feel pain, and she would have died in peace and with dignity. However, despite Martha's strong argument for legalizing euthanasia, I find it wrong.

Dao's Paper—"Summary/ However" Paragraph

The first sentence of this introduction poses the question that the essay addresses. The main body of the paragraph summarizes Martha's opposing view on euthanasia, and the final sentence, introduced by the transition "however," presents Dao's thesis.

FOR WRITING AND DISCUSSION

For this exercise, assume that you favor development of wind-generated electricity. Use the summary/however move to acknowledge the view of civil engineer David Rockwood, whose letter opposing wind-generated electricity you read in Chapter 1 (pp. 11–12). Assume that you are writing the opening paragraph of your own essay. Follow the pattern of Dao's introduction: (a) begin with a one-sentence issue or question; (b) summarize Rockwood's view in approximately one hundred words; and (c) state your own view, using "however" or "in contrast" as a transition. Write out your paragraph on your own, or work in groups to write a consensus paragraph. Then share and critique your paragraphs.

The Division-into-Parallel-Parts Move

Among the most frequently encountered and powerful of the set plays is the *division-into-parallel-parts move.* To initiate the move, a writer begins with an umbrella sentence that forecasts the structure and creates a frame. (For example, "Freud's theory differs from Jung's in three essential ways" or "The decline of the U.S. space program can be attributed to several factors.") Typical overview sentences either specify the number of parts that will follow by using phrases such as "two ways," "three differences," "five kinds," or they leave the number unspecified, using words such as *several, a few,* or *many.* Alternatively, the writer may ask a rhetorical question that implies the frame: "What are some main differences, then, between Freud's theory and Jung's? One difference is . . . ."

To signal transitions from one part to the next, writers use two kinds of signposts: transition words or bullets and parallel grammatical structure.* The first kind of signpost can use transition words to introduce each of the parallel parts.

first . . . , second . . . , third . . . , finally . . . .

first . . . , another . . . , still another . . . , finally . . . .

to begin . . . , likewise . . . , in addition . . . , lastly . . . .

either . . . or. . . .

one . . . , in addition . . . , furthermore . . . , also . . . .

Or, instead of transition words, writers can also use a series of bullets followed by indented text.

The Wolf Recovery Program is strictly opposed by a large and vociferous group of ranchers who pose numerous objections to increasing wolf populations.

- They perceive wolves as a threat to livestock
- They fear the wolves will attack humans
- etc.

The second kind of signpost uses the same grammatical structure to begin each parallel part, creating a parallel, echolike effect.

*Note how this sentence itself initiates a division-into-parallel-parts move.

> I learned several things from this class. First, *I learned that* . . . . Second, *I learned that* . . . . Finally, *I learned that* . . . .

A typical version of this move is embedded in the following single paragraph taken from a long professional essay. The author is discussing the impact of an article in which psychologist George Miller shows that a person's short-term memory capacity is "seven plus or minus two" pieces of information.* This paragraph uses a rhetorical question as the umbrella sentence that initiates the move.

> Why did this apparently simple point have a decidedly major impact within [cognitive psychology]? First, Miller's essay brought together a large amount of hitherto dispersed data and suggested that they pointed to a common conclusion. Second, it suggested that the number 7 was no mere accident: it designated genuine limitations in human information-processing capacities. . . . Third, as indicated, the message in the paper was not without hope, for Miller indicated ways by which humans ingeniously transcend this limitation.
>
> —Howard Gardner, *The Mind's New Science: A History of the Cognitive Revolution*

Using the Parallel-Parts Move on a Large Scale

The division-into-parallel-parts move is also frequently used to control larger stretches of text in which a dozen or more paragraphs may work together to complete a parallel series of parts. For example, you are currently in part three of a stretch of text introduced by the mapping sentence on page 455: "Next we describe four of the most powerful set plays." In fact, the division-into-parallel-parts move often forms the major organizational strategy of the whole essay. Here are some examples of common situations in which writers use this move on a large scale.

Classification   When writers want to divide a concept into various categories—a thinking process often called *classification*—they regularly devote a major piece of the essay to each of the classes or categories.

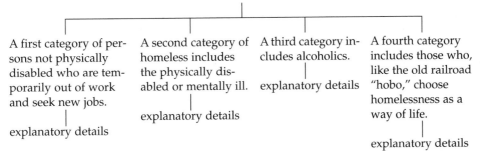

Political solutions to homelessness must take into account four categories of homeless people.

A first category of persons not physically disabled who are temporarily out of work and seek new jobs.	A second category of homeless includes the physically disabled or mentally ill.	A third category includes alcoholics.	A fourth category includes those who, like the old railroad "hobo," choose homelessness as a way of life.
explanatory details	explanatory details	explanatory details	explanatory details

---

*We demonstrated the significance of Miller's article for writers in the discussion of why writers revise in Chapter 17.

Exemplification   A process sometimes called *exemplification* or *illustration* occurs when a writer illustrates a point with several extended examples.

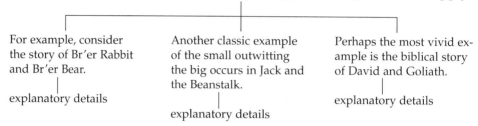

Many of our stories and legends depict cunning little guys outwitting dull-brained big guys.

For example, consider the story of Br'er Rabbit and Br'er Bear.

explanatory details

Another classic example of the small outwitting the big occurs in Jack and the Beanstalk.

explanatory details

Perhaps the most vivid example is the biblical story of David and Goliath.

explanatory details

Causal Analysis   Writing that analyzes causes of a phenomenon is also often organized into parallel parts, with each part developing a single cause.

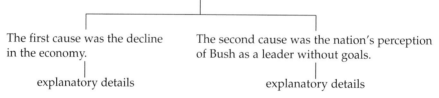

Despite George Bush's enormous popularity following the Gulf War, he nevertheless lost the presidency to Bill Clinton. His decline in popularity can be attributed to two causes.

The first cause was the decline in the economy.

explanatory details

The second cause was the nation's perception of Bush as a leader without goals.

explanatory details

Process Analysis   Writers often explain a process by dividing it into a number of separate stages or steps.

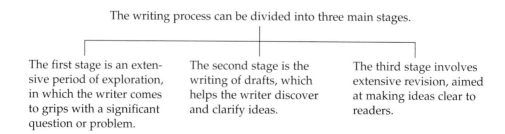

The writing process can be divided into three main stages.

The first stage is an extensive period of exploration, in which the writer comes to grips with a significant question or problem.

The second stage is the writing of drafts, which helps the writer discover and clarify ideas.

The third stage involves extensive revision, aimed at making ideas clear to readers.

Argumentation   When writers of arguments offer two or more parallel reasons for adhering to a particular view or course of action, they typically use the division-into-parallel-parts move. Dao used this large-scale strategy to organize her argument against euthanasia.

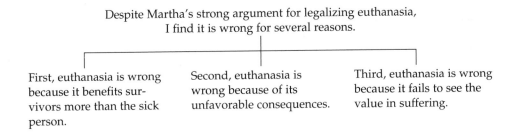

Despite Martha's strong argument for legalizing euthanasia,
I find it is wrong for several reasons.

First, euthanasia is wrong because it benefits survivors more than the sick person.

Second, euthanasia is wrong because of its unfavorable consequences.

Third, euthanasia is wrong because it fails to see the value in suffering.

Using the Parallel-Parts Move to Generate Ideas

The division-into-parallel-parts move can serve as a particularly powerful engine for idea generation. When displayed in a tree diagram, the parallel branches created by the move invite you to think of ideas that will fit laterally and vertically into the diagram. For example, in your first draft you might identify two causes of a phenomenon, but in the act of drafting you might think of a third or even a fourth cause. Simultaneously, you might think of more or stronger ways to develop each of the causes. The number of main branches and supporting branches can be expanded or contracted as you think of new ideas or see ways to combine or recombine old ones.

Ordering the Parallel Parts

Whenever you create two or more parallel parts, you must decide which to put first, which to put in the middle, and which to put last. If the parts are of equal weight and interest, or if you are just exploring their significance, the order doesn't much matter. But if the parts are of different importance, significance, or complexity, their order can be rhetorically important. As a general rule, save the best for last. What constitutes "best" depends on the circumstances. In an argument, the best reason is usually the strongest or the one most apt to appeal to the intended audience. In other cases, the best is usually the most unusual, the most surprising, the most thought provoking, or the most complex, in keeping with the general rule that writers proceed from the familiar to the unfamiliar, from the least surprising to the most surprising.

FOR WRITING AND DISCUSSION

Working individually or in small groups, use the division-into-parallel-parts move to create, organize, and develop ideas to support one or more of the following point sentences. Try using a tree diagram to help guide and stimulate your invention.

1. To study for an exam effectively, a student should follow these (specify a number) steps.
2. Why do U.S. schoolchildren lag so far behind European and Asian children on standardized tests of mathematics and science? One possible cause is . . . (continue).
3. There are several ways for an individual to help the homeless without giving money to panhandlers.
4. TV advertisements for male-oriented products, such as beer, razors, and aftershaves, reflect several different kinds of gender stereotypes.
5. Constant dieting is unhealthy for several reasons.

The Comparison/Contrast Move

A common variation on the division-into-parallel-parts move is the *comparison/contrast move*. To compare or contrast two items, you must first decide on the points of comparison (or contrast). If you are contrasting the political views of two presidential candidates, you might choose to focus on four points of comparison: differences in their foreign policy, differences in economic policy, differences in social policy, and differences in judicial philosophy. You then have two choices for organizing the parts: the *side-by-side pattern,* in which you discuss all of candidate A's views and then all of candidate B's views; or the *back-and-forth pattern,* in which you discuss foreign policy, contrasting A's views with B's views, then move on to economic policy, then social policy, and then judicial philosophy. Here is how these two patterns would appear on a tree diagram.

Side-by-side pattern

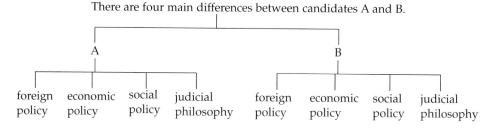

Back-and-forth pattern

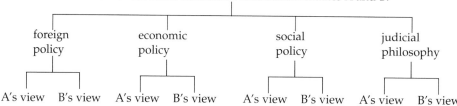

There are no cut-and-dried rules that dictate when to use the side-by-side pattern or the back-and-forth pattern. However, for lengthy comparisons the back-and-forth pattern is often more effective because the reader doesn't have to store great amounts of information in memory. The side-by-side pattern requires readers to remember all the material about A when they come to B, and it is sometimes difficult to keep all the points of comparison clearly in mind.

FOR WRITING AND DISCUSSION

Working individually or in groups, create tree diagrams for possible paragraphs or essays based on one or more of the following point sentences, all of which call for the comparison/contrast move. Be sure to make at least one diagram follow the back-and-forth pattern and make at least one diagram follow the side-by-side pattern.

1. There are several significant differences between childbirth as it is practiced by middle-class American women today and childbirth as it was practiced by middle-class American women prior to the women's liberation movement.
2. To understand U.S. politics, an outsider needs to appreciate some basic differences between Republicans and Democrats.
3. Although they are obviously different on the surface, there are many similarities between the Boy Scouts and a street gang.
4. There are several important differences between closed-form and open-form writing.
5. There are significant differences between the classic 1931 film *Frankenstein* and Mary Shelley's original novel by the same title. (You can substitute any other film/novel comparison.)

A WORD ABOUT STYLE: THE PLAIN VOICE

In Chapter 4 we saw how writers vary their style according to their purpose, their intended audience, and their genre. The closed-form style relies on points-first organization, along with other structural devices that are discussed in Chapter 19, such as forecasting, transitions, and placement of old and new material. The effect of closed-form style is to focus the reader's attention on the subject matter and to achieve maximum clarity, coherence, and transparency. At the extreme closed end of the closed-to-open-form continuum, the writer *as writer* strives to disappear altogether, leaving the reader absorbed exclusively in the essay's subject matter.

Even though closed-form writers share a common desire to stay out of the reader's way, they do vary their voices to suit the rhetorical context. In most cases, they shift voices to *meet* their readers' expectations rather than to defy them, as is common in open-form prose. For example, the prose in an academic journal article can be extremely dense in its use of technical terms and complex sentence structure, but expert readers in that field understand and expect this voice. When writers wish to reach a wider range of readers, they take on a plainer voice, using simpler diction and less complex syntax.

This *plain voice* is well suited to most of the writing you do in college. And, if you are attuned to the natural rhythms and language of your own voice, you should be able to write in the plain style and to sound like a real human being genuinely engaged with a topic.

This plain voice not only helps your readers understand your ideas better, it can even help you create clearer ideas. Sometimes students (and occasionally colleagues) come to our offices with convoluted, confusing drafts—larded with jargon or thesaurus-induced bafflegab that they would never use in real conversation. We get lost, so we ask them to read their drafts aloud and to listen to their voices, hearing whether it sounds like a conversation they might have with a friend. They usually laugh and say no. We then ask them to put the draft down and just *say* what they mean. Inevitably, the oral version is much clearer and more graceful than the draft. We send them back to their desks to write what they said in this plain voice. If you trust your ideas, and trust your reader to be an interested listener who values your ideas, then just talk to that reader when you write. The resulting plain voice will serve you and your audience well.

Summary

This chapter has focused on the structure and style of closed-form writing. We examined how writers organize closed-form prose by stating a risky thesis and then supporting it in a series of paragraphs that place points first and develop them with particulars. This kind of writing is different from the riskless and surpriseless prose that we called "and then," "all about," and engfish writing. To compose tightly constructed closed-form pieces, writers often use the visual power of tree diagrams and the predictive power of set play organizational moves: the for example move; the summary/however move; the division-into-parallel-parts move; and the comparison/contrast move. These structural devices contribute to a clear, coherent style that draws minimal attention to the writer and puts maximum attention on the subject matter. Although closed-form writers vary their voices to fit rhetorical context, a plain voice that sounds like the writer's speaking voice often works best.

The next chapter describes ways to revise closed-form writing. In it we show you how to use organizational principles that ensure clarity, coherence, and transparency by guiding readers smoothly through the sequence of concepts in a closed-form piece.

chapter 19

Revising
Closed-Form Prose

I think the writer ought to help the reader as much as he can without damaging what he wants to say; and I don't think it ever hurts the writer to sort of stand back now and then and look at his stuff as if he were reading it instead of writing it.

—James Jones, *Writer*

In the previous chapter, we explained how closed-form writers organize their material into a hierarchical structure of points and particulars. We also explained that readers transfer material into their long-term memory only when they perceive how particulars are related to a point. In their attempt to perceive meaning, readers have only so much *reader energy*, which they can use either to understand the writer's ideas or to figure out where the writer is going.* When readers get lost, it's often because the relationship between old and new material is confusing. "Whoa, you lost me on the turn," a reader might say. "How does this passage relate to what you just said?" Whereas open-form writers often leave gaps between old and new material on purpose, increasing the reader's active involvement as interpreter of the text, closed-form writers consider such confusions fatal. Their goal is for the reader *not* to get lost. In this chapter, we show you how to revise your rough drafts to ensure that your readers will stay on track.

Studies of reading comprehension suggest that readers can comprehend the meaning of a text more easily when the writer follows four basic principles.

1. *Start and end with the big picture.* Tell readers where they are going before they start the journey, refer to this big picture at key transition points, and refocus on the big picture in your conclusion.

---

*For the useful term *reader energy*, we are indebted to "The Science of Scientific Writing" by George Gopen and Judith Swan, *American Scientist*, 78, 1990, pp. 550–559. In addition, much of our discussion of writing in this chapter is indebted to the work of Joseph Williams, George Gopen, and Geoffrey Colomb. See especially Gregory G. Colomb and Joseph M. Williams, "Perceiving Structure in Professional Prose: A Multiply Determined Experience," in *Writing in Nonacademic Settings*, eds. Lee Odell and Dixie Goswami. New York: The Guilford Press, 1990, pp. 87–128.

2. ***Place points before particulars.***   This principle is closely related to principle 1. Just as readers need to see the whole essay before proceeding to the body paragraphs, they need to see points before particulars, the meaning before the support.

3. ***Signal relationships with transitions.***   Like signposts on a highway, transition words keep the reader on track by indicating relationships among sentences, paragraphs, and larger parts. In longer texts, writers provide resting places that sum up what has been covered so far and show readers their current location in the big picture.

4. ***Bind sentences together by following the old/new contract.***   Clear sentences typically proceed from old to new material. Similarly, the whole text proceeds from the familiar to the unfamiliar, from the simple to the complex, from the common ground to the surprise.

The rest of this chapter discusses ways to apply these principles as you revise.

PRINCIPLE 1: START AND END WITH THE BIG PICTURE

As writing teachers, we are often asked by colleagues to help edit drafts of their articles or books before they submit them for publication. These colleagues usually expect us to ferret out their grammatical mistakes, but grammar is almost never a problem. The most common problem we find is that we can't figure out the big picture. As readers, we need a preview of the whole argument in the introduction, and then we need frequent transitions along the way to keep us on track. In the absence of a big picture, we have to make provisional guesses about what's coming and why. The more reader energy we divert from understanding the writer's ideas to figuring out how the parts relate to each other, the more we feel like a motorist stuck behind a huge truck in a traffic jam, baffled and frustrated by the delays. Passages that give us the big picture lift us up for a brief bird's-eye view of the traffic ahead, giving us hope and helping us understand where we are going.

We mention our colleagues' drafts to assure you that failure to provide the big picture is common in any writer's early drafts. As we explained in Chapter 17, writers often don't know the big picture when they begin drafting so that they must wait until late in the writing process before they can provide the big picture for readers. In the rest of this section we explain how to sketch out the big picture for readers through an effective title and introduction and how to return to the big picture in the essay's conclusion.

Writing Effective Titles

The reader's first indication of an essay's big picture is its title. It is through titles that most writers attract their readers. People typically scan tables of contents, bibliographies, and indexes to select what they want to read by title alone. In a magazine's table of contents, imagine how unhelpful a title such as "My Paper," "Essay 3," or "Democracy" would be. Yet inexperienced writers, forgetting to think about how readers use titles, sometimes select ones such as these.

Your title should provide a brief but detailed overview of what your paper is about. Academic titles are typically longer and more detailed than are titles in popular magazines. They usually follow one of four conventions.

1. Some titles simply state the question that the essay addresses ("Will Patriarchal Management Survive Beyond the Twentieth Century?").
2. Some titles state, often in abbreviated form, the essay's thesis ("The Writer's Audience Is Always a Fiction").
3. Very often the title is a summary of the essay's purpose statement ("The Relationship Between Client Expectation of Improvement and Psychotherapy Outcome").
4. Many titles consist of two parts separated by a colon. To the left of the colon the writer presents key words from the essay's issue or problem or a "mystery phrase" that arouses interest; to the right the author places the essay's question, thesis, or summary of purpose ("Money and Growth: An Alternative Approach"; "Deep Play: Notes on a Balinese Cockfight"; or "Fine Cloth, Cut Carefully: Cooperative Learning in British Columbia").

Although such titles might seem stuffy or overly formal to you, they indicate how much a closed-form writer wishes to preview an article's big picture. Although their titles may be more informal, popular magazines often use these same strategies. Here are some titles from recent issues of *Redbook* and the business magazine *Forbes.*

"Is the Coffee Bar Trend About to Peak?" (question)

"A Man *Can* Take Maternity Leave—And Love It" (abbreviated thesis)

"Why the Department of Education Shouldn't Take over the Student Loan Program" (summary of purpose statement)

"Feed Your Face: Why Your Complexion Needs Vitamins" (two parts linked by colon)

Composing a title for your essay can help you find your focus when you get bogged down in the middle of a draft. When students come to our offices for help with a draft, we usually begin by asking them their proposed title. Such a question forces them to "nutshell" their ideas—to see their project's big picture. Talking about the title inevitably leads to a discussion of the writer's purpose, the problem to be addressed, and the proposed thesis. Having invested all this conceptual effort, students can appreciate how much information their title provides their readers.

Writing Effective Introductions

Introductions serve two purposes—to hook the reader's interest, if such a hook is necessary, and then to pick up where the title leaves off in sketching in the big picture. Closed-form introductions typically describe the problem to be addressed, provide needed background, state the essay's thesis or purpose, and preview the essay's structure, sometimes including a summary of its argument. In a short essay, the introduction may comprise simply the opening paragraph, but in longer essays introductions typically require several paragraphs. Writers often wait until late in the writing process to draft an introduction because, as you saw in Chapter 17, these big-picture features are often in flux during the writer's early drafts.

Whether you do it early in the process as a way to focus your initial plan or late in the process after your ideas have solidified, writing the introduction forces you to focus on your essay's big picture. If you have trouble writing introductions—and many writers do—guide questions can help. Before writing your introduction, take fifteen minutes or so to write out exploratory answers to the following questions.

1. What is your thesis statement?
2. What question does your thesis answer?
3. Why is this a problematic and significant question? What attempts have others made to answer it (include your own previous attempts)? (Freewrite for at least three to four minutes on this one.)

4. Do you imagine that your reader is already interested in this question? If not, how could you make this question interesting for your reader? (Freewrite for several minutes.)

5. How much prior knowledge do you think your reader has about this topic? How much background information will your reader need to understand the problem and appreciate the conversation that your paper is joining?
6. Finish this sentence: My purpose in this paper is

   _____ .

7. Fill in the blanks: Before reading my essay, I expect my reader to believe this about my topic: _____ ;
   after reading my essay, I want my reader to believe this about my topic:

   _____ .

8. Finish this sentence: I can describe the structure of my essay as follows:

   _____ .

These questions will help you get unstuck because they generate all the information you will need to write an initial draft of your introduction.

Typical Features of a Closed-Form Introduction

In Chapter 2 we noted that a typical introduction to an academic article has three basic features: a question or problem to be investigated, a tentative answer to the question, and a structural or organizational map of the article. As we promised, we will now examine these features—along with a few others—in more detail.

Feature 1: An Opening Lead or Hook Appropriate to Your Rhetorical Context

The lead or hook comprises the opening sentences of the essay and is aimed at capturing the reader's interest in the subject. In the Thomas Szasz's introduction you examined in Chapter 2 (p. 26), the thesis was so revolutionary that the writer did not need any other devices to snag his readers' interest. But when you are writing for general audiences, you may need to hook your readers in the opening sentences through a dramatic vignette, a startling fact or statistic, an arresting quotation, or an interesting scene. *Reader's Digest* articles are famous for their interest-grabbing leads. Here is a typical opening from a *Reader's Digest* article.

> The first faint tremor rippled through the city just before ten o'clock that warm summer night. Then came the sound—as if something heavy was rolling along the ground. The tremor intensified into a rapid jerking, sending dishes crashing and tables and chairs dancing. Thousands of frightened people ran out of their houses into the darkness.
>
> Dawn's light showed the earthquake's horror. At least 60 lay dead, many buried under collapsed buildings. Virtually every home was damaged.
>
> This wasn't just another trembler along one of California's many faults, like the devastating quake that shook the Los Angeles area last January 17. It was one that rocked Charleston, S.C., on August 31, 1886.
>
> While many Americans believe serious earthquakes happen only in California, scientific research confirms that the risk in other states may be higher than anyone thought.
>
> —Lowell Ponte, "Earthquakes: Closer Than You Think"

With its dramatic account of an actual earthquake, and its subsequent revelation that the earthquake occurred in South Carolina a century ago, this opening could prove irresistible to readers suddenly concerned about their own risk of being caught in an earthquake. Done responsibly, such leads can generate readers' interest in significant topics that they might otherwise ignore. Done irresponsibly, such leads can divert readers' attention from weaknesses in the rest of the article (shaky claims, scanty evidence). A boffo lead ought to be followed by a responsible treatment of its subject.

Most academic writing opens less dramatically than does this example, usually beginning directly with the next feature—the problem to be examined.

Feature 2: Explanation of the Question to Be Investigated Readers are intrinsically interested in questions; once they become engaged with the question you address, most will read on to see how you answer it. The question is the common ground that you share with your reader at the outset; it summarizes the conversation that your essay joins. You may want to state the question directly, or you may want to imply it, letting the reader formulate it from context.

Unless the problem or question is very familiar, you will need to show your readers both what makes the question problematic, that is, why it hasn't already been solved, and what makes it significant, that is, why it is a problem worth solving. As Chapter 1 showed, to demonstrate why a question is problematic, writers often summarize differing views of experts, show why a commonly posed answer to the question is unsatisfactory, or otherwise show what aspects of the problem need more attention, often through a review of the literature. To reveal a problem's significance, writers point either to the benefits that will come from solving it or to the negative consequences of leaving it unsolved. (See Chapter 1 for further discussion of academic problems.)

Feature 3: Background Information   Sometimes your readers may need background information before they can appreciate the problem your paper addresses or the approach you take—a definition of key terms, a summary of events leading up to the problem at issue, factual details needed for basic understanding of the problem, and so forth. When readers need extensive information, writers sometimes provide it in the first main section of the paper *following* the introduction.

Feature 4: A Preview of the Whole Through a Thesis Statement, Purpose Statement, Blueprint Statement, or Actual Summary of What's Coming   As you saw in Chapters 2 and 3, a thesis statement summarizes the writer's answer to the problem, usually in a single sentence.* A *purpose* statement, in contrast, announces the writer's intention without necessarily summarizing the argument. A purpose statement typically begins with a phrase such as "My purpose is to . . . " or "In the following paragraphs I wish to . . . " and provides a statement of the author's reasons for writing the essay—the purpose or intention. A *blueprint* statement describes the form of the upcoming essay, usually announcing the number of main parts and describing the function or purpose of each one. In long articles, authors may provide a full-scale summary of what's coming. Explicit purpose statements, blueprint statements, and full-scale summaries are common in academic and business writing, but are less common in informal or popular essays.

For a simple illustration of this feature, let's return to Dao's essay on euthanasia from Chapter 18. In her introduction, Dao could have used any of the following options for previewing the whole:

Brief thesis statement (main point only, with no summary of supporting argument)

Example   Euthanasia is wrong.

Detailed thesis statement (summarizes whole argument)

Example   Although my friend Martha presents good arguments in favor of euthanasia, I am opposed to euthanasia because it benefits the living more than the sick, because it leads to dangerous consequences, and because it fails to appreciate the value of suffering.

Purpose statement

Example   My purpose in this essay is to present several reasons that euthanasia is wrong.

---

*Sometimes a writer will lay out only the question or problem that the essay addresses and delay the thesis until later in the essay. This powerful structure, which lets the argument slowly unfold and keeps its final point a mystery, is discussed in Chapter 20 (p. 512). Such a strategy moves the essay's structure closer to the open end of the closed-to-open continuum.

Blueprint statement

Example   First I show how euthanasia benefits the living more than the sick; then I discuss the bad consequences of euthanasia; finally I argue that euthanasia fails to acknowledge the value of suffering.

But which of these options should Dao choose? A rule of thumb is to provide the least amount of mapping necessary for reader comprehension, especially for writing aimed at popular audiences. Hence Dao elected to place only a brief thesis statement in her introduction.* However, academic writing, as well as most legal, technical, and business prose, tends to include explicit mapping in the introduction.

FOR WRITING AND DISCUSSION

What follows is the introduction to a closed-form essay by paleontologist Stephen Jay Gould. Gould writes for general audiences interested in the philosophy and history of science, especially the field of evolutionary biology. Read the introduction carefully. Then, working in small groups or as a whole class, answer the questions that follow.

The human mind delights in finding pattern—so much so that we often mistake coincidence or forced analogy for profound meaning. No other habit of thought lies so deeply within the soul of a small creature trying to make sense of a complex world not constructed for it.... No other error of reason stands so doggedly in the way of any forthright attempt to understand some of the world's most essential aspects—the tortuous paths of history, the unpredictability of complex systems, and the lack of causal connection among events superficially similar.

Numerical coincidence is a common path to intellectual perdition in our quest for meaning. We delight in catalogs of disparate items united by the same number, and often feel in our gut that some unity must underlie it all. [Gould then gives numerous examples of people's fascination with certain "mystical" numbers, such as the numbers seven and five.]

In this essay, I shall discuss two taxonomic systems (theories of classification of organisms) popular in the decades just before Darwin published the *Origin of the Species*. Both assumed reasons other than evolution for the ordering of organisms; both proposed a scheme based on the number five for placing organisms into a hierarchy of groups and subgroups. Both argued that such a simple numerical regularity must record an intrinsic pattern in nature, not a false order imposed by human hope upon a more complex reality. I shall describe these systems and then discuss how evolutionary theory undermined their rationale and permanently changed the science of taxonomy by making such simple numerical schemes inconsistent with

---

*Another choice would be to ask a *thesis question:* "The case of Martha's grandmother raises a troubling question: Should euthanasia be legalized?" Using this approach, Martha wouldn't tell readers where she stood until later in her essay, treating the body of her essay as exploration. On our continuum from closed-to-open forms of writing (p. 14), this approach would create a *delayed-thesis* essay, or, if Dao truly couldn't make up her mind, it might create a thesis-seeking exploratory essay rather than a thesis-asserting argument.

a new view of nature. This important change in scientific thought embodies a general message about the character of history and the kinds of order that a world built by history, and not by preordained plan, can (and cannot) express.

—Stephen Jay Gould, "The Rule of Five"

1. What question or problem does this article address?
2. What makes this problem both problematic and significant? In Gould's view, why should anyone care that scientists used to interpret the universe as governed by a preordained plan based on the number five?
3. What strategy does Gould use in the opening lead to engage readers' interest?
4. Identify the previewing features in this introduction (thesis statement, purpose statement, blueprint statement, partial summary of what's coming).
5. What is the predicted organization of Gould's article?

The following passage occurred at the end of the introduction for a college research paper on theories of education. Using cues about structure and meaning in this previewing passage, create the top branches of a tree diagram for this essay.

My purpose in the following paragraphs is to reveal the complexity of the arguments surrounding the open curriculum controversy. I will examine first the view of three educators influenced by Rousseau--A. S. Neill, John Holt, and Jerry Farber. Each of these people believes that the goal of education should be the joyful pursuit of self-discovery and that children should be free to explore their own natural interests. I will then turn to two opponents of the open curriculum--Max Rafferty and B. F. Skinner. Rafferty believes that the goal of education is the acquisition of intellectual skills rather than self-discovery. B. F. Skinner believes that the concept of freedom is an illusion and thus opposes the notion that students can "choose" their own curriculum.

Writing Effective Conclusions

Although it may seem odd to include conclusions in a discussion about starting with the big picture, it's really not. Conclusions and introductions aren't so much opposites as complements. In both, writers are concerned with the essay as a whole more than with any given part. In a conclusion, the writer attempts to bring a sense of completeness and closure to the profusion of points and particulars laid out in the body of the essay. The writer is particularly concerned with helping the reader to move from the parts back to the big picture and to understand the importance or significance of the essay.

If you are having trouble figuring out how to conclude an essay, consider the following guide questions, which are designed to stimulate thought about how to conclude and to help you determine which model best suits your situation.

1. How long and complex is your essay? Is it long enough or complex enough that readers might benefit from a summary of your main points?
2. What's the most important point (or points) you want your reader to remember about your essay? How long ago in the essay did you state that point? Would it be useful to restate that point as succinctly and powerfully as possible?
3. Do you know of an actual instance, illustration, or example of your main point that would give it added heft?
4. What larger principle stands behind your main point? Or, what must your audience accept as true in order to accept your main point? How would you defend that assumption if someone were to call it into question?
5. Why is your main point significant? Why are the ideas in your paper important and worth your audience's consideration? What larger issues does your topic relate to or touch on? Could you show how your topic relates to a larger and more significant topic? What might that topic be?
6. If your audience accepts your thesis, where do you go next? What is the next issue or question to be examined? What further research is needed? Conversely, do you have any major reservations, unexpressed doubts, or "All bets are off if X is the case" provisos you'd like to admit? What do you *not* know about your topic that reduces your certainty in your thesis?
7. How much antagonism or skepticism toward your position do you anticipate? If a great deal, would it be feasible to delay your thesis, solution, or proposal until the very end of the paper?

Because many writers find conclusions challenging to write, we offer the following six possible models.

The Simple Summary

The most common, though often not the most effective, kind of conclusion is a simple summary, in which the writer recaps what has just been said. This approach is useful in a long or complex essay or in an instructional text that focuses on concepts to be learned. We use summary conclusions for most of the chapters in this text. In a short, easy-to-follow essay, however, a summary conclusion can be dull and may even annoy readers who are expecting something more significant, but a brief summary followed by a more artful concluding strategy can often be effective.

The Pan-to-a-Larger-Landscape, or Web, Conclusion

A particularly effective concluding strategy is to draw the reader's attention to the importance or significance of your topic or issue by showing how it fits into the larger scheme of things. This strategy is analogous to a filmmaker's pan-to-a-larger-landscape ending. Two lovers, having struggled heroically throughout the film to achieve union with one another, finally kiss as the camera slowly pulls away, showing them situated against the sea, mountains, or sky. The lovers' feelings for each other are, by implication, as timeless and grand as nature itself. By analogy, when you pan to a larger landscape, you show your topic against a background of a larger and more significant topic, revealing the importance or relevance of your own topic.

Another metaphor for this effect is a spider web. If you touch a spider web at any point, your touch can be felt at other points on the web. By analogy, the question or issue you examine is connected to a web of other questions and issues. If your essay focuses on one part of the web, you can show in your conclusion how your issue touches another part of the web. You see your essay as a whole, but place it in the context of a still larger whole, just as one intersection on a spider web is part of a much larger structure.

An essay analyzing the effectiveness of pass-fail grading could conclude by tying that particular issue to the larger context of the success of the school system and the values it is trying to instill in students. Alternatively, the same issue might be tied to a philosophic question about human motivation: Do humans require extrinsic rewards and punishments to pursue learning or can they pursue it for its own sake? To take another example, an essay on gun control could conclude by relating gun control to the larger issue of congressional independence versus the influence of lobbies or of individual rights versus the authority of government.

Although a web conclusion can provide a particularly satisfying form of closure, you need to use this strategy carefully. One danger of shifting to a larger context is that the reader may perceive it as a new, unrelated topic unless you make the connection between your thesis and your larger context explicit.

The Proposal Conclusion

Another option, often used in analyses and arguments, is a *proposal conclusion,* which calls for action. A proposal conclusion states the action that the writer believes needs to be taken and briefly demonstrates the advantages of this action over alternative actions or describes its beneficial consequences. If your paper analyzes the consequences of shifting from a graduated to a flat-rate income tax, your conclusion may recommend an action, such as adopting, modifying, or opposing the flat tax. A slight variation is the *call-for-future-study conclusion,* which indicates what else needs to be known or resolved before a proposal can be offered. Such conclusions are especially common in scientific writing.

The Scenic or Anecdotal Conclusion

Popular writers often use a *scenic* or *anecdotal conclusion,* in which a scene or brief story illustrates a theme's significance without stating it explicitly. A paper examining the current trend against involuntary hospitalization of the mentally ill homeless might end by describing a former mental patient, now an itinerant homeless person, collecting bottles in a park. Such scenes can help the reader experience directly the emotional significance of the topic analyzed in the body of the paper.

The Hook and Return

A related variety of conclusion is the *hook and return,* in which the ending of the essay returns to something introduced in the opening hook or lead. If the lead of your essay is a vivid illustration of a problem—perhaps a scene or an anecdote—then your conclusion might return to the same scene or story, but with some variation to illustrate the significance of the essay. This sense of return can give your essay a strong feeling of unity.

The Delayed-Thesis Conclusion

This variety of conclusion delays the thesis until the end of the essay. Rather than stating the thesis, the introduction merely states the problem, giving the body of the essay an open, exploratory, "let's think through this together" feel. Typically, the body of the paper examines alternative solutions or approaches to the problem and leaves the writer's own answer—the thesis—unstated until the end. This approach is especially effective when writing about highly complex or divisive issues on which you want to avoid taking a stand until all sides have been fairly presented.

These six types of conclusion are neither exhaustive nor mutually exclusive. It is possible to imagine a conclusion that mixes several of these types—a few sentences summarizing your essay, a short passage showing the relationship of your topic to some broader issues, a brief call to action, and a final concluding scene. In determining an effective conclusion, you need to assess your audience's attitude toward your thesis, its understanding of your topic, the length and complexity of your essay, and what you want to happen as a result of people's reading your essay. Review the guide questions at the beginning of this section to help determine the most appropriate conclusion for you.

PRINCIPLE 2: PLACE POINTS BEFORE PARTICULARS

We have discussed strategies for providing the big picture at the beginning and end of the essay through effective titles, introductions, and conclusions. Now we turn to a key strategy for helping the reader see the big picture throughout the middle of the essay. In this section we show how closed-form prose is most clear when the writer places topic sentences near the beginning of each paragraph. Such sentences not only predict the particulars that are to come in the paragraph, but also provide links back to the essay's big picture, thereby helping the reader relate each new paragraph to the writer's evolving argument.

Although closed-form paragraphs generally open with topic sentences, writers' rough drafts often lack them. In rough drafts point sentences are sometimes missing entirely; at other times they are misplaced or they misrepresent what the paragraph actually does or says. In such cases, readers momentarily lose the connection between what they are reading and the big picture. The reader's energy is divided between trying to understand the particulars and trying to determine what point they support. During revision, you should check your body paragraphs carefully to be sure you have written clear topic sentences and placed them strategically.

Putting Topic Sentences at the Beginning of Paragraphs

To see why writers place topic sentences at the beginnings of paragraphs, consider the revisions in the following paragraph from an early draft of the student essay opposing carpeting dorm rooms (Chapter 17, pp. 439–40).

*Carpet Paper—
Revised Draft*

Another reason for the university not to buy carpets is the cost.
∧ According to Rachel Jones, Assistant Director of Housing Services, the initial purchase and installation of carpeting would cost $300 per room. Considering the number of rooms in the three residence halls, carpeting amounts to a substantial investment. Additionally, once the carpets are installed, the university would need to maintain them through the purchase of more vacuum cleaners and shampoo machines. This money would be better spent on other dorm improvements that would benefit more residents, such as expanded kitchen facilities and improved recreational ~~space. Thus carpets would be too~~ expensive.

In the original draft, the writer states the point at the end of the paragraph. In his revision he states the point in an opening topic sentence that links back to the thesis statement, which promises "several reasons" that the university should not buy carpets for the dorms. The words "another reason" thus link the topic sentence to the argument's big picture.

Revising Paragraphs for Unity

In addition to placing topic sentences at the heads of paragraphs, writers often need to revise topic sentences to better match what the paragraph actually says, or revise the paragraph to better match the topic sentence. Paragraphs have unity when all of their sentences develop what is predicted in the topic sentence. Paragraphs in rough drafts are often not unified because they reflect the writer's shifting, evolving, thinking-while-writing process. Consider the following paragraph from an early draft of Dao's argument (see Chapter 18) against euthanasia, which her peer reviewer labeled "confusing." What makes it confusing?

*Dao's Paper—Early
Draft Paragraph*

First, euthanasia is wrong because no one has the right to take the life of another person. Some people say that euthanasia or suicide will end suffering and pain. But what proofs do they have for such a claim? Death is still mysterious to us; therefore, we do not

```
know whether death will end suffering and pain or not. What seems to

be the real claim is that death to those with illnesses will end our

pain. Such pain involves worrying over them, paying their medical

bills, and giving up so much of our time. Their deaths end our pain

rather than theirs. And for that reason, euthanasia is a selfish act,

for the outcome of euthanasia benefits us, the nonsufferers, more.

Once the sufferers pass away, we can go back to our normal lives.
```

The paragraph opens with an apparent topic sentence: "Euthanasia is wrong because no one has the right to take the life of another person." But the rest of the paragraph doesn't focus on that point. Instead, it focuses on how euthanasia benefits the survivors more than the sick person. Dao had two choices: to revise the paragraph to fit the topic sentence or to revise the topic sentence to fit the paragraph. Here is her revision, which includes a different topic sentence and an additional sentence mid-paragraph to keep particulars focused on the opening point.

```
      First, euthanasia is wrong because it benefits the survivors more than the sick person.
      ₳First, euthanasia is wrong because no one has the right to take

the life of another person. Some people say that euthanasia or sui-
                    the sick person's
cide will end₳suffering and pain. But what proofs do they have for

such a claim? Death is still mysterious to us; therefore, we do not
            Moreover, modern pain killers can relieve most of the pain a sick person has to endure.
know whether death will end suffering and pain or not.₳What seems to

be the real claim is that death to those with illnesses will end our

pain. Such pain involves worrying over them, paying their medical

bills, and giving up so much of our time. Their deaths end our pain

rather than theirs. And for that reason, euthanasia is a selfish act,

for the outcome of euthanasia benefits us, the nonsufferers, more.

Once the sufferers pass away, we can go back to our normal lives.
```

Dao unifies this paragraph by keeping all its parts focused on her main point: "Euthanasia . . . benefits the survivors more than the sick person." You may not be persuaded by her argument, but at least her point is now clear.

A paragraph may lack unity for a variety of reasons. It may shift to a new direction in the middle, or one or two sentences may simply be irrelevant to the point. The key is to make sure that all the sentences in the paragraph fulfill the topic sentence's prediction.

PRINCIPLE 3: SIGNAL RELATIONSHIPS WITH TRANSITIONS

One of the best ways to keep readers on track is to signal the relationship between sentences and larger parts with transitions. Transitions are like signposts that signal where the road is turning. Without them, a reader can't predict where an argument might be headed. Transitions limit the possible directions that an unfolding argument might take. Consider how the use of "therefore" and "nevertheless" limits the range of possibilities in the following examples:

While on vacation, Suzie caught the chicken pox. Therefore, _____ .

While on vacation, Suzie caught the chicken pox. Nevertheless, _____ .

"Therefore" signals to the reader that what follows is a consequence. Most readers will imagine a sentence similar to this one:

Therefore, she spent her vacation lying in bed itching, feverish, and miserable.

In contrast, "nevertheless" signals an unexpected or denied consequence, so the reader might anticipate a sentence such as this:

Nevertheless, she enjoyed her two weeks off, thanks to a couple of bottles of calamine lotion, some good books, and a big easy chair overlooking the ocean.

Using Common Transition Words to Signal Relationships

Transition words, such as "therefore" and "nevertheless," signal logical relationships between sentences and paragraphs and help to speed readers' comprehension of texts. Here is a list of the most common transition words and phrases and what they signal to the reader*:

Words or Phrases	What They Signal
first, second, third, next, finally, earlier, later, meanwhile, afterwards	*sequence*—First we went to dinner; then we went to the movies.
that is, in other words, to put it another way, — (dash) , : (colon)	*restatement*—He's so hypocritical that you can't trust a word he says. To put it another way, he's a complete phony.
rather, instead	*replacement*—We shouldn't use the money to buy opera tickets; rather, we should use it for a nice gift.
for example, for instance, a case in point	*example*—Mr. Carlysle is very generous. For example, he gave the janitors a special holiday gift.
because, since, for	*reason*—Taxes on cigarettes are unfair because they place a higher tax burden on the working class.

*Although all the words on the list serve as transitions or connectives, grammatically they are not all equivalent; some are coordinating conjunctions, some are subordinating conjunctions, and some are transition adverbs. Each different kind of word requires a different grammatical construction and punctuation.

Words or Phrases *(cont.)*	What They Signal *(cont.)*
therefore, hence, so, consequently, thus, then, as a result, accordingly, as a consequence	*consequences*—I failed to turn in the essay; therefore I flunked the course.
still, nevertheless	*denied consequence*—The teacher always seemed grumpy in class; nevertheless, I really enjoyed the course.
although, even though, granted that (with still)	*concession*—Even though the teacher was always grumpy, I still enjoyed the course.
in comparison, likewise, similarly	*similarity*—Teaching engineering takes a lot of patience. Likewise, so does teaching accounting.
however, in contrast, conversely, on the other hand, but	*contrast*—I disliked my old backpack immensely; however, I really like this new one.
in addition, also, too, moreover, furthermore	*addition*—Today's cars are much safer than those of ten years ago. In addition, they get better gas mileage.
in brief, in sum, in conclusion, finally, to sum up, to conclude	*conclusion or summary*—In sum, the plan presented by Mary is the best choice.

FOR WRITING AND DISCUSSION

This exercise is designed to show you how transition words govern relationships between ideas. Working in groups or on your own, finish each of the following statements using ideas of your own invention. Make sure what you add fits the logic of the transition word.

1. Writing is difficult; therefore _____ .
2. Writing is difficult; however, _____ .
3. Writing is difficult because _____ .
4. Writing is difficult. For example, _____ .
5. Writing is difficult. To put it another way, _____ .
6. Writing is difficult. Likewise, _____ .
7. Although writing is difficult, _____ .
8. _____ . In sum, writing is difficult.

In the following paragraph, various kinds of linking devices have been omitted. Fill in the blanks with words or phrases that would make the paragraph coherent. Clues are provided in brackets.

Writing an essay is a difficult process for most people. _____ [contrast] the process can be made easier if you learn to practice three simple techniques. _____ [sequence] learn the technique of nonstop writing. When you are first trying to think of ideas for an essay, put your pen on your paper and write nonstop for ten or fifteen minutes without ever letting your pen leave the paper. Stay loose and free. Let your pen follow the waves of thought. Don't worry about grammar or spelling. _____ [concession] this technique won't work for everyone, it helps many people get a good cache of ideas to draw on. A _____ [sequence] technique is to write your rough draft rapidly without worrying about being perfect. Too many writers try to get their drafts right the first time. _____ [contrast] by learning to live with imperfection, you will save yourself headaches and a wastepaper basket full of crumpled paper. Think of your first rough draft as a path hacked out of the jungle—as part of an exploration, not as a completed highway. As a _____ [sequence] technique, try printing out a triple-spaced copy to allow space for revision. Many beginning writers don't leave enough space to revise. _____ [consequence] these writers never get in the habit of crossing out chunks of their rough draft and writing revisions in the blank spaces. After you have revised your rough draft until it is too messy to work from any more, you can _____ [sequence] enter your changes into your word processor and print out a fresh draft, again setting your text on triple space. The resulting blank space invites you to revise.

Writing Major Transitions Between Parts

In long closed-form pieces, writers often put *resting places* between major parts—transition passages that allow readers to shift their attention momentarily away from the matter at hand to a sense of where they've been and where they're going. Often such passages sum up the preceding major section, refer back to the essay's thesis statement or opening blueprint plan, and then preview the next major section. The longer the essay, the more readers appreciate such passages. Here are three typical examples.

> So far I have looked at a number of techniques that can help people identify debilitating assumptions that block their self-growth. In the next section, I examine ways to question and overcome these assumptions.

> Now that the difficulty of the problem is fully apparent, our next step is to examine some of the solutions that have been proposed.

> These, then, are the major theories explaining why Hamlet delays. But let's see what happens to Hamlet if we ask the question in a slightly different way. In this next section, we shift our critical focus, looking not at Hamlet's actions, but at his language.

Signaling Transitions with Headings and Subheadings

In many genres, particularly scientific and technical reports, government documents, business proposals, textbooks, and other long articles in magazines or scholarly journals, writers conventionally break up long stretches of text with headings and subheadings. Headings are often set in different type sizes and fonts, and mark transition points between major parts and subparts of the argument.

Headings serve some of the same purposes served by the title of the essay or article; they encapsulate the big picture of a part or section and preview its contents. They may also relate back to the thesis statement, but sometimes, especially in scientific and social scientific articles, they are generic section markers, such as

"Introduction," "Methods," "Findings," and so forth. Writers are apt to compose their headings late in the writing process, and the act of doing so may lead to further revisions. When you add headings, ask yourself questions such as these: Just where *are* the major transition points in the text? What would be a good title or umbrella that summarizes or previews this part? How clearly do my levels of headings relate to each other?

Writing descriptive headings is almost as demanding as writing a thesis statement. Because composing headings and subheadings is such a powerful exercise, we often ask our students to write headings for their papers, even if headings are not conventionally used for the type of writing they are doing. (For an example of headings in a student paper, see Mary Turla's research paper in Chapter 23, pp. 583–96.)

PRINCIPLE 4: BIND SENTENCES TOGETHER BY FOLLOWING THE OLD/NEW CONTRACT

The final principle for writing clear closed-form prose is the *old/new contract*. The old/new contract asks writers to begin sentences with something old—something that links back to what has gone before—and then to end sentences with new information that advances the argument. Following this principle creates an effect called *coherence*, which is closely related to unity. Whereas *unity* refers to the clear relationship between the body of a paragraph and its topic sentence, between the parts and the whole, *coherence* refers to the clear relationship between one sentence and the next, between part and part.

FOR WRITING AND DISCUSSION

To understand how the old/new contract makes reading easier, read the following version of the paragraph you just read, deliberately revised to violate the old/new contract.

> The old/new contract is a final principle for writing clear closed-form prose. Beginning your sentences with something old—something that links back to what has gone before—and then ending your sentence with new information that advances the argument is what the old/new contract asks writers to do. An effect called *coherence*, which is closely related to *unity*, is created by following this principle. Whereas the clear relationship between the topic sentence and the body of the paragraph, between the parts and the whole, is what *unity* refers to, the clear relationship between one sentence and the next is what *coherence* refers to.

In your own words, write out a brief explanation of the old/new contract and illustrate it with one example from this last passage. Describe the difference between the original version of your example and the altered version and explain what makes the original version easier to follow.

Then, in small groups or as a whole class, share your explanations and examples.

If you are like most readers, you have to concentrate much harder to understand the altered version because it violates the way your mind normally processes information. If a writer doesn't begin a sentence with old material, readers have to hold the new material in suspension until they have figured out how it connects to what has gone before. Eventually they can make sense out of the passage, but doing so expends considerably more reader energy by shifting readers' concentration from what's being said to how the parts connect.

Placing Old Information in the Topic Position

The key to making the old/new contract work is placing old information near the beginning of sentences in what we call the *topic position*. Readers associate topics with the beginnings of sentences simply because in the standard English sentence the topic (or subject) comes before the predicate—hence the notion of a "contract" by which writers agree not to fool or frustrate their readers by breaking with the normal order of things. The contract dictates that the writer put the new material, which advances the argument, in the last part of the sentence—the *stress* position—only after starting readers off with familiar material.

What exactly do we mean by "old" or "familiar" information? We don't mean material that readers have known about for a long time. We mean material that readers have just read and stored in memory. When the writer provides a previewing or mapping passage in the introduction, part of what the reader stores as old information is expectation for what's coming—an empty array to be filled in later in the essay. When you follow the old/new contract, each new sentence in your essay must in some way link itself back to this old, familiar material. You can create these links in one of three ways: (1) linking back to a key word or concept in the immediately preceding sentence; (2) linking back to a key word or concept in an earlier point (or subpoint) sentence; or (3) linking back to a previous prediction about structure, perhaps in a thesis or blueprint statement. We used all three linking devices in the opening paragraph of this section.

> The final principle for writing clear closed-form prose [links back to our opening blueprint statement (p. 465) telling readers we are going to discuss "four principles" for creating closed-form prose; "final" tells readers that we are starting the last main part of the chapter] is the *old/new contract*. The old/new contract [links back to key word in preceding sentence] asks writers to begin sentences with something old—something that links back to what has gone before—and then to end sentences with new information that advances the argument. Following this principle [links back to a key word in the paragraph's opening (topic) sentence] creates an effect called *coherence*, which is closely related to *unity*. Whereas *unity* [repeats last word of previous sentence] refers to the clear relationship between the body of a paragraph and its topic sentence, between the parts and the whole, *coherence* refers to the clear relationship between one sentence and the next, between part and part.

Since English sentences divide into two main parts—the subject and the predicate—the old information most commonly goes in the subject slot and the new information in the predicate slot.

> A useful strategy for improving the coherence of your prose is to follow the old/new contract. *The old/new contract* means . . . .

However, there are alternative ways of putting old information at the front of a sentence. You can place it in an introductory clause—

> A useful strategy for improving the coherence of your prose is to follow the old/new contract. *When you follow the old/new contract*, you . . . .

—or in a phrase, such as a prepositional phrase, near the beginning of the sentence—

> A useful strategy for improving the coherence of your prose is to follow the old/new contract. The advantage *of such a contract* is that . . . .

In the rest of this section we provide advice on how to use the old/new contract as you revise for clarity and coherence.

Using a Variety of Strategies to Link Back to Old Information

To illustrate in greater detail various strategies for linking sentences according to the old/new contract, we use the following passage from an *Atlantic Monthly* article on a proposed federal crime-prevention program using community policing. The paragraph that precedes this passage describes a plan to help cities hire 100,000 new police officers.

> The 100,000 new officers are specifically intended to help revitalize neighborhood life; they're supposed to be trained in community policing, a progressive model of police work embraced, at least rhetorically, by practically everyone. Community policing calls for a partnership of the police and local residents, and expands the focus of the police from arrests to intervention and preventive "problem solving." In its most reductive form, this approach is viewed as a shift from deploying police officers in patrol cars that randomly cruise the streets and answer calls for assistance to deploying them on the street and encouraging them to establish ongoing relationships with residents. Community policing is often described simplistically as a return to cops on the beat who are integral parts of the neighborhood.
>
> In its sophisticated form, however, community policing entails what William Bratton, formerly Boston's and now New York City's police commissioner, has called a "sea change" in the concept of policing, from reactive, "incident-oriented" law enforcement to a hybrid of enforcement and community-service work aimed at crime prevention. It envisions the demilitarization of police departments, a shifting of authority down through management to the ranks, so that cops on the street will have more discretion and can go beyond making arrests to analyzing underlying problems and responding to them with community cooperation. At its most cosmic, community policing requires teaching critical-thinking skills to peo-

ple who have traditionally been taught to play by the book. Advocates of community policing stress that it is not simply a new program or strategy but a transformative new philosophy—what a New Age cop might call a paradigm shift.

—Wendy Kaminer, "Crime and Community"

Let's look at various sentence-level strategies used by this writer to link back to old information.

Repeating a Key Word

The most common way to open with something old is to repeat a key word from the preceding sentence or an earlier point sentence. Let's look at the construction of sentences in the *Atlantic Monthly* passage. The paragraph that precedes our quoted passage describes a new federal crime bill that will help cities hire 100,000 police officers. The next paragraph therefore opens with old information: "The 100,000 new officers are specifically . . . ." The new information in this sentence is that these officers are to be trained in community policing. Subsequently, the concept of community policing, which is new information in the first sentence, becomes old information in the rest of the passage. Six of the eight sentences in the passage repeat the phrase "community policing" early in the sentence either as the subject or as the object of an opening prepositional phrase (for example, "advocates of community policing"). The remaining two sentences open with "it" or "this approach," both of which refer to "community policing"—see the next two strategies.

Using Pronouns to Refer to Key Words

Another strategy is to use pronouns that refer to a key earlier noun. In our sample passage the words "community policing" recur six times; the pronouns "it" and "its," referring to community policing, recur five times. "In *its* most reductive form," "In *its* sophisticated form," "*It* envisions the demilitarization," "At *its* most cosmic," and "Advocates of community policing stress that *it* is . . . ."

Summarizing, Rephrasing, or Restating Earlier Concepts

Writers can link back to a preceding sentence by using a word or phrase that summarizes or restates it. A good example of this strategy occurs near the beginning of the sample passage.

> Community policing calls for a partnership of the police and local residents, and expands the focus of the police from arrests to intervention and preventive "problem solving." In its most reductive form, *this approach* is viewed as a shift from . . . .

The words "this approach" summarize the whole concept conveyed in the preceding sentence.

Echoing an Earlier Sentence Structure

Another strategy for linking back to old information is to echo an earlier sentence structure rather than to repeat a key word. The reader's memory of the earlier structure helps tie the new back to the old. In our passage, note how a sequence of prepositional phrases creates an echolike effect linking new back to old.

> Community policing calls for a partnership of the police and local residents. . . . *In its most reductive form,* this approach . . . . *In its sophisticated form,* however, . . . *At its most cosmic,* community policing . . . .

These strategies give you a powerful way to check and revise your prose. Comb your drafts for gaps between sentences where you have violated the old/new contract. If the opening of a new sentence doesn't refer back to an earlier word, phrase, or concept, your reader could derail, so use what you have learned to repair the tracks.

FOR WRITING AND DISCUSSION

Here is an early draft paragraph from a student's essay in favor of building more nuclear reactors for electricity. This paragraph attempts to refute an argument that building nuclear power plants is prohibitively expensive. Read the draft carefully and then do the exercises that follow.

[1] One argument against nuclear power plants is that they are too expensive to build. [2] But this argument is flawed. [3] On March 28, 1979, Three Mile Island (TMI) Nuclear Station suffered a meltdown. [4] It was the worst accident in commercial nuclear power operation in the United States. [5] During its investigation of TMI the Presidential Commission became highly critical of the U.S. Nuclear Regulatory Commission (NRC), which responded by generating hundreds of new safety regulations. [6] These regulations forced utility companies to modify reactors during construction. [7] Since all the changes had to be made on half-completed plants, the cost of design time, material, and personnel had to be very large. [8] The standards set by the NRC would not be acceptable to a utility company. [9] All reactors now being built had been ordered before 1973. [10] With all the experience gained by research here in the U.S. and overseas, the licensing process can be cut in half without reducing the safety of the plant. [11] A faster approval rate could lower the cost of the construction of a plant because it eliminates all the delays and cost overruns.

1. Working on your own, place a vertical slash in front of any sentence that doesn't open with some reference back to familiar material.
2. See if your class or small group agrees on the location of these slashes. In each case, how does the writer's violation of the old/new contract create confusion?
3. Working individually or in small groups, try to revise the paragraph by filling in gaps created by violation of the old/new contract.

Avoiding Ambiguous Use of *This* to Fulfill the Old/New Contract

Some writers—often those with a good intuitive feel for the old/new contract—try to achieve coherence by using the pronoun *this* by itself to refer back to a broad concept in the previous sentence or group of sentences. The result—although not usually a grammatical error—is flabby and often ambiguous. Consider how the opening paragraph of this main section (p. 481) might read if some of the explicit links were replaced by "this."

Original	The final principle for writing clear closed-form prose is the *old/new contract*. The old/new contract asks writers to begin sentences with something old—something that links back to what has gone before—and then to end sentences with new information that advances the argument. Following this principle creates an effect called *coherence*, . . .
Ambiguous Use of *This*	The final principle for **this** is the *old/new contract*. **This** asks writers to begin sentences with something old—something that links back to what has gone before—and then to end sentences with new information that advances the argument. Following **this** creates an effect called *coherence*, . . .

Perhaps this passage helps you see why we refer to *this* (used as a pronoun) as "the lazy person's all-purpose noun-slot filler."

The Old/New Contract, Weak Repetition, and Passive Voice

As we have emphasized throughout this text, it is difficult to lay down rules for writing—even for closed-form, thesis-based prose. Inevitably, in some rhetorical context, it will be desirable to break any rule that a grammarian or rhetorician might devise. In this final section, we look at ways in which the old/new contract bumps up against two well-known rules for good writing and overrides them.

The Old/New Contract Qualifies "Avoiding Weak Repetition"

Many of you have been warned against frequent repetition of the same word (or "weak repetition," as your teacher may have called it). You may not be aware that repetition can also be strong when it's used for emphasis ("You're wrong. Dead wrong.") or as part of the glue that holds stretches of prose together. Repetition is a strategy that writers use to link sentences. Remember that the *Atlantic*

Monthly passage on police reforms repeated the phrase "community policing" six times. Imagine how much more difficult this passage would be to follow if, fearful of weak repetition, the author had pulled her thesaurus down from the shelf and begun sticking in synonyms.

> The 100,000 new officers are specifically intended to help revitalize neighborhood life; they're supposed to be trained in *community policing,* a progressive model of police work embraced, at least rhetorically, by practically everyone. *Operating a neighborhood constabulary* calls for a partnership of the police and local residents. . . . *Employing a confraternity of law enforcement agents* is often described simplistically as a return to cops on the beat who are integral parts of the neighborhood.
>
> In its sophisticated form, however, *social group gumshoeing* entails . . . . At its most cosmic, *running a communal peace officer program* requires teaching . . . . Advocates of the *neighborly cop approach* stress that . . . .

You get the picture. Keep your reader on familiar ground through repetition of key words.

The Old/New Contract Qualifies "Prefer Active over Passive Voice"

Another rule that you may have learned is to use the active voice rather than the passive voice. In the active voice the doer of the action is in the subject slot of the sentence and the receiver is in the direct object slot, as in the following examples:

The dog caught the Frisbee.

The women wrote letters of complaint to their boss.

The landlord raised the rent.

In the passive voice the receiver of the action becomes the subject and the doer of the action either becomes the object of the preposition *by* or disappears from the sentence.

The Frisbee was caught by the dog.

Letters of complaint were written (by the women) to the boss.

The rent was raised (by the landlord).

Other things being equal, the active voice is indeed preferable to the passive because it is more direct and forceful. But in some cases other things *aren't* equal, and the passive voice is preferable. What the old/new contract asks you to consider is whether the doer or the receiver represents the old information in a sentence. Consider the difference between the following passages.

Second Sentence, Active Voice	My great-grandfather was a skilled cabinetmaker. He made this dining-room table near the turn of the century.
Second Sentence, Passive Voice	I am pleased that you stopped to admire our dining-room table. It was made by my great-grandfather near the turn of the century.

In the first passage, the opening sentence is about "my great-grandfather." To begin the second sentence with old information ("he," referring to "grandfather"), the writer uses the active voice. The opening sentence of the second passage is about the dining-room table. To begin the second sentence with old information ("it," referring to "table"), the writer must use the passive voice, since the table is the receiver of the action. In both cases, the sentences are structured to begin with old information.

Summary

Chapters 18 and 19 have focused on strategies for composing and revising closed-form, thesis-based writing. In this chapter, we discussed four principles of revision to apply to your drafts to help readers stay on track.

1. Start and end with the big picture.
2. Place points before particulars.
3. Signal relationships with transitions.
4. Bind sentences together by following the old/new contract.

In the next chapter we turn from closed-form writing, which aims primarily to support a thesis as efficiently and clearly as possible, to open-form writing, which is more expressive and exploratory, less hierarchical, and more stylistically varied.

c h a p t e r 20

Creating Open Forms

Several weeks ago a friend and I drove up to Seattle for the annual meeting of the National Council of Teachers of English: five thousand name-tagged English teachers milling around book displays or sitting in close, thick-carpeted conference rooms listening to papers with titles like "Ideology and Praxis in the Postmodern Classroom" or "Sentence Combining Revisited." We spent the first afternoon walking along Lake Washington, talking about our lives and looking at the houses crowded on the shore, glimpsing interiors. The Burke-Gilman Trail lay in shadow, banked by tangled blackberries. A seaplane skidded on the brilliant lake. Mount Rainier hung over the Naval Air Station. . . . At the window counter of a little cafe we ate eggs and hashbrowns and watched the ferries come in.

It's not that the concurrent sessions back at the Conference Center were unimportant. I admire scholars, more and more since I admitted I'm not one. It's a question of natural tendency, and in a sense, of specialization. Somewhere a few years ago I stopped checking my instincts and let my mind work the way it works and more and more I think I've entirely lost the knack of identifying issues, making arguments, and joining the debate. I've veered off toward the particular, the peripheral, accelerating so fast in that direction that sometimes I feel myself lost in a kind of aphasia, my left hemisphere almost dormant. All I'm interested in, all I seem to process, are moods and moments, atmosphere, sudden scenes and faces. I'm swept along at the market, dazed, sometimes elated, and the fish are flying around me and the ferries are coming and going and sometimes the mountain appears from behind the clouds and sometimes it doesn't. . . .

My reading has become purely "literary" in the sense of dwelling in the kind of visceral world only literary detail can re-create, the impulse for meaning and extraction suspended. I sit in the easy chair in the livingroom, in front of the maple tree and the picture window, the trees all around me, and I drink coffee and read and the afternoon fades to evening and I reach up to turn on the light.

—Chris Anderson, *English Teacher and Writer*

In the epigraph, Chris Anderson describes a shift in his interests from one kind of prose to another. Less and less interested in academic writing and its concern for "identifying issues, making arguments, and joining the debate," Anderson chooses to dwell in a more visceral world, to suspend "the impulse for meaning and extraction."

What Anderson turns away from is the very kind of writing we've just spent two chapters discussing—lucid, clear, thesis-governed prose. In making this shift, he expresses a desire we probably all share, to do something with words other than to support a thesis in a clear and organized way. He longs to let the particulars of his experience—eggs and hash browns, flying fish, and the dimming late-afternoon light—into his prose.

Here we, too, shift our focus from closed- to open-form writing. But we must first acknowledge that our discussion of open-form writing is necessarily more tentative and less complete than was our discussion of closed-form writing. Whereas closed-form prose is governed by a few widely accepted conventions, open-form writing plays with those conventions in a bewildering variety of ways. Consequently, we don't claim to treat open-form writing exhaustively. We review a few of the major differences between open- and closed-form writing and offer some advice on how to open up your own prose when your purpose, audience, and genre call for an open form.

THE NARRATIVE BASE OF OPEN-FORM WRITING

Closed-form writing is, above all else, reader friendly. By laying out the whole, putting points first, using clear transitions, and following the old/new contract, closed-form writers place maximum emphasis on ease of reading. In contrast, open-form writers, by violating, ignoring, or simply stretching those same conventions, demand more of their readers—more patience, more flexibility, more tolerance for ambiguity. But as you will see, there are rewards for readers who make the effort to engage fully with open-form prose.

Both the difficulties and the pleasures of open-form writing derive from its narrative base, its tendency to convert explicit theses and conceptual issues into implicit themes and dramatic tensions. This narrative base forces the reader to have a different sort of engagement with the text and a different sort of relationship with the author. Open-form reading affords pleasures akin to game playing or puzzle solving. The price readers pay for this recreation is the expenditure of considerable intellectual energy as they become active interpreters—even cocreators—of the text.

Thesis-based writers typically reach their conclusions offstage. They analyze particulars and test ideas during drafting, delete irrelevant and unsuccessful notions, and then rearrange their remaining ideas and particulars under a hierarchy of points and subpoints in a final draft. Closed-form writers typically begin by telling the audience what conclusion they've reached about the topic, and then use most of the rest of the paper to justify that conclusion, taking care to minimize self-reference along the way.

Open-form writers, meanwhile, are just as likely to take readers backstage to share the process that led to their conclusion. They often cast themselves in the role of participants reporting their quest for understanding and all the coincidences, disappointments, snatches of conversation, puzzling advice, and confusion they experienced along the way. Because readers share the writer's experiences and fallibility and witness the confounding of the writer's hypotheses and predictions, they feel free—impelled in some cases—to formulate their own hypotheses and predictions. This tendency of open-form prose to give prominence to the particulars that writers experience during the process of understanding is captured neatly in Chris Anderson's vivid comparison of narrative-based essays with old-growth forests.

> All the dead and dying ideas, all the ideas abandoned or modified in the course of the writing, are left lying on the page, not revised away, the tentative conclusions rising up from that previous thinking. The levels are there. Gaps open. . . .
>
> Details make sense. The trivial has meaning.

Of the many kinds of open-form prose, one of the most common is an autobiographical narrative that combines an expressive purpose (writing that emphasizes the writer's experiences and feelings) with a literary purpose (writing that uses strategies of literature for an aesthetic effect). To help you understand open-form writing, we begin with an example of an autobiographical narrative written by a student.

After reading the essay, respond to the questions that follow.

Patrick Klein

Berkeley Blues

1   It was a cold night. That is nothing new in San Francisco, but something made this night particularly frigid. It was early February and the whole city, including the Berkeley section where we were staying, was still held tight in the firm grip of winter. It had also rained that afternoon and the air, having been cleared by the storm, was cold and sharp. It hurt the back of your throat when you inhaled and turned into mist when you exhaled. As the six of us hurriedly walked in a huddled mass, the water that was lying in puddles on the dimly lit sidewalk jumped out of our way as we slammed our dress shoes down into its dregs. We silently decided on our destination and slipped into the grungy, closet-like pizza joint. We took the only seats the place had and as we pulled them into a circle, we all breathed a sigh of relief.

Student Essay

This was our first night at Berkeley. We were there for a debate tour- 2
nament to be held the next day at the university. On this night, however,
we were six high school sophomores in search of food. So, dressed in our
suits and ties (we were required to wear them) and heavy coats, we ventured
out of the university and entered the city of Berkeley.

Berkeley is an interesting place. Many might have romantic notions of a 3
bunch of shaggy intellectuals discussing French existentialism while sipping cappuccino, but while this might have been the case a few decades ago,
the reality is that Berkeley is a ghetto. The place is filled with grungy
closet shops while newspapers cover the sidewalks and the people lying on
them. The university is divided from this ghetto by a two-lane street.

As the six of us crossed the two-lane street that fateful night, my 4
thoughts drifted to my own neighborhood, which up until that moment had been
the extent of my world.

McCormick Ranch, Arizona, is a sheltered place. To a certain extent it's 5
mostly white, with little crime and few domestic problems. Everybody has a
pool, at least two cars, and a beautiful desert sunset every night. I had
everything I ever wanted. It seemed very gentle and dreamlike compared to
the harsh slum we found ourselves in.

When we made it into the pizza place and moved the chairs into a pro- 6
tective circle around a square table, anxiety about our "hostile" environment was quickly swept away with hot, greasy pizza. We ate until we were
content and were trying to decide how to divide the few remaining pieces
among ourselves when it happened.

The pizza place was separated from the rest of humanity by a large win- 7
dow. Our table was directly in front of that window and two feet from the
door. People had been passing the window and probably remarking on the six
well-dressed kids inside, but we paid them no mind and they all walked by
without incident. Still, our hearts were seized with terror every time a
human being would pass that window, and we hoped with all that we could
muster that every one of them would continue on. We were almost right.

8   On this night, when six young yuppie kids from an upper middle-class world decided to risk it and go eat pizza in a ghetto, he walked by. He didn't look any different from others we'd seen that night. Black. Dirty. Tired. Cold. His clothes consisted of a grimy, newspaper-stained jacket, a T-shirt with who-knows-how-old dirt on it, flimsy pants with holes at the knees, and tattered excuses for shoes. He was not quite up to par with our Gucci loafers and Armani jackets.

9   He shuffled past the window and glanced in. We didn't notice. He stopped. We noticed. Twelve eyes glanced up as casually as they could and six hearts stopped beating for a second. Yep, still there. All eyes went back to the floor, except for two. Those eyes belonged to Chad, and in some act of defiance, his eyes met the poor man's eyes and glared.

10   The man opened the door. "We're all going to die," I thought. "All my hopes and dreams are going to end here, in a stupid pizza place, at the hands of a crazy black bum."

11   He took something out of his pocket.

12   It was shiny.

13   I couldn't look.

14   A knife.

15   No. It was a flask. He took a swig from it, and, still propping the door open with his sagging frame, spoke the most jolting, burning words I've ever heard.

16   "I love you," he said. "All of you." He glanced at Chad, "Even you." He stepped back and said, "I know what you think of me, but I still love you." I will probably never forget those words or how he said them with a steady, steely voice.

17   Then he left. That was it. Gone. It took about five minutes for anyone to talk. When the talking started, we exchanged jokes and responded with empty, devastating laughter.

18   We soon left the shop. It had grown colder outside and we quickly returned to our climate-controlled hotel room. We had just eaten a filling

meal and paid for it with our own money. We were all about fifteen. The man
we had encountered was probably in his fifties. He had no roof, no money,
or food. It seemed strange that I owned more than an adult, but in truth,
he had more than I. He was able to love us when we ostracized him and thought
stereotypically about him.

I remember later trying to rationalize my sickening behavior by think-   19
ing that there is nothing wrong with being and acting afraid in a strange
environment. I tried to use my age as an excuse. Nothing worked. I was guilty
of fearing a fellow human being because of his color and my preset notions
of bums.

To this day I still think about what difference, if any, it would have   20
made if we had given him our leftover pizza. It might have eased my conscience. It was a very cold night and we had made it colder.

FOR WRITING AND DISCUSSION

1. A piece of advice often given to open-form writers is "Above all else, be interesting." How does student writer Patrick Klein hook and sustain readers'
   interest?
2. This essay does not assert a thesis statement in the introduction, yet the narrative has a focus and a point that becomes increasingly clear near the end.
   What do you see as the point of this essay?
3. According to his teacher, Patrick was at first unable to think of a topic to
   write about. (The assignment was to write an autobiographical narrative
   about an event that made a difference in your life.) "But I can't think of anything that made a big difference in my life!" he commented. Then his teacher
   asked him to write a journal entry in which he looked at some event, situation, or behavior, however minor, that he now regretted. This journal entry
   led him to remember the incident in the pizza joint, which he still thought
   was no big deal and too minor to write about. What Patrick came to understand is the point that Chris Anderson made about open-form writing:
   "Details make sense. The trivial has meaning" (see p. 489). How has Patrick
   invested a seemingly trivial event with meaning?

The Core of Narrative: The Minimal Story

A humbler word for the academic term *narrative* is *story*. As we show in this
section, what distinguishes a story from chronologically organized "and then"
writing is *significance,* or *meaning*. (See Chapter 18, pp. 446–48 for a discussion of

"and then" writing.) To help you appreciate the essential criteria that make a piece of writing a story, consider the following brief passages, all of which meet our definition of minimal story.

> I have been so totally erased from nature lately, like a blackboard before school starts, that yesterday when I was in the Japanese section of San Francisco, Japantown, I saw the sidewalk littered with chocolate wrappers.
> There were hundreds of them. Who in the hell has been eating all these chocolates? I thought. A convention of Japanese chocolate eaters must have passed this way.
> Then I noticed some plum trees on the street. Then I noticed that it was autumn. Then I noticed that the leaves were falling as they will and as they must every year. Where had I gone wrong?
>
> —Richard Brautigan, "Leaves"

> A crow stole a large chunk of cheese off a windowsill and flew away to a high tree to eat it. A fox witnessed the theft and trotted over beneath the tree. As the crow prepared to eat the cheese, the fox watched quietly. Finally, the fox cleared his throat and caught the crow's attention.
> "Excuse me, sir. I couldn't help but notice the lovely black sheen of your feathers. Really quite striking. And the graceful lines of your body, the perfect proportions. One just doesn't see that sort of beauty around here everyday."
> The crow listened closely, puffing himself up with each of the fox's compliments.
> "I also can't help wondering if your voice is as beautiful as your body. If it is, you are, to be sure, the king of birds in these woods."
> The crow, eager to affirm the fox's high opinion of him, broke out in a raucous, cawing serenade. The moment he opened his beak, the cheese fell to the ground at the fox's feet. The fox promptly ate the morsel and trotted away, calling out over his shoulder as he left:
> "So much for your beauty; next time we meet, let's discuss your brains."
> *Moral:* "It is a maxim in the schools,
>   That Flattery's the food of fools;"
>   And whoso likes such airy meat
>   Will soon have nothing else to eat.
>
> —Oliver Goldsmith, "The Crow
> and the Fox," *Aesop's Fables*

A strange old man
stops me,
Looking out of my deep mirror.

> —Hitomaro, *One Hundred Poems from the Japanese*

Despite their differences, all these pieces—a slice-of-life vignette, a fable, and a poem—are stories, very brief stories, to be sure, but stories nonetheless. To illustrate what we mean by the term *story*, let's consider a cartoon (see p. 496), the "Cathy" cartoon.

In the cartoon, Cathy's boyfriend, Irving, offers to dispose of her Christmas catalogs; Cathy emphatically rejects his offer. Undeterred, Irving suggests throw-

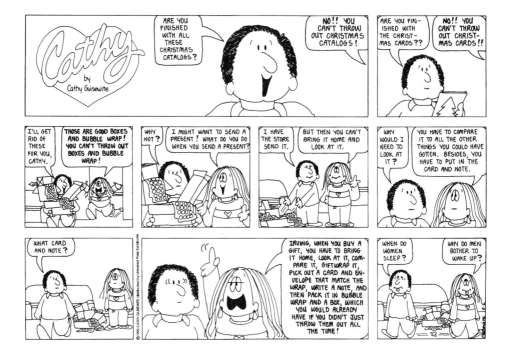

ing out a bunch of old Christmas cards; again, Cathy nixes his suggestion. Still game, Irving announces that he is throwing out empty Christmas boxes, so sure of his ground this time that he doesn't even ask. When Cathy rejects Irving's attempt to be helpful for a third time, he finally asks for a reason. In what follows, they become increasingly baffled about each other. An exasperated Cathy delivers a finger-wagging speech on the "right" way to buy and send gifts. In the final panel, they walk off in opposite directions, asking questions that express their almost perfect mutual miscomprehension.

What makes this a story? In a nutshell, it is a story because it depicts a series of connected events that create a sense of tension or conflict that is resolved through insight, understanding, or action. Each event depicted in its individual panel is connected to events depicted in the adjacent panels; in turn, all the panels have to do with Christmas gift giving and expressions of thoughtfulness. The cartoon depicts tension created by the contrary attitudes toward gift giving. Finally, there is a resolution of that tension in the form of a recognition or generalization about the meaning or significance of the experience: specifically, that different beliefs about gift giving point toward much larger differences in worldviews. These four criteria—depicted events, connectivity, tension, and resolution—must be met to create a *minimal story*. (As always with open-form writing, there's an escape clause to this contract. Struggling against and violating conventions is central to open-form writing. Consequently, many serious writers intentionally snub one or more of these criteria on the way to producing serious open-form writing. But they realize they are working against powerful conventions.)

Depiction of Events

Each of our minimal stories depicts events in a narrative sequence: a man walking down a street and awakening to his surroundings; a crow stealing a piece of cheese and confronting a fox; an old man looking in a mirror and momentarily not recognizing his face. The depiction of events is the defining feature of narrative. Whereas thesis-based writing descends from questions to theses to supporting reasons and evidence, stories unfold linearly, temporally, from event to event over time. The classic fairy-tale opening, "Once upon a time," underscores the importance of this temporal unfolding to a story and simultaneously underscores the importance of "onceness." Things that happen at a point in time, happen only once. One reason that the concept of "story" is so important is that a writer uses a story to preserve events and experiences that, however common, happened to the writer, and to the writer alone, just as the writer describes it. To be sure, many people get married or enter college every day, but no one else's account of that experience can be substituted for your account of your own experience of universal events.

Connectivity

The events of a story must be connected, not merely spatially or sequentially connected, but causally or thematically connected as well. They must affect each other. Stories are more than just chronicles of events. Novelist E. M. Forster offered the simplest definition of a true narrative when he rejected "The king died and then the queen died," but accepted "The king died and then the queen died . . . of grief." The last two words in the second version connect the two events to each other in a causal relationship. By the same token, Brautigan's "Leaves" becomes a story only when you realize that the "chocolate wrappers" are really plum leaves, a recognition that changes your understanding of all that precedes it.

Tension or Conflict

The third criterion for a minimal story, tension or conflict, creates the sense of anticipation and potential significance that keeps the reader reading. In an obvious case, the whodunit story, the tension follows from attempts to identify the murderer or to prevent the murderer from doing in yet another victim. In many comic works, such as the "Cathy" cartoon, the tension is generated by confusion or misunderstanding that drives a wedge between people who would normally be close. Will the relationship survive? is a key source of comic tension. Tension always involves contraries, such as those between one belief and another, between opposing values, between the individual and the environment or the social order, or between where I am now and where I want to be or used to be. The contrary in "Leaves" is between the old self, who sees chocolate wrappers and the new self, who sees plum leaves; in the fable the tension is between the crow and the fox; in the haiku it's between the "me" who looks into the mirror and the old man who looks back.

Resolution, Recognition, or Retrospective Interpretation

The final criterion for a minimal story is the resolution or retrospective interpretation of events. The resolution may be stated explicitly or implied. Fables typically sum up the story's significance with an explicit moral at the end. In contrast, the interpretation of events in poetry is almost always implicit. The sample haiku includes only two events, which are really one event: the narrator is stopped by a "strange old man," and the narrator looks into a mirror. The narrator's *recognition* is that he is that same old man. This recognition—"That's I in the mirror; when I wasn't looking, I grew old!"—in turn ties the singular events of the story back to more universal concerns and the reader's world. The usual direction of a story, from singular event(s) to general conclusion, reverses the usual points-first direction of closed-form essays. Stories force readers to read inductively, gathering information and looking for a pattern that's confirmed or disconfirmed by the story's resolution. This resolution is the point *toward* which readers read. Typically, a person's satisfaction or dissatisfaction with a story hinges on how well the resolution manages to explain or justify the events that precede it and how it fits with the resolution the reader has been forming while reading through the events.

FOR WRITING AND DISCUSSION

Working as a whole class or in groups, explain how the student essay "Berkeley Blues" qualifies as a minimal story. How does it meet the four basic criteria: depiction of events, connectivity, tension, and resolution? In contrast, how does the stolen watch "and then" narrative (pp. 446–48) fail to meet the criteria for a minimal story? How does your experience as a reader differ as you ponder "Berkeley Blues" versus the stolen watch story?

The Elements of Literary Narrative

In this section, we turn from the functional criteria for a story—the things a story is supposed to do—to the elements of a literary narrative—what it's made of. We examine the concepts of plot, character, scene, and theme.

Plot

By *plot* we mean the basic action of the story, including the selection and sequencing of scenes and events. Often, stories don't open with the earliest chronological moment, but start *in media res* ("in the middle of things") and then flash backward to fill in needed earlier details. What you choose to include in a story and where you place it are concerns of plot. Generally, writers develop some scenes or events in detail and hurry over others in summary form. Variation in the amount of detail devoted to scenes determines the plot's *pacing*.

Although plots can unfold in a variety of ways, the following stages represent a universal plot sequence:

1. Arresting opening
2. Introduction of characters and filling in of background
3. Building of tension or conflict through oppositions embedded in a series of events or scenes
4. Climax, or pivotal moment, when the tension or conflict comes to a head
5. Reflection on the events of the plot and what they might mean

You can see this basic pattern in Patrick Klein's "Berkeley Blues." In the opening scene, a group of high school students, in Berkeley for the first time, find a pizza joint on a frigid night. Gradually, Patrick introduces the characters (six middle-class students, dressed in suits, from an affluent Arizona suburb) and fills in the background (they are in Berkeley for a debate tournament and have wandered into a seedy neighborhood). He slowly builds the tension, which is created by oppositions embedded in the story (threatening inner-city versus pleasant suburbs; wealth versus poverty; white kids in Gucci loafers and Armani jackets versus old black man in grimy jacket). The tension reaches its climax when the old man pulls out a (knife?) flask and says . . . "I love you." In the rest of the narrative, Patrick reflects on the meaning of this experience and comes to some understanding of his own fear and guilt and the power of stereotyping.

Character

A second essential element of narrative is character—the people the story is about. Characters sometimes function both as unique individuals and as symbolic representatives of some quality, trait, or value. The six students in "Berkeley Blues" are simultaneously real individuals and symbols of privilege. So, too, the old man is both a real individual and a symbol of The Other—those remote from us whose differences from us frighten us. Major characters tend to forward or to frustrate the narrator's or central character's growth in a significant way, thereby contributing to the story's sense of tension.

How you present characters in your personal narrative also depends on the role they play in your story. In Patrick's story, the old man appears only briefly and says just a few words. However important the old man is to the narrator's growth, the story isn't about him, but about the narrator's sudden recognition of why he was fearful and the effects of that fearfulness on his perception of reality. In this regard, the awakening of "Berkeley Blues" resembles the awakening in Brautigan's "Leaves."

Setting

The setting of a narrative is the physical location in which events occur. Writers choose the elements of setting that are important to understanding the conflict or tension that drives a story. The setting often relates thematically to the other elements of the story. In "Berkeley Blues," the setting—a cold February night in a seedy urban neighborhood where "newspapers cover the sidewalks and the people [lying] on them"—is juxtaposed with the narrator's own "home" setting—a white neighborhood where everyone "has a pool, at least two cars, and a beautiful desert sunset every night"—to embody visually the story's primary tension.

Theme

The word *theme* is difficult to define. It is analogous to the thesis statement of a closed-form essay, but it is seldom stated explicitly and it is never proved with reasons and evidence. One way to define theme is to say that it denotes the generalizable significance of a story. The theme of "Berkeley Blues," baldly stated, might be "It is bad to stereotype people." But the story resonates more deeply than this. The story looks at the source of stereotyping—superficial knowledge, social and economic difference, and the fear that results from ignorance—as well as at its effects. Moreover, it juxtaposes middle-class students' fearfulness to the black man's confounding message of love. Whereas the old man is an impenetrable mystery to the students, their thoughts are apparently transparent to him. It would be difficult to put all this into a one-sentence moral like the moral of a fable. And so it would be with most good stories, no matter how simple they appear.

STRUCTURAL CHARACTERISTICS
OF OPEN-FORM WRITING

Patrick Klein's autobiographical narrative serves as a good example of narrative-based, open-form prose. Many other kinds of open-form prose share some but not all of the features of "Berkeley Blues." In this section we examine the surprising twists and turns of structure that characterize most pieces of open-form writing.

What makes a structural twist surprising is the way in which it violates the conventions of closed-form prose. For example, Patrick breaks the cardinal closed-form rule that pronouns should refer only to previously stated antecedents; he introduces the stranger only as a "he" and gradually reveals his identity. The violation creates an aura of mystery and suspense.

When open-form prose is successful, the effect of breaking closed-form rules isn't so much confusion as delayed gratification. In this example, the reader eventually finds out who "he" is, thereby meeting a definition of form offered by philosopher Kenneth Burke in the epigraph to Chapter 18: "the arousal and fulfillment of desire." In closed-form prose, we can easily see this process at work: The writer previews what he or she is going to say, arousing the reader's desire to see the general statement translated into specifics, and then fulfills that desire speedily through a presentation of pertinent points and particulars.

In more open-form prose the fulfillment of desire follows a less straightforward path. Writers offer fewer predictions, leaving readers less sure of where they're headed; or, writers make a prediction and then put it aside for a while as they pursue some other point, whose relevance may seem tenuous. In other words, the period of arousal is longer and more drawn out; the fulfillment of desire is delayed until the end, when the reader finally sees how the pieces fit together. Next we describe some of the sudden turns open-form writers take to surprise their readers and delay the fulfillment of their readers' desires.

Failure to Predict

Open-form writers regularly violate the principle of forecasting and mapping that we stressed in Chapter 19 (start with the big picture). Consider the following introduction to an essay.

> This is a story about love and death in the golden land, and begins with the country. The San Bernardino Valley lies only an hour east of Los Angeles by the San Bernardino Freeway but is in certain ways an alien place: not the coastal California of the subtropical twilights and the soft westerlies off the Pacific but a harsher California, haunted by the Mojave just beyond the mountains, devastated by the hot dry Santa Ana wind that comes down through the passes at 100 miles an hour and whines through the eucalyptus windbreaks and works on the nerves. October is the bad month for the wind, the month when breathing is difficult and the hills blaze up spontaneously. There has been no rain since April. Every voice seems a scream. It is the season of suicide and divorce and prickly dread wherever the wind blows.
>
> —Joan Didion, *Slouching Toward Bethlehem*

The opening of the first sentence seems straightforward enough: the essay will have something to do with "love and death in the golden land." But then things go a bit awry from the perspective of closed-form prose. The reader is expecting a thesis of some sort, a point about love and death. Instead, the essay seems to veer off into a concern with the geography of San Bernardino. In the end, all this description—and the description that follows for three lengthy paragraphs—is relevant. Didion is panning the landscape, offering, quite literally, a big picture, which is the backdrop for her story about a murder that took place here. But the reader must take this relevance mostly on trust and must read the description carefully to pick up clues to its relevance.

Sudden Gaps

An important convention of closed-form prose is the old/new contract, which specifies that the opening of every sentence should link back in some way to what has gone before. Open-form prose often violates this convention by leaving gaps in the text, forcing the reader to puzzle over the connection between one part and the next.

Almost any sequence of sentences in Annie Dillard's "Living Like Weasels" (which you can read in its entirety on pp. 132–34) violates this convention. The following example begins after Dillard has startled a weasel and exchanged glances with it.

> He disappeared. This was only last week, and already I don't remember what shattered the enchantment. I think I blinked, I think I retrieved my brain from the weasel's brain, and tried to memorize what I was seeing, and the weasel felt the yank of separation, the careening splashdown into real life and the urgent current of instinct. He vanished under the wild rose. I waited motionless, my mind suddenly full of data and my spirit with pleadings, but he didn't return.
>
> Please don't tell me about "approach-avoidance conflicts."

Dillard suddenly shifts, without transition, from a narrative about the weasel to a conversation with the reader about "approach-avoidance conflicts." Many other paragraphs open with similar gaps. Here is another example.

> What goes on in [a weasel's] brain the rest of the time? What does a weasel think about? He won't say. His journal is tracks in clay, a spray of feathers, mouse blood and bone: uncollected, unconnected, loose-leaf, and blown.
>
> I would like to learn, or remember, how to live. I come to Hollins Pond not so much to learn how to live as, frankly, to forget about it.

Here Dillard switches, again without transition, from musing about the mental life of a weasel to asserting that she would like to learn how to live. What is the connection between her encounter with the weasel and her own search for how to live? Dillard's open-form prose leaves these gaps for the reader to ponder and fill in.

Unstable or Ironic Points of View

Whereas the closed-form style encourages a single sort of viewpoint—rational, trustworthy, thoughtful—the open-form style tolerates a variety of viewpoints, including some that are more perplexing than reassuring. In open-form prose, writers are free to don masks and play around with different personae, including some that the writer may question or even loathe. A particular favorite of open-form writers is the ironic point of view. In this context, *irony* means saying one thing while intending other things, one of which may be the exact opposite of what's being said.

Consider the following bit of irony from eighteenth-century writer Jonathan Swift:

> I have been assured by a very knowing American of my acquaintance in London, that a young healthy child well nursed is at a year old a most delicious, nourishing, and wholesome food, whether stewed, roasted, baked, or boiled; and I make no doubt that it will equally serve in a fricassee or a ragout.

The shock of this passage comes in part from the narrator's sudden change of direction. The opening seemingly points toward some elevating discussion of child wellness. Then, without warning, the reader is mired in a grotesque treatise on the tastiness of cooked children.

Clearly the narrator's values are not shared by Swift, a religious Irishman who spent much of his life protesting the very sort of inhumanity he presents in this passage. What does Swift gain by adopting the persona of a moral monster and proposing that poor Irish people sell their children to English gentry for food in order to reduce Ireland's population and make some money? For one thing, he gains immediacy.

By stepping inside the persona that he reviles, Swift dramatizes what he sees as the snobbish, self-assured, and predatory English "gentleman." He doesn't talk about his enemy; he *becomes* that enemy so that the reader can see him as Swift sees him. Swift could have written an essay condemning the callous attitudes that were causing the Irish people so much suffering. But consider what would happen to the passage if Swift were to speak for himself.

> The landed English gentry who control Ireland treat the Irish people like consumer goods to be bought, sold, and used up in the service of their self-interests.

For all the English care, we Irish could be chunks of mutton to be tossed into their nightly stew.

That's still pretty strong, but it leaves the reader outside the evil that Swift describes. The audience hears about "landed English gentry" but doesn't experience their attitudes, values, and language directly, as in the original passage. The difference in the two passages is the difference between being told that someone is really hideous and spending half an hour trapped in a phone booth with that person.

Unstable viewpoints aren't always this dramatic. But they always offer writers the freedom to present directly, through dialogue and perspective, points of view that they might otherwise have to re-present via summary and argument. Such viewpoints also require readers to be more attentive in order to distinguish the author's point of view from that of the narrator.

STYLISTIC CHARACTERISTICS OF OPEN-FORM PROSE

Perhaps the first thing you notice about open-form prose is its great range of styles. In many cases, you can read a paragraph of open-form prose and identify the writer solely by the style. In contrast, closed-form writing has a much narrower range of stylistic variation. Closed-form style is mostly invisible; you tend not to notice *how* the writer says things unless the writer says something perplexing or confusing. If you notice the language in a closed-form essay, it often signals a lapse on the writer's part. In open-form writing, though, you may well be arrested by a writer's peculiar use of language—a striking phrase, an unexpected metaphor, or an unusual construction.

Let us consider more closely some of the ways in which open-form writers play with their medium.

Specific Words

According to the poet William Blake, "To Generalize is to be an Idiot." Open-form writers don't usually go that far, but they do tend to stay at a fairly low level of abstraction, typically eschewing a hierarchy of points, subpoints, and particulars in favor of an artful array of particulars.

To illustrate what might constitute "an artful array of particulars," consider the case of writer John McPhee. When asked why he wrote the sentence "Old white oaks are rare because they had a tendency to become bowsprits, barrel staves, and queen-post trusses" instead of a more generic sentence, such as "Old white oaks are rare because they used to be so valuable as lumber," he responded in a way that reveals his love of the particular.

> There isn't much life in [the alternative version of the sentence]. If you can find a specific, firm, and correct image, it's always going to be better than a generality, and hence I tend, for example, to put in trade names and company names

and, in an instance like this, the names of wood products instead of a general term like "lumber." You'd say "Sony" instead of "tape recorder" if the context made it clear you meant to say tape recorder. It's not because you're on the take from Sony, it's because the image, at least to this writer or reader, strikes a clearer note.

Some readers might complain that the particulars "bowsprits, barrel staves, and queen-post trusses" aren't helpful in the way that particulars in closed-form prose are. In closed-form prose, examples clarify and support points. McPhee, on the other hand, uses three unusual examples that will give most readers a moment's pause. Today most barrel staves and bowsprits are made of metal, not oak, and few contemporary readers encounter them on a regular basis no matter what they're made of. Furthermore, few readers at any time could readily identify "queen-post trusses," a technical term from the building trade. Instead of smoothly completing the reader's understanding of a point, McPhee's particulars tend to arrest and even sidetrack, sending the reader in pursuit of a dictionary.

But if McPhee's examples momentarily puzzle, it's the sort of puzzlement that can lead to greater understanding. Precisely because they are exotic terms, these words arouse the reader's curiosity and imagination. "[E]xotic language is of value," says McPhee. "A queen-post truss is great just because of the sound of the words and what they call to mind. The 'queen,' the 'truss'—the ramifications in everything."

For McPhee, the fact that these words trip up the reader is a point in their favor. If McPhee had said that old white oaks are rare these days because they became parts of "floors, buckets, and fences" no one would blink or notice. If you were to visualize the items, you'd probably call up some ready-made pictures that leave little trace in your mind. You also wouldn't hear the sounds of the words. (In this regard, notice McPhee's emphasis on images sounding "a clearer note.") Your forward progress toward the point would be unimpeded, but what would be lost? A new glimpse into a lost time when oak trees were used to make exotic items that today exist mostly in old books and memories.

Another quality also recommends words that readers trip over, words such as "bowsprit," "barrel stave," and "queen-post truss": their power to persuade the reader to believe in the world being described. Tripping over things, whether they're made of steel or words, forces the reader to acknowledge their independence, the reality of a world outside the reader's own head. For this reason, writers of formula fiction—thrillers, westerns, romances, and the like—will load their texts with lots of little details and bits of technical information from the time and place they describe. Because their stories are otherwise implausible (e.g., the description of the Evil Empire's doomsday machine) they need all the help they can get from their details (the size of the toggle bolts used to keep the machine in place while it's blasting out intergalactic death rays) to convince readers that the story is real.

Revelatory Words

We use the term *revelatory words* for specific details that reveal the social status, lifestyle, beliefs, and values of people. According to writer Tom Wolfe, carefully chosen details can reveal a person's "status life"—"the entire pattern of behavior and possessions through which people express their position in the world or what they think it is or hope it to be."

Wolfe favors writing that records "everyday gestures, habits, manners, customs, styles of furniture, clothing decoration, styles of traveling, eating, keeping house, modes of behaving toward children, servants, superiors, inferiors, peers, plus the various looks, glances, poses, styles of walking and other symbolic details that might exist within a scene." For example, Patrick Klein and his classmates are economically revealed as middle class by their attire—"Armani jackets" and "Gucci loafers."

Revelations of status life through the judicious selection of details are readily found in popular magazines. In the following opening to a *Gentleman's Quarterly* article about Bob Guccione, Jr., the entrepreneurial son of *Penthouse* publisher Bob Guccione, author Eric Konigsberg selects details about Bob Jr.'s choices of restaurant and dining companion to reveal "his position in the world or what [he] think[s] it is or hope[s] it to be."

> Dinner at Nobu, Robert De Niro's newest TriBeCa property, a polished but frenetic sushi temple replete with onyx bar, curved walls and patrons clutching Kate Spade handbags. The restaurant is the choice of Bob Guccione Jr., who has brought along a companion for the evening. He has the chef order for us, commands "your finest sake" and tells the waiter to put a beer for himself on our tab.

In the next paragraph we learn that "Bobby's date is a blonde woman from England named Suzanne. She is very tan and wears a mummuu with no bra."

FOR WRITING AND DISCUSSION

1. Based on this opening, write a brief response to the question, What sort of person is Bob Guccione, Jr.? In your response, avoid using any words that appear in the excerpt. Compare your response to those of your fellow group members. On what points do you agree? Disagree? On what items in the opening did you formulate your response?
2. Try your own hand at using descriptive details that reveal status life. Working in small groups or as a whole class, create a list of specific details that you might associate with each of the following: junior-high boys standing on a street corner; college professors; the kitchen of an upscale apartment of a two-professional couple; the kitchen of a lower-middle-class blue-collar family; the kitchen of an apartment shared by college students; people sitting in a dentist's office.

Memory-Soaked Words

Wolfe offers a psychological explanation for the pleasure people take in exotic or revelatory language: "Print (as opposed to film or theater) is an indirect medium that does not so much 'create' images or emotions as jog the reader's memories." The best way to jog that memory and evoke sensations, according to

Wolfe, is through careful selection of very specific words and images that evoke complex responses in the brain; the "human memory seems to be made up of *sets of meaningful data*" (emphasis ours) as opposed to separate bits of data that people consciously combine. In the following passage, Wolfe describes the complex interplay between writers' words and readers' responses.

> These memory sets often combine a complete image and an emotion. The power of a single image in a story or song to evoke a complex feeling is well known. I have always enjoyed the opening lines of a country and western song by Roger Miller called "King of the Road." "Trailers for Sale or Rent," it begins, "Room to Let Fifty Cents." It is not the part about trailers that I enjoy so much as the "Room to Let." This is the sort of archaic wording that, in my experience, is found only in windows or on door frames in the oldest and most run-down section of a city. It immediately triggers in my memory a particular view of a particular street near Worcester Square in New Haven, Connecticut. The emotion it calls up is one of loneliness and deprivation but of a rather romantic sort (bohemia). One's memory is apparently made up of millions of such sets, which work together. . . . The most gifted writers are those who manipulate the memory sets of the reader in such a rich fashion that they create within the mind of the reader an entire world that resonates with the reader's own real emotions.
>
> —Tom Wolfe, *New Journalism*

Had Miller opened his song with "Room *for Rent* Fifty Cents," there would have been no loss of clarity; if anything, most people would process the more familiar "rent" more rapidly than "let." The loss would have been associational and emotional. "For Rent" signs are too common to evoke any particular set of associations for most people. "To Let" signs, however, are rare enough that they are much more likely to evoke particular times and places for those who've encountered them. People who have never heard the phrase "to let" will either puzzle over it and eventually experience the pleasure of making sense of it or not notice the substitution and pass over it.

FOR WRITING AND DISCUSSION

Make a list of words and names associated with your childhood that you now rarely hear or use. Share your list with others in your group and identify the items that provoke the strongest associations. Examples include "Flexible Flyer" for those who remember those old sleds; "tetherball," for those who have played that game on a playground; "Cookie Monster" from *Sesame Street*; "Pez guns"; "Mister Bill"; or "8-track tapes." The idea is to think of specific words that are soaked with memories. Identify the emotions you associate with these words.

Figurative Words

Open-form writers often use figurative language in situations in which closed-form writers would use literal language. When journalist Nicholas Tomalin describes a captured Vietnamese prisoner as young and slight, the reader understands him in a literal way, but when he compares the prisoner to "a tiny, fine-boned wild animal," the reader understands him in a different way; the reader understands not only what the subject looks like—his general physical attributes—but how that particular boy appears in that moment to those around him—fierce, frightened, trapped.

Metaphors abound when literal words fail. When writers encounter eccentric people or are overwhelmed by the strangeness of their experiences, they use metaphors to try to explain the situation and their reactions to it. Writers use metaphors the way travelers sometimes use cameras in distant places—to record not only their journey, but themselves on the journey, in the snapshot. Consider Annie Dillard's account of a full solar eclipse, which she witnessed in 1979 in the state of Washington. Metaphors form the spine of her description.

> It began with no ado. It was odd that such a well-advertised public event should have no starting gun, no overture, no introductory speaker. . . . Seeing a partial eclipse bears the same relation to seeing a total eclipse as kissing a man does to marrying him, or as flying in an airplane does to falling out of an airplane. . . . However, during a partial eclipse the air does indeed get cold, precisely as if someone were standing between you and the fire. . . .
>
> I turned back to the sun. It was going. The sun was going and the world was wrong. The grasses were wrong; they were platinum. Their every detail of stem, head, and blade shone lightless and artificially distinct as an art photographer's platinum print. . . . The hillside was a nineteenth-century tinted photograph from which the tints had faded. All the people you see in the photograph, distinct and detailed as their faces look, are now dead. . . . I looked at Gary [her husband]. He was in the film. Everything was lost. He was a platinum print, a dead artist's version of life. . . . We had all started down a chute of time. At first it was pleasant; now there was no stopping it. Gary was chuting away across space, moving and talking and catching my eye, chuting down the long corridor of separation. The skin on his face moved like thin bronze plating that would peel. . . . From all the hills came screams. . . . At once this disk of sky slid over the sun like a lid. The sky snapped over the sun like a lens cover. The hatch in the brain slammed. . . . In the sky was something that should not be there. In the black sky was a ring of light. It was a thin ring, an old, thin silver wedding band, an old, worn ring. It was an old wedding band in the sky, or a morsel of bone.
>
> —Annie Dillard, "Total Eclipse"

In trying to describe a one-of-a-kind experience—the total eclipse of the sun—Dillard faces a special kind of writing problem. Many of her readers won't have shared the experience she describes. For them, her words could be empty referents, unless she can enable her readers to experience the event through her description. To do so, Dillard uses metaphors that link the unique experience of a solar eclipse to a set of equivalent experiences (old photographs and lids slamming shut, wedding bands) that most of her readers will share. Through these figures, she captures not merely the generic fearsomeness of the experience, but the particular terror this event evoked for her.

Notice how Dillard allows the reader to share her experience by letting it unfold in stages, marked by the development of her metaphors. She moves from casually noting that a total eclipse is different from other public events (an eclipse starts unannounced), to contrasting it to a partial eclipse (a partial eclipse is like flying in an airplane whereas a total eclipse is like falling out of an airplane), to a detailed description of her "eclipsed" surroundings (which are like a faded tint photograph of long-dead people), to an image of her husband (who hurls through space while his skin peels off like bronze plate), to an image of the moon blocking the sun (which resembles a lens cover being snapped shut), to the resultant appearance of the sun in the sky (the corona of the eclipsed sun is like a wedding band or morsel of bone floating in the sky).

Each successive metaphor is more ominous, leading up to the grotesque image of her husband, the one person she feels closest to, receding rapidly into space while his skin peels off. Dillard puts the reader inside the dramatic situation, the uncertainty of an unfolding event, and re-creates the sense of estrangement until even a wedding band, displaced in the sky, becomes an eerie symbol of things going wrong. If she were describing this event to an audience in closed-form style, most of these images would probably be discarded as too private, too idiosyncratic. They would in all likelihood be treated as distractions or interferences blocking the reader by substituting an account of what an eclipse was like for a given writer for an account of what an eclipse truly *is.*

COMBINING CLOSED AND OPEN ELEMENTS

So far we have been talking about features of open-form prose in its purer forms. Sometimes, however, writers wish simply to loosen basically closed-form prose by combining it with some features of open-form prose. If, for example, an academic wanted to share new developments in a field with a popular audience, he or she would be well advised to leaven his or her prose with some elements of open-form writing. In this final section, we offer several pieces of advice for loosening up closed-form prose.

Introducing Some Humor

Humor is rare in tightly closed prose because humor is nonfunctional—it doesn't *have* to be there for a writer to make a point—and closed-form prose values efficiency, getting what you have to say said in the most economical fashion. Also, closed-form writers are concerned with being taken seriously, and for some readers, serious writing and humorous writing are incompatible. Writers who make people laugh may find themselves being taken less seriously, no matter how unfair that may be.

Humor is closely related to one of the mainsprings of open-form style, surprise. Humor typically depends on sudden twists and abrupt changes in direction. In physical comedy, pratfalls are funny in direct proportion to the audience's inability to see them coming. In verbal humor, the less clearly the audience sees the punch line coming, the more it makes the audience laugh.

Humor is particularly valuable in that it can make imposing subjects more manageable for readers. Just as humor can deflate pretensions and bring down the high and the mighty in an instant, it can make arcane, difficult, and foreign subjects less anxiety producing. Formal, abstract language can put readers off, estranging them from the subject; humor has the power to "de-strange" a subject, to allow the audience to look at it long enough to understand it. Many popular books on science and many of the best instructional books on car repair, cooking, money management, and other of life's drearier necessities use a humorous style to help their phobic readers get on with life.

To appreciate the effect of humor, consider the following passages from two different instructional books on how to operate the database program Paradox. The first passage, from *Windows in 21 Days*, uses a clear, humor-free, closed-form style.

> In this book, you learn by following detailed step-by-step exercises based on real-world problems in database application design. Every exercise leads you further into the power of "Paradox for Windows" as you develop the components of an automated application. This section does the following: explains the assumptions and conventions used in this book; lists the hardware and software requirements and setup needed to run Paradox for Windows and use this book efficiently; and offers some suggestions for strategies to get the most from this book. The step-by-step exercises make it easy.

Now note the different effect produced by the following passage from one of the hugely popular *Dummies* books:

> Welcome to *Paradox for Windows for Dummies*, a book that's not afraid to ask the tough questions like "When's lunch?" and "Who finished the cookie dough ice cream?" If you're more interested in food (or Australian Wombats, for that matter) than you are in Paradox for Windows, this book is for you. If you're more interested in Paradox for Windows, please get some professional help before going out into society again.
>
> My goal is to help you get things done despite the fact that you're using Paradox. Whether you're at home, in your office, or at home in your office (or even if you just *feel* like you live at work) *Paradox for Windows for Dummies* is your all-in-one guidebook through the treacherous, frustrating, and appallingly technical world of the relational database.

FOR WRITING AND DISCUSSION

1. Which of these two instructional books would you prefer to read?
2. The second passage says that the world of relational databases is "treacherous, frustrating, and appallingly technical," whereas the first stresses that the "step-by-step exercises [in the book] make it easy." Why do you suppose the humorous passage stresses the difficulty of databases whereas the

humorless passage stresses the ease of a step-by-step approach? Is it good strategy for the humorous writer to stress the difficulty of Paradox?

3. Under what rhetorical circumstances are humorous instructions better than strictly serious instructions? When is a strictly serious approach better?

Using Techniques from Popular Magazines

Writers who publish regularly for popular audiences develop a vigorous, easy-reading style that differs from the style of much academic writing. The effect of this difference is illustrated by the results of a famous research study conducted by Michael Graves and Wayne Slater at the University of Michigan. For this study, teams of writers revised passages from a high school history textbook.* One team consisted of linguists and technical writers trained in producing closed-form texts using the strategies discussed in Chapter 19 (forecasting structure, putting points first, following the old/new contract, using transitions). A second team consisted of two *Time-Life* book editors.

Whereas the linguists aimed at making the passages clearer, the *Time-Life* writers were more concerned with making them livelier. The result? One hundred eleventh grade students found the *Time-Life* editors' version both more comprehensible and more memorable. Lack of clarity wasn't the problem with the original textbook; unbearable dryness was the problem. According to the researchers, the *Time-Life* editors did not limit themselves

> to making the passages lucid, well-organized, coherent, and easy to read. Their revisions went beyond such matters and were intended to make the texts interesting, exciting, vivid, rich in human drama, and filled with colorful language.

To see how they achieved this effect, let's look at their revision. Here is a passage about the Vietnam War taken from the original history text.

> The most serious threat to world peace developed in Southeast Asia. Communist guerrillas threatened the independence of the countries carved out of French Indo-China by the Geneva conference of 1954. In South Vietnam, Communist guerrillas (the Viet Cong) were aided by forces from Communist North Vietnam in a struggle to overthrow the American-supported government. . . .
>
> Shortly after the election of 1964, Communist gains prompted President Johnson to alter his policy concerning Vietnam. American military forces in Vietnam were increased from about 20,000 men in 1964 to more than 500,000 by 1968. Even so, North Vietnamese troops and supplies continued to pour into South Vietnam.

Here is the *Time-Life* editors' revision.

> In the early 1960's the greatest threat to world peace was just a small splotch of color on Kennedy's map, one of the fledgling nations sculpted out of French Indo-China by the Geneva peacemakers of 1954. It was a country so tiny and remote that most Americans had never uttered its name: South Vietnam. . . .

---

*The study involved three teams, but for purposes of simplification we limit our discussion to two.

Aided by Communist North Vietnam, the Viet Cong guerrillas were eroding the ground beneath South Vietnam's American-backed government. Village by village, road by road, these jungle-wise rebels were waging a war of ambush and mining: They darted out of tunnels to head off patrols, buried exploding booby traps beneath the mud floors of huts, and hid razor-sharp bamboo sticks in holes. . . .

No sooner had Johnson won the election than Communist gains prompted Johnson to go back on his campaign promise. The number of American soldiers in Vietnam skyrocketed from 20,000 in 1964 to more than 500,000 by 1968. But in spite of GI patrols, leech-infested jungles, swarms of buzzing insects, and flash floods that made men cling to trees to escape being washed away—North Vietnamese troops streamed southward without letup along the Ho Chi Minh Trail.

What can this revision teach you about loosening up prose? What specifically are the editors doing here?

First, notice how far the level of abstraction drops in the revision. The original is barren of sensory words; the revision is alive with them ("South Vietnam" becomes a "small splotch of color on Kennedy's map"; "a struggle to overthrow the American-supported government" becomes "[They] buried exploding booby traps beneath the mud floors of huts and hid razor-sharp bamboo sticks in holes").

Second, notice how much more dramatic the revision is. Actual scenes, including a vision of men clinging to trees to escape being washed away by flash floods, replace a chronological account of the war's general progress. According to the editors, such scenes, or "nuggets"—vivid events that encapsulate complex processes or principles—are the lifeblood of *Time-Life* prose.

Finally, notice how the revision tends to delay critical information, moving information you would normally expect to find in the subject position into the stress position. In the first paragraph, the *Time-Life* writers talk about "the greatest threat to world peace" in the early 1960s for five lines before revealing the identity of that threat—South Vietnam.

FOR WRITING AND DISCUSSION

Here is a passage from a student argument opposing women's serving on submarines. Working individually or in small groups, enliven this passage by using some of the techniques of the *Time-Life* writers.

```
Not only would it be very expensive to refit submarines for women

personnel, but having women on submarines would hurt the morale of

the sailors. In order for a crew to work effectively, they must have

good morale or their discontent begins to show through in their per-

formance. This is especially crucial on submarines, where if any

problem occurs, it affects the safety of the whole ship. Women would

hurt morale by creating sexual tension. Sexual tension can take many
```

forms. One form is couples' working and living in a close space with all of the crew. When a problem occurs within the relationship, it could affect the morale of those directly involved and in the workplace. This would create an environment that is not conducive to good productivity. Tension would also occur if one of the women became pregnant or if there were complaints of sexual harassment. It would be easier to deal with these problems on a surface ship, but in the small confines of a submarine these problems would cause more trouble.

Delaying Your Thesis

In Chapter 8, we described a strategy for taking your reader on an exploratory journey toward a thesis rather than stating the thesis explicitly in the introduction. The effect is twofold. First, the *problem*, not the writer's solution, is put in the foreground. Second, readers are invited to co-investigate the mystery, which increases their delight in discovering a resolution. When making an argument, the writer might propose several opposing theses or review several other people's theses without committing to one until late in the essay. Or, the writer might simply reject all the arguments and choose to end in a quandary. In either case, the writer enlists the reader in a hunt for closure. Although such essays still have theses at their hearts, they follow the pattern of quest narratives and can possess all the compelling readability of a mystery tale.

FOR WRITING AND DISCUSSION

Let's return to the words of Chris Anderson, whose forestry analogy began this chapter. In the quotation that follows, Anderson argues the need for forest engineers to write essays (what we would call open-form writing) as well as articles (closed-form writing) because the two ways of writing entail two different ways of seeing.

> It may even be that the essay is the only form that can honestly and accurately reflect the complexities and the dynamics that the New Forestry [forestry with a strong ecological/environmental bent] is trying to understand. It may be that only the structure of the essay can communicate the larger ecologies, natural and personal. It may be that scientists should be writing essays in addition to articles because in writing them they would be forced in a stance of wonder, humility, tentativeness, attention.

Put into your own words what you think Chris Anderson is getting at when he says that foresters should write essays as well as articles. What would it be like for an article writer, such as civil engineer David Rockwood (whose letter opposing wind power you read in Chapter 1, pp. 11–12), to turn from the closed-form article mode to the open-form essay mode? How might such a person's thinking be changed?

Summary

Open-form writing tries to do more with language than state a thesis and support it. We have shown how open-form writing uses a narrative base. When narrative is effective, it meets the criteria for a minimal story—depiction of events, connectivity, tension, and resolution—and uses the elements of plot, character, setting, and theme. Typically, open-form writers create surprising structural twists by failing to predict what's coming, by leaving intentional gaps in the text, and by adopting various points of view, including, on occasion, unstable viewpoints, such as irony. Open-form writers also have a penchant for concrete, sensory language—specific details, revelatory words, and memory-soaked words. We suggested several ways of loosening up closed-form prose by writing midway along the continuum: using humor, trying out some of the strategies of popular writers (using concrete language, dramatic construction, and belated placement of a subject in the stress position), or delaying the thesis.

c h a p t e r 21

Working in Groups to Pose and Solve Problems

> The consensual process of truth seeking is based on the simple assumption that all of us thinking together are smarter than any one of us thinking alone.
>
> —Parker Palmer, *Educator*

> For excellence, the presence of others is always required.
>
> —Hannah Arendt, *Philosopher*

At first glance, group work and writing may seem to be totally unrelated, even irreconcilable, activities. Group work typically involves lots of motion, noise, and (usually) purposeful activity—making decisions, planning events, distributing tasks—whereas writing is something that most people do on their own, in a quiet room, curled up with a yellow legal pad or seated in front of a humming word processor, often for less clear-cut ends. But precisely because the two processes are so different, they can complement and support each other in particularly powerful ways.

Even in the world of creative writing, long thought to be the most reclusive and solitary of pursuits, few authors operate in strict isolation. Most seek out the company of other writers to converse informally about their craft, share manuscripts, and discuss the work of their contemporaries and their predecessors.

Writing communities are even more important in business and professional settings. The vast majority of scientific and technical articles are team written, often by three or more authors. And few major reports or proposals in the business or academic world are the product of a single author. In these settings writing is becoming more, rather than less, communal. Increasingly, legal briefs, ad campaigns, articles, brochures, letters to customers, memos to stockholders, and so forth are the products of team efforts.

The reasons for this trend are not hard to trace. First, much of contemporary work is so complex and technical that no single person has enough expertise to compose a nonroutine document. Second, many large businesses, for reasons of economy and employee morale, use self-directed teams to accomplish tasks that in the past were assigned to middle managers overseeing hierarchically organized staffs. Perhaps most important, much professional writing is now produced on networked computers. Writers on a network can easily transfer files to team members, who can enter changes electronically, without having to convert the file to paper or redo the entire draft.

Clearly, the ability to write effectively as part of a team is an increasingly critical skill for career advancement. Many businesses regard group skills as one of the three or four most important determinants of employee success. But perhaps you are not concerned with this brand of success. Maybe you envision yourself as a lone wolf operating on the fringes of—even at odds with—the corporate world. Well, don't stop reading. This chapter will still be of great value to you. The ability to form and operate within communities is important for reasons that transcend economics and career ambitions.

Human beings construct knowledge through interaction with others. Throughout this text we have said that to write an essay is to join a conversation about a topic. The back-and-forth dialogue involved in group work is a real-time version of the conversations embodied in printed texts. Through discourse with others, you gather multiple perspectives on phenomena, which you synthesize through the filter of your own perspective. In other words, you construct your knowledge by exposing yourself to alternative views. Moreover, purposeful, thoughtful group interaction is a source not only for knowledge of the world around you, but also for self-knowledge. It allows you to stand outside yourself, to see the products of your mind the way that others see them. The kind of thinking that you practice in a group is the kind of thinking you need to exhibit in writing.

In the rest of this chapter, we offer advice on how to work effectively in groups and to become more adept at critical thinking, composing, and revising. We examine some basic principles of group interaction, explore some typical problems that small groups encounter, and provide strategies for accomplishing three common kinds of group tasks—general problem solving to develop critical thinking skills, brainstorming to generate ideas for essays, and peer reviewing to facilitate revision of rough drafts.

BASIC PRINCIPLES OF SUCCESSFUL GROUP INTERACTION

If the thought of group work makes you uncomfortable, you are not alone. Most people have had unpleasant or unproductive experiences working in groups. Jokes about committees ("Committees keep minutes and waste hours," or "A zebra is a horse designed by a committee") attest to the innate distrust of groups felt by most born in the United States. Middle-class popular literature, film, and media all lionize the exploits of the single individual working apart from the herd.

Keep in mind, however, that small groups in writing classrooms are less like unwieldy, bureaucratic committees than they are like problem-solving design teams analogous to the engineering teams that design cars or the marketing teams that plan new sales strategies. And recall that one of the world's most influential documents—the Declaration of Independence—was written as a small-group project.

To help you form efficient and productive teams, we recommend that you and your teammates practice the following principles.

Avoid Clone-Think and Ego-Think

Many group tasks ask you to propose and justify a solution to a problem by consensus. As we will show later in this chapter, a group consensus is not the same as a majority view. Although a consensus is a form of agreement, a good one grows out of respectful and productive *disagreement*. The best small groups build solutions thoughtfully, beginning with different points of view and encouraging dissent along the way. Weak groups either reach closure too early or bicker endlessly, never building on disagreement to reach consensus.

To steer a middle ground between early closure and endless bickering, you need to avoid two common problems of group interaction: clone-think and ego-think. When groups lapse into clone-think, discussions degenerate into "feel-good sessions" guaranteed to produce safe, superficial solutions. Everyone agrees with the first opinion expressed to avoid conflict and difficult work. At the other extreme is the ego-think group, in which group members go their own way, producing a collection of minority views. Whereas clone-thinkers view their task as conformity to a norm, ego-thinkers see their goal as safeguarding the autonomy of individual group members. At both extremes, group members fail to take one another's ideas seriously.

When we talk about taking other people's ideas seriously or about reaching consensus, we don't mean that group discussions should transform people's fundamental values and attitudes. But we do mean that they should bring about realistic changes: softening a position, complicating an understanding, or simply acknowledging an alternative possibility. These sorts of changes in understanding happen only when people learn how to present and consider alternative views in a constructive, nonthreatening manner. One approach to avoiding both clone-thinking and ego-thinking is to practice our next principle, empathic listening.

Listen Empathically

Sometimes called Rogerian listening, after the psychologist Carl Rogers, who popularized the technique, empathic listening is a powerful strategy for helping people resolve conflicts. To be *empathic* is to try to stand in the other person's shoes—to understand the values, beliefs, and fears underlying that person's position. Empathic listeners are *active*, not passive; they interpret not only the speaker's words, but also the speaker's tone of voice, body language, and even silences. Empathic listeners invite speech from others by maintaining eye contact, avoiding disapproving frowns or gestures, asking clarifying questions, and nodding or taking notes.

The rules of empathic listening are simple. Before you respond to someone else's position on an issue, summarize that person's viewpoint fairly in your own words. Carl Rogers discovered that when negotiating parties in a dispute (or couples in marital therapy) were required to summarize each other's views, the experience often defused their anger and encouraged them toward compromise or synthesis. In small groups, empathic listening can deepen conversation. If there is a dispute, the acting group leader might ask one disputant to summarize the other's position. For example: "Irwin, what do you understand Beth's position to be here and how do you see your position differing from hers?" Once Irwin and Beth understand their differences, they will be better able to reconcile them.

When a group becomes skilled at listening, here's what happens.

1. *There are fewer interruptions.* Group members have more "space" in which to complete their thoughts. They take turns speaking. To get the floor, one person doesn't have to interrupt another.
2. *Participation is more equitable.* Group discussions are less apt to be dominated by one or two group members. The group draws out shy or quiet group members and values their contributions.
3. *Discussions are more connected.* Speakers are apt to begin their contributions by referring to what previous speakers have said. "I really liked Pam's point about . . . " or "I see what Paul was saying when . . . , but . . . ."

FOR WRITING AND DISCUSSION

Freewrite your response to the following questions:

1. In the group work we have done so far in this class, how well do I think the group members have listened to and understood my views?
2. How good a listener have I been?
3. What might our group do differently to promote better listening?

Then, share your freewrites in groups and take turns summarizing each other's views. Reach consensus on several ways in which the group might improve its listening skills.

Play Assigned Roles

Writing groups accomplish tasks more efficiently when members take turns playing two distinct roles.

1. *Leader/Coordinator.*   This person's job is to ensure that the assigned task is clearly understood by all, to set clear goals for the session, to monitor the time, to keep the group on task, and to make sure that the group has its assigned product completed in the time allocated by the instructor. To prevent

early closure or endless bickering, the leader/coordinator must draw out divergent views, promote good listening, and help the group achieve a consensus, without ever being dictatorial.

2. *Recorder/reporter.* The recorder keeps notes on the group's decision-making process, constantly asking group members for clarification, and reads back what he or she understands group members to have said and decided. The recorder also synthesizes the group's deliberations and reports the results to the class.

In writing classrooms, we have found that groups work best when each student takes a rotation in each of these roles. Some instructors prefer to combine the two roles so that a group recorder serves as both leader and note taker.

Be Sensitive to Body Language

Groups can often learn to function more effectively by reading body language. Groups that draw their chairs close together are more effective than groups that maintain distance from each other or marginalize some members through irregular placement of chairs. Group members should note potential problems signaled by body language. A person who sits with arms folded across the chest staring out a window is signaling alienation. Other signs of dysfunction include side conversations, division of the group into subgroups, and domination of the discussion by one or two people who ignore others.

Invest Time in Group Maintenance

Group members periodically need to reflect on and think critically about their performance, a process called *group maintenance.* Group maintenance may be as simple as taking several minutes at the completion of a task to discuss the things the group did well or not so well and to identify steps for improvement.

Occasionally a more extensive and formal sort of group-maintenance task is required. One such task calls for each member to do a self-assessment by freewriting responses to questions such as the following:

Our group performs best when _____.

Our group's effectiveness could be improved if _____.

My greatest strength as a group member is _____.

Another thing I could contribute is _____.

The members then share these self-assessments with the whole group.

An even more ambitious group-maintenance project involves an ethnographer, a student from another group who observes the group in action and writes up a report on his or her observations. Figure 21.1 is a list of items we ask ethnographers to look for when observing a group.

After responding to these questions, the ethnographers should present the observations to the group and answer any questions the group may have about

---

1. How much time did the group spend reviewing the instructions before plunging into discussion?
2. How were the coordinator and recorder chosen? Had they fulfilled these responsibilities previously?
3. Describe how the group undertook its task. How did it begin the actual work?
4. On average, how long did each group member speak? What was the total amount of time that each group member spoke during the entire session?
5. How many times did group members interrupt each other?
6. How often did group members refer to what others had said before presenting their own contributions?
7. How were disagreements resolved or not resolved?
8. How well did the coordinator and recorder perform their functions?

FIGURE 21.1   Ethnographer's Questionnaire

them. Later, the group should discuss the report on its own. Finally, the group should present to the whole class a brief summary of what it learned from being observed and how it intends to improve its processes.

SOME SPECIAL PROBLEMS IN MAKING GROUPS WORK

How groups handle problem situations is crucial to their success. In this section we suggest how an understanding of the effects of learning style and cultural background on group behavior can alleviate potential problems. We also discuss ways of handling an "impossible" group member.

Recognizing How Personality and Culture Affect Group Participation

Group interaction can often be improved if group members understand the influence of personality and culture on a person's behavior in a group. Psychologists have discovered that people with different personality types have different reactions to working in groups. According to interpreters of the Myers–Briggs Type Indicator,* one of the most highly regarded personality assessment tests, people who test as *extroverts* like to think through an issue by talking out their ideas with

*The Myers–Briggs Type Indicator locates persons along four different continuums: introversion/extroversion, thinking/feeling, sensing/intuition, perceiving/judging. Composition researchers have used the Myers–Briggs inventory to reveal fascinating differences among writers that throw valuable light on students' behavior in groups. (See Jensen, G. H., and DiTiberio, J. K. *Personality and the Teaching of Composition.* Norwood, N.J.: Ablex Publishing, 1989.)

others; they tend to be vocal and highly engaged during group discussions. People who test as *introverts* prefer thinking privately about an issue before talking about it and are often uncomfortable discussing their ideas in groups, although they listen carefully and take in what everyone is saying. Often, quiet group members are listening more carefully and thinking more deeply than more vocal people realize. Until the group gently encourages them to contribute, however, they may be silent.

Judgers like to reach decisions rapidly, and they often grow impatient if the group wants to extend discussion of an issue. In contrast, *perceivers* resist early closure and want to talk through all possible points of view on an issue before reaching a decision. If you understand such personality differences, then you might better tolerate classmates' behaviors that are different from your own.

Other important differences are related to culture. Most U.S.-born students are used to talking in class, holding class debates, and even disagreeing with the teacher. In many cultures, however, it is disrespectful to argue with the teacher or to speak in class unless called on. Students are socialized to listen and not to talk. They can find group work in a North American college extremely painful.

Speech habits also vary widely. Typically, North Americans state their desires bluntly and assertively in ways that would seem rude to people from Asian cultures, who are taught to mask their statements of desire in roundabout conversation. Some cultures have a strong oral tradition of storytelling or speech making, whereas others have a tradition of silence. If your institution has a diverse student body that includes members of ethnic minority groups and international students, then group work can be a fascinating laboratory for the study of cultural differences.

FOR WRITING AND DISCUSSION

Your instructor or institution might arrange for your class to take the Myers–Briggs Personality Inventory or the Kolb Learning Style Inventory. If so, then you can share what these tests reveal about you with other members of your group. If not, then you can take your own mini-inventory by checking off the description in Table 21.1 that best represents you for each of the pairs listed. After you have made your choices, share your self-assessment with other members of your group. How do the differences in your responses account for the different ways in which you behave in the group?

Dealing with an "Impossible" Group Member

Occasionally groups face a critical test of their ability to manage conflict: the Impossible Group Member, or IGM. IGMs may dominate group discussions; they may be rude or intimidating, trying to turn every discussion into a conflict; they may sit sullenly, draining off group enthusiasm; or they may be generally unprepared or fail to do the work assigned to them outside class.

TABLE 21.1 Mini–Personality Inventory

Do you like to:

_____ Organize the discussion		_____ Go with the flow	
_____ Assert your own views and rights		_____ Compromise	
_____ Stick to the central issue		_____ Examine all facets of a problem	
_____ Reach a firm decision		_____ See merit in all sides of an issue	
_____ Think out your own position before talking		_____ Think by talking now	
_____ Reason problems out logically		_____ Trust your instincts and feelings	
_____ Get serious		_____ Lighten up	
_____ Show passion		_____ Stay calm	
_____ Reach a resolution		_____ Talk for talk's sake	
_____ Follow teacher's instructions carefully		_____ Value spontaneity	
_____ Apply rules rigorously		_____ Allow exceptions to rules	

Although it's not easy to deal with an IGM (sometimes the instructor has to intervene), most impossible group members are really possible group members who need encouragement and direction. The root of most IGMs' problems is their difficulty in recognizing the effects they're having on other people. Direct criticism of their behaviors will likely surprise them—they won't see it coming—and cause them to react defensively. IGMs need to see the consequences of their actions and they need to see positive behaviors modeled for them. If IGMs dominate discussions, they need to learn to listen. If they are sullenly silent, they need to have their input actively solicited and their responses taken seriously. They have to take their turns in leadership positions and learn to appreciate the difficulties of consensus building and decision making. And they must be made aware that their actions are bothering the other group members.

The best way to deal with IGMs is to discuss the problem candidly, perhaps during a group-maintenance session (see pp. 518–19). If group members reflect on and evaluate *how* the group did its task, focusing on group shortcomings ("What could we do better next time?") rather than on individuals' failures ("Martine, you drive me crazy!"), then it becomes easier for errant group members to accept responsibility for their actions. In explaining a problem to an IGM, try using what communication experts call "I statements" rather than "you statements." Keep the focus on your own feelings and avoid launching accusations. Note the different tones in the following examples:

You Statement Martine, you're always insulting us by looking out the window.

I Statement Martine, when you look out the window, it makes me feel like I'm a boring person.

You Statement	Pete and Valencia are always dominating the discussion.
I Statement	On some days I want to say something in the group but there is never a break in the conversation where I can join.

Using "I statements" helps defuse defensiveness by calling attention to the consequences of behaviors without attaching blame or censure.

We are now ready to turn to productive group strategies for addressing three kinds of tasks: general problem solving, idea generating, and peer reviewing.

SOLVING CRITICAL-THINKING PROBLEMS IN SMALL GROUPS

Many of the group tasks in this text pose a critical-thinking problem. Your group must develop a consensus solution for the problem and your group recorder must present and justify the solution to the whole class. These tasks help to develop your skills as a critical thinker while deepening your knowledge of rhetorical principles. Later, you can apply what you learn to more formal writing tasks.

Seeking Consensus

The problems we pose in this text have alternative solutions—there is no single right answer. When different group members propose different answers to the same problem, how does a group reach a consensus decision?*

First of all, don't assume that every group member has to be completely satisfied with the group's final solution. Instead, everyone should agree that the proposed solution is feasible and rationally supportable. Your solution must be achieved through *consensus* rather than through majority vote, coin flip, or turn taking. This approach means that each group member has veto power over the final solution. But this option should be used sparingly, and only if a person truly cannot live with the proposed solution. After an initial discussion to ensure that everyone fully understands the task, you can use the following guidelines to embark on a problem-solving procedure that encourages consensus.

1. Ask every group member to propose at least one tentative solution for discussion. Members should present justifying arguments as well, so that group members can appreciate the reasoning behind each approach.
2. Once you have presented a possible solution, avoid arguing for it a second time. Your goal is now to be flexible and listen to other viewpoints rather than to press for adoption of your own position. Remember, however, not to give up your viewpoint quickly just to avoid conflict. Yield only if you see legitimate strengths in other approaches.

---

*The discussion of consensus making is adapted from Parker Palmer *To Know as We Are Known: Education as a Spiritual Journey.* San Francisco: Harper and Row, 1983, pp. 94–96.

3. If none of the proposed solutions wins everyone's approval, begin brainstorming for alternatives that synthesize good features from various proposals. Sometimes you can formulate a lowest-common-denominator solution—one that everyone grudgingly accepts but that no one really likes—and brainstorm ways to improve it.

4. Don't think in terms of winners and losers ("If Lenore's solution wins, then Pete's must lose"). Rather, try to negotiate win/win solutions in which all parties give up something but also retain something.

5. Accept disagreement and conflict as a strength rather than a weakness. Chances are that the disagreements in your group mirror disagreements in the larger community to which your solution must appeal. From these disagreements you can forge a synthesis that is much stronger than any individual's private solution. As Parker Palmer says in the epigraph to this chapter, "The consensual process of truth seeking is based on the simple assumption that all of us thinking together are smarter than any one of us thinking alone."

GENERATING IDEAS IN SMALL GROUPS

The previous section focused on using small groups to propose a consensus solution to a critical-thinking problem. In this section we turn to a second kind of problem that groups can address in a writing course—helping each group member to generate ideas and arguments for an essay. Brainstorming and invention tasks are built into all the assignments in Part Two of this book. Some involve brainstorming for topics or converting broad topic areas into focused problems. Others involve brainstorming for supporting arguments and details. This section describes various ways in which students can work in pairs or small groups to help one another perform these tasks.

Group Brainstorming

Group brainstorming uses intuitive, unstructured thinking. During a brainstorming session, everyone is encouraged to suggest ideas, however outlandish they may seem on the surface, and to build on, without criticizing or questioning, all other suggestions generated by group members. Groups often begin brainstorming by asking individual members to take turns offering ideas. Frequently, a high-energy, almost frantic atmosphere develops. In its zanier moments, brainstorming crosses over into free association.

For a writer exploring topic ideas, brainstorming sessions can provide a variety of options to consider as well as clues about an audience's potential reaction to a topic and ideas about how the writer might change those views. Brainstorming can also generate arguments in support of a thesis. When the class is assigned a persuasive paper, playing the believing-or-doubting game (pp. 39–42) with each group member's proposed thesis can help writers anticipate alternative possibilities and counter-evidence as well as new support for a position. In the believing/ doubting game, group members alternate between brainstorming every reason they can think of for supporting a classmate's thesis and brainstorming every reason they can think of for opposing the thesis or finding the thesis inadequate. In a few minutes' time, a productive believing-or-doubting session can produce numerous points for a writer to use or reasons that might lead the writer to modify the thesis.

Interviewing in Pairs or Triads

Interviewing one another in pairs or in groups of three early in the writing process can help generate ideas. One-on-one or one-on-two interviews that enable writers to talk through their ideas can help clarify their sense of direction and stimulate new ideas. When you are the interviewer, use the set of generic questions in Figure 21.2, modifying them to fit each assignment.

When you conduct your interview, get the writer to do most of the talking. Respond by offering suggestions, bringing up additional ideas, playing devil's advocate, and so forth. The goal is for the writer to rehearse the whole paper orally. Whenever the writer gets stuck for ideas, arguments, or supporting details, help to brainstorm possibilities.

During these sessions, it is best for writers not to look at notes or drafts. They should try to reformulate their ideas conversationally. We recommend that each student talk actively for fifteen to twenty minutes as the interviewer asks probing questions, plays devil's advocate, or helps the writer think of ideas.

PEER REVIEW WORKSHOPS

Later in the writing process, after classmates have produced solid rough drafts, small peer review groups can be effective at stimulating revision. In a typical composition-class workshop, classmates working in pairs, triads, or groups of four to six respond to each other's rough drafts and offer suggestions for revision. These workshops are most helpful to writers when group members have developed sufficient levels of professionalism and trust to exchange candid responses.

FIGURE 21.2   Guide Questions for Interviewers

- What problem or question is your paper going to address?
- Why is this an interesting question? What makes it problematic and significant?
- How is your paper going to surprise your readers?
- What is your thesis statement? (If the writer doesn't have a good thesis statement yet, go on to the next question and then come back to this one. Perhaps you can help the writer figure out a thesis.)
- Talk me (us) through your whole argument or through your ideas so far.

A frequent problem in peer review workshops is that classmates try so hard to avoid hurting each other's feelings that they provide vague, meaningless feedback. Saying, "Your paper's great. I really liked it. Maybe you could make it flow a little better" is much less helpful than saying, "Your issue about environmental pollution in the Antarctic is well defined in the first paragraph, but I got lost in the second paragraph when you began discussing penguin coloration."

Responsibilities of Peer Reviewers and Writers

Learning to respond conscientiously and carefully to others' work may be the single most important thing you can do to improve your own writing. When you review a classmate's draft, you should prepare as follows:

1. *Understand how experienced writers revise their drafts.* Prior to reviewing a classmate's draft, read Chapter 17, which describes the writing process. Pay particular attention to pages 437–38, which provide general guidelines about what to look for when reading a draft and summarize the kinds of changes writers often make in response to reviews: additions, deletions, re-ordering, complete refocusing and rewriting, and so forth.
2. *Understand the assignment and the guidelines for peer reviewers.* For assignments in Part Two of this text, carefully read both the assignment itself and the guidelines for peer reviewers at the end of the chapter in which the assignment appears. These guidelines will help both the writer and you, as peer reviewer, to understand the demands of the assignment and the criteria on which it should be evaluated.
3. *Understand that you are not acting as a teacher.* A peer reviewer's role is that of a fresh reader. You can help the writer appreciate what it's like to encounter his or her text for the first time. Your primary responsibility is to articulate your understanding of what the writer's words say to you and to identify places where you get confused, where you need more details, where you have doubts or queries, and so on. Although the specific kinds of evaluations called for in the Guidelines for Peer Reviewers will also be helpful, you don't need to be an expert who is offering solutions to every problem.

When you play the role of writer during a workshop session, your responsibilities parallel those of your peer reviewers. You need to provide a legible rough draft, preferably typed and double-spaced, which doesn't baffle the reader with illegible handwriting, cross-outs, arrows, and confusing pagination. Your instructor may ask you to bring photocopies of your draft for all group members. During the workshop, your primary responsibility is to *listen,* taking in how others respond to your draft without becoming defensive.

Exchanging Drafts

An excellent method of exchanging drafts is to have each writer read his or her draft aloud while group members follow along in their own photocopies. We value reading drafts aloud when time allows. Reading expressively, with appropriate emphasis, helps writers distance themselves from their work and hear it anew. When you read your work silently to yourself, it's all too easy to patch up bits of broken prose in your head or to slide through confusing passages. But if you stumble over a passage while reading aloud, you can place a check in the margin to indicate where further attention is needed. Another benefit to reading aloud is perhaps more symbolic than pragmatic. Reading your work to others means that you are claiming responsibility for it, displaying your intention to reach a range of readers other than the teacher. And knowing that you will have to read your work aloud will encourage you to have that work in the best possible shape before bringing it to class.

Types of Peer Review Workshops

After you've read your draft aloud, the next stage of your peer review may take one of several forms, depending on your instructor's preference. We describe here three basic strategies: response-centered workshops, advice-centered workshops, and out-of-class reviews. Additional strategies often build on these approaches.

Response-Centered Workshops

This process-oriented, nonintrusive approach places maximum responsibility on the writer for making decisions about what to change in a draft. After the writer reads the draft aloud, group members follow this procedure.

1. All participants take several minutes to make notes on their copies of the manuscript. We recommend using the "Good!" wavy line, "?" system described in Chapter 17, pages 437–38.
2. Group members take turns describing to the writer their responses to the piece—where they agreed or disagreed with the writer's ideas, where they got confused, where they wanted more development, and so forth. Group members do not give advice; they simply describe their own personal response to the draft as written.
3. The writer takes notes during each response but does not enter into a discussion. The writer listens without trying to defend the piece or explain what he or she intended.

No one gives the writer explicit advice. Group members simply describe their reactions to the piece and leave it to the writer to make appropriate changes.

Advice-Centered Workshops

In this more product-oriented and directive approach peer reviewers collaborate to give advice to the writer. This method works best if group members use the Guidelines for Peer Reviewers that conclude each chapter in Part Two. Here is one way to conduct an advice-centered workshop.

1. The instructor divides the class into groups of four. Each student reads his or her paper aloud to the group. (This step can be omitted if time is limited.)
2. Each group divides into pairs; each pair exchanges drafts with the other pair.

3. The members of each pair collaborate to compose jointly written reviews of the two drafts they have received. These reviews should present the pair's collaborative responses to the questions in the Guidelines for Peer Reviewers in the assignment's chapter.
4. The drafts and the collaboratively written reviews are then returned to the original writers. If time remains, the two pairs meet jointly to discuss their reviews.

Since advice-centered reviews take longer than response-centered reviews, the instructor may ask writers to supply copies of their drafts to their peer reviewers at the class meeting prior to the workshop. The reviewers can read the drafts carefully and come to the review session with critiques already in mind. When two students work together to share observations about a draft, they often produce more useful and insightful reviews than when working alone.

Out-of-Class Peer Reviews

A variation on the advice-centered approach can be used for out-of-class reviews.

1. The instructor divides the class into pairs; each pair exchanges drafts with another pair.
2. Each pair meets outside class to write its collaborative review based on the Guidelines for Peer Reviewers. Then pairs exchange their reviews the next day in class.

This method allows reviewers to spend as long as they need on their reviews without feeling rushed by in-class time constraints.

How to Use the Guidelines for Peer Reviewers

The Guidelines for Peer Reviewers at the end of each chapter in Part Two are designed to help you review a writer's draft step-by-step. Each set of guidelines follows the same four-part structure: section I asks you to read the draft all the way through at normal speed, putting "Good!" in the margin next to passages you like and wavy lines next to passages that confuse you. Section II asks you to describe what you currently see in the draft. Section III asks you to offer suggestions for improvement, focusing on the higher-level concerns of ideas, organization, and development. Finally, Section IV asks you to note problems of editing and mechanics.

As you can see, the questions focus first on higher-order concerns and then on lower-order concerns (see Chapter 17, pp. 437–38). They also emphasize understanding rather than criticism. Before you evaluate the draft (Section III), you are asked simply to observe carefully what's in the draft (Section II) by describing, summarizing, or listing its features. Writing out what you see in this way will help you and the writer test whether you have a common understanding of the text. Discrepancies between your perceptions and those of the writer are an implicit form of judgment, a warning that the writer may need to clarify his or her intentions. Inevitably, some of the questions in these guidelines will be more fruitful than others for any particular paper. Don't worry if you find yourself spending as much time on one or two items as on all the rest combined.

Responding to Peer Reviews

After you and your classmates have gone over each others' papers and walked each other through the responses, everyone should identify two or three things about his or her draft that particularly need work. Before you leave the session, you should have some notion about how you want to revise your paper.

You may get mixed or contradictory responses from different reviewers. One reviewer may praise a passage that another finds confusing or illogical. Conflicting advice is a frustrating fact of life for all writers, whether students or professionals. Such disagreements reveal how readers cocreate a text with a writer: each brings to the text a different background, set of values, and way of reading.

It is important to remember that you are in charge of your own writing. If several readers offer the same critique of a passage, then no matter how much you love that passage, you probably need to follow their advice. But when readers disagree, you have to make your own best judgment about whom to heed. In our own writing—including the writing of this text—we tend to follow the advice that is presented to us most fully and rationally. We value most a well-explained sense of the reader's difficulty, an explanation of what causes the problem, and a specific suggestion about how to solve it.

Once you have received advice from others, sit down alone and reread your draft again slowly, "re-visioning" it in light of that feedback. Note especially how different readers responded to different sections of the draft. Then, based on your own responses as well as theirs, develop a revision plan, allowing yourself time to make sweeping, global changes if needed. You also need to remember that you can never make your draft perfect. Plan when you will bring the process to a close so that you can turn in a finished product on time and get on with your other classes and your life (see our advice on satisficing in Chapter 17, p. 442).

Summary

This chapter has looked at various ways of using small groups in a writing classroom, examining general principles of effective group interaction and discussing ways for groups to handle special problems. Working effectively in groups means learning to appreciate the dialectic nature of knowledge, recognizing that understanding is synthesized from conversations with people who have differing perspectives. Because to write is also to join a conversation, working in groups teaches the kind of thinking writers need to do.

We described how groups can solve problems together—learning how to build consensus and vary perspectives—and how groups can help their members generate ideas for essays through brainstorming or interviewing. Finally, we explained how to conduct effective peer review workshops using either response-centered or advice-centered approaches.

A Guide to
Research

part **FOUR**

c h a p t e r **22**

Focusing a Problem and Finding Sources

College writers regularly use research information in their work, whether it is a short analytical or persuasive piece that cites one or two sources or a longer research paper that cites dozens of sources. A research paper, although longer than many other kinds of papers, follows the same principles of writing discussed throughout this text. In a research paper, the writer poses an interesting and significant problem and responds to it with a surprising thesis. However, in a formal research paper, the writer is expected to use extensive research data for support and to cite and document all sources in a formal academic style.

Much popular writing takes on the characteristics of a research paper, but without the documentation. Consider the following excerpt from an article in *Glamour.*

> Subliminal self-help tapes—which promise everything from instant relaxation to higher earning power—are a big business: Industry watchers estimate they generate about $60 million in sales annually. But a number of recent studies show no evidence that they work.
>
> . . . Philip Merkle, Ph.D., of the University of Waterloo, analyzed commercially available tapes using a spectrograph that reveals patterns of auditory signals. He found no evidence of speech-associated patterns on the tapes. The messages embedded in the tapes are so completely masked by the other sounds that they cannot be heard *even subliminally.*
>
> —Pamela Erens, "Are Subliminal Self-Help Tapes a Hoax?"

As does a good research paper, this article has a thesis (subliminal self-help tapes are not effective) and uses research data for development and support (a statistic about the size of the subliminal self-help tape industry and a summary of the research by Philip Merkle). But if you doubt the figure of $60 million, you have no way to check the author's accuracy. Nor can you find Merkle's work to read it for yourself. You might be able to contact the researcher at the University of Waterloo, but that would be an inefficient approach to tracking down his work.

The purpose of citing sources and giving complete bibliographic information in academic research papers is to enable readers to follow the trail of the author's research. Although the conventions for documentation seem cumbersome at first, they are designed to give readers essential information about a source quickly and efficiently.

The three chapters in Part Four give you the information you need to produce an effective research paper. This chapter guides you through the process of posing and focusing a good research problem and shows you how to find sources by unlocking the resources of your library and community. Chapter 23 takes you through the process of writing a research paper, teaching you skills for summarizing, paraphrasing, and quoting sources (and for avoiding plagiarism). Chapter 23 also explains how to cite and document your sources according to the conventions of two primary academic systems—those of the Modern Language Association (MLA) and of the American Psychological Association (APA). Chapter 24 discusses how to make active use of computers and networking technology to find and retrieve sources and to manage the research process and explains specifically how to conduct electronic searches and how to use the Internet to converse with others interested in your research area.

WHAT DO WE MEAN BY SOURCES?

Before starting a research project, you need to know what researchers mean by the word *sources*. There are two kinds of sources. *Primary sources* include newspaper articles, letters, diaries, eyewitness accounts, laboratory notes, interviews, court records, government data, historical documents, and the like, and *secondary sources* are articles and books written by investigators who have themselves analyzed and evaluated the primary sources. For Mary Turla's research project on mail-order brides (pp. 583–96), for example, a catalog distributed by a mail-order bride service would be a primary source, whereas a book on culture in the Philippines would be a secondary source.

Understanding how secondary sources get published may also be helpful to you. When scholars undertake a research project, they generally record their findings first as field notes, exploratory entries in research logs, write-ups of interviews, computer spreadsheets of statistics, and so forth. Other scholars can occasionally access these immediate data if the researcher is willing to share it informally in personal letters, E-mail postings, interviews, or casual discussions. The first formal sharing of research data often takes place at academic conferences, when scholars with similar interests get together to present papers orally and to participate in discussions. A paper presented orally often becomes a first draft, which the researcher will revise as an article for a scholarly journal. Sometimes conferences publish their proceedings in a microfilm format or in an electronic forum, such as a World Wide Web site. Conference presentations usually occur within six months to a year following completion of the research.

Research results deemed important by the scholar's research community are often published as articles in specialized scholarly journals, usually one to three years after completion of the research. Most academic research is published in scholarly journals rather than in books. Scholarly journals are usually refereed—

an editorial board evaluates submissions and accepts or rejects them on the basis of their scholarly merit. Because prestigious journals have a high rejection rate, acceptance of an article by an important journal marks a high point in a scholar's academic career.

Later—three to six years after completion of the research—a fraction of the research published in journals finds its way into books. Many scholarly books are reworkings of material originally published as articles in scholarly journals. These books are typically aimed at more general audiences than are scholarly articles and usually integrate more material, giving readers a more complete view of a topic and a much richer sense of context. The bibliographies in the back of scholarly books are often an excellent resource for further research.

Finally, when ideas and information have been established as central to a discipline, they are published in reference sources, such as encyclopedias. Later in this chapter we list a variety of specialized encyclopedias that will enable you to get a quick overview of any topic.

In summary, you will find the newest information on a topic in the papers presented at recent scholarly conferences. The next most recent sources are articles in academic journals, and then information and ideas in recent scholarly books. The currently accepted ideas of a field—its established and less controversial tenets—can be found in reference books, such as encyclopedias. In addition, much of the research generated by academic institutions is picked up by the popular media and reported in newspapers or integrated into feature articles in popular magazines, such as *Scientific American*, *Psychology Today*, or *The Atlantic Monthly*.

FOR WRITING AND DISCUSSION

Prior to class, go to your college's library and ask the reference librarian for a recently acquired scholarly book in a field you find interesting. (Many libraries have special shelves for new acquisitions.) Look at the copyright date of the book. Then look at the bibliography in the back of the book. What is the most recent date of the sources cited in the bibliography? What can you surmise about the lag time between the last research the writer was able to do and the time the book was actually published? Peruse the book's preface to see if the writer gives any overview of his or her research process. Whom does the writer thank in the acknowledgments section, usually placed near the end of the preface? Does the writer mention debts to previous researchers? What can you surmise about how this book came to be published?

In class, share your findings with your classmates.

BEGINNING A RESEARCH PAPER

Your first goal in writing a research paper is to convert a general topic area into a research question. The research question focuses your investigation, and later, when your answer to that question emerges as a thesis, it focuses your writing.

Developing Your Research Question

How do you choose a topic and develop it into a significant research question? First, you need to choose something that interests you. Your initial interest in a subject is likely to be broad and unfocused. For instance, you may be interested in eating disorders, say, or homelessness, but you may not be ready or able to pose specific research questions. To formulate questions, you need to do some preliminary reading. We recommend the following strategy:

- Read an overview of your topic in an encyclopedia.
- Skim a recent book related to your topic, looking carefully at its table of contents and examining the titles in its bibliography.
- Locate and read a recent scholarly article related to your topic (later in this chapter we show you how to find articles in academic journals). Note carefully the problem that the article addresses, and peruse the titles in its bibliography.
- Find and read a popular article related to your topic from the kinds of magazines indexed in *The Reader's Guide to Periodical Literature* or INFOTRAC.

This preliminary reading should give you some initial insights into the kinds of questions or controversies that writers are investigating or debating. The bibliographies in your sources may lead you to other books or articles that spark your interest. After doing this preliminary reading, try freewriting your answers to probe questions.

- What problems, questions, or issues about my topic are examined in the material I have read?
- What problems or questions does this material raise for me?
- When people discuss my topic, what questions do they ask or what do they argue about?

Another way to develop a research question is to discuss your topic with friends, trying to discover issues that particularly interest you. You don't need to know the answer to your question right away; your research will help you find a response. But until you settle on a research question, you won't know what part of your reading will be useful in your paper. Once you develop a research question—for example, "What is the current thinking about in-patient versus out-patient treatment of anorexia nervosa?" or "Should eating disorders be covered by insurance policies?" or "What role did the deinstitutionalization of the mentally ill play in the increase in homelessness?"—your research efforts can become focused and efficient.

In Chapter 1 we illustrated the development of a research question by following the exploratory process of student writer Mary Turla, who had selected the topic "mail-order brides." As we explained, Mary was attracted to this topic by a notorious murder case in Seattle in which an American husband gunned down his Filipina mail-order bride outside the courtroom where she was filing for divorce. Mary's initial abhorrence of the mail-order bride industry was later tempered when her mother commented that becoming a mail-order bride might be the only way for many young Filipina woman to escape abject poverty in the Philippines. Mary then posed her research problem this way: Should the mail-order bride industry be made illegal? (See Chapter 1, pp. 8–9.) We return to Mary's story later.

Evaluating Your Research Question

Once you have posed an initial research question (remember that your question may evolve considerably as your research progresses), test it for feasibility by considering the following questions:

- Are you personally interested in this question?
- Is the question both problematic and significant?
- Is the question limited enough for the intended length of your paper?
- Is there a reasonable possibility of finding information on this question?

This last question is particularly crucial. Good research writers depend on their skill at sleuthing out sources from a wide variety of places—college library, specialized libraries in the community, government and industry reports, nonprint media such as radio and television, the Internet, personal correspondence and interviews, or your own field research using observation and questionnaires. The rest of this chapter shows you how to unlock the resources of your library and your community. (For advice on using the Internet, see Chapter 24, pp. 613–19.)

FOR WRITING AND DISCUSSION

Review the criteria for evaluating research questions. Working as a whole class or in small groups, discuss each of the following research questions, evaluating them against the criteria. Does the question seem interesting? Is it problematic and significant? Is it limited enough for a short research project? Will there be information available on the topic? Is the question clear and precise? If a question doesn't meet the criteria, try revising it.

1. Do students work better if they don't work for grades?
2. Should pregnant women receive prenatal care?
3. Are helmet laws for motorcyclists effective in preventing injuries?
4. Is education good for children?
5. Why are there so many wars?
6. Why don't we do something about the welfare system?
7. Does a low-fat diet increase life expectancy?
8. Is Western medicine superior to traditional nonwestern medicine?
9. Should the United States limit immigration?
10. Does birth order affect children's development?

FINDING LIBRARY SOURCES

To be a good researcher, you need to know how to find materials in your college's or university's library. Because most people think "books" when they enter a library, they tend to focus on the bookshelves and neglect the wealth of other resources available. Much of the valuable—and the most up-to-date—information in a library resides in articles in newspapers and periodicals (magazines and academic journals). Libraries also contain a wealth of special reference tools, ranging from specialized encyclopedias to vital statistics.

Searching for Books

Until recently, a library's holdings were listed in a card catalog. Today, most libraries use on-line catalogs. A library's catalog, whether accessed by cards or by computer, is the guidepost to its books as well as to its magazines, journals, newspapers, dissertations, major government documents, and multimedia (videos, cassettes, and microform collections).

The basic logic of card catalogs—author cards, title cards, and subject cards—is retained in on-line systems. In both systems, books are listed by author, title, and subject. Our discussion of card catalogs highlights the logic of this approach. We provide brief additional information about card catalogs here, and additional information about on-line catalogs in Chapter 24 (p. 613).

In a card catalog, the author card (the main entry card) displays the author's name in the top left just under the call number. Other cards for the same work are identical to the author card but have a line added above for the title or subject. Because many famous authors not only write books but also have books written about them, their names may be on cards both as authors and as subjects. On a subject card the subject heading—in this case a proper name—is written in capital letters or typed in red above the author of the work. Author cards—books by a person—are filed in front of subject cards—books about a person. In a library with a large collection, remembering how to navigate around these similar-looking cards can help you avoid becoming confused. Sometimes files include cards for editors, coauthors, illustrators, or translators as well. Individual essays, stories, or plays in an anthology may also have separate cards.

Making Shrewd Use of Subject Headings

At the start of a research project, when you have only a topic area in mind, the subject cards (or subject entries in an on-line catalog) are probably your most important resource. Subject headings used for the subject entries are logical, uniform, and consistent. Most libraries use the headings established by the Library of Congress, which you can find listed in a four-volume reference book entitled *Library of Congress Subject Headings* (ask your librarian where this source is located in your library). This book can be especially helpful if you have trouble finding a subject heading that fits your topic.

Suppose that you are researching the effectiveness of state-run alcohol-treatment programs for street people. What subject heading do you start with? Alcoholism? Treatment programs? Homeless? Let's say you decide to begin with "alcoholism." You discover in the *Library of Congress Subject Headings* that "alcoholism" is a mammoth topic, with more than a page of subheadings. You then try "street people." Under that heading you find the instruction "USE Homeless persons." So you look up "homeless persons," where you find the following listing:

Homeless persons *(May Subd Geog)*	*Means that the subject heading "homeless persons" is used for (UF) these other three terms.*
UF Homeless adults	
Homeless people	
Street people	
BT Persons	*Means that "persons" is a broader term (BT).*
RT Homelessness	*Means that "homelessness" is a related term (RT).*
NT Church work with the homeless	
Homeless aged	*Means that all these headings are narrower terms (NT).*
Homeless children	
Homeless students	
Homeless veterans	
Homeless women	
Homeless youth	
Libraries and the homeless	
Police services for the homeless	
Rogues and vagabonds	
Shelters for the homeless	
Social work with the homeless	
Tramps	
Underground homeless persons	
Mental health services *(May Subd Geog)*	*Indicates subheadings under "homeless persons."*
Law and legislation *(May Subd Geog)*	

These listings use several abbreviations. *(May Subd Geog)* stands for "may be subdivided geographically" and indicates that listings under this category may be further subdivided by state or region. UF means "used for." The remaining abbreviations classify other subject headings that you might want to call up in your search: BT = "broader term"; RT = "related term"; and NT = "narrower term." In this case, because you are interested in treatment programs for homeless alcoholics, you might decide to try the subject headings "Social work with the homeless" and "Homeless mental health services."

In traditional card catalogs, subject headings place the most important or general word first and list specific qualities or subdivisions next. For example, the topic "the government of France" is listed under "France—Politics and government." Be creative as you look for subject headings, and use the helpful hints provided by the card or on-line catalog. A "See" or "Use" reference will lead you from an unused heading to a used heading. A "See also" reference suggests other related subject headings. Finally, when you find a book on your topic, look at the bottom of the card, which lists all the subject headings under which your book is filed. An on-line catalog usually provides the same information, but its location on the screen may vary from library to library. These other subject headings may lead you to other books.

In an on-line catalog, you don't need to worry about alphabetizing. With a card catalog, however, the following alphabetizing rules will be helpful.

■ Headings are alphabetized word by word rather than letter by letter. For example, *New Zealand* comes before *Newark.* Remember the rule "Nothing before something."

■ Articles (*a, an,* and *the*) at the beginning of headings or titles are ignored.

■ Abbreviations are alphabetized as if they were spelled out. For example, *St.* is filed under *Saint.*

■ Names beginning with *Mc* and *M'* are grouped with names beginning with *Mac.*

■ Chronological order is used for historical subheadings. "Great Britain—Literature—Sixteenth Century" precedes "Great Britain—Literature—Eighteenth Century."

The Logic of Shelving Systems

Once you have found a book in your library's catalog, you use the call number to locate the book in the library. Most libraries have open stacks, allowing you to go to the shelf and pick up a book yourself. Take advantage of your trip to the shelf to browse through the nearby volumes because other books on the same subject will be housed in the same area. Often your best sources turn up through casual browsing.

The call number will be either a Dewey Decimal number, generally used in elementary, high school, and local public libraries, or a Library of Congress (LC) number, generally used in academic libraries. Some older libraries have books shelved under both systems. Following is an overview of each system.

Dewey Decimal System

000	General Works
100	Philosophy and Related Disciplines
200	Religion
300	Social Sciences
400	Language
500	Pure Science
600	Technology and Applied Science
700	The Arts
800	Literature and Rhetoric
900	General Geography and History

Library of Congress System

A	General Works
B	Philosophy, Psychology, and Religion
C	Auxiliary Sciences of History
D	General and Old World History (except America)
E–F	American History
G	Geography, Anthropology, Manners and Customs, Folklore, Recreation
H	Social Science, Statistics, Economics, Sociology
J	Political Science
K	Law
L	Education
M	Music
N	Fine Arts
P	Language and Literature
Q	Science
R	Medicine
S	Agriculture, Plant and Animal Industry, Fish Culture, Fisheries, Hunting, Game Protection
T	Technology
U	Military Science
V	Naval Science
Z	Bibliography and Library Science

These numbers and letters represent general categories that are further subdivided as other letters and numerals are added. A book titled *Familiar Trees of America*, by William C. Grimm, for instance, has the Library of Congress call number QK481 (Q=science; K=botany; 481=North American trees). If you are aware of the system's logic, you can browse more productively.

Searching for Articles in Periodicals

Most of the information in periodicals (magazines and academic journals) and newspapers never finds its way into books. You can find articles in these important sources either through computerized indexes or through traditional printed indexes. (For information on computerized searches, see Chapter 24, pp. 613–19.) This section explains traditional indexes, which remain an important resource even if your library offers on-line searching of periodicals.

Before discussing how to use the indexes, let's review some of the most useful ones. We have divided them into two categories. The indexes listed under Current Affairs cover a variety of subjects and lead the researcher to current controversies and issues in numerous fields. The specialized indexes focus on individual areas of study.

Current Affairs

Readers' Guide to Periodical Literature.   The best-known index, the *Readers' Guide* covers popular magazines for a general audience including such topics as current events, famous people, movie reviews, and hobbies. It focuses primarily on nonscholarly publications, such as *Time, Newsweek, Popular Mechanics,* and *People,* but it also indexes many highly respected intellectual sources such as *Foreign Affairs* and *Scientific American.*

New York Times Index.   The subject index to the *New York Times* includes brief synopses of articles and gives exact references to date, page, and column. Its wide circulation, comprehensive coverage, and extensive indexing make this publication especially useful. Once you have found the date of an event through this index, you can search the back issues of other papers for their coverage of the same event.

Wall Street Journal Index.   A monthly and annual guide to the *Wall Street Journal,* this index is organized in two parts: (1) corporate news indexed by name of company and (2) general news indexed by subject.

Business Periodical Index.   This index leads you to articles on marketing, management, public relations, advertising, and economics.

Biography Index. This quarterly and annual index lists for biographical material in current books and periodicals.

Public Affairs Information Service (P.A.I.S.) Bulletin.   Serving as a guide to articles, pamphlets, and books on economic and social issues, public administration, politics, and international relations, this index is useful for finding information on current public policy, both domestic and international.

General Science Index.   This index to general science periodicals covers topics such as biology, botany, chemistry, environment and conservation, medicine and health, physics, and zoology.

Education

Education Index.   This index includes more than 300 periodicals, proceedings, and yearbooks covering all phases of education, organized by author and subject. It also has good coverage of sources related to children and child development.

Current Index to Journals in Education.   This index lists more than seven hundred education and education-related journals, organized by author and subject.

History and Literature

MLA (Modern Language Association) International Bibliography of Books and Articles in Modern Language and Literature.   This comprehensive index of scholarly articles on languages and literature of various countries is arranged by national literatures with subdivisions by literary periods.

Annual Bibliography of English Language and Literature. A subject index of scholarly articles on English language and literature, this index covers major writers and is arranged chronologically.

Humanities Index. This subject index covers topics in archeology, classics, folklore, history, language and literature, politics, performing arts, philosophy, and religion. It was called the *Social Sciences and Humanities Index* until 1974.

Historical Abstracts. This work includes abstracts of scholarly articles on world history, excluding the United States and Canada, covering the period from 1775 to 1945.

America: History and Life. This work comprises abstracts of scholarly articles on the history of the United States and Canada.

Nursing and Medical Sciences

Cumulative Index to Nursing and Allied Health Literature. This major index covers topics on nursing and public health.

Index Medicus. This monthly subject index includes periodical literature on medicine and related topics published in all principal languages.

Philosophy and Religion

Philosopher's Index. Scholarly articles in books and periodicals are indexed by author and subject. The subject section includes abstracts.

Religion Index One: Periodicals. This index has a Protestant viewpoint, but includes Catholic and Jewish periodicals as well. It provides a subject and author index of scholarly articles on topics in religion.

Physical and Social Sciences

Social Sciences Index. This index covers all subjects and disciplines in the social sciences, including anthropology, area studies, psychology, political science, and sociology. It concentrates on scholarly journals, but includes some popular magazines. The title was *Social Sciences and Humanities Index* until 1974.

Psychological Abstracts. This subject and author index covers books, journals, technical reports, and scientific documents and includes an abstract of each item.

Applied Science and Technology Index. This work is a subject index to periodicals in the fields of aeronautics and space sciences, automation, earth sciences, engineering, physics, telecommunications, transportation, and related topics.

Biological and Agricultural Index. This subject index covers English-language periodicals in agricultural and biological sciences.

General Science Index. See under Current Affairs.

Using Periodical Indexes

Although there are many periodical indexes, they are all organized similarly and include clear directions for use in the front of each volume. The key to using these indexes efficiently is thinking of good subject headings. Be creative and persistent. Most indexes have extensive cross-references that will eventually lead you to the heading you need. Keeping a list of the subject headings you use can save you time if you return to the indexes a second time or if you use more than one index for the same topic.

Once you have found appropriate articles listed under a subject heading, copy the bibliographic information you will need to find the articles. The library will have a list of its periodicals; check that list to see whether the journal or magazine you need is in the library. If it is, note its call number. Periodicals are often shelved by call number in the stacks just as books are shelved, although some libraries have a separate periodicals section arranged alphabetically.

Your library may also store some periodicals on microfiche (a small card containing page-by-page photographic negatives of a journal or magazine) or microfilm (a roll of film, similar to a traditional filmstrip). Your librarian will help you use machines that allow you easily to read the text and even copy pages that you will need for further reference. If your library does not have the article you need in any form, ask your librarian about getting the article through an interlibrary loan—an increasingly quick and common practice.

Finding Information in Special Reference Materials

Reference works are usually kept in a special section for use in the library only. They offer excellent help, ranging from background information as you begin your reading to statistics that provide hard evidence related to your thesis. The following list gives you some examples of reference works. Be sure to ask your librarian for other suggestions.

Encyclopedias.   Encyclopedias are extremely helpful for background reading in the initial stages of research. By giving you the big picture, encyclopedias provide a context for better understanding articles and books. In addition to general encyclopedias, you will find many specialized encyclopedias, among them the *Dictionary of American History, The International Encyclopedia of the Social Sciences,* the *McGraw-Hill Encyclopedia of Science and Technology,* and the *Encyclopedia of World Art.*

Book Review Digest.   This reference work provides a summary of the reviewed book and excerpts from a variety of reviews so that you can gain an understanding of controversies and issues in a given field. To use the *Book Review Digest* efficiently, you need to know the publication date of the book in question, as reviews are published the year the book is published and in the two to three succeeding years.

Congressional Record.   The *Congressional Record* contains the transcript of what is said on the floors of the Senate and the House of Representatives. It also contains an appendix of materials that members have asked to be included as part of the permanent record. Its index allows you to trace every reference to a given subject and to find out who discussed or acted on a bill. Many reference libraries carry this useful tool for people interested in history, politics, biography, and current events.

Statistical Abstract of the United States.   This publication dates back to 1879 and contains statistical tables on birthrates, abortion, marriage, divorce, health care, employment, nutrition, and so forth. It is a good primary source on life in the United States.

Facts on File.   Summaries of news stories in this publication show the development of events so that you see how they played out over the space of a year. Stories are arranged by subject, person, and country.

At each step of your library search, remember that your best aid is your librarian. Librarians are experienced in helping you find the right subject headings, pointing out nonbook holdings in the library, leading you through the interlibrary loan process, and introducing you to less-known resources in the library. Librarians will also steer you to the most helpful of the various reference tools designed for research projects such as yours.

FOR WRITING AND DISCUSSION

Working in groups, choose a current issue about public affairs (for example, global warming, gangs, or the federal deficit) that will allow you to use a wide range of library resources, including the *New York Times Index* and *Congressional Record.* With your group, go to your college library and use indexes to find titles of articles on the issue you selected; also locate relevant information from specialized references, such as encyclopedias, *Facts on File,* and *Statistical Abstracts of the United States.* You will probably want to divide up the work, having each group member become familiar with several sources in order to teach them to the rest of the group. When the group has finished, everyone should have a good idea of how to use these sources.

SPECIALIZED LIBRARIES AND LOCAL ORGANIZATIONS

Sometimes a search of your college library doesn't give you the information you need. In these cases, don't give up too quickly. Mary Turla, whose freewriting on mail-order brides we have been following, found little information in two academic libraries, even though one of them is the largest academic library in her part of the country. Instead, she was able to find the material she needed at a small specialized library devoted to Filipino culture and history. The public libraries in many cities house directories of specialized libraries.

Businesses and organizations also have libraries and information services. Public relations departments can provide brochures and pamphlets. For example, if you were writing about diabetes, you could ask the American Diabetes Association for books and articles available to the public. Check the Yellow Pages of your telephone directory for businesses or organizations that might be good sources of information. Student writer Sheridan Botts, who wrote an exploratory paper (pp. 170–72) and a research paper (pp. 401–13) on the funding of hospices, obtained much of her information from materials provided by local hospices and insurance companies.

Be aware, however, that businesses and organizations that provide information to the public do so for a reason. Often the reasons are benign. The American Diabetes Association, for example, wants to provide helpful information to persons afflicted with diabetes. But it is wise to keep in mind the bias of any organization whose information you use. Bias does not mean that the information is wrong, but bias will affect the slant of writing and the choice of aspects of a question that will be discussed. A good researcher looks at many points of view with an open and questioning mind. If you are researching whether to cut old-growth timber, you will want to read publications of both the environmentalists and the timber industry, keeping in mind the goals and values of each group. If the "facts" of either group seem hazy, you will need to seek more reliable data from a disinterested source. In one respect, you have an advantage when working with data provided by organizations because their biases are readily visible.

FINDING INFORMATION THROUGH INTERVIEWS AND PERSONAL CORRESPONDENCE

Interviews and personal correspondence can often provide special perspectives as well as the most current look at what is happening in an area.

Interviews

An interview is often a highly effective way to gather specialized information. Although asking a busy professional for an interview can be intimidating, many experts are generous with their time when they encounter a student who is truly interested in their work. Depending on circumstances, your interview can be formal or informal; you may even conduct an interview over the telephone, without a face-to-face meeting. No matter what the format, all interviews benefit from the following practices:

1. Be prepared for the interview. Be professional as well as friendly. Explain what you are working on and why you are asking for an interview. Know in advance what you hope to learn from the interview.
2. Be sure you have done background reading before the interview. Ideally, interviews should give you knowledge or perspectives unavailable in books or

articles. The interview should supplement what you have learned from your reading, not take the place of your reading. Although you needn't be an expert at the time of the interview, you should be conversant about your subject.

3. Have well-thought-out questions ready. Be as thorough with your questions as possible. Most likely you will have only one chance to interview this person. Although you may include some short-answer questions, such as "How long have you been working in this field?" the heart of your interview should focus on open-ended questions, such as "What changes have you seen in this field?" "What solutions have you found to be most successful in dealing with . . . ? or "What do you see as the causes of . . . ?" Questions framed in this way will elicit the information you need but still allow the interviewee to range freely. Avoid yes-or-no questions that can stall conversation with a one-word answer. Also try to avoid leading questions. For example, instead of asking a social worker, "What do you think about infringing on the rights of the homeless by making some of them take antipsychotic medication?" ask instead, "What are your views on requiring the mentally ill homeless to take antipsychotic medications as a condition for welfare assistance?" The more you lead the interviewee to the answers you want, the less valid your research becomes.

4. If the interviewee rambles away from the question, don't jump in too fast. You may learn something valuable from the seeming digression. You may even want to ask unanticipated questions once you have delved into new ideas. In short, be prepared, but also be flexible.

Before you conduct an interview, consider how you plan to record the information. Many people like to use a portable tape recorder, but be sure to ask your interviewee's permission if you plan to do so. You may still want to take notes, but taping allows you to focus all your attention on the interaction, following the speaker's train of thought and asking yourself what else you need to know. If you do not tape-record the interview, try to get all the main ideas down on paper and to be accurate with quotable material. Don't hesitate to ask if you are unsure about a fact or statement or if you need to double check what the person intended to say.

You will probably leave the interview feeling immersed in what you heard. No matter how vivid the words are in your mind, take time *very* soon after the interview to go over your notes or to transcribe your tape. What may seem unforgettable at the moment is all too easy to forget later. If you do your checking soon, you can usually fill in gaps in your notes or explain unclear passages on the tape. Do not trust your memory alone.

FOR WRITING AND DISCUSSION

You can practice interview techniques by interviewing fellow students. Imagine that your class is conducting field research to answer the following question: What are the chief problems that students encounter in producing college-level research papers? Working in small groups, develop a short sequence of interview questions that will elicit the information you seek. Outside class, each class member should interview a fellow student, preferably one not in your current writing class. The next day, you should all report the results of your interviews to the class, discussing any difficulties in conducting the interviews and sharing insights into how to improve interviewing techniques.

Personal Correspondence

Occasionally, it is appropriate to write a letter requesting information from an individual or organization. In the letter, state who you are and explain the purpose of your request. Make your request clear and concise. Enclose a stamped, self-addressed envelope for the reply.

GATHERING INFORMATION THROUGH QUESTIONNAIRES

The results of a questionnaire can often add weight to your argument. Although questionnaires always raise problems of bias and statistical validity, careful planning, decision making, and accurate reporting can alleviate most of the problems. You must first decide whether to make your questionnaire anonymous. Although respondents are likely to answer more honestly when the questionnaire is anonymous (for instance, a person is not likely to admit having plagiarized a paper if you are watching him or her fill out the questionnaire), anonymous questionnaires often have a low rate of return. Typically, those who feel strongly on an issue are most likely to fill out and return an anonymous questionnaire, so the returned questionnaires may not accurately reflect a random sampling of opinions. Choose carefully what group of people receive your questionnaire. In your paper, you have an obligation to describe your sample accurately and to state your rate of return.

Finally, the construction of the questionnaire is crucial to its success. Experts work days or weeks perfecting survey questions to avoid bias in answers. Including your questionnaire as an appendix to your paper will lend credibility to your evidence because readers will then be able to check the quality of your questions. Keep your questionnaire clear and easy to complete. Proofread it carefully, and try it out on a guinea pig respondent before you make your final version. Once your questionnaire is complete, type it neatly and write an introduction that explains its purpose. If possible, encourage response by explaining why the knowledge gained from the questionnaire will be beneficial to others.

CONCLUDING YOUR INFORMATION GATHERING

Once you have posed an interesting research question, your search for sources can take on the fascination of a detective puzzle. For many students it is difficult to bring the process of information gathering to a close and to begin the process of reading, note taking, exploratory writing, and drafting. But it is important to do some actual writing early in the process because only by producing a preliminary draft will you detect gaps in your knowledge that require additional research. Exploratory writing and drafting help you focus and increase the efficiency of your information gathering.

Summary

This chapter has discussed the purpose of citing sources and introduced the terms *primary source* and *secondary source*. We presented strategies for converting a general topic into a research question, including preliminary reading and discussions with friends. Once a research question has been chosen, we suggested testing it by posing a series of questions, considering especially the availability of sources. We also described library sources and suggested ways to use them effectively. We pointed out additional sources of information, such as specialized libraries and local organizations. Finally, we addressed strategies for information gathering through interviewing, correspondence, and questionnaires.

The next chapter guides you through the process of reading, note taking, reflecting, and drafting, showing you how to incorporate research information into your own prose.

chapter 23

Using and
Citing Sources

The previous chapter helped you pose a good research question and begin unlocking the resources of your library and community. This chapter helps you continue the research process, focusing on the purposeful use of sources. First we look at ways to read source material and to take notes that alternate between recording and reflecting. Then we examine strategies for integrating research information gracefully into your paper, using quotations, paraphrases, and summaries. Finally, we discuss conventions for crediting sources through citations and documentation.

FOCUSING AND REFINING YOUR RESEARCH QUESTION

In the last chapter, we reviewed Mary Turla's thinking as she settled on her research question: Should the mail-order bride industry be made illegal? In this section we follow her process through the next stages as she works to focus and refine the question.

Mary began researching her question by looking for newspaper and magazine articles, but she found only occasional references to the subject of mail-order brides. Nor did she find many direct references to the subject in her college library's catalog or periodical indexes. Apparently, this topic had rarely been addressed by academic writers.

Mary turned to creative searching in special libraries and was finally able to locate some articles on mail-order brides as well as some books on Filipino culture that helped her understand the psychology of Filipina women. (See Mary's exploratory essay, pp. 167–69.) Soon she had amassed a considerable amount of information about the mail-order bride industry. The more she read, the more Mary decided that she was totally opposed to it. Despite her mother's argument in its favor (that it helped Filipina women escape poverty), Mary planned to oppose the industry. She felt that the information she had gathered would serve as condemning evidence.

At this point, Mary was following two lines of thought for her paper, both supporting her view that the mail-order bride industry was harmful. First, she believed that the industry posed dangers both for the would-be husband and, especially, for the would-be wife, whose immigrant status and isolation from family made her extremely vulnerable. Second, Mary felt that the industry had a detrimental effect on the image of all Asian women. She planned to use both lines of reasoning to support her initial thesis that the industry should be abolished.

As Mary began to draft her paper, however, she found that she could not cover both areas adequately within the page limit set by her instructor. In addition, the volume of information on the two lines of reasoning was skewed; Mary found more articles on the fate of mail-order brides than on the image of Asian women. Most important, she began to appreciate more fully the potentially positive benefits of the industry. So, she altered her thinking and her thesis—perhaps the mail-order bride business should remain legal but should be strictly regulated.

Mary's case is instructive to all research writers. Often when you begin to write—or even before that, while you are doing research—you discover that you must change your focus, by narrowing it, expanding it, or shifting it in some other way. Sometimes you must alter your purpose as well and adopt a different approach to your problem. Mary started out thinking that she would be an advocate in a public controversy; her thesis was that the mail-order bride business should be made illegal. But when she began searching for materials she discovered that the controversy had not yet made it into the public consciousness. So, she had to amplify her purpose. Her first task became to bring the controversy to people's attention; *then* she could advocate a position. However, as her research progressed, Mary became less certain of her stance and began to see both sides of the controversy more fully. Hence she changed her thesis to "The mail-order bride industry should be regulated." We discuss the relationship between research and purpose more fully later.

What Mary's example shows is that, as a researcher, you must walk a fine line. You must not be so fickle as to shift direction each time you gather information from a new source, but you must be flexible enough to deviate from your original plans when substantial information urges you to go in a new direction.

READING, THINKING, AND NOTE TAKING

As you read through your sources, you should engage in two intertwined tasks. First, you need to take effective notes so that you can retrieve information efficiently when you begin drafting. Second, you need to reflect on your reading, imagining how each particular source might be used in your paper and how it influences your thinking about your topic.

There is no one right way to conduct these two activities, but we can offer two techniques that have worked for other writers. First, you can try using a dialectic, or double-entry, journal. Divide a page in half, entering notes on one side and writing reflections about what you've read on the other (see Chapter 2, pp. 37–38); for an example, see Chapter 8, pp. 184–87). Or, you can take notes on index cards and then do your reflective thinking in a separate research journal. We suggest that you try both techniques and perhaps experiment with a method of your own to discover what works best for you.

One common practice that does *not* work for most writers is *not* to take notes as you read and *not* to do any exploratory writing. We've seen students check out numerous books from the library and photocopy a dozen or more articles, but then write nothing as they read (sometimes they highlight passages with a marker), hoping to rely on memory to navigate through the sources later. This practice can lead to severe writer's block and often results in a cut-and-paste, "all about" report rather than in a focused, well-developed paper.

In this section we want to show you how to take purposeful notes on your readings and how to use exploratory writing to discover your purpose. Because the value of any source depends on your purpose for using it, and because your purpose evolves as your research progresses, taking notes on your readings requires looping back and forth between recording and reflecting.

The Logic of Note Taking

What kind of notes should you take? You can answer this question only in the context of your own research question, purpose, and thesis. To help you appreciate the logic of note taking, we begin by describing some typical roles that you might adopt when writing an academic research paper.

Synthesizer of current best thinking on a problem. In this role, you research the current thinking of experts on some important problem and report what the experts currently think. Your paper has primarily an informative purpose. Examples of research questions: What is the current thinking on the value of insulin pumps in managing Type I diabetes? What is the current view of experts on the causes of homosexuality?

Problem-solving detective or critical analyst. You seek a satisfactory answer that resolves the research question. You may find information that answers the question directly (informative purpose), or you may need to analyze primary sources or other data (analytical purpose). Examples of questions that require you to take this role: What were orphanages like in the nineteenth-century United States? To what extent has the North American Free Trade Agreement (NAFTA) caused U.S. jobs to go to Mexico?

Original field researcher. You pose an original research problem and conduct field research through observation, interviews, or questionnaires to gather data. You may also do library research to review what others have said about the problem. Such papers generally combine an informative and an analytical purpose and often take the form of a five-section scientific report. Examples of field research questions: What effect has the new Student Union building had on commuter students' bonding with the university? What is our campus environment like for gay and lesbian students?

Analytical thinker who must position himself or herself in a critical conversation. In this case much of your paper depends on your original analysis of a phenomenon, but you must relate your views to others who have addressed the same or similar questions. Examples: What is the function of violence in fairy tales for children? What effect do beauty and fashion magazines have on the identity and values of teenage girls?

Reviewer of a controversy. In this role, you report the arguments on various sides of a controversy (informative purpose). For example: What are the current arguments for and against the single-payer health-care system? What are the arguments for and against creating a five-year undergraduate engineering curriculum?

Advocate in a controversy. You shift from an informative to a persuasive purpose—your paper becomes a researched argument. Examples: Should the United States permit managed harvesting of old-growth forests? Should the United States adopt a single-payer health-care system?

Once you understand the typical roles that academic researchers play, it is easy to see the logic of note taking, which is a function of your purpose in using a source. As a writer, you read sources for two main reasons.

1. ***To gather data and information.*** Often you read sources to find data and information relevant to your research question—facts, statistics, examples, anecdotes, testimony, and so forth. If your purpose is informative, you will select and organize this information for readers; if your purpose is analytic, you will use the data in more complex ways, seeking to find meaningful patterns that lead to a surprising answer to your research question; if your purpose is persuasive, the data will become supporting evidence for your argument or counterevidence that complicates the issue and may support opposing views.
2. ***To understand other voices in the conversation.*** You also read sources to find out what others have said about your research question, to learn who the experts are, to discover various perspectives and points of view, to find out what is accepted and what is controversial, and so forth. Often your notes in this category will be summaries or paraphrases of a writer's argument, sometimes including brief quotations. As you learn about different points of view, you also try to determine how each writer's perspective on an event, analysis of a phenomenon, or position on an issue may be similar to or different from your own.

Taking Purposeful Notes

To make your notes purposeful and hence efficient, rather than randomly selective or needlessly exhaustive, you need to imagine how a given source might be used in your research paper. Table 23.1 shows how research notes are a function of your purpose.

Purposeful note taking entails looping back and forth between recording and exploratory reflection. Exploratory writing lets you imagine how a given source might be used in your paper and thus guides your note taking. In turn, reading and note taking might cause you to discover new ideas that lead to further exploratory reflection.

TABLE 23.1   Note Taking According to Purpose

Informative/Analytical Purpose	
How Source Might Be Used in Your Paper	**Notes to Take**
For background information about your topic or for new information used in the body of your paper	Summarize the information; record specific data
As part of a section reviewing previous research on your question	Summarize the problem addressed, the findings, and the conclusions (review of literature for experimental report)
As part of a section describing differing analyses or perspectives related to your research question	Summarize the writer's perspective, analysis, or point of view; in your reflection notes, explore how and why the sources disagree

Persuasive Purpose	
For background information about your issue	Summarize the information; record specific data
As data, information, or testimony to be used as supporting evidence for your position	Record the data or information; summarize or paraphrase supporting argument with occasional quotes of key phrases; directly quote short passages for supporting testimony; note the credentials of writer or person quoted
As data, information, or testimony that counters your position and supports opposing views	Take notes on counterevidence; in your reflection notes, speculate on how you might respond to counterevidence
As an opposing or alternative position on your issue	Summarize the argument fully and fairly; in your reflection notes, explore causes of disagreement (disagreements about facts, values, beliefs, assumptions) and speculate whether you can refute argument, concede to it, or compromise with it

Strategies for Taking Notes

When you take notes, keep a few general principles in mind. First, take notes that are complete. Going back to the library to check for accuracy or to get a fact that you have forgotten wastes time. Also, make sure that when you have used a source's exact words you mark the quoted passage with prominent quotation marks. If you don't intend to quote from the source, be sure that you record the information you need, restating it completely in your own words (we discuss summarizing and quoting later in this chapter).

If you are fairly certain that you plan to use a source extensively in your paper, you might want to photocopy it to facilitate quoting and citing later. As we have explained, however, it is both expensive and inefficient to substitute photocopying for note taking. The time you save early on by not taking notes will be eaten up later by your confusion over what to use and by your insufficient tilling of the soil through exploratory writing.

In many cases, particularly early in the research process, you might not know whether a source will be useful or how you might want to use it. In these cases, you could include a brief summary of the source's contents in your notes, indicating what kinds of data it offers. Later, when you are more sure of your purpose, you can make an informed decision about whether to use the source.

Next, check that you have all the bibliographic information needed for a citation, including the page numbers for each entry in your notes. It's a good habit to write down the author, title, and other bibliographic data before you begin to take notes. Whether you quote or summarize, you will need to cite the source if you use the writer's ideas (we discuss how to cite sources and avoid plagiarism later in this chapter).

You can record your notes in a journal-style notebook, on cards, or on a computer disk. Many students find that a spiral notebook is efficient for note taking; it keeps everything together and offers the option of putting exploratory writing next to notes in the form of a dialectic notebook (see pp. 37–38). When you use a notebook, place bibliographic information at the top of the first page of notes from a particular book or article; then include page references in parentheses after each quotation or paraphrase.

Some students prefer to use note cards. Some writers put bibliographic information on three-by-five-inch cards and the actual notes on five-by-eight-inch cards. The advantage to this system is that you can use subject headings on the cards and arrange them in various categories when you are planning and writing your paper. The disadvantage is that you might mix up or lose cards; also, some students feel that the cards are cumbersome to carry.

You can also use a computer for recording notes. Depending on the capabilities of your software and your own facility with computer technology, you can take advantage of the speedy data-entry-and-retrieval systems that computers offer.

Reflecting on Your Notes

You should use the strategies for active reading and response discussed in Chapter 6 to reflect on your notes. Exploratory writing will not only help you imagine how a given source might be used in your argument, but it will also help you deepen and complicate your thinking and begin formulating a thesis and a plan for support.

For each set of notes you take on a source, consider doing exploratory writing to answer one or more of the following questions:

- How might I use this source in my own paper?
- How does this source affect my thinking about my subject?
- How reliable and credible is this source? What are its limitations and biases? (See next section.)
- What new questions does this source raise?

Analyzing Bias in Sources

When you read sources for your research project, you always need to consider their trustworthiness, limitations, and biases. Follow our advice in Chapter 6 on reading with and against the grain. When you read against the grain, consider the following issues:

- How up-to-date is this source? Recent sources are usually better than older ones, so check the publication date. However, many older sources are highly respected and influential. Generally, you can gauge an older source's credibility by seeing how often it is referred to by recent writers in the field.
- What is the writer's point of view? Most closed-form writers attempt to change a reader's view in some way. As you read a source, identify the writer's thesis and ask questions about the writer's use of evidence to support it. What is omitted? What differing viewpoints have other writers taken?
- How credible is this writer? What are the writer's political views? What are the writer's credentials and affiliations? Is the writer affiliated with an organization known for its advocacy of certain positions or viewpoints? For example, scientists and engineers employed by the nuclear power industry are apt to have different views about nuclear energy from those of scientists affiliated with sun- or wind-power research. Knowing a writer's organizational affiliation doesn't mean you can discount the writer's arguments and data; it just means that you need to raise appropriate questions.
- What is the reputation and editorial slant of the publication in which the source appears? Editorial slants can range from liberal (*Utne Reader, Mother Jones, The Nation*) to conservative (*National Review, Reader's Digest*). Likewise, publications affiliated with advocacy organizations (the Sierra Club, the American Association of Retired People, the National Rifle Association) will have a clear editorial bias. If you are uncertain about the editorial bias of a particular magazine or newspaper, consult the *Gale Directory of Publications and Broadcast Media* or *Magazines for Libraries,* which, among other things, identifies the intended audience and political biases of a wide range of magazines and newspapers.

The value of our advice on purposeful note taking will become clearer in the following section, as we show you how writers can use the same source in different ways for different purposes.

CONTEXT AND PURPOSE IN THE USE OF SOURCES

One of the most useful skills you can learn as a research writer is how to incorporate sources smoothly into your own prose. Your decisions about what to borrow from another writer will be shaped by your own context and purpose. To begin our examination of how writers incorporate sources into their prose, let's look at how three hypothetical writers might use the following article about violence in the old West.

ROGER D. MCGRATH
THE MYTH OF VIOLENCE IN THE OLD WEST

1   It is commonly assumed that violence is part of our frontier heritage. But the historical record shows that frontier violence was very different from violence today. Robbery and burglary, two of our most common crimes, were of no great significance in the frontier towns of the Old West, and rape was seemingly nonexistent.

2   Bodie, one of the principal towns on the trans-Sierra frontier, illustrates the point. Nestled high in the mountains of eastern California, Bodie, which boomed in the late 1870s and early 1880s, ranked among the most notorious frontier towns of the Old West. It was, as one prospector put it, the last of the old-time mining camps.

3   Like the trans-Sierra frontier in general, Bodie was indisputably violent and lawless, yet most people were not affected. Fistfights and gunfights among willing combatants—gamblers, miners, and the like—were regular events, and stagecoach holdups were not unusual. But the old, the young, the weak, and the female—so often the victims of crime today—were generally not harmed.

4   Robbery was more often aimed at stagecoaches than at individuals. Highwaymen usually took only the express box and left the passengers alone. There were eleven stagecoach robberies in Bodie between 1878 and 1882, and in only two instances were passengers robbed. (In one instance, the highwaymen later apologized for their conduct.)

5   There were only ten robberies and three attempted robberies of individuals in Bodie during its boom years, and in nearly every case the circumstances were the same: the victim had spent the evening in a gambling den, saloon, or brothel; he had revealed that he had on his person a significant sum of money; and he was staggering home drunk when the attack occurred.

6   Bodie's total of twenty-one robberies—eleven of stages and ten of individuals—over a five-year period converts to a rate of eighty-four robberies per 100,000 inhabitants per year. On this scale—the same scale used by the FBI to index crime—New York

City's robbery rate in 1980 was 1,140, Miami's was 995, and Los Angeles's was 628. The rate for the United States as a whole was 243. Thus Bodie's robbery rate was significantly below the national average in 1980.

Perhaps the greatest deterrent to crime in Bodie was the fact that so many people   7
were armed. Armed guards prevented bank robberies and holdups of stagecoaches carrying shipments of bullion, and armed homeowners and merchants discouraged burglary. Between 1878 and 1882, there were only thirty-two burglaries—seventeen of homes and fifteen of businesses—in Bodie. At least a half-dozen burglaries were thwarted by the presence of armed citizens. The newspapers regularly advocated shooting burglars on sight, and several burglars were, in fact, shot at.

Using the FBI scale, Bodie's burglary rate for those five years was 128. Miami's   8
rate in 1980 was 3,282, New York's was 2,661, and Los Angeles's was 2,602. The rate of the United States as a whole was 1,668, thirteen times that of Bodie.

Bodie's law enforcement institutions were certainly not responsible for these low   9
rates. Rarely were robbers or burglars arrested, and even less often were they convicted. Moreover, many law enforcement officers operated on both sides of the law.

It was the armed citizens themselves who were the most potent—though not the   10
only—deterrent to larcenous crime. Another was the threat of vigilantism. Highwaymen, for example, understood that while they could take the express box from a stagecoach without arousing the citizens, they risked inciting the entire populace to action if they robbed the passengers.

There is considerable evidence that women in Bodie were rarely the victims of   11
crime. Between 1878 and 1882 only one woman, a prostitute, was robbed, and there were no reported cases of rape. (There is no evidence that rapes occurred but were not reported.)

Finally, juvenile crime, which accounts for a significant portion of the violent crime   12
in the United States today, was limited in Bodie to pranks and malicious mischief.

If robbery, burglary, crimes against women, and juvenile crime were relatively rare   13
on the trans-Sierra frontier, homicide was not: thirty-one Bodieites were shot, stabbed, or beaten to death during the boom years, for a homicide rate of 116. No U.S. city today comes close to this rate. In 1980, Miami led the nation with a homicide rate of 32.7; Las Vegas was a distant second at 23.4. A half-dozen cities had rates of zero. The rate for the United States as a whole in that year was a mere 10.2.

Several factors contributed to Bodie's high homicide rate. A majority of the town's   14
residents were young, adventurous, single males who adhered to a code of conduct that frequently required them to fight even if, or perhaps especially if, it could mean death. Courage was admired above all else. Alcohol also played a major role in fostering the settlement of disputes by violence.

If the men's code of conduct and their consumption of alcohol made fighting   15
inevitable, their sidearms often made it fatal. While the carrying of guns probably reduced the incidence of robbery and burglary, it undoubtedly increased the number of homicides.

For the most part, the citizens of Bodie were not troubled by the great number of   16
killings; nor were they troubled that only one man was ever convicted of murder. They accepted the killings and the lack of convictions because most of those killed had been willing combatants.

Thus the violence and lawlessness of the trans-Sierra frontier bear little relation to   17
the violence and lawlessness that pervade American society today. If Bodie is at all representative of frontier towns, there is little justification for blaming contemporary American violence on our frontier heritage.

What we want to show in this section is how there is no one right way to use this article in your own research paper. What you use depends on your own research question and your own purpose in using the source. Sometimes you will summarize a source's whole argument; sometimes you will summarize only a part; at still other times you will use an isolated fact or statistic from the source or quote a sentence or two as testimonial evidence. In what follows we show how three hypothetical writers, addressing three different research questions, use this source in different ways.

Writer 1: Summary for an Analytical Paper

Our first hypothetical writer is analyzing the causes of violence in contemporary U.S. society. She wants to reject one possible cause—that contemporary violence grows out of our violent past. To make this part of her argument, she summarizes McGrath's article.

> Many people believe that violence is part of our Wild West heritage. But Roger McGrath, in his article "The Myth of Violence in the Old West," shows that frontier violence was very different from contemporary violence. He explains that in a typical frontier town, violence involved gunslingers who were "willing combatants," whereas today's typical victims—"the old, the young, the weak, and the female"—were unaffected by crime. Because the presence of an armed populace deterred robbery and burglary, theft was much less common in the old West than today. On the other hand, McGrath explains, killings were fueled by guns, alcohol, and a code of conduct that invited fighting, so murders were much more frequent than in any U.S. city today (6). Thus, according to McGrath, there is little resemblance between violence on the frontier and violence in today's cities, so we cannot blame current violence on our tumultuous frontier past.

In this passage the author summarizes McGrath's argument in order to refute the violent frontier theory about the causes of contemporary violence. Presumably, this author will proceed to other causes of violence and will not return again to McGrath.

Writer 2: Partial Summary for a Persuasive Paper

In our next case, our hypothetical writer uses McGrath's article in an argument supporting gun control. He wants to refute the popular anti-gun-control argument that law-abiding citizens need to be armed to protect themselves against crime.

> Opponents of gun control often argue that guns benefit society by providing protection against intruders. But such protection is deadly, as Roger McGrath shows in his study of violence in the frontier town of Bodie, California. Although guns reduced theft, as seen in the low rate of theft in the well-armed town of Bodie, the presence of guns also led to a homicide rate far above that of the most violent city in the U.S. today. The homicide rate in the frontier town of Bodie, California, for example, was 116 per 100,000, compared to the current national average of 10.2 per 100,000 (McGrath 20). True, Bodie citizens reduced the theft rate by

being heavily armed, but at a cost of a homicide rate more than ten times the current national average. To protect our consumer goods at the cost of so much human life is counter to the values of most Americans.

McGrath's article contains data that could be used on either side of the gun control debate. This writer acknowledges the evidence showing that gun possession reduces theft and then works that potentially damaging information into an argument for gun control. How might you use the McGrath article to oppose gun control?

Writer 3: Partial Summary for an Analytical Paper

Looking at another facet of McGrath's article, our last hypothetical writer summarizes part of McGrath's article to support her thesis that a community's definition of crime is constantly shifting.

> Our notion of criminal activity shifts over time. For example, only a short time ago on the American frontier, murder was often ignored by law enforcement. Roger McGrath, in his discussion of violence in the frontier town of Bodie, California, during the 1870's and 1880's, showed that the townspeople accepted homicides as long as both the murderer and the victim were "willing combatants" who freely participated in gunfights (McGrath 20). These young males who were the "willing combatants" in Bodie share many characteristics with modern gang members in that they were encouraged to fight by a "code of conduct": "A majority of the town's residents were young, adventurous, single males who adhered to a code of conduct that frequently required them to fight even if . . . it could mean death" (20). Today's gang members also follow a code of conduct that requires violence—often in the form of vengeance. Although joining a gang certainly makes a youth a "willing combatant," that status doesn't prevent prosecution in court. Today's "willing combatant" is a criminal, but yesterday's "willing combatant" was not.

This writer uses McGrath's article to make a point completely different from McGrath's. But by extending and applying information from McGrath's article to a new context, the writer gathers fuel for her own argument about shifting definitions of the word *criminal*.

FOR WRITING AND DISCUSSION

Each of our hypothetical writers uses McGrath's article for a different purpose. Working individually or in groups, answer the following questions. Be ready to elaborate on and defend your answers.

1. What are the differences in the ways the writers use the original article? How are these differences related to differences in each writer's purpose?
2. What differences would you expect to find in the research notes each writer took on the McGrath article?
3. What makes each writer's passage different from a purposeless listing of random information?

Next, read Edward Abbey's article, "The Damnation of a Canyon," in Chapter 14 (pp. 349–52). Imagine that you are going to use Abbey's article in an essay of your own. Working individually or in small groups, write an appropriate passage for each of the following scenarios. Note: For more help in writing your passages, read the next section on summarizing, paraphrasing, and quoting.

Scenario 1   You are a supporter of dams and wish to write an article supporting the Glen Canyon Dam and opposing Abbey's article. Write a one-paragraph summary of Abbey's views to include in your own essay.

Scenario 2   You are doing research on the ecological effects of dams and want to use Abbey's article as one source. For your essay, write a paragraph, citing Abbey's article, on how building the Glen Canyon Dam changed the river's ecology.

Scenario 3   You are investigating the socioeconomic status of people who use Powell Lake for recreation. You particularly want to investigate Abbey's claim that the lake is used only by the wealthy. For your essay, write a short passage that reports Abbey's view of the socioeconomic status of the lake's recreational users.

SUMMARIZING, PARAPHRASING, AND QUOTING

In this section we examine some of the techniques our three hypothetical writers used to adapt the McGrath article to their own purposes: summarizing, paraphrasing, and quoting.

Summarizing and Paraphrasing Sources

A common way to work a source into your own prose is to summarize its thesis or argument. This is an especially useful strategy when the source's argument can directly support your own or when the source represents an opposing or alternative view. You may summarize only a portion of the source's argument if only that portion is relevant. Summaries can be as short as a single sentence or as long as a paragraph. The passage by Writer 1 is a good example of how to use a summary gracefully. (See Chapter 6, pp. 109–12, for detailed advice on summary writing.)

Another effective way to use sources is to paraphrase. *Paraphrasing* means "restating in your own words." Unlike a summary, which condenses the original, a paraphrase is approximately the same length as the original. The writer of a paraphrase keeps the source's original ideas and information but changes the wording. Because it is about the same length as the original, a paraphrase usually covers only a small section of the original source. You paraphrase when you want to include the actual details of the source's argument. To avoid plagiarism, you must transform the writer's original words entirely into your own language as well as acknowledge the source in a citation. (See the discussion of plagiarism later in this chapter.)

Attributive Tags and Citations

Whenever you summarize or paraphrase, you will need to use *attributive tags,* phrases that indicate that material is from another source; "according to Mc-Grath," "McGrath contends," and "in McGrath's view" all serve this purpose. In most documentation systems the source of the quoted or paraphrased material is cited in parentheses at the end of the borrowed material. (We discuss citation of sources later.) The attributive tag, together with the parenthetical citation, helps the reader distinguish between the writer's own ideas and those borrowed from sources. In the following excerpt from Mary Turla's paper, note how she uses attributive tags and parenthetical citations to acknowledge her sources. Attributive tags and citations are underlined in color.

Mary's Paper—Paragraph with Attributive Tags

> Based on ancient Malay tradition, Filipina women, compared to Chinese or Japanese women, have historically enjoyed full equality with the Filipino male. Guthrie and Jacobs describe this equality, relating several aspects of the culture that indicate equal status of men and women. They note that in the Philippines daughters and sons traditionally share equally in inheritance. Within the family, children owe some respect and obedience to all older family members; age, not necessarily sex, is what commands respect in the culture. Guthrie and Jacobs also point to the important position of numerous women in business and government in the Philippines (42). . . . . Stanley Karnow also stresses the powerful position of women both in past and present. He states that. . . .

Quoting a Source

A good rule of thumb for research writers is to use quotations sparingly. In-experienced writers usually quote too often, filling their paper with so many others' voices that their writing loses its own voice and sense of purpose. Quotations are important when you use another author as testimony; they are also useful for imparting the flavor and tone of an original source; and they can enhance your credibility. Often a quotation of just a few words, worked smoothly into the syntax of your own prose, is as effective as a longer quotation. We demonstrate how to work quotations into your own prose after we discuss plagiarism in more detail.

AVOIDING PLAGIARISM

Before we proceed to the nuts and bolts of quoting and citing sources, we will take a brief excursion into the realm of ethics to explain plagiarism. As you know from writing your own papers, developing ideas and putting them into words is hard work. Plagiarism occurs whenever you take someone else's work and pass it off as your own. Plagiarism has two forms: borrowing another person's ideas without giving credit through proper citation and borrowing another writer's language without giving credit through quotation marks or block indentation.

The second kind of plagiarism is far more common than the first, perhaps because inexperienced writers don't appreciate how much they need to change the wording of a source to make the writing their own. It is not enough just to change the order of phrases in a sentence or to replace a few words with synonyms. In the following example, compare the satisfactory paraphrase of a passage from McGrath's piece with a plagiarized version.

Original	There is considerable evidence that women in Bodie were rarely the victims of crime. Between 1878 and 1882 only one woman, a prostitute, was robbed, and there were no reported cases of rape. (There is no evidence that rapes occurred but were not reported.)
Acceptable Paraphrase	According to McGrath, women in Bodie rarely suffered at the hands of criminals. Between 1878 and 1882, the only female robbery victim in Bodie was a prostitute. Also, rape seemed nonexistent, with no reported cases and no evidence that unreported cases occurred (McGrath 20).
Plagiarism	According to McGrath (20), there is much evidence that women in Bodie were seldom crime victims. Between 1878 and 1882 only one woman, a prostitute, was robbed, and there were no reported rapes. There is no evidence that unreported cases of rape occurred (McGrath 20).

FOR WRITING AND DISCUSSION

This writer of the plagiarized passage perhaps assumes that the accurate citation of McGrath is all that is needed to avoid plagiarism. Yet this writer is guilty of plagiarism. Why? How has the writer attempted to change the wording of the original? Why aren't these changes enough?

The best way to avoid plagiarism is to be especially careful at the note-taking stage. If you copy from your source, copy exactly, word for word, and put quotation marks around the copied material or otherwise indicate that it is not your own wording. If you paraphrase or summarize material, be sure that you don't borrow any of the original wording. Also be sure to change the grammatical structure of the original. Lazy note taking, in which you follow the arrangement and grammatical structure of the original passage and merely substitute occasional synonyms, leads directly to plagiarism.

Also remember that you cannot borrow another writer's ideas without citing them. If you summarize or paraphrase another writer's thinking about a subject, you should indicate in your notes that the ideas are not your own and be sure to record all the information you need for a citation. If you do exploratory reflection to accompany your notes, then the distinctions between other writers' ideas and your own should be easy to recognize when it's time to incorporate the source material into your paper.

CONVENTIONS FOR QUOTING AND CITING SOURCES

We discuss next conventions for using source material in your research paper. These rules are specified by two organizations whose style manuals are followed by academic writers everywhere: the MLA, or Modern Language Association, for papers in the arts and humanities, and the APA, or American Psychological Association, for papers in the social sciences and education. Other disciplines may use their own conventions, so before you begin drafting a research paper, check to see which system your instructor recommends.

Long Quotations

Writers typically distinguish long quotations from the rest of the text by using block indentation. If a quoted passage is more than four lines long (MLA system) or more than forty words (APA system), use block indentation rather than quotation marks. The quoted material should be indented one inch (or ten spaces if you are using a typewriter) from the left margin for the MLA system and one-half inch (or five spaces) from the left margin for the APA system. For quotations of only one paragraph or less, do not add an additional indentation to mark the start of a paragraph. For a quotation of two or more paragraphs, indent an additional one-half inch (or five spaces if you are using a typewriter) more for the first line of each paragraph. List the citation in parentheses two spaces after the punctuation at the end of the quotation. Do not use quotation marks at the beginning and end of the passage because the block format itself indicates a quotation. Here is an example of a block quotation indented ten spaces per the MLA system.

```
McGrath describes the people most affected by violence in the fron-

tier town of Bodie:

          Fistfights and gunfights among willing combatants--gam-

          blers, miners, and the like--were regular events, and

          stagecoach holdups were not unusual. But the old, the
```

```
young, the weak, and the female--so often the victims of

crime today--were generally not harmed. (18)
```

Short Quotations

When a quotation is too short for the block method, it should be inserted directly into your own sentences and set off with quotation marks. The attributive tag may be put at the beginning, middle, or end of your sentence.

Beginning	McGrath claims, "It was the armed citizens themselves who were the most potent—though not the only—deterrent to larcenous crime" (19).
Middle	"Rarely were robbers or burglars arrested," says McGrath, "and even less often were they convicted" (19).
End	"Robbery was more often aimed at stagecoaches than at individuals," McGrath asserts (18).

Note that the parenthetical citation follows the closing quotation mark and precedes the period ending the sentence.

In these examples, the quotations are complete sentences. The opening word of the sentence is capitalized, and a comma separates the attributive tag from the quotation. Often, however, you'll choose not to quote a complete sentence but to weave a quoted phrase or clause directly into your own sentence.

> McGrath contrasts frontier violence to crime today, pointing out that today's typical crime victims are "the old, the young, the weak, and the female" (19) and showing that these groups were not molested in Bodie.

Here no comma precedes the quotation; the writer is not quoting a complete sentence introduced by an attributive tag. Rather, the quotation becomes part of the grammar of the writer's own sentence.

Modifying Quotations to Fit Your Grammatical Structure

Occasionally the grammar of a desired quotation won't match the grammatical structure of your sentence or a word, such as a pronoun, will not be clear if it is taken out of its original context. In these cases, you change the quotation or add a clarifying word, placing brackets around the changes to indicate that the material is not part of the original wording. You also use brackets to show a change in capitalization.

Original Passage	The newspapers regularly advocated shooting burglars on sight, and several burglars were, in fact, shot at.

Quotation Modified to Fit Grammar of Writer's Sentence

In Bodie, an armed citizenry successfully eliminated burglaries, with "newspapers regularly advocat[ing] shooting burglars on sight" (McGrath 206).

Original   Highwaymen, for example, understood that while they could take
                the express box from a stagecoach without arousing the citizens,
                they risked inciting the entire populace to action if they robbed the
                passengers.

Use of Brackets to Change Capitalization and to Explain Missing Referents

            Public sentiment influenced what laws were likely to be broken.
            "[W]hile they [highwaymen] could take the express box from a
            stagecoach without arousing the citizens, they risked inciting the en-
            tire populace to action if they robbed the passengers" (McGrath 19).

Perhaps the most frequent modification writers make is to omit portions of a
quotation. To indicate an omission in a quotation, use an ellipsis (three spaced
periods).

Original   Finally, juvenile crime, which accounts for a significant portion of
Passage   the violent crime in the United States today, was limited in Bodie to
                pranks and malicious mischief.

Ellipses Used to Indicate Omission

            "Finally, juvenile crime . . . was limited in Bodie to pranks and ma-
            licious mischief" (McGrath 20).

If the omission occurs between two sentences, use an additional period to indicate
the sentence boundary.

According to McGrath, "Bodie was indisputably violent and lawless, yet most
people were not affected. . . . [T]he old, the young, the weak, and the female—so
often the victims of crime today—were generally not harmed" (18).

Quotations Within Quotations

Occasionally a passage that you wish to quote will already contain quotation
marks. If you use block indentation, keep the quotation marks exactly as they are
in the original. If you set the passage within your own quotation marks, however,
change the original double marks (") into single marks (') to indicate the quotation
within the quotation. The same procedure works whether the quotation marks are
used for quoted words or for a title.

Original Passage: Robert Heilbroner Quoting William James

            And finally, we tend to stereotype because it helps us make sense
            out of a highly confusing world, a world which William James once
            described as "one great, blooming, buzzing confusion."

Quoted Passage: Writer Quoting Heilbroner

            Robert Heilbroner explains why people tend to create stereotypes:
            "And finally, we tend to stereotype because it helps us make sense
            out of a highly confusing world, a world which William James once
            described as 'one great, blooming, buzzing confusion' " (22).

CONVENTIONS FOR DOCUMENTING SOURCES

Documentation often seems like a thankless chore after the long effort of thinking, researching, and writing, but it is a valuable service for readers; it also gets easier with time and practice. In general, you should cite any information that you have taken from others with the exception of commonly known or commonly available knowledge (the birthdate of John F. Kennedy, the boiling point of water).

In the recent past, writers documented their work with footnotes or endnotes. Academic writers now use new conventions that greatly simplify documentation. They place citations in parentheses in the text just after the material requiring documentation, and they place the complete source information in a bibliography at the end of the paper.

The MLA and the APA specify slightly different forms for this purpose. For an example of MLA documentation, see Mary Turla's paper on pages 583–96, for APA documentation see Sheridan Botts' paper on pages 401–13.

Next we illustrate how to use both systems.

In-Text Citations

To cite sources in your text using the *MLA system,* place the author's name and the page references in parentheses immediately after the material being cited. If an attributive tag already identifies the author, give only the page number in parentheses. Once you have cited the author and it is clear that the same author's material is being used, you need cite only the page references in parentheses. The following examples show parenthetical documentation with and without an attributive tag. Note that the citation precedes the period. If you are citing a quotation, the parenthetical citation follows the quotation mark but precedes the final period.

> The Spanish tried to reduce the status of Filipina women who had been able to do business, get divorced, and sometimes become village chiefs (Karnow 41).

> According to Karnow, the Spanish tried to reduce the status of Filipina women who had been able to do business, get divorced, and sometimes become village chiefs (41).

> "And, to this day," Karnow continues, "women play a decisive role in Filipino families" (41).

A reader who wishes to check up on the source will find the bibliographic information in the Works Cited section by checking the entry under Karnow. If more than one work by Karnow was used for the paper, the writer would include in the in-text citation an abbreviated title of the book or article following Karnow's name.

> (Karnow, "In Our Image" 41)

In the *APA system,* the parenthetical reference includes the author's name and the date of the source as well as the page number if a particular passage or table is cited. The elements in the citation are separated by commas and a "p." or "pp." precedes the page number. If a source has more than one author, you use an ampersand (&) to join their names. When the author is mentioned in an attributive tag, you include only the date and page. The following examples show parenthetical documentation with and without attributive tags according to APA style.

> The Spanish tried to reduce the status of women who had been able to do business, get divorced, and sometimes become village chiefs (Karnow, 1989, p. 41).

> According to Karnow, the Spanish tried to reduce the status of women who had been able to do business, get divorced, and sometimes become village chiefs (1989, p. 41).

> "And, to this day," Karnow continues, "women play a decisive role in Filipino families" (1989, p. 41).

Just as with MLA style, with APA style readers will look for sources in the list of references at the end of the paper if they wish to find full bibliographic information. In the APA system, this bibliographic list is titled "References." If your sources include two works by the same author published in the same year, you place an *a* after the date for the first work and a *b* after the date for the second, ordering the works alphabetically by title. If Karnow had published two different works in 1989, your in-text citation would look like this:

> (Karnow, 1989b, p. 41)

Citing a Quotation or Other Data from a Secondary Source

Occasionally you may wish to use a quotation or data from a secondary source. If possible, find the quotation in its original source and cite that source. If the original source is not available, you should cite the secondary source and indicate that you have taken the material from a secondary source by using "qtd. in" (MLA) or "cited in" (APA). List only the secondary source in your Works Cited or References section. In the following example, the writer wishes to use a quote from a book entitled *Living Buddha, Living Christ,* written by a Buddhist monk, Thich Nhat Hanh. The writer is unable to locate the book and instead has to quote from a book review by Lee Moriwaki. Here is how the in-text citations will look.

> **MLA**   A Buddhist monk, Thich Nhat Hanh, stresses the importance of inner peace: "If we can learn ways to touch the peace, joy, and happiness that are already there, we will become healthy and strong, and a resource for others" (qtd. in Moriwaki: C4).

> **APA**   A Buddhist monk, Thich Nhat Hanh, stresses the importance of inner peace: "If we can learn ways to touch the peace, joy, and happiness that are already there, we will become healthy and strong, and a resource for others" (cited in Moriwaki, 1995, p. C4).

In the next section we describe the format for the bibliographic entries under Works Cited in the MLA system and under References in the APA system.

Bibliographic Listings at the End of Your Paper

Both the MLA and APA systems specify a complete list of all items cited, placed at the end of the paper. The list should comprise all sources from which you gathered information, including articles, books, videos, letters, and electronic sources. The list should not include works you read but did not cite. In both systems, all works are listed alphabetically by author, or by title if there is no author.

In the *MLA system* the title of the list, "Works Cited," is centered one inch from the top of the page. Sources are listed alphabetically, the first line flush with the left margin and succeeding lines indented one-half inch (or five spaces if you are using a typewriter). Here is a typical example of a work cited in MLA form.

Karnow, Stanley. In Our Image: America's Empire in the Philippines.

New York: Random, 1989.

The same information with a slightly different arrangement is used in the *APA system.* The title "References" is centered at the top of the page. Entries for sources are listed alphabetically. After the first line, which is flush at the left margin, succeeding lines are indented three spaces.

Karnow, S. (1989). In our image: America's empire in the Philippines.

New York: Random House.

The remaining pages in this section show examples of MLA and APA formats for different kinds of sources, including the electronic sources described in Chapter 24. Following these examples is a typical page from a Works Cited or References list that features formats for the most commonly encountered kinds of sources.

General Format for Books

MLA: Author. Title. Edition. City of Publication: Publisher, year

of publication.

APA: Author. (Year of Publication). Title. City of Publication:

Publisher.

One Author

MLA: Coles, Robert. The Spiritual Life of Children. Boston:

Houghton, 1990.

APA: Coles, R. (1990). The spiritual life of children. Boston:

Houghton Mifflin.

In the MLA style, author entries include first names and middle initials. In the APA style only the initials of the first and middle names are given, unless full names are needed to distinguish persons with the same initials. In the APA style only the first word and proper names in a title are capitalized. Note also that the year of publication follows immediately after the author's name. In the MLA system, names of publishers have standard abbreviations, listed on pages 218–20 in the *MLA Handbook for Writers of Research Papers.* In the APA system, names of publishers are not usually abbreviated, except for the elimination of unnecessary words such as *Inc., Co.,* and *Publishers.* Note also that in the MLA style, punctuation following the underlined title is not underlined, but in the APA style, punctuation following the underlined title *is* underlined.

Two Listings for One Author

MLA: Doig, Ivan. <u>Dancing at the Rascal Fair</u>. New York: Atheneum,

1987.

---. <u>English Creek</u>. New York: Atheneum, 1984.

In the MLA style, when two or more works by one author are cited, the works are listed in alphabetical order by title. For the second and all additional entries, type three hyphens and a period in place of the author's name. Then skip two spaces and type the title.

APA: Doig, I. (1984). <u>English Creek</u>. New York: Atheneum.

Doig, I. (1987). <u>Dancing at the rascal fair</u>. New York:

Atheneum.

Selfe, C. L. (1984a). The predrafting processes of four high-

and four low-apprehensive writers. <u>Research in the Teaching</u>

<u>of English, 18,</u> 45-64.

Selfe, C. L. (1984b). <u>Reading as writing and revising strat-</u>

<u>egy.</u> (ERIC Document Reproduction Service No. ED 244-295)

In APA style, when an author has more than one entry in "References," the author's name is repeated and the entries are listed chronologically (oldest to newest) rather than alphabetically. When two entries by the same author have the same date, they are then listed in alphabetical order. Lowercase letters are added after the year of publication to distinguish them from each other when cited by date in the text.

Two or More Authors

> MLA: Ciochon, Russell, John Olsen, and Jamie James. The Search for
>
> the Giant Ape in Human Prehistory. New York: Bantam,
>
> 1990.

> APA: Ciochon, R., Olsen, J., & James, J. (1990). The search for the
>
> giant ape in human prehistory. New York: Bantam Books.

Note that the APA style uses the ampersand (&) to join the names of multiple authors.

Using *et al.* for Works with Several Authors

> MLA: Maimon, Elaine P., et al. Writing in the Arts and Sciences.
>
> Cambridge, MA: Winthrop, 1981.

In the MLA system, if there are four or more authors, you have the option of using the form *et al.* (meaning "and others") after the name of the first author listed on the title page.

> APA: Maimon, E. P., Belcher, G. L., Hearn, G. W., Nodine, B. F., &
>
> O'Connor, F. W. (1981). Writing in the arts and sciences.
>
> Cambridge, MA: Winthrop.

APA style calls for you to write out the names of all authors, no matter how many, for one work.

Anthology with an Editor

> MLA: Rabkin, Norman, ed. Approaches to Shakespeare. New York:
>
> McGraw, 1964.

> APA: Rabkin, N. (Ed.). (1964). Approaches to Shakespeare. New York:
>
> McGraw-Hill.

Essay in an Anthology or Other Collection

> MLA: Stein, Robert B., Lon Polk, and Barbara Bovee Polk. "Urban
>
> Communes." Old Family/New Family. Ed. Nona Glazer-Malbin.
>
> New York: Nostrand, 1975. 171–88.

APA: Stein, R. B., Polk, L., & Polk, B. B. (1975). Urban communes.

In N. Glazer-Malbin (Ed.), Old family/new family

(pp. 171-188). New York: Van Nostrand.

Book in a Later Edition

MLA: Valette, Rebecca M. Modern Language Testing. 2nd ed. New York:

Harcourt, 1977.

Williams, Oscar, ed. A Little Treasury of Modern Poetry.

Rev. ed. New York: Scribner's, 1952.

APA: Valette, R. M. (1977). Modern language testing (2nd ed.). New

York: Harcourt, Brace, Jovanovich.

Williams, O. (Ed.). (1952). A little treasury of modern

poetry (Rev. ed.). New York: Scribner's.

Multivolume Work

Cite the whole work when you have used more than one volume of the work.

MLA: Churchill, Winston S. A History of the English-Speaking Peo-

ples. 4 vols. New York: Dodd, 1956-58.

APA: Churchill, W. S. (1956-1958). History of the English-speaking

peoples (Vols. 1-4). New York: Dodd, Mead.

Include the volume number when you have used only one volume of a multivolume work.

MLA: Churchill, Winston S. The Great Democracies. New York: Dodd,

1957. Vol. 4 of A History of the English-Speaking Peo-

ples. 4 vols. 1956-58.

APA: Churchill, W. S. (1957). A history of the English-speaking peo-

ples: Vol. 4. The great democracies. New York: Dodd, Mead.

Reference Work with Frequent Editions

MLA: Pei, Mario. "Language." World Book Encyclopedia. 1976 ed.

In citing familiar reference works under the MLA system, you don't need to include all the normal publication information.

APA: Pei, M. (1976). Language. In <u>World book encyclopedia</u> (Vol. 12,

pp. 62-67). Chicago: Field Enterprises.

APA does not give a specific example for use of a reference book. The APA manual directs the writer to follow an example similar to the source and to include more information rather than less.

Less Familiar Reference Work Without Frequent Editions

MLA: Ling, Trevor O. "Buddhism in Burma." <u>Dictionary of Comparative</u>

<u>Religion</u>. Ed. S. G. F. Brandon. New York: Scribner's,

1970.

APA: Ling, T. O. (1970). Buddhism in Burma. In S. G. F. Brandon

(Ed.), <u>Dictionary of comparative religion</u>. New York:

Scribner's.

Edition in Which Original Author's Work Is Prepared by an Editor

MLA: Brontë, Emily. <u>Wuthering Heights</u>. 1847. Ed. V. S. Pritchett.

Boston: Houghton, 1956.

APA: Brontë, E. (1956). <u>Wuthering Heights</u> (V. S. Pritchett, Ed.).

Boston: Houghton, Mifflin. (Original work published 1847)

Translation

MLA: Camus, Albert. <u>The Plague</u>. Trans. Stuart Gilbert. New York:

Modern Library, 1948.

APA: Camus, A. (1948). <u>The plague</u> (S. Gilbert, Trans.). New York:

Modern Library. (Original work published 1947)

In APA style, the date of the translation is placed after the author's name; the date of original publication of the work is placed in parentheses at the end of the reference. In text, this book would be cited as follows:

(Camus, 1947/1948)

Corporate Author (a Commission, Committee, or Other Group)

MLA: American Medical Association. <u>The American Medical Associa-</u>

<u>tion's Handbook of First Aid and Emergency Care</u>. New

York: Random, 1980.

APA: American Medical Association. (1980). <u>The American Medical</u>

   <u>Association's handbook of first aid and emergency care.</u> New

   York: Random House.

Anonymous Work

MLA: <u>The New Yorker Cartoon Album: 1975–1985</u>. New York: Penguin, 1987.

APA: <u>The New Yorker cartoon album: 1975–1985.</u> (1987). New York:

   Penguin Books.

Republished Work (For Example, a Newer Paperback Published After the Original Hardbound)

MLA: Sagan, Carl. <u>The Dragons of Eden: Speculations on the Evolution</u>

   <u>of Human Intelligence</u>. 1977. New York: Ballantine, 1978.

APA: Sagan, C. (1978). <u>The dragons of Eden: Speculations on the</u>

   <u>evolution of human intelligence.</u> New York: Ballantine.

   (Original work published 1977)

General Format for Articles

MLA: Author. "Article Title." <u>Magazine or Journal Title</u> volume

   number (Date): inclusive pages.

APA: Author. (Date). Article title. <u>Magazine or Journal Title,</u>

   <u>volume number,</u> inclusive pages.

Scholarly Journal with Continuous Annual Pagination

MLA: Barton, Ellen L. "Evidentials, Argumentation, and Epistemologi-

   cal Stance." <u>College English</u> 55 (1993): 745–69.

APA: Barton, E. L. (1993). Evidentials, argumentation, and epistemo-

   logical stance. <u>College English, 55,</u> 745–769.

Scholarly Journal with Each Issue Paged Separately

MLA: Pollay, Richard W., Jung S. Lee, and David Carter-Whitney.

   "Separate, but Not Equal: Racial Segmentation in Cigarette

   Advertising." <u>Journal of Advertising</u> 21.1 (1992): 45–57.

APA: Pollay, R. W., Lee, J. S., & Carter-Whitney, D. (1992). Racial

segmentation in cigarette advertising. Journal of Advertis-

ing, 21(1), 45-57.

Note that in both systems when each issue is paged separately, both the volume (in this case, 21) and the issue number (in this case, 1) are given.

Magazine Article

MLA: Fallows, James. "Vietnam: Low-Class Conclusions." Atlantic

Apr. 1993: 38-44.

APA: Fallows, J. (1993, April). Vietnam: Low-class conclusions.

Atlantic, 38-44.

Note that this form is for a magazine published each month. The next entry shows the form for a magazine published each week.

Anonymous Article

MLA: "The Rebellious Archbishop." Newsweek 11 July 1988: 38.

APA: The rebellious archbishop. (1988, July 11). Newsweek, 38.

Review

MLA: Bliven, Naomi. "Long, Hot Summer." Rev. of We Are Not Afraid:

The Story of Goodman, Schwerner, and Cheney and the Civil

Rights Campaign of Mississippi, by Seth Cagin and Philip

Dray. New Yorker 11 July 1988: 81+.

This is a review of a book. The "81+" indicates that the article begins on page 81 but continues later in the magazine, perhaps on pages 83, 87, and 89. For both movie and book reviews, if the reviewer's name is not given, begin with the title of the reviewed work, preceded by "Rev. of" in the MLA system or "[Review of *title*]" in the APA system. Begin with the title of the review if the review is titled but not signed.

APA: Bliven, N. (1988, July 11). Long, hot summer [Review of the

book We are not afraid: The story of Goodman, Schwerner,

and Cheney and the civil rights campaign of Mississippi].

The New Yorker, 81-86.

Newspaper Article

MLA: `Healy, Tim. "The Politics of Real Estate." Seattle Times 14`

`June 1988: 1E.`

APA: `Healy, T. (1988, June 14). The politics of real estate. The`

`Seattle Times, p. 1E.`

Note that the section is indicated if each section is paged separately.

Newspaper Editorial

MLA: `Smith, Charles Z. "Supreme Court Door Opens for a Minority."`

`Editorial. Seattle Times 14 July 1988: 18A.`

APA: `Smith, C. Z. (1988, July 14). Supreme Court door opens for a`

`minority [Editorial]. The Seattle Times, p. 18A.`

Letter to the Editor of a Magazine or Newspaper

MLA: `Fleming, Deb. Letter. Ms. July 1988: 14.`

APA: `Fleming, D. (1988, July). [Letter to the editor]. Ms., 14.`

Include a title if one is given to the letter in the publication.

Information Service such as ERIC (Educational Resources Information Center) or NTIS (National Technical Information Service)

MLA: `Eddy, P. A. The Effects of Foreign Language Study in High`

`School on Verbal Ability as Measured by the Scholastic`

`Aptitude Test-Verbal. Washington: Center for Applied Lin-`

`guistics, 1981. ERIC ED 196 312.`

APA: `Eddy, P. A. (1981). The effects of foreign language study in`

`high school on verbal ability as measured by the Scholastic`

`Aptitude Test-Verbal. Washington, DC: Center for Applied`

`Linguistics. (ERIC Document Reproduction Service No. ED 196`

`312)`

Formats for Electronic Sources

You should list source information if you incorporate material from any of the electronic sources described in Chapter 24, including interactions on the Internet.

The following categories cover electronic materials that the MLA and APA have specified as of this writing.

Books, Pamphlets, or Texts in On-line Databases or CD-ROMs That Are Also Available in Print

> MLA: Melville, Herman. <u>Moby-Dick, or The White Whale</u>. Ed. Howard
>
>   Vincent. New York: Viking, 1957. Online. U of Virginia
>
>   Lib. Internet. 10 Mar. 1995. Available FTP: etext.
>
>   virginia.edu.

Note that the last two lines list the medium, archive name, computer network, date of access, and supplementary electronic access information.

> APA: NCTE. (1987). <u>On writing centers</u> [CD-ROM]. Urbana, IL: ERIC
>
>   Clearinghouse for Resolutions on the Teaching of Composi-
>
>   tion, II. SilverPlatter.

Include the medium in brackets next to the title, the location, and then the name of the publisher, producer, or distributor.

The entry in "Works Cited" or "References" should document the electronic source, not the printed one. Even if the material is available in printed form, the electronic version may be substantially different.

Journals or Periodicals in On-line Databases or CD-ROMs That Are Also Available in Print

> MLA: Kettel, Raymond P. "An Interview with Jerry Spinelli: Thoughts
>
>   on Teaching Writing in the Classroom." <u>English Journal</u> 83
>
>   (1994): 61–64. Urbana: ERIC Clearinghouse on Elementary
>
>   and Early Childhood Educ., 1966–1995/Feb. <u>ERIC</u>. CD-ROM.
>
>   SilverPlatter. 21 Mar. 1995.

List the medium, vendor name, and issue date. You should list supplementary electronic access information if it is available.

> APA: Kettel, R. P. (1994). An interview with Jerry Spinelli:
>
>   Thoughts on teaching writing in the classroom. <u>English</u>
>
>   <u>Journal</u> 83 (1994): 61–64. Urbana, IL: ERIC Clearinghouse on
>
>   Elementary and Early Childhood Educ. 1966–1995/Feb. <u>ERIC</u>
>
>   ipps.lsa.uminn.edu

Note that the last item in this format is a retrieval location.

Books, Journals, or Periodicals in On-line Databases or CD-ROMs That Are Not Available in Print

> MLA: Knuuttila, Simo. "Remarks on Induction in Aristotle's Dialectic
>
> and Rhetoric." Revue Internationale de Philosophie 47
>
> (1993): 78-88. CD-ROM. Bowling Green: Bowling Green State
>
> University, 1980.

Include the medium, vendor name, and date of issue. You should also list supplementary electronic access information if it is available.

The APA style follows the specifications for on-line journals available in print.

Computer Disks That Are Not Available in Print

> MLA: Microsoft Word. Vers. 6.0. Diskette. Everett: Microsoft, 1994.

> APA: Microsoft Word 6.0 [Computer software]. (1994). Everett, CA:
>
> Microsoft.

Include the medium, city of issue, vendor name, and date of issue.

The APA style follows the specifications for on-line books available in print.

Information Service Data Bank

> MLA: Department of Labor. "U.S. Population by Ethnic Origin: Urban
>
> and Urbanized Areas." 1990 U.S. Census of Population and
>
> Housing. Online. Human Resource Information Network. 10
>
> Apr. 1995.

Include the medium, network name, and date of issue. You should also include supplementary access information if it is available.

> APA: Shimabukuru, J. (Ed.). (1995, February). Internet in ten
>
> years-Essays [62 paragraphs]. Electronic Journal on Virtual
>
> Culture, 3(1). Available FTP: 138.122.118.1

Note that this format lists retrieval information, including the server and retrieval path.

Electronic Newsletter or Conference

> MLA: Meynell, H. A., ed. "Grace, Politics and Desire: Essays on
>
> Augustine." Bryn Mawr Medieval Review 93, 8.2 (1990): 7
>
> pp. Online. Internet. 10 Mar. 1995.

Include the medium, network name, and date of access. You should also include supplementary access information if it is available.

The APA style follows the specifications for material from an information service data bank.

E-mail, Listservs, and Other Nonretrievable Sources

> MLA: Rushdie, Salman. "My Concern About the Fatwa." E-mail to the
>
> author. 1 May 1995.

Note that this format specifies that the document is an E-mail letter, to whom it was addressed, and the date of transmission.

In APA style, this material is not listed in "References." You should, however, acknowledge it in in-text citations.

> The novelist has repeated this idea recently (Salman Rushdie, E-mail
>
> to the author, May 1, 1995).

Bulletin Board or Newsgroup Posting

> MLA: MacDonald, James C. "Suggestions for Promoting Collaborative
>
> Writing in College Composition." 10 Nov. 1994. Online
>
> posting. NCTE Forum/current topics/bulletin posting.
>
> America Online. 12 Mar. 1995.

Include the date of transmission or posting, the medium, network name, location information, an address or path for electronic access, and date of access.

In APA style, this material is acknowledged in in-text citations only. See the specifications for E-mail, listservs, and other nonretrievable sources.

Miscellaneous Materials

Films, Filmstrips, Slide Programs, and Videotapes

> MLA: Chagall. Dir. Kim Evans. Ed. Melvyn Bragg. Videocassette. Lon-
>
> don Weekend Television, 1985.

> APA: Evans, K. (Director), & Bragg, M. (Editor). (1985). Chagall
>
> [Videocassette]. London: London Weekend Television.

Television and Radio Programs

> MLA: Korea: The Forgotten War. Narr. Robert Stack. KCPQ, Seattle.
>
> 27 June 1988.

APA: Stack, R. (Narrator). (1988, June 27). The forgotten war.

Seattle: KCPQ.

Interview

MLA: Deltete, Robert. Personal interview. 27 Feb. 1994.

APA: Deltete, R. (1994, February 27). [Personal interview].

The APA publication manual says to omit nonrecoverable material—such as personal correspondence, personal interviews, lectures, and so forth—from "References" at the end. However, in college research papers, professors usually like to have such information included.

Lecture, Address, or Speech

MLA: North, Oliver. Speech. Washington Policy Council. Seattle. 20

July 1988.

APA: North, O. (1988, July 20). Speech presented to Washington Pol-

icy Council, Seattle, WA.

In the MLA system, if the title of the speech is known, give the title in quotation marks in place of "Speech." The *Publication Manual of the American Psychological Association* has no provisions for citing lectures, addresses, or speeches because these are nonrecoverable items. However, the manual gives authors leeway to design citations for instances not covered explicitly in the manual. This format is suitable for college research papers.

For more complicated entries, consult the *MLA Handbook for Writers of Research Papers*, fourth edition, or the *Publication Manual of the American Psychological Association*, fourth edition. Both books should be available in your library or bookstore.

Quick Check Reference: MLA and APA Bibliographic Entries

As a handy reference to the most commonly encountered kinds of entries in college research papers, see pages 579–80. These two pages illustrate a "Works Cited" list (MLA format) and a "References" list (APA format). These lists give you a quick summary of the formats for the most commonly used sources.

Works Cited: MLA Style Sheet for the Most Commonly Used Sources

Author's last name and page number in upper right corner. → Ross 27

Works Cited

Book entry, one author. Use standard abbreviations for common publishers. → Adler, Freda. <u>Sisters in Crime</u>. New York: McGraw, 1975.

Andersen, Margaret L. <u>Thinking About Women: Sociological Perspectives on Sex and Gender</u>. 3rd ed. New York: Macmillan, 1993.

Book entry in a revised edition.

Bart, Pauline, and Patricia O'Brien. <u>Stopping Rape: Successful Survival Strategies</u>. New York: Pergamon, 1985.

Book with two or three authors. With four or more authors use "et al.," as in Jones, Peter, et al.

Durkin, Kevin. "Social Cognition and Context in the Construction of Sex Differences." <u>Sex Differences in Human Performances</u>. Ed. Mary Anne Baker. New York: Wiley, 1987. 45-60.

Article in anthology; author heads the entry; editor cited after the title. Inclusive page numbers come two spaces after the period following year.

Fairburn, Christopher G., et al. "Predictors of 12-month Outcome in Bulimia Nervosa and the Influence of Attitudes to Shape and Weight." <u>Journal of Consulting and Clinical Psychology</u> 61 (1993): 696-98.

Article in scholarly journal paginated consecutively throughout year. This article has four or more authors.

Kantrowitz, Barbara. "Sexism in the Schoolhouse." <u>Newsweek</u> 24 Feb. 1992: 62.

Weekly or biweekly popular magazine; abbreviate all months except May, June, and July.

Langeweische, William. "The World in Its Extreme." <u>Atlantic</u> Nov. 1991: 105-40.

Monthly, bimonthly, or quarterly magazine.

Taylor, Chuck. "After Cobain's Death: Here Come the Media Ready to Buy Stories." <u>Seattle Times</u> 10 Apr. 1994: A1+.

Newspaper article with identified author; if no author, begin with title.

References: APA Style Sheet for the Most Commonly Used Sources*

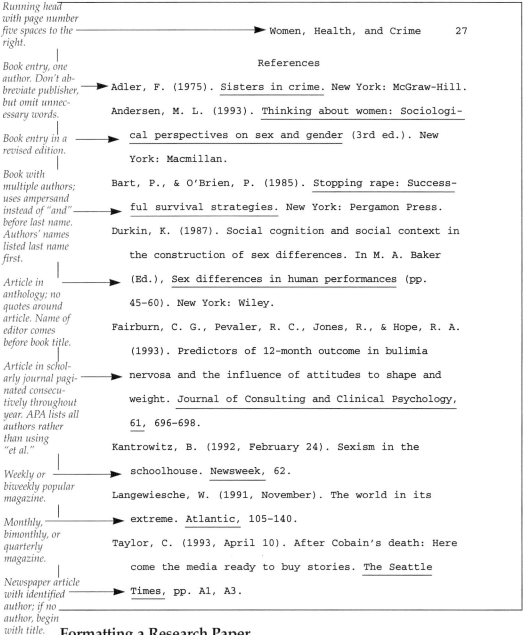

Running head with page number five spaces to the right.

→ Women, Health, and Crime   27

                              References

Book entry, one author. Don't abbreviate publisher, but omit unnecessary words.

→ Adler, F. (1975). Sisters in crime. New York: McGraw-Hill.

Andersen, M. L. (1993). Thinking about women: Sociologi-

Book entry in a revised edition.

→   cal perspectives on sex and gender (3rd ed.). New

      York: Macmillan.

Book with multiple authors; uses ampersand instead of "and" before last name. Authors' names listed last name first.

Bart, P., & O'Brien, P. (1985). Stopping rape: Success-

→ ful survival strategies. New York: Pergamon Press.

Durkin, K. (1987). Social cognition and social context in

      the construction of sex differences. In M. A. Baker

Article in anthology; no quotes around article. Name of editor comes before book title.

→ (Ed.), Sex differences in human performances (pp.

      45–60). New York: Wiley.

Fairburn, C. G., Pevaler, R. C., Jones, R., & Hope, R. A.

      (1993). Predictors of 12-month outcome in bulimia

Article in scholarly journal paginated consecutively throughout year. APA lists all authors rather than using "et al."

→ nervosa and the influence of attitudes to shape and

      weight. Journal of Consulting and Clinical Psychology,

      61, 696–698.

Kantrowitz, B. (1992, February 24). Sexism in the

Weekly or biweekly popular magazine.

→ schoolhouse. Newsweek, 62.

Langewiesche, W. (1991, November). The world in its

Monthly, bimonthly, or quarterly magazine.

→ extreme. Atlantic, 105–140.

Taylor, C. (1993, April 10). After Cobain's death: Here

      come the media ready to buy stories. The Seattle

Newspaper article with identified author; if no author, begin with title.

→ Times, pp. A1, A3.

Formatting a Research Paper

College instructors usually ask students to follow standard academic conventions for formatting research papers. Although conventions vary from discipline

*Note that many instructors in the social sciences prefer that student papers be prepared as a final copy and therefore use the hanging indent format in the Reference list.

to discipline, the most common formatting styles are the MLA or the APA. The MLA formatting style is illustrated in Mary Turla's paper on pages 583–96. The APA formatting style is illustrated in Sheridan Botts's paper on pages 401–13.

Formatting features common to both MLA and APA

- Double-space the text throughout, including quotations and notes.
- Use one-inch margins top and bottom, left and right.
- Indent five spaces at the beginning of every paragraph.
- Number pages consecutively throughout the manuscript including the bibliographic section at the end.
- Begin the bibliographic section (called "Works Cited" in MLA and "References" in APA) on a separate page.

Distinctive formatting features for MLA

- Do not include a cover page. Type your name, professor's name, course number, and date in the upper left-hand corner of your paper (all double-spaced) beginning one inch from the top of the page; then double-space and type your title, centered, without underlines, boldface, or all caps (capitalize first word and important words only); then double-space and begin your text (see page 583 for an example).
- Page numbers go in the upper right-hand corner flush with the right margin and one-half inch from the top of the page. The page number should be preceded by your last name (see pp. 583–96). The text begins one inch from the top of the page.
- Start a new page for your bibliography, which is titled "Works Cited" (centered, one inch from top of page, without underlining, quotation marks, bold face, or all caps). Format each entry according to the instructions on pages 567–78 (see pp. 595–96 for an example; also see p. 579).

Distinctive formatting features for APA

- Has a separate title page, numbered page 1, and a 100–150 word Abstract, numbered page 2 (the main body of your text begins with page 3). Approximately one-third from the top of the page, type your title centered and double-spaced, without underlines or all caps (capitalize first word and important words only). Two spaces below the title type your name (centered). Two spaces below your name, type your course number (centered), and two spaces below that type the date (for an example of an APA title page, see page 401).
- Page numbers go in upper right-hand corner, flush with right margin. Five spaces to the left of your page number, type your running head (a short version of your title), capitalizing only the first letters. Note that the first page of the main text is numbered page 3 (see pp. 402–13).
- Start a new page for your bibliography, which is titled "References" (centered, one inch from top of page, without underlining, quotation marks, bold face, or all caps). Format each entry according to the instructions on pages 567–78 (see pp. 412–13 for an example; also see p. 580).

Summary

This chapter has shown that research writing is a variation on the thesis-governed writing with which you are already familiar. We have discussed how to focus and refine your research question, suggesting that you remain flexible throughout your research process so that your purpose and thesis can evolve as you discover new information. The chapter has explained purposeful strategies for reading, thinking, and note taking to help you avoid random inclusion of data and keep all research information focused on your own thesis. The chapter has also discussed methods of summarizing, paraphrasing, and quoting through the effective use of attributive tags, quotation marks, and block indentation. These methods enable you to work research sources smoothly into your own writing, distinguish your ideas from those of your sources, and avoid plagiarism. Finally, the chapter has explained how to use the MLA and the APA systems to cite and document your sources.

Student Example

We conclude with a sample of a successful effort: Mary Turla's research paper on mail-order brides. She uses the MLA system for citing and documenting her sources.

½"

Turla 1

Mary Turla

Professor Nichols

English 125

30 May 1995

Mail-Order Bride Romances: The Need for Regulation

On March 2, 1995, an angry and outraged Timothy Blackwell took the law into his own hands. Packing a 9mm Taurus semiautomatic handgun, he walked into a Seattle courthouse and gunned down his wife, Susanna Remarata Blackwell, a mail-order bride. According to The Seattle Times, the couple were nearing the end of a year-long annulment case when the murder took place. Timothy wanted the marriage annulled, claiming that his wife, a native of the Philippines, had used him to get money and to gain U.S. citizenship. Susanna, however, filed for divorce, alleging physical and emotional abuse. She was also seeking residency under a battered-wife exception to deportation law. Seated outside the Seattle courtroom with two supportive friends, Susanna was awaiting the final proceedings in the legal dispute when Timothy shot all three (Haines and Sevens A1, A8).

The Blackwell case highlights the complex issues surrounding the controversial mail-order bride industry. Their tragic marriage illustrates the potential frustra-tion and turmoil for both partners in a mail-order match. They were victims of an industry that exploits

Turla 2

the poverty of third-world women and the romantic fantasies of American men. To build clientele and profits, the agencies employ marketing techniques that promote inaccurate and harmful stereotypes of both men and women, particularly Asian women. Therefore, regulations and controls must be implemented to control the problems and abuses that result.

Background: How Mail-Order Bride Agencies Work

Despite bad press, the mail-order bride business has grown into a thriving multi-million-dollar industry (Henderson A8). Over a thousand organizations in the United States, Canada, Western Europe, and Australia peddle mail-order introductions (Krich 36). Most of the agencies are "struggling, small-time operations, run out of a post-office box," some started by couples who had met through another pen-pal service (Krich 36). However, there are other agencies that are long-established and more successful. One of the largest and most successful agencies is California-based Rainbow Ridge Consultants, owned by Harvard Ph.D. John Broussard and his wife, Kelly Pomeroy. Begun in 1974, Rainbow Ridge Consultants publishes three separate bimonthly directories. The catalogs, running up to 48 pages, feature Philippine "Island Blossoms," Asian women in general, and random brides-to-be from Peru to Yugoslavia (Krich 36).

Most agencies follow the operating pattern established by Rainbow Ridge Consultants. At the supply end,

Turla 3

agencies place ads in local papers to lure women into
sending pictures with pertinent biographies and personal
information to the mail-order service--usually at no
charge (Krich 44). This information is then placed in
catalogs with names like "Jewel of the Orient," "Asian
Sweethearts," and "East Meets West Club." The agencies
then advertise their catalogs to men in magazines such
as Psychology Today, Playboy, and Rolling Stone (Mochizuki 1). In 1984 alone about 7,000 Filipino women married Australians, Europeans, and Americans through this
system (Agbayani-Siewert and Revilla 158). Despite their
claim that the only service their agencies offer is a
"pen-pal service," their wide variety of fees and services indicates deliberate efforts to arrange marriages.

How the Agencies Justify Their Services

5   The proliferation of agencies demonstrates what is
perhaps the strongest argument for the existence of
mail-order bride agencies--that there is at present a
strong demand for their services. Villipando cites a
1983 study that surveyed 265 men actively seeking brides
from Asia. According to this study, the typical men who
use the service were middle aged, had a good income, and
were often professionals or managers, but they were
burnt out by this society's high-pressure singles' scene
and were in search of a woman who was traditional and
family oriented rather than feminist and career oriented
(Villipando 6). As another researcher puts it, men seek-

ing mail-order brides are tired of American women, whom they find "too aggressive, too demanding, and too career-oriented" (Valdez 5).

While the men approach the agencies in search of emotional fulfillment, poverty appears to be the major reason that potential brides enter the market. For many, any option is better than the economic desperation found in much of the third world. For example, although the Philippine government has outlawed agencies from openly advertising catalog services and recruiting women, the practice remains and flourishes (Henderson 48). Poverty and improvement of the bride's and her family's economic status are the main reasons why Filipinas join mail-order clubs (Yuchengco 28). "These women are likely to turn to a correspondence marriage as a way to escape the poverty and lack of economic opportunity in the Philippines" (Agbayani-Siewert and Revilla 158).

Moreover, in some cases the mail-order bride system leads to satisfactory marriages. If a couple views their mail-order marriage as a practical partnership rather than as an "emotional cure-all" (Krich 46), it can sometimes succeed. Filipina Juliet Manalo Boxall is the director of the Filipino Friendship Club, the same mail-order service through which she met her English husband, Geoff Boxall. Their marriage has, thus far, lived up to their expectations. Boxall argues for the advantages of a "long-distance romance." (She feels that

6

7

Turla 5

the use of the terms "mail-order bride" or "mail-order
marriage" is a damaging mis-labeling of the service.)
She believes that time, distance, and shared values help
ensure a couple's compatibility. Because they write and
phone for months before they meet, she says, the couple
often "knows each other" better than couples whose
courtship is "ordinary." She adds that without the constant pressures of sex or "instant gratification" from
the ordinary dating scene or services, "a couple can get
to know each other without the distractions of sex and
how to handle it" (Boxall 27).

Rebuttal: "Fantasy Catalogs," Not a Pen-Pal Service

    Although the agencies claim to be just a pen-pal
service, the agencies use the catalogs to attract and
entice would-be suitors by playing up the advantages of
marrying a third-world bride. The language and imagery
found in most of the bride catalogs not only demonstrate
the white man's fantasy of a submissive and erotic Oriental woman, but it also promotes the image that the
women featured are sexual and economic commodities. "The
bride catalogs are frank: virginity, subservience, pow-
erlessness," writes Filipina activist Ninotchka Rosca
(48). American Asian Worldwide Service perpetuates the
stereotypes when it says in its brochure: "Asian ladies
are faithful and devoted to their husbands" (Villipando
13). "Like the Filipina, Malaysian and Indonesian women
are raised to respect and defer to the male. . . . The

Turla 6

young Oriental woman . . . derives her basic satisfaction from serving and pleasing her husband," states a
Broussard catalog (Villipando 13). Agencies use such
marketing techniques because they work. The earlier mentioned 1983 study cited by Villipando showed that 80
percent of the active foreign-bride seekers accept this
false image as true (Villipando 13).

On the other side of the world, the prospective
brides initially seem ideally prepared for life in the
West, especially if the bride is Filipina. (According to
Agbayani-Siewert and Revilla, 75 percent of mail-order
brides come from the Philippines.) The Pinay (or Filipina), compared with many of her third-world counterparts, is westernized, educated, and conservative as
well as Roman Catholic. Many speak English reasonably
well. Some women may also possess the "colonial mentality" so that for them "anything or anyone that comes
from the West is good" (Yuchengco 28). They also believe
strongly in marriage and family.

However, the man expecting a docile "Island Blossom"
may be in for quite a surprise if he chooses a Filipina
to fulfill his dreams. So warns David Watkins:

> Yet the writer would caution any Australian
> male who is seeking "a meek, obedient slave"
> that he may well be in for a rude awakening if
> he sees a Filipino bride as the answer to his
> dreams. . . . [M]any of the girls are well

9

10

Turla 7

educated professionals. . . . More importantly,

every Filipina is used to being treated with

respect and is very capable of making life

very uncomfortable for a husband who treats

her as a (sexy) domestic helper. (82)

Based on ancient Malay tradition, Filipino women, com-

pared with Chinese or Japanese women, have historically

enjoyed full equality with the Filipino male. Guthrie

and Jacobs describe this equality, noting several as-

pects of the culture that indicate equal status of men

and women. In the Philippines, daughters and sons tradi-

tionally share equally in inheritance. Within the fam-

ily, children owe respect and obedience to all family

members who are <u>older</u>; age, not gender, is what commands

respect in the culture. Guthrie and Jacobs also point to

the important position of numerous women in business and

government in the Philippines. And even the language

carries a sense of gender equality. In Tagalog, the most

important Filipino language, the words <u>he</u> and <u>she</u> are

both expressed by the one word <u>siya</u> so that, unlike many

languages, Tagalog makes it unlikely for one sex to be

considered superior to the other (Guthrie and Jacobs

42). Stanley Karnow also stresses the powerful position

of women both in the past and present. He states that

the Spanish tried to reduce the status of women who

could do business, get divorced, and sometimes become

village chiefs, but that the image of the Virgin Mary

Turla 8

upheld the force of women though limiting their power
more to the family (41). In addition to having women in
strong economic and political roles, the Philippines
provides similar educational opportunities for males and
females. This egalitarian tradition doesn't create a
spineless, weak wife.

Echoing the words of Watkins, Filipina activist Ellen
Ayaberra argues that mail-order catalogs' misrepresentation of the Filipina may lead not only to a grossly distorted image of the Filipina, but also to a disastrous
marriage. As she told me in a private interview:

> The mail-order bride industry should be abol-
> ished, one reason being that it misrepresents
> Asian women as being stupid and dumb. . . .
> The truth is that many Filipinas are hardwork-
> ing, degree-holding professionals who want to
> excel in both the workplace and the home.

As the warnings above suggest, both the men and women
involved would do well to be critical of advertisements
and catalogs that attempt to reduce the lives and
personalities of real people into two-dimensional
fantasies.

The Dark Side of Mail-Order Romance: The Wife's
Helplessness and the Man's Power

Although mail-order agencies claim that they build
lasting friendships, the truth is that they exploit
fantasies. When reality sets in, what happens to the

11

12

Turla 9

marriage? Whether the man turns violent, as did Timothy

Blackwell, or simply uses other forms of power, the in-

herent inequality in the mail-order marriage places the

bride in a vulnerable position. Even before addresses

are exchanged, the men have a significant advantage.

In most cases, only the woman is subjected to a lengthy

investigation before she can be featured in a catalog.

One catalog, for example, requires that a woman submit

proof of single status, vital statistics, and other in-

formation about her education, career interests, and

hobbies (Yuchengco 25). On the other hand, the inter-

ested male customer is not required to undergo an

inquisition. Some companies even discourage men from

"revealing certain types of information in their let-

ters, including such negative characteristics as being

black or physically disabled" (Krich 36). Krich con-

cludes, "The inequity of power is heightened by the

inequity of knowledge" (36).

13   The bride's vulnerability is intensified when she

marries her American husband, moves to the United

States, and assumes immigrant status. Marriage to an

American enables the bride to apply for permanent resi-

dent status, commonly known as "the green card," in

three years. Because the husband can deport her, he

holds tremendous power in their relationship. "If becom-

ing an American is their main aim, they are at the com-

plete mercy of their spouse for the three years until

Turla 10

citizenship is granted--and the husband holds the power to deport her if she doesn't play by his rules" (Krich 45).

Although it is difficult to document that domestic violence is a direct result of the mail-order marriage, victims, social workers, and women's rights' activists around the world have voiced their outrage, concerns, and fears. Donna Lewen, an advocate for the Northwest Immigration Rights Project and the woman who also handled Susanna Blackwell's case, claims that the connection between abuse and the fear of being deported is a familiar pattern in mail-order marriages. "In every case I've handled in which the immigrant woman is being abused, the threat of deportation is part of the cycle," she commented (qtd. in Haines and Sevens A1). Ignorance of immigration laws, little or no access to resources, and little or no community support are among the other forces that keep these immigrant women vulnerable to and dependent on their husbands. Asian victims of abuse are also reluctant to seek help because their failed marriage is often a source of shame (Mochizuki 25).

It should also be noted that males, as well as females, suffer from mail-order romance. "Challenged with evidence of abuse, the mail-order husbands like to cite rumors they've heard of brides who take their American men for all the money they're worth, then disappear once they've got their citizenship papers" (Krich 46).

Turla 11

Timothy Blackwell felt justified in his anger at his
wife. He wanted the marriage annulled on the basis that
she had used him only to gain citizenship. During the
proceedings, he "complained bitterly throughout his testimony about the money he had sent to her" (Haines and
Sevens A8).

The Need for Regulation

16   Unfortunately, because there is such a great demand
for mail-order bride services and because some mail-
order marriages are successful, total prohibition of the
mail-order bride industry seems unlikely. However, governmental regulation may prevent some of the abuses.

17   The industry thrives on desperate circumstances and
false expectations. Yet with most agencies unregulated,
the potential for abuse and exploitation is great, so
measures must be taken to protect the interests of the
men and women whose futures are at stake. For example,
agencies should be required to provide education concerning the realistic consequences of pursuing a mail-
order marriage. Brides should be supplied with realistic
explanations of what life is like in America and understand thoroughly how American immigration and citizenship laws work. Grooms should have detailed information
about the cultural backgrounds of the women they see in
the catalogs. Brides should be aware of programs and
support services available to immigrant wives. Another
safeguard for potential abuse would be to require a

background check on the male clients before they begin
to correspond. Furthermore, the agencies should perform
a follow-up service to see how the mail-order marriages
work out. Most important, however, is that both the men
and women are fully aware of the issues involved. Before
correspondence begins, the couples must be educated
enough to have formed realistic expectations concerning
people, cultures, and relationships.

The horrible ending of the Blackwell marriage demonstrates the potentially tragic outcome of mail-order
dating and marriages. Blackwell was a lifelong bachelor
when he met and married Susanna. He was drawn in by the
fantasy of the Asian woman as the ideal mate who would
satisfy his every wish. During the annulment proceedings, he testified, "I had heard so much that these
women were very sincere, very loving, very faithful. And
I always admired Polynesian-type women, with very long,
straight, black hair and very light brown skin" (Haines
and Sevens A8). Both Timothy and Susanna Blackwell
bought into the fantasy portrayed through the catalogs.
For the Blackwells, pain and frustration resulted when
fantasy and reality collided. Their dream world eventually turned into a nightmare.

18

Turla 13

Works Cited

Agbayani-Siewert, Pauline, and Linda Revilla. "Filipino
    Americans." Asian Americans. Ed. Pyong Gap Min.
    Thousand Oaks: Sage, 1995. 135-65.

Ayaberra, Ellen. Personal interview. 26 Apr. 1995.

Boxall, Juliet. "The Filipino Friendship Club and the
    Courtship of a Filipino Bride" Filipinas Oct. 1992:
    27-29.

Guthrie, George M., and Pepita Jimenez Jacobs. Child Rear-
    ing and Personality Development in the Philippines.
    Philadelphia: Pennsylvania State UP, 1967.

Haines, Thomas W., and Richard Sevens. "Gunman Felt
    Duped by Bride from the Start." Seattle Times 4
    Mar. 1995: A1+.

Henderson, Diane. "Mail-Order Bride Industry Thrives."
    Seattle Times 4 Mar. 1995: A1.

Karnow, Stanley. In Our Image: America's Empire in the
    Philippines. New York: Random, 1989.

Krich, John. "The Blooming Business of Imported Love."
    Mother Jones Feb.-Mar. 1986: 34-46.

Mochizuki, Ken. "I Think Oriental Women Are Just Great."
    International Examiner 7 May 1986: 25.

Rosca, Ninotchka. "Skin Trade Adventures." Special Edi-
    tion Press Spring 1984: 46-49

Valdez, Marybeth. "Return to Sender: The Mail-Order
    Bride Business in the Philippines." The Philippine
    Review May 1995: 5.

Villipando, Venny. "The Business of Selling Mail-Order
      Brides." San Diego Asian Journal 1 Feb. 1990: 6–16.

Watkins, David. "Filipino Brides: Slaves or Marriage
      Partners?" Australian Journal of Social Issues 17.1
      (1982): 73–84.

Yuchengco, Mona Lisa. "The Changing Face of the Filipino
      Woman." Filipinas Oct. 1992: 24+.

chapter 24

Electronic Writing and Research

When most people think about writing with a computer, the first thing that comes to mind is a word processor, equipped with a spell checker and a thesaurus. However, today's computer technology offers writing students countless options for exploring ideas, writing collaboratively, and conducting research. On-line interest groups exchange information about topics ranging from aliens to zygotes. Writers can compose modular contributions to a text and instantaneously distribute them to coauthors around the world. On-line archives offer resources from the world's greatest libraries at the touch of a finger. In this chapter we introduce you to some of these new options. Given the rapid pace of technological change, more resources will probably be available by the time you are reading this book, but the information here should serve as a guide to potential uses for these new resources.

OPPORTUNITIES FOR EXPLORING IDEAS WITH OTHERS

Many colleges and universities provide students with some form of access to the global network of computers called the Internet, either in the writing classroom or through a computer center or lab. Some institutions use independent personal computers (PCs), whereas others rely on workstations connected to a central computer. In either case, you need instructions from an experienced user on how to access the Internet from your system.

In this section, we look closely at some of the resources available to you via the Internet and discuss strategies for accessing these resources in ways that will be useful to you as a writer. We focus first on E-mail, Usenet newsgroups, and local and global chat, and then we turn to electronic collaboration possibilities and new forms of writing that use hypermedia, such as the World Wide Web.

E-mail and Listservs

You may already be using electronic mail (E-mail) at school, at work, or at home. E-mail sends messages from one network user to another around the globe in a matter of seconds. Many college instructors use E-mail as a way to enable student-to-student and student-to-instructor contact. For people with access to the Internet, E-mail has largely replaced traditional letters. This medium differs from traditional correspondence in that it is less formal; E-mail correspondents abbreviate more and labor less over grammar and spelling. However, in E-mail as in traditional correspondence, the appropriate level of formality is a function of the rhetorical situation. A quickly written response to a suggested meeting can consist of a simple "yes, OK at 10," whereas a job inquiry should be crafted more carefully.

Some people have likened E-mail to a written phone call. But unlike phone or face-to-face conversations, E-mail conversations can't rely on tone of voice or gesture to convey meaning. To compensate, E-mail users employ "emoticons"—symbols constructed from keyboard characters—to express emotion or sarcasm. Figure 24.1 provides a sampling of these symbols; mentally rotate each symbol a quarter turn to the right to get the picture right side up.

To use E-mail you need an address and you need to know the addresses of people whom you want to contact. E-mail addresses have three components: the individual account, or mailbox name; the @ sign; and the name of a mail server or domain. The mail server gathers messages sent to a network and then delivers them to individual users. Figure 24.2 shows a sample E-mail address.

You may choose your own account or mailbox name, but you must use the preassigned name for your server. Check with your instructor or computer center about setting up your Internet account and E-mail address.

Once your account is set up, you can send messages to anyone who has an Internet account. Your computation center may offer you a choice of mail-reading programs, which transfer messages back and forth from the campus mail server to your own PC or terminal. Some programs require you to type or enter textual commands to read your mail; others provide a point-and-click interface. To send E-mail, you need to know (a) the command for opening new messages; (b) the pro-

FIGURE 24.1   Sampling of E-mail "Emoticons"

:-)	basic smiley—indicates a joke or playfulness
;-)	winking smiley—indicates irony or sarcasm
:-O	surprised smiley
:-<>	angry smiley
:-(	sad smiley
:-/	smirking smiley
:-[	pouting smiley

FIGURE 24.2   A Sample E-mail
Address

mailbox/account
name ↓

server/domain
name ↓

billybob@mail.armadillo.edu

cedures for configuring recipients' addresses in the header of your message; and
(c) the "send" command for transferring your messages.

Messages you receive will likely be stored in an in-box. To read E-mail, you
open the in-box or mailbox in which it is stored and select the messages you want
to read. To respond to a message, you use a "respond" or "reply" command. When
you choose to "reply" to a message, a new message format is set up for you, usually with the original author's address and the text of the original message quoted
in a response window. Most mail-reading programs have on-line help for these
basic commands. After you have mastered the logistics of E-mail, you can incorporate it into your writing process. We describe two means of doing so here, but
you may find other possibilities as well.

E-mail Thought Letters

If you're just beginning to explore a topic for a paper or if you're wrestling
with a major supporting point, try doing an E-mail freewrite and sending it to one
or more friends or classmates. E-mail's spontaneity will encourage them to respond quickly and informally, and you can begin an easygoing exchange that you
may choose to sustain until you've finished your essay.

Since most mail programs quote the original message (signified by > on the
screen) in a response, your partners can easily comment on thought letters. Here
is an example of a freewrite about Internet media and the responses received. At
2:17 P.M. on 10/24/95, Jaime Garza wrote:

```
>From my limited experience of newsgroups and
>MOOs and MUDs,* it seems to me that the
>newsgroups offer more insightful information and
>the people who post attempt to put forth
>legitimate information more so than those in
>MOOs or other real time communication media. Of
>course there are vast differences among
>newsgroups and among MOOs . . .

Good point. I'm glad you qualified your
assessment of the real-time media, because, to
me, it seems like the purpose of the discussion
and the investment of the participants will
```

*MOOs and MUDs are on-line meeting spaces. We will discuss them later in this chapter.

```
influence the quality of the exchanges that take
place.

>Anyway, the MOOs, etc . . .   don't allow a user
>to think about an argument and then make a well
>thought out rebuttal. The real time media also
>seem more social than the newsgroups . . .

I see your point now. The pace of the real-time
discussion prevents people from gathering their
thoughts and composing in-depth replies. I am
curious about the way you describe MOOs as more
social, though. What do you mean by social? Don't
people on newsgroups also socialize? Do you think
it is the pace of real-time media that makes
things more social, or something else?
```

The original quoted message is indicated by the greater than signs (>) in front of each line. With E-mail, you can write freely in a message and your peers can easily refer to specific points or ideas as they respond.

Listserv Discussions

Another potentially productive way to use E-mail is to join a listserv interest group. A listserv compiles any number of E-mail accounts into a mailing list and forwards copies of messages to all people on the list. There are thousands of well-established listservs about a wide variety of topics. You need to know the address of a list in order to join. Specific information about joining various listservs and an index of active lists can be found by entering the Uniform Resource Locator (URL) address "http://tile.net/lists/" once you are on the World Wide Web in a browser.* Once you have subscribed to a listserv, you receive all messages sent to the list and any message you send to the list address will be forwarded to the other members.

A message sent to a listserv interest group is sure to find a responsive audience because all members on the list have chosen to take part in an ongoing discussion on the list's specific topic. Often lists archive and periodically post important messages or frequently asked questions (FAQs) for you to study. Most lists are for serious students of the list's topic, so to avoid offending any list members, learn the conventions for posting a message before you jump in.

Although you might find all kinds of interactions on a listserv, many users expect thoughtful, well-organized statements. If you are posting a message that introduces a new thread of discussion, you should clearly state your position (or

---

*Each file on the World Wide Web has a unique address, or URL, which allows writers to link to information on the Web and lets users move to specific sites. *http* stands for hypertext transfer protocol. There are a number of different systems, or protocols, on the Internet that facilitate the sharing of information. E-mail, for example, is often transferred using the simple mail transfer protocol. Since all the servers and clients that E-mail users work with understand this particular protocol, messages can be exchanged. The http protocol is more advanced and subsumes many earlier Internet protocols.

question) and summarize those of others. Here is a sample posting to a listserv on the environment.

```
To: environL@brahms.usdg.org
From: alanw@armadillo.edu (Alan Whigum)
Subject: Acid Rain and Action

I've been doing research on acid rain and am
troubled by some of the things I've found. For
instance, I've learned that washing coal gases
with limestone before they are released could
reduce sulfur emissions. I know that the
government has the power to mandate such devices,
but the real problem seems to be lack of public
pressure on the government. Why don't people push
for better legislation to help end acid rain? I
suppose it's an economic issue.
```

In turn, you can expect cogent, thoughtful responses from the list members. Here's a possible reply to the preceding message.

```
To: environL@brahms.usdg.org
From: bboston@armadillo.edu
Subject: Re Acid Rain and Action

I think you are right in pointing out that it is
ultimately public pressure that will need to be
applied to reduce acid rain. I've heard the
argument that it is cost that prevents steps from
being taken; people will pay more for goods and
services if these measures are taken, so they
resist. However, judging from the people I've
talked to about the subject, I would say that a
bigger problem may be knowledge. Most of them
said they would be willing to pay a little bit
more for their electricity if it meant a safer
environment. People aren't aware that action needs
to be taken now, because the problem seems remote.
```

When you join a listserv, you are granted instant access to a discourse community that is committed and knowledgeable about its topic. You can join one of the discussions already taking place on the list or post a request to get information and clarification about your own interests.

Listservs can take your ideas through a productive dialectic process as your message is seconded, refuted, complicated, and reclarified by the various list members. They also afford valuable opportunities to practice your summarizing skills as you respond to messages or provide additional information in a second posting. For example, suppose you take issue with a long message that placed the blame for homelessness on Reagan administration policies during the 1980s.

Rather than reproduce that entire message, you might provide a brief summary of the main points. The summary would not only give the readers enough background information to appreciate fully your response, it would also help you determine the main points of the original message and pinpoint the issues on which you disagree.

Usenet Newsgroups

Among the most useful sections of the Internet for writers are the bulletin-board-like forums of Usenet newsgroups. Newsgroups are electronic forums that allow you to post or respond to messages about virtually any topic imaginable. Newsgroups can be powerful tools for exploring problems and considering alternative viewpoints. The news server at your school determines the organization and number of groups available to you. Some schools carry groups that provide articles from professional news services, such as AP, Reuters, and UPI. Others provide topic-centered discussion groups. Your campus system may also offer class newsgroups for exchanging messages and drafts with others at your school. Check with your instructor or computer center to find out how to access the groups available to you.

Newsgroups feature messages that remain posted for a relatively long time, depending on the amount of traffic in the group. This practice allows for the development of various threads of discussion in response to the postings. An example, shown in Figure 24.3 shows both the nested postings to a newsgroup and an excerpt from one of the postings. Matt Giwer's posting mentions revisionists who want to reduce the estimates of the number of Holocaust victims. A response from William C. Anderson asks for a source. Giwer then claims that the information is common knowledge. The posting by John Morris again challenges Giwer for a source. Finally, Giwer responds to the challenges by citing the source for his information. Although this thread was continued after these postings and Giwer was further challenged, you can see that the postings constitute a kind of dialectic that interrogates the initial assumption.

Although you may be tempted to join such a thread immediately, you should familiarize yourself with some of the style conventions and the audience for that particular newsgroup before jumping in. Take time to read and listen in (lurk) to the group's postings. Debate on Usenet can become fairly heated, and a message that ignores previous postings can elicit angry responses ("flames"). In addition, a message that doesn't consider the newsgroup's audience or its favored style will likely be challenged. For example, if you want to post something in the "alt.fan.rush-limbaugh" group, you should be cautious about composing a message that openly contradicts Rush Limbaugh's brand of politics. If you send a message to the newsgroup "soc.history," you might be able to tread less carefully—this list is more politically diverse—however, members of this group might take offense if asked an obvious factual question.

Regardless of their makeup, most groups resent being asked questions that have already been answered. Some groups provide an archive of frequently asked

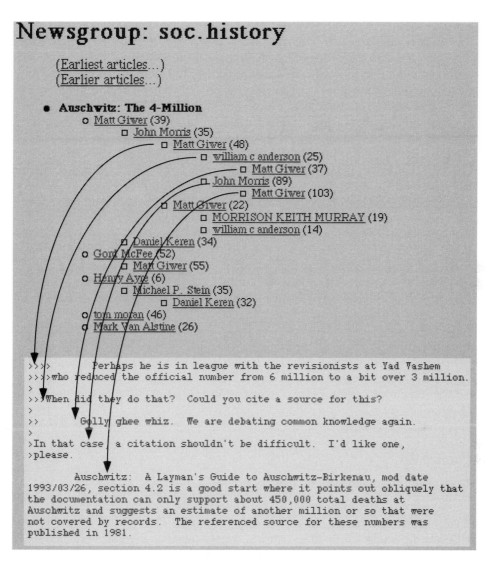

Newsgroup: soc.history

(Earliest articles...)
(Earlier articles...)

● **Auschwitz: The 4-Million**
   ○ Matt Giwer (39)
      □ John Morris (35)
         □ Matt Giwer (48)
           □ william c anderson (25)
              □ Matt Giwer (37)
           □ John Morris (89)
              □ Matt Giwer (103)
         □ Matt Giwer (22)
           □ MORRISON KEITH MURRAY (19)
           □ william c anderson (14)
         □ Daniel Keren (34)
   ○ Gord McFee (52)
         □ Matt Giwer (55)
   ○ Henry Ayre (6)
         □ Michael P. Stein (35)
           □ Daniel Keren (32)
   ○ tom moran (46)
   ○ Mark Van Alstine (26)

```
>>>>       Perhaps he is in league with the revisionists at Yad Vashem
>>>>who reduced the official number from 6 million to a bit over 3 million.
>
>>>When did they do that?  Could you cite a source for this?
>
>>       Golly ghee whiz.  We are debating common knowledge again.
>
>In that case a citation shouldn't be difficult.  I'd like one,
>please.

        Auschwitz:  A Layman's Guide to Auschwitz-Birkenau, mod date
1993/03/26, section 4.2 is a good start where it points out obliquely that
the documentation can only support about 450,000 total deaths at
Auschwitz and suggests an estimate of another million or so that were
not covered by records.  The referenced source for these numbers was
published in 1981.
```

FIGURE 24.3   A Sample Newsgroup Thread

questions (FAQs). If your interest is in something practical that is likely to be covered in the FAQ files, refer to them before posting a query. You should use the expertise of the group to find information that you might not be able to uncover otherwise.

When you are ready to post a message, use of some of the strategies outlined for composing a message to a listserv: try to summarize and synthesize your own position as well as those of others; highlight what you see as the most problematic or murky aspects of the topic. Carefully constructed messages are more likely to receive useful responses.

When you do receive feedback, evaluate it with special care. The unfiltered nature of all Internet media makes critical reading an essential skill. Because anyone with an Internet connection can take part in a discussion or post a message or article, you need to evaluate this information differently than you would articles from national newsmagazines, which are professionally written, edited for clarity, and checked for accuracy.

Although most postings are thoughtful, you will also find carelessly written messages that misconstrue an argument, personal rants that offer few, if any, stated reasons for their claims, and propaganda and offensive speech of many kinds in certain newsgroups. It is your responsibility, and unique opportunity, to read newsgroup messages critically, looking for their various biases and making decisions about their relative authority.

Of course, printed sources are marked by their own biases. Deadlines and space constraints may limit the depth and accuracy of printed coverage, and first-hand insights may be screened by authors and editors. If you were studying attitudes toward the Middle East peace process, a newsgroup exchange between a conservative Jew in Israel and a Palestinian student in the United States might provide better insight than a news article for your work. As you read through newsgroup messages, take time to evaluate the users' personal investments in the issue. Compare their comments to those in traditional sources, check for accuracy, and look for differing perspectives. Work these perspectives into your own thinking and writing about the topic. Treat information and points of view gathered from the Internet as primary rather than as secondary material; many of the people who contribute such material care passionately about an issue. It is up to you to place this material in context and edit it for your own audience.

Real-Time Discussion or Chat

Real-time discussions, or "chat," are synchronous exchanges that take place on a network—meaning that messages are transferred instantly back and forth among members taking part in the discussion. We focus on real-time interactions that take place on the Internet, but you can apply many of the strategies outlined here to local chat programs in your writing class. One of the most popular forms of real-time interaction takes place in the various channels of Internet Relay Chat (IRC). As with newsgroup and listserv communications, in chat you compose messages on your own computer and send them through the chat program to other users on the network. Some schools allow you to connect directly to a computer-center server and issue a command that will activate an IRC program. You may also have an IRC program on your workstation or PC that will make the connection for you. Once you are connected, you will want to issue a "list" command to see which topics are being discussed. You can then use the "join" command to log on to a particular channel. Since the specifics for connecting and issuing the various commands vary, you will need to check with your instructor or an experienced user for information about using IRCs at your school.

Like other Internet forums, chat groups are organized around common interests; but IRC sessions are more spontaneous and informal than is communication through newsgroups or listservs, because they consist of exchanges from people who are logged on at the same time. Moreover, in most cases, anyone can drop in on a chat, so the composition and focus of the group shifts from moment to moment. In these conversations, typographical and spelling errors are mostly overlooked, and abbreviations are an acceptable part of real-time style. The pace can be extremely fast, so users generally focus on getting their thoughts out rather than on producing highly polished messages.

IRC conversations and many other real-time exchanges also allow users to act as characters and to include scripted actions in the conversations. Imagine three users discussing flag burning.

```
William: I'm studying the constitutionality of flag-
burning amendments. Does anybody have any opinions?

Pat Buchanan: I think that if you are an
American, you should respect the country enough
not to deface her symbols.

*Thomas Jefferson takes out a match and sets fire
to the corner of an old thirteen star flag. It's
probably more important to respect the underlying
principles of our country than its symbols.
```

The asterisk denotes that the user Thomas Jefferson has issued an "action" command. By putting his name at the beginning of the message, other users see whatever follows as an action performed by that character. Users can construct a third-person narrative by mixing speech with the actions of their characters. You may use this feature in role-playing exercises or to explore some open-ended thinking about your topic.

When you join an IRC channel, you will be asked to choose a nickname. As you ponder your choice, think about some of the issues of persona that we discussed in Chapter 4. How do you want others to perceive you? How will your persona affect what you write? As you work in IRCs, you will refine your ability to weave various personae into your writing.

Perhaps even more than newsgroup or listserv discussions, chat sessions tend to heat up easily. Many real-time forums on the Internet allow users to take on pseudonyms, and some people use the opportunity to become irresponsible in what they say and write.

IRCs give rise to several ethical issues. In these uncensored forums, you will undoubtedly encounter discussions and materials that aren't appropriate for your assignments and class work. You may be challenged to assess your own feelings about censorship, pornography, hate speech, and free speech. And you will need to consider the impact of your persona and words on others as you take on a character or act out an idea.

Perhaps the most useful function of chat sessions is that they promote brain-storming and freewriting. When you are writing in a real-time environment, treat the activity as an exploratory one. Expect the message that you send to be challenged, seconded, or modified by the other writers in the session. Keep an open mind about the various messages that fly back and forth and be sure to respond to points that you find particularly useful or problematic. If you are using a local classroom chat program, you will be talking to people you know, so the conversation will be more predictable. When it's over, you might ask your instructor for a transcript of a chat session; reading it later will help solidify the free thinking that goes into a real-time discussion.

OPPORTUNITIES FOR COLLABORATIVE DISCUSSION AND WRITING

In many ways, all of the Internet is a medium for collaboration. Whether you use E-mail, postings to a newsgroup, or on-line chat, working with the Internet involves interaction with others. There are some specific approaches to using forums such as E-mail and chat for productive collaborative work; and there are other electronic forums specially designed for collaborative efforts.

E-mail and Newsgroups

If you are undertaking a group project, you can use E-mail lists to facilitate discussion. You should familiarize yourself with the "nickname" function of your mail reader. After converting members' E-mail addresses into nicknames, you can send messages directly to the nickname without having to write out the entire address. E-mail is also an excellent vehicle for conducting peer reviews. Not only can reviewers easily react to a paragraph or essay, but they can also work at their convenience and take as much time as they need to write their response. If a piece is long or contains special formatting, you will probably want to send it as an attached file that will be downloaded along with your message. Check the documentation for your mail program or see your instructor or computer center if you need help with nicknames and attachments.

It can be difficult to comment on a draft sent via E-mail. Some people insert comments in parentheses or use boldface or capital letters within the text of an assignment. But sentence-level changes are generally difficult to note. E-mail draft exchanges are probably more beneficial in the development stage than in the final stages of polishing a paper. You can focus on larger issues of organization, style, readability, and coherence by writing a paragraph or two at the end of the draft.

Newsgroups provide an excellent space for posting drafts, collaborating, and sharing class work. You may also be able to share work with other classes through a designated newsgroup. If you are working with other classes on a newsgroup, you might be tempted to respond mostly to members of your own class, but you'll get more out of the experience if you treat the members of the other courses as equal partners. There is value for writers in communicating with people who don't share all their assumptions, values, and language. In this regard, international newsgroups can be especially worthwhile. But you should take care not to flood your international partners with your assignments. Instead, perhaps working in smaller groups, brainstorm about an interpretation or stance on an issue before posting to your foreign partners.

On-Line Meeting Spaces and Specialized Software

Whereas chat forums such as IRCs can be useful for collaborating on the Internet, many people prefer to use another forum for multiple users, a MU* site.[†] Most MU*s are text-based virtual environments that allow users to meet, construct spaces and objects, and chat with each other. You are most likely to participate in a MU* to meet and converse with your peers, probably through a MU* designed for class interaction. Diversity University, for example, is a MOO that offers meeting spaces for students. Figure 24.4 (on p. 608) shows a section of the campus.

Notice that the virtual environment of the campus is conveyed through textual description. As you move through the campus, you take in and interact with the environment through writing. Typing "Look Board" will bring a description of the Learning Hall notice board to your screen. Commands such as "out" or "east" let you navigate to different sections of the campus. These environments, with their vivid textual descriptions, lend a sense of reality to the interactions that take place. They also provide unique spaces, such as the Learning Hall or the Student Union Lounge, for groups to meet to converse about writing projects.

After you've learned how to navigate the virtual environment of a MU*, you might try your hand at building your own environment. Describing MU* environments can help you create experiences for your readers. Authors of successful MU* spaces know that their descriptions must show, not tell their readers something about their message or argument. In this sense, MU* construction falls along the open end of the writing continuum. A MU* project should deliver information about an issue in story form. For example, a group of students at the University of Texas built a model town in a MU*. The town was caught up in a controversy over the opening of an adult bookstore. Users who logged on to the MU* could meet community leaders offering different perspectives on the issue of free speech and could also interact with objects in the village. Figure 24.5 (on p. 609) shows how these objects can shed light on an issue. Creating MU* spaces requires learning advanced MU* commands; hence your instructor or an experienced user will need to help you along the way. For more information about MU* building commands and philosophy and about accessing MU*s, you can consult the University of

---

[†]Originally specific to one type of computer game, Dungeons and Dragons, the acronym MU* has been adopted by others to designate the various multiple-user virtual environments. Variants of on-line meeting spaces include MUDs (Multiple User Domains), MUSHs (Multiple User Shared Hallucination sites), and MOOs (MUD Object Oriented sites).

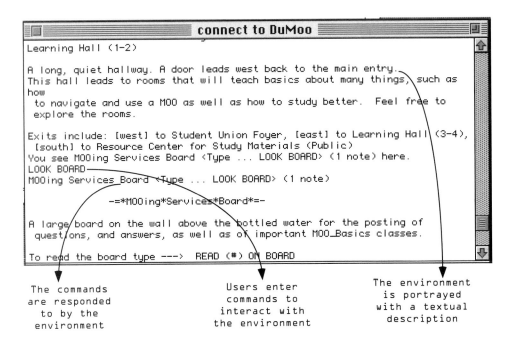

The commands are responded to by the environment

Users enter commands to interact with the environment

The environment is portrayed with a textual description

FIGURE 24.4 A Screen from the MOO Diversity University

Texas Austin's Computer Writing and Research Labs on the World Wide Web (http://www.cwrl.utexas.edu/moo/).

In most cases you can connect to a MU* as a guest. If you are planning to spend any length of time in a MU*, however, we recommend that you log on as a character. The opening screen will help you create a character and get connected. Again, consider the issues of persona discussed in Chapter 4 as you select a name for your MU* character. MU*s also let you assign a textual description to your character. Other MU* users can then consult your description and gain a better understanding of your character's role and motivation. Check the on-line help for instructions on setting your description, and use this opportunity to further your understanding of personae and how they influence your readers' perceptions.

Once you are on a MU*, you can both speak to people and emote, that is, perform actions that will be displayed as third-person narratives. Speaking and acting are accomplished with the "say" (usually a quotation mark ["]) and "emote" (usually a colon [:]) commands. To interact, you type one of these commands followed by text. For example, if Alan types

```
"I can't get a handle on my research topic.
```

then

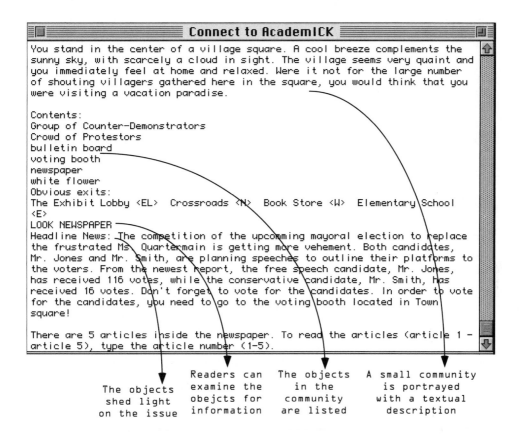

FIGURE 24.5   A Screen from a MU* Simulating a Model Town

```
Alan says, "I can't get a handle on my research
topic."
```

appears on all users' screens. If Carla types

```
:furrows her brow and asks, "what do people
usually disagree about when they talk about it?
```

then

```
Carla furrows her brow and asks, "what do people
usually disagree about when they talk about it?
```

appears. These messages and actions appear instantaneously.

When you interact on a MU*, keep in mind some of the strategies for real-time discussion that we presented earlier, including brainstorming activities. Always consider the impact of the personae that you adopt, and take steps to write responsibly.

PC software programs offer another option for collaborative work. Some enable writers to mark up and annotate on-line texts; others allow multiple users to work on a document simultaneously. NCSA has a program called Collage, which provides a common screen for users over the Internet so that they can work together; users can type text or place graphics in a document from any computer with an Internet connection. You can also find collaboration programs for local networks. Programs such as Timbuktu let students share their screens as they work together on projects. Your instructor or computer-center consultant may recommend one of these programs.

Hypertexts

The term *hypertext* refers to projects that use electronic links to construct documents containing both text and nontextual elements. Hypertexts that incorporate video, graphical, and audio files are sometimes called *hypermedia documents.* Composing with hypermedia often involves learning some form of programming language or developing expertise with special software. For most writing projects, however, you can easily use the World Wide Web and such programs as ToolBook or HyperCard to create a hypertext.

Traditional essays are linear—a reader starts at the beginning and reads through the document until the end. A hypertext project can be nonlinear. You can visualize a hypertext as a network of different paths that lead a reader through a landscape of information. For example, a project on capital punishment might use a menu that offers a choice of perspectives or information about the topic. One reader could choose the path that talks about deterrence; another might take a path that begins with background information and the history of capital punishment. Along the way, authors repeat or summarize information, provide easy ways for readers to travel further in the document by charting possible routes, and provide explicit connections and transitions between chunks of information.

The various chunks of information in hypertexts are called *nodes* rather than pages or chapters. The connections between the nodes are called *links.* If you picture the models of molecules you have seen in science classes, you can get a feel for the construction of a hypertext.

Hypertext is an excellent medium for a group writing project. Different writers—sometimes continents apart—can create different nodes and pursue separate but related lines of thought. Typically one writer coordinates the project and keeps track of the various nodes that are created. This project coordinator composes a map for readers on the opening, or index, page that describes the information at the various nodes and shows connections among them. This initial screen is something like the introduction or topic paragraph of a traditional essay—it should chart the direction of the project and whet the reader's interest.

Figure 24.6 shows how separate hypertextual nodes can be presented in a map for a project on the environment. Brief descriptions about the project's nodes include *hot text* (indicated by underlined text). The reader clicks on this text to choose a path. The hot text should deliver key information about the link so that

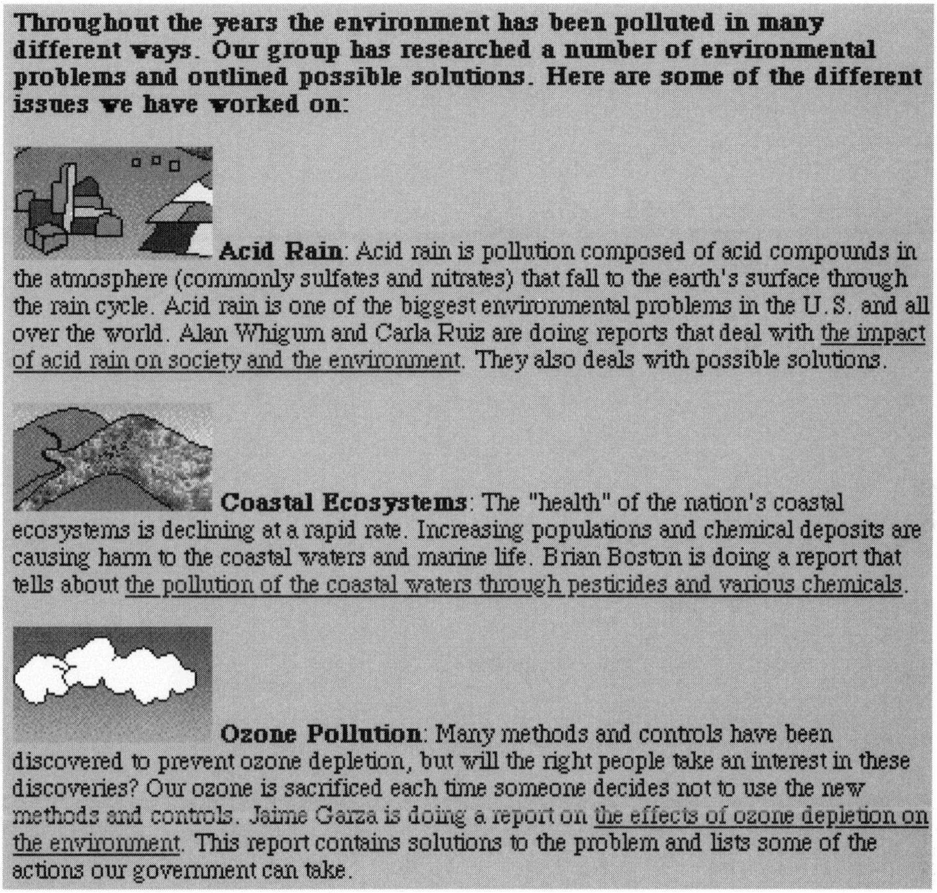

Throughout the years the environment has been polluted in many different ways. Our group has researched a number of environmental problems and outlined possible solutions. Here are some of the different issues we have worked on:

Acid Rain: Acid rain is pollution composed of acid compounds in the atmosphere (commonly sulfates and nitrates) that fall to the earth's surface through the rain cycle. Acid rain is one of the biggest environmental problems in the U.S. and all over the world. Alan Whigum and Carla Ruiz are doing reports that deal with the impact of acid rain on society and the environment. They also deals with possible solutions.

Coastal Ecosystems: The "health" of the nation's coastal ecosystems is declining at a rapid rate. Increasing populations and chemical deposits are causing harm to the coastal waters and marine life. Brian Boston is doing a report that tells about the pollution of the coastal waters through pesticides and various chemicals.

Ozone Pollution: Many methods and controls have been discovered to prevent ozone depletion, but will the right people take an interest in these discoveries? Our ozone is sacrificed each time someone decides not to use the new methods and controls. Jaime Garza is doing a report on the effects of ozone depletion on the environment. This report contains solutions to the problem and lists some of the actions our government can take.

FIGURE 24.6   Sample Screen Showing Hypertextual Nodes

readers can make well-informed choices as they move through the project. Constructing such a map and refining your links is a great way to assess the project. The process will encourage you to clarify the relationships among different pieces of information and to determine which lines of thought might be under- or overdeveloped.

Creating documents with links and nodes takes practice, but composing in this way also frees you from some of the constraints of linear texts. You can create interesting avenues for readers to explore at their own pace without interrupting the flow of a narrative or argument. You can also offer your readers a selection of different versions of a document so that they can make choices about language, length, or level of difficulty as they read.

In many ways, the structure of hypertext reflects the kind of nonlinear thinking you do when you are dwelling on a problem. Your thoughts take leaps—perhaps to an analogous situation, a similar event, an article or a book, even a familiar association. Hypertexts allow you to develop several streams of thought simultaneously. Readers make leaps as they explore the text, skipping familiar territory and following links within the document that inspire greater interest.

Hypertexts can be confusing if they are not carefully charted. In the introduction to each node, you will want to provide a statement of purpose as well as to clarify connections among the major ideas in your project. Figure 24.7 shows an example of a statement of purpose.

If your instructor assigns an individual or group project using a hypertextual program, such as ToolBook or HyperCard or the World Wide Web, be sure to ask for clear instructions and be sure that you will have access to other resources, such as tutorials, handouts, and manuals.

FIGURE 24.7   Sample Hypertext Screen Providing Statement of Purpose

Air Pollution

Solutions: Why Now?

This page discusses why we should enact some of the possible solutions to the problem of air pollution. The solutions are outlined in more detail in the previous section. To better understand why taking action is so important, you may want to return to our section outlining the problems caused by pollution. We're still discovering negative consequences of air polluution. We need to take action now.

The question is do the solutions cost a lot of money? Yes, they do. In order to apply all of the above methods it can cost the factory and businesses millions. The estimated costs are $800,000,000 alone from public sectors. For private sectors it can cost up to $17,000,000,000. Reducing pollution might cut salaries for many workers due to the cost of expenses which would rise (Hodges 582).

The estimations of the cost of devices to reduce pollution are accurate, but what about the money it takes to repair the damages caused by air pollution? The annual total for air pollution is $16 billion in the U.S. The amount spent dealing with air pollution leaves less money for cures for diseases, military expenses, or for government debt. It is like throwing away money just because factory and business owners do not want to take the time and money and invest in new methods and devices to prevent air pollution.

OPPORTUNITIES FOR CONDUCTING RESEARCH

We've been talking so far about ways in which networked computers can change how you interact and write. Next we discuss how computers can alter your approach to research. You have instant access to a vast array of information through electronic catalogs, archives, and Internet resources. We provide here an introduction to electronic research capabilities, although many more resources will undoubtedly be available by the time this book is in your hands. (For information on citing sources described here, see Chapter 23, pp. 574–77.)

On-Line Catalogs and Electronic Databases

Most libraries today offer on-line catalogs. In years past, researchers had to flip through rows and rows of card-catalog drawers to find a source; today you can type in a few words on a computer keyboard and produce a comprehensive listing of the library's resources on your topic. Most on-line catalogs will tell you which items are available and where they can be found.

To use an on-line catalog—or most other electronic research technology—effectively, you need to be adept at keyword searching. As we suggested in Chapter 22, you may want to begin by checking the *Library of Congress Subject Headings* for your initial keyword entry. You will need to be persistent and flexible. For example, if you are trying to find information on the economic influence of the timber industry in South America, you might enter the keywords "timber and economics." If these keywords produce numerous entries on the spotted owl controversy in the Pacific Northwest, you might alter your keywords to "timber and economics not owl" and free your screen of owl references. Most on-line catalogs allow you to refine keyword searches in a similar way, but you should check the options available before you begin working with an unfamiliar system.

Many libraries also provide computerized indexes that tap into international databases of articles and information or that are built around specific subject areas, and most of these indexes offer the option of keyword searching. The Lexis Nexis catalog, which provides information about, and access to, news and legal publications, is particularly useful for writers. Many schools charge a fee to use these resources, but the breadth of information they offer makes the fee worthwhile. Other subject-area indexes useful to writers include the Modern Language Association's bibliographic listings (see Chapter 22 for a brief description), the ERIC abstracts of articles on education, the General Science Index (see Chapter 22), and the Academic Periodical index. Check with the reference desk in your library to learn how to make the best use of the indexes available. Many of these indexes are moving to the Internet via the World Wide Web.

Listservs, Newsgroups, and Chat as Resources

One of the most important steps in the research process is to convert your topic into a workable research question. Internet forums offer an opportunity for you to place your question before an interested and knowledgeable audience and to receive feedback. By posting your question to a newsgroup, for example, you can test your thinking about the issue through dialogue and also get suggestions for resources from subject-area experts in the group.

Interactions on the Internet can provide valuable source material, and you should use the same sort of care you use with traditional sources when you incorporate these into your projects. Treat conversational resources as interviews. If you are involved in a chat session, let the participants know what you are working on and request their permission if you think you might cite any of the discussion. For material from a listserv or newsgroup, try to contact personally (via E-mail) any individuals whose comments or postings you might later incorporate into your work. In general, items posted to the Internet are considered in the public domain and available for your use, but as a responsible writer you should make every effort to obtain permission before using on-line materials. You should also respect the privacy of individuals who do not want their on-line writing used in your paper.

If you are using an Internet forum for research, it is crucial for you to save and document any items you might use because information comes and goes on the Internet. When you save material on a diskette or drive, jot down or append information about when and where you found it so that you can document the item properly later on; note the name of the chat session, listserv, or newsgroup, the identity of the poster, and the date.

The World Wide Web and Gopher

In addition to the many conversational resources that we've mentioned, the Internet offers an unsurpassed collection of government documents, on-line articles, and other useful files. In the past, researchers had to use several different programs to find these files and to wade through the information; today, technologies such as Gopher and the World Wide Web offer far more efficient options for searching the Internet.

Gopher is designed to tunnel through archives of information. Many institutions have cataloged Gopher resources under large geographic or subject headings. With Gopher, you can tap into these categories and browse through items logically. Most Gopher programs are set to open at a site that lists these useful categories. As Figure 24.8 shows, a Gopher listing typically includes a "search" option. Within this category, you should be able to find a powerful search engine called Veronica. Veronica uses keywords to find information on the net, so you can refine your searches as you would a search using an on-line catalog. The help files within Veronica provide more information about performing keyword searches.

If you have access to the World Wide Web, we recommend that you do most of your searching there. The web has a number of powerful search engines. In a similar manner to Gopherhosts, these search engines have collected and categorized a large number of Internet files and will perform keyword searches. Most of these search engines will find not only text files, but also graphical, audio, and

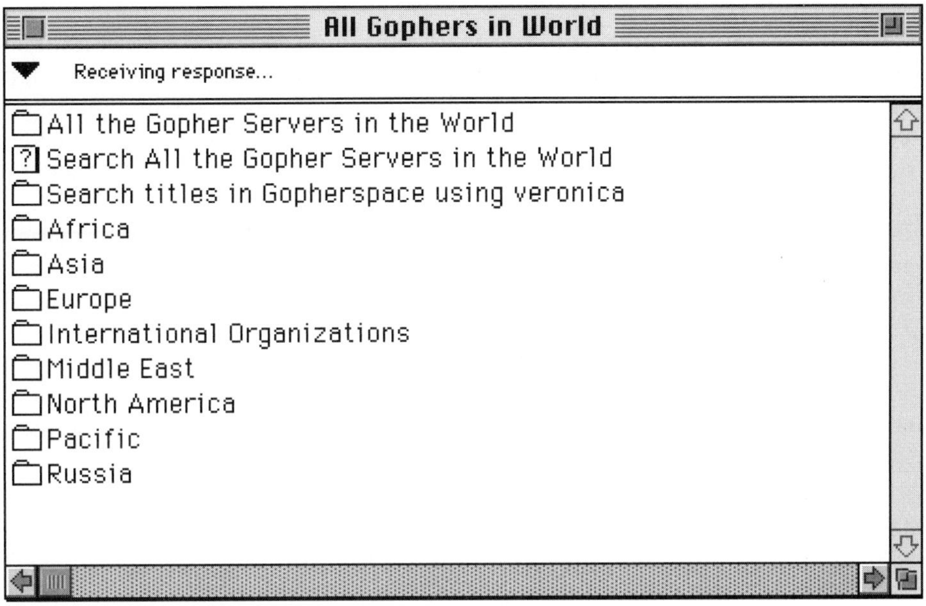

```
╔══════════════════════════════════════════════════════════════╗
║ ▤▢         ════  All Gophers in World  ════             ▣ ║
╠══════════════════════════════════════════════════════════════╣
║ ▼      Receiving response...                                  ║
╟──────────────────────────────────────────────────────────────╢
```

FIGURE 24.8   A Gopher Site Listing Geographical Resource Categories

video files. Some look through the titles of files, whereas others scan the entire text of documents. Different search engines can scan different resources, so it is important that you try a variety of searches when you look for information. Although the web is evolving rapidly, some of the best search engines are fairly stable. For starters, you might try the following:

Yahoo (http://www.yahoo.com)

Lycos (http://www.lycos.com)

Webcrawler (http://www.webcrawler.com)

These search engines will also let you browse through large subject categories, or trees. Subject trees often incorporate resources from both Gopher and web sites, but browsing on the web is the easiest way to navigate through them. The most important thing to keep in mind as you move through these trees (or do any browsing on the web) is that it is easy to lose track of where various resources are located. Most Internet software allows you to compile lists of locations that you've visited. These lists—usually referred to as *Bookmarks* or *Hotlists*—allow you to return quickly to previously visited sites. We recommend that you save on a diskette or drive any items that you think are particularly valuable. Web and Gopher sites can disappear over time; the only way to ensure that an item will be available for you to use later is to save a copy.

Browsing the web is an excellent way to help focus your thinking about an issue or topic. For example, suppose that you were searching for information about mining and its impact on Third World countries. As you browsed through some subject trees related to the environment, you might discover an item listing a protest over human rights abuses at Third World mining sites. If you followed the thread of information in the protest listing, you might find out that American students were upset because they felt that an international mining corporation was using their university as part of a public relations effort. This information might prompt you to reconsider your topic; you might decide to broaden your focus to include ways in which mining firms try to shape perceptions at home of their activities abroad.

As you search the Internet for resources, you will be exposed to new information and perspectives. You will want to remain flexible in the early stages of your research effort so that you can reap the benefits of the wealth of information available on-line. You will also want to play both the explorer and the investigator as you move through the research process. Your initial searches on the web can help you scout for resources. Some of the links that you follow will be dead ends; others will lead to new discoveries and useful collections of subject-related resources.

Once you've arrived at a topic and gathered some resources, you'll need to investigate them with care. Just as anyone with a connection can post thoughts to a newsgroup or chat forum, anyone can put up a web page that furthers his or her own agenda. Flashy graphics and other design elements on web pages can sometimes overwhelm the information that is being presented or lend an air of authority to an otherwise suspect argument or position. Judge these sites critically, with an eye on both the presentation and the reliability of the information.

Sample Research Sessions

The best way to get a feel for how to use the Internet for research is to try a search yourself. To get you started, we describe what we found when we experimented with two topics: international mining operations and mail-order brides (Mary Turla's topic discussed in Chapters 22 and 23). Let's review your hypothetical interest in international mining and its impact on the Third World. After a brief search on the web, you broadened your focus to include how public perception of mining operations is shaped in the United States. Then you decided to work on a specific controversy involving a protest at a U.S. university. The protest was staged by students at the University of Texas at Austin against Freeport McMoRan, Incorporated. With your focus in mind, we began a search of the net.

Using a combination of search engines on the World Wide Web and the keywords "Freeport and protest," "mining and protest," and "McMoRan," we were able to locate hundreds of files with potential information. One search for "McMoRan" alone produced ninety-eight items. By following some of these links we found United Nations documents, company statements, articles by professors at the university, articles from newspapers and magazines, firsthand accounts of the impact of mining on indigenous people, and web sites devoted entirely to the controversy.

The large number of items in this search highlights a potential problem for researchers working on the Internet—too much information. You would need to narrow this search to make the resources more manageable. Using the refined keywords "McMoRan and UT," we found only two items, both related directly to the controversy. Since two files aren't likely to provide enough information to fully understand a topic, you would probably want to wade through some of the longer lists of results to get a wider angle on the controversy and to read critically the most likely sources. You would look for biases in the files distributed by Freeport McMoRan, Inc. and those written by students and professors. You might compare files originating in the mainstream press with firsthand items found on the net. Critically reading through the resources would sharpen your thinking and help you determine what items to use in your research project.

When we researched the mail-order bride topic, we discovered that many of the pen-pal operations Mary mentions in her paper had already set up shop on the web. Rather than returning a list of useful articles, our search found links to home pages set up by these services.

Figure 24.9 illustrates one of our keyword searches and some of the returns from our query. Note that the keywords "marriage and philippines" helped us limit our search. This query returned 36 items; a search for the term "philippines" alone returned more than 1,700 items.

Our search returned few published articles and excerpts from books and little critical information on mail-order bride services, but we did stumble across some interesting items, such as government information about the validity of overseas

FIGURE 24.9   Screen from a Keyword Search on "Marriage and Philippines"

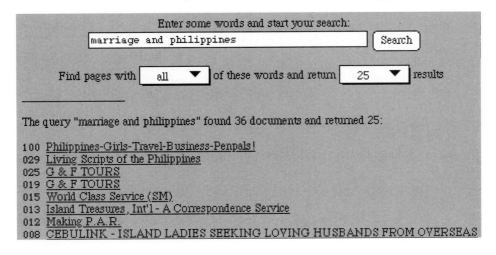

marriages and Immigration and Naturalization Services forms that could be downloaded.

We also found information about, and a link to, the newsgroup "soc.culture.filipino." This newsgroup is devoted to discussion of issues related to Filipino culture. We took our research question to the newsgroup by posting the following query:

```
Hi all. I'm trying to come to grips with the
mail-order bride phenomenon, especially in the
Philippines. I am writing from an entirely
American perspective, so I have no idea what
other views might be, but browsing on the web for
information on mail-order brides, all I found
were services that offered everything from
X-rated tours to instant marriages.

At first I suspected that someone was preying on
poor women, but when I looked at some of the
personals I realized that many of the women were
educated and professional. Is the mail order
bride exploitation, a worthwhile service, or
both? Can anyone give me some more insight? I'm
not interested in a pen-pal or bride, just trying
to use the net to find out about another culture
and clarify this topic.
```

We received responses later that day from several members of the group. One response in particular shows the resource power of Internet dialogue.

```
I happened to read your posting at
soc.culture.filipino.

The  mail-order bride  phenomenon is a complex
issue. There are genuine people (professionals or
not) who seek friendship with a view to meeting
the right person by mail or through the net, or
introduction through friends and relatives who
are already overseas. These are the people who
find no difference in meeting someone special in
life whether it be through mail or the net or
others or in person. Their reasons are varied, as
varied as in any culture, but as a Filipino
myself, and as someone who had worked as a social
worker for the immigration department here in
Australia, I find that majority are sincere and
looking for friends or future partners. . . .

My work at Immigration [also] showed me a black
picture of this mail-order bride phenomenon. That
is because I have dealt with a lot of the
victims--mostly innocent, sincere loving wives
```

```
beaten up or maltreated by their usually much
older partners. There was a study here in
Australia which looked into Australian-Filipino
marriages, and it revealed that more than 70
percent of those who had found their partners
through this means are happy.

One can go on and on, for such is the complexity
of the issue. . . .
```

So, although we did not find articles about the topic, we did gather responses from well-informed respondents; some had firsthand knowledge of the topic and broadened our thinking in useful ways. These samples should demonstrate to you that the Internet can be used to gather conventional research data as well as informal exchanges that are potentially valuable resources.

Summary

In this chapter, we discussed uses for networked computers beyond word processing for writers. Computer networks can provide entry into important discourse communities, offering a unique opportunity to examine various rhetorical situations and explore ideas through ongoing electronic conversations. Each of the forums for exploration—E-mail, listservs, newsgroups, and on-line chat—provides opportunities to hone such rhetorical skills as synthesizing, problem posing, and critical reading. Because each of these forums also has particular conventions and unique memberships, you need to study the rhetorical situation carefully before you join the conversation. We also discussed using the Internet for collaboration. We suggested how you can use E-mail and newsgroups to work with your peers; we looked at MU*s—virtual realities on the Internet that provide on-line spaces for writers to meet and work; we showed how hypertextual media, such as the World Wide Web, can be used to construct collaborative projects. Finally, we examined the research potential of electronic resources both as repositories for on-line texts and documents and as rich sources of dialogue that can help stimulate and refine ideas and also serve as primary sources for a paper.

A Guide
to Writing
Under Pressure

part F I V E

c h a p t e r 25

Essay Examinations
Writing Polished Prose in a Hurry

I'm pretty good at writing term papers, but when I have to write under pressure, I freeze. Last time I took an essay test, I wrote two pages before I realized that I'd left out an important piece of my argument. By the time I had scratched out, made additions, and drawn arrows all over the page, my paper was such a mess that I couldn't decipher it. Needless to say, the instructor couldn't either.

For me, the worst thing about exams is trying to figure out what the professor wants. The final in my European literature course was a perfect example: There was only one question. It started with a difficult-to-follow quotation from an author we hadn't studied, which we were supposed to apply to a whole slew of questions about novels we had read during the semester. The question went on for half a page (single spaced!) and had at least five or six subsections. By the time I finished reading it, I didn't have a clue about where to start or how to cover so much ground in a single essay.

> —Anonymous undergraduate students at the University of Oklahoma, paraphrased from responses written when asked to comment on their experiences with essay examinations

We have focused thus far on writing assignments that you complete outside class over a period of days or weeks. This amount of time allows you to plan, explore, draft, and revise through a process that is something like the following:

- You receive an open-ended assignment well in advance of its due date and mull it over until you find an interesting angle to pursue
- You explore the ongoing arguments about your issue, immersing yourself in reading, research, coffeehouse conversations with your classmates, and exploratory writing—perhaps changing your view along the way
- As the deadline approaches, you revise through several drafts until you arrive at a satisfactory final product

However, much of the writing you do in college doesn't allow for the luxury of extended exploration and revision. According to researcher Mary Meiser, as much as 50 percent of academic writing in college consists of timed essay examinations. For such writing, your composing scenario will probably be something like the following:

- You arrive in a classroom with your brain crammed full with facts, theories, and arguments
- Your instructor asks a narrowly focused question that you've never seen before and may not have much interest in addressing
- Working in a relatively uncomfortable, stressful classroom setting, you have an hour or so to shape your knowledge into a polished single draft that convinces your professor you've mastered the material

The writing you do during this hour may count for as much as half your course grade. Challenging? Undoubtedly. Rewarding? Yes, but not in the same way in which writing papers is rewarding.

WRITING UNDER PRESSURE

When instructors give essay exams, they want to see how well students can restate, apply, and assess course material. Just as important, they want to see whether students can discuss what they have studied in their own words—whether they can participate in that discipline's discourse community. These twin demands make essay exams doubly challenging. Not only must you master course material, but you must also write about it quickly and confidently. Some students have trouble streamlining their writing process to fit a strict time limit (see the first epigraph for this chapter). Others students have problems understanding complicated essay prompts or shaping their knowledge to fit the assignment (see the second epigraph for this chapter). Still others find it difficult to study effectively, recall information, or organize their essay responses.

Even students who perform adequately on essay tests often dislike them. They see essay exams as rigid exercises that stifle intellectual exploration or as artificial busywork unrelated to the real writing they will do outside school. Although you will rarely take exams once you leave college (unless you plan to attend graduate school—and both the LSAT and the MCAT exams have essay components), writing essay tests can help you develop skills relevant to many real-world situations. In such fields as journalism, advertising, marketing, publishing, engineering, teaching, you will need to compose documents on tight deadlines. In the following excerpt, journalist Linda Ellerbee describes her audition for a job as anchor of the NBC weekend news. She was required to write a feature story under pressure.

> I spent hours . . . running the film back and forth, stopping and starting, trying to figure out what to say in this 15.5-second gap, that 6-second pause, how to arrange the information I had so that it wove smoothly in and out of interviews, music, and background noise. . . . The whole time, I felt like a cowboy heading for the shootout at high noon.

Ellerbee argues that her college training in English helped her handle the stress; she ultimately won the job.

Although you probably accept that it's important to learn how to write essay exams, you may still ask, "Aren't some people simply bad test takers?" or "Professors and courses are so diverse—can any approach work for all of them?" No single method can guarantee a high grade in every subject. You will always have to adapt your exam response to the course, the instructor, and the test question. But this chapter shows you how to plan and draft an exam essay and how to adapt to the unique requirements of in-class essay writing. Practice exercises will also help you identify features of successful essay responses and let you try your hand at writing under pressure.

First, though, take a few minutes to think about your past experiences with writing under pressure.

FOR WRITING AND DISCUSSION

Freewrite for five or ten minutes in response to the following questions, then share your responses with classmates.

1. Think of a timed writing assignment that you wrote particularly well or one that ended in disaster. What happened? Which parts of the task caused you particular trouble, and which seemed easy? How might you approach future assignments differently?
2. Which do you think is more difficult, writing an essay exam or writing a research paper? Explain why, focusing on the different thinking, writing, and revision skills each requires.

HOW ARE EXAMS DIFFERENT FROM OTHER ESSAYS?

Essay exams do share similarities to other assignments. Most of the instruction in this book applies to exam writing. For instance, you already know how to respond to rhetorical context—audience, style, and genre—as you write a paper. You can transfer this ability to a test situation by analyzing your instructor's expectations. What theories or arguments does your instructor seem to favor or dislike? Does your instructor encourage individual interpretations and opinions? In the movie *Dead Poets Society*, Robin Williams plays an English literature teacher who, in the very first class, tells students to tear out and destroy the introductory section of their poetry textbooks. His students learn quickly that they need to develop independent insights about the material in order to pass the course. Although most professors don't communicate their preferences so dramatically, knowing what your professor expects can help you focus exam responses much as analyzing an audience can help you focus an out-of-class paper.

You also know the importance of knowing what you're talking about. Even the most brilliant writers will stumble on a test if they haven't bothered to attend class regularly, take notes, participate in class discussions, and keep up with the reading. Familiarity with the material lays the groundwork for a successful exam performance, just as thorough research and exploratory writing grounds a good paper.

However, not all the writing strategies you use for papers will serve you well in a test situation. Writing researcher Randall Popken, after reviewing more than two hundred sample exams in various disciplines, identified three skills unique to essay exam writing.

1. The ability to store, access, and translate appropriate knowledge into an organized essay
2. The ability to analyze quickly the specific requirements of an exam question and formulate a response to fit them
3. The ability to deal with time pressure, test anxiety, and other logistical constraints of the exam situation

We examine each of these skills in the next section.

PREPARING FOR AN EXAM: LEARNING AND REMEMBERING SUBJECT MATTER

One of the biggest differences between writing a paper and writing an exam essay involves how you access subject matter. Think about the last time you wrote a paper outside class. You may have used your memory to search for ideas or to explore personal knowledge about the topic, but you also had access to other sources—the library, course readings, your classmates' and instructor's input. In an exam, you're on your own. You won't know beforehand which of the many pages of material you'll be asked to synthesize and comment on. Although you may have studied hard and learned a great deal, you may not know how to display your knowledge in writing. Many inexperienced undergraduates fail exams either because they scribble down everything they can remember, however remotely related to the topic, or because they agonize so much over what to include that they write very little. Preparing for an exam involves finding efficient ways to organize and recall your knowledge so that you can easily construct an intelligent argument on paper.

Identifying and Learning Main Ideas

No instructor will expect you to remember every single piece of information covered in class. Most teachers are happy if you can remember main ideas and theories, key terminology, and a few supporting examples. The best strategy when you study for an essay exam is to figure out what is most important and learn it first.

How do you determine the main ideas and key concepts? Sometimes they're obvious. Many professors outline their lectures on the board or distribute review sheets before each exam. If your professor does not provide explicit instructions, listen for a thesis statement, main points, and transitions in each lecture to determine the key ideas and relationships among them. For example,

> The *most important critics* of the welfare state are . . .
>
> *Four developments* contributed to the re-emergence of the English after the Norman invasion . . .
>
> Hegel's dialectic was *most influenced by* Kant . . .
>
> *Three major interpretations* of Grant Wood's *American Gothic* are . . .

Look for similar signals in your textbook and pay special attention to chapter summaries, subheadings, and highlighted terms. If the course involves a lot of discussion or if your professor prefers informal remarks to highly structured lectures, you may have to work harder to identify major points. But streamlining and organizing your knowledge in this way will keep you from feeling overwhelmed when you sit down to study.

Most instructors expect you to master more than the information they cover in class. Essay exams in humanities, social science, and fine arts courses often ask for an individual interpretation, argument, or critique. To prepare for such questions, practice talking back to course readings by developing your own positions on the viewpoints they express. If the professor has lectured on factors involved in mainstreaming schoolchildren with physical disabilities, look at your notes and try to define your own position on mainstreaming. If the textbook identifies salient features of Caravaggio's art, decide how you think his paintings compare to and differ from his contemporaries' work. Questioning texts and lectures in this way will help personalize the material and expand your understanding. In feminist scholar Adrienne Rich's words, it will allow you to "claim your education" rather than to passively accept what's taught. Remember, though, that professors won't be impressed by purely subjective opinions; as you explore your views, search for evidence and arguments, not just from your own experience, but from the course as well, that you can use to support your ideas in the exam. For specific strategies to help you understand and respond to reading material review Chapter 6.

Applying Your Knowledge

In business, science, social science, and education courses, professors may ask you to apply a theory or method to a new situation; for example, they might ask you to show how first in, last out accounting might work in bookkeeping for a washing machine factory or how you might use Freudian concepts to analyze a hypothetical psychiatric case. If you suspect that such a question might appear, use some study time to practice this kind of thinking. Brainstorm two or three current situations to which you could apply the theories or concepts you've been learning. Check local newspapers or browse the World Wide Web for ideas. Then freewrite for a few minutes on how you might organize an essay that puts the theory to work. For instance, if you've studied federal affirmative action law in a public administration course you might ask the following questions: How does the law apply to the recent decision by the California regents to abolish race as a factor in college admissions? How might it apply to a local controversy over hiring female firefighters? You won't be able to predict exactly what will appear on the exam, but you can become skilled at transferring ideas into new settings.

Making a Study Plan

Once you've identified crucial subject matter, you need to develop a study plan. If you're a novice at studying for a major exam, try following some tried-and-true approaches. Review your instructor's previous exams. If you can't obtain an old exam, don't be afraid to ask your instructor for general guidelines about the type, length, and format of questions he or she normally includes on tests. Then generate your own practice questions and compose responses. If you can, organize group study sessions with two to four classmates. Meet regularly to discuss readings, exchange practice questions, test each other informally, and critique each other's essays.

Avoid study techniques that are almost universally ineffective. Don't waste time trying to reread all the material or memorize passages word for word (unless the exam will require you to produce specific formulas or quotations). Don't set an unreasonable schedule. You can seldom learn the material adequately in one or two nights, and the anxiety produced by cramming can hurt your performance even more. Most important, don't stay up all night studying. Doing so can be worse than not studying at all, since sleep deprivation impairs your ability to recall and process information.

No matter how you decide to study, remember that the point of developing exam-preparation strategies isn't simply to do well on a single test, but to become comfortable with learning difficult, complex material and to acquire a level of intellectual confidence that will help you grow as a writer.

ANALYZING EXAM QUESTIONS

Whereas paper assignments typically ask you to address broad problems that can be solved in numerous possible ways, essay exams usually require much more narrowly focused responses. Think about some of your paper assignments. They might have read, "Write a persuasive research paper in which you propose a solution to a current local controversy" or "Write a 10-page essay exploring an ethical issue in the field of vertebrate biology"; they might have called for either closed- or open-form prose; but in virtually all cases you were free to choose from among several possible approaches to your topic. Essay exams, in contrast, feature well-defined problems with a very narrow range of right answers. They require you to recall a particular body of information and present it in a highly specific way. However, what your instructors are asking you to recall and how they want it presented will not always be clear to you. Exam questions often require interpretation.

Although the language of essay exams varies considerably across disciplines, professors typically draw on a set of conventional moves when they write exam prompts. Consider the following question from an undergraduate course in the history of the English language:

> Walt Whitman once wrote that English was not "an abstract construction of dictionary makers" but a language that had "its basis broad and low, close to the ground." Whitman reminds us that English is a richly expressive language because it comes from a variety of cultural sources. One of these is African American culture. Write an essay discussing the major ways in which African American culture and dialect have influenced the English language in the United States. Identify and illustrate at least three important influences: What were the historical circumstances? What important events and people were involved? What were the specific linguistic contributions?

This question presents an intimidating array of instructions, but it becomes manageable if you recognize some standard organizational features.

Outside Quotations   First, like many exam questions, this sample opens with a quotation from an author or work not covered in the course. Many students panic when they encounter such questions. "Whitman?! We didn't even study Whitman. What am I supposed to do now?" Don't worry. The primary function of such quotations is to encapsulate a general issue that the instructor wants you to address in your response. When you encounter an unfamiliar quotation, look carefully at the rest of the question for clues about what role it should play in your essay. The point of the Whitman quotation is restated in the very next sentence—English is shaped by numerous cultural influences—and the function of the quotation is simply to reinforce that point. Because the rest of the question tells you specifically what kinds of cultural influences your response should address (African American culture, three major linguistic contributions), you don't need to consider this quotation when you write your essay.

Sometimes professors will ask you to take a position on an unfamiliar quotation and support your argument with material covered in the course. Suppose that the question was, What is your position on Whitman's view? Do you believe that English is enriched or corrupted by multicultural influences? In this case the quotation is presented as the basis for a thesis statement, which you would then explain and support. A successful response might begin, "Whitman believes that multicultural influences make our language better, but this view is hopelessly naive for the following reasons. . . ." or "Whitman correctly argues that the contributions of different cultures enrich our language. Take these three examples. . . ."

Organizational Cues   The question itself can show you the best way to organize your response. Questions tend to begin with general themes, which often suggest a thesis statement. Subsequent divisions tell you how to organize the essay into sections and in what order to introduce supporting points. For example, a successful response that follows the organization of our sample might be arranged as follows:

- A thesis stating that several contributions from African American language and culture have enriched English
- Three supporting paragraphs, each discussing a different area of influence by
    1. summarizing historical circumstances
    2. noting important people and events
    3. providing one or two examples of linguistic contributions

Key Terms   As do all exam questions, this one asks you to write about a specific body of information in a specific way. When you encounter a lengthy question such as this, first pick out the *noun phrases* that direct you to specific areas of knowledge: "African American culture," "major influences on the English language in the United States," "historical circumstances," "important events and people," "linguistic contributions." Pay careful attention to words that modify these noun phrases. Does the question tell you how many influences to discuss? What kinds of examples to cite? Does the instructor include conjunctions, such as "or," to give you a choice of topics, or does he or she use words such as "and" or "as well as" that require you to address all areas mentioned? Pronouns, such as "who," "what," "where," and "why," also point to particular kinds of information.

After you've determined the specific areas you will need to address, look for *directive verbs* that will tell you what to do: "discuss," "identify," or "illustrate," for example. These verbs define the horizons of your response: some mandate detailed responses, others don't; some ask for personal insights, others don't; some, such as "list" and "construct," even suggest the form your answer should take. Table 25.1 defines some key directives that frequently appear in essay exams and provides sample questions for each.* Meanings vary somewhat according to the course, the context of the question, and the professor's expectations, but you'll feel more confident if you have basic working definitions.

In some questions, directives are implied rather than stated directly. If a question asks, "Discuss the effects of Ronald Reagan's tax policies on the U.S. economy during the 1980s," you'll need to summarize what those policies were before you can assess their effects. Before you can take a position on an issue, you have to define what the controversy is about. In general, when you answer any question, you should include sufficient background information about the topic to convince your instructor that you're making an informed argument, whether or not the question specifically asks for background information.

FOR WRITING AND DISCUSSION

Bring in an exam question from another class or choose one of the sample questions from Table 25.1. In collaboration with one or two classmates, analyze the

*Our thanks to Michael C. Flanigan, who suggested the format and some of the terms for this table.

TABLE 25.1   Some Common Question Verbs

Analyze—asks you to break an argument, concept, or approach into parts and examine the relations among them; discuss causes and effects; evaluate; or explain your interpretation or judgment. Look carefully at the rest of the question to determine which of these strategies to pursue in your response. Example: *Analyze the various technical, acoustic, and aesthetic factors that might lead a musician to choose analogue over digital recording for a live performance. Be sure to include the strengths and weaknesses of both methods in your discussion.*

Apply—asks you to take a concept, formula, theory, or approach and adapt it to another situation. Example: *Imagine that you've been hired to reengineer the management structure of a major U.S. automaker. How might you apply the principles of Total Quality Management in your recommendations?*

Argue—asks you to take a position for or against an issue and give reasons and evidence to support that position. Example: *Argue whether you believe that cloning should be pursued as a method of human reproduction. Be sure to account for the relationship between cloning and mitosis in your discussion.*

Compare—asks you to note similarities between two (or more) objects or ideas. Example: *Compare the leadership styles of Franklin Delano Roosevelt, John F. Kennedy, and Ronald Reagan, focusing particularly on their uses of popular media and political rhetoric.*

Construct—asks you to assemble a model, diagram, or other organized presentation of your knowledge about a concept. Example: *Construct a model of the writing process that illustrates the major stages writers go through in developing an idea into a finished text.*

Contrast—asks you to point out differences between two or more objects or ideas. Example: *Contrast the use of religious imagery in Edward Taylor's "Upon Wedlock, and Death of Children" and Anne Bradstreet's "Before the Birth of One of Her Children." Then identify and discuss some possible sources of these differences.*

Critique—asks you to analyze and evaluate an argument or idea, pointing out and explaining both strengths and weaknesses. Example: *Dinesh D'Souza's "Illiberal Education" sparked widespread controversy when it was published in 1991. Write an essay critiquing D'Souza's arguments against affirmative action, identifying both the strengths and the weaknesses of his position. Use examples from the text, class discussion, and other class readings to illustrate your points.*

Define—asks you to provide a clear, concise, authoritative meaning for an object or idea. Your response may include describing the object or idea, distinguishing it clearly from similar objects or ideas, and providing one or more supporting examples. Example: *How was "equality" defined by the Supreme Court in Plessy v. Ferguson (1896)? How did that definition influence subsequent educational policy in the United States?*

Discuss—asks you to provide a comprehensive presentation and analysis of important concepts, supported by examples or evidence. These questions generally require detailed responses, so be sure to cover several key points or to examine the topic from several perspectives. Refer to the rest of the essay question for more detailed guidelines about what information to include in your response. Example: *Discuss the controversy that surrounded Stanley Milgram's studies of authority and state your own position on the relevance and validity of the experiments.*

Enumerate—asks you to list steps, components, or events pertaining to a larger phenomenon, perhaps briefly explaining and commenting on each item. Example: *A two-year-old child falls from a swing on the playground and lies unconscious. As the head preschool teacher, enumerate the steps you would take from the time of the accident until the ambulance arrives.*

continued

TABLE 25.1 Some Common Question Verbs *continued*

Evaluate—asks you to make a judgment about the worth of an object or idea, examining both strengths and weaknesses. Example: *Evaluate William Whyte's "Street Corner Society" as an ethnographic study. What are its methodological strengths and weaknesses? Do you believe the weaknesses make Whyte's research obsolete?*

Explain—asks you to clarify and state reasons to show how some object or idea relates to a more general topic. Example: *Explain the relationship of centripetal force to mass and velocity and give an example to illustrate this relationship.*

Identify—asks you to describe some object or idea and explain its significance to a larger topic. Example: *Identify the major phonetic characteristics of each of the following language groups of southern Africa, and provide illustrative examples of each: Koisan, Niger-Kordofanian, and Nilo-Saharan.*

Illustrate—asks you to give one or more examples, cases, or other concrete instances to clarify a general concept. Example: *Define "monopoly," "public utility," and "competition," and give specific illustrations of each.*

List—asks you to name a series of related objects or concepts one by one, perhaps briefly explaining each. Example: *List the major sampling designs used in communications research and briefly identify their advantages and disadvantages. Which of these designs would you use to conduct a market test of a new children's television program for Nickelodeon? Why?*

Prove—asks you to produce reasons and evidence to establish that a position is logical, supportable, or factual. Example: *Use your knowledge about the findings of the 1991 National Assessment of Educational Progress to prove either that (1) public schools are doing an adequate job of educating children to become productive U.S. citizens, or (2) public schools are doing an inadequate job of educating children to become productive U.S. citizens.*

Review—asks for a quick survey or summary of something. Example: *Review the major differences between Socrates' conception of ethics and the ethical theories of his contemporaries in the fifth century* B.C.E.

Summarize—asks you to lay out the main points of a theory, argument, or event in a concise and organized manner. Example: *Summarize Mill's definition of justice and explain how it differs from Kant's. Which definition comes closest to your own, and why?*

Trace—asks you to explain chronologically a series of events or the development of an idea. Example: *Write an essay that traces the pathway of a nerve impulse through the nervous system, being sure to explain neuron structure, action potential, and the production and reception of neurotransmitters in your discussion.*

question, then construct a potential thesis and scratch outline for a successful response. Be prepared to share your work with the class.

This next exercise will hone your ability to analyze essay questions. Each of the following student essays received an A as a response to one of the four closely related questions that follow it. Each essay may address issues raised in two or more questions, but each is an A response to only one. Your task is to figure out which question the essay answers best. Although you have not read the specific material on which each essay draws, you should nonetheless be able to match the responses based on the kinds of information included and how the information is used.

Decide on your answer independently, then compare answers in small groups. Try to come to a group consensus, referring to Table 25.1 to help resolve disagreements. As you discuss your responses, note any successful strategies that you may be able to adapt to your own writing.

From a library science course

1   Bandura's social learning theory breaks from the behaviorist learning theory developed by B. F. Skinner. Behaviorists believe that humans learn only those behaviors which are positively reinforced; behaviors which are not reinforced become "extinct." Bandura, however, argued that some learning happens vicariously, as a child models the behaviors of people around him or her. Such learning does not depend on direct reinforcement, but on observation and imitation. For example, a child from a violent family may behave aggressively toward his or her friends, not because there is a reward for behaving that way, but because he has seen the behavior continually at home.

2   Many variables affect whether a child will learn from a model, according to Bandura. These include the type of behavior, whether the model is someone the child admired, and whether the behavior is punished or reinforced. For example, if a movie villain slapped a woman, a child might not imitate the behavior, since the model is not someone he or she wants to identify with. But if the hero of the movie did the same thing, especially if the woman responded by passionately kissing him (a reward), the child would be more likely to repeat the behavior.

3   Bandura's theory has clear implications for library staff in selecting children's books. It is important that children have available a variety of positive role models to identify with and imitate--especially to provide a balance to the violent, sexist role models often presented in television and movies. School-age boys who survive on a t.v. diet of Arnold Schwarzenegger and Power Rangers need to also read about males who are admirable without being violent. Biographies of men like Abraham Lincoln and Mahatma

Gandhi, and novels like <u>Johnny Tremain</u> and <u>Encyclopedia Brown</u> that show characters who succeed by helping others, give boys some positive behaviors to
imitate. Stories about strong, independent girl characters, such as <u>Caddie</u>
<u>Woodlawn</u> and <u>The Summer of the Swans</u>, give young girls whose ideas are shaped
by Barbie and <u>Beverly Hills 90210</u> more admirable role models.

　　These are just a few examples. Many books give both boy and girl read-　　4
ers characters to look up to. Bandura's theory shows us just how important
that is to children's social learning.

Which question does this response address most successfully?

1. Summarize the learning theories of Skinner and Bandura, and explain how
   each might inform book selections at a children's library.
2. Review the major components of Bandura's theory of social learning. Then
   discuss the following: How might these principles apply if you were responsible for selecting children's books for a public library system? What kinds
   of books might Bandura's theory lead you to choose?
3. Bandura's social learning theory proposes that children learn partly from
   imitating the behavior of role models. Based on what you know about children's reading preferences, do you believe this is the case? Support your position with examples of particular books, characters, and themes.
4. Compare and contrast Skinner's learning theory, Bandura's theory of social
   learning, and current theories on children's book selection.

From a British literature course

　　<u>Gulliver's Travels</u> and <u>Frankenstein</u> portray characters whose adventures　　1
bring them face to face with the innate weaknesses and limitations of hu-
mankind. Victor Frankenstein and Lemuel Gulliver find out during their travels that humans are limited in reasoning capacity and easily corruptible,
traits that cause even their best intentioned projects to go awry. These
characters reflect the critical view that Swift and Shelley take of human
nature. Both believe that humans have a "dark side" that leads to disastrous effects.

　　In <u>Gulliver's Travels</u>, Gulliver's sea voyages expose him to the best and　　2
worst aspects of human civilization. Through Gulliver's eyes, readers come

to share Swift's perception that no matter how good people's original intentions, their innate selfishness corrupts everything they attempt. All the societies Gulliver visits give evidence of this. For example, Lilliput has a system of laws once grounded on justice and morality, but which slowly were perverted by greedy politicians into petty applications. Even the most advanced society, Brobdingnag, has to maintain a militia even though the country is currently peaceful--because they acknowledge that because humans are basically warlike, peace can't last forever. By showing examples of varied cultures with common faults, Swift demonstrates what he believes to be innate human weaknesses. He seems to believe that no matter how much progress we make, human societies will eventually fall back into the same old traps.

3   Victor Frankenstein also experiences human limitations, this time in his own personality, as he pushes to gain knowledge beyond what any human has ever possessed. When he first begins his experiments to manufacture life in the laboratory, his goals are noble--to expand scientific knowledge and to help people. As he continues, he becomes more concerned with the power that his discovery will bring him. He desires to be a "god to a new race of men." Later, when the creature he creates wreaks havoc, Frankenstein's pride and selfishness keep him from confessing and preventing further deaths. Like the societies Gulliver observed, Frankenstein is a clear example of how human frailties corrupt potentially good projects.

4   Even though Swift and Shelley wrote during two different historical periods, they share a critical view of human nature. However, several unambiguously good characters in <u>Frankenstein</u>--including the old man and his daughter--suggest that Shelley feels more optimism that people are capable of overcoming their weaknesses, while Swift seems adamant that humans will eternally backslide into greed and violence. Basically, however, both works demonstrate vividly to readers the ever present flaws that prevent people and their societies from ever attaining perfection.

Which question does this essay address most successfully?

1. Contrast Swift's and Shelley's views of human nature, illustrating your points with specific examples from *Gulliver's Travels* and *Frankenstein.*
2. Analyze the use Swift and Shelley make of scientific knowledge to show the limits of human progress in *Gulliver's Travels* and *Frankenstein,* citing specific illustrations from each work.
3. Discuss the characters of Lemuel Gulliver in *Gulliver's Travels* and Victor Frankenstein in *Frankenstein:* What purpose does each serve in the text? How does each author use the character to illustrate important traits or concepts?
4. Many of the writers we've studied this semester explored the limitations of human potential in their work. Write an essay showing how any two of the following works deal with this idea: William Blake's *Songs of Innocence and Experience,* Jonathan Swift's *Gulliver's Travels,* Mary Shelley's *Frankenstein,* Percy Shelley's "Prometheus Unbound." Does each writer suggest a pessimistic or optimistic view of human nature? Be sure to support your argument with specific illustrations from each test.

DEALING WITH CONSTRAINTS: TAKING AN ESSAY EXAM

Suppose that you've organized the course material, studied faithfully, analyzed the exam questions, and know generally how you'll respond. You still need one more skill to succeed: the ability to thrive within the limits of a test situation. You will be confined in a classroom with no computer and given an extremely short amount of time in which to write, with little opportunity to correct mistakes or revise. How can you overcome these logistical hurdles?

First, you need to minimize test anxiety. Many students feel anxious if a test question looks unfamiliar or difficult. Others freeze up if they lose their train of thought midway through an essay. Still others panic when time begins to run out. You can't control the level of difficulty of test questions; you will lose your train of thought occasionally; and time will run out. But you don't have to respond by collapsing. You can learn to anticipate potential disasters and brainstorm ways to handle them. If you tend to panic when a test question looks impossible on first reading, make a deal with yourself to close your eyes and count to ten, then read it again and try to screen off the parts that you don't have to consider. If you usually run out of time, set a time limit for writing some practice questions so that you can get used to performing under pressure. Finally, make sure that you're in top form to take the exam: organize your supplies, including extra exam booklets and scratch paper, pens, and any testing aids your instructor allows, the night before; get plenty of sleep; eat breakfast; arrive at class a few minutes early; give yourself a pep talk. These measures will increase your confidence and head off debilitating nerves.

Lack of time when writing an essay exam is perhaps the hardest constraint for most people to deal with. Most writers produce their best work only after writing several drafts. You won't be able to compose a perfectly polished essay in an exam—there simply isn't time—so you will need to streamline your writing process through planning. After you have analyzed the exam question carefully, take a few minutes to jot down a quick outline or a list of key concepts you want to discuss. Exploratory writing techniques, such as tree diagrams and freewriting, can help you generate and arrange ideas. Prewriting gives you a sense of direction and helps you remember where the essay is going as you write.

For example, one undergraduate student jotted down this five-minute scratch outline in response to the following exam question in a Texas government course:

> What are the relative advantages and disadvantages of the district method versus the at-large method in municipal elections? Analyze the strengths and weaknesses of each and then either argue in favor of one method over the others or propose a different plan that avoids the limitations of both.

➤ Thesis
District method
Advantages--history of discrimination and underrepresentation of minorities (examples)
             --race consciousness important for overcoming injustice
Disadvantages--encourages racial divisions
             --not necessary because much racism has been overcome; minorities may now be freely elected (ex. Sen. Barrientos, Ann Richards) <u>BUT</u>
At-large
Advantages--all citizens can work together for common good, not just concerned with narrow group interests
Disadvantages--majority rule may ignore important minority needs (ex. East Austin)◄
THESIS--B/c minorities have been and are still underrepresented in local government, the district method of local elections, while flawed, offers the best chance for these communities' voices to be heard.

Once you have a plan, you need to determine how much time to give to each answer. Many students' grades suffer because they blow all their time on the first question and then race through the rest of the exam. To determine how much time to allot each response you need to solve a quick ratio problem. Divide the points assigned to a given question by the points for the whole exam; the result equals the percentage of time you should spend on that question. When you write your answer, follow the example of journalists and load critical information in your lead. Write a first paragraph that nutshells your whole answer (the second student response in the For Writing and Discussion exercise on pages 634–35 does this beautifully). Add examples and details to the extent that you have time, moving from more important to less important. If you can't finish a response in time, stop, but don't panic. You may have time to return to it later. If not, write a brief note directing the professor to your original notes or outline; let your professor know that you intended to write more but ran out of time. Many instructors will award partial credit for outlined responses.

You can save time by focusing only on elements important to your grade. Instructors don't expect dramatic, polished introductions and conclusions or artistically constructed sentences in an exam. They would rather you provide a clear thesis statement and explain your main points fully. Most instructors also value organization, although some grade almost entirely on content.

Instructors differ in how they treat errors in grammar, spelling, and punctuation. Some believe it's unfair to expect students to edit their work thoroughly in a short time and don't penalize such errors unless they interfere with the argument (as do garbled or fragmented sentences, for example). Other instructors deduct points for grammatical errors on the grounds that correct usage is always important. You should know your instructor's position on this issue. If your instructor is a stickler for these details, you may want to save the last five or ten minutes of the exam period for proofreading. Even the strictest professor, however, is unlikely to penalize you heavily for minor errors (such as writing "to" for "too," minor comma errors, misplaced modifiers).

Even if you know a lot about a question, avoid writing more than it asks—unless, perhaps, you know absolutely nothing about one question and want to demonstrate extreme depth of understanding about the others to compensate. It may be intellectually rewarding to showcase additional insights, examples, or arguments, but you'll squander time that you need for other questions. Also, remember that your instructor has lots of exams to read. Extraneous material may make it difficult for your instructor to find the core of your argument.

Producing a quality first draft is a reasonable goal for you to have when you write an exam essay. A disorganized, poorly thought-out, or scratched-up response is likely to land you in trouble, but a clear, reasonably organized, readable response will fare well in virtually any course.

Guidelines for Producing Successful Responses

No matter how committed you are to studying, planning, analyzing exam questions, and managing time constraints, your worries about essay tests probably come down to a single, inevitable question: What does an A response look like? Research suggests that most professors want closed-form, thesis-based prose that develops key ideas fully, drawing on supporting facts and examples. Although your essay's shape will be influenced by your individual writing style and the particular rhetorical context, the following summary of the points covered in this chapter can serve as a template for a successful essay.

> *Clear thesis statement.*   Show your professor that you understand the big picture the question addresses by including a thesis statement early on. Many professors recommend that you state your thesis clearly, though not necessarily stylishly, in the very first sentence.

> *Coherent organization.*   Although a few instructors will read your essay only to see whether you've included important facts and concepts, most ex-

pect a logical presentation. Each paragraph should develop and illustrate one main point. Use transition words and phrases to connect each paragraph clearly to the thesis of the essay ("Another factor that led to the economic decline of the South was . . . "; "In contrast to Hegel, Mill believed . . . "). Show your instructor that you know where the essay's going, that you're proving your thesis.

Support and evidence.   When the question calls for supporting facts and examples, be specific. Don't assert or generalize unless you present names, dates, studies, examples, diagrams, or quotations from your reading as support.

Independent analysis and argument.   Your response should not be a pedestrian rehash of the textbook. When the question allows, present your own insights, criticisms, or proposals, making sure to support these statements with course material and relate them clearly to your thesis.

Conclusion.   Even if you're running short of time, don't leave the instructor wondering at the end of your essay, "What does all this mean?" Write a sentence or two to tie together main points and restate your thesis. Your conclusion, even if brief, serves an important rhetorical function. It confirms that you've dealt adequately with the question and proved your point.

Clearly we can't teach you everything you need to know about exam writing in one chapter. Becoming comfortable with any genre of writing requires patience and experience. To familiarize you with important differences between successful and unsuccessful exam essays, we offer two activities. The first asks you to rank a range of sample student papers and to suggest how the weakest ones might be improved. The evaluative criteria you develop in this exercise will help you succeed in the second activity, which asks you to write a practice essay exam.

FOR WRITING AND DISCUSSION

The following essays were written anonymously by first-year undergraduate English students at the University of Oklahoma as part of a research study on writing under pressure. The students had studied portions of Robert McCrum, William Cran, and Robert MacNeil's *The Story of English,* a text on the history of the English language.* Students wrote for one hour on the following essay question:

> The English language is a product of wide-ranging cultural and historical influences, from the Anglo-Saxon invasion of Celtic Britain in 449 to William Caxton's introduction of the printing press in 1476. Write an essay tracing the development of English through the Middle English period: What cultural influences and historical events do you believe were most important? How did each of these contribute to the English we speak today—grammar, vocabulary, pronunciation? Be sure to identify at least four major influences and to support your arguments with

*The results of this study are discussed in Christy Friend, "Research on Essay Exams: Using Inquiry to Enhance Students' Learning and Performance," unpublished master's thesis, University of Oklahoma, 1990. The five student papers have been edited to eliminate minor mechanical errors.

specific historical details and examples of borrowed words, phrases, and linguistic structures.

The four responses presented here represent a range of weak, adequate, and strong responses as evaluated by a panel of writing instructors. Even though all the information in each response is substantially correct—that is, the responses contain no major factual errors—the panel gave one of the essays the equivalent of an A, one a B, one a C, and one a D/F. Your task is threefold:

1. Read the essays. Rank them from weakest to strongest, based on the exam question, the criteria developed in this chapter, and any other features you think are important. Remember, there are no major factual errors in these essays, so don't worry if you don't know much about the topic. Justify your rankings.
2. Compare your rankings with those of a group of your classmates. Try to come to a consensus about the relative success of each essay and about the criteria you think are most important.
3. Share your group's rankings with the entire class and discuss areas of agreement and disagreement. Then make suggestions for improving the weakest response.

Response 1

The English language is a hearty one, having survived the beatings of   1
time. Indeed, it is a melting pot of different people, cultures, and geographical locations. In particular, four different societies helped spawn
the language we know today. Each played a specific role in bringing about
English. However, important roles were also played by circumstance, for example: the invasion of Celtic Britain, the 100 Years War, and St. Augustine's dramatic conversion of Europe to Christianity.

Philosophers argue that at some time there was one source, a common   2
source of many modern languages. It has been labeled Indo-European. Many ar-
chaeologists have traced the roots of the English language to this point.
Many different cultures have found striking similarities: "mater," the word
for mother among the Romans, and the word for mother among the people of
Denmark, for example. As people began to migrate the language changed due
to differences in environment and culture. A tribe that lived by a water
source would have a different vocabulary due to their resources, in comparison to one that didn't live near a common water source. The Angles,

Saxons, and Jutes were three major tribes which were related to the Indo-Europeans. There were other influential tribes as well, the Danes and the Celts, for example. The Celts were the first to settle Britain, and the Danes migrated and settled in Denmark. King Alfred the Great was a key figure in the growth of English. He began a book of Chronicles which kept a record of England's history. He also helped restore the popularity of the English language.

3   Around the year 597 A.D. Christianity was introduced to England by St. Augustine. He brought amazing results, converting many to Christianity, and with that brought a wealth of Latin and even some Greek. Biblical scholars all spoke and wrote in Latin, and Latin became the language of the scholarly. New words like "cross" and "baptism" were introduced. Monks set up monasteries, which trained young men, teaching them Christian values, theology, ethics, and Latin.

4   Many other historical events influenced and enforced the English language. The 100 Years War, for example, dramatically increased the use of English. English was the only language spoken by the common people during this war. French was at this time the language of the rich. Latin was the language of the church and scholars, and English was the language of the common people.

5   Another boost the language got was when literary authors began to write in English as opposed to Latin. People enjoyed humor, as they do today, and Geoffrey Chaucer's works in English became extremely popular. His Canterbury Tales were masterpieces, and they remain popular today.

6   When the printing press was invented in 1476, the English language had proved hearty enough to stand the test of time. English quickly took to print, was standardized, and was well on its way to becoming what we speak and write today. The English we speak today brings to mind our freedom and pride in America. The pride we hold in our form of language is evident.

Response 2

"Speak correct English," your kindergarten teacher used to say when you   1
made a grammar mistake or used a make-believe word. Since we were children,
we are told that the language we speak follows unchanging rules that have
been there since the beginning of time. Nothing could be further from the
truth. The English language was formed through a long series of events from
the time of the Anglo-Saxon invasion to the 100 Years' War and the development of the printing press. During this time, four cultures influenced the
language and created the basis for the English we speak today.

The original people to live on the British Isles were the Celts, a group   2
of tribes who spoke a group of languages called "Cymraeg." The Celts had a
peaceful farming culture, but invasion cost them much of their identity. All
of the groups which invaded Britain were after the mineral wealth and rich
land found there.

The first roots of English arose in 449 A.D. with the arrival in Britain   3
of the Anglo-Saxons and the Jutes. The language these people spoke scholars now call "Old English." Old English was a language which sounded very
much like Dutch, except for a few Welsh (as the Celts came to be called)
words which represented things that the Anglo-Saxon language didn't have
words for. For instance, the Welsh word for a marshy, low place was called
a "crag." The Anglo-Saxons, a Germanic people from the coast of Denmark and
Germany, had no word for this; therefore they used the Celtic word for it.
But the Anglo-Saxons were the ones that provided the "guts" of the English
language, like "is," "the," and "I." They drove the Celts to the "Celtic
Fringe" and did not bother to learn the Celtic languages. Sometimes towns
would have two names because the Anglo-Saxons never bothered to learn the
original name.

However, the war between the Anglo-Saxons and the Celts did not last   4
forever. After the Anglo-Saxons had conquered, they settled down and began
to farm and be relatively peaceful again. A Roman Catholic priest named St.

Augustine saw two Anglo-Saxon slave boys on sale in Rome. He wrote that it was ironic that such beautiful and innocent children were pagan and didn't have the opportunity to become Christian. After seeing the boys, Augustine decided that the British Isles needed conversion to Christianity. The conversion was slow but peaceful. The Christians brought words like "angel" and "psalm" to the Saxons. Therefore Christianity became the cornerstone of Anglo-Saxon life and set the stage for the next big event, the Viking invasion.

5   The Vikings, also called the Danes, conquered the country around the 5th century A.D. Their victory was complete and nearly destroyed the English language forever. However, the young King of Wessex, Alfred, fought back. Driven to a marshy town called Somerset, he negotiated a treaty so that the Danes controlled Northern England and the Anglo-Saxons controlled the southern part of England. For a while the Danes stayed on their side and the Saxons theirs. However, the walls slowly fell and the Scandinavian culture and the Anglo-Saxon culture mixed, as did the languages. The Danish language helped simplify Old English. All was well until the Normans arrived.

6   The Norman Invasion also seemed like the end for English. All business and scientific communication was done in Latin and French. English was reduced to the commoners' language. However, it did not die because it was too well established. Also, the Normans immediately began to take English wives and had to learn English to communicate. When English emerged during the 13th century, it had changed to the form scholars call Middle English.

7   In retrospect, the successive conversions and invasions of England shaped the language into what it is today. If all of these had not occurred, the English we speak today may have sounded more like German than English.

Response 3

1   English was really a melting pot of many events and cultures combined to make a very versatile language. Many English words can be traced by being

similar to words in different languages. The tracing of English goes as far back as 6000 B.C. Many peoples were involved in the development of English, as well as many different events. During the earliest times there were the Jute, Angle, Saxon, and Welsh (Celtic) cultures, who contributed indirectly to form some of the words we use today. Some of the major events were the Viking invasions, revolutions, and a very significant thing was the 100 Years' War, which produced one of the greatest English writers: Geoffrey Chaucer. Chaucer was born in 1340 to a middle class family; when he got older he became a squire and learned how to read and write. He wrote many literary works in English, and the greatest of these was probably the Canterbury Tales.

There were also many other great people who contributed. Henry III sup-   2
ported the French system and was opposed to English. Edward V started the turnabout of the English language. Some of the greatest stories ever written show the way that other cultures influenced English. Beowulf is one example.

Although English is now the main common language in most of Britain, the   3
Welsh are bilingual and like this system. The linguistic effects of other cultures, like Latin, French, and Scandinavian, have been extraordinary. They brought new words, new meanings, and new pronunciation and grammar to English. These contributions often times sound and are spelled very similarly, and that is why it is easy for scholars to trace the ancestry of certain words and grammatical features just by going back to these other languages and making comparisons to the English language we speak today.

Another important cultural impact is names. Many people's names describe   4
an aspect of their heritage. "Mac" (meaning "son of") is a common prefix in Scottish last names. Other last names pinpoint where the person's family is from or their occupation ("baker"). Even the person's geographical location or their religious values could be indicated. From the earliest times to the modern era, there are so many cultures involved in the English language

that it would be nearly impossible to find every root, but with what scholars know now, many of these questions about "why" and "how" may be answered one day.

Response 4

1   The English language has evolved from many cultural and historical influences. Four major developments that have contributed to the evolution of the English language are: the invasion of Celtic Britain by the Anglo-Saxons; the Viking invasions; the Norman French invasion; and finally, the cultural revolution, which was an indirect result of the Norman French occupation of England. However, the cultural influences on the English language include not only the conquerors of Britain but also the Romans, who made their contribution through the Christian faith during the Anglo-Saxon era.

2   The Anglo-Saxons invaded Britain in A.D. 449. These first invaders came from Denmark and the coastal part of Germany in search of rich farming land. They refused to adopt or learn the native Celtic language and so soon they were combining words of both the Celts and their language. For example, "cheet" is Celtic for "wood," but the Anglo-Saxons formed constructions like "cheetwood." So English vocabulary expanded, but only by a few words. The Celts did not have any major linguistic influence, except for a few geographical and place names. The Anglo-Saxons, however, provided the core of modern English. They spoke what scholars now call "Old English," a Germanic language which is grammatically the basis for the English we speak today. The one hundred most common words in modern English come from the Anglo-Saxons, words like "the," "you," and "is."

3   An indirect contribution by the Anglo-Saxons was the decision by Anglo-Saxon rulers to allow the conversion of England to Christianity around A.D. 579. Christianity, or the Latin language, enriched English with many new words, particularly words that express abstract religious thoughts--like "angels" and "discipline." It also introduced new words from the Eastern side of the world, like "cedar," "camel," and "lion," since the missionar-

ies came from Rome. Besides that, it encouraged the application of old English words to new meanings (for example, "heaven," "hell," and "God"). The linguistic impact of Christianity was firmly established when monks set up monastery schools throughout the country to train boys as priests. Many of the words we use today have Latin roots.

The next invaders of England, the Vikings, were Scandinavians from Iceland, Sweden, and Norway who spoke Old Norse. Their first raids on England began in A.D. 793. The King of Wessex, Alfred the Great, fortunately, managed to drive the Vikings to the north while he and other Saxon rulers occupied the south. This situation created the need for a national identity, and Alfred was able to create patriotism by supporting the English language. He began writing a chronicle of English history, in English, to show his support for English culture. The presence of the Vikings therefore consolidated English as a source of common identity. Contact with the Danes also simplified English. The grammar of English until this time had a complicated system of inflections (the meaning of the word was determined by its prefix or ending rather than its position in a sentence). But to ease communication, most of the inflections dropped out, and the grammar began to rely on word order. 4

The Norman French attacked England in 1066. After their conquest they took control of all the important positions in the church and the state, so that French became the official language. English remained the vernacular language, but because it was not recognized by the government, it was rarely written down, and there was a real danger that the language would be lost. Although many French words entered into English during the years of French occupation, it was probably because of this humiliation (that the French caused the British) that led to the anti-French sentiment that resulted in the cultural revolution that followed the defeat of the French in England. 5

By the fourteenth century, the emergence of Chaucer and other poets initiated a cultural revolution by turning old, spoken English into a written 6 form. This was made easier by the introduction of the printing press in 1476. As printed works became available, regional differences in vocabulary, spelling, and pronunciation became standardized and the resulting form became known as Middle English--which is very similar to modern English. By the sixteenth century, the stage was set for the English of William Shakespeare and the Elizabethans, which was even more closely related to modern English.

7   Through these historical events, wars, and occupations by the Anglo-Saxons, Vikings, and Normans, English evolved through the Middle Ages and set the stage for the language we speak today.

To gain some practical experience, your instructor may ask you to write an essay exam on one of the following topics. Use the preparation and prewriting strategies you've practiced in this chapter and any other strategies you find useful to prepare for the exam. Review the guidelines for writing a successful response presented on pages 638–39 and, if possible, organize and conduct group study sessions with your classmates.

Exam Option 1   Imagine that you've been appointed to a campus committee charged with developing minimum requirements for writing assignments in undergraduate courses. Specifically, the committee is trying to decide whether to require professors to assign a final essay exam or a major research paper in core-curriculum courses. Write an essay in which you argue in favor of mandatory essay exams or mandatory research papers, using examples from your own experience and material from Chapters 1 through 4 and this chapter to support your position. You may want to consider some or all of the following questions in your discussion: Which kind of writing helps students learn the most? Which kind of writing most accurately gauges how well students know course material? Which kind of writing develops skills students are most likely to need in the future?

Exam Option 2   Explain the difference between closed-form and open-form prose as presented in Chapter 1 and Chapters 18–20. Illustrate your answer with examples taken from Sharon Lerner's "If We've Come Such a Long Way, Why Are We Still Smoking?" (pp. 123–27) and Annie Dillard's "Living Like Weasels" (pp. 132–34). Why does Lerner choose to write near the closed end of the closed-to-open continuum, whereas Dillard chooses to write near the open end?

Exam Option 3   Write an essay on a topic of your instructor's choice.

Summary

This chapter has discussed strategies for writing effective examination essays under time pressure. We have shown how exam essays differ from essays written outside class and have suggested strategies for learning and remembering subject matter, for analyzing exam questions, and for dealing with the constraints of an exam situation. We have also provided guidelines for producing successful examination essays: a clear thesis statement, coherent organization, support and evidence, independent analysis and argument, and an effective conclusion. Finally, the chapter provides exercises to help you improve your own ability to understand the criteria for a good exam answer and to produce a good answer yourself.

Acknowledgments *(continued from copyright page)*

Page 4.   Andrea Lunsford and Lisa Ede, *Singular Texts/Plural Authors: Perspective on Collaborative Writing.* Carbondale and Edwardsville, IL: Southern Illinois University Press, 1992, p. 21.

Page 11.   David M. Rockwood, letter to editor, *The Oregonian,* January 1, 1993, E4. Reprinted with the permission of the author.

Page 12.   Minnie Bruce Pratt, excerpt from "Identity: Skin Blood Heart," in *Yours In Struggle: Three Perspectives on Anti-Semitism and Racism* by Elly Bulkin, Minnie Bruce Pratt, and Barbara Smith. Copyright © 1984 by Elly Bulkin, Minnie Bruce Pratt, and Barbara Smith. Reprinted with the permission of Firebrand Books, Ithaca, New York.

Page 20.   Stephen Bean, "The Starling Mystery" (previously unpublished student essay). Reprinted with the permission of the author.

Page 21.   David Wallechinsky, "This Land of Ours," *Parade Magazine,* July 5, 1992, p. 4.

Page 21.   A. Kimbrough Sherman, in *Thinking and Writing in College: A Naturalistic Study of Students in Four Disciplines* by Barbara E. Walvoord and Lucille P. McCarthy, Urbana, IL: NCTE, 1990, p. 51.

Page 26.   Thomas S. Szasz, *The Myth of Mental Illness.* New York: Harper & Row, 1974, p. 8.

Page 35.   "Proposed Law Calls for Fines, Arrests," *Seattle Times,* October 1, 1993. Copyright © 1993 Seattle Times Company. Used by permission.

Page 39.   Peter Elbow, *Writing Without Teachers.* New York: Oxford University Press, 1973, pp. 147–90.

Page 40.   Paul Theroux, *Sunrise with Seamonsters.* Boston: Houghton Mifflin, 1985.

Pages 43 and 45.   Peter Elbow, *Writing Without Teachers.* New York: Oxford University Press, 1973, pp. 14–15.

Page 54.   James Moffett, *Active Voice: A Writing Program Across the Curriculum.* Montclair, NJ: Boynton/Cook Publishers, 1981.

Page 71.   Penny Parker, "For Teeth, Say Cheese," *Readers Digest,* October 1991. Copyright © 1991. Reprinted with permission from the October 1991 *Reader's Digest.* Originally appeared in *New Scientist,* April 6, 1991, p. 15. Reprinted with permission from New Scientist.

Page 71.   Carlo Patrono, "Aspirin as an Antiplatelet Drug," *The New England Journal of Medicine, 330,* May 5, 1994, pp. 1287–94. Copyright © 1994 by the Massachusetts Medical Society. Reprinted by permission of *The New England Journal of Medicine.*

Page 78.   Randal Rubini, "A Vicious Cycle," *Seattle Times,* August 27, 1992, G1+.

Page 80.   Lorna Marshal, *The !Kung of Nyae Nyae.* Cambridge: Harvard University Press, 1976, pp. 177–78.

Page 80.   P. Draper, "!Kung Women: Contrasts in Sexual Egalitarianism in Foraging and Sedentary Contexts," in R. Reiter (Ed.), *Toward an Anthropology of Women.* New York: Monthly Review Press, 1975, pp. 82–83.

Page 83.   Sarah Bean, "Contrasting Descriptions" (previously unpublished student essay). Reprinted with the permission of the author.

Page 86.   Mike Royko, *Seattle Times,* April 7, 1995, B11.

Page 86.   Mark Twain, "Two Ways of Seeing a River," in *Life on the Mississippi.* New York: Harper & Row, 1899.

Page 88.   S. I. Hayakawa, excerpt from "Reports, Inferences, Judgments," in *Language in Thought and Action, 4th ed.* by S. I. Hayakawa, copyright © 1978 by Harcourt Brace & Company, reprinted by permission of the publisher.

Page 100.   Marcia Angell, "Disease as a Reflection of the Psyche," *The New England Journal of Medicine, 312,* 1985, pp. 1570–72. Copyright © 1985 by the Massachusetts Medical Society. Reprinted by permission of *The New England Journal of Medicine.*

Page 105.   Robert B. Cullen with Sullivan, "Dangers of Disarming," *Newsweek,* October 27, 1986. Copyright © 1986 by Newsweek Inc. All rights reserved. Reprinted by permission.

Page 115.   Jane Tompkins, " 'Indians': Textualism, Morality, and the Problem of History." *Critical Inquiry, 13,* no. 1, Autumn 1986. Copyright © 1986 by The University of Chicago. Reprinted with the permission of the author and The University of Chicago Press.

Page 119.   Joan Didion, "On Going Home," in *Slouching Toward Bethlehem* by Joan Didion. Copyright © 1966, 1968 by Joan Didion. Reprinted by permission of Farrar, Straus & Giroux, Inc.

Page 123.   Sharon Lerner, "If We've Come Such a Long Way, Why Are We Still Smoking?" *Ms.*, May/June, 1995. Reprinted by permission of *Ms.* Magazine, © 1995.

Page 128.   Florence King, "I'd Rather Smoke Than Kiss," *National Review,* July 9, 1990, pp. 32–36. Copyright © 1990 by National Review, Inc., 150 East 35th Street, New York, NY 10016. Reprinted by permission.

Page 132.   Annie Dillard, "Living Like Weasels," in *Teaching a Stone to Talk: Expeditions and Encounters.* Copyright © 1982 by Annie Dillard. Reprinted with the permission of HarperCollins Publishers, Inc.

Page 143.   Richard Wright, *Black Boy.* New York: Harper & Row, 1966, pp. 216–17.

Page 146.   Bill Russell, excerpt from *Second Wind: The Memoirs of an Opinionated Man* by Bill Russell with Taylor Branch. New York: Random House, 1979. Copyright © 1979 by William F. Russell. Reprinted with the permission of The Robbins Office.

Page 147.   Maureen Howard, excerpt from *Facts of Life.* Copyright © 1978 by Maureen Howard. Reprinted with the permission of Little, Brown and Company.

Page 153.   Sheila Madden, "Letting Go of Bart," *Santa Clara Magazine,* Summer, 1994. Copyright © 1994 by Sheila Madden. Reprinted with the permission of the author.

Page 161.   "Essay A/Essay B" from "Inventing the University," in *When A Writer Can't Write* by David Bartholomae. Reprinted with the permission of The Guilford Press.

Page 167.   Mary Turla, "Mail-Order Bride Romances: Fairy Tale, Nightmare, or Somewhere in Between?" (previously unpublished student essay). Reprinted with the permission of the author.

Page 170.   Sheridan Botts, "Exploring Problems About Hospice" (previously unpublished student essay). Reprinted with the permission of the author.

Page 173.   Jane Tompkins, " 'Indians': Textualism, Morality, and the Problem of History," *Critical Inquiry, 13,* no. 1, Autumn 1986. Copyright © 1986 by The University of Chicago. Reprinted with the permission of the author and The University of Chicago Press.

Pages 183 and 188.   Stephen Bean, "Sam" journal entries and "Should Women Be Allowed to Serve In Combat Units?" (previously unpublished). Reprinted with the permission of the author.

Page 196.   Article abstract of "Reefer Madness" by Eric Schlosser, August 1994. Abstract reprinted with the permission of *The Atlantic Monthly.*

Page 196.   Article abstract of "The Sex-Bias Myth in Medicine" by Andrew G. Kadar, M.D., August 1994. Abstract reprinted with the permission of *The Atlantic Monthly.*

Page 196.   Article abstract of "It's Not the Economy, Stupid" by Charles R. Morris, July 1993. Abstract reprinted with the permission of *The Atlantic Monthly.*

Page 197.   Article abstract of "Midlife Myths" by Winifred Gallagher, May 1993. Abstract reprinted with the permission of *The Atlantic Monthly.*

Page 198.   Leo Banks, "Not Guilty: Despite Its Fearsome Image, the Tarantula Is a Benign Beast," *America West Airlines Magazine,* February 1988. Copyright © 1988 by Leo Banks. Reprinted with the permission of the author.

Page 199.   Cheryl Carp, "Behind Store Walls" (previously unpublished student essay). Reprinted with the permission of the author.

Page 202.   David Quammen, "The Face of a Spider: Eyeball to Eyeball with the Good, the Bad, and the Ugly," *Outside Magazine,* March 1987. Reprinted by permission of the author. All rights reserved. Copyright © 1987 by David Quammen.

Page 214.   Sut Jhally, *The Codes of Advertising: Fetishism and Political Economy of Meaning in the Consumer Society.* New York: St. Martins, 1987, p. 2.

Page 215.   "Attention Advertisers: Real Men Do Laundry," *American Demographics,* March 1994, pp. 13–14.

Page 220.   Coors advertisement: "Sam and Me." Courtesy Coors Brewing Co.

Page 223.   Zenith advertisement: "Of Sound Body." Courtesy SDI Technologies, Inc.

Page 224.   Hennessy advertisement: "The World's Most Civilized Spirit." Courtesy Schieffelin & Somerset Co., 2 Park Avenue, New York, NY 10016.

Page 226.   Vance Packard, excerpt from *The Hidden Persuaders.* Copyright © 1957 and renewed 1985 by Vance Packard. Reprinted with the permission of the author.

Page 227.   Gillian Dyer, "On Manner and Activity," in *Advertising as Communication.* Copyright © 1982 by Gillian Dyer. Reprinted with the permission of Methuen & Co., International Thomson Publishing Services, Andover, UK.

Page 230.   Mark Crispin Miller, "Getting Dirty," in *Boxed In: The Culture of TV.* Copyright © 1989 by Mark Crispin Miller. Reprinted with the permission of Northwestern University Press. See also Fred Danzig's article in *Advertising Age,* June 7, 1982, in which he lampoons Miller's essay.

Page 235.   Stephen Bean, "How Cigarette Advertisers Address the Stigma Against Smoking: A Tale of Two Ads" (previously unpublished student essay). Reprinted with the permission of the author.

Page 241.   "Minimum Wage Called Defining Issue," *Tempe Tribune,* February 4, 1995. Reprinted with the permission of the Associated Press.

Page 242.   "Minimum Wage" bar graphs. Reprinted with permission of the Associated Press.

Page 243.   "Minimum-Wage Raise Would Buy Extra Bag of Groceries a Week," *Tempe Tribune,* February 4, 1995. Reprinted with the permission of the Associated Press.

Page 244.   "GOP Cool to Clinton Call to Raise Minimum Pay," *Arizona Republic,* February 4, 1995. Copyright © 1995. Reprinted with the permission of Tribune Media Services.

Page 245.   "Minimum Wage" pie charts. Reprinted with permission of AP/Wide World Photos.

Page 260.   "The 3% Solution" graph by Elys A. McLean, *USA TODAY,* April 17, 1995. Copyright © 1995, USA TODAY. Reprinted with permission.

Page 261.   "Collection of Child Support" graph by Cliff Vancura, *USA TODAY,* April 18, 1995. Copyright © 1995, USA TODAY. Reprinted with permission.

Page 266.   Robert Wright, "What Do 167 Deaths Justify?" *Time,* May 15, 1995.

Page 267.   Bryant Stamford, "Understand Calories, Fat Content in Food," *Seattle Times,* July 27, 1995. Copyright © 1995. Reprinted with the permission of Gannett News Service.

Page 268.   John Paulos, "Recession Forecast If Steps Not Taken," in *A Mathematician Reads the Newspaper.* Copyright © 1995 by John Paulos. Reprinted with the permission of HarperCollins Publishers, Inc.

Page 280.   Evelyn Dahl Reed, "Medicine Man." This story from *Coyote Tales from the Indian Pueblos* by Evelyn Dahl Reed appears courtesy of Sunstone Press, P. O. Box 2321, Sante Fe, NM 87504-2321. Copyright © 1988 by Evelyn Dahl Reed.

Page 289.   Guy de Maupassant, "Moonlight," Robert Scholes, Trans., in *Elements of Literature,* 4th ed. New York: Oxford, 1991.

Page 292.   Alice Walker, "Everyday Use (for your grandmama)," in *In Love & Trouble: Stories of Black Women,* copyright © 1973 by Alice Walker, reprinted by permission of Harcourt Brace & Company.

Page 298.   Holly Burkett, "The Julian Within" (previously unpublished student essay). Reprinted with the permission of the author.

Page 308.   Monica Yant, "Many Female Athletes at Risk of 'Triad' of Health Problems," *Seattle Tribune,* June 18, 1992, B14.

Page 315.   Stephen Jay Gould, "Sex, Drugs, Disasters, and the Extinction of Dinosaurs," in *The Flamingo's Smile: Reflections on Natural History* by Stephen Jay Gould. Copyright © 1984 by Stephen Jay Gould. Reprinted by permission of W. W. Norton & Company, Inc.

Page 320.   Ron Witten, "Suns Set in West: Wait Until Mourning" (previously unpublished student essay). Reprinted with the permission of the author.

Page 332.   Stephen Toulmin, *The Uses of Argument.* Cambridge: Cambridge University Press, 1958.

Page 345.   Robert Reich, "Companies are Cutting Their Hearts Out," *The New York Times Magazine,* December 19, 1993. Copyright © 1993 by The New York Times Company. Reprinted with the permission of *The New York Times.*

Page 349.   Edward Abbey, "The Damnation of a Canyon," in *Beyond the Wall: Essays from the Outside* by Edward Abbey. Copyright © 1971, 1977, 1979, 1984 by Edward Abbey. Reprinted by permission of Henry Holt and Co., Inc.

Page 353.   David S. Bennahum, "Getting Cyber Smart," *The New York Times,* May 22, 1995. Copyright © 1995 by The New York Times Company. Reprinted with the permission of *The New York Times.*

Page 355.   Walt Spady, "A Misguided Ban on Personal Watercraft," *Seattle Times*, February 1996, written by John Wood, edited by Walt Spady. Reprinted with the permission of Walt Spady.

Page 357.   Elijah Isaacson, "The Proposed 'Block Schedule' Is a Bad Idea" (previously unpublished student essay). Reprinted with the permission of the author.

Page 375.   Gabriel Judet-Weinshel, "Inadequacies of the DARE Program" (previously unpublished student essay). Reprinted with the permission of the author.

Page 377.   Charles Krauthammer, "B-2 or Not B-2?: That's an Important Question," *The Washington Post*, July 1995. Copyright © 1995 Washington Post Writers Group. Reprinted with permission.

Page 379.   Corby Kummer, "Is Coffee Harmful?" *The Atlantic Monthly*, July 1990. Copyright © 1990. Reprinted by permission.

Page 395.   Theresa LaPorte, "A Proposal to Create a Quiet Study Lounge" (previously unpublished student essay). Reprinted with the permission of the author.

Page 401.   Sheridan Botts, "Saving Hospices: A Proposal for Per Diem Funding" (previously unpublished student essay). Reprinted with the permission of the author.

Page 413.   Richard Wade, "Reduce Jail Terms in Exchange for Becoming Literate" (editors' title; originally titled "Reading, Writing, Rehabilitation"), *The New York Times*, May 29, 1992. Copyright © 1992 by The New York Times Magazine. Reprinted with the permission of *The New York Times*.

Page 415.   Stephen Moore and Dean Stansel, "Let's Stop Corporate Welfare," *USA TODAY*, September 1995. Reprinted from USA TODAY magazine, copyright © 1995 by the Society for the Advancement of Education.

Page 427.   Jonathan Swift, quoted in Jon Winokur (Ed.), *Writers on Writing*. Philadelphia: Running Press, 1986.

Page 443.   Kenneth Burke, *The Grammar of Motives*. Berkeley: University of California Press, 1969.

Page 443.   Norman Mailer, *Of a Fire on the Moon*. Boston: Little, Brown, 1970, p. 52.

Pages 456 and 457.   Dao Do, "Choose Life" (previously unpublished student essay). Reprinted with the permission of the author.

Page 459.   Howard Gardner, *The Mind's New Science: A History of the Cognitive Revolution*. New York: Basic Books, 1985, p. 90.

Page 465.   James Jones, quoted in Jon Winokur (Ed.), *Writers on Writing*. Philadelphia: Running Press, 1986.

Page 469.   Lowell Ponte, "Earthquakes: Closer Than You Think," *Reader's Digest*, April 1994.

Page 471.   Stephen Jay Gould, "The Rule of Five," in *The Flamingo's Smile: Reflections in Natural History*.

Page 476.   Dao Do, "Choose Life" (previously unpublished student essay). Reprinted with the permission of the author.

Page 483.   Wendy Kaminer, "Crime and Community,"*The Atlantic Monthly*, May 1994, pp. 111–12.

Pages 489 and 491.   Chris Anderson, excerpt from *Edge Effects: Notes from an Oregon Forest*. Copyright © 1993 by University of Iowa Press. Reprinted with the permission of the publisher.

Page 491.   Patrick Klein, "Berkeley Blues," in *University of Arizona First Year Composition Guide*. Copyright © 1995 by University of Arizona First Year Composition Program. Reprinted with the permission of Burgess Publishing Company.

Page 495.   Richard Brautigan, "Leaves," in *The Tokyo-Montana Express* by Richard Brautigan. Copyright © 1980. Reprinted by permission.

Page 495.   Oliver Goldsmith, "The Crow and the Fox," in *Aesop's Fables*.

Page 495.   Hitamaro, "A strange old man," haiku translated by Kenneth Rexroth, in *One Hundred Poems from the Japanese*. Copyright © 1956. All rights reserved by New Directions Publishing Corp. Reprinted by permission of New Directions Publishing Corp.

Page 496.   Cathy cartoon, "Are you finished with all these Christmas catalogs?" Copyright Cathy Guisewite. Reprinted with permission of Universal Press Syndicate. All rights reserved.

Page 501.   Joan Didion, "On Going Home," in *Slouching Toward Bethlehem* by Joan Didion. Reprinted by permission of Farrar, Straus & Giroux, Inc.

Page 502.   Jonathan Swift, "A Modest Proposal," in *The Prose Works of Jonathan Swift*. London: Bell, 1914.

Page 503.   *College Composition and Communication,* Viponid Interview with John McPhee, May 1991, pp. 203–04.

Page 504.   Tom Wolfe, "New Journalism," introduction to *New Journalism,* Tom Wolfe and E. W. Johnson, Eds. New York: Harper & Row, 1973, p. 32.

Page 505.   Eric Konigsberg, "Dad Always Liked You Best," *GQ,* June 1995, p. 48.

Page 506.   Tom Wolfe, "New Journalism," introduction to *New Journalism,* Tom Wolfe and E. W. Johnson, Eds. New York: Harper & Row, 1973, p. 32.

Page 506.   Nicolas Tomalin, in *New Journalism,* Tom Wolfe and E. W. Johnson, Eds. New York: Harper & Row, 1973, p. 201.

Page 507.   Annie Dillard, "Total Eclipse," in *Teaching a Stone To Talk: Expeditions and Encounters.* Copyright © 1982 by Annie Dillard. Reprinted with the permission of HarperCollins Publishers, Inc.

Page 509.   *Windows in 21 Days*

Page 509.   *Paradox 5 for Windows for Dummies,* by John Kaufeld. San Mateo, CA: IDG Books Worldwide, Inc., 1994.

Page 510.   Michael F. Graves and Wayne H. Slater, "Could Textbooks Be Better Written and Would It Make a Difference?" *American Educator,* Spring, 1986, pp. 36–42.

Page 514.   Parker Palmer, *To Know as We Are Known: Education as a Spiritual Journey.* San Francisco: Harper and Row, 1983.

Page 514.   Hannah Arendt, *The Human Condition.* Chicago: University of Chicago Press, 1958.

Page 531.   Pamela Erens, "Are Subliminal Self-help Tapes a Hoax?" *Glamour,* October 1994, p. 62.

Page 555.   Roger D. McGrath, "The Myth of Violence in the Old West," in *Gunfighters, Highwaymen, and Vigilantes.* Copyright © 1984 by The Regents of the University of California. Reprinted with the permission of University of California Press.

Page 583.   Mary Turla, "Mail-Order Bride Romances: The Need for Regulation" (previously unpublished student essay). Reprinted with the permission of the author.

Page 623.   Mary Meiser, "Survival Skill: Learning to Write the Essay Exam," *Wisconsin English Journal,* 21, 1982, p. 20–23.

Page 624.   Linda Ellerbee, *"And So It Goes": Adventures in Television.* New York: Putnam, 1986.

Page 626.   Randall Popken, "Essay Exams and Papers: A Contextual Comparison," *Journal of Teaching Writing,* 8, 1989, pp. 51–65.

Page 626.   Michael C. Flanigan, "Processes of Essay Exams" (unpublished manuscript). University of Oklahoma, 1991.

Page 639.   Robert McCrum, William Cran, and Robert MacNeil, *The Story of English.* Kingsport, TN: Penguin, 1985.

Index

Arguments *(continued)*
  pro/con, 331, 332, 332,
    360–61
  qualifiers in, 336
  reason in, 368
  rebuttal conditions in,
    335–36, 337, 368–69
  stated reason in, 368
  structure of Greek, 339–41
  subclaims in, 331
  summary of, 557
  supporting position, 338–43,
    362
  truth issues in, 330–31
  value issues, 331
  warrants in, 333, 334, 335,
    368
Articles
  academic, introductions to,
    26–27
  citation styles for, 572–74
  newspaper. *See* Newspaper
    articles
  researching, 539–42
"Aspirin as an Antiplatelet
    Drug" (Patrono), 71
Attributive tags
  author mention in, 565–66
  with parenthetical documen-
    tation, 565
  for research paper, 111
  in short quotations, 563
  summarizing/paraphrasing
    for, 560
  without parenthetical docu-
    mentation, 565
Audience
  academic, 61
  affect on writing, 60
  appeal, 215
  assessment of, 61–62
  assumptions about, 205–06
  beliefs of, 340–41
  changes in, 60–61
  clarification, revising for, 431
  classical arguments and, 333
  intended
    articulation of differences
      from, 113–14
    surprise for, 207
  reading, 60
  target, 215, 218, 237, 352
  values of, 340–41
Author
  citations, 567–69

corporate, citations for,
    571–72
  mention, in attributative
    tags, 565–66
  version of truth of, 81
Autobiographical narratives
  essays, 57
  intimacy in, 138
  as open-end writing, 138–45
  opposition of contraries in,
    139
  pivotal moments in, 142
  techniques for, 138
Autobiographical tension, 141

Background
  information, on essay exam,
    627–28
  material, in arguments, 382
Background information
  in introductions, 469–70
  lack of, 108
Bandwagon appeal fallacy, 344
Banking method of education,
    7–8
Banks, Leo ("Not Guilty: De-
    spite Its Fearsome
    Image, the Tarantula Is a
    Benign Beast"), 198–99
Bartholomae, David, 165
Bean, John ("How Do You Get
    Rid of Your Dog's
    Fleas?"), 17–18
Bean, Stephen (student), "How
    Cigarette Advertisers
    Address the Stigma
    Against Smoking: A Tale
    of Two Ads," 235–37
"Behind Stone Walls" (Carp),
    199–201
Believing-doubting game,
    39–42, 274
Belletristic prose, 59
Bennahum, David ("Getting
    Cyber Smart"), 353–55
"Berkeley Blues" (Klein), 491–94
Bias
  in newsgroup messages, 604
  in research material, 544
  in sources, 554–55
Bibliography
  citation for, 553
  listings, MLA form for,
    567–80
  in periodical indexes, 542

search through INFOTRAC,
    184
Biography Index, 540
Biological and Agricultural Index,
    541
Block indentation, *vs.* quota-
    tion marks, 562
Blueprint statement, 471
Body language, 518
Bookmarks, on Internet, 615
Book Review Digest, 542
Books
  citation styles for, 567–72,
    575, 576
  commonplace, 37–38
  search for, in libraries, 536
"B-2 or Not B-2? That's an Im-
    portant Question"
    (Krauthammer), 377–78
Botts, Sheridan (student), 544
  "Exploring Problems About
    Hospice," 170–72
  "Saving Hospices: A Pro-
    posal for Per Diem
    Funding," 401–21
Brainstorming
  in groups, 523–24
  on Internet, 606
  trigger questions for, 194,
    209–10
Brautigan, Richard ("Leaves"),
    495
Brookfield, Stephen, 3
Bulletin board, 577
Burke, Kenneth, 443, 500
Burkett, Holly (student) ("The
    Julian Within"), 298–99
Business Periodical Index, 540

Card catalogs, *vs.* on-line cata-
    logs, 538
Career
  advancement, group skills
    and, 515
  success, writing for, 4–5
Carp, Cheryl (student) ("Behind
    Stone Walls"), 199–201
"Cathy" cartoon, as minimal
    story, 495–96
Causal analysis
  case study, 311–13
  definition of, 305
  exploration of, 309–10
  free writing in, 324
  idea maps in, 323

Editing and Revision Symbols

AB	Faulty or inappropriate abbreviation
ACT/PASS	Weak use of the passive voice
ADJ-F	Incorrect form for adjective
ADV-F	Incorrect form for adverb
AGR-PN	Faulty pronoun-antecedent agreement
AGR-SV	Faulty subject-verb agreement
AWK	Awkward wording
BIAS?	Language seems biased; use inclusive language
CAP	Misused capitalization
CASE	Wrong pronoun case
CS	Comma splice
DANG	Dangling modifier
FP	Faulty predication
FRAG	Sentence fragment
GRAM	Sentence structure is not grammatical
ITAL	Italics or underlining is misused or needed
LANG/STYLE	Style is dull; consider ways to enliven passage
MC	Mixed construction
MF	Inappropriate manuscript form
MM	Misplaced modifier
NUM	Misuse of words/figures in representing numbers
O/N	Passage violates old/new contract